WRITING HANDBOOK

SECOND EDITION

WRITING HANDBOOK

BERNARD J. STREICHER, S.J.

MICHAEL P. KAMMER, S.J.

CHARLES W. MULLIGAN, S.J.

 Loyola Press
Chicago

Loyola Press
3441 North Ashland Avenue
Chicago, Illinois 60657
Phone: (800) 621-1008
Fax: (312) 281-0555

Cover design: Jill Mark Salyards

Library of Congress Cataloging-in-Publication Data

Streicher, Bernard J.
    Writing Handbook / Bernard J. Streicher, Michael P. Kammer,
Charles W. Mulligan. —2nd ed.
        p.   cm.
    Rev. ed. of: Writing Handbook / Michael P. Kammer, Charles W.
Mulligan.
    Includes index.
    ISBN 0-8294-0910-6
    1. English language—Rhetoric—Handbooks, manuals, etc.
2. English language—Grammar—Handbooks, manuals, etc. 3. Academic
writing—Handbooks, manuals, etc.   I. Kammer, Michael P., 1914-
II. Mulligan, Charles W.   III. Kammer, Michael P., 1914- Writing
Handbook. IV. Title.
PE1408.S768 1996
808' .042—dc20

PREFACE

Writing Handbook by Kammer and Mulligan was first published in 1953. With expansion of the exposition section and rearrangement of some other materials, the book appeared in an alternate form in 1960 under the title *For Writing English.* These two handbooks have continued in print to the present day, without revision, and still account for modest annual sales. Their appeal rests upon a remarkably thorough treatment of grammar and usage. Some of the rules are written with such prevision that they appear enlightened even today. Nevertheless, it became apparent that the book as a whole, dealing as it does with a living and changing language, needed updating.

This second edition of *Writing Handbook* represents a major revision. Incorporated are hundreds of minor changes in the usage sections (including updated capitalization of religious terms) and the rearrangement of some of the original material. An already thorough section on paragraph development has been expanded. The essay section now includes not only a discussion of the formal essay but also the critical essay, review, and essay examination. Checklists on essay writing and on sentence structure and diction have been added and are keyed to the appropriate rules and statements in the text for easy reference. Also expanded are the argumentation and narration sections and the list of library resources for research writing. Since the formats for both research papers and business correspondence have undergone major changes in recent years, these two sections have been completely rewritten. There are also new sections: the word processor, a glossary of frequently misused words and phrases, and sentence exercises in grammar, usage, style, and diction keyed to the text for convenient study.

This is an editor's and a writer's handbook: both a reference book and a guide to effective composition. It is particularly distinctive in two ways. First, the book eschews lengthy explanations on points of language and composition in favor of numbered rules and statements followed by examples. Second, it is as thorough as possible within the limitations of a handbook. It would, for example, be difficult to find a general handbook with a more thorough coverage of grammar, usage, and diagraming. In addition, the section on research writing presents detailed information and models on three widely used styles of format and documentation advanced, respectively, in *MLA Handbook for Writers of Research Papers, Publication Manual of the American Psychological Association,* and *A Manual for Writers of Term Papers, Theses, and Dissertations* (University of Chicago). There is also extensive coverage of various styles of business letters and proper forms of address. As a refresher in essentials, the exercises on correct and effective sentences provide a convenient review of some basic writing skills. Finally, as with the first edition, the book is carefully and thoroughly indexed. Users possessing only general knowledge of terminology will be readily able to find the material they are looking for.

A number of my fellow Jesuits contributed to this revision. I am especially indebted to Daniel L. Flaherty, former director of Loyola University Press, who suggested and supported the project; to George A. Lane, the current director, for continuing that support; and to Joseph F. Downey, editorial director at Loyola University Press, and John A. St. George for their careful work with the text at every stage. Other Jesuits read one or more sections of the text and made valuable suggestions: Francis F. Burch, St. Joseph's University; James H. Donahue, Loyola College; Fred M. Henley, University of Detroit Mercy; William B. Hill, University of Scranton; Joseph P. Hopkins, University of Detroit Jesuit High School and Academy; Donal T. MacVeigh, St. Peter's College; John P. Murphy, Loyola University of Chicago; William J. O'Malley, Fordham Preparatory; Philip C. Rule, College of the Holy Cross; Joseph D. Scallon, Creighton University; D. Clayton Schario, University of Detroit Mercy; Edward V. Stackpoole, University of San Francisco; Thomas J. Steele, Regis College; Leonard A. Waters, Creighton University.

B. J. S.

CONTENTS

This table of contents lists matter by pages;

but the index found at the back of the book

lists them by rule, with letter and number.

A | Parts of speech

B | **The sentence—use and structure**

C | **Syntax**

Syntax, continued

D | Punctuation

E | **Division of words** 253

F | **Abbreviations** 256

G | **Numbers** 262

H | **Capitals**

I | **Spelling**

J | **Diagraming**

K | The sentence — structure and diction

L | The paragraph

M | The essay

N | The research paper

O | Definition

P | Argument

Q | Description

R | **Narrative Writing**

S | **Letters, résumés, and memos**

T | Word processing

| U | **Glossary of usage** | 781 |

| V | **Sentence exercises** |

A Word on Grammar and the Type of Grammar Used in This Handbook

A grammar provides a precise way of talking about language. It studies the various classes of words, their functions, and relations as they occur in sentences. In American schools the English language has traditionally been studied and taught to native speakers of English from the point of view of how the words, their arrangements, and functions contribute to the meanings of the commonly accepted form of English. Such *traditional* grammar is prescriptive; that is, it attempts to teach how to speak and write correctly according to socially accepted standards. This kind of grammar usually presumes that a student knows the meaning of a sentence and then, by logical analysis, attempts to show how the elements can be said to contribute to that meaning. In other words, it begins with meaning and only subsequently considers how the forms contribute to the meaning.

Traditional grammar has roots in eighteenth-century English grammar and, even earlier, in the classical models of Latin grammar used during the Renaissance. In turn, this grammar can ultimately be traced through Donatus to an early Latin grammarian, Priscian, who taught Latin to Greeks in sixth-century Constantinople. For the most part he discussed Latin in the meaning categories used in Greek (the language of his students), which were different from the meaning categories and arrangements of forms used in Latin. Although this kind of grammar has been called traditional, it is really quite different from what earlier Sanskrit, Greek, and Roman grammarians attempted—howsoever imperfectly; namely, to write structural or descriptive grammars.

Rather than beginning with meaning, *structural* grammar attempts to describe the patterned system of signals which convey meaning. It thus tends to be descriptive rather than prescriptive and concentrates on formal patterns rather than on the meaning which individual languages may convey in different and often contrasting ways. This sort of grammar tends, as traditional grammar does, to be synchronic rather than diachronic; that is, it describes how the language works now rather than how the patterns or mechanisms developed historically.

Historical grammars explore language change; they attempt to explain the current patterns of a language in terms of the historical influences which affected the phonological, morphological, syntactic, lexical, and cultural levels of that language. These studies made exceptional progress during the nineteenth century and in the first quarter of the twentieth century.

More recently *transformational-generative* grammar has attempted to account for language phenomena by viewing language as a set of rules which specify the competence of a speaker of a particular language. This grammar shows how basic sentences can be changed and combined and also gives insight into the creative mind and the way language is learned. *Sociolinguistics* examines the complex relationships which exist between language and society.

Each of the various types of grammars just described has different objectives, focus, and methodology; and each has made its contribution to an understanding of the English language. In recent times structural and transformational-generative grammars have been particularly useful. But because their methods of analysis are relatively complex, traditional grammar (often with modifications) is still taught in most schools in the United States today. In addition, traditional grammar terminology is commonly used in foreign-language instruction. For its general utility, then, traditional grammar is used in this handbook.

A

Parts of speech

In general

A1 Words are classified as parts of speech chiefly according to the way in which they are used in sentences, though they can be classified to some extent according to what they mean outside sentences.

A2 There are eight parts of speech: nouns,[1] pronouns, verbs, adjectives, adverbs, prepositions, conjunctions, and exclamatory words (interjections). Other elements of speech are the expletives (*it* and *there*) and the verbals (gerunds, participles, and infinitives).

A3 The same word, spelled the same way, can sometimes be several parts of speech in turn.

The *little* man was peering at me again.	*Little* is an adjective.
The cymbal player cared *little* for music of any kind.	*Little* is an adverb.
Let me have a *little*, please.	*Little* is a pronoun.

The noun

A4 A noun is the name of a person, place, or thing. ("Thing" includes not only objects, but also qualities or conditions, actions, ideas, and so on.)

Janet doesn't like that *color*.
Look at this *picture* of the *Kennedy Space Center*.

---

[1] Nouns are called substantives; so are other words or groups of words that function as nouns.

A
B

Kinds of nouns

A5 A common noun is the name shared by all persons or things of the same kind. It can be applied to every member of a group or class of things.

girl	knife
house	dog

A6 A proper noun is the particular name of a particular person, place, or thing.

Daniel Boone   Chicago   Buick

A7 A concrete noun is the name of something that exists by itself. Often, not always, such a thing is perceived by the senses.

mountain	soul
violin	angel
flame	air

A8 An abstract noun is the name of a quality or an attribute apart from any object. It sometimes names the general as opposed to the particular.

whiteness	courage
humanity	sport
person (in general, as opposed to a particular person like Martha Washington)	

A9 A collective noun is the name of a group of persons or a group of things.

team	herd
army	school (of fish)

Gender of nouns

A10 Nouns are of masculine gender when they carry with them the notion of the male sex.

The *boy* looked searchingly at me.
My *uncle* really did intend to pay the rent.
The *stallion* reared his fine head.

A11 Nouns are of feminine gender when they carry with them the notion of the female sex.

The *girl* says she heard no call.
The *waitress* sniffed and disappeared.
My *aunt* hopes to attend the classes for adults.
The *mare* was altogether proud of the colt and showed it.

A12 Many feminine and masculine gender nouns are gradually being replaced by words that have become gender inclusive.

heroine	—>	hero
police woman	—>	police officer
stewardess	—>	flight attendant
fireman	—>	firefighter
mailman	—>	letter carrier
workman	—>	worker

A13 Nouns are of common (masculine or feminine) gender when they do not distinguish between the sexes.

People are funny.

Parents often have no way of letting a child know how completely they understand the problems of young social life.

It is dangerous to take a bone from a *dog.*

The *flight attendant* was very helpful.

A14 Nouns are of neuter gender when they name things that have no sex.

A great *rock* lay some yards to the left.
The *idea* was new to me.

A15 Some sexless entities are given masculine or feminine gender by tradition or necessity.

We have much in common with our *sister* school.

She loved God because *he* first loved her.

A16 Some sexless things are sometimes given a gender in lively or poetic writing.

She was a graceful *ship*, much in love with speed.

That ol' *man river, he* don't say nuthin'.

A17 The vegetable kingdom is ordinarily treated as neuter.

The *tree* lay in ruins, *its* upended roots high in the air.

Now here is a *blossom* that certainly has not wasted *its* sweetness on the desert air.

A18 Collective nouns naming groups as groups (not as individuals) are treated as neuter.

The *crowd* had *its* attention diverted by the frantically waving man on the fire escape.

As usual, the *army* overextended *its* supply lines.

A19 The common-noun names of very young children are often treated as neuter in passages where the sex of the child has no bearing on the thought.

A *child* [an *infant*, a *baby*] has *its* rights no less than an adult.

A20 The common-noun names of animals are often treated as neuter regardless of the thought of the passage.

A *hen* is perfectly happy trying to hatch a darning egg along with *its* own real eggs.

Person of nouns

A21 A noun that designates the speaker is in the first person.

This revolver belongs to me, *James Horder.*

A22   A noun that designates the person or thing spoken to is in the second person.

I mean you, *Bill.*
For you, my *country*, I will gladly die; but I had rather live.

A23 A noun that designates the person or thing spoken of is in the third person.

St. Barbara is the patron of gunners and miners.

Number of nouns[2]

A24 A singular noun names one person or thing; a plural noun names more than one person or thing.

Singular	Plural
girl	girls
tree	trees

A25 Some nouns are plural in form but singular in meaning; other nouns are singular in form and either singular or plural in meaning.

The *news is* all good.
Measles is catching.
Physics is my most difficult subject.
Politics is not my field.
The *sheep is* lost.
The *scissors is* in the drawer.
The *sheep have been* slaughtered.
Moose are to be found in Canada and the northern United States.

The pronoun

A26 A pronoun is a word that is used in place of a noun or other substantive.

Helen said *she* would make ham sandwiches.

She is used in place of *Helen.*

Tom made this bow. *He* is clever with tools but so hasty that *he* cut *himself* a number of times.

The two *hes* and *himself* take the place of *Tom.*

My uncle has an unconventional spaniel *that* does not sit up and beg.

That takes the place of *spaniel.*

---

[2] See I4-12 on the formation of plurals of nouns.

A27 The antecedent of the pronoun is the noun whose place the pronoun takes.

Helen said she would make ham sandwiches.	Helen is the antecedent of *she.*
Tom made this bow. He is clever with tools but so hasty that he cut himself a number of times.	*Tom* is the antecedent of the two *hes* and *himself.*

A28 Some words may be thought of as nouns, pronouns, or adjectives. They differ from ordinary pronouns in this, that they can modify an implied but unexpressed noun.

The *good* enjoy two worlds.	As an adjective, *good* modifies the absent noun *people.*
They enjoy two worlds.	*They* is a pronoun. It cannot modify *people. Good people* makes sense, but *they people* does not.

Personal and possessive pronouns

A29 The personal pronouns indicate the speaker (first person), the person or thing spoken to (second person), or the person or thing spoken of (third person).

The personal pronouns are—

	First person	
	Singular	*Plural*
Nominative	I	we
Possessive	my	our
Objective	me	us
	Second person	
	Singular	*Plural*
Nominative	you (thou)	you (ye)
Possessive	your (thy)	your
Objective	you (thee)	you (ye)

8

	Third person	
	Singular	*Plural*
Nominative	he, she, it	they
Possessive	his, her, its	their
Objective	him, her, it	them

Personal pronouns in the possessive case are always used as adjectives: "This is *my* hat." (They are sometimes called possessive adjectives. See A83.)

A30 The possessive pronouns denote either ownership or origin or source.

The possessive pronouns are—

First person	
Singular	*Plural*
mine	ours

Second person	
Singular	*Plural*
yours (thine)	your

Third person	
Singular	*Plural*
his, hers, its	theirs

The possessive pronouns are always used as nouns, or substantives, and are always in either the nominative or the objective case: "This hat is *mine* ; give him *his*."[3]

A31 *He, his,* and *him* are used when the antecedent is masculine or common; *she, hers,* and *her,* when the antecedent is feminine; *it* and *its,* when the antecedent is neuter. The rest of the personal pronoun forms are used no matter what the gender of the antecedent.

On the witness stand the police officer testified that *he* had fired in self-defense.

Grace decided to buy the orange hat, even though *she* thought it was rather expensive.

---

[3] In many cases, perhaps most, *his* and *its* can be taken either as a personal pronoun in the possessive case (that is, an adjective) or as a possessive pronoun (that is, a substantive).

Demonstrative pronouns

A32   The demonstrative pronouns are—

Singular	*Plural*
this	these
that	those

A33   The demonstrative pronouns are used to specify, to point out, to call attention to their antecedents with special emphasis.

This is my choice.
I did not say *that.*
This is fine; *that* simply will not do.
Deliver *those* to my home; *these* I'll take with me.

A34   The demonstrative pronouns take the place of their antecedents; they do not accompany and modify nouns as the demonstrative adjectives do.

This is my home.

This—demonstrative pronoun —takes the place of *house* or *home* as subject of the predicate verb *is.*

This home is mine.

This—demonstrative adjective —is not the subject or object but accompanies and modifies the noun *home.*

A35   The demonstrative pronouns have the same forms for all persons, genders, and cases.

A36   *This* and *these* ordinarily refer to what is present, near, just referred to, or about to be referred to; *that* and *those* to what is more remote in time or place.

Look at *this* [referring to something near the speaker].
Look at *that* [referring to something across the room].

People call me stupid. *This* would anger me if I did not reflect that they would call me something worse if they knew me better.

And now *this* is what I am going to say to you.

A37 Demonstrative *that* and *those* are used to refer to the thing or idea indicated or understood from the situation or context.

The writing is *that* of Claiborne, but the sentiments are not hers.

[The first word spoken to a man who has just entered a room:] *That* is why I like you—you are always prompt.

Self-Pronouns

A38 The *self*-pronouns (compound personal pronouns) are—

	First person	
	Singular	*Plural*
Nominative and objective	myself	ourselves
	Second person	
	Singular	*Plural*
Nominative and objective	yourself	yourselves
	Third person	
	Singular	*Plural*
Nominative and objective	oneself	themselves
	himself	
	herself	
	itself	

A39 *Himself* is used when the antecedent is masculine or common; *herself,* when the antecedent is feminine; *itself,* when the antecedent is neuter. The rest of the *self*-pronouns are used no matter what the gender of the antecedent.

It has been said of Abe Lincoln that *he* pulled *himself* up by his own bootstraps.

My sister climbed the tree *herself* and rescued *her* kitten before the fire truck arrived.

A large *boulder* detached *itself* from the mass atop the hill and began to roll down toward us with increasing momentum.

I found *myself* wishing that we had not involved *ourselves* with such a reckless group.

A40   When a *self*-pronoun is used to show that the action is reflected upon the doer of the action, it is called a reflexive pronoun.

Feavy hurt *himself.*

He wrote *himself* a note.

She wrote a note to *herself.*

They are sitting by *themselves.*

A41   As reflexives, the *self*-pronouns can be used only in the objective case as direct objects, indirect objects, or the objects of prepositions.

Turner has betrayed *herself* [direct object].
That week Rossiter gave *himself* [indirect object] no peace.
Of *ourselves* [object of a preposition] we can do nothing.

A42   When a *self*-pronoun is not used as described in A40 but merely in apposition as reinforcement for another word in the sentence, it is called an intensive pronoun.[4]

He *himself* trained the seals.
He trained the seals *himself.*

A43   As intensives, the *self*-pronouns may be used in apposition with a word in the nominative or objective case.

She herself voted against the proposal twice.
We met none other than our *neighbors themselves* downtown.
Here is a picture of *Mary herself* when she was two.
I myself have no objections to the plan.
It was necessary that the *captain himself* set the course.

---

[4] Some grammarians call intensive pronouns adjectives.

Relative pronouns[5]

A44 The relative pronouns are—

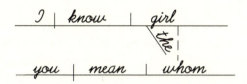

	Singular or plural		
Nominative	who	that	which
Possessive	whose[6]		
Objective	whom		which

A45 The relative pronouns take the place of nouns and join or relate a dependent (adjective) clause to an antecedent in another clause.

I know the girl *whom* you mean.

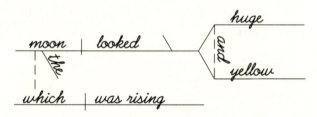

The moon, *which* was rising, looked huge and yellow.

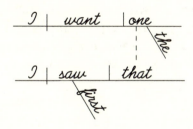

I want the one *that* I saw first.

---

[5] Relative pronouns are sometimes used as indefinites: "*Whom* I marry is my business."

[6] *Whose* is often used as the possessive of *that* and *which* : "I was blinded by the sun, *whose* light was intense."

A46 In general, use relative *who* and *that*[7] when the antecedent is a person or a personification, and *which* and *that* when the antecedent is not a person.[8]

> That *boy whom* I considered so worthless turned out to be the most reliable back on the team.
> That *boy that* I considered so worthless turned out to be the most reliable back on the team.
> The *wheel, which* fell off, rolled into the canal and sank.
> The *wheel that* fell off rolled into the canal and sank.

A47 Relative *which* is often preferred to *who* when the antecedent is a collective noun naming a group of persons as a group and not as individuals.

> The committee, *which* met regularly, deserved its pay.
> I consulted the family, *which* didn't like the idea at all.
> The crowd, *which* had been quiet, broke into a roar.
> The audience, *which* was larger than expected, filled the hall.

A48 Where the antecedent nouns are both persons and things, use relative *that* when you can; use *which* when you cannot use *that*, or reword the sentence.

> Where are the people and the money *that* will save our school?
>
> Judy Kerr and her dogs, of *which* I have spoken so often, have gone to Hollywood.
>
> Judy Kerr, of *whom* I have spoken so often, has gone to Hollywood with her dogs.

A49 The relative pronouns have the same form for all persons and numbers. (In other words, *who, that,* and *which* have only one form for first, second, and third person and for singular and plural number.)

---

[7] There is a tendency to use *that* only when the antecedent is not a person.

[8] In restrictive clauses, *that* is preferred to *which.*

A50 A relative pronoun refers to an antecedent in another clause. This fact makes a relative pronoun and its adjective clause easy to distinguish from (a) an interrogative or indefinite pronoun or adjective and its noun clause, (b) the demonstrative-pronoun and demonstrative-adjective *that*, and (c) the conjunction *that*.

I know the *girl whom* you refer to.	*Whom* is a relative pronoun because it has an antecedent, *girl*, in the independent clause of the sentence.
Tell me, *whom* do you mean?	*Whom* does not have an antecedent in the independent clause of the sentence. It is, therefore, an interrogative pronoun.
I know *whom* you mean.	*Whom* does not have an antecedent in the sentence. It is, therefore, an indefinite pronoun.
I know *what* man you mean.	*What* does not have an antecedent in the sentence. It is an indefinite adjective.
Here are the *blueprints that* you were looking for.	*That* is a relative pronoun because it has an antecedent, *blueprints*, in the independent clause of the sentence.
I was looking for the blueprints when I found *that* on the floor.	*That* has no antecedent in the independent clause. *That* is a demonstrative pronoun.
I was looking for something else when I found *that* blueprint on the floor.	*That* has no antecedent in the independent clause. *That* is a demonstrative adjective.
I knew *that* you were looking for the blueprints.	*That* has no antecedent in the independent clause of the sentence. This time, however, it is a conjunction.

A
B

Interrogative pronouns

A51   The interrogative pronouns are—

	Singular or plural		
Nominative	who	which	what
Possessive	whose	whose	
Objective	whom	which	what

A52   The interrogative pronouns are so called because they ask questions.

Whom do you want?
No one asked me, *What* did I want?
No one asked me *what* I wanted.
Who wrote *Moby Dick?*
Whose is that beautiful dog?
Which is the one you like?

A53   Use interrogative *who* in any kind of question when the antecedent is a person. Use interrogative *what* when the antecedent is not a person.

Whom do you want?
Whose is this pastrami sandwich?

What are you carrying?
What do you think of these?

A54   You may use interrogative pronoun *which* whether or not the antecedent is a person, but only in questions involving a choice.[9]

Which did you choose (Myron or Clark)?
Which did you choose (the trip to Miami or the scholarship)?

In ascending order of good English:

Which is the better quarterback?
Which of the two is the better quarterback?
Who is the better quarterback?

---

[9] Many good writers will not use the interrogative pronoun *which* when the antecedent is a person, unless the pronoun is followed by an *of* phrase. See model sentences in A55.

A55   The interrogative pronouns are all third person.

> *Who* of us *is* brave enough to take the man's dare?
> *Who* of us *are* brave enough to take *their* places?
> *Which* of us *are* going?
> *Whose are* these?

Indefinite pronouns[10]

A56   Some common indefinite pronouns are—

Singular		Plural	Singular or plural
another	one	both	all
anybody	other	few	any
anything	somebody	many	more
each	someone	others	none
either	something	several	some
everybody	what		
everyone	whatever		
everything	whatsoever		
little	which		
much	whichever		
neither	whoever		
nobody	whomever		
nothing	whosoever		

A57   The indefinite pronouns are so called because they often take the place of antecedents that are not named and that cannot be pinned down to any particular persons, places or things.

> *Anybody* coming through the door would trip.
> *One* of these has onions on it.
> I found *nobody* with *whom* to play cricket.
> *Whatsoever* you do, do it from the heart.
> In this business *anything* can happen.
> I want *whatever* you want.

---

[10] Relative pronouns are sometimes used as indefinites: "*Whom* I marry is my business."

A58 *All, any, more, none,* and *some* are singular pronouns if they indicate how much; they are plural if they indicate how many.[11]

All of the cake *was* burned.
All of the cakes *were* burned.

Was any of the cake burned?
Were any of the cakes burned?

Some of the cake *was* burned.
Some of the cakes *were* burned.

We looked for crepe paper, but there *is none.*
None of the people you expected *have* come.

A59 If the antecedent is exclusively masculine, treat the indefinite pronoun as masculine; if the antecedent is exclusively feminine, treat the indefinite pronoun as feminine.

Everybody at the stag party made his contribution to the welfare fund.	Exclusively masculine.
Has *anybody* lost her purse?	Exclusively feminine.

A60 In formal writing and speaking, when the antecedent is both masculine and feminine, you may treat the indefinite as masculine. Most writers today, however, use an inclusive gender form in such cases when this can be done *without awkwardness and without loss of meaning.*

Everyone has *his* own share of joys and sorrows.
All people have *their* share of joys and sorrows.

---

[11] *None* can indicate how many and yet be singular if there is good reason for stressing the notion of "not a single one." For example, "I went to the dog pound today and looked at every dog there, but *none* of them *was* mine." The same is true of *any* when there is reason to stress the notion of "a single one": "*Any* at all—the red, the maroon, or the vermilion—*is* good enough." See also C16.

A majority of these gender-problem sentences can either be rephrased into the plural or reworded in such a way in the singular that the problem is eliminated. See C239.

A61 Singular indefinites are all third person. Plural indefinites get their person (also number and gender) from their antecedents (usually found in a following prepositional phrase).

Each of you has a funny look on *his* face.
All of you have funny looks on *your* faces.
All of us have funny looks on *our* faces.

Reciprocal pronouns

A62 The reciprocal pronouns are *each other* and *one another.* They are called reciprocal because they are used in pairs to show an interaction.

The twins helped *each other.*
Each helped the *other.*

The soldiers slaughtered *one another* mercilessly.
One slaughtered *another.*

A63 Use *each other* to refer to only two; *one another* to refer to more than two.

The verb

A64 A verb is a word that expresses the actuality of its subject. Either it shows the subject as acting or as being acted upon; or it shows the subject as possessing an attribute, or character, or a relation; or it shows the subject as having actuality.

Tim *ran* forward and *was shot.*
You *have* good looks and good manners; you *have* good clothes.
God *exists.*

Conjugation of verbs

A65   Model conjugation of the verb *praise*:

ACTIVE VOICE
INDICATIVE MOOD

	Regular form	*Progressive form*	*Emphatic form*
Present	I praise	I am ⎤	I do ⎤
	you praise	you are	you do
	he praises	he is	he does
		⎬ praising	⎬ praise
	we praise	we are	we do
	you praise	you are	you do
	they praise	they are ⎦	they do ⎦
Past	I ⎤	I was ⎤	I did ⎤
	you	you were	you did
	he	he was	he did
	⎬ praised	⎬ praising	⎬ praise
	we	we were	we did
	you	you were	you did
	they ⎦	they were ⎦	they did ⎦
Future	I ⎤	I ⎤	
	you	you	
	he ⎱ shall *or*	he ⎱ shall *or* will	
	⎬ will praise	⎬ be praising	
	we	we	
	you	you	
	they ⎦	they ⎦	
Present perfect	I have ⎤	I have ⎤	
	you have	you have	
	he has	he has	
	⎬ praised	⎬ been praising	
	we have	we have	
	you have	you have	
	they have ⎦	they have ⎦	

(The progressive form is used to denote continuing action; see C41. See also C44. The emphatic form is used for emphasis and as a substitute for regular forms when those would be awkward; see C49-52.)

	Regular form	Progressive form
Past perfect	I you he we you they } had praised	I you he we you they } had been praising
Future perfect	I you he we you they } shall *or* will have praised	I you he we you they } shall *or* will have been praising

SUBJUNCTIVE MOOD[12]

	Regular form	Progressive form	Emphatic form
Present	I you he we you they } praise	I you he we you they } be praising	I you he we you they } do praise
Past	I you he we you they } praised	I you he we you they } were praising	I you he we you they } did praise

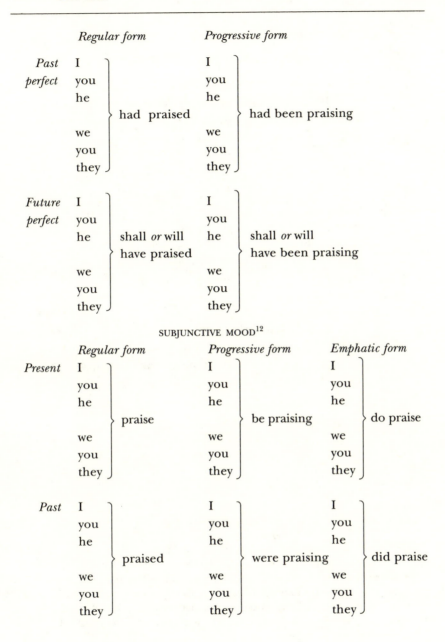

---

[12] Some word like *although, if, in order that, lest, that, though, till,* or *unless* is regularly used with the subjunctive mood. See C108-15.

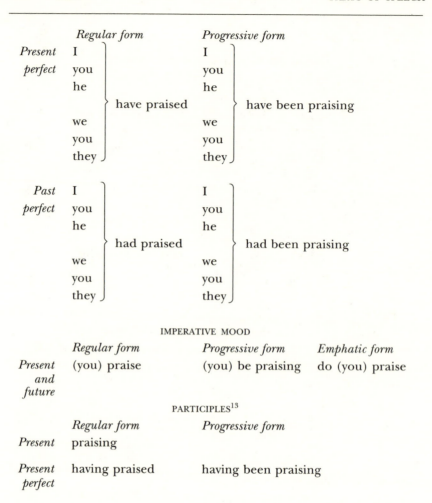

	Regular form	*Progressive form*
Present perfect	I you he we you they } have praised	I you he we you they } have been praising
Past perfect	I you he we you they } had praised	I you he we you they } had been praising

IMPERATIVE MOOD

	Regular form	*Progressive form*	*Emphatic form*
Present and future	(you) praise	(you) be praising	do (you) praise

PARTICIPLES[13]

	Regular form	*Progressive form*
Present	praising	
Present perfect	having praised	having been praising

---

[13] Some grammars maintain that there is an active past participle, as, for instance, *returned* in the following sentence, "Recently returned from Denver, Mr. Alton had some interesting things to say about the Western dispute over water rights. WRITING HANDBOOK takes the traditional view that such a participle is the present perfect, with *having* implied but not expressed in the sentence.

The participles are verbals, half adjective and half verb. They are used in conjugating verbs, however, primarily in their verb sense, which stresses actuality, rather than in their adjective sense, which stresses modification—changing the meaning—of nouns.

INFINITIVES

	Regular form	*Progressive form*
Present	(to) praise	(to) be praising
Present perfect	(to) have praised	(to) have been praising

GERUNDS

| *Present* | praising | |
| *Present perfect* | having praised | having been praising |

PASSIVE VOICE

INDICATIVE MOOD

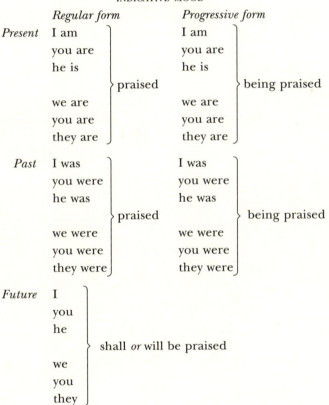

	Regular form	*Progressive form*
Present	I am you are he is we are you are they are } praised	I am you are he is we are you are they are } being praised
Past	I was you were he was we were you were they were } praised	I was you were he was we were you were they were } being praised
Future	I you he we you they } shall *or* will be praised	

Regular form

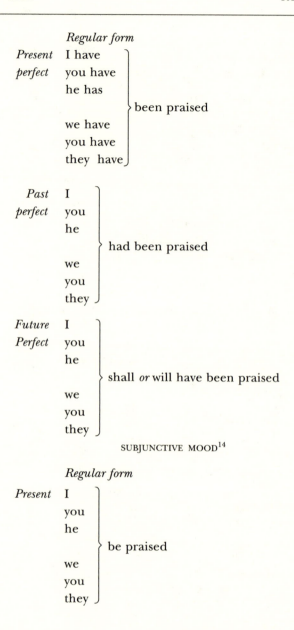

Present perfect	I have you have he has we have you have they have } been praised
Past perfect	I you he we you they } had been praised
Future Perfect	I you he we you they } shall *or* will have been praised

SUBJUNCTIVE MOOD[14]

Regular form

Present	I you he we you they } be praised

[14] Some word like *although, if, in order that, lest, that, though, till,* or *unless* is regularly used with the subjunctive mood. See C108-15.

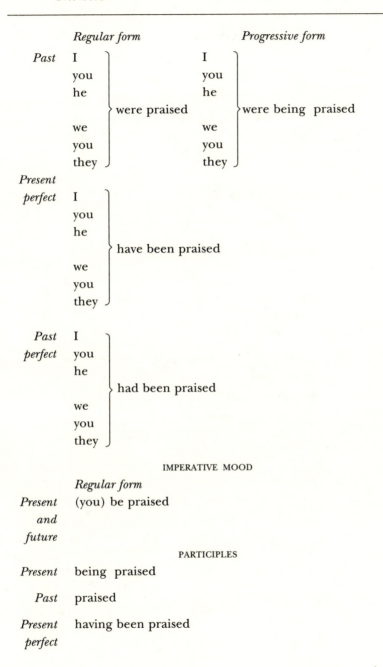

	Regular form	Progressive form
Past	I you he we you they } were praised	I you he we you they } were being praised
Present perfect	I you he we you they } have been praised	
Past perfect	I you he we you they } had been praised	

IMPERATIVE MOOD

Regular form

Present and future   (you) be praised

PARTICIPLES

Present   being praised

Past   praised

Present perfect   having been praised

INFINITIVES

Present   (to) be praised

Present   (to) have been praised
perfect

GERUNDS

Present   being praised

Present   having been praised
perfect

A66   Conjugation of the verb *be:*

INDICATIVE MOOD

Present	I am	*Past*	I was
	you are		you were
	he is		he was
	we are		we were
	you are		you were
	they are		they were
Future	I will be	*Present*	I have been
	you will be	*perfect*	you have been
	he will be		he has been
	we will be		we have been
	you will be		you have been
	they will be		they have been

Past	I	*Future*	I will have been
perfect	you	*perfect*	you will have been
	he		he will have been
	$\left. \begin{array}{c} \\ \\ \\ \end{array} \right\}$ had been		
	we		we will have been
	you		you will have been
	they		they will have been

SUBJUNCTIVE MOOD[15]

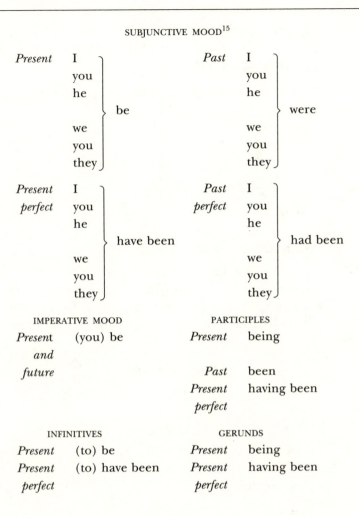

Present	I you he we you they	be	*Past*	I you he we you they	were
Present perfect	I you he we you they	have been	*Past perfect*	I you he we you they	had been

IMPERATIVE MOOD		PARTICIPLES	
Present and future	(you) be	*Present*	being
		Past	been
		Present perfect	having been

INFINITIVES		GERUNDS	
Present	(to) be	*Present*	being
Present perfect	(to) have been	*Present perfect*	having been

---

[15] Some word like *although, if, in order that, least, that, though, till,* or *unless* is regularly used with the subjunctive mood. See C108-15.

A67 A progressive form of the verb *be* (usually followed by a predicate adjective) exists, but as a general rule only in the following moods and tenses:

Present indicative		Past indicative		Past subjunctive	
I am		I was		I	
you are		you were		you	
he is		he was		he	
	being		being		were being
we are		we were		we	
you are		you were		you	
they are		they were		they	

The principal parts of verbs

A68 The principal parts of a verb are those forms from which all the voices, moods, and tenses of the verb can be formed. They are the present infinitive; the past indicative, first person singular; and the past participle.

Present infinitive	Past indicative first person singular	Past participle
be	was	been
praise	praised	praised
begin	began	begun

A69 The greater number of verbs regularly form their past indicative and past participle by adding *d, ed,* or *t* to the present infinitive.

Present	Past	Past participle
praise	praised	praised
guide	guided	guided
rip	ripped	ripped
bless	blessed	blessed
bend	bent	bent
kneel	kneeled *or* knelt	kneeled *or* knelt

A70 The principal parts of the following verbs sometimes cause difficulty.

	Present	Past	Past participle
1	arise	arose	arisen
2	attack	attacked	attacked
3	awake	awaked *or* awoke	awaked *or* awoke(n)
4	awaken	awakened	awakened
5	be	was	been
6	bear[16]	bore	borne *or* born[17]
7	beat	beat	beat *or* beaten
8	become	became	become
9	begin	began	begun
10	bend	bent	bent[18]
11	beseech	besought	besought
12	bid	bade *or* bid[19]	bidden *or* bid[19]
13	bind	bound	bound
14	bite	bit	bitten *or* bit
15	bleed	bled	bled
16	blow	blew	blown
17	break	broke	broken
18	bring	brought	brought
19	broadcast	broadcast *or* broadcasted[20]	broadcast *or* broadcasted[20]
20	build	built	built
21	burn	burned *or* burnt	burned *or* burnt
22	burst	burst	burst
23	buy	bought	bought

[16] Carry, suffer, tolerate, give birth to.

[17] When applied to pregnancy or birth, *borne* can be used as part of verbs in the passive only when they are followed by *by*, expressed or implied. *Born* means only brought into life, is always passive, and is never followed by *by*.

[18] The archaic *bended* is used in expressions like "on bended knee."

[19] Use *bid, bade, bidden* only in some sense of command or order; use *bid, bid, bid* in all senses—command, offer a price for something, name a number and a suit in cardplaying.

[20] *Broadcast* is preferred to *broadcasted* in referring to television and radio. Use only *broadcast* in all other senses.

	Present	*Past*	*Past participle*
24	carry	carried	carried
25	catch	caught	caught
26	choose	chose	chosen
27	climb	climbed	climbed
28	cling	clung	clung
29	come	came	come
30	deal	dealt	dealt
31	dig	dug	dug
32	dive	dived *or* dove	dived
33	do	did	done
34	drag	dragged	dragged
35	draw	drew	drawn
36	drink	drank	drunk
37	drive	drove	driven
38	drown	drowned	drowned
39	eat	ate	eaten
40	fall	fell	fallen
41	feed	fed	fed
42	fight	fought	fought
43	find	found	found
44	flee	fled	fled
45	fling	flung	flung
46	flow	flowed	flowed
47	fly	flew	flown
48	forbid	forbade *or* forbad	forbidden
49	forget	forgot	forgotten *or* forgot
50	forsake	forsook	forsaken
51	freeze	froze	frozen
52	get	got	got *or* gotten
53	give	gave	given
54	go	went	gone
55	grind	ground	ground
56	grow	grew	grown

	Present	Past	Past participle
57	hang	hanged[21]	hanged[21]
58	hang	hung	hung
59	hold	held	held
60	kill	killed	killed
61	kneel	knelt *or* kneeled	knelt *or* kneeled
62	know	knew	known
63	lay[22]	laid	laid
64	lead	led	led
65	lean	leaned *or* leant	leaned *or* leant
66	leap	leaped *or* leapt	leaped *or* leapt
67	learn	learned	learned
68	leave	left	left
69	lend	lent	lent
70	let	let	let
71	lie[23]	lay	lain
72	lie[24]	lied	lied
73	light	lighted *or* lit	lighted *or* lit
74	loose	loosed	loosed
75	lose	lost	lost
76	mean	meant	meant
77	meet	met	met
78	pay	paid	paid
79	prove	proved	proved *or* proven
80	raise[25]	raised	raised
81	read	read	read
82	ride	rode	ridden
83	ring	rang	rung
84	rise	rose	risen
85	run	ran	run

[21] *Hanged* is preferred to *hung* for putting to death by suspending.
[22] Transitive; to set or put something down.
[23] Intransitive; to recline.
[24] To tell an untruth.
[25] Do not confuse with *arise* or *rise*. (See list.)

	Present	Past	Past participle
86	say	said	said
87	seal	sealed	sealed
88	see	saw	seen
89	seek	sought	sought
90	sell	sold	sold
91	set[26]	set	set
92	sew[27]	sewed	sewed *or* sewn
93	shake	shook	shaken
94	shine	shone *or* shined[28]	shone *or* shined[28]
95	shoot	shot	shot
96	show	showed	shown *or* showed
97	shrink	shrank *or* shrunk	shrunk *or* shrunken
98	sing	sang	sung
99	sink	sank *or* sunk	sunk
100	sit	sat	sat
101	slay	slew	slain
102	sleep	slept	slept
103	slide	slid	slid
104	slink	slunk *or* slinked	slunk *or* slinked
105	smite	smote	smitten
106	sneak	sneaked *or* snuck	sneaked *or* snuck
107	sow[29]	sowed	sowed *or* sown
108	speak	spoke	spoken
109	split	split	split
110	spring	sprang *or* sprung	sprung
111	steal	stole	stolen
112	stick	stuck	stuck
113	sting	stung	stung
114	stink	stank *or* stunk	stunk
115	stride	strode	stridden
116	string	strung	strung
117	strive	strove *or* strived	striven *or* strived
118	swear	swore	sworn

---

[26] Do not confuse with *sit.* (See list.)
[27] As with thread.
[28] *Shined* means to make shiny or bright by polishing.
[29] As for example, seed or, figuratively, discord.

	Present	Past	Past participle
119	sweat	sweat *or* sweated	sweat *or* sweated
120	swim	swam	swum
121	swing	swung	swung
122	take	took	taken
123	teach	taught	taught
124	tear	tore	torn
125	tell	told	told
126	thrive	thrived *or* throve	thrived *or* thriven
127	throw	threw	thrown
128	tread	trod	trodden *or* trod
129	wake	waked *or* woke	waked
130	wear	wore	worn
131	weave	wove	woven
132	win	won	won
133	work	worked *or* wrought[30]	worked *or* wrought[30]
134	wring	wrung	wrung
135	write	wrote	written

A71 Do not use the past participle for the past indicative.

drank
He ~~drunk~~ the poison.

saw
I ~~seen~~ it myself.

came
The cold drinks ~~come~~ earlier than we expected.

swam
She ~~swum~~ across the river on her way to freedom.

---

[30] The past verb-form *wrought,* always transitive, is nowadays heard only in such an expression as "The hurricane wrought great havoc," which is a cliché, or "The chain was wrought in gold throughout." The ordinary, though not frequent, use of *wrought* is as an adjective: *wrought* iron which refers to iron which has been fashioned or worked into shape.

A72 Do not use the past indicative but the past participle with helping verbs.

run

The ink had ~~ran~~ down the length of the paper.

fallen

Snow had ~~fell~~ all night.

A73 Do not invent parts for verbs.

brought

Rodney ~~brung~~ the beer.

thrown

The test papers were ~~throwed~~ out during the summer.

broke

The blast ~~busted~~ the window.

Helping verbs[31]

A74 Helping verbs are verbs that are used together with other verbs to express changes of thought such as voice, mood, tense, and other shades of meaning. The principal helping verbs are—

be	must
can *and* could	ought
do	shall *and* will
have	should *and* would[32]
may *and* might	

---

[31] Helping verbs are treated in general in C36-39. Particular helping verbs are treated in C40-93.

[32] *Should* and *would* are sometimes called past-tense forms of *shall* and *will.* But they are very frequently used to express a great deal more than mere past time. The same is true of *might* and *could,* which are considered past-tense forms of *may* and *can.* See C70-93.

Verb person and number

A75 Verbs have person only to agree with their subjects; that is, in some moods and tenses verbs show a change of form to indicate that the subject noun or pronoun is the speaker (first person), the person or thing spoken to (second person), or the person or thing spoken of (third person).

I *am* humble [first person].
You *are* humble [second person].
She *is* humble [third person].

A76 Verbs have number only to agree with their subjects; that is, in certain moods and tenses verbs show a change of form to indicate that the subject noun or pronoun is singular or plural.

I am humble [singular].
We are humble [plural].

The adjective

A77 An adjective is a word that modifies a noun or some other substantive.[33]

That is *dangerous* fun.
Do you want to see something *strange?*
Who is *this wonderful* "she" you're talking about?

A78 An adjective can be distinguished from an adverb by the fact that an adjective always modifies a noun or a pronoun never a verb, an adjective, or an adverb.

[Adjective:] She is known for her *quick* rejoinders.
[Adverb:] Turn *quick* or be sorry.

---

[33] In sentences like "The *good* die young," words ordinarily used as adjectives are sometimes said to be nouns or pronouns. They may be considered as nouns or pronouns or as adjectives modifying an implied word like *people.*

Descriptive and limiting adjectives

A79   A descriptive adjective gives a word picture of (describes) the appearance or character or condition of the noun or pronoun it modifies.

> *green* apples   *young* thief   *sick* boy

A80   A limiting adjective modifies a noun or pronoun by narrowing down (limiting) or enlarging or multiplying the person or thing without describing it.

this street	*five* girls
his shirt	*triple* play
some games	*second* trial
any trick	*no* chance

A81   The limiting adjectives are these: possessive, demonstrative, relative, interrogative, indefinite, and numeral (cardinal and ordinal); the articles *a, an, the.*

A82   The possessive, demonstrative, relative, interrogative, indefinite, and numeral adjectives are called pronominal adjectives because they are part pronoun: they modify noun and pronouns or are used as substantives.

Possessive adjectives

A83   The possessive adjectives are in fact the personal pronouns in the possessive case (see A29).[34]

First person		*Second person*		*Third person*	
Singular	*Plural*	*Singular*	*Plural*	*Singular*	*Plural*
my	our	your (thy)	your	his	
				her	their
				its	

Here is *my* contribution.
Here is *our* contribution.
Your make-up is very heavy.
Its name is Shep.
Their name is well known.

---

[34] Any substantive in the possessive case functions as an adjective.

A84 The possessive adjectives (since they are pronouns) show person, number, and gender to agree with their antecedents as far as they can.

My plan is to train myself little by little to do without sleep altogether.

The first person is used because the antecedent is the speaker.

As for Grace and me, *our* plan is to see Europe while there is something left of it.

Our is plural because the compound antecedent, *Grace and me*, is plural.

This stone has *its* story to tell to the person who can read it.

Its is neuter gender because the antecedent, *stone*, is neuter gender.

A85 Do not use the apostrophe with the possessive adjectives.

his
He spends ~~his'~~ holidays playing golf.

its
It's a friendly little beast. What's ~~it's~~ name?

your
Is that ~~you're~~ blouse?

A86 Do not use *there* or *they're* for *their.*

their
Isn't that ~~there~~ swimming pool?

Their
~~They're~~ trouble is pride.

Demonstrative adjectives

A87 The demonstrative adjectives are—

Singular	*Plural*
this	these
that	those

The is considered a weak demonstrative adjective.

A88 The demonstrative adjectives specify the nouns (or, rarely, the pronouns) they modify, point them out, or call attention to them.

These people around us, I feel, are not friendly.
No, *those* permits; not the ones in your hand.

A89 *This* and *these* ordinarily refer to what is present, near, just referred to, or about to be referred to; demonstrative *that* and *those* ordinarily refer to what is more remote in time or place.

Look at *that* new Cadillac [referring to an automobile passing in the street].

And now *this* proverb may interest you: God's help is nearer than the door.

Centuries ago someone first said, "An argument cannot batter down a fact." *That* statement is still true.

A90 Do not use *them* as a demonstrative adjective.

those
Give me ~~them~~ pliers that you borrowed from me.

A91 Do not say *this here* and *that there*, *these here* and *those there*.

This ~~here~~ bed is not nearly as comfortable as that ~~there~~ one.

A92 Use *this* and *that* with singular nouns, *these* and *those* with plural nouns.

That   *makes*
~~Those~~ sort of people ~~make~~ me ill.

This   *is an*
~~These~~ kind of ~~words are~~ adjective~~s~~.

This   *burns*
~~These~~ make of automobile~~s burn~~ alcohol.

*T*hose *sorts* of candy—peppermints and chocolates—make me ill.
These kinds of words are called adjectives and pronouns.
These makes of automobile—Mercedes and Subaru—are foreign.

Relative adjectives

A93 The relative adjectives are—

which   whose

A94 Relative adjectives modify a noun (or, rarely, a pronoun) and also connect the dependent clause in which they stand with an antecedent in another clause.

The man *whose* window we broke just went into the police station.

We spent more than seven years in Juarez, in *which* city, by the way, we met Tracy.

A95 The relative adjective *which* seldom makes for pleasant reading. It is usually best to avoid it when you do not have to use it.

[Unpleasant:] I met a stranger in Miami, *which stranger* turned out to be a man with an indifferent attitude toward money.

[Better:] I met a stranger in Miami who turned out to be a man with an indifferent attitude toward money.

Interrogative adjectives

A96 The interrogative adjectives are—

whose   which   what

A97 The interrogative adjectives modify a noun (or, rarely, a pronoun) and also ask a question.

Whose picture is that?

Vickie asked *which* show we intended to see.

What sort of technician is your friend?

Indefinite adjectives

A98   Some common indefinite adjectives are—

Singular	Singular or plural	Plural
a, an[35]	all	both
another	any	few
each	no	many[36]
either	other	several
every	such	
neither	what	
	whatever	
	whatsoever	
	which	
	whichever	

A99   The indefinite adjectives modify nouns (or, rarely, pro-nouns) by limiting the nouns somewhat vaguely, saying indefinitely which one, how many, or how much.

Let me have *another* chance.

Any kind of yacht will do.

Both eyes are blue, of course.

No one has ever seen the *other* sisters.

Someone should have told the general *what* password was being used that night.

Slice it in any way *whatsoever*, it's still cold pheasant.

Whichever road you take, you will have a lonely journey.

Several people escaped through the tunnel.

Either kind will cost a small fortune.

Every attempt to dissuade them will meet with failure.

---

[35] *A, an* are indefinite adjectives; but they may also be called indefinite articles.

[36] In the expression *many a* ("Many a soldier has been a hero"), *many* may most conveniently be considered an adverb modifying *a.*

Numeral adjectives

A100 A numeral adjective limits a noun by stating its number.

A101 The cardinal numeral adjectives give the amount, tell how many. They are *one, two, three,* and so on.

I have *six* dollars.

A102 The ordinal numeral adjectives give the rank or place in an order or line-up.

Franklin, by carefully concealing his brilliance, managed to rank *twenty-ninth* in a class of thirty.

By the *sixth* day we were getting a little weary of pork chops.

If you sail from New York on the *fifth*, you should dock at Southampton on the *eleventh*.

Articles

A103 The articles are limiting adjectives. *The*, the weak demonstrative akin to *this* and *that*, might be called a definite adjective; *a* and *an*, indefinite.

A104 *A* is used before a word beginning with a consonant sound, *an* before a word beginning with a vowel sound.[37]

a drugstore	a one [sound of *w*]
a hawk	an apple
a historian	an hour [sound of *o* (*ou*)]
a union [sound of *y*]	

The adverb

A105 An adverb is a word that modifies a verb, an adjective, or another adverb.

Ferdinand growls *fiercely*.

---

[37] For further discussion of *a* and *an* before a word beginning with a consonant or vowel, see the Glossary.

A *very* high wall surrounded the place.

Jeanne was *not* entirely surprised.

A106 Whether a word is an adverb or not depends upon the work it does. Thus not every word that ends in *ly* is an adverb, nor must every adverb end in *ly*; *lovely* is an adjective, for instance, and *slow* may be an adverb. Again, a word ordinarily used as an adverb may sometimes be used as an adjective or a noun.

Here [adverb] is the woman who rules cosmetics.
Our property runs to *here* [noun].

A107 An adverb adds affirmation, negation, degree, manner, time, place, doubt, conclusion, and so on, to the word that it modifies.

[Affirmation:] yes, surely, certainly, indeed
[Negation:] no, not, hardly, scarcely, never
[Degree:] almost, barely, hardly, scarcely, completely, entirely,
    merely, only, partially, mainly, little, much, more, less, very
[Manner:] well, fast, slowly, lazily, busily, badly
[Time:] now, yesterday, immediately, always, recently, daily
[Place:] here, there, within, behind, everywhere
[Doubt:] maybe, perhaps, possibly, probably
[Conclusion:] consequently, therefore, hence, wherefore [but
    these words are usually conjunctive adverbs][38]

A108 Some adverbs have two forms, one like the adjective and the other in *ly*; for example, *slow, slowly; sharp, sharply; cheap, cheaply.* You may use the briefer form where it does not sound awkward, usually in imperative sentences.

Drive *slow*.
Look *sharp*!
Slowly the marquis mounted the guillotine.
Scrooge looked *sharply* at Marley's ghost.

---

[38] See A120.

A109 An adverbial noun is a noun in the objective case that modifies a verb, an adjective, or an adverb.

Rita went *home.*
The *Cyprus* sank ninety *feet* deep.

A110 A conjunctive adverb is an adverb that has a connective function (see A120).

The habit is a bad one; *consequently,* it must be broken.
Mullins is a lunatic; he is, *moreover,* a dangerous lunatic.

The preposition

A111 A preposition is a word that always has a noun or other substantive as its object and along with that object forms a single unit, which is used as a modifier or, infrequently, a substantive.

The vertical lines *in* newspapers are column rules.	*In* has an object, *newspapers,* and together with *newspapers* makes one adjective phrase modifying *lines.*
She left *with* me.	*With* has an object, *me,* and together with *me* makes one adverb phrase modifying *left.*
Over the fence is out.	*Over* and its object, *fence,* form a substantive (a noun phrase) that is the subject of *is.*

A112 Some of the more common prepositions are—

about	besides	notwithstanding	through
above	between	of	throughout
across	beyond	off	till
after	but [except]	on	to
against	by	onto	touching
along	concerning	out	toward
amid	considering	outside	towards
among	despite	over	under
around	down	past	underneath

at	during	pending	until
barring	except	regarding	unto
before	for	respecting	up
behind	in	round	upon
below	inside	save	with
beneath	into	saving	within
beside	like	since	without

A113 Some words are called participial prepositions because they are participles given a prepositional use but keeping the *-ing* form. Some common participial prepositions are *concerning, including, notwithstanding, pending.*

I should like to talk to you *concerning* your passport.

Everyone, *including* the captain, thought the ship had sailed.

We shall have to proceed *notwithstanding* your objections.

Why don't you write your memoirs, *pending* your release from the penitentiary?

To determine whether you are dealing with a participial preposition or a verbal, substitute *about* for *concerning*; *with* for *including*; *in spite of* for *notwithstanding*; and *until* for *pending*. If the sentence makes sense after the substitution, the chances are good that you have a participial preposition.

We shall have to proceed *notwithstanding* your objections.	Substitute *in spite of* for *notwithstanding* and the sentence makes sense. *Notwithstanding* is, consequently, a participial preposition here.
I am afraid, sir, that we shall have to proceed, your objections *notwithstanding*.	Substitute *in spite of.* The substitution makes nonsense of the end of the sentence. *Notwithstanding* is not a participial preposition here.

A114 A compound preposition is a preposition that is made up of more than one word; for example, *because of, on account of, along with, in spite of, in order to, with a view to.*[39]

The conjunction

A115 A conjunction is a word or group of words whose function is to connect words with words, phrases with phrases, clauses with clauses, sentences with sentences, and paragraphs with paragraphs.

Sheila *and* I are the pleasantest people!

It is impossible for her to talk to you *or* for me to give you the least information.

I hope that you have a good trip *and* that you enjoy your vacation.

The rest, I'm afraid, is up to you. *For* you will be alone, quite alone, with no one to turn to.

At length it was decided to strike for Kotuk afoot. ¶ *But* that decision turned out to be a mistake and a bad one.

A116 A coordinating conjunction connects words, phrases, and clauses that are of the same order or rank: two subject nouns, two predicate verbs, two adjective modifiers, two independent clauses, two dependent clauses, and so on.

A117 The common simple coordinating conjunctions[40] are—

and	but not	neither	or
but	for[41]	nor	

---

[39] It is equally common, however, to treat *on account, in spite, in order,* and *with a view* as preposition and object followed by another phrase.

[40] Some other conjunctions, such as *so* and *yet,* are more properly called semi-coordinators. Because of certain adverbial characteristics, still other conjunctions with strong coordinating functions (e.g., *furthermore, however*) are classified as conjunctive adverbs.

[41] When *for* introduces a dependent clause of cause or reason, it functions as a subordinating conjunction, not as a coordinating conjunction.

Raphael *and* Michael were originally Jewish names.	*And* connects the two subjects.
It should rain, *for* the wind has shifted to the south.	*For* connects the two independent clauses.
They do not toil, *neither* do they spin.	*Neither* connects the two independent clauses.
The explanation was not that Austin was cold *but* that he was bashful.	*But* connects the two dependent clauses.

A118 The correlative coordinating conjunctions are so called because they are used in split pairs.

The common correlatives are—

both . . . and	neither . . . nor
either . . . or	not only . . . but (also)
if [in the sense of *whether*]	whether . . . or
. . . or	

Both the children *and* the adults of the tribe are adept in the use of the blowgun.

Not only did we lose the supplies, *but* our guide came down with cholera just beyond Mamba.

Either Carmichael is telling the truth, *or* we have been cruelly unjust to Williams.

It is difficult to decide *whether* to abandon the prisoners *or* to send them back with an inadequate guard.

A119 Use *neither . . . nor,* not *neither . . . or.*

nor
Gilbert was neither strong ~~or~~ intelligent.

nor
Neither affirm ~~or~~ deny that you are a Wiffenpoof.

46

A120 Conjunctive adverbs[42]—and a few phrases that serve as conjunctive adverbs—are those that have only a connective function. They have no grammatical connection with the sentence; they are used independently (or absolutely) and connect independent clauses logically, in thought. The common ones are—

accordingly	further	nevertheless
again	furthermore	nonetheless
also	hence	otherwise
as a matter of fact	however	still
at any rate	in brief	then
besides	in fact	therefore
consequently	indeed	thereupon
finally	likewise	thus
first (second, etc.)	moreover	

The job had to be done; *consequently,* the Marines did it.

Whirligig beetles can skitter fast across the surface of the water; *furthermore,* they can dive.

Verano likes flattery; *indeed,* she thrives on it.
Verano likes flattery; she, *indeed,* thrives on it.

I haven't a dollar; *as a matter of fact,* I haven't any money at all.
I haven't a dollar; I haven't any money at all, *as a matter of fact.*

A121 Do not confuse conjunctive adverbs with subordinating conjunctions or relative adverbs. Conjunctive adverbs are never used in dependent clauses unless some subordinating connective is also expressed or implied.

Now you contradict yourself; *before,* you said that you could not possibly have overheard the accused.	Conjunctive adverb. Independent clause.

---

[42] Such words are called conjunctive *adverbs* because, in certain contexts, they may be moved—unlike coordinating and subordinating conjunctions, but like typical adverbs—to various positions in a clause. See the model sentences in A120.

The experiment took place on the day *before* Mr. Kenna and his son disappeared.	Relative adverb. Dependent adjective clause.
We had left *before* you and Aleck arrived.	Subordinating conjunction. Dependent adverb clause.

A122 Subordinating conjunctions are those that connect sentence parts that are not of the same order or rank. Most importantly, they connect noun and adverb clauses with independent clauses or subordinate them to other dependent clauses.

A123 The following subordinating conjunctions are commonly used to connect noun clauses with independent clauses or with other dependent clauses.

how	where
that	whether
when	why

I don't know *whether* Caroline has the popcorn concession.

Tell me *where* we can vote.

A strutting, apoplectic little man in a faded black suit asked *why* the doors had been locked and *how* he was supposed to get home in time for dinner.

A124 The following subordinating conjunctions are commonly used to connect adverb clauses with independent clauses or with other dependent clauses.

after	if	till
although	in order that	unless
as	least	until
as . . . as	now that	when
as if	provided (that)	whence
as though	since	whenever
because	so as (so . . . as)	where
before	so that (so . . . that)	wherever
even if	that	while
even though	though	whither

No one looked up *when* I tripped on the rug.

I feel a kinship with Achilles *because* he also had difficulty with a heel.

Everything was fine *until* the dog, excited by the jarring start of the train, barked once and attracted the attention of the conductor.

A125 Some subordinating conjunctions usually introducing adverb clauses are also used to introduce adjective clauses. These conjunctions are called relative adverbs.

after	since	whence	whither
before	when	where	why

This is the place *where* I always hide the money.

Holt told us the reason *why* the fan belt had broken.

This is the hour *when* witches brew.

The exclamatory word

A126 Exclamatory words are words or groups of words that express feeling, usually strong feeling, but have no grammatical connection with the rest of the sentence.

Oh, someone will take care of it.

Ah! There's the sniveling little ape.

A127 Some common exclamatory words are—

ah	for heaven's sake	oh	tut
aha	gee	oh my	ugh
boo	good grief	oops	well
bravo	ha	ouch	whew
darn	hey	shucks	wow
dear me	hurrah	tch	yippee

A128 *O,* without *h,* is nowadays capitalized and used almost exclusively with nouns in direct address in rather formal and poetic contexts.

O Diana, these are your forests!

The expletive

A129 The expletives are the words *it*[43] and *there* standing before the verb in place of the real subject, which usually follows the verb.

It is evident that your rifle needs cleaning.	*That your rifle needs cleaning* is the subject noun clause.
There will be a concert next Saturday.	*Concert* is the subject noun.
How many cats *there* are in Farrell's cabin!	*Cats* is the subject noun.
Was *it* very difficult to scrape the paint off?	*To scrape the paint off* is the subject noun phrase.

The gerund

A130 A gerund is a verbal that is part noun and part verb. It contains an *-ing* ending and is always used as a noun.

Smoking is not permitted here.

My husband has never really enjoyed *hiking*.

The fun of *waiting* is yours.

Their occupation is *mining*.

Jan specializes in careful *planning*.

A131 Since a gerund is part noun, it can do what any substantive does in a sentence: be a subject, an object, or a complement; and it can have an adjective modifier.

Smoking is not permitted here.	*Smoking* is the subject.
My husband has never really enjoyed *hiking*.	*Hiking* is the object.

---

[43] It is easy to distinguish expletive *it* from impersonal *it,* for the latter is the subject pronoun of its predicate verb; for example, "*It* snowed heavily."

Similar to *it* as an anticipatory subject is the *it* that serves as an anticipatory object: "I take *it* that you are happy?" "Bruno found *it* easy to agree."

The fun of *waiting* is yours.	*Waiting* is the object of *of*.
Their occupation is *mining*.	*Mining* is the predicate complement after *is*.
Jan specializes in careful *planning*.	*Planning* is modified by *careful*.

A132 Since a gerund is part verb, it has voice and tenses; it can take a direct or indirect object or a complement; and it can be modified by an adverb.

Having been praised once made Alex conceited.	*Having been praised* is passive voice, present perfect tense.
There is no question of her *having given* me help.	*Me* is the indirect object and *help* the direct object of *having given*.
His *being* a butler does not disturb Catherine.	*Butler* is a complement after *being*.
God *gave* Fritzl the equipment for *talking* loudly.	*Talking* is modified by the adverb *loudly*.

The participle

A133 A participle is a verbal that is part adjective and part verb. It is always used as an adjective.

A *roaring* wind swept through the valley.
Returning, she bolted the door.
The principal looks *pleased*.
The others, highly *dissatisfied* with the result, stalked off.

A134 Since a participle is part adjective, it can modify a noun or pronoun, be a complement, or take an adverb modifier.

A *roaring* wind swept through the valley.	*Roaring* modifies *wind*.
Returning, she bolted the door.	*Returning* modifies *she*.
The principal looks *pleased*.	*Pleased* is the predicate complement after *looks*.

The others, highly *dissatisfied* with the result, stalked off.	*Dissatisfied* is modified by the adverb *highly* and the adverb phrase *with the result.*

A135 Since a participle is part verb, it has voice and tenses; it can take a direct or indirect object or a complement; and it can be modified by an adverb.

Having buried his treasure and *feeling* tired, Rip curled up for a nap.	*Having buried* is present perfect tense and *feeling* present tense; both are active voice.
There sat Siegel *selling* Itzy a broken penknife.	*Selling* has *Itzy* as an indirect object and *penknife* as a direct object.
Fleetwood, *feeling* angry, stiffened and frowned.	*Feeling* has *angry* as a complement.
Rising slowly, the old man put out a hand for the paper.	*Rising* is modified by the adverb *slowly.*

A136 Occasionally it is difficult to know whether the participle is being used with adjective force or merely as part of the predicate verb. In such cases only the writer's intention or the context can decide.

Florence was surprised.

Florence | was surprised

Florence | was \ surprised

The infinitive

A137 An infinitive is a verbal that is used as a noun, or substantive, as an adjective, or as an adverb. (Sometimes *to*, the sign of the infinitive, is omitted, especially after verbs like *make, see,* and *hear.* See infinitive phrases, C385-86.)

A138 When used as a noun, an infinitive can do what any substantive does in a sentence: be a subject, an object, or a complement; and it can have a predicate adjective.

To lie avails you nothing.	*To lie* is the subject of the verb *avails.*

Karen wanted *to leave*.	*To leave* is the object of the verb *wanted*.
Our best plan now is *to hide*.	*To hide* is the complement after *is*.
To err is human.	*To err* has the predicate complement *human*.

A139 When used as an adjective, an infinitive can modify a noun or other substantive.

The will to *conquer* can be highly important.	*To conquer* modifies *will*.
To eat *to live* is what matters.	*To live* modifies the substantive *to eat*.

A140 When used as an adverb, an infinitive can modify a verb, an adjective, or another adverb.

We hurried *to be seated*.	*To be seated* modifies *hurried*.
Are you ready *to return?*	*To return* modifies *ready*.
Max did not wait long enough *to hear*.	*To hear* modifies *enough*.

A141 Since an infinitive is part verb, it has voice and tenses; it can have a subject (which is always in the objective case) and take a direct or indirect object or a complement; and it can be modified by an adverb.

It started *to rain*.	*To rain* is active voice, present tense.
We considered him *to be* almost negligible.	*To be* has the subject *him*.
If you want *to give* yourself a fright, look down.	*To give* has *yourself* as the indirect object and *fright* as the direct object.
Once again the bull began *to struggle* violently.	*To struggle* is modified by the adverb *violently*.

B

The sentence — use and structure

Definition

B1 A sentence is a judgment that is expressed in words and stands as an independent statement. It makes an affirmation or a denial, asks a question, or gives a command.

Lights were burning in the house.
We are not amused.
Did Plato learn nothing in Syracuse?
Stand right there.

B2 An elliptical sentence is a sentence from which words have been omitted that can be *easily and naturally* supplied by the reader or listener.

Meeting tonight at eight-fifteen.
A smart child!
Anybody home?
Happy birthday!

[In answer to a question:] Three o'clock.
[In answer to a question:] No.
O to be in England, now that April's there!

Why is *The Nigger of the Narcissus* one of the world's great sea stories? Because Conrad, the author, put into this novel all his love and understanding of ships, sailors, the winds, and the great sea.

The missing words in the elliptical sentence are *easily and naturally* supplied from the preceding sentence.

Sentence sense

B3 A half-sentence is not a complete judgment and cannot stand as an independent statement.[1]

You mean that you have not read the famous Father Brown detective stories? Father Brown, a jovial, keen-witted little priest, being one of the great fictional detectives, much beloved not only by readers but by writers of mysteries.

A nominative absolute poses as a complete sentence.

From boyhood Howard Pyle was captivated by the daredevil spirit of pirates. Being able, moreover, to express his dreams with the pen.

A participial phrase poses as a complete sentence.

Although he was born in the humblest surroundings and reared almost without schooling, Mark Twain lived to achieve world-wide fame. To be honored by generations of people, many of whom never noted his pessimism.

An infinitive phrase poses as a complete sentence.

Damon Runyon made himself a national reputation as a journalist. Before writing the now-famous stories of the bandits of Broadway and adding many a word to the American language.

A prepositional phrase poses as a complete sentence.

I found Mr. Canterbury at work in his place at the very

---

[1] The half-sentence is also known as the incomplete sentence, the sentence fragment, and the period-fault sentence.

end of Fordham Road. A peculiar establishment, uncluttered by anything but Mr. Canterbury, an oriental rug, and a telephone.

An appositive poses as a complete sentence.

Treason and loyalty, mystery and adventure, tragedy and comedy—all play their part in making *Ivanhoe* a romantic book. Which should be read by everyone.

An adjective clause poses as a complete sentence.

B4 A runover is a sentence that runs over into the next sentence, being stopped only by a comma or by no punctuation at all.[2]

He enjoyed reading *Captain Blood,* it is a book of adventure.

B5 Correct runovers by (a) putting a period and a capital between the sentences, (b) inserting a semicolon, if there is sufficient unity in the thought, (c) inserting a comma and a coordinating conjunction, or (d) subordinating the less important idea.

He enjoyed reading *Captain Blood.* It is a book of adventure.
He enjoyed reading *Captain Blood*; it is a book of adventure.
He enjoyed reading *Captain Blood*, for it is a book of adventure.
He enjoyed reading *Captain Blood*, which is a book of adventure.

Sentences according to use

B6 According to use, sentences are declarative, interrogative, imperative, and exclamatory.

B7 A declarative sentence makes a statement.

The noises began at midnight.

---

[2] If a runover (run-on sentence) is stopped inadequately by a comma, the sentence is called a comma-splice sentence; if a runover is not stopped by any punctuation, it is called a fused sentence.

Charles asked when the noises began.

"When did the noises begin?" asked Charles.

"The man is dangerous!" cried Evanston with what seemed to be genuine alarm; and, I must admit, I was inclined to agree.

"Go at once," said Emily, quietly but with unmistakable determination; so Charles went—at once.

B8 An interrogative sentence asks a direct question.[3]

When did the noises begin?

Now that I come to think of it, why would anyone wish to fish the snapper banks at a season when the snappers will not bite?

B9 An imperative sentence in general gives a command. The command may be an entreaty, a warning, a prohibition, and so on.

Stop.
Come.
Save me!
Please come!
Proceed at your own risk.
Thou shalt not kill.
You shall not pass.

B10 An exclamatory sentence expresses a sudden or strong emotion.

Mother!
Patriots, arise!
Must I see this!
Yes! Essex still rebels!

---

[3] A direct question is a question expressed in the words of the speaker; for example, "Where is the platypus?" An indirect question gives the sense of the speaker's question without quotation; for example, "She asked where the platypus was." An indirect question does not make an interrogative sentence, since it involves rather a statement about a question than the mere question itself.

Sentences according to structure

B11   According to structure, sentences are classified as simple, compound, complex, and compound-complex.

B12   A simple sentence is a sentence that has only one subject and one predicate.

Witch doctors howled.

Herman Melville published *Moby Dick*, his greatest and best-known novel, in 1851.

Starvation affects a person's mind as well as body.

It was a peculiar place of business, uncluttered by furniture, files, secretaries, or anything but Mr. Canterbury and a telephone.

B13   The subject of a simple sentence can be a noun or any other substantive except a clause.[4]

Frogs [noun] croak.
They [pronoun] croak.
To croak dismally [noun phrase] is natural to frogs.

B14   The subject of a simple sentence may be simple or compound. The predicate of a simple sentence may be simple or compound.[5]

Chieftains pranced.
Witch doctors and chieftains howled.
Witch doctors pranced and howled.
Witch doctors and chieftains pranced and howled.

B15   A compound sentence is a sentence made up of two or more independent clauses properly connected.[6]

The cougar looked down, and I shot it.	Independent clause: *The cougar looked down.* Independent clause: *and I shot it.*

---

[4] A substantive is a noun or any other word or group of words that is used as a noun.
[5] See C4 and C6.
[6] For independent and dependent clauses, see C391-92. For proper connection of the clauses of compound sentences, see D43-45.

A
B

| The cougar looked down; I shot it. | Independent clause: *The cougar looked down.* Independent clause: *I shot it.* |

B16 A complex sentence is a sentence made up of one independent clause and one or more dependent clauses.[7] (See B17.)

| When the cougar looked down, I shot it. | Independent clause: *I shot it.* Dependent clause: *when the cougar looked down.* |
| I shot the cougar as it looked down and before it was aware of the child. | Independent clause: *I shot the cougar.* First dependent clause: *as it looked down.* Second dependent clause: *and before it was aware of the child.* |

B17 The definition of a complex sentence in B16 is true in only a general sense, for a complex sentence with a noun clause as the subject or complement or object of the verb does not contain an independent clause at all. In such sentences there is no independent clause distinct from the dependent clause. (See C398 and C402.)

Where Terry is going concerns only him.	The noun clause, *where Terry is going*, is the subject of *concerns*; and *concerns only him*, the predicate, passes for the independent clause.
Candy is what I like.	The noun clause, *what I like*, is the predicate complement after *is*; and *candy is* must pass as the independent clause.
You get what you pay for.	The noun clause, *what you pay for*, is the object of *get*; and *you get* must pass for the independent clause.

---

[7] For independent and dependent clauses, see C391-95.

B18   A compound-complex sentence is a sentence that contains two or more independent clauses and one or more dependent clauses.

Magellan was killed in the Philippines; nevertheless, his companions, eager to prove that the world is round, continued their westward journey until their ships at length cast anchor off the coast of Spain.	Independent 1: *Magellan was killed in the Philippines.* Independent 2: *nevertheless, his companions, eager to prove . . . continued their westward journey.* Dependent 1: *that the world is round.* Dependent 2: *until their ships at length cast anchor off the coast of Spain.*

Syntax

Subjects and predicates

C1   The subject is the part of a clause or sentence that is talked about. The predicate is the part of a clause or sentence that talks about the subject.[1]

	Subject	Predicate
Kathy prays.	Kathy	prays.
Were you waiting for me?	You	were waiting for me?

---

[1] Many grammars call subject and predicate in this general sense *complete subject* and *complete predicate*. This book distinguishes between *subject* and *subject noun* or *substantive* and between *predicate* and *predicate verb*. In one-word subjects and predicates, of course, *subject* and *subject noun* or *substantive* will coincide, as will *predicate* and *predicate verb*.

	Subject	Predicate
The man in the bowler hat was leaning against the lamppost, waiting for me.	The man in the bowler hat waiting for me.	was leaning against the lamppost . . .
Go!	[You]	go!
There is something very strange about you tonight, Count Dracula.	Something very strange	is about you tonight, Count Dracula.
Squatting on the sandy ground, his eyes looking off beyond us to the hills, the wrinkled old Indian took the drum between his knees and began to beat a hypnotic rhythm.	Squatting on the sandy ground, his eyes looking off beyond us to the hills, the wrinkled old Indian	took the drum between his knees and began to beat a hypnotic rhythm.

C2 The subject noun or other substantive is the word in the subject that governs the predicate verb.

	Subject noun	Predicate
Kathy prays.	*Kathy*	prays.
Marcia sneered.	*Marcia*	sneered.
Were you waiting for me?	*you*	were waiting for me?
The man in the bowler hat was leaning against the lamppost, waiting for me.	*man*	was leaning against the lamppost . . .
Squatting on the sandy ground, his eyes looking off beyond us to the hills, the wrinkled old Indian took the drum between his knees.	*Indian*	took the drum between his knees.

61

C3 Do not insert immediately after a subject noun a subject pronoun meaning exactly the same thing.[2]

Jules ~~he~~ wants to be a chemical engineer.

Willa Cather and Edna Ferber ~~they~~ are American novelists.

C4 A compound subject is a subject that is made up of two or more subject nouns or other substantives. (See C6.)

Johnson and *Powers* disappeared.
He and *you* and *I* are the winners.
To play records and *to go to shows* are all Jack cares about.

C5 The predicate verb is the verb in the predicate that is governed by the subject noun(s) or other substantive(s).

	Subject noun	*Predicate verb*
Kathy prays.	Kathy	*prays*
Marcia sneered.	Marcia	*sneered*
Were you waiting for me?	you	*were waiting*
The man in the bowler hat was leaning against the lamppost, waiting for me.	man	*was leaning*
Squatting on the sandy ground, his eyes looking off beyond us to the hills, the wrinkled old Indian took the drum between his knees.	Indian	*took*

C6 A compound predicate is a predicate that is made up of two or more predicate verbs. Note that some sentences have a compound subject and a compound predicate.

Johnson bowed *and* disappeared.

---

[2] This does not affect those constructions in which a speaker is represented as mulling over names; for example, "Willa Cather and Edna Ferber —they were American novelists, weren't they?"

The ship *sank* at the bow, then *heeled* a little to port, and finally *plunged* beneath the surface.

John and Mary *sang* and *danced*.

Verb agreement in general

C7 Make a predicate verb agree with its subject noun(s) or other substantive(s) in person and number.[3]

John *sings* like an excited bullfrog.
This machine *crushes* rock.
Sandra and Julia *have* a new computer.
Everybody is to be inoculated, *say* the authorities.
An excellent athlete and a good student *is* Marilyn.

C8 Make the predicate verb agree with the real subject substantive after the expletive *there*.[4] (But see C34.)

There is only one glass.

There *is* others besides you. *are*

There are a lot of reasons for the conpany's failures. (See C16.)

C9 Make the predicate verb agree with the subject substantive and not with words in apposition.

I, your commanding officer, ~~orders~~ this retreat. *order*

The doubles team, Ogden and McCarthy, ~~have~~ not won a set. *has*

C10 Make the predicate verb agree with the subject substantive and not with words introduced by *with, along with, including, as well as, no less than, of,* and so on.

I, together with my dog, ~~has~~ hunted these woods for five years. *have*

---

[3] For the notion of person, see A21-23. For the notion of number, see A24-25.

[4] For sentences like "There *is* more than one way to solve a problem" and "There *are* more than two ways to solve a problem," see C18.

has

Joe, as well as I, ~~have~~ stayed up, getting the annual ready for the printer's deadline.

has

Bad health, along with many years, ~~have~~ weakened poor Featherstonhaugh.

has

The light on the new Raleigh bicycles ~~have~~ a generator.

C11 The number and person of a relative pronoun depend upon its antecedent. Make sure you have the right antecedent, according to sentence sense, before you make the predicate verb agree with a relative-pronoun subject.

Pasteur was one of those men who *are* not easily discouraged.

Pasteur was the only one of those men who *was* not easily discouraged.

The only one of his stories that *was* amusing was a tale of three men locked in an elevator.

One of the people who *were* present was Donna Gilbreth.

The number of members who *were* absent was truly deplorable.

I who *am* the leader will decide.

You who *are* irresponsible will simply have to follow.

C12 Always use a third-person singular predicate verb after *it*, whether expletive or pronoun.

It *is* fun swimming and sailing.
It *was* they; it *was* not I.
It *was* two hours before he returned.

C13 When a collective noun names a group acting as a unit, use a singular predicate verb with it.[5]

is
The committee ~~are~~ angry.

has
The jury ~~have~~ been out an hour and a half.

sings
The congregation ~~sing~~ badly.

C14 When a collective noun names a group acting as individuals, use a plural predicate verb with it.[6]

have
The jury ~~has~~ disagreed among themselves.

are
The crew ~~is~~ not yet all in their places.

were guests
The senior class ~~was guest~~ of the Stoneleighs.

C15 Use a singular predicate verb with the singular indefinite pronouns and adjectives.

was
Each of the thieves ~~were~~ caught.

---

[5] At times, deciding whether a collective noun names a group acting as a unit is difficult. Use a singular or plural verb depending on what you want to say.

[6] See the footnote above. Often, changing the sentence is better than using such awkward expressions as this: "The class are each sitting in a different seat." Say rather: "Each member of the class is sitting in a different seat."

is
Everyone ~~are~~ asked to be there.

Neither plan is worth anything.

sparkles
Each wave and ripple ~~sparkle~~.

C16 Use a plural predicate verb with expressions like *the rest, a part, half, two thirds, all, any, none, some, a lot,* and *a variety* when they indicate how many, and a singular predicate verb when they indicate how much.

Half of the exercises *were burned* by the janitor.
Half of the exercise *was burned* by the janitor.

The rest of the books *are* trash.
The rest of the book *is* trash.

Part of the horses *were shipped* to Miami.
Part of the horse *was shipped* to the glue factory.

A *lot* of opportunities *were* available.
A *lot* of time *is being spent* on this project.

A wide *variety* of phenomena *were* evident.
A wide *variety* of phenomena *was* evident.

C17 Use a plural predicate verb with *a number* (meaning several, quite a few), but a singular predicate verb with *the number*. (See also C16.)

have
A number of people ~~has~~ asked us for the recipe.

has
The number of people ~~have~~ increased greatly.

C18 If a noun or pronoun following *more than* is singular, use a singular predicate verb. If it is plural, use a singular predicate verb if it indicates how much, a plural predicate verb if it indicates how many.

There *is* more than one way to solve a problem.

There *are* more than two ways to solve a problem.
There *is* more than two gallons in the tank.
There *is* more than ten dollars in the billfold.
There *are* more than ten one-dollar bills on the counter.

C19 Use a plural predicate verb when adjectives connected by *and* so modify a subject noun or other substantive as to show that it means more than one thing.

are
Both good and bad butter ~~is~~ sold here.

have
The chocolate and the pound cake ~~has~~ been won.

C20 Use a singular predicate verb with words that are plural in form but singular in meaning.[7]

was
The gallows ~~were~~ erected beside the road.

is
Measles ~~are~~ catching.

was
The news ~~were~~ good.

was
Physics ~~were~~ my easiest subject.

C21 Ordinarily use a singular predicate verb with the names of sciences like *mathematics, physics,* and *economics.*

Mathematics *is* my downfall.
Physics *is* the study of matter and motion.
Economics *is required* in third year.

C22 Ordinarily use a plural predicate verb with the names of practical affairs like *politics* and *athletics.* (But see C23.)

Athletics *are* much *fostered* at North High.
Politics *play* havoc with a policy based on principle.

---

[7] See C21-23.

Gymnastics *have been* highly *developed* by some nations.
Foreign affairs *are* much *debated* in the Senate.

C23 In sentences where the notion of one thing is emphasized, use a singular predicate verb even with words like
politics and *athletics*.

Politics *has become* a complicated study.
Athletics *wastes* too much of a student's time.
Foreign affairs *offers* real opportunity for a fascinating career.

C24 Use a singular predicate verb with plural nouns that are
felt to express a single unit.[8]

isn't
Four gallons ~~aren't~~ much gas.

is
Ten miles ~~are~~ too far on worn-out tires.

was
There ~~were~~ five hundred dollars in his pocket.

C25 Use a singular predicate verb with a word that is discussed as a word.

They is a pronoun.
Lilacs has a very pleasant sound.

C26 Use a singular predicate verb with plural titles and plural
proper names used to designate one person or one
thing.

has
The United States ~~have~~ great responsibilities.

is
The Fishermen ~~are~~ an interesting book.

---

[8] Occasionally—but not always—the predicate complement will indicate that the plural subject noun is expressing a single unit. In some
sentences, however, the singular or plural predicate verb is a matter of the
writer's choice; for example, "Clothes absorb [*or* absorbs] too much of a
girl's thinking and planning."

has

The *Times* ~~have~~ a full sports coverage.

has

Shelley, Shark, and Shumack [one business firm] ~~have~~ gone into bankruptcy.

Twin Oaks *is* a ramshackle house at the bend of the river.

Verb agreement with compound subjects

C27   Use a plural predicate verb with a compound subject whenever *and* is used or implied between the words.[9]

have

Johnson and Powers ~~has~~ disappeared.

were

The water polo and the diving contest ~~was~~ called off.

Three sandwiches and a quart of milk *are* waiting for you.
Knapp, Wallace, Berger *are* the leaders.
Cal and Haas, Wills and Smith *are* our tennis teams.

C28   When a compound subject has both affirmative and negative parts, make the predicate verb agree in person and in number with the affirmative rather than with the negative part. (But see C29.)

am

I, not you, ~~are~~ deciding.

are

You, not I, ~~am~~ deciding.

are

Terry and Bill, hardly Ken, ~~is~~ to be relied on.

C29   When awkwardness results from carrying out C28, rewrite the sentence.

I am deciding, not you.

---

[9] See C35 for an exception.

You are deciding, not I.

Terry and Bill are to be relied on. Ken seems less trustworthy.

C30 When the parts of a compound subject are of different person or number and are connected by *or, either . . . or, not only . . . but also, neither . . . nor,* and other disjunctives,[10] make the predicate verb agree in person and number with the nearer part. (But see C31.)

Either they or I *am* to go.

Not only Jean but also Jane and Paul *are* invited.

Not only you but also Jim *was* mistaken.

Neither the mother nor the daughters *were* invited.

Neither the daughters nor the mother *was* invited.

C31 When awkwardness arises from carrying out C30, re-write the sentence.

If they don't go, then I must.

Jean, Jane, and Paul are invited.

You were not the only one who was mistaken; Jim was too.

The mother was not invited; but neither were the daughters.

The daughters were not invited; but neither was the mother.

C32 When the parts of a compound subject represent one person or thing, or are felt to make up one collective idea, use a singular predicate verb.

plays

My friend and neighbor, Kittredge, ~~play~~ the flute.

was

A coach and four ~~were~~ rattling down the King's Road.

is

The hop, skip, and jump ~~are~~ no longer a common event at track meets.

---

[10] Disjunctives are coordinating conjunctions that separate, or offer a choice between, the words that they connect. Grammatically, they connect; in thought, they separate. They connect because they show that words go together as subject nouns or objects and so on; but they also separate, offer a choice between, or break into units, the meanings of those same words.

Rioting and violence often leads [*or* lead] to tyranny.

He was of the old school, and maintained that a blackboard and a switch was [*or* were] all that any teacher needed to turn dullards into scholars.

[Singular verb would be incorrect:] A destroyer and a cruiser were standing by.

C33 When each of the singular parts of a compound subject is considered separately, make the predicate verb agree with the nearest. (To decide whether or not you have such a case, mentally insert *or* before the last part. If *or* makes sense in the sentence, each part of the subject is being considered separately. If it does not, then they are being taken together.)

A shred of a tune, a face vaguely familiar, the *odor* of a hallway, *unleashes* a flood of memory to sicken or delight us.

A shred of a tune, a face vaguely familiar, *or* the odor of a hallway *unleashes* a flood of memory to sicken or delight us.	*Or* makes good sense here.
A pitcher, a catcher, a batter, *or* a fielder-baseman *is* all one needs to play a simple form of baseball.	*Or* makes nonsense of this sentence. Change *is* to *are*.

C34 When several words separate the subject nouns or pronouns of a compound subject, the predicate verb after expletive *there* may agree with the nearer subject noun or pronoun.

There *was* a plain, unpainted wooden *table* in a corner of the kitchen under the window and, near the stove, two ancient and scabrous wicker *chairs* of doubtful comfort and uncertain strength.	A good many words intervene between *table* and *chairs*.

There *is* only modest *talent* and even less *desire* to produce this show.

There *are* a *hammer, pliers,* and *screw driver* in that drawer.

C35 When a whole compound subject is modified by *each, every, many a, such a, and no,* use a singular predicate verb.[11]

Each man, woman, and child *has* received some sort of souvenir to take home.

Each back, *each* lineman, and *each* coach *was* quizzed before the ruling was changed.

Every officer and member *was* there to answer roll call.

Many a man and woman *is* allergic to ragweed.

Such an idea and attitude *is* unworthy of you.

No hat and *no* purse *was* to be found.

Verb use

Helping verbs in general

C36 Helping verbs are verbs that are used together with other verbs to express changes of thought such as voice, mood, tense, and other shades of meaning. The principal helping verbs are —

be	must
can *and* could	ought
do	shall *and* will
have	should *and* would[12]
may *and* might	

---

[11] When *each* follows a plural subject but precedes the verb, the verb is plural; for example, "They each *have* their reasons." When *each* follows the verb, subsequent elements are usually singular; for example, "Mary, Jane, and Alice have scholarships each to *her* favorite university."

[12] *Should* and *would* are sometimes called past-tense forms of *shall* and *will.* But they are used to express a great deal more than mere past time. The same is true of *might* and *could,* called past-tense forms of *may* and *can.*

C37 Helping verbs together with the verb they help, form one predicate verb—even when the helpers are separated from the rest of the verb. (The one predicate verb in each of the following examples is italicized.)

Poison *was mentioned.*
The three tethered horses *must have been frightened.*
Did he *call* ?
Are you *coming* ?
Isn't all this mournful talk *depressing* you?
Copperheads *have* often *been seen* in this swamp.
May I—excuse this interruption—*make* a remark?
This code *has* twice *been* completely *lost.*
Should not Del *have been* more quickly *alerted* ?

C38 Do not separate parts of the predicate verb when awkwardness results.

[Awkward:] They referred to the speech which the president *had* late this past summer *delivered.*

[Better:] They referred to the speech which the president *had delivered* late this past summer.

C39 Do not use the past indicative active but the past participle with helping verbs.

run
The ink had ~~ran~~ down the length of the paper.

fallen
Snow had ~~fell~~ all night.

I had never before *swum* so far.

Helping verb **be**

C40 Helping verb *be* is used to make up its own progressive form and the progressive form of other verbs.

The Gutowskis *will* be here soon.
The Gutowskis *were* apologizing for being late.

C41   The progressive form of a verb presents the action not merely as something that happens but as something that continues to happen or that progresses.

[Regular form:] She *sews.*
[Progressive form:] She *is sewing.*

C42   The progressive form of the present tense of verbs is commonly used as a substitute for the future tense.

[Future:] I *will return* tomorrow.
[Progressive present:] I *am returning* tomorrow.

C43   The progressive present of the verb *go* is commonly used as a substitute for the future tense.

[Future:] You *will regret* this.
[Progressive present of go:] You *are going* to regret this.

[Future:] I *will go.*
[Progressive present of *go:*] I *am going* to go.

C44   The progressive form of the present tense active is used to avoid awkwardness or archaic formality in asking direct questions.

[Regular form, to be avoided:] *Swim* you with us today?
[Progressive form:] *Are* you *swimming* with us today?

C45   The progressive form of the past tense active of *go* is sometimes used to express supposition, expectation, intention, or purpose.

Hilton *was going* with us, but at the last moment he found that he could not go.

I thought Reinke *was going* to scream.

C46   Helping verb *be* is used to form the passive voice.[13]

The tree *was* hit by lightning.
You *will be* sued for gross negligence.

---

[13] See A65 and C94.

C47 Helping verb *be,* followed by an infinitive with *to,* is used to express futurity, obligation, expectation, supposition, or an indirect command.

[Futurity:] I *am to be* queen of the festival.

[Obligation:] We *are to obey* God in all things.

[Expectation:] A department store *is to be built* on the site of the finest old theater that this section of the country possessed.

[Supposition:] You are basing your investment on the guess that there *is to be* a new market for boomerangs.

[Indirect command:] You *are* all *to be* up and dressed by four-thirty tomorrow morning.

Helping Verb *do*

C48 Helping verb *do* is used to make up its own emphatic form and the emphatic form of other verbs.

C49 The emphatic form of a verb lends insistence or emphasis to what the verb asserts.[14]

[Regular form:] I *finished* my homework.
[Emphatic form:] I *did finish* my homework.

C50 Helping verb *do* is used with the present and past active to avoid awkwardness or archaic formality when *not* is used with regular forms of *do.*

[Regular form, to be avoided:] I *did* not what I was told.

[With helping verb:] I *did* not *do* what I was told.

[Regular form, to be avoided:] Did she complain about the extra charge? No, she *complained* not.

[With helping verb:] Did she complain about the extra charge? No, she *did*n't.

---

[14] In older verse and in some modern verse, helping verb *do* is often used simply for rhythm or sound, with no note of emphasis.

C51   Helping verb *do* is used with the present and past active to avoid awkwardness or archaic formality when asking direct questions.

[Regular form, to be avoided:] *Play* you the saxophone?
[With helping verb:] *Do* you *play* the saxophone?

[Regular form, to be avoided:] *Heard* you Buster calling?
[With helping verb:] *Did* you *hear* Buster calling?

C52   Helping verb *do* is used in the imperative to express polite insistence or to avoid awkwardness.

Do sit down, Mr. Topeavy.

Do tell us, Father Smithers, whether we will have to associate with, well, all sorts of people in heaven.

Do have a fifth helping of the turkey, Alfred; we weren't really planning on serving it cold for supper this evening.

Don't cry [instead of *Cry not*].

Helping verb **have**

C53   Helping verb *have* is used to form the perfect tenses.

C54   Helping verb *have,* followed by an infinitive with *to,* is used to express obligation or necessity.

We *have to leave* everything just as we found it.

Marie, please try to understand that Sheila *had to do* what she did.

If you *had had to earn* your money as a boy, you might now have more respect for other people's property.

C55   Do not use *of* for *have* or *'ve,* and do not insert an *of* after *had.*

have
You should ~~of~~ seen the crowd at Dinny's last night.

have

They ought to ~~of~~ gone to a vocational school.

would have

If Duke had ~~of~~ let go, the rest of us ~~would of~~ fallen.

Helping verb **must**

C56 Helping verb *must* has only one form for all tenses, persons, and numbers.

C57 Helping verb *must* is most commonly used to express obligation or necessity.

Someone *must stay* with Phineas until the doctor comes.

When you increase the pressure to that point, then something *must give* somewhere.

To win the jackpot you *must answer* four of the five questions.

C58 Since helping verb *must* has only one form, it is often wise to substitute another verb for it in order to avoid ambiguity or awkwardness.

[Ambiguous and awkward:] Marie, please try to understand that Sheila *must have done* what she did.

[Better:] Marie, please try to understand that Sheila *had to do* what she did.

C59 Helping verb *must* is used with other verbs to express supposition or speculation.

Someone *must have broken* the news to my father before I finally arrived home.

The window *must have been broken* by the storm.

Whoever it was *must have worn* gloves.

It *must have been* about three o'clock before the courier finally brought the package to the office.

Helping verb **ought**

C60   Helping verb *ought* has only one form for all tenses, persons, and numbers.

C61   Use the infinitive with *to* after *ought;* without *to* after *ought not.*

C62   Do not use *had ought.*

ought to have seen

You ~~had ought to see~~ the people at the festival.

ought not

You ~~hadn't ought to~~ be disrespectful.

C63   Helping verb *ought* expresses obligation, supposition, expectation, speculation, or fitness.

[Obligation:] You *ought to set* an example to your children if you expect good conduct from them.

[Supposition, expectation, speculation:] There *ought to be* another train in ten minutes.

[Fitness:] I *ought to have been told* of the family's plans even if I am the black sheep.

Helping verbs **shall** and **will**

C64   Helping verbs *shall* and *will* have only one form for all tenses, persons, and numbers.

C65   Helping verbs *shall* and *will* are used to form the future and the future-perfect tenses.

C66   Although you may use *shall* in all persons to express simple futurity, expectation, or mere statement of fact, in such instances *will* is more common.[15]

At this rate I *will (shall) graduate* in three years.

---

[15] Formerly, *shall* was used with the first person and *will* with the second and third.

If things happen as they usually do, you *will (shall)* some day *regret* your silly threat.

Tchaikovsky, the copyright owner, *will (shall) give* us no trouble.

C67 Although you may use *shall* with all persons to express intention, purpose, or determination on the part of the speaker, in such instances *will* is more common.[16]

I *will (shall) cut* right through all this red tape.	Clearly determination, intention, or purpose.
You *will (shall) go* where you're told!	Spoken in reprimand.
They *will (shall)* not *pass.*	Spoken by a general rallying his troups against an enemy.

C68 In questions, ordinarily use *shall* (rather than *will*) with the first person.

Shall I or *shall I* not *eat* another peanut?
Shall we *dance,* or are you tired?

C69 Use *shall* (rather than *will*) to express obligation—especially in legal matters.

The debt *shall* be repaid in full.

Helping verbs **should** and **would**

C70 Helping verbs *should* and *would* have only one form for all moods, tenses, persons, and numbers.

C71 Use *should* after *if* in all persons to express a supposition or imagined conditions or a condition contrary to fact.[17]

---

[16] Formerly, *will* was used with the first person and *shall* with the second and third.

[17] This rule holds, of course, in conditions where *if* is implied but not expressed; for example, "*Should* he come, we would be delighted."

C72   If *if . . . should* has been used in a condition, then in the conclusion use *would* to express intention, willingness, or simple future result.

If Barbara should sing, I *would make* for that exit.
If I should ask you, I'm sure you *would oblige* me.
If Tom should not return, then you *would be* one of the six to share the pie.

Such conditions are usually expressed today by the present and future indicative.

If Barbara *sings*, I *will make* for that exit.
If I *ask* you, I'm sure you *will oblige* me.
If Tom *returns*, then you *will be* one of the six to share the pie.

C73   Use *would* after *if* in all persons to express imagined or supposed willingness or a condition of willingness that is contrary to the facts.

If *I would* [usually expressed today by *if I wanted to*], I could take the day off.

If you *would try*, you could become a very effective speaker.

If Evans *would* only *talk* to me, I think I could persuade her to buy an advertisement in the *Post*.

C74   Use *should* or *would* with the first person and *would* with the second and third to express a modest opinion.

I should (or *would*) *say* that this oyster is asserting itself.
You would hardly *say*, would you, that I look like a criminal?
One would imagine that O'Leary dislikes talking in public.

C75   Use *should* or *would* with the first person, *would* with the second and third with *prefer, care, like, be glad, be inclined*.

I should (or *would*) *prefer*, of course, to breathe.

You would be inclined, I think, to consider mayhem good fun.

The *Millers would* not *care* to have their goldfish pond used as a wading pool.

C76   Use *should* with all persons to express duty, obligation, desirability, expectation, doubtful necessity.

[Duty or obligation:] If you are going to join us, *you should be* here before ten o'clock.

[Desirability:] I think it better that *someone* known to the family *should attend* the funeral.

[Expectation:] There *should be* another *car* in ten minutes.

[Doubtful necessity:] Ordinarily, a *rock* of that size *should fall* with terrific force.

C77   Use *would* with all persons to express habit or inclination.

I would put my foot in the bucket every time at bat.

Even as a baby, *you would take* Homer down from the shelf and gaze at the beautiful Greek words.

But an *American would think* that there is nothing more delicious than steak and potatoes.

C78   Use *would* with all persons in a polite expression of a desire.

I would make a final remark.
Would you come this way, please?
Mr. and Mrs. Bright would have you join them at their table.

C79   Questions with *should* and *would* are governed by C71-78.

C80   Use *should* as a past of *shall* and *would* as a past of *will*.

I asked you what *we should do* to overcome our problems.
At that time you were sure that *you would be* a lawyer some day.
At that time she was sure that *she would be* a lawyer some day.

Helping verbs *may* and *might*

C81   Helping verbs *may* and *might* have only one form for all tenses, persons, and numbers.

c

C82   Use *may* to express permission.[18]

Please, Ma, *may* I *keep* the puppy?
You *may stay* in swimming until the car comes back.

C83   Use *might* as a past of *may.*

Mother said that I *might keep* the puppy; but when I returned to look for it, it was gone.

The coach had told us that we *might stay* in swimming until the car came back.

C84   When no *if* clause is involved, use *may* to express a near possibility, *might* to express a remote one.

It *may* rain. [The sky is cloudy.]

It *might* rain. [The climate is treacherous.]

They *may go*; in fact, I should not be surprised if they did.

They *might go*; but, judging by the way that Steve was talking at lunch, I don't think they will.

C85   When an *if* clause expresses a supposition, an imagined condition, or a condition that is contrary to fact, use *might* in the independent clause even to express a near possibility. Do not use *may.*

If you were more careful, you *might be allowed* to use the drill press.

If Creon would control his temper, we *might be* able to use him as the father in the play.

If she could recite the Declaration of Independence by heart, I *might change* her grade.

If you should answer all the questions correctly, you *might make* the quiz bowl team.

---

[18] In the United States many writers tend to make *can* do *may's* work as well as its own, especially in informal usage.

C86 When an *if* clause does not fall under C85, use either *may* or *might* in the independent clause.

> If she recites the Declaration of Independence by heart, I *may* (or *might*) *change* her grade.

C87 Use *may* and *might* (*might* for the past) to express purpose or intention.

> I'm working in order that I *may encourage* the others.
> I worked in order that I *might encourage* the others.

Helping verbs *can* and *could*

C88 Helping verbs *can* and *could* have only one form for all tenses, persons, and numbers.

C89 Use *can* or *could* to express power, ability, skill: *can* suggesting a near possibility and *could* a more remote one.[19]

> I don't know whether I *can sail* so large a boat by myself.
> I don't know whether I *could sail* so large a boat by myself.

C90 Use *could* as a past of *can*.

> I didn't know whether I *could sail* so large a boat by myself.

C91 When an *if* clause expresses a supposition, an imagined condition, or a condition that is contrary to fact, use *could* in the independent clause.

> If there were less talk, we *could finish* the cracker-eating contest.

> He really believes that he *could sing* the title role [if he should be asked to do so].

> If we had had a third, we *could have played* three-man territory, a game invented by a madman.

> If nobody would object, we *could leave.*

---

[19] In the United States even the best writers use *can* and *could* to express permission. See C82.

c

C92 If *if... could* has been used in the condition, then in the conclusion use *would* (not *will*).

Even if they *could reach* Sagrado by Tuesday, it *would be* too late.

C93 Use *could* as a softer, more polite, more indirect form of *can*.

Could you *get* me another table, please?

Active and Passive Voice

C94 Voice is that form which a verb takes to show whether the subject is acting or being acted upon. The active voice is the form of the verb that shows that the subject is acting. The passive voice is the form of the verb that shows that the subject is being acted upon.

[Active:] Herbert *teased* the lion.
[Passive:] The lion *was teased* by Herbert.

C95 Do not confuse passive voice with past time (tense).

C96 Avoid awkward passives.

[Awkward:] The streets *are being walked* by restless crowds.
[Use the active:] Restless crowds *are walking* the streets.

C97 A verb used in an intransitive sense cannot usually be changed into the passive voice. But sometimes a preposition and an intransitive verb are so closely associated that together they become a compound transitive verb and can be put into the passive.[20]

[Active:] The truck *ran into* the bus.
[Passive:] The bus *was run into* by the truck.

[Active:] Julie's friends *thought* well *of* her.
[Passive:] Julie *was* well *thought of* by her friends.

---

[20] When such constructions are used, it is sensible to think of the word that was a preposition in the active as part of a compound verb in the passive and to analyze it and diagram it accordingly. However, it may justly be considered a preposition retained from the active and diagramed to one side.

C98 A verb in the passive may have a predicate complement; that is, a predicate noun or predicate adjective.

> Mervin was elected *treasurer.*
> Ursula is considered *clever.*

C99 A predicate complement results in the passive when the verb in the active has an objective complement.

> The committee elected Mervin *treasurer* [objective complement in the active].

> Mervin was elected *treasurer* [predicate noun in the passive].

> Everyone considers Ursula *clever* [objective complement in the active].

> Ursula is considered *clever* [predicate adjective in the passive].

C100 Although a verb cannot have an ordinary direct object when it is in the passive, it can yet have an object held over from the active and called a "retained object." [21]

> We were asked the *price.*

> We were given *directions* by a security officer.

> Someone must have been given a *warning,* for the enemy artillery was waiting for us.

C101 A retained object results in the passive when the verb in the active has two direct objects, one of which is made the subject noun or pronoun of the active.

[Active:] The customer immediately asked *us* the price.	*Us* and *price* are the double object of *asked.* (Do not confuse with compound object.)

---

[21] Ordinarily, retained objects are not pronouns; but, if one were, it should of course be put in the objective case. Since retained objects are so seldom pronouns, and hence case is not involved, the retained object is of no consequence in English and, along with a good number of other fine points of grammar, is treated in this book only because it may give difficulty from time to time in the analysis of a sentence.

c

[Passive:] We were immediately asked the *price*.	*Us* has been made the subject pronoun (*we*), and *price* is the retained object, held over from the active.

C102 A retained object results in the passive when the indirect object of the active (or the object of *to* or *for* acting as an indirect object) is made the subject noun or pronoun in the passive. For then the direct object is retained in the passive.

[Active:] A security officer gave us *directions*.

[Passive:] We were given *directions* by a security officer.	Indirect object *us* has been made the subject pronoun (*we*), and *directions* is the retained object, the direct object held over from the active.

[Passive:] Just outside the library, I was handed a *summons*.

The three moods

C103 The mood of a verb is the grammatical form that shows how the verb expresses the actuality of its subject— whether as a fact, as a possibility, as a doubt, as a wish, and so on.

C104 In English there are three moods: the indicative, the imperative, and the subjunctive.[22] Each of the three verb moods conveys a particular manner of doing or being. See C105-15.

---

[22] Some grammars list also an optative mood, a potential mood, and so on. This book acts on the principle that all the manners of expression of a verb are well accounted for by the three moods given here and by the helping verbs.

C105 Use the indicative mood to state something as a fact, to deny that something is a fact, or to ask questions about it as a fact.

> Robert W. Service *was born* in England in 1874.
> The sun *is* not *shining*.
> *Will* the dog *bite*?
> I wonder whether there *is* any use in waiting.

C106 Use the imperative mood to give commands. (*Command* is here taken to include direct second-person orders, pleas, warnings, instructions, and so on.)

> *Honor* thy father and thy mother.
> *Save* me!
> *Proceed* at your own risk.
> *Let's* go.[23]

C107 The present and future indicative are frequently used as substitutes for the imperative mood.

This is my command: Malcolm Guerny *dies*.	Substitute for *execute Malcolm Guerny*.
Thou *shalt* not *kill*.	Substitute for *do not kill*.
You *will be* here tomorrow at eight.	Substitute for *be here at eight*.

C108 In general, use the subjunctive mood to show that conditions, concessions, and wishes are contrary to the facts. The subjunctive mood indicates that what is said is in some way not actual or certain but is imagined or wished or desired or conceived as possible. Subjunctive forms have fallen into rather general disuse in spoken English. The following particular rules, however, are observed in formal written English.

---

[23] Some grammars treat this as a hortatory (exhorting) subjunctive. Calling it an imperative seems more realistic and accurate.

C109 Use the present subjunctive after verbs of ordering, willing, resolving, and proposing, and after expressions of necessity when these are followed by the conjunction *that*.

God *wills that* everyone *be saved.*

We *are determined that* no one *be admitted* who cannot speak persuasively.

The rule *requires that* a person *reach* his twenty-first year before he may apply for admission.

It *is necessary that* Igor *play* loud enough to cover the noise of shifting the set.

Mrs. Reingold *asks that* a guest not only *enjoy* her parties but also *work* hard at doing so.

I *move that* Mr. Hall *represent* us in Washington.

In most instances other forms of the verb may take the place of the formal construction of *that* followed by the present subjunctive. (It is better, however, to keep the formal construction in sentences beginning *Resolved.*)

God *wills that* everyone *should be saved.*

The dean *has ordered that* Fleming *should take* (or *shall take*) another examination *Friday.*

The dean *has ordered* Fleming *to take* another examination on Friday.

Resolved, That the secretary *take* our complaint to the president.

C110 Use *were* (past subjunctive) to indicate that what you are saying is contrary to present or future fact.

If only I *were* class president. [I'm not.]

Even if she *were* to beg me, I wouldn't drive my car to the beach. [And she hardly will.]

If I *were* you, I would apologize. [But I'm not.]

C111 Use *had* plus the past participle, either the regular or progressive form (past-perfect subjunctive), to indicate that what you are saying is contrary to past facts.

If only *I had been* at home! [But I was not.]

Even if she *had begged* me, I wouldn't have driven my car to the beach. [But she didn't.]

If I *had been listening* to the radio, I'd have won a prize. [But I was not.]

C112 Do not use *would have* (for *had* plus the past participle) to express a wish, a concession, or a condition that is contrary to past facts.

had

If the apartment ~~would have~~ been on the first floor, we would have taken it.

C113 When using the subjunctive after *as if* and *as though*, use *were* to express an action or state that is simultaneous with that of the main verb; use *had* plus the past participle to express an action or state that is prior to that of the main verb.

Simultaneous

Douglas { acts / acted / will act / has acted / had acted } as if he *were* owner of the place.[24]

Prior

Douglas { acts / acted / will act / has acted / had acted } as if he *had been* owner of the place.

---

[24] In conversational English the indicative is now regularly used in such instances to express both possible and contrary-to-fact statements; for example, "He acts as if he is the owner of the place."

C114 Nowadays the present and present-perfect subjunctives are scarcely used. The indicative, the past and the past-perfect subjunctive, and helping verbs are used instead.

Instead of—
If Meg *be* here, she will answer for me.

Ordinarily use—
If Meg *is* here, she will answer for me. [Indicative.]

If Meg *have been here,* she will have left a note for us.

If Meg *has been* here, she will have left a note for us. [Indicative.]

If Meg *had been* here, she would have left a note. [Past-perfect subjunctive.]

C115 When they carry the sense and do not sound awkward, helping verbs (like *shall, should, would,* and *could*) may be substituted for the subjunctive forms of C109-11 and C113.

Instead of—
Even if you *were* to pay me, I would tell the truth.[25]

You may find—
Even if you *should pay* me, I would tell the truth.

If Tooky *were* here, he would prove that I caught that fish.

If Tooky *could be* here, he would prove that I caught that fish.

We are determined that no one *be admitted* who cannot speak persuasively on many subjects.

We are determined that no one *shall be admitted* who cannot speak persuasively on many subjects.

If you *played* [past subjunctive] your cards right, you might get Mr. Acton to equip the darkroom.

If you *should* [or *would,* depending on the meaning] *play* your cards right, you might get Mr. Acton to equip the darkroom.

---

[25] Notice the change in meaning in this version: "Even if you pay me, I will have to tell the truth."

The tenses

C116   The tenses are the different forms that a verb takes to indicate the time of an action or state.

C117   In general, the present tense indicates that something is happening now.

> I *eat* now.
> I *am eating* now.
> I *do eat* now.

C118   The present (indicative, chiefly) is used to express facts and truths that are independent of time.

> The human soul *is* immortal.
> She said that blue and yellow *make* green.

C119   The present (indicative) is used to indicate habitual action that still continues.

> He *takes* a nap in the afternoon.
> Alison *is* always here by four o'clock.

C120   The present (indicative) is sometimes used for vividness in narratives about the past. Once introduced into a narrative, this present-for-past device must be kept until there is a reason within the narrative for changing to a past tense.

> Booth *shoots* Lincoln and *leaps* to the stage.

C121   The present tense of all moods, and of the participle, gerund, and infinitive is frequently used with a future meaning.

> When *does* this morning's mail *get* in?
> Max's ship *sails* at midnight.
> We *may*—we're not sure—*have* a meeting next Monday.
> Someone said that we *might be asked* to repeat the performance.
> I suggest that he *see* Mrs. Carroll, who handles all such complaints.

C122 In general, the past tense (indicative) is used to indicate that something happened in the past and is no longer happening now.

> I *came*, I *saw*, I *conquered.*
> I *was hoping* to find a small sailboat for my youngest daughter.
> The wailing *began* yesterday at sunset and *stopped* just a moment or two ago.

C123 The past (indicative), usually the progressive form, may indicate an action or state that was the background of another action or state in the past.

> I *was swimming* alone when the shark attacked me.

C124 The past (indicative) may indicate past habitual action.

> Moreland *ate* twice a day.
> Moreland *used* to eat twice a day.

C125 The past subjunctive is used to express present and future time.

> If you *were* interested, I would show you a quicker method of factoring.

> If you *sang* the song with the same naturalness during the performance tomorrow, we should have a hit. But I'm afraid you will be a little tense.

C126 The future tense indicates that something will take place later.

> The rest *will be sent* out later.
> I *will phone* for a taxi this minute.

C127 The present perfect (indicative) indicates that something has taken place in the past but continues into the present or has consequences that continue into the present. Use the present perfect when you wish to stress a link between the present time and what happened in the past.

> No one *has heard* from Bud since he went away.
> The examinations *have begun.*
> I *have been* ill for two months.

There *has been* a riot.

Obviously the war *has been* a sorry failure.	The war is definitely over, but the writer wishes to stress that it was recent and that its consequences are still present.

C128 The past perfect (indicative) indicates that an action or state took place prior to some other past action or state.

Father De Smet learned that the tribe *had retreated* farther west.

The fire *had been burning* briskly for an hour or more when we began to see some change in the glowing metal.

Ms. Kane *had* already *bought* her ticket before she went to the station.

C129 The past perfect (indicative) is used with *before* to indicate that an action or state that was begun in the past and that might, could, should, or would have been completed in the past was not completed.

He was interrupted before he *had finished* the story.

We were ready an hour before anyone *had arrived.*	The past perfect implies that people might, could, or should have arrived. If a mere statement of fact is wanted, the past should be used: *before anyone arrived.*

C130 The past may properly be used for the past perfect when it is not important to show that one action has preceded another.

Weeks was discharged because he *washed* the dishes too hastily.	Although the dishwashing preceded the discharging, the statement is clear without using the past perfect.
We changed our plans after we *got* the message.	Although receiving the message preceded the changing of plans, the statement is clear without the past perfect.

C131 The past should be used for the past perfect when the latter would detract from the thought of the sentence.

Children *heard* the news and leaped into the air for joy.

"Children *had heard* the news" would be distracting here. The writer wants to stress the sudden impact of the news and the children's almost simultaneous reaction to it.

C132 The future perfect is used to indicate that something will already have happened before something else will happen.

I *shall have finished* this typing before night [falls].
They *will have left* before you arrive.

C133 Sometimes the future perfect is used in a sentence to go with a future thought that is not expressed but merely implied.

If Tom has been here, he *will have left* a note.

Implied thought: as we *shall discover* later.

By now Grandmother Webster *will have arrived* at the farm.

Implied thought: as we *shall find* out later. (Here the future perfect also carries a connotation of *should or ought to have arrived.*)

C134 The future perfect is not much used in the United States today. For it are substituted the present, the future, or the present perfect.

Instead of—
I *will have finished* the typing before night.

You may find—
I *will finish* the typing before night.

Please telephone me as soon as you *will have heard.*

Please telephone me as soon as you *hear.*

Please telephone me as soon as you *have heard.*

Sequence of tenses

C135 The tense of verbals and subordinate predicate verbs frequently depends on the tense of the main verb.

C136 If the main verb is present, the subordinate verbs are usually present, present perfect, or future.

Jane *says* that tea *is* ready.	Both the saying and the being ready occur at the same time.
Buddy *will* not *talk* now because he *is* afraid.	The talking and the being afraid occur at the same time. *Will* not *talk* is present here.
The examination *seems* easy because we *have studied* hard.	The studying preceded the examination; so the present perfect is used.
We *have* some fine indoor games ready so that the rain *will* not *spoil* the children's fun.	The rain is a future possibility, so the future is used here.
[Exception:] The examination *seems easy* because we *studied* hard.	The rule is not ironclad. Here the past is used rather than the present perfect because the writer does not wish to present the studying as something recent or not yet over.
[Exception:] I *believe* that Columbus *discovered* America in 1492.	The rule is not ironclad. Here the sense simply demands the past rather than the present-perfect tense.

C137 If the main verb is past or past perfect, make the subordinate verbs past or past perfect if you can do so and still express your meaning fully and accurately. (See also C361.)

Margate *said* that he *was* too busy to come and hear what you *might propose* at the meeting.	*Was* indicates the same time as the main verb, *said.* And the past, *might propose,* is better than

So don't expect him.

the present, *may propose*, after the past.

Margate *said* that he *would be* out of town and hence *could* not *attend* tomorrow's meeting. So don't expect him.

Would and *could* are better than *will* and *can* to express the proper time relation.

Whenever she *heard* an owl hoot, she *remembered* that fateful night.

Hears would be quite incorrect, since it would give no full hint of the time relation of one act to the other.

Joshua *could conquer* the city only after God *had come* to his aid.

At the time Joshua was able to conquer the city, God's help had already been given.

[Exception:] Tavitt *ordered* that I *report* for KP.

The present, *report*, is called for, according to C109, after verbs of ordering, and so on. *Should report*, however, could also be used.

C138 Do not keep the sequence of tenses asked for in C137 if the dependent clause is intended to present something as usual, characteristic, or always true.

Did you *ask* when the eastbound train *comes* in?

I *have told* you that Nigel *studies* hard, *plays* hard, and *is making* good grades in school.

Junior *had* never *heard* that the earth *is* round.

C139 In a single sentence or in a series of sentences or paragraphs connected by one line of thought, do not change the verb time unless you have to.

[Wrong:] When first we meet him, he is lying on the cropped grass in front of the grandstand watching with an idle eye the afternoon scrimmage of the football team. His pose is altogether graceful and seems to imply relaxed power rather than lethargy or weakness. He *had* a good head, strong, with features cleanly but not sharply chiseled.

[Right:] When first we meet him, he is lying on the cropped grass in front of the grandstand watching with an idle eye the afternoon scrimmage of the football team. His pose is altogether graceful and seems to imply relaxed power rather than lethargy or weakness. He *has* a good head, strong, with features cleanly but not sharply chiseled.

[Right:] When first we met him, he was lying on the cropped grass in front of the grandstand watching with an idle eye the afternoon scrimmage of the football team. His pose was altogether graceful and seemed to imply relaxed power rather than lethargy or weakness. He *had* a good head, strong, with features cleanly but not sharply chiseled.

C140 Use the present participle if the action of the participle takes place at the same time as that of the predicate verb.

Working for thirty-six hours hand running, that single shift cleared the ways of three oil tankers.

Being a little uncomfortable even in my sleep, I was not able to get the rest I needed.

Leaving the parking lot, you will hand your ticket to the attendant.

I am without a care in the world, *sailing* along between the islands that wall off the sound.

C141 Use the present-perfect participle if the action of the participle is prior to the action of the predicate verb.

Having scuttled the clipper, Johannsen sat in the dory planning her next move.

Having been refused by every publisher in the city, Schmidt may buy his own printing press.

Having paced sixty feet from the shore, we came to the mound and began to dig feverishly.

C142 Use the past participle regardless of the time of the predicate verb.

Delighted with my job, I see no reason to change.

Wearied with waiting, the dog had curled up on a seat of the ferris wheel and gone to sleep.

Given half a chance, she will win the TV contest hands down.

Frightened by the deafening crash, he jumped from his chair and ran to the window.

C143 Use the present-perfect infinitive if the action of the infinitive is prior to that of the predicate verb. Use the present infinitive in all other cases.

He is said to *have died* of apoplexy while delivering a frenzied television commercial.

The doctor was reported to *have come* to Tranquillity Beach to study the effects on the human body of sand in picnic lunches.

I want to *leave* now.
I wanted to *leave* yesterday.
I had expected to *leave* tomorrow.

C144 Use the present or present-perfect gerund if the action of the gerund is prior to that of the predicate verb. Use the present gerund in all other cases.

Noble was accused of *having written* a ditty lampooning the dean.
Noble was accused of *writing* a ditty lampooning the dean.
"I have no intention of *budging*," said the immovable object.

Transitive verbs and objects

C145 A transitive verb is one that requires an object to complete its meaning.

The Ford ▷— hit —▷ Jimmy.	*Hit* is transitive; *Jimmy* is the object needed to complete the meaning of *hit*.
We ▷— enjoy —▷ music.	*Enjoy* is transitive; *music* is the object needed to complete the meaning of *enjoy*.

C146 The same verb may be transitive in one sentence and intransitive in another.

> Jack ▷— is dancing —▷ a polka.
> Jack ▷— is dancing ⌐.

C147 A direct object is the noun or other substantive that completes the meaning of the verb and is directly governed by it.

The Ford hit *Jimmy.*	The Ford hit whom? Jimmy.
We enjoy *music.*	We enjoy what? Music.
I hate *lying.*	I hate what? Lying (gerund).
I like *to loaf.*	I like what? To loaf (infinitive).
She prefers *that you remain.*	She prefers what? That you remain (noun clause).

C148 A direct object may be compound.

We bought *caramels* and *liverwurst.*

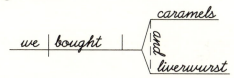

C149 In some sentences, some verbs—like *ask, teach, lead,* and *hear*—take two direct objects. (Do not confuse two direct objects with a compound object.)

You led *us* a merry *chase.*

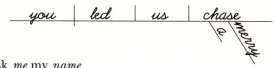

Ask *me* my *name.*

Hear *me* my *lessons.*

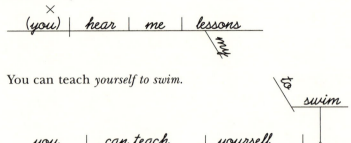

You can teach *yourself to swim.*

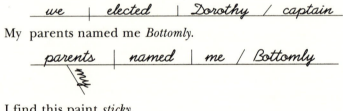

C150 In some sentences, some verbs—like *name, choose, elect, deem,* and *find*—take both a direct object and an objective complement.

C151 An objective complement is a noun, pronoun, or adjective (in the objective case) referring to the direct object and filling out the meaning of the verb.

We elected Dorothy *captain.*

$$\underline{\text{we} \quad | \quad \text{elected} \quad | \quad \text{Dorothy} \ / \ \text{captain}}$$

My parents named me *Bottomly.*

$$\underline{\text{parents} \quad | \quad \text{named} \quad | \quad \text{me} \ / \ \text{Bottomly}}$$

I find this paint *sticky.*

$$\underline{\text{I} \ | \ \text{find} \quad | \quad \text{paint} \quad / \ \text{sticky}}$$

C152 Put a pronoun which is being used as a direct object in the objective case.

I rather like *her.*

                              him   her
Did I miss anyone? Yes, ~~he~~ and ~~she~~.

whom

I don't know ~~who~~ I invited.[26]

C153 Expressions like *I believe* and *do you suppose* complicate the use of the proper case of *who* or *whom*.[26] Whenever in doubt, diagram the sentence and see where *who* or *whom* falls in the diagram.

This is the gentleman whom, I believe, you distrust.

Whom is the direct object of the verb *distrust*.

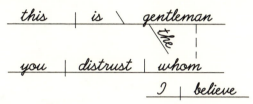

Who do you suppose ate the icing?

Who is the subject pronoun of the verb *ate*.

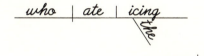

I must find someone whom I can believe.

Whom is the direct object of the verb *can believe*.

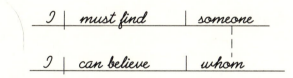

C154 The indirect object of a transitive verb names the person or thing that receives the direct object. In other words, the indirect object names the person or thing to, for, or toward whom an action is done.

---

[26] In informal writing and speaking, *who* is regularly used instead of *whom* as direct object. Even in informal communication, however, the objective *whom* is commonly used when it immediately follows a preposition. *Who* are you talking to? To *whom* it may concern.

Professor Trinkle gave *me* a retort.

I only told *Roddy* and *Allen* the time.

They handed *Jim* and *me* a bowl of watery soup.

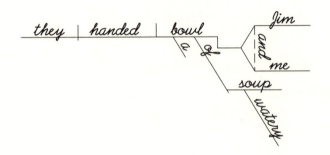

C155 Insert the preposition *to* or *for* before a likely object. If the insertion makes good sense, the chance is excellent that you have an indirect object.

Virginia brought Mother a birthday gift.	Insert *to* before *Mother*, and you make sense. *Mother* is the indirect object.
A taxi brought Mother home.	Insert *to* before *Mother*, and you do not make good sense. *Mother* is not the indirect object in this sentence.
Dad bought us round-trip tickets.	Insert *for* before *us*, and you make sense. *Us* is the indirect object.

C156 Put a pronoun that is the indirect object in the objective case.

[Answering the question, "Did Denise give anybody a piece?":] Not *me.*

Intransitive verbs and complements

C157 An intransitive verb is a verb that does not have a direct object.

Who *is singing?*
The plot *thickens.*
My blood *boiled* when he told me to bring him his slippers.
The wind *is blowing.*

C158 Some verbs—like *be* and *seem*—cannot be used transitively; other verbs may be transitive in one sentence and intransitive in another.

[Transitive:] Jack ▷— is dancing →▷ a polka.
[Intransitive:] Jack ▷— is dancing ⌐.

C159 A linking verb is an intransitive verb that only connects its subject with another substantive or an adjective, which is in the nominative case.

Peggy *is* president.   *Is* connects *Peggy* with *president,* a noun in the nominative case.

You *seem* strange.

Seem connects *you* with *strange,* an adjective in the nominative case.

you | seem \ strange

103

C160 A predicate complement is a substantive or an adjective in the nominative case *(a)* that is used with a linking verb or a verb in the passive voice and *(b)* that represents, describes, or refers to the subject noun or pronoun.

They are *brothers.*	Predicate noun.
That is *what I asked.*	Predicate noun clause.
The artist was really *she,* Charlotte Burns.	Predicate pronoun.
The iron is becoming *red.*	Predicate adjective.
Kurt was appointed *waterboy.*	Predicate noun after a passive predicate verb.

C161 Put the predicate pronoun of a predicate verb in the nominative case.[27]

It is *I.*
This should be *he.*
Was it *they?*

C162 All linking verbs carry some sense of the verb *be.* So, in deciding whether you should use an ordinary intransitive verb with an adjective modifier, or a linking verb with a predicate adjective, do this: Substitute a corresponding form of the verb *be* for the predicate verb and use an adjective complement. If the substitution carries the sense you want, then the linking verb plus a predicate adjective is probably the correct construction.

Suppose you are deciding whether to say "A rose smells sweet" or "A rose smells sweetly." Say "A rose is sweet." Does that carry the rough sense of what you want to say? Yes. So "A rose smells sweet" is quite correct. (As a matter of fact, "A rose smells sweetly" would mean that a rose looks charming when it is smelling something else.)

---

[27] In informal writing and speaking, the objective case of the predicate pronoun is regularly used after *it is, it was,* and so on. In some other instances the objective is clearly preferable; for example, "That picture isn't really *him*" [instead of *he*].

C163 Say *feel bad, ill, well, good, right* (adjectives after linking verb). Do not say *feel badly, rightly* (adverbs).

bad

I don't feel ~~badly~~ about voting the Republican ticket.

After working all afternoon laying pipes, I had a swim that felt very good indeed.

C164 Say *do well, badly* (adverbs), since *do* in the sense of *succeed* is not a linking verb. Do not say *do good, bad, nice.*

well

I did very ~~good~~ in my examination.

nicely

This will do [succeed, fill the bill] very ~~nice~~.

C165 The following verbs are frequently used as linking verbs.

act [*in the sense* of pretend to be] (stupid)	look (funny)
appear (strange)	loom (large)
bang (shut)	play (dead)
be (sure)	prove (worthwhile)
become (wise)	rank (fifth)
break (free)	remain (puzzled)
burn (blue)	rest (assured)
burst [out] (singing)	ring (true)
continue (agreeable)	rise (triumphant)
fall (dead *or* sick)	run (true [to form])
feel (bad)	seem (odd)
flame (red)	shine (golden)
get (sick)	show (cowardly [*adjective*])
go (mad)	smell (sweet)
go [on] (studying)	sound (harsh)
grow (ridiculous)	stand (corrected)
hold (true)	stay (united)
keep (honest)	take (sick)
lie [*in the sense of* remain] (quiet)	taste (strong)
	turn [out] (delicious)
	turn (white)

Verbs confused

C166 Do not confuse—

Lie—meaning to recline. (Intransitive.)

Present	Past	Past participle
lie	lay	lain

lie

People ~~lay~~ down when they're tired.

lay

The bicycle ~~laid~~ in the weeds for three days.

lain

I had scarcely ~~laid~~ down on my bed when the alarm rang.

Lay—meaning to put *something* down. (Transitive.)

Present	Past	Past participle
lay	laid	laid

lay

Now I ~~lie~~ me down to sleep.

laid

Hollings ~~lay~~ his big hand on my rifle.

laid

Christ has ~~lain~~ down his life for his friends.

C167 Do not confuse—

Sit—meaning to be seated. (Intransitive.)

Present	Past	Past participle
sit	sat	sat

sit

Don't ~~set~~ in that chair; that's the cat's.

sat

Imperturbable Jones has ~~set~~ so long in front of the department store window that people think he is part of the display.

sat

Kings have *set* on that bench you are polishing your boots on, soldier.

sat

[Exceptional, transitive use:] Ichabod *set* his horse like a loose-jointed scarecrow athwart a great beer barrel.

sat

[Exceptional, transitive use:] Mr. Northrup *set* himself down and chatted for an hour.

Set—meaning to put, place, or fix *something*. (Transitive.)

Present	Past	Past participle
set	set	set

Janet had *set* a pail of water on the lowest step to catch a thief but caught her own astonished father.

Set the coffeepot on the stove, Sam.

Set your watches to agree with mine; we attack in exactly six minutes.

Set—meaning chiefly to sit on eggs as does a fowl. (Intransitive.)

Present	Past	Past participle
set	set	set

set

Hens will *sit* on darning eggs or light bulbs.

C168 Do not confuse—

Hang—meaning to suspend or be suspended (but preferably not used of putting to death by suspending).

Present	Past	Past participle
hang	hung	hung

Hang your clothes on a hickory limb; the water's fine.

hung

We ~~hanged~~ our clothes on a hickory limb but found crocodiles in the water.

hung

You should have ~~hanged~~ your clothes on a higher limb where the goat couldn't have reached them.

hung

That suit ~~hanged~~ on Longjohn like a slack tepee around a tent pole.

Hang—meaning to put to death by suspending.

Present	Past	Past participle
hang	hanged	hanged

Hang your friend from a hickory limb; he used up all the hot water.

hanged

Tommers was ~~hung~~ from a hickory limb for confusing other ranchers' brands with his own.

hanged

Before they ~~hung~~ him, they put Edmund Campion through a mock trial whose verdict was set before its date.

C169 Do not confuse—

Rise—meaning to ascend, to get up, or to emerge. (Intransitive.)

Present	Past	Past participle
rise	rose	risen

rose

The sun ~~raised~~ at about four-thirty that morning.

rise

Come on, marine; ~~raise~~ and shine!

rising

There we saw peak ~~raising~~ above peak sharply, till the last seemed a pinnacle upon which no one could ever stand.

risen

We had ~~raised~~ early, for fish greet the dawn hungry.

You could almost see the dough *rising* in the pan.

Raise—meaning to make something rise. (Transitive.)

Present	Past	Past participle
raise	raised	raised

raised

The sun had ~~risen~~ itself for a look over the rim of the world.

raised

Our Lord ~~rose~~ Lazarus from the tomb.

raise

Here's a story that may ~~rise~~ a laugh.

C170 Do not confuse—

Lose—meaning to fail to keep, to suffer defeat.

Present	Past	Past participle
lose	lost	lost

lose

I am afraid you are going to ~~loose~~ a hubcap.

lose

Leoville should ~~loose~~ to Damien by six points.

Loose and *loosen*—meaning to free, to untie, to relax.

Present	Past	Past participle
loose	loosed	loosed
loosen	loosened	loosened

Loose

~~Lose~~ the prisoners and let them go.

Loosen

~~Losen~~ the girth on the black stallion.

C171 Do not confuse—

Teach—meaning to attempt to cause someone to learn.

taught
Miss McBride ~~learned~~ us how to square dance.

teaching
Christ had a difficult time ~~learning~~ the apostles.

Learn—meaning to acquire knowledge or skill.

We *learn* that Richelieu had some good points.
Why should a boy *learn* to cook?

C172 Do not confuse—

Effect—meaning to bring about or cause something.

Present	*Past*	*Past participle*
effect	effected	effected

effected
My white mouse, Squeaky, has ~~affected~~ his escape.

effect
If Marilyn shows up, we can ~~affect~~ a compromise.

Affect—meaning to influence, to move the emotions; to pretend or feign something.

Present	*Past*	*Past participle*
affect	affected	affected

affected
Too much sun has ~~effected~~ poor Maddern's brain.

affected
All the coarse louts in the crowd were visibly ~~effected~~ by the sentimental movie.

affect
Mr. Pringle tried to ~~effect~~ surprise; but he was a poor actor, and so he deceived nobody.

C173 These are the principal parts of *let* and *leave*:

Present	*Past*	*Past participle*
let	let	let
leave	left	left

C174 Use *let*, not *leave*, with *be*.

Let
~~Leave~~ me be.

C175 Use *let*, not *leave*, in the sense of *permit*.

Let
~~Leave~~ me tell you.

Let
~~Leave~~ them enter.

Let
~~Leave~~ us know if there are any changes.

C176 Use *let*, not *leave*, to give a sense of exhortation to a verb.

Let
~~Leave~~ us go to the matinee.

Let
~~Leave~~ us answer tyranny with a smile.

C177 Use *leave*, not *let*, in the sense of *abandon, forget*.

left
I must have ~~let~~ the keys in the car.

left
Who ~~let~~ his ice cream on top of the stove?

C178 Ordinarily use either *let* or *leave* with *alone*.

Let me *alone*.
Leave me *alone*.

[Exception:] Two people, *let alone* one, would be unable to budge him if he fell down. Only *let alone* may be used in this peculiar, idiomatic sense of *not to mention*.

111

Case

C179 Case is the form of a substantive that indicates its sense relation to other words in a sentence. The nominative shows that the substantive is the subject or predicate complement of a verb; the objective, that it is the object of some other word; and so on.

C180 There are three cases in English: the nominative, the possessive, and the objective.

C181 Nouns in English have a distinctive form only for the possessive case. Sense and position indicate the nominative and objective relationships.

C182 Some pronouns have distinctive forms for all three cases. (See A29, A30.)

Nominative	I	we
Possessive	mine	ours
Objective	me	us

Possessive of nouns and pronouns

The possessive case

C183 If a noun or pronoun denotes ownership, origin, source, right, responsibility, and so on, put it in the possessive case.

Mrs. Witherspoon's car is here.	The possessive here denotes ownership.
Michael's jokes are dull.	Michael does not strictly own the jokes, but he tells them or originates them.
Hilda's father delights in doing the unexpected.	In the strict sense Hilda does not own her father, and yet he does belong to her.

This is all *Hillman's* fault.

In the strict sense Hillman does not possess the fault; and yet it does belong to him, for he is responsible for it.

C184 The possessive case is an adjective case, and any substantive in the possessive case is ordinarily used as an adjective.

This is *Hillman's* fault.

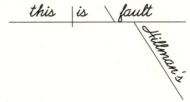

C185 A noun or pronoun may be in the possessive case and at the same time, from another point of view, in the nominative or objective case.

That hat is *mine.*

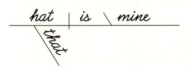

Mine is the possessive case of *I,* but also predicate pronoun in the sentence and, therefore, nominative case.

The **of** Possessive[28]

C186 *Of* followed by a noun or pronoun is frequently used to show ownership.

The clamor *of the alarm* finally awakened them.	The alarm's clamor.
The Mohicans tortured the brother of *Andaiuga.*	Andaiuga's brother.
That old Model T *of Henry's* should be laid to rest in a junk yard.	Henry's old Model T.

---

[28] This is commonly called the possessive genitive.

C187 When the owner is a living thing, the *of* possessive is used where it sounds better or is clearer than the ordinary possessive.

For the life *of me,* I could not think of the answer [rather than *for my life*].

C188 A combination of the *of* possessive and the ordinary possessive is very common, especially when the object possessed is modified by a demonstrative. This combination is known as the double possessive. Notice that in this instance a noun that is possessive in form does not function as an adjective but as a substantive.

That old hat *of Father's* might fit you.

Father's, though possessive in form, is a substantive, the object of *of.*

She is a friend *of mine.*
Those remarks *of Colby's* have cost us a holiday.

Sometimes the form affects the meaning.

[Compare:]   She lost that snapshot *of Joe.*
She lost that snapshot *of Joe's.*

C189 The *of* possessive is the more common form when the owner is not a living thing.

[Common:] the back *of the chair*
[Less common:] the *chair's* back

[Common:] the pleasure *of reading*
[Unusual, because awkward and ambiguous:] *reading's* pleasure

[Common:] the call *of the sea*
[Unusual, because awkward:] the *sea's* call

[Common:] the end *of the line*

[Unusual, because awkward:] the *line's* end

C190 Inanimate objects that are personified use the possessive case and the *of* possessive with equal ease.

> the *wind's* murmur
> the murmur *of the wind*
>
> *death's* cold fingers
> the cold fingers *of death*
>
> the *rose's* breath
> the breath *of the rose*
>
> *autumn's* winds
> the winds *of autumn*

C191 The possessive case is more common than the *of* possessive with the following expressions and some others.

the law's delay	a three-days' drive
for pity's sake	the year's events
two-hours' walk	six-months' interest
a stone's throw	the world's work
a day's work	fifty-cents' worth
a month's notice	a dollar's worth

Some of the expressions above consist of a numeral plus a measure of time, like *a two-hours' walk*. These expressions may be written in three ways:

> a two-hours' walk
> a two-hour's walk
> a two-hours walk

Many authors and editors prefer *a two-hour* walk, which is classical English.

When the numeral in these expressions is *one* or less than one, they are written thus: *a one-hour's walk*, a *half-hour's walk*. (Here *'s* is not required, but it is recommended.)

Nominative absolutes

C192 A nominative absolute is a peculiar kind of phrase related to the rest of the sentence in sense but not in grammar and made up of a noun or pronoun plus a participle or a participial phrase.

Classes having been dismissed, we found time heavy on our hands.

C193 Elliptical nominative absolutes, with the participle omitted but understood, are rather common.

(being)

The game ₍ₐ₎ over, Marty collapsed in the locker room.

(standing)

The dog ₍ₐ₎ at her side, Beth unlocked the door.

C194 Put the "subject" pronoun of a nominative absolute in the nominative case.

He

~~Him~~ absent, there was no one to play the piccolo.

Direct address

C195 A noun in direct address is a noun used to address someone or something, or to attract a person's attention. A noun in direct address is related to the rest of the sentence in sense but not in grammar; that is, it is not subject noun, object, modifier, and so on.

Drop that, *junior*!
Pulasko, where's your story?
Remember, *sister dear*, the times I've done the dishes for you.
Sorry, *friend*, you'll just have to look for the gold by yourself.

C196 Words that are usually adjectives may be used as nouns in direct address.

Turn on the ignition, *stupid*.
Where, my *sweet*, did you hide my pipe?
Those are my feet you're stepping on, *graceful*.
Well, *speedy*, what took you so long?

Appositives

C197 An appositive is a word, phrase, or clause used only to explain another substantive and meaning practically the same thing.

Our neighbors, the *Tuttles,* raise vultures.	The head word[29] is *neighbors*; the appositive noun, explaining *neighbors*, is *Tuttles.*
Bwana has gone with my brother, the witch *doctor.*	The head word is *brother*; the appositive noun, explaining *brother*, is *doctor.*
Whom did you forget — *me* ?	The head word is *whom*; the appositive pronoun, explaining *whom*, is *me.*
Her favorite sport, *sailing,* turned out to be very expensive.	The head word is *sport*; the appositive gerund, explaining *sport*, is *sailing.*
My job, *to sing two songs a night,* is pleasant.	The head word is *job*; the appositive infinitive phrase, explaining *job*, is *to sing two songs a night.*
The fact *that you are here* proves your innocence.	The head word is *fact*; the appositive clause, explaining *fact*, is *that you are here.*

C198 Except for the cases in C199, put appositive substantives into the same case as the head word.[30]

This is Stoat's [possessive], the catcher's [possessive], expensive new chest protector.

Did you see my cousin's [possessive], Monica's [possessive], new car?

---

[29] For convenience, the noun that is explained by an appositive is called "head word."

[30] See footnote 29.

Whose [possessive] is this—yours [possessive]?

Whom [objective] did you forget—me [objective]?

C199 Do not use the possessive case for both head word and appositive when *(a)* agreement would sound awkward or *(b)* head word and appositive are treated as a unit.

The next two meetings will be held at *Smith's*, the best *host* among us.	*Host's* would sound awkward.
I bought this pith helmet at *Carlton* the *Hatter's*.	*Carlton the Hatter's* is the trade name used by the company; therefore, it is considered a unit.
Have you seen *Brando the Great's* new trick—the one in which she pulls a hat out of a rabbit?	*Brando the Great's* is a unit.

C200 Some appositives are introduced by *or, namely*, and similar expressions.

A pirogue, or *dugout,* is the main means of transportation on some bayous.	*Dugout* is used to explain *pirogue* and means practically the same thing; therefore it is clearly an appostive.
A pirogue or a *raft* was what we needed.	*Raft* does not explain *pirogue* or mean the same thing; therefore it is clearly not an appositive.
There is only one person for whom I would vote; namely, my *uncle.*	*Uncle* explains *person* and in this sentence means the same thing; therefore it is clearly an appositive.
For your information those are flying mammals, or *bats.*	*Bats* is used to explain *flying mammals* and in this context means practically the same thing; therefore it is clearly an appositive.

C201 An appositive may be accompanied by objects, modifiers, and other words closely associated with it.

Her favorite sport, *hunting lost documents*, led to some surprising discoveries.	The whole noun phrase, *hunting lost documents*, is the appositive.

Restrictive and nonrestrictive appositives[31]

C202 Appositives are restrictive when the writer uses them as necessary to the sense or identity of the head word.

The very fact *that you are here* proves that you did not telephone me from Washington just now.	Suppose that you have not told the reader previously what fact you are talking about; *that you are here* is necessary to the sense. Therefore, you want *that you are here* joined very closely to the head word. The noun clause is restrictive.
At that moment, someone at the back of the hall raised the cry *"Down with Carrigan!"*	Suppose that you have not previously told the reader what the cry was; the sense would be incomplete without *down with Carrigan*. So you want *down with Carrigan* joined very closely to the head word. The noun phrase, therefore, is restrictive.
My cousin *John Keating* is brighter than all the rest of my cousins put together.	Suppose that you have several cousins and you want the reader to know that none of the others is meant but only John Keating. Then you must join *John Keating* very closely to the head word *cousin*. In other words, the noun *John Keating* is restrictive.

---

[31] The various rules for punctuation of appositives are treated in Section D and referenced in the index under Appositives, punctuation.

C203 Appositives are nonrestrictive when the writer joins them loosely to the head word merely as added information, as a point worth bringing in but not very necessary to the thought.

Let me tell you how lucky is your presence here at this moment. This fact, *that you are here,* proves that you did not telephone me from Washington just now.

Suppose that you have already told the reader what fact you mean and only add *that you are here* for emphasis and unmistakable clearness or even just for better rhythm. Then you want *that you are here* joined only loosely to the head word. In this case the noun clause is nonrestrictive.

This cry, *"Down with Carrigan!"* was taken up first by one voice, then by another, until it swelled into a hoarse, frightening chant.

Suppose that you have already told the reader what the cry was in an earlier sentence (not given here). Here you mention it only to remind the reader what it was and to emphasize it. So you do not want *down with Carrigan* joined very closely to the head word. The noun phrase is just added information and hence nonrestrictive.

A young cousin of mine, *John Keating,* stumbled upon the hide-out quite by accident.

Suppose that you add the information that your cousin is named John Keating simply because the addition might please a reader who knows him or might brighten the sentence by adding a bit of identification. Then you do not want *John Keating* joined very closely to the head word *cousin.* The noun *John Keating* is nonrestrictive.

C204 Often context or circumstances force a writer to use an appositive restrictively.

[If there has been no previous mention of the word *garrison*, then it must be restrictive in this sentence:] The word *garrison* does not sound Anglo-Saxon to me.

[If *novelist* and *statesman* were nonrestrictive in this sentence, the result would be nonsense:] I believe you are talking about Churchill the *novelist* rather than Churchill the *statesman*.

C205 Use this test: Read the sentence without the appositive. If the sentence still says basically what you want it to, the appositive is nonrestrictive (nonessential). If the sentence does not say what you want it to but something else, the appositive is restrictive (essential).

The butcher, Abell Miller, won't give us any credit.

[Without the appositive:] The butcher won't give us any credit.

Suppose that you are chiefly interested in saying that the butcher cut off your credit. You add *Abell Miller* not from need but as an extra. The sense does not change. The appositive is nonrestrictive.

Shirley was fond of the expression "you guys."

[Without the appositive:] Shirley was very fond of the expression.

Suppose that you chiefly intend to tell which expression Shirley was fond of. The omission changes the sense entirely. The appositive *you guys* is clearly restrictive.

I dropped the rescue note from the window on the chance that someone might be passing below.

[Without the appositive:] I dropped the rescue note from the window on the chance.

Suppose that you chiefly wish to state what it was that made you drop the rescue note from the window. The omission changes the sense entirely and leaves the sentence puzzling and incomplete. The appositive noun clause *that someone might be passing below* is clearly restrictive.

Pronoun use

Pronouns in general

C206 A pronoun is a word that is used in place of a noun or other substantive.

Frances was expected to object, but *she* didn't.

C207 Do not use *same* as a pronoun unless you wish to stress identity or similarity.

I have received your letter and thank you for ~~same~~ *it*.	Here there is no reason to stress identity. *It* carries the full meaning perfectly.
Water seeks its own level. The *same*, I think, may be said of mean characters.	Here there is reason to stress identity or similarity.

C208 Do not insert immediately after a subject noun a subject pronoun meaning exactly the same thing.[32]

Jules ~~he~~ wants to be a chemical engineer.
Willa Cather and Edna Ferber ~~they~~ are American novelists.

C209 Do not say *let's us*, which is the same as saying *let us us*.

~~Let's us~~ *Let us* be very careful in using contractions.

C210 Politeness usually requires that the personal pronouns *I* and *we* be placed last in a compound subject.

Mary and I [*not* I and Mary] have a suggestion.

[Poor:] Janice and I and Fred spent the entire day cleaning out the attic.
[Better:] Janice and Fred and I spent the entire day cleaning out the attic.

---

[32] Not affected by this rule are those rare constructions in dialogue in which a person is represented as thinking over names and then breaking off into a statement about them. Such a construction requires a dash; for example, "Willa Cather and Edna Ferber—they were American novelists, weren't they?"

Pronoun subjects, objects, and complements

C211 Put the subject pronoun of a predicate verb in the nominative case.

> *He*   *she*
> ~~Him~~ and ~~her~~ will come at eight.

> *they*
> Would Charles or his brother take a catfish off a hook? Not ~~them~~.

C212 Put the "subject" pronoun of a nominative absolute in the nominative case.

> *He*
> ~~Him~~ absent, there was no one to play the piccolo.

> *They* being what they are, I'm afraid that you will simply have to make allowances for them.

C213 Put the subject pronoun of an infinitive in the objective case.

The judges expected *him* to be nervous.

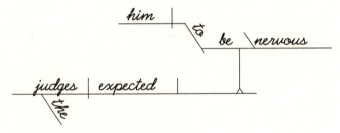

For *her* to object is unusual.

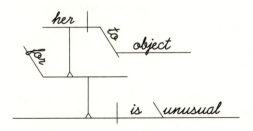

C214 In general, put the subject of a gerund in the possessive case or use the possessive adjective. When this is impossible or awkward, use the objective case. (See C379.)

Laura's coming home was a surprise.

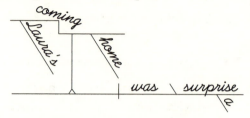

There is no doubt about *her* being elected.

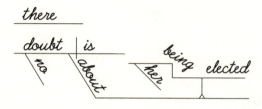

I can't conceive of *him*, a man we trusted, saying such a thing.

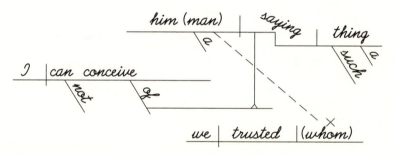

C215 Put the predicate pronoun of a predicate verb in the nominative case.[33]

It is *I.*

$$it \mid is \setminus I$$

---

[33] In informal writing and speaking, the objective case of the predicate pronoun is regularly used after *it is, it was,* and so on. An expression like "it is I" is appropriate in a formal context. In some other instances the objective is the only sensible form; for example, "That picture isn't really *him*" [instead of *he*].

This should be *she*.

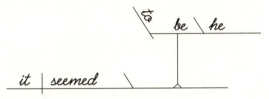

C216 Put the predicate pronoun of an infinitive in the nominative case if a nominative precedes the infinitive; put it in the objective case if an objective precedes the infinitive.

It [nominative] seemed to be *he* [nominative].

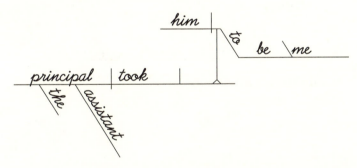

The assistant principal took him [objective, subject of the infinitive] to be *me* [objective].

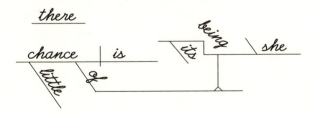

C217 Put the predicate pronoun of a gerund in the nominative case if a possessive precedes the gerund; put it in the objective case if an objective precedes the gerund.

There is little chance of *its* being *she*.

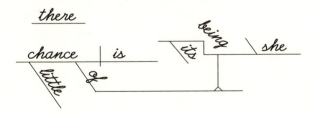

125

There is no doubt about *this* being *her*.

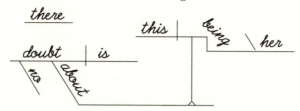

C218 Put a pronoun used as direct object of a predicate verb or of a verbal in the objective case.

Did I miss anyone? Yes, ~~he~~ and ~~she~~.

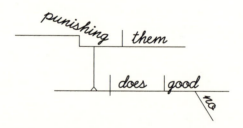

Who did you invite?[34]

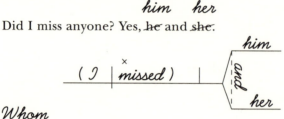

Punishing *them* does no good.

C219 Expressions like *I believe* and *do you suppose* complicate sentences containing *who* or *whom* and make it difficult to apply C218. Whenever you are in doubt, mentally diagram the sentence and see where *who* or *whom* falls in the diagram.

---

[34] In informal writing and speaking, *who* is regularly used instead of *whom* as direct object.

This is the gentleman whom, I believe, you distrust.

Whom is the direct object of the verb *distrust*.

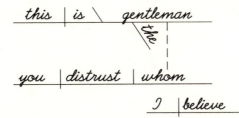

Who do you suppose ate the icing?

Who is the subject pronoun of the verb *ate*.

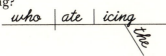

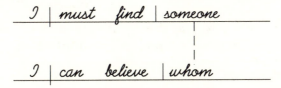

I must find someone *whom* I can believe.

Whom is the direct object of the verb *can believe*.

C220 Put a pronoun that is the indirect object in the objective case.

Generous though she usually is, Denise did not give *me* a piece of cake.

[Answering the question, "Did Denise give anybody a piece?":] Not *me*.

C221 Put the object pronoun of a preposition in the objective case.

me
Between you and I̶, I think Marty's personality is his new Lincoln.

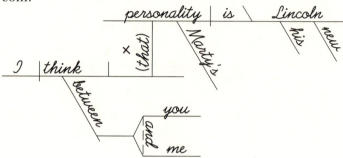

whom
I'm sure I gave the carbolic acid to someone. Now to w̶h̶o̶?

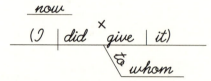

C222 In order to use the right case of a personal pronoun after *than* or *as*, mentally complete the elliptical sentence.

Tush, you are much stronger than *he* [is strong].
I'd trust Marcus sooner than [I'd trust] *her*.
I'd trust Marcus sooner than *she* [would trust Marcus].
There is no other so strong as *he* [is].

Pronouns and antecedents

C223 The noun whose place a pronoun takes is called the antecedent of the pronoun.

Helen said she would make ham sandwiches.   *Helen* is the antecedent of *she*.

C224 Sometimes a pronoun takes the place of another pronoun. The latter is then called the intermediate antecedent.

Each of the boys has his own way of making a bed.   *Each* is the intermediate antecedent of *his*.

C225 Except for the instances discussed in C226, make sure that every pronoun and possessive adjective has an antecedent.

Lack of antecedents

I want to tell you about a little experience I had while driving from Albuquerque to Santa Fe last week. They don't have culverts to carry off rain under the road. They just dip, and rain rushes down from the hills and over the road, usually leaving a lot of sand and gravel on them. We were driving too fast, I'll admit, when he shouted, "Look out! There's a dip." Well, the other didn't see the dip in time; and so it plowed right into the sand, skidded off the road, and stopped on the brink of a ravine some twenty feet deep. It is certainly dangerous, and I'll tell you it taught us a lesson.

Proper use of antecedents

I want to tell you about a little experience I had while driving from Albuquerque to Santa Fe last week. There are no culverts to carry off rain under the road. The highway just dips, and rain rushes down from the hills and over the road, usually leaving a lot of sand and gravel in the depressions. My companions and I were driving too fast, I'll admit, when one of them —not the driver—shouted, "Look out! There's a dip." Well, the driver didn't see the dip in time; and so the car plowed right into the sand, skidded off the road, and stopped on the brink of a ravine some twenty feet deep. Driving fast, especially over such treacherous roads, is certainly dangerous; and I'll tell you it taught us a lesson.

C226 In some expressions it is impossible and undesirable to give a definite antecedent for a pronoun. This, for instance, is true with the interrogative pronouns, the indefinite pronouns, and with *they* or *we* when the pronoun means "people in general," or *one* when it means "a person."

I say, *somebody* knocked.	The antecedent must be kept indefinite until it is disclosed who did knock.
Who is behind you?	It is impossible to give the antecedent of *who*—at least until the person being questioned answers.
[Right:] *It* is raining.	This is impersonal *it*, an idiomatic use. No antecedent can be named.
[Wrong:] *It* explains radar in this book.	*It* lacks an antecedent, and there is no reason for the construction. Say "This book explains radar."
[Wrong:] *It* says in the paper that the game was rained out.	Say "The paper says."
[Right:] *We* are all inclined to like people who like us.	*We* needs no antecedent here, because it means "people in general."
[Right:] *One* does not notice the rapid calculations the eye makes when one is guiding a bulky automobile through close-packed traffic.	*One* means "a person" here; hence no antecedent is needed.
[Wrong:] A pronoun is *one* that takes the place of a noun.	*One* should have a clear antecedent here, or it should be replaced by *a word*.
[Right:] *He* who prays is [*They* who pray are] certainly blessed.	*He* and *they* need no antecedent here, for the pronouns are the equivalent of "any person" or "people in general."
[Wrong:] I went down to the shop, and *she* gave me a brief tour.	*She* should have an antecedent in an earlier sentence.

C227 *You* is quite commonly used in the sense of "people in general," but it is so frequently confusing that it should be avoided in this sense as far as it can be without considerable awkwardness. Make all references clear.

Vague reference

"That old pinchbeak, Mrs. Snoop, and the other two neighborhood busybodies, Miss Small and Miss Prim, caught us just as we were about to leave."

"I'll bet she told you off about teasing her old cat."

"Yes. Well, you know what I told her? I told her if she didn't stop scratching my dog when she's asleep and harming nobody, I'd take her to the quarry pond and drown her in a sack."

"The old cat!"

"She is. She's an old cat."

Clear reference

"That old pinchbeak, Mrs. Snoop, and the other two neighborhood busybodies, Miss Small and Miss Prim, caught Johnny and me just as we were about to leave."

"I'll bet Mrs. Snoop told you two off about teasing her old cat."

"Yes. Well, you know what I told her? I told her that if her cat didn't stop scratching my dog when the dog is asleep and harming nobody, I'd take the cat to the quarry pond and drown her in a sack."

"Mrs. Snoop is an old cat herself."

"She is. She's an old cat."

C228 If a pronoun might cause confusion, do one of these things:

A. Put the pronoun so close to its antecedent that the reader must see without any trouble that the two go together.

B. Repeat the antecedent or use another noun.

C. Avoid the antecedent-pronoun arrangement altogether.

[Wrong:] On my last visit to Seaux, before it was bombed off the map, I saw a thing that moved me very much. *It* was a

It is not immediately clear whether *it* refers to Seaux or to the thing that moved the writer so much.

little town in the South of
France, hardly more than a
village. *It* moved me so deeply
because *it* was unexpected
and at the same time thoroughly American.

[Correction by moving antecedents and pronouns closer together:]
I remember my last visit to *Seaux* before it was bombed off the
map. *It* was a little town in the South of France, hardly more than
a village. My recollection is vivid because while I was there I saw
a *thing* that moved me very much. *It* moved me so deeply because
it was unexpected and at the same time thoroughly American.

[Correction by repeating the antecedent or using another noun:]
On my last visit to Seaux, before it was bombed off the map, I
saw a thing that moved me very much. *Seaux* was a little town in
the South of France, hardly more than a village. The *incident*
moved me so deeply because it was unexpected and at the same
time thoroughly American.

[Correction by rewriting so as to avoid the antecedent-pronoun
arrangement:]
On my last visit to Seaux (until it was bombed off the map,
Seaux was a little town in the South of France, hardly more
than a village), I saw a thing that moved me very much. *I was
moved* so deeply because what happened was unexpected and at
the same time thoroughly American.

C229 The case of a pronoun depends on how the pronoun is
used in its own clause or sentence.

We met an Eskimo ~~whom~~ *who* had been converted by Father Buliard.

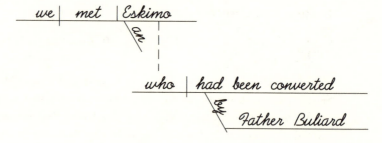

The Eskimo *whom* we met had been converted by Father Buliard.

C230 Make a pronoun agree with its antecedent in person, number, and gender.

Nora [second-person antecedent], you [second person] put those books behind you [second person].

My fellow *officers* and *I* [plural antecedents (*I* is an intermediate antecedent)] promise that we [plural] will give safe-conduct to any messenger sent to us [plural].

The *tree* [neuter antecedent], strong as it [neuter] looked, splintered as it [neuter] fell.

C231 When the antecedent is the context or situation, make the pronoun third person, singular number, neuter gender.

It's Anna coming up the stairs, isn't *it*?
It was another sales representative at the front desk.

C232 Use a singular pronoun with a singular collective noun, unless the members of the group are clearly acting as separate individuals.

its
The *team* lost ~~their~~ second game through sheer nervousness.

their
The *team* were either standing, kneeling, or lying at ~~its~~ ease in the end zone.

C233 Use a singular pronoun when the antecedent is two or more singular nouns or pronouns joined by *or, nor, either . . . or, neither . . . nor,* or other disjunctives.

his
Have you no pen? *Joe or Ted* will lend you ~~theirs~~.

hers
Whose hat is this? *Neither Lou nor Meg* left ~~theirs~~.

c

C234 Use a plural pronoun when the antecedent is made up of a plural and a singular word.

My *brothers* and *I* have *our* quarrels, but *we* get along.

If *Mary* and her *friends* come in after school to make fudge, tell *them* not to use all the sugar.

C235 When an antecedent is made up of words in the first and the second or third persons, put the pronoun in the first person.

You, your *sister,* and *I* are to wait for *our* group captain on the corner of Washington and Beloit.

You and *I* are to wait for *our* group captain on the corner of Washington and Beloit.

My *teammates* and *I* met *our* match at bowling last night; *we* lost.

C236 When an antecedent is made up of words in the second and third persons, put the pronoun in the second person.

You and *Clifford* ought to wait for *your* group captain on the corner of Washington and Beloit.

You and your *teammates* certainly met *your* match at bowling last night; *you* lost.

C237 When agreement is complicated by an *of* expression *(the number of, best of, one of,* and so on), make sure that you select the right antecedent according to the meaning you wish to convey.

The only one of his stories that *was* amusing was a tale of three men locked in an elevator.	*One* is the antecedent, not *stories,* since all of the stories but one were dull.
One of the people who *were* present was a Don Q.	*People* is the antecedent, not *one.*
This was the best of the stories that *were* told.	*Stories* is the antecedent, not *best* or *this.*

The number of members, *which runs* [or *who run*] into the thousands, surprises me.	Either *number* or *members* may be the antecedent.
The number of members who *were* absent was truly deplorable.	*Members* is the antecedent, not *number.*

C238 Except for the cases in C240, make a pronoun agree in person, number, and gender with an indefinite pronoun that is the (intermediate) antecedent.

> As for schedule cards, *all* of us lost *ours.*
> I remembered my lines, but *several* forgot *theirs.*
> *Someone* left *her* earrings at our house.

C239 When the antecedent is both masculine and feminine, you may treat the indefinite pronoun as masculine. Most writers today, however, use an inclusive gender form in such cases when this can be done *without awkwardness or loss of meaning*.

> *Each* and *every* person here must do *his* own fair share.
> [Acceptable:] *Everyone* has *his* share of joys and sorrows.
> [Improved:] *All people* have *their* share of joys and sorrows.

Most writers today avoid use, where possible, of masculine gender forms with words such as *everybody, everyone, each, person* when the meaning includes both feminine and masculine genders. In such cases, the best solution is either to rephrase the sentence into the plural or to reword the singular in order to eliminate unnecessary gender problems.

> A. Give *each* student *his* paper when *he* is ready.
>   Give students *their* papers when they are ready.

> B. The average *person* is concerned about *his* taxes.
>   The average *person* is concerned about taxes.

C240 When a singular reference after *everybody* or *everyone* is awkward or meaningless, the plural should be used.

When I came out of the dark cellar, *everybody* was laughing at me; but even so I was glad to see *them*.

The candidate made an excellent impression on *everyone*, and *they* cheered her wildly.

[Formal:] *Everybody* has a right to *his* opinion.
[Informal:] *Everybody* has a right to *their* opinion.

C241 When the indefinite pronoun *one* is the (intermediate) antecedent, put the pronoun in the third person, singular number.

[Wrong:] One does *their* [or *your*] best in life by serving God.
[Right:] One does *one's* best in life by serving God.
[Right:] One does *his* [or *her*] best in life by serving God.

C242 Put a pronoun in the third person singular when its antecedent is modified by a singular indefinite adjective.

Each truck and *each* trailer must have *its* proper license.
Neither one looks like *his* mother.

Personal-pronoun use

C243 Do not write *theres* or *there's* for *theirs*.

The money is *theirs*, belongs to them.
There's [there is] food enough for everybody. Please take your time.

theirs

These must be friends of ~~theres~~.

C244 Do not write *it's* or *its'* for *its*.

its

What a pretty kitten! What's ~~it's~~ name?

Demonstrative-pronoun use

C245 Do not use *them* where you should use a demonstrative.

[Homemaker, pointing to the cheapest grapefruit on the counter:]

those

"I'll take a dozen of ~~them~~."

Those

~~Them~~ are just the words I expected to hear, Clarence.

C246 Do not say *this here, that there, these here,* and *those there.*

These ~~here~~ will fit, but those ~~there~~ will not.

C247 If you insert words between the demonstrative and *here* or *there,* the expression can stand in good writing but should not be used unless the rhythm or some other quality of the sentence will be helped.

"Now *these melons here,*" said Mr. Grover, leading me down the row of exhibits, "are about the size of a healthy California grape."

Self-Pronoun use

C248 Do not use a *self*-pronoun where a personal pronoun can carry the full meaning without sounding awkward.

[Wrong:] Susan and *myself* were here at seven-thirty.
[Right:] Susan and *I* were here at seven-thirty.

[Wrong:] Robert gave the old bicycle to my brother and *myself.*
[Right:] Robert gave the old bicycle to my brother and *me.*

[Wrong:] *Ourselves* and the others made twenty people.
[Right:] *We* and the others made twenty people.

[Right:] There goes Careless Smith hurting *himself* again.	If you used the personal pronoun here, you would change the meaning of the sentence to something else.
[Right:] Finally the guard left us to *ourselves.*	*Left us to us* would sound strange indeed.
[Right:] They are quite able to get along by *themselves.*	*By them* would sound strange and mean nothing.

C249 Do not write *ourselfs* for *ourselves, hisself* for *himself,* or *theirselves* for *themselves.*

ourselves

We are proud of ~~ourselfs~~.

himself

I think he hurt ~~hisself~~ badly.

themselves

I say let them take care of ~~theirselves~~.

Relative-pronoun use

C250 The relative pronouns are used only to introduce (dependent) adjective clauses.

I know the girl *whom* you mean.	*Whom you mean* is a dependent adjective clause modifying the noun *girl* in the independent clause.
We found the weapon *that* he probably used.	*That he probably used* is an adjective clause modifying *weapon.*
The newspaper account, *which* I read last night, didn't give her name.	*Which I read last night* is an adjective clause modifying *account.*

C251 A relative pronoun refers to an antecedent in another clause. This fact makes a relative pronoun and its adjective clause easy to distinguish from (a) an interrogative or indefinite pronoun or adjective and its noun clause, (b) the demonstrative-pronoun and demonstrative-adjective *that,* and (c) the conjunction *that.*[35]

I know the *girl whom* you mean.	*Whom* is a relative pronoun. It has an antecedent, the noun *girl,* in the independent clause of the sentence.

---

[35] A relative pronoun sometimes has as its antecedent the whole idea expressed in the independent clause; for example, "She sang badly, which made the maestro wince." But it is difficult to use this construction without awkwardness and confusion. Avoid it until you are a professional writer.

c

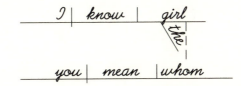

I know *whom* you mean.

Whom is not a relative pronoun. It does not have an antecedent in the independent clause.

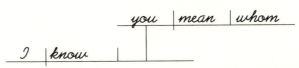

Here are the *blueprints that* you were looking for.

That is a relative pronoun. It has an antecedent in the independent clause: *blueprints*. So the dependent clause is an adjective clause.

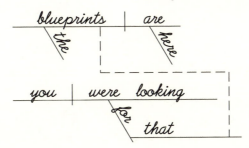

I was looking for the blueprints when I found *that* on the floor.

That is not a relative pronoun. It has no antecedent in the independent clause.

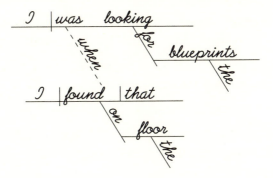

I was looking for something else when I found *that* blueprint on the floor.

That is not a relative pronoun. It has no antecedent in the independent clause.

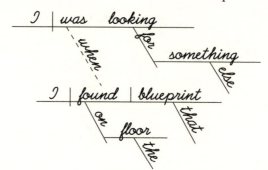

I knew *that* you were looking for the blueprints.

That is not a relative pronoun. It has no antecedent in the other clause (the independent clause).

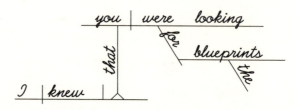

C252 Ordinarily use *that* to introduce restrictive adjective clauses and *which* to introduce nonrestrictive adjective clauses. (If, however, awkwardness results, simply ignore this rule and use whichever word seems better.)

[Restrictive:] The bike *that* I sold is very different from the bike *that* you sold.

[Nonrestrictive:] The bike, *which*, by the way, I sold the other day, had become an object of envy among the children.

[Restrictive:] The competition was as fierce as that *which* (not *that*) the team had experienced in Barcelona.

The introductory *that* is frequently omitted from such clauses (though, of course, it is still understood).

This is the only dictionary *(that)* I have.

C253 The case of the relative pronoun does not depend on the case of the antecedent but is determined by the way the relative is used in its own clause.

who

We met an Eskimo ~~whom~~ had been converted by Father Buliard.

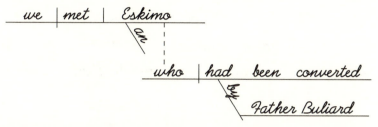

C254 Parenthetical clauses that intervene between the relative pronoun and the rest of its own clause do not affect the case of the relative.

who

Tim is a man ~~whom~~ we know will fight for us.

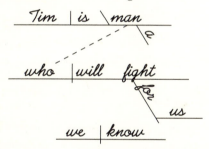

C255 To determine whether a clause is parenthetical or not, read the sentence omitting the clause in question. If the sentence continues to say what you want it to, the clause is parenthetical.

Tim is a man who ~~we know~~ will fight for us.

Cancel the clause *we know* and the sentence still makes easy, good sense; and the meaning is largely unchanged. It is clear, therefore, that *we know* is parenthetical.

Interrogative-pronoun use

C256 Do not use an apostrophe with *whose* when it is used as an interrogative pronoun, and do not confuse *whose* (of whom) with the contraction *who's* (who is).

Whose
~~Who's~~ are you wearing?

Indefinite-pronoun use

C257 Use *less* to indicate how much, *fewer* to indicate how many.

Fewer   *are*
~~Less~~ than five instructions ~~is~~ insufficient.
Less than a bushel is insufficient.
There is *less* time and *fewer* workers than we had expected.

Adjective and adverb use

Adjective use

C258 A predicate adjective is one that follows a linking verb, whose subject it modifies.

The iron is becoming *red*.
You are called *lucky*.

C259 An attributive adjective is one that modifies its substantive directly, without the intervention of any sort of a linking verb.

Don't eat *green* apples.
There is a *happy* girl.

C260 Attributive adjectives are often used as objective complements, directly modifying the object of a verb or preposition.

I find this paint *sticky*.
Simpson dropped his chin like a man *shot*.
We all found the play *humorous*.
She fought back like a person *possessed*.

C261 An appositive adjective is an attributive adjective that is used in an appositive way; that is, it is loosely attached to its substantive as a kind of afterthought, an extra description, an added detail. Ordinarily an appositive adjective follows the substantive it modifies, though it may sometimes precede.

The wind, *mournful* and *desolate*, howled all night through the branches of the empty trees.

Long, gleaming, two-edged, a knife stuck in the wall.

C262 Clarity often requires that the article be used with each substantive or adjective to show that more than one person or thing is meant.

The secretary and *the* treasurer *were* arrested. [Two people.]
The secretary and treasurer *was* arrested. [One person.]

A black and *a* white purse *were* lost. [Two purses.]
A black and white purse *was* lost. [One purse.]

Adverb use

C263 Do not use *most* (to the maximum degree) for *almost* (not quite).

almost
The milk is ~~most~~ gone.

C264 Do not use two negatives.

anything
I didn't do ~~nothing~~ wrong!

C265 In connection with C264, remember that words like *scarcely, hardly, barely, nothing, nobody*, and *never* are negative.

was
There ~~wasn't~~ scarcely any recoil.

was
For the tenth consecutive day there ~~wasn't~~ hardly any breeze.

barely recognized

His face was so battered I ~~didn't barely recognize~~ him.

any

There was hardly ~~no~~ water in the radiator.

anybody

No, sir, I didn't see ~~nobody~~.

anything

In her whole life she never did ~~nothing~~ to harm anyone.

C266   Do not use *never* when you mean simply *not*.

didn't take

I ~~never took~~ those letters for you this afternoon.

C267   Do not add an *s* to *somewhere, anywhere, nowhere,* or *anyway*.

somewhere

Let's go ~~somewheres~~ else.

C268   Do not use *kind of* or *sort of* as an adverb; use *somewhat, rather, fairly,* and so on.

a little

I'm ~~kind of~~ tired.

rather

It is ~~sort of~~ absurd for her to challenge the coach.

C269   Do not use *real* either for *really* or for *very* or *extremely*.

very

The coffee is ~~real~~ hot.

C270   Do not use *some* for *somewhat* or *a little*.

somewhat

He reads ~~some~~ faster than he used to.

I'm *a little* perplexed by your argument.

C271 Do not use *sure* but *surely* to mean undoubtedly, indeed, yes indeed.

surely
You ~~sure~~ told her.

Surely
Will I work for five dollars an hour? ~~Sure!~~

C272 Do not place *too* or *very* immediately before a past participle that usage has not as yet established as an adjective. Between *very* or *too* and the past participle insert an appropriate adverb, like *deeply, genuinely, greatly, much.*

Questionable	*Preferable*
Yes, indeed, we were *very* impressed.	Yes, indeed, we were *very much* impressed.
But, sir, I am *too* indebted to you already.	But, sir, I am *too deeply* indebted to you already.

[Correct:] You could hardly expect her to admit that she is a *very* distinguished person.

C273 It is preferable, ordinarily, not to use *up* after such verbs as *ascend, connect, cripple, divide, end, finish, open, rest,* and *settle.*

All the candidates ascended ~~up~~ the platform.
Please connect me ~~up~~ with the superintendent.
Poor Mother is all crippled ~~up~~ with rheumatism.
Let's divide ~~up~~ the candy now!
Where does this highway end ~~up~~?
At last Angus has finished ~~up~~ drying the dishes.
Don't open ~~up~~ this package until Christmas.
It will take me a long time to rest ~~up~~ completely.
Why don't these people settle ~~up~~ their bills?

[Not affected by this rule, because *up* is necessary:] On the seventh day we broke *up* several packing cases for fuel.

Confusion of adjective and adverb

C274 Do not use adjectives to modify verbs, adjectives, or adverbs.[36]

well
I didn't do very ~~good~~ in the physics test.

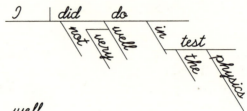

well
This is a ~~good~~-built house.

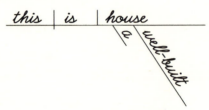

nicely
She played a bit of Chopin very ~~nice~~.

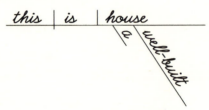

heavily
Don't walk about so ~~heavy~~.

---

[36] For the use of adjectives with linking verbs and for problem sentences like "I feel bad" or "I feel badly," see C163-65.

Robert behaved very ~~bad~~ *badly* at Mrs. Snifton's tea.

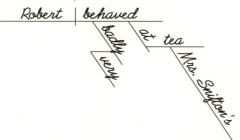

C275 Do not use *this* or *that* for the adverbs *so* or *very*.

He was ~~that~~ *so* happy he could only cry.

I have never seen the lake ~~this~~ *so* blue as this.

Comparison of adjectives and adverbs

The three degrees of comparison

C276 Comparison is the change made in the form of adjectives and adverbs to show that the word they modify is greater or less in quantity or quality than something else.

C277 The positive degree indicates that the substantive modified is not being compared with anything else. The comparative and superlative degrees indicate that the substantive modified is being compared with something else. (The comparative involves only two things; the superlative, at least three.[37])

[Positive degree:] A hamburger is a *beautiful* thing.
[Comparative degree:] A hamburger is *more beautiful* than anything else I know.

---

[37] The superlative degree of an adjective or adverb (usually with *most*) may be used without any suggestion of comparison to express a high degree of perfection, imperfection, and the like. For examples see C301.

[Superlative degree:] A hamburger is the *most beautiful* thing in the world.

[Positive degree:] What a *large* onion that is.
[Comparative degree:] Bermuda onions are a great deal *larger* than chives.
[Superlative degree:] This is the *largest* onion of the three.

[Positive degree:] Ms. Marble closed the store *early*.
[Comparative degree:] Ms. Marble closed the store *earlier* than Mr. Kemp closed his.
[Superlative degree:] Of all the merchants on Clay Avenue, Ms. Marble closed her store *earliest*.

Forming the comparative and superlative

C278 Many adjectives (and some adverbs) of one and two syllables form the comparative by adding *er,* and the superlative by adding *est,* to the positive.

Positive	*Comparative*	*Superlative*
dull	dull*er*	dull*est*
small	small*er*	small*est*
large	larg*er*	larg*est*
few	few*er*	few*est*
humble	humbl*er*	humbl*est*
flighty	flight*ier*	flight*iest*
high	high*er*	high*est*
near[38]	near*er*	near*est*
early	earl*ier*	earl*iest*

C279 If the adjective or adverb ends in *e*, drop that *e* before *er* and *est*. If the adjective ends in *y* preceded by a consonant, change the *y* to *i*.

humble	humbler	humblest
flighty	flightier	flightiest

---

[38] A number of adverbs have alternate forms that are identical with the corresponding adjectives; for example, *near, quick, sharp, slow.*

C280 If the adjective or adverb is of one syllable, double a final consonant after a vowel that is short in sound.

fat	fa*tt*er	fa*tt*est
wet	we*tt*er	we*tt*est
thin	thi*nn*er	thi*nn*est
hot	ho*tt*er	ho*tt*est

C281 Many adjectives and adverbs of one and two syllables and all adjectives and adverbs of more than two form the comparative by placing *more* or *less,* and the superlative by placing *most* or *least,* before the positive.

Positive	*Comparative*	*Superlative*
dull	*more* dull	*most* dull
dull	*less* dull	*least* dull
humble	*more* humble	*most* humble
humble	*less* humble	*least* humble
softly	*more* softly	*most* softly
softly	*less* softly	*least* softly
absurdly	*more* absurdly	*most* absurdly
absurdly	*less* absurdly	*least* absurdly
delightfully	*more* delightfully	*most* delightfully
delightfully	*less* delightfully	*least* delightfully
elaborate	*more* elaborate	*most* elaborate
elaborate	*less* elaborate	*least* elaborate
joyously	*more* joyously	*most* joyously
joyously	*less* joyously	*least* joyously
admirable	*more* admirable	*most* admirable
admirable	*less* admirable	*least* admirable
near	*less* near	*least* near
close	*less* close	*least* close

C282 The following adjectives and adverbs form the comparative and superlative irregularly as shown.

ADJECTIVES

Positive	Comparative	Superlative
good	better	best
well	better	best
bad	worse	worst
ill	worse	worst
little	smaller [size]	smallest [size]
	less [quantity]	least [quantity]
much	more	most

ADJECTIVES

Positive	Comparative	Superlative
many	more	most
far	further	furthest
	farther	farthest
	[distance only]	[distance only]

ADVERBS

Positive	Comparative	Superlative
well	better	best
ill	worse	worst
badly	worse	worst
much	more	most
little	less	least
	further	furthest
far	farther	farthest
	[distance only]	[distance only]

C283 Note that the comparison of *few* is *fewer* and *fewest* (C278), not *less* and *least*. Do not say "Less people came than were expected." Say "Fewer people came than were expected."

C284 Of their very nature some adjectives and adverbs have, strictly speaking, no comparative or superlative. Such are *unique, dead, circular, triangular.* Some of them, however, are used in loose or figurative comparisons; for example, *deader than a doornail.* But it is considered a blunder to attribute any degree whatever to *unique* or *peerless*, since *unique* means the only one of its kind and *peerless* means without equal. So do not say "very unique" or "more peerless."

Using the comparative

C285 Use the comparative with *than*.

Horrowitz is a *better* quarterback *than* Flugel.
Chetwood was hurt *less severely than* Tracy or Cameron.
Schmidt proved *more obstreperous than* we expected.

C286 Do not use the comparative if you are comparing more than two persons or things or more than two groups of persons or things.

Geraldine is clearly the *most* bashful of the three Hollingsworth girls.

If you are talking about the Sneeds, the Clarks, and the Lapierres, the Clarks are to my mind the *most* charitable couple of the three.

C287 Finish a comparison involving *than* before beginning one involving *as* or *so*, and vice versa.

[Wrong:] She is prettier but not so entertaining as her sister.
[Right:] She is prettier *than* her sister but not so entertaining.[39]

C288 Keep balance in a comparison.

[Wrong:] The freshmen's awards are far, far handsomer than the sophomores.	Awards are compared with sophomores.
[Right:] The freshmen's awards are far, far handsomer than the sophomores'.	Freshmen's awards are compared with sophomores' awards.

---

[39] The adverb *so* may be used in a negative statement; *as* is equally correct in such instances.

C289 Do not use double comparatives.

Wait! I know a ~~more~~ better way.

C290 When using the comparative with things of the same group, use *other, else,* or an equivalent word.

[Wrong:] Dr. Black has more elaborate gadgets than any dentist in town.	This compares Dr. Black with himself and says that he has more elaborate gadgets than he himself has.
[Right:] Dr. Black has more elaborate gadgets than any *other* dentist in his town.	This compares Dr. Black with the rest of his group—the dentists in his town. *Other* keeps the doctor from being compared with himself.

[Wrong:] I have made larger contributions to the United Way drive than anybody in my class.
[Right:] I have made larger contributions to the United Way drive than anybody *else* in my class.

[Wrong:] I like tutti-frutti better than any flavor.
[Right:] I like tutti-frutti better than any *other* flavor.

C291 When using the comparative with things of different groups, do not use the words *other, else,* or some other equivalent expression.

[Wrong:] This steam engine develops as much power as any *other* diesel.	This statement implies that a steam engine is a diesel engine. The word *other* illogically puts the two engines in the same group or class.

[Right:] This steam engine develops as much power as any diesel.

[Wrong:] Without training, Stani sings as well as somebody *else* with years of music school behind him.	This statement implies that the untrained Stani has had years of music school. *Else* puts Stani in the group of those who have had training.

[Right:] Without training, Stani sings as well as somebody with years of music school behind him.

[Wrong:] This plane is as big and comfortable as any *other* moderate-sized ocean liner.
[Right:] This plane is as big and comfortable as any moderate-sized ocean liner.

C292 In order to use the right case of a personal pronoun after *than* or *as*, mentally complete the elliptical sentence.

Tush! You are much stronger than *he* [is strong].
I'd trust Marcus sooner than [I'd trust] *her*.
I'd trust Marcus sooner than *she* [would trust Marcus].
There is no other so strong as *he* [is].

C293 Do not substitute *all the farther, all the further, all the faster, all the longer, all the quicker,* and similar expressions for *as far as, as fast as, as long as, as quick as,* and similar expressions of comparison.

as long as
This is ~~all the longer~~ I can wait.

the fastest
Four knots an hour is ~~all the faster~~ that the *Q* will sail.

[Right, since it is not a substitute for *as soon as*:] If you leave now, you will get to Covington all the sooner.

Using the superlative

C294 Use the superlative degree when *than* is not used and more than two persons or things or groups of persons or things are compared.[40]

---

[40] There are idiomatic uses of the superlative with only two involved; for example, "Put your best foot forward" or [said to two prizefighters:] "May the best man win."

greatest

There are faith, hope, and charity, of which the ~~greater~~ is charity.

fattest

Which was the ~~fatter~~—Cassius, Casca, or Caesar?

most

Of the five tennis players, who is the ~~more~~ talented?

C295 When an *of* phrase limits an adjective or adverb in the superlative degree, do not use *other, else,* or an equivalent word.

[Wrong:] That suggestion is the most cowardly of all the *others*.
[Right:] That suggestion is the most cowardly of all.

[Wrong:] I am the least known of all the *other* poets in my class.
[Right:] I am the least known of all the poets in my class.

C296 When an *of* phrase limits an adjective or adverb in the superlative degree, make the object of *of* a plural noun or a collective noun.

[Wrong:] Paul has the sincerest friends of any *boy* in our class.
[Right:] Paul has the sincerest friends of all the *boys* in our class.

[Wrong:] You are the least responsible person of *anybody* I know.
[Right:] You are the least responsible of all the people I know.

[Wrong:] Rover has the best qualities of any *dog* in the show.
[Right:] Rover has the best qualities of all *the dogs* in the show.

C297 When an *of* phrase limits an adjective or adverb in the superlative degree, make sure that the object of *of* includes the person or thing to be compared.

[Wrong:] Nolan Kane is the most talented of his brothers, Kerry and "Sugar" Kane.   This sentence says that Nolan is one of his two brothers, which is absurd.

[Right:] Of the three Kane brothers—Nolan, Kerry, and "Sugar"—Nolan is the most talented.

[Wrong:] of all the cities along the Mississippi, the people of Natchez seem to me the most charming. | This sentence compares cities with people, instead of people with other people.

[Right:] Of all the *dwellers* in the cities along the Mississippi, the *people* of Natchez seem to me the most charming.

[Wrong:] You are the least responsible of all the *others* I know.
[Right:] You are the least responsible of all the boys I know.

C298 Do not use a superlative where the comparative is called for and is sufficient.

Of the two plans, this is the ~~least~~ *less* effective.

C299 Do not use double superlatives.

You do the ~~most~~ oddest things!

C300 Make all comparisons grammatical and complete.

[Wrong:] She maintained that Rudolph Valentino was one of the handsomest actors, if not the handsomest, of modern times.
[Right:] She maintained that Rudolph Valentino was one of the handsomest actors, if not the handsomest *actor*, of modern times.

[Wrong:] Oil is one of the greatest, if not the greatest, export commodities of Alaska.
[Right:] Oil is probably the greatest export commodity of Alaska.

[Wrong:] One of, if not the oldest, ministers in the city is Pastor James Hardy.
[Right:] Pastor James Hardy is either the oldest minister in the city or one of the oldest.

C301 The superlative degree of an adjective or adverb (usually with *most*) may be used without any suggestion of comparison to express a high degree of perfection, imperfection, and the like.

This cowardly remark is *most unworthy* of you.

I must say he was a *most unruly* little boy.

And, of course, all of your teachers have treated you *most kindly?*

Restrictive and nonrestrictive modifiers

C302 Modifiers are classified as restrictive and nonrestrictive. By modifiers are meant adjectives (including participles used adjectivally) and adjective phrases and clauses, adverbs and adverb phrases and clauses.

C303 Modifiers are called restrictive (essential) when the writer wants them joined very closely in sense to the words that they modify.

The accountants *that I know* dress fastidiously.

C304 Modifiers are called nonrestrictive (nonessential) when the writer wants them joined loosely to the words that they modify—as added information, as a by-the-way thought, as a point worth bringing in but not necessary to the chief notions of the sentence.

A comb—*which, by the way, costs very little*—is equipment that you should have and even use.

C305 To determine whether a modifier is restrictive or not, read the sentence without the modifier. If the sentence still says essentially what you want it to, the modifier is nonrestrictive (nonessential). If the sentence is changed—if it does not say what you want it to but something else—the modifier is restrictive (essential).

I prefer freshmen, enthusiastic and willing.

[Without the modifier:] I prefer freshmen.

Suppose that you wish mainly to say that you had rather teach freshmen than other classes. Suppose you add *enthusiastic and willing* as extra and secondary information explaining why you prefer freshmen. The adjectives, then, are nonrestrictive.

I prefer freshmen enthusiastic and willing.

[Without the modifier:] I prefer freshmen.

Suppose you wish to say that you like freshmen better when they are enthusiastic and willing than when they are lazy. The omission of *enthusiastic* and *willing* would change this sense. Here the adjectives are restrictive.

Johnson, blubbering, was a sight to behold.

[Without the modifier:] Johnson was a sight to behold.

Suppose your chief thought is that Johnson was a sight to behold. You add *blubbering* as an interesting detail, unnecessary to the main idea. In this sentence the participial adjective is nonrestrictive.

Johnson blubbering was a sight to behold.

[Without the modifier:] Johnson was a sight to behold.

Suppose that you wish to say that it was an astonishing thing to see an ordinarily brave man like Johnson mumbling tearfully. Omit *blubbering* and the sentence no longer expresses your meaning. In this sentence the participial adjective is restrictive.

Joan Drew was, probably, the only person at the table who had ever tasted enchiladas.

[Without the modifier:] Joan Drew was the only person at the table who had ever tasted enchiladas.

Suppose that your main point is that Joan was the only one who had tasted enchiladas. You add *probably* as an afterthought, just to be accurate. Omit *probably* and your chief thought is unchanged. The adverb is nonrestrictive.

Joan Drew was probably the only person at the table who had ever tasted enchiladas.

[Without the modifier:] Joan Drew was the only person at the table who had ever tasted enchiladas.

The column of Allen's, about fast driving, made Oliver Hornsby angry.

[Without the modifier:] That column of Allen's made Oliver Hornsby angry.

The column of Allen's about fast driving made Oliver Hornsby angry.

[Without the modifier:] That column of Allen's made Oliver Hornsby angry.

I did take the car back, right after the dance.

[Without the modifier:] I did take the car back.

I took the car back right after the dance.

[Without the modifier:] I took the car back.

Suppose that you want as part of your chief thought that you are not certain but nearly so that only Joan has tasted enchiladas. Omit *probably*. The sentence is not what you intend. The adverb is restrictive.

Suppose your chief thought is that Allen's column made Hornsby angry. Your readers know the column you refer to. You add *about fast driving* only to be sure they remember. The phrase is nonrestrictive.

Suppose you are sure that your readers will not know which column you are talking about unless you name it. *About fast driving* is necessary to your chief thought. The adjective phrase is restrictive.

Suppose your chief thought is that you took the car back. You add *right after the dance* only as some extra information that might impress your readers. The adverb phrase is nonrestrictive.

Suppose your chief purpose is to tell *when* you took the car back. In this sentence the adverb phrase is restrictive.

Mr. Ruhlman, who was here less than an hour ago, has just died.

[Without the modifier:] Mr. Ruhlman has just died.

The Mr. Ruhlman who was here less than an hour ago just died.

[Without the modifier:] The Mr. Ruhlman just died.

No one will be in the office on the Fourth, because that's a holiday.
[Without the modifier:] No one will be in the office on the Fourth.

No one would commit murder just because he did not like a hat.

[Without the modifier:] No one would commit murder.

The politician, whom we both admire, spoke to the crowd.

The politician whom we both admire spoke to the crowd.

Suppose your chief thought is that Mr. Ruhlman just died. *Who was here less than an hour ago* is an interesting, but extra, detail. The adjective clause is nonrestrictive.

Suppose that you are using the dependent clause to distinguish the dead Mr. Ruhlman from another Mr. Ruhlman. It is necessary to your thought. In this sentence the adjective clause is restrictive.

Suppose that you add *because that's a holiday* only to emphasize what has already been made clear. The adverbial clause is nonrestrictive.

Suppose that you are discussing motives for murder. The motive is then part of the chief thought. Omit *just because he did not like a hat* and you say something you do not intend —something silly, in fact. The adverbial clause is restrictive.

Suppose your chief thought is that the politician spoke. *Whom we both admire* is an extra bit of information. The adjective clause is nonrestrictive.

Suppose you want to distinguish this politician from others. *Whom we admire* is a restrictive adjective clause.

C306 Adjectives that precede their nouns must, in most cases, be restrictive if they are to make any sense at all. But there are exceptions.

[Restrictive:] The *perfect* friend is a hard one to find.
[Restrictive:] We heard the news on an *old* and *asthmatic* radio.
[Restrictive:] A *black* limousine stopped at the *neighborhood* Dairy Queen.

[Nonrestrictive:] *Unafraid*, Germaine faced the crowd.
[Nonrestrictive:] The last balloon popped and, *dismayed*, Joey burst into tears.

[Nonrestrictive:] The ice cream, *melted*, and the sandwiches, *hard* and *stale*, proved unappetizing fare.

C307 Articles are always restrictive.

The solution did not appeal to Blackbeard.
A bat and *an* eagle should not be kept in *the* same cage.

C308 Almost all adverbs that precede and modify adjectives or adverbs must be restrictive if they are to make sense.

The fumes were *quite* strong.
I have never seen you behave *more* disagreeably.
Millie delivered a *very* impassioned speech to her classmates.

C309 *Possibly, probably, certainly, perhaps, therefore, consequently, doubtless,* and some other adverbs expressing certainty, doubt, or conclusion almost always modify verbs and hence may be used restrictively or nonrestrictively.

[Restrictive:] The boy was tall and *probably* strong.
[Nonrestrictive:] The boy was tall and, *probably*, strong.

C310 Introductory phrases have their own rules of punctuation (D60-65), regardless of whether they are restrictive or nonrestrictive.

C311 Adverb clauses that precede their independent clause have their own rule of punctuation (D57), regardless of whether they are restrictive or nonrestrictive.

Dangling, misplaced, and squinting modifiers

Dangling modifiers

C312 Modifiers that seem to modify no word (or no word sensibly) are called dangling modifiers.

[Dangling adjective:] *Curious,* the forbidden door loomed as a challenge.
[Right:] The forbidden door loomed as a challenge to the two curious children.

[Dangling participle:] *Exhausted,* the bed looked inviting.
[Right:] Since I was exhausted, the bed looked inviting.

[Dangling participial phrase:] An hour later, *strolling the beach and climbing the sand dunes,* an outrigger canoe emerged from behind Starvation Point.
[Right:] An hour later, while Mary and Steve were strolling the beach and climbing the sand dunes, an outrigger canoe emerged from behind Starvation Point.

[Dangling phrase with gerund:] *After having been in the sun for two hours,* the punch tasted cool and refreshing.
[Right:] After having been in the sun for two hours, Janet and Tom found that the punch tasted cool and refreshing.

[Dangling infinitive phrase:] *To sing well,* the diaphragm should be extended.
[Right:] To sing well, extend your diaphragm.

[Dangling elliptical dependent clause:] *When a year old,* it is possible to learn to swim.
[Right:] When children are a year old, it is possible for them to learn to swim.

[Dangling elliptical dependent clause:] *When acting like a fool,* you should be patient.
[Right:] When he is acting like a fool, you should be patient.

C313 Make sure that every modifier modifies a definite word expressed in the sentence.

C314 Do not use a dangling elliptical dependent clause. The omitted subject noun or pronoun of an introductory elliptical dependent clause must be the same as the subject noun or pronoun of the independent clause.

[Dangling elliptical dependent clause:] *When two days old,* my mother died.
[Right:] When I was two days old, my mother died.

[Dangling elliptical dependent clause:] *Although in very good shape,* the hike was exhausting.
[Right:] Although he was in very good shape, the hike was exhausting.
[Right:] Although in very good shape, he was exhausted by the end of the hike.

C315 An introductory infinitive used as an adverb expressing purpose must logically refer to the subject noun or pronoun even though grammatically the infinitive modifies the predicate verb.

one must read books
To be educated, ~~books must be read~~.

breathe from
To sing well, ∧ the diaphragm ~~must be used~~.

learn
To judge fairly, ∧ the facts ~~must be learned~~.

C316 A few participial and infinitive phrases are said to be used in the absolute construction when they have no grammatical connection with the rest of the sentence. But do not make use of such a construction unless you are certain that it is common in good writers.

Talking of football, who won the Nebraska game?
Coming to the point, the answer is no.
She may be wrong—*granting,* of course, her basic honesty.
Granted that he is a persuasive speaker, will he be a steady worker?
Allowing for minor errors, the experiment can be called a success.

To judge from her looks, she's about forty years old.
To think you'd be so unmannerly!

Misplaced modifiers

C317 Misplaced modifiers are modifiers—whether words, phrases, or dependent clauses—so awkwardly placed (usually so far from the word they should modify) that they seem to modify the wrong word.

[Misplaced adjectives:] *Orange and crimson*, the poet gazed long at the sunset.
[Right:] The poet gazed long at the orange and crimson sunset.

[Misplaced adjective phrase:] *With the face of a dinosaur*, the hunter killed the prehistoric monster.
[Right:] The hunter killed a prehistoric monster with the face of a dinosaur.

[Misplaced adjective clause:] She hid the oriental jewel in a fragile cigar box, *which was worth many fortunes.*
[Right:] She hid the oriental jewel, which was worth many fortunes, in a fragile cigar box.

C318 Place modifying words, phrases, and clauses as near as you reasonably can to the words they modify.

Squinting modifiers[41]

C319 Squinting modifiers—often adverbs, adverb phrases, or adverb clauses—are modifiers so placed that they seem to modify either of two expressions.

frequently
I was ˄ advised ~~frequently~~ to review Latin.

Without the correction it is difficult to tell whether *frequently* modifies *advised* or *to review.*

---

[41]A squinting modifier is simply a special kind of misplaced modifier. A modifier is said to squint when one cannot tell whether it is looking toward the expression that precedes it or toward the expression that follows.

On the following day
   ᴧFrank was told ~~on the fol-~~ ~~lowing day~~ to enlist.

Without the correction it is difficult to tell whether *on the following day* modifies *was told* or *to enlist.*

When I was too tired to think,
   ᴧI agreed ~~when I was too tired~~ ~~to think~~ to work on Saturdays.

Without the correction it is difficult to tell whether *when I was too tired to think* modifies *agreed* or *to work on Saturdays.*

C320   Place a modifier so that it unmistakably modifies only the word or expression that you want it to.

Preposition use

Correct preposition use

C321   You may end a sentence with a preposition, unless such use is awkward or lacking in euphony.

I can tell you what the shouting is *about.*
Craig has nobody to eat lunch *with.*

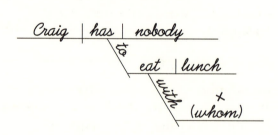

C322   Do not make a preposition do its own work and that of a different preposition as well.

to
She is willing to listenᴧbut not to argue with you.

with
I have correspondedᴧbut never spoken to the president.

C323 Do not omit a preposition when the omission dulls the parallel between the sentence elements or makes the sentence a little difficult to understand at first reading.

by

Seven of us will be back by nine if not ˄ eight.

C324 Do not use *of* for *have* or *'ve*, and do not insert an *of* after *had*.

have

You should ~~of~~ seen the crowd at Dinny's last night.

have

They ought to ~~of~~ gone to a vocational school.

would've

If Duke had ~~of~~ let go, the rest of us ~~would of~~ fallen.

C325 *Upon* and *on* may be used interchangeably, except where one or the other sounds unpleasant.

C326 Use *into* for entrance, not *in*.

into

Janet *dropped* the bucket ~~in~~ the well.
That Porsche has been *parked in* the same place all day.

C327 *Onto* (one word) may be used whenever it functions as a preposition. (Very often *to* alone is sufficient—and preferred.)

Wales climbed *onto* the top of the shed.
Invite His Excellency *onto* the platform.
All the climbing equipment fell *onto* the ledge below.

C328 Use *on to* (two words) whenever *on* is an adverb, *to* being a preposition.

We must walk *on to* the next town.
Play *on to* the end of the song.
The sailors were lured *on to* destruction.

C329 Use *beside* when you mean at the side of or next to; use *besides* when you mean in addition to.

Beside

~~Besides~~ the ice cream there stood a mountain of cookies.

Besides

~~Beside~~ ice cream there were mountains of cookies.

C330 Use *different from* before a noun or pronoun.

Oh, she is entirely *different from* other girls.
You are *different from* him in many ways.

(In these cases *different than* is sometimes used and cannot be censured; but *different from* is more widely established in current American usage. *Different to* is British usage.)

C331 Use *different than* before a clause, whether complete or elliptical.

Vincent uses the word in a *different* sense *than* it was used a generation ago.
At night the world appears *different than* in the day.

C332 When *differ* means to be different, use *from* after it.

You differ a great deal *from* your studious brother.

C333 When *differ* means to disagree, use *with* for persons and *on, about,* and so on, for things.

I differ *with* you *about* the oddest things!
We differ *on* the need for environmental laws.
We differ *about* many things, especially politics.
In my opinion we have always differed *over* trivial matters.

C334 Use *part from* to mean leave or bid farewell to; use *part with* to mean give up.

She parted *from* her parents.
She parted *with* her last cent.

C335 Use *agree with* with persons; use *agree on, to,* and so on, with things.

> I don't agree *with* you.
> Let us all agree *to* her nomination.
> I cannot agree *on* that plan of action.

C336 Do not use *at* or *to* after *where.*

> Now where on earth can he have gone to?

> I don't know exactly where I am at.

C337 Do not use *off* where *from* will make sense.

> *from*
> Jerry bought the motorcycle off a friend.

C338 Do not use *of* after *remember, recollect,* or *recall.*

> I don't remember of hearing him say that.

> Do you recollect of the days when we used to gig frogs in this same pool?

> I don't recall of that incident.

C339 Use *between* in reference to two; use *among* in reference to more than two.[42]

> *between* *among*
> The disagreement was among Tom and James, not between the entire club membership.

> *among*
> The old man divided his wealth between his four sons.

Between is also used to show the relationship of one thing to many generally or individually.

> Talks continued between France and other members of the Common Market.

---

[42] See Glossary for a further distinction.

C340 Do not use the expression *want in (out, off, through, up, down,* and so on)* or one like *want next the window.*

to get
This woman wants‸off at the next stop.

to sit
Does little Herbie want‸near the window?

Polished preposition use[43]

C341 Use *like* as a preposition, not as a conjunction. (In other words, always use *like* with an object.)

mine
You have a jacket like ~~I have.~~

as
Put a little alcohol into the tank ~~like~~ he told you.

C342 Do not use *inside of* for *within* in reference to time, or *outside of* for *aside from.*

within
We should finish ~~inside of~~ a day.

Aside from
~~Outside of~~ a month of zero weather, the winter has been mild.

C343 Do not use *around* when you actually wish to mean *nearly* or *about.*

about
The baby weighs ~~around~~ eight pounds.

nearly
We had to paddle ~~around~~ seven miles for food.

---

[43]These rules are sometimes ignored, even by writers and speakers of note. If, however, you keep them, your writing will gain in simplicity, clarity, and elegance.

C344 Do not use *on* after *continue* unless you need it to make sense.

Then we continued ~~on~~ walking for another day.
Paul continued *on* the road to Damascus.

C345 Say *forbid to* and *prohibit from*.

to hold

The constitution forbids a person ~~from holding~~ two offices at once.

from parking

People are prohibited ~~to park~~ their cars on these narrow streets.

C346 Do not use *of* after *off*.

The maid knocked the picture off ~~of~~ the table.
They took his name off ~~of~~ the roster of candidates.

C347 Do not use *of* after *inside* and *outside*.

Dent was trapped inside ~~of~~ the burning hotel.
We had locked ourselves outside ~~of~~ the house.

C348 Omit the prepositions in such expressions as these: *cover over, over with*, and *start in*.

Cover ~~over~~ the stew.
Thank the Lord the war is over ~~with~~.
John had better start ~~in~~ to read his book.

C349 Use *at* or *about* but not *at about*.

[Poor:] This snapshot was taken at about ten o'clock.
[Better:] This snapshot was taken at ten o'clock.
[Better:] This snapshot was taken about ten o'clock.

C350 In expressions like *angry with* and *angry at* use *with* for persons, *at* for things.

The block leader was angry *with* me *at* my carelessness.
The detective was angry *about* many things.
I am angry *at* all bureaucratic incompetence.

C351 Since *due* is an adjective, use it only as a predicate complement or the modifier of a noun; do not use it as a preposition. (See Glossary.)

Because of
Due to the holiday, offices will be closed tomorrow.
[Predicate complement:] The applause was *due* to her.
[Adjective:] I am waiting for the discount *due* to me.

C352 Do not say *back behind,* and use *behind* rather than *back of* or *in back of.*

Behind
Back behind me sat the Martins.

Behind
Back of me sat the Martins.

Behind
In back of me sat the Martins.

Conjunction use

C353 Use *neither . . . nor,* not *neither . . . or.*

nor
Gilbert was neither strong or intelligent.

C354 Do not use *because* to introduce a noun clause that is the subject of a sentence. Use *that* or *the fact that.*

That
Because you are sleepy does not exempt you from the examination.

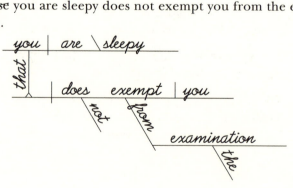

The fact that

~~Because~~ you are sleepy does not exempt you from the examination.

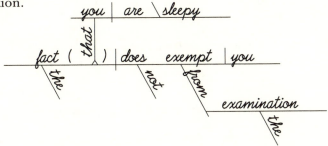

C355 Do not use *because* to introduce a noun clause that is the predicate complement after *the reason is*. Use *that* or *the fact that*.

that

The reason for his broad smile is ~~because~~ he won the essay contest.

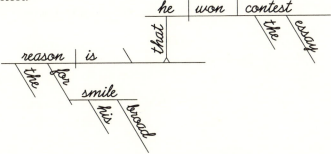

the fact that

The reason for his broad smile is ~~because~~ he won the essay contest.

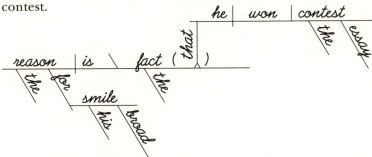

The reason why I've changed my mind is *that* this horse is absolutely uncontrollable.

The reason why I've changed my mind is *the fact that* this horse is absolutely uncontrollable.

C356 Do not use *when* or *where* to introduce a predicate complement in definitions or explanations.

the senior dance

The big event of the year is ~~when the seniors have their dance.~~

the refraction and reflection of the sun's rays

A rainbow is ~~when the sun's rays are refracted and reflected~~ by raindrops.

The jackknife is *a dive in which you bend from the waist and touch your ankles while keeping your knees unflexed.*

Most people will agree that one of the loveliest times of the year is *the coming of spring.*

C357 Do not use *where* for *that* in object clauses.

that

I saw in the bulletin ~~where~~ Jones was appointed.

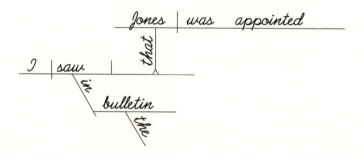

Did you hear *that* Mrs. Wipperman keeps more than fifty cats in her house?

C358 Do not use *as, as if,* or *as though* to introduce an object or predicate noun clause after verbs of thinking, saying, or feeling. Use *that.*

It seems to me [same as *I think*] *that* ~~as if~~ that's a great deal of automobile for so small a boy.

That that's a great . . . a boy is the predicate noun of *seems.*

that
Well, she didn't say ~~as~~ she agreed with me.

That she agreed with me is the object of *say.*

that
Mother doesn't feel ~~as though~~ she should go without a particular invitation.

That she should go without a particular invitation is the object of *doesn't feel.*

C359 Do not use *being as* or *being that* when you should use *since* or *because.*

Since
~~Being as~~ you are my brother, you should lend me the tie.

Because
~~Being that~~ I have no ticket, I shall have to watch from the doorway.

C360 As a conjunction, *since* may indicate cause or time. Because of this dual capability and possible ambiguity, avoid *since* in sentences that could indicate either cause or time.

[Ambiguous:] Since they left, I have been unhappy.
[Clearly cause:] Because they left, I have been unhappy.
[Clearly time:] Ever since they left, I have been unhappy.

[Ambiguous:] Since she passed the examination, she has been celebrating.
[Clearly cause:] Because she passed the examination, she has been celebrating.
[Clearly time:] After passing the examination, she celebrated.

C361 When a clause introduced by *since* indicates time and has its verb in the past tense, the verb in the independent clause is in a perfect tense.

Since the war *ended,* there *has been* (not *was*) no real progress in solving the country's internal problems.

C362 Do not use *except* for *unless.*

unless

You will get nowhere ~~except~~ you talk to a powerful man like Rooney.

C363 Do not use *without* as a conjunction.

[Wrong:] Don't leave without you pay your dues.
[Right:] Don't leave *before* you pay your dues.

[Wrong:] There's no hope without they find another halfback.
[Right:] There's no hope *unless* they find another halfback.

[Wrong:] I seldom eat peanuts without I think of the circus.
[Right:] I seldom eat peanuts *that I do not think* of the circus.

C364 Do not omit the second *as* when expressing a comparison.

[Wrong:] Donna's average is as good if not better than mine.
[Right:] Donna's average is as good *as* mine, if not better.

C365 Do not omit *than* when it is needed to complete a comparison.

[Wrong:] Your explanation is more convincing but altogether different from his.

[Right:] Your explanation is more convincing *than,* but altogether different from, his.

C366 Do not use *as* ambiguously, so that it could indicate either time or cause or reason or circumstance.

[Ambiguous:] *As* Blackie was being pommeled, Mary was smiling coldly.   Time or cause.

[Clearly time:] *When* Blackie was being pommeled, Mary was smiling coldly.

[Clearly cause:] *Because* Blackie was being pommeled, Mary was smiling coldly.

[Ambiguous:] *As* I was talk-   Time or cause.
ing, my wife left the room.
[Clearly time:] *While* I was talking, my wife left the room.
[Clearly cause:] *Because* I was talking, my wife left the room.

[Ambiguous:] As you are go-   Reason or circumstance.
ing downtown, please leave
this prescription at the hospital.
[Clearly reason:] *Since* you are going downtown, please leave this prescription at the hospital.
[Clearly circumstance:] *As* you go downtown, please leave this prescription at the hospital.

[Clearly time:] *As* I lay on the beach, someone stole my watch and class ring.
[Clearly cause:] *As* I was very late, I took a short cut through Forest Park.

C367 Do not use *on account of* or *on account of because* as a conjunction.

because

I play the oboe ~~on account of~~ I like to play the oboe.

because

Olive fell ~~on account of because~~ the stairs were slippery.

C368 Do not use *while* in place of *although* unless the meaning is perfectly clear.

Although

~~While~~ John was only two months old, his aunt read him the Bible.

C369 Do not use *directly* or *immediately* in place of the conjunction *as soon as*.

As soon as
~~Immediately~~ volunteers were called for, Wanda stepped forward.

As soon as
~~Directly~~ the painters left, little Maury, with a gleam in his eye, raised his dirty hands to the wall.

C370 *So that* is preferred to *so* in expressing purpose.

[Doubtful:] Chris built a shelter up in the tree *so* he could have a place to himself.
[Better:] Chris built a shelter up in the tree *so that* he could have a place to himself.

C371 *When* is preferred to *than* after *scarcely, hardly, barely*.

when
The Greshams had *scarcely* met her ~~than~~ she began to rearrange their lives for them.

C372 *And* is clearer and is considered better usage than *while* for expressing addition.

and
A book lay open on his knees, ~~while~~ a blanket was wrapped about his feet.

C373 Use *different from* before a noun or pronoun. See also C330–31.

Oh, she is entirely *different from* other girls.

Phrases

In general

C374 A phrase is a group of words not containing a predicate verb and used as a noun, an adjective, or an adverb.

C375 According to their form phrases are divided into prepositional, gerund, participial, and infinitive phrases.

Prepositional Phrases

C376 A prepositional phrase consists of a preposition plus its object and whatever modifiers there may be.

Caesar was certainly a master *of men.*

C377 A prepositional phrase can be used (uncommonly) as a noun,[44] as an adjective modifying a noun or pronoun, or as an adverb modifying a verb, an adjective, or an adverb.

[Adjective phrase:] The girl *in blue* is Sid's cousin.

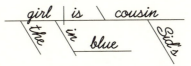

[Adjective phrase:] The house *to the left* is going to be the parish youth center.

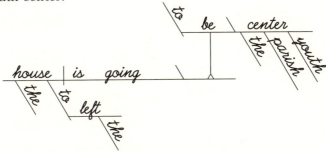

[Adverb phrase:] Mr. Clark lost his billfold *in the rain barrel.*

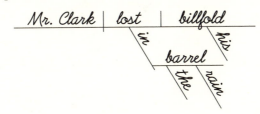

---

[44] Prepositional phrases are sometimes nouns rather than modifiers. In "Over the fence is out," *over the fence* is a substantive, the subject of the predicate verb. This, however, is not a common use of a prepositional phrase.

[Adverb phrase:] This is very good *of you.*

Gerund phrases

C378 A gerund phrase is a gerund and any subject, objects, complements, or modifiers it may have. A gerund phrase is always used as a noun.

[Noun, subject of predicate verb:] *Ellen's crawfishing* has disgraced her.

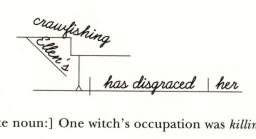

[Predicate noun:] One witch's occupation was *killing swine.*

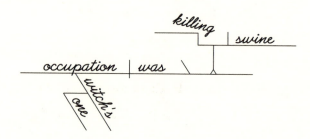

[Noun, object of a verb:] She resents *his having been a butler.*

[Noun, object of preposition:] Volpone was punished for *playing sick.*

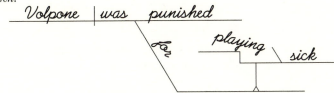

C379 Ordinarily use a possessive form of an adjective modifier with the gerund.[45] Sometimes, however, another form must be used either because there is no possessive form of the word or because the word is modified by a phrase or clause. (See C214.)

None were moved by *John's* pleading.

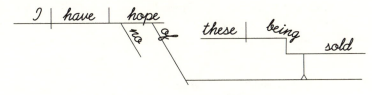

Her singing was a mistake.

I have no hope of *these* being sold.

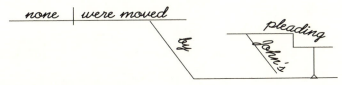

---

[45] Grammarians speak of this possessive as the subject of the gerund.

I can understand *young and old* falling under her spell.

On the *permission to go* being repeated, she gathered together her things and left the room.

Have you discussed *Dr.Lynch,* who used to be on the faculty here, publishing her memoirs?

C380 After a preposition, use the possessive with the gerund when this can be done and when it will not hurt the sense that you intend. At other times use the objective with the participle.

[Not very good:] There is some hope of *him* paying what he owes.	*His* could be used instead of *him* without awkwardness and without loss of meaning.

[Better:]There is some hope of *his* paying what he owes.

[Bad:] The sight of *his* waiting so coolly infuriated me.	One sees a person waiting, not the waiting itself.

[Better:] The sight of *him* waiting so coolly infuriated me.

C381 Sometimes it is hard to tell the difference between a gerund phrase and a participial phrase. In such instances the writer's thought must be sought out. (In your own writing rearrange the sentence so as to leave no room for ambiguity.)

[Clearly a gerund phrase:] There is no question of *our leaving today.*	Evidently the question is not about us but about leaving today.
[Clearly a participial phrase:] Can't you see *Gus running for a bus!*	Evidently Gus is not the kind of person who would or could attempt to catch a bus by running for it.
[Uncertain:] Martin was surprised at *her talking so sharply.*	Martin could be surprised at her or at her sharp words. What the writer means can be determined only by considering the sentence in its context in the paragraph.

The choice between the possessive with a gerund and a noun or pronoun with a participle frequently depends on what is to be emphasized. The more important word functions as a noun and the other word functions as an adjective.

Joe's *studying* [*studying* as noun (gerund) modified by possessive]
Joe studying [*Joe* as noun modified by an adjective (participle)]

Participial phrases

C382 A participial phrase is a participle plus the words that accompany it as object, predicate complement, or adverb modifier. [46]

A man *fighting an octopus* gets wrapped up in his work.

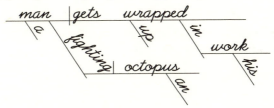

Fargrave, *looking rather pale*, stepped back from the balcony.

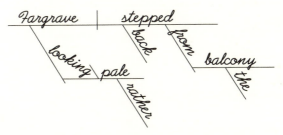

C383 Participial phrases are used only as adjectives.

A man *fighting an octopus* gets wrapped up in his work.

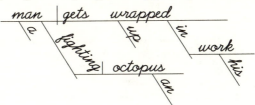

---

[46] See C381.

C384 After a preposition, use the possessive with the gerund rather than the objective with the participle, when this can be done and when it will not hurt the sense that you intend. (See also C381.)

[Not very good:] There is some hope of *him* paying what he owes.

His could be used instead of *him* without awkwardness and without loss of meaning.

[Better:] There is some hope of *his* paying what he owes.

[Bad:] The sight of *his* waiting so coolly infuriated me.

One sees a person waiting, not the waiting itself.

[Better:] The sight of *him* waiting so coolly infuriated me.

Infinitive phrases

C385 An infinitive phrase is an infinitive—with or without *to*—plus the words that accompany it as subject substantive, object, predicate complement, or adverb modifier.[47]

The other choice is *to apologize immediately.*

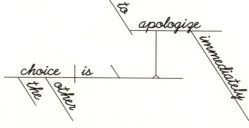

Adam Boyd planned *to betray John Ogilvie.*

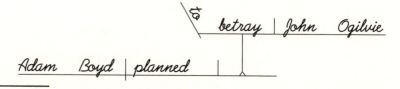

---

[47] Put the subject of an infinitive in the objective case (C213). Note that the subject of an infinitive is quite often preceded by the preposition *for,* as, for example, "*For* her to lose courage now would be fatal." Put the predicate pronoun of an infinitive in the nominative case if a nominative precedes the infinitive; put it in the objective case if an objective precedes the infinitive (C216).

C

I never manage *to look neat.*

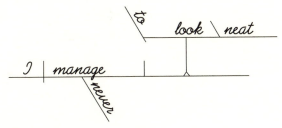

I heard *the motor roar.*

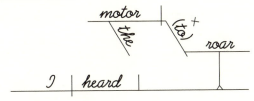

It is absurd for *you to like only funeral marches.*

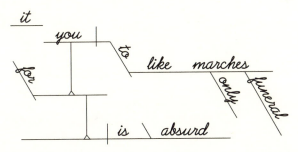

C386 Infinitive phrases are used as nouns, as adjectives, and as adverbs.

[Noun:] *To return now* would be impossible.

[Noun:] The other choice is *to apologize immediately.*

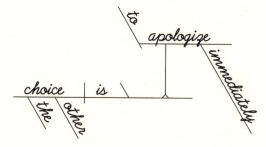

[Noun:] My new glasses make *me feel uncertain* about steps and curbings.

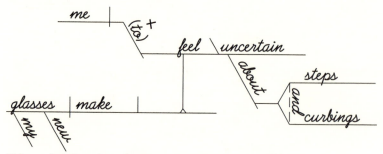

[Noun:] Adam Boyd planned *to betray John Ogilvie.*

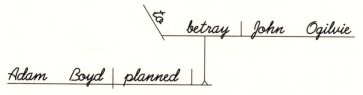

[Adjective:] A desire *to run far away* took hold of me.

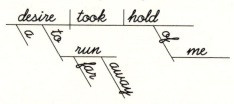

[Adjective:] I don't doubt your ability *to thrash me.*

[Adverb:] The filly seemed ready *to obey promptly.*

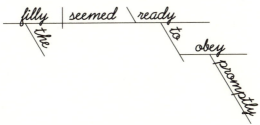

[Adverb:] The little fellow slipped from his horse to *retrieve the gun.*

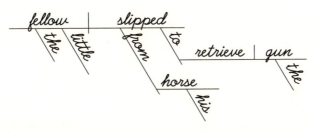

C387 Since *to* and the infinitive form one unit, they should not be split without reason. For the sake of clarity or force, however, *to* and the infinitive are frequently separated.

[Poor:] Rita was able *to quickly adjust* to the unusual circumstances.
[Better:] Rita was able *to adjust quickly* to the unusual circumstances.

[Poor:] Now is the time *to begin formally* the campaign.
[Better:] Now is the time *to formally begin* the campaign.

Clauses

In general

C388 A clause is a judgment that either can stand alone as an independent statement (an independent clause) or cannot stand alone as an independent statement but is part of a sentence (a dependent clause).

Three men left last night, | and three will leave today.
    Clause 1   *Clause 2*

My hope has sickened, | but it has not died.
    Clause 1   *Clause 2*

C389 The predicate of a clause must contain a predicate verb, not merely a verbal.

Three men left last night, *and three will leave today.*

And three will leave today is a clause. *Will leave* is the predicate verb.

Three men left last night, *slipping away in the dark.*

Slipping away in the dark is not a clause. There is no predicate verb, merely the participle *slipping.*

Three men left last night *to destroy the main span.*

To destroy the main span is not a clause. There is no predicate verb, merely the infinitive *to destroy.*

C390 The subject substantive and the predicate verb of a clause may either or both be compound.

Three men and a child left last night, and another man will leave today.

Three men and a child left last night is one clause. It has only one (compound) subject: *three men and a child.*

Three men and a child packed and left last night, and another man will leave today.

Three men and a child packed and left last night is one clause. It has only one (compound) subject and one (compound) predicate.

Independent clauses

C391 An independent clause is a related group of words that contains a subject and a predicate and can stand alone as a sentence. (See B17 and C402.)

Three men left last night, | and three will leave today.
    Independent clause   *Independent clause*

[*Three men left last night* could make a simple sentence by itself. *And three will leave today* could make a simple sentence by itself.]

While we were sleeping, | three of the men left.
Dependent Clause | *Independent clause*

[*Three of the men left* could make a simple sentence by itself: independent clause. *While we were sleeping* could not make a simple sentence by itself. It is a clause, but not an independent clause.]

C392 A second independent clause may be connected to the first by punctuation alone or by punctuation and coordinating conjunctions or conjunctive adverbs.

Dependent clauses

C393 A dependent clause is a related group of words that contains a subject and a predicate and cannot stand alone as a sentence. It is used in a sentence as a noun, adjective, or adverb.

While we were sleeping, | three of the men left.
Dependent clause | *Independent clause*

[*While we were sleeping* is a clause. But were it standing alone, it would make only a half-sentence; so it is a dependent clause.]

C394 An essential part of every dependent clause is either a subordinating conjunction; a relative or interrogative pronoun, adjective, or adverb; or indefinite *who, which, what,* or *whose.* Be sure never to leave them out when you are reading a clause to determine whether it is a dependent or an independent clause.

Barbara didn't say *that* she would return.
Barbara didn't say *when* she would return.
This is *what* I want.
Ask Allison *what* she is doing here.
We paid ten dollars, *which* price was not exorbitant.
There is the car *that* I want.

C395 Since the connective is often omitted from an elliptical sentence, be sure to insert it mentally before deciding whether a clause is independent or dependent.

that

I say ∧ you're not going.

that

That little box ∧ you hold contains death.

The other box, he said, would not hold so much.

He said is independent. No connective can be inserted.

C396 An elliptical clause is a dependent clause that is grammatically incomplete but nonetheless clear in meaning.

[Elliptical:] Mary Ann is younger *than Pat.*
[Complete:] Mary Ann is younger *than Pat is young.*

[Elliptical:] *When only a child,* Marsha spoke both English and Spanish.
[Complete:] *When she was only a child,* Marsha spoke both English and Spanish.

C397 Avoid dangling elliptical clauses by supplying the omitted words (usually subject or predicate) or by rephrasing the sentence.

[Wrong:] *Though rare in this part of the country,* my neighbor saw a hummingbird the other day.
[Right:] *Though hummingbirds are rare in this part of the country,* my neighbor saw one the other day.

[Wrong:] *Although in very good shape,* the mountain seemed formidable, even invincible.
[Right:] *Although she was in very good shape,* the mountain seemed formidable, even invincible.

Noun clauses

C398 A noun clause is a dependent clause that is being used as a noun.

[Noun clause, subject:] *What you are saying* does not interest me.

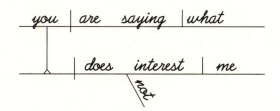

[Noun clause. direct object:] I see *that you are determined.*

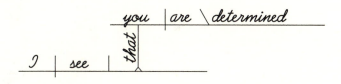

[Noun clause, object of a preposition:] Nothing is clear except *that Flau has escaped.*

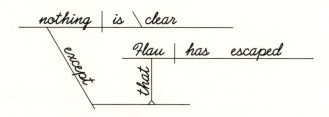

C399 The following subordinating conjunctions are commonly used to connect noun clauses with independent clauses or with other dependent clauses.

how	when
if [in the sense	where
of *whether*]	whether
that	why

I don't know *whether* Alice has the popcorn concession.
Tell me *where* we can vote.
It is certain *that* ground-controlled approach was inadequate.
Where she could have hidden is the question.

C400 The interrogative and indefinite relative pronouns and adjectives *who, whose, whom, which,* and *what* introduce noun clauses.

What you mean is not clear.

The question is, *who* has the chipmunk?

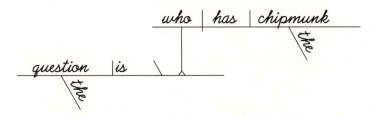

Russ would not say to *whom* he had given his ring.

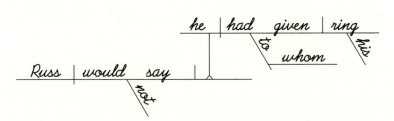

We had an argument about *whose* snapshot should be submitted.

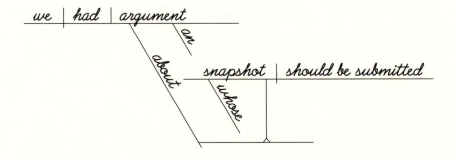

Mr. Ebbetts couldn't decide *which* was the worst.

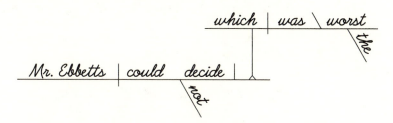

Mr. Ebbetts couldn't decide *which* trombonist was the worst.

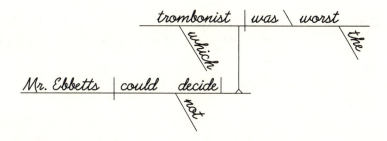

C401 Subject noun clauses are frequently preceded by the expletive *it*.

It is clear *that a crowbar was used.*

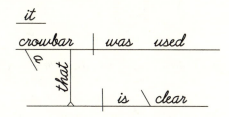

C402 It is a peculiarity of some sentences that the independent clause cannot be stated without the inclusion of the noun clause. (See B17.)

What you have said to me is frightening.	Noun clause: *what you have said to me.*
	Independent clause: *what you have said to me is frightening.*

Adjective clauses

C403 An adjective clause is a dependent clause that modifies a substantive.

The one *that sneezed* is a penguin.

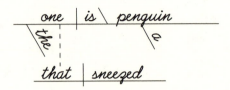

C404 Adjective clauses are relative clauses; that is, they are introduced by relative adverbs, relative pronouns, and relative adjectives.

[Relative adverb:] I have been quite busy in the time *since* I got my new job.

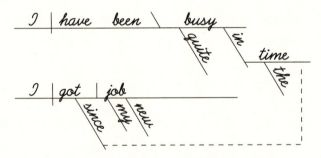

[Relative pronoun:] I know the girl *whom* you mean.

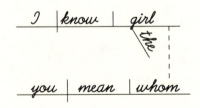

[Relative adjective:] We spent seven years in Juarez, in *which* city, by the way, we met Mark Tracy.

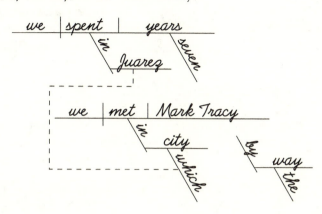

C405 A relative adverb refers to an antecedent in another clause.

I can remember the *period* *when* no one took computers seriously.

When is a relative adverb. It refers to the noun *period* in the independent clause. The dependent clause is an adjective clause.

There was a great deal of talk *when* you left.

When is not a relative adverb. It does not refer to a noun in the independent clause; so the dependent clause is not an adjective clause.

I don't know *why* you should worry.

Why is not a relative adverb here. It does not refer to a noun in the independent clause; so the dependent clause is not an adjective clause.

C406 A relative pronoun refers to an antecedent in another clause. (See A50 and C251.)

I know the *girl whom* you mean.

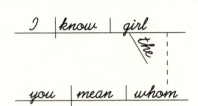

Whom is a relative pronoun. It has an antecedent in the other clause (the independent clause): *girl.* So the dependent clause is an adjective clause.

I know *whom* you mean.

Whom is not a relative pronoun. It does not have an antecedent in the independent clause.

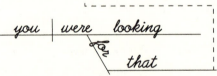

Here are the *blueprints that* you were looking for.

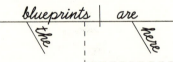

That is a relative pronoun. It has an antecedent in the independent clause: *blueprints.* So the dependent clause is an adjective clause.

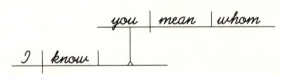

C407 The case of the relative pronoun has nothing to do with the antecedent but depends on how the relative is used in its own clause.

We met an Eskimo ~~whom~~ *who* had been converted by Father Buliard.

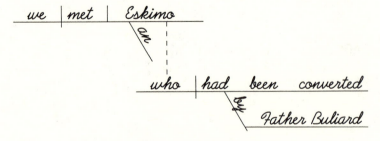

C408 The relative adjective *which* seldom makes for pleasant reading. It is usually best to avoid it when you do not have to use it.

I met a stranger in Miami, who [*not* "which stranger"] turned out to be a man with an easygoing attitude toward money.

[All right, because it somehow increases the humor:] Demarre made a bombastic speech about Demarre; and then Horner proclaimed him the modern Aeolus, *which* term Demarre did not understand and so took for a compliment.

Adverb Clauses

C409 An adverb clause is a dependent clause that modifies a verb, an adjective, or an adverb.

[Modifying a verb:] *When he had revived,* he said a strange thing.

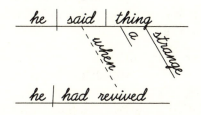

[Modifying an adjective:] Television long remained unsatisfactory *because it could be transmitted only some fifty miles.*

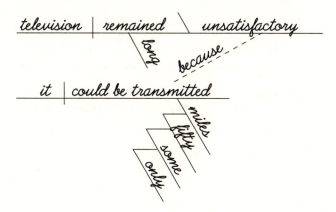

[Modifying an adverb:] Charles behaved so badly *that we had to put him into a padded cell.*

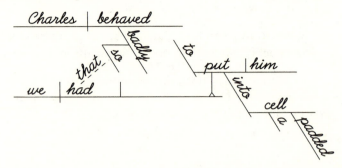

C410 Adverb clauses are introduced by subordinating conjunctions.

Because Anita had the only automobile, we elected her president of our travel club.

After the death of their leader in 1521, Magellan's men continued their westward journey *until* their ships at length cast anchor off the coast of Spain.

C411 Do not confuse subordinating conjunctions with conjunctive adverbs, which cannot be used in dependent clauses unless a subordinating connective is present; or with relative adverbs, which must have an antecedent in some other clause of the sentence.

C412 If an elliptical adverb clause dangles—modifies or seems to modify nothing or the wrong thing—simply fill in the missing words.

When ˄ *the pot is* simmering, carefully remove ˄ *it* from the stove.

C413 *If* is sometimes omitted from conditional clauses, and the subject noun or pronoun is put after the predicate verb.

Had Father the means, he most certainly would give us children an education.   Same as *if Father had the means.*

Should you ever come West, be sure to visit us.   Same as *if you should ever come West.*

Punctuation

End punctuation

D1 Every sentence must end with a period, a question mark, or an exclamation point.[1]

D2 Put a period at the end of a declarative sentence.

The sun is shining.

D3 Put a period at the end of an imperative sentence if the feeling expressed is mild. (See D16.)

Do what I tell you.
Close the door when you leave.
Don't forget to remind me.

D4 Put a period at the end of a request, order, or command that—for the sake of courtesy—is phrased as a question.

Will you please see me before you go home.
Would you type this letter before any of the others.
May I have a reply by tonight.
Will the witness take the stand, please.

D5 Put a period at the end of an indirect question.[2]

A man asked me where I was going.

---

[1] For punctuation of sentences that are interrupted or that trail off, see D20 and D23.

[2] A direct question is a question expressed in the words of the speaker; for example, "Where is the widget?" An indirect question gives the sense of the speaker's question without quotation; for example, "She asked where the widget was." Indirect questions are frequently introduced by *whether* and by *if* in the sense of *whether*.

D6 Put a question mark at the end of a direct question.[3]

Where are you going?
Who wrote "To a Skylark"?
"Where are you going?" a man asked me.
She asked, "What do you think you're doing?" in a threatening
tone of voice.

D7 Use a question mark after a sentence that is interrogative in meaning though declarative in form.

The executioner is ready?
Paris calls *that* a hat?

D8 Words or phrases or clauses in a series may each be followed by a question mark if each is equivalent to a fully expressed question.

Where did you come from? why? how?[4]
Where did you find this dog? at what time of day?
Shall I tell Mother you called? that you will return again?[5]

D9 When an emphatic question that is not a quotation occurs within a sentence or at the end of a sentence, use a question mark after it. Often, however, when the question is not felt as emphatic, only a comma is used after it.

Have we enough gasoline for the trip? is always the first question.

To the question, Where are you going? she had no answer.

---

[3]A direct question is a question expressed in the words of the speaker; for example, "Where is the widget?" An indirect question gives the sense of the speaker's question without quotation; for example, "She asked where the widget was." Indirect questions are frequently introduced by *whether* and by *if* in the sense of *whether*.

[4]When the questions consist of single words and are part of the basic structure of a single sentence, they are usually italicized and the question marks omitted; for example, "The question is *when* not *where*."

[5]In a series of longer interrogative elements within one sentence, a single question mark at the end of the sentence is preferred.

The first thing you will be asked is this: What are you qualified to do?

How can I arrange my schedule, is what I must think of next.

D10 Use a question mark at the end of a question within parentheses or dashes.

His first name was just plain C (can you imagine it?), the third letter of the alphabet.

Truffles—have you ever eaten any?—are a subterranean fungus.

D11 If a question mark belongs to both the parenthesis and the rest of the sentence, or only to the rest of the sentence, place the mark outside the parenthesis at the end of the sentence.

Would you care to join us (in other words, will you take the dare)?

Can you tell me where Ribbon Parkway is (it's the road to the Tallons')?

D12 Do not use a question mark if an exclamation point or another question mark would precede it. (See D13.)

Where is the fool who cried, "Fire! Fire!"
Who asked, "What is truth?"

D13 Do not end a sentence with two terminal punctuation marks. Retain only the more important of the two marks.[6]

[Wrong:] She quietly asked, "Where is the Jungfrau?".
[Right:] She quietly asked, "Where is the Jungfrau?"

[Wrong:] Why did he repeatedly shout, "This is absurd!"?
[Right:] Why did he repeatedly shout, "This is absurd!"

D14 For the use of a question mark with quotation marks, see D129.

---

[6] If a question mark or an exclamation point ends a sentence preceded by an abbreviation with its period, keep both marks.

D15 Put an exclamation point after a word, a phrase, a statement or command or question (exclamatory elements) to indicate strong feeling.

What! You wouldn't dare!
Jump!
How splendid!
The safe was empty!
The ghost was gone!

D16 Put an exclamation point at the end of an imperative sentence if the feeling expressed is strong. (See D3.)

Do what I tell you!
Help!
Call the police!
Drop it!

D17 Use an exclamation point at the end of an exclamation within parentheses or dashes.

His first name (imagine!) was just plain C, the third letter of the alphabet.

D18 For the use of exclamation points with quotation marks, see D129.

D19 Do not use exclamation points often.

D20 Use a dash (—) to show that a sentence is interrupted before its close. (See D23.)

Besides, I see no reason for thinking that we must have the Merkels over just because— You are not listening to me, George Lindquist!

Anyone can fix an electrical outlet like this. I suggest that you watch me, and you will learn what—. Why are you staring like that?

[Either method used above is acceptable for ending an interrupted sentence.]

D21   Use three spaced ellipsis points (periods) to indicate an omission of words or sentences from a quotation.[7]

A. *Ellipsis points at the beginning of a sentence.*

> " . . . [T]here was not the slightest trace of fear; indeed, he was smiling a slight, amused smile."

(Brackets enclosing a letter indicate a change from the original text.)

B. *Ellipsis points within a sentence.*

> "On the brown face . . . there was not the slightest trace of fear; indeed, he was smiling a slight, amused smile."

 If other punctuation occurs immediately before or after the ellipsis, it is included provided that it helps the meaning or better shows what has been omitted.

> "The play left much to be desired . . . ; however, it also left much to be pondered."

(The semicolon shows that *however* contrasts the two independent clauses. Without the semicolon the function of *however* would be ambiguous.)

C. *Ellipsis points at the end of a sentence.* (Compare with D23.)

> "On the brown face of the fellow there was not the slightest trace of fear. . . . "[8]

D. *Ellipsis points between sentences.*

1. The first sentence not finished (with ellipsis points after the end punctuation of the sentence).

    > "Within an hour it was apparent that he was meeting the full resistance. . . . No one was creating a diversion at the eastern end of the little town."

2. The first sentence finished (place ellipsis points after the end punctuation of the sentence, whatever that punctuation may be — period, question

---

[7] There is a space before, between, and after ellipsis points.
[8] The first period ends the original sentence.

mark, exclamation point), the following sentence (or sentences) omitted.

"Within an hour it was apparent that he was meeting the full resistance of Templi. . . . Hard pressed for a decision, he fanned his men out in a quarter circle in the south-west."

3. The first sentence finished (place the ellipsis points after the end punctuation of the sentence, whatever that punctuation may be — period, question mark, exclamation point), the next quoted sentence beginning after its opening.

"Within an hour it was apparent that he was meeting the full resistance of Templi. . . . [so] he fanned his men out in a quarter circle in the southwest."

(Brackets enclosing a word indicate an insertion into the quotation. See D115.)

4. The first sentence unfinished, the next quoted sentence beginning after its opening.

"Within an hour . . . he fanned his men out in a quarter circle in the southwest."

D22 Use a full line of spaced ellipsis points (periods) to indicate the omission of one or more paragraphs from prose or a line or more from poetry. (The omission of one or more paragraphs may also be adequately indicated by a period and three ellipsis points at the end of the paragraph preceding the omission.)

I have tried to show you how you may enrich your life by giving yourself seriously to the pursuits of knowledge.

. . . .

How different is the view of past life in the person who has grown old in knowledge and wisdom from that of one who has grown old in ignorance and folly!

Shall I compare thee to a summer's day?

. . . .

Rough winds do shake the darling buds of May,
And summer's lease hath all too short a date.

D23 Use three spaced ellipsis points (periods) to show that a sentence, while not abruptly interrupted, trails off with words left unsaid. (See D20.)

> Trevor was there when the letter was stolen. Trevor was recognized by old Marsden, and now Marsden has been killed. Trevor spends a good deal of money but never seems to earn any. I'm beginning to wonder whether Mr. Trevor . . .

D
E
F
G

D24 Do not use any punctuation to mark the end of the lines in the various headings and addresses of a letter or envelope.

The Donner Publishing Co.	709 Webster Street
1544 Banks Street	Troy, Maine 04987
Salem, MA 01970	January 18, 1990

D25 Use a comma after the salutation of an informal letter. Use a colon after the salutation of a formal letter. (See D90.)

Dear Jane,	Dear Father Raymond,
Dear Mother,	Dear Grandpa,

D26 Use a comma after the complimentary close of a letter.

Yours truly,	Sincerely yours,
Very truly yours,	Yours sincerely,

D27 Do not use a period or a comma at the end of a literary title that is set off on a line by itself (for example, the title of an essay). You may use a question mark, or, if it is really needed, an exclamation point.

They Live on a Volcano

A Short Dissertation
On Buying Pigs in a Poke
by Norman Coles

Did Nero Burn Rome?

A Rat! A Rat!

The comma

D28 If words, phrases, or dependent clauses occur in the form *a, b, c*—if, that is, there are no conjunctions between them—use commas between them.[9]

The leaders in this movement are Kerry, Scott, Ryan.

A long, gleaming, two-edged knife stuck in the wall.

His words rang out coldly, sharply, threateningly.

This is a government of the people, by the people, for the people.

The charges against you are that you were driving without a license, that you were exceeding the speed limit, that you drove through a red light.

D29 If an *a, b, c* (no conjunction) series precedes a verb or clause that stands in the same relation to each member of the series, use a comma after each member, including the last. (Such items in series are usually substantives, appositive adjectives, adverbs, or dependent clauses.)

We, you, they, want the same thing.

To work, to pray, to play, to rest, are most people's life.

Seeing what you see, hearing what you hear, doing what you do, are the way to peace and tranquility of heart.

Long, gleaming, two-edged, a knife stuck in the wall.

Sharply, coldly, threateningly, his words rang out.

The prime minister cleverly, adroitly, accepted the issue.

That you were driving without a license, that you were exceeding the speed limit, that you drove through a red light, are the charges against you.

---

[9] A comma alone may be used in a series of independent clauses if they are short; for example, "I came, I saw, I conquered."

This rule does not apply to attributive adjectives.

A long, gleaming, two-edged knife stuck in the wall.

The one serviceable, safe, certain, remunerative, attainable quality in every study and in every pursuit is the quality of attention.

D30 Separate by a comma only adjectives equal in rank (co-ordinate adjectives). (They are equal in rank if they can be joined by *and* or if their positions can be reversed without loss of meaning.)

> a truthful, courageous answer [truthful *and* courageous answer; courageous, truthful answer]

> a dingy, evil-smelling hallway [dingy *and* evil-smelling hallway; evil-smelling, dingy hallway]

> [Wrong:] a variety of small, Alaskan salmon

D31 Often an adjective is so closely united to a noun that the two are equivalent to one word. If such an expression is preceded by another adjective, do not separate the two adjectives by a comma.

> fur coat—cheap fur coat
> industrial park—large industrial park
> brick house—new brick house

D32 If there is a conjunction between only the last two words, phrases, or dependent clauses in a row—if, that is, they occur in the form *a, b, and c*—separate them by commas, placing the last comma before the conjunction.[10] An exception to this rule is such an expression as "and so forth," "and so on," which is followed by a comma.

Were they red, yellow, *or* white roses?

She was always running from office to office, laughing uproariously at nothing, *and* shouting at the top of her voice.

---

[10] This is not the only system used in the United States, but it has the advantage of clarity in particular instances.

If you are back here by four o'clock, if you have half of the money with you, *and* if you have a note from Mr. Farmer that he will take the rest from your wages, then you may have the drawing board and the compass and the dividers.

The comma, the semicolon, the dash, and so forth, are matters that concern editors.

Books, magazines, pamphlets, maps, and so on, are kept in the library.

D33 If all the words, phrases, or dependent clauses in a row are connected by conjunctions—if, that is, they occur in the form *a and b and c*—do not separate them by commas.

Men *and* women *and* children wandered through the ruins looking for scraps that might be sold to buy food.

If you mean that Heflin was negligent *or* that the radar was defective *or* that your information was incomplete, then we shall have to ask you for evidence.

D34 Where a conjunction makes one unit of two things, use no comma before the conjunction.

I ordered soup, salad, *ham and eggs.*

Ham and eggs is considered one dish, one unit.

Sink or swim, fail or succeed, and *live or die,* for all I care.

D35 Do not put a comma before a coordinating conjunction that connects only two words, two phrases, or two dependent clauses.

[Wrong:] To the end of the line she attached a wire leader, *and* a hook about two inches long.
[Right:] To the end of the line she attached a wire leader *and* a hook about two inches long.

[Wrong:] He was a tall, *and* gawky lad.
[Right:] He was a tall *and* gawky lad.

D36 Use a comma before a single coordinating conjunction whenever (a) it is preceded by a similar conjunction joining two parallel elements—for instance, two nouns— and (b) it itself is joining two other parallel elements— for instance, two verbs.

We begin our lives on earth in a world of glory *and* inexplicable wonder, *and* end them in a world that has grown sere and old.

We know Jules *and* Frances, *and* feel they would be good company.

I do not like spaghetti *or* sauerkraut, *or* want any beer.

D37 Do not separate the last attributive adjective of a series from the substantive it modifies.[11]

[Wrong:] The boatswain of the *Cleopatra* was a squat, shifty-eyed, *soft-spoken, fellow.*
[Right:] The boatswain of the *Cleopatra* was a squat, shifty-eyed, *soft-spoken fellow.*

[Wrong:] Hers is a merry, wholesome, *hearty, laugh* that makes you want to laugh too.
[Right:] Hers is a merry, wholesome, *hearty laugh* that makes you want to laugh too.

D38 Unless an interrupter occurs, do not separate a conjunction from what follows it.

[Wrong:] Ed was riding a sleek, young, *and*, spirited palomino.
[Right:] Ed was riding a sleek, young, *and* spirited palomino.
[Right:] Ed was riding a sleek, young, *and*—unless it was merely restless—spirited palomino.

[Wrong:] They said they wouldn't come, *but*, they did.
[Right:] They said they wouldn't come, *but* they did.
[Right:] They said they wouldn't come; *but*, if Alcide is to be believed, they did.

---

[11] Appositive adjectives that precede their substantive are separated from it by a comma; for example, *"Humble, happy, and kind*, Philip brought out the best in all of us." See D29.

D39 Use commas to set off the second and subsequent items in a reference, a geographical name, a date, an address, personal titles.[12]

Look up Shakespeare's *Hamlet,* Act III, scene 2, line 14.

Shreveport, Louisiana, is very different from New Orleans.

Earthquakes shook Los Angeles on Friday, November 14, 1941.

Jean Dickson lives at 2115 Pershing Drive, Waterford, Maryland, in a walk-up apartment on the second floor.

William Watson, Jr., will speak at the luncheon.

The Reverend John Blake, O.P., S.T.D., Ph.D.

D40 When a period of time is identified only by a month and a year, do not separate the year with commas.

The events of August 1945 are of great historical importance.

The dropping of the first atomic bomb on August 6, 1945, is a significant historical event.

D41 Do not use a comma before the first item of a series.

[Wrong:] Bilstein was thinking of, *driving home,* getting out of his wet clothes, taking a hot bath, and going directly to bed.
[Right:] Bilstein was thinking of *driving home*, getting out of his wet clothes, taking a hot bath, and going directly to bed.

[Wrong:] Graves grew up in, *Elsford,* Friar, and Hope, Rhode Island.
[Right:] Graves grew up in *Elsford,* Friar, and Hope, Rhode Island.

[Wrong:] All you have to do is, *dial this number,* ask for Mrs. Scribner, and mention my name.
[Right:] All you have to do is *dial this number,* ask for Mrs. Scribner, and mention my name.

---

[12] For semicolons with items in a series, see D81.

D42 Unless an interrupter occurs, do not use a comma to separate a subject from its predicate verb or a predicate verb from its complements or objects.

[Wrong:] *Fishing, swimming, and woodcraft, took* a lot of our time.
[Right:] *Fishing, swimming, and woodcraft took* a lot of our time.
[Right:] Fishing, swimming, and woodcraft, *all under the direction of the cabin counselors,* took a lot of our time.

[Wrong:] His particular aversions *are, work, study, and excercise.*
[Right:] His particular aversions *are work, study, and exercise.*
[Right:] His particular aversions are, *as you know,* work, study, and exercise.

D43 Use a comma before *and, but, or, for, nor, so,*[13] and *yet* when they join independent clauses of a compound sentence.[14] (But see D44, D45.)

The siren cried out, *and* instantly a narrow lane was opened for the ambulance.

The concert was almost over, *so* he decided to leave.

Neither was the coffee hot, *nor* were the doughnuts fresh.

D44 Use a semicolon rather than a comma before *and, but, or, for, nor, so,*[13] and *yet* in a compound sentence if—(a) either clause is long—say, three or four lines; (b) the sentence already contains commas;[15] or (c) either clause contains a colon, dash, or semicolon.

Ted was reared in the country and lived on a farm for eighteen years; but in spite of that he cannot recognize the common trees and flowers, and seems to know nothing of the care and feeding of livestock and poultry.

---

[13] *So* in the sense of *and so,* not in the sense of *so that* (subordinate conjunction).

[14] Exception: you may omit the comma before *and, but, or, for, nor, so,* and *yet* if both clauses are short; for example, "I shall go but you must stay."

[15] You may use a comma between such independent clauses if there are one or two other commas in the sentence and clarity is not compromised. See footnote 24 to D78.

You may take the six-o'clock local train, slow-traveling but comfortable; or you may take the express, less convenient, perhaps, but faster.

It all came to one thing: mutiny; but some of the crew were not quite ready for that.

D45 Under three conditions a comma may be used in a compound sentence even when *and, but, or, for, nor, so,*[16] or *yet* is not present: (a) if the clauses are short (say, three or four words); (b) neither of them contains a comma, colon, or dash; (c) if they are closely allied in thought and construction. For example, "United we stand, divided we fall" or "I came, I saw, I conquered" or "His voice trembled, his knees shook, his face paled."

D46 In a sentence beginning with a *that* clause from which the *that* is omitted, a comma is sufficient between the *that* clause and the principal clause.

Gerald has made himself sick, he played so hard.	[Usual phrasing:] Gerald played so hard that he has made himself sick.
Our vacation is over, I am sorry to say.	[Usual phrasing:] I am sorry to say that our vacation is over.
She will stay a week longer, she tells me.	[Usual phrasing:] She tells me that she will stay a week longer.
He did not understand a word of her talk, it could clearly be seen.	[Usual phrasing:] It could clearly be seen that he did not understand a word of her talk.
You are really not at fault, you know.	[Usual phrasing:] You know that you are really not at fault.

---

[16] *So* in the sense of *and so,* not in the sense of *so that* (subordinate conjunction).

D47   Set off words in direct address by commas.

> *Barbara,* I want to apologize for what I said.
> Come this way, *my friend,* to see the giraffe.
> Here's a letter for you, *Michelle.*

D48   Set off an ordinary nonrestrictive (nonessential) appositive by commas.[17]

> The first letter of the alphabet, *a,* was all that Marko learned in the first eight weeks.

> This is a bluebottle, *or buzzing,* fly.

> The Turkish government sternly forbade the wearing of the fez, *or tarboosh.*

> This ambition you mentioned, *to make people notice you,* is selfish and will make you unhappy.

> You are simply repeating the most important of all truths, *that there is a God.*

D49   Do not set off restrictive (essential) appositives.

> I mean Churchill *the novelist,* not Churchill *the statesman.*
> The word *affect* is often confused with the word *effect.*
> He made the claim *that he was not responsible for his brother.*

D50   Do not set off appositives or adjectives that are part of a proper name.

> Robert *the Strong* was a great warrior.
> This is a statue of Alexander *the Great.*
> Pepin *the Short* was the father of Charlemagne.
> In 875 Charles *the Bald* was king of France and Holy Roman Emperor.
> To his friends he was known as Willie *the Wizard.*
> Hagar *the Horrible* is a cartoon character.
> We call her Dorothy *the Diplomat.*

---

[17] For dashes, especially with long nonrestrictive appositives or those that contain their own punctuation, see D97-102; for colons see D83; for parentheses see D106.

D51 Set off ordinary nonrestrictive (nonessential) modifiers by commas.[18]

A young man, *tall and handsome,* waved to me from his table across the room.

There is no point in asking, *probably.*

Baker will be the first to avoid punishment, *begging off somehow.*

Mrs. Pierce is as pleasant a person, *in her own way,* as you would care to meet.

The pilot, *as if he had gone mad,* headed the plane straight into the mountain.

Our team, *which had not practiced in a week,* played poorly.

D52 Before setting off a modifier, make sure that you intend it to be nonrestrictive (nonessential). If you are in doubt, use no punctuation. Too many commas are worse than too few.

D53 Do not set off restrictive (essential) modifiers.

He entered *trembling with emotion.*
The woman *with the red hat* is my wife.
Boys *who tell lies* should be reprimanded.

D54 Ordinarily use commas (or an exclamation point) with *oh* and other exclamatory or parenthetical words, phrases, and clauses.[19]

Oh, what's the use?

It was a deep, blue pool in a kind of grotto; and, *oh,* was the water cold.

If you don't have the car—*oh!* you do have it.

Well, that's just about it.

---

[18] For dashes and parentheses with nonrestrictive modifiers, see D102 and D106. For commas with clauses introduced by *which,* see C252 and Glossary.

[19] For dashes and parentheses with parenthetical expressions, see D94 and D105.

It seemed like a short swim; and, *well,* I certainly didn't want to seem a coward.

Next, there is a little matter of timing that I want to take up with the sound crew.

Try the recipe for, *say,* a week.

Where, *pray tell,* are the keys?

Red, *to be sure,* never knew that he had been cheated.

You have a reason, *I suppose,* for the charges you make?

He would have come, *he explained,* if his aunt had not hidden his clothes.

Then you do agree with me, *don't you?*

John Hamilton, *Jr.,* is nauseated.

Sister Joan Acker, *S.N.D.,* is on the forum.

A Julie Peck, *M.A., Ph.D.,* wants to sell you and me a carload of breakfast food.

The contracts, blueprints, *etc.,* call for a room without doors.

Flowers, magazines, ash trays, *and so on,* cluttered every available table and chair.

Punctuation may be omitted if an exclamatory or parenthetical expression can be clearly and easily read without pause.

Oh what's the use?
Well that's just about it.

D55 Do not set off *O* (which is nowadays always capitalized and reserved for rather poetic use with nouns in direct address).

O Diana, these are your forests!

D56 Set off a nominative absolute by commas.

The danger signal ringing, we stopped the car.

I cannot tell you, *my parents being away,* whether I can go bowling or not.

Nothing extra was served at dinner, *the supplies being lower than they had been for months.*

D57 When an adverb clause precedes an independent clause, set off the adverb clause by a comma.

Although the road was icy and snow was falling, the doctor got to our house in time.

Finally, *when order had been completely restored,* the cowardly judge crept from behind his desk.

While you are baiting my hook, I'll dig for more worms behind the boathouse.

The comma may be omitted, however, if the adverb clause is short and the meaning is clear and does not run into the independent clause, or if the subject of the adverb clause and the subject of the independent clause are the same.

Before the bus leaves ask the driver what time it is.
Since Mr. Crane came to Maryvale last year he has made many friends.

D58 If an introductory adverb clause is preceded by a coordinating conjunction, do not use a comma after the conjunction unless the clause is long.

And if you see your sister Marcella, ask her to the party.

But before you both leave, your wife must register at the office.

Nor, unless the governor can be persuaded to use his full power and intervenes before the end of the month, can we have any hope of getting what we want.

D59 Use a comma or commas to set off a terminal or internal nonrestrictive (nonessential) adverbial clause. (If such an adverbial clause is essential, do not use a comma or commas.)

[Nonessential:] Bill did not play yesterday, *since he had injured his knee.*

[Nonessential:] Alfredo began to study French, *although he has difficulty with languages,* in order to read Camus in the original.

[Essential:] They have been anxious to sell their house *ever since they decided to move to Arizona.*

[Essential:] Carolyn came *when she was ready.*

D60 In general, use a comma after an introductory phrase or series of phrases of five words or more.

To see the West as it really is, drive your own car and spend several days in each place.

Returning from a walk late last night, I heard the angry voices of some neighbors quarreling in their back yard.

Quite a while before dark, bats began to dip, circle, and glide through the long avenue of oaks.

After dinner we plan to entertain you with some home movies.

D61 Even if it is less than five words, use a comma after an introductory phrase that is only loosely connected with the sentence (for example, a bridging phrase like *after all* or *for that matter*).

After all, I'm only human.
For one thing, grey and *gray* are spelled differently.
For the last time, the answer is no!
For that matter, Russia was a dictatorship too.
For goodness' sake, stop dawdling.
Simply put, poverty and hardship need not be part of the human condition.

D62   Even if it is longer than five words, an introductory adverbial phrase related to the adjoining part of the sentence need not be followed by a comma unless clarity is compromised.[20]

On the way home after the party we met the Joneses.
Before the basketball game at the coliseum some clowns entertained the crowd.

D63   If an introductory phrase in the second half of a compound sentence is preceded by a coordinating conjunction, use a comma after the conjunction only if the phrase is parenthetical.[21]

Some people have poor memories, but *with a measure of effort and resourcefulness,* they can make up for that deficiency.

Many people have allergies, but *in most cases* the allergies are not serious.

Many people have allergies; but, *for the most part,* those allergies are not serious.

D64   Do not use a comma after an introductory adverbial phrase when it immediately precedes the verb it modifies.

To the west of the river is another golf course.

Among these bits of crystalline carbon may be hidden a valuable diamond.

D65   If an introductory phrase is preceded by a coordinating conjunction, do not use a comma after the conjunction unless the phrase is long or parenthetical.

And with the help and encouragement of all of you, the staff can finish the assignment in a short time.

---

[20] When such a phrase ends with a verb or a preposition, a comma is used before a following noun to preserve clarity (otherwise the noun might be taken as an object).

[21] This comma rule applies to similarly placed adverbial clauses.

But owing to heavy rains and bad roads, I was delayed a week in Arizona.

Nor, granted all the pleasant people you will meet and the multitude of things you can see and do, will you fail to enjoy yourself on the cruise.

Nor, by the way, is there much hope for the rescuers.

D66 Use a comma after *namely, for example, for instance, that is,* and so on, when they introduce an appositive. (See also D82.)

One city—*namely,* Brooklyn—was not represented.

Some social studies (*for example,* history and civics) are taught in all high schools.

Sammy paid the same fee; *that is,* five dollars.

D67 *Namely, for example, for instance, that is,* and so on, may be preceded by either a comma, a semicolon, a colon, or a dash according to the magnitude of the break with the rest of the sentence. The colon and dash are to be preferred when what follows is either emphatic or lengthy.

One city was not represented, *namely,* Brooklyn.

Sammy paid the same fee; *that is,* five dollars.

One kind of guest we do not want: *namely,* a person who is boisterous, loud, and careless.

D68 Use a comma after a conjunctive adverb.[22]

Cindy likes flattery; *indeed,* she thrives on it.

The job had to be done; *consequently,* the Marines did it.

---

[22] In general, place a semicolon before a conjunctive adverb and a comma after it. Short conjunctive adverbs (e.g., *then, thus*) are not always followed by a comma.

Whirligig beetles can skitter fast across the surface of the water; *furthermore,* they can dive.

D69 Use a comma (or commas) with absolute expressions like *first, now, perhaps, thus,* and so on.

First, your comment was unsolicited; *second,* it lacks all pertinency.

Now, it is easier to talk about millions than to make them.

Marsha will maintain, *perhaps,* that she does not want the job.

Thus, a child that has been burned is afraid of fire.

D70 Many words function either as conjunctive adverbs or as absolute expressions; and these same words can be adverbs in the strict sense. How they are used in a sentence determines whether they are to be punctuated or not.

First, your scheme is impractical. [Absolute expression]

First catch your rabbit; then cook it. [Adverb]

Now, it is easier to talk about millions than to make them. [Absolute expression]

Now comes a point that is hard to explain. [Adverb]

Ravelon, *however,* was not on time. [Absolute expression]

Ravelon promised to be here at ten; *however,* he was late. [Conjunctive adverb]

Ravelon cannot be on time, *however* hard he tries. [Adverb]

D71 Do not confuse a phrase that is really the subject or object with an introductory phrase.

Bringing wood into the house every evening is a sheer waste of time.	Subject of the sentence. No comma here.

Bringing wood into the house every evening, she used up what little strength and energy she had left.	Introductory phrase. Use a comma here.

D72 Set off by commas a contrasting expression introduced by *not, but not, certainly not, never,* and so on, if you want it read with a preceding or following pause.

Only a lawyer or a doctor, *but not a tradesman*, would so pepper his language with Latin expressions.

Because he had power, *not of course because he was astute,* Tag's word was received with respect by the Randall politicos.

I have decided to lend the car to Shirley *but not to you.*

She is very kind *not because she is a queen*; many a woman has been a queen and has not been kind.

D73 Use commas to set off a suspended expression.

During, *and for a long time after*, the famine, the people were desperately poor.

In his fright the man began swimming away from, *not toward*, the dock.

Audrey looks like, *but is quite different from*, her twin sister.

Our old house was as large as, *but less conveniently arranged than*, this new one.

D74 Use a comma before a single, complete, directly quoted sentence that occurs within another sentence.

Herbert answered, "I don't know."

D75 Do not use a comma before an indirect quotation or an indirect question.

[Wrong:] Herbert answered, that he didn't know.
[Right:] Herbert answered that he didn't know.

[Wrong:] She asked, whether anybody else had noted a change in the frequency.

[Right:] She asked whether anybody else had noted a change in the frequency.

D76 Use a comma to separate those parts of a sentence that would be confusing if read together without pause.

Two hours before, the fire broke out.

Within, the box was lined with satin.

To fleas, fleas are not offensive.

Whatever is, is not necessarily right.

Instead of hundreds, thousands came.

To John, Matthew was always kind.

When the cyclone hit, the Ryans were away from home.

By striking, the members of the union forced a reluctant recognition of their rights.

To escape, a small, enterprising mouse chewed his way through *Mrs. Rancy's Cookbook.*

Fifteen people loaded with Christmas presents and bustling about exchanging greetings and inquiries about friends, and five neighbors cutting sandwiches in the tiny kitchen crammed the capacity of the little cottage to bursting.

He's going to go, crazy or not crazy.

There was a small, fluffy poodle with the attendant, barking in miniature frenzy.

D77 Do not use unnecessary commas; that is, commas for which you cannot cite a rule or give a good reason.

The semicolon

D78 Use a semicolon rather than a comma before *and, but, or, for, nor, yet,* and *so* in a compound sentence if (a) *either* *clause is long*— say, three or four lines;[23] (b) the sentence already contains commas,[24] or (c) either clause contains a colon or a dash.

Ted was reared in the country and lived on a farm for eighteen years; but in spite of that he cannot recognize the common trees and flowers, and seems to know nothing of the care and feeding of livestock and poultry.

You may take the six-o'clock local train, slow-traveling but comfortable; or you may take the express, less convenient, perhaps, but faster.

It all came to one thing: mutiny; but some of the crew were not quite ready for that.

The town—a little one-street affair suddenly cropping up on the prairie—was not the place to look for Reggie; nor did our first day of inquiry there achieve any results.

D79 Use a semicolon before a conjunctive adverb[25] that joins independent clauses.[26]

Pat is the sort to plan a thing thoroughly; moreover, she has the personality to win support for the new constitution.

There was no point in taking a loss year after year; consequently, we sold the presses and the equipment in the bindery.

I bowled 225; however, I don't do that every day.

---

[23] A line here means the length of line found on single-column pages (for example, the pages of most books). Certainly three or four lines in the double-column width of *Reader's Digest* is not to be considered long.

[24] You may use a comma between independent clauses if there are one or two other commas in the sentence and clarity is not compromised. Sometimes a single comma within an independent clause necessitates a semicolon between clauses: *If this is so, desist at once; the alternative is chaos.* At other times a sentence with one or even two commas in an independent clause is better served by a comma between clauses: *By the way, Jim stopped at our house this afternoon, and he asked about you. Joan, our neighbor, knows almost everything about bonzai trees, and she will gladly tell you all about them.*

[25] For a list of conjunctive adverbs, see A120.

[26] Conjunctive adverbs joining two independent clauses are regularly followed by a comma. Short conjunctive adverbs such as *then* and *thus* are not always followed by a comma.

D80 Use a semicolon between independent clauses that have no connective between them. (But see D45.)

Fran Karney was supposed to arrive this morning; she arrived last night instead.

I can't leave the house this morning; I have too much to do.

D81 Use a semicolon to set off the items of a series if the items contain commas.

The Dana Company has branch offices in Billings, Montana; Santa Fe, New Mexico; and Tucson, Arizona.

Tell what is significant about these dates in the life of Julian Randolph: January 4, 1900; September 27, 1902; March 1, 1904; and December 9, 1908.

D82 A semicolon may be used before *namely, for example, for instance,* and similar expressions when they introduce an appositive. (See also D66.)

Chrysler introduced something new in 1951; *namely,* the spark plug in the center of the cylinder.

Rodent is a name that includes a number of little beasts besides rats; *for instance,* squirrels.

Tippy has quite redeemed himself; *for example,* he behaved like a human being at lunch today.

The colon

D83 Use a colon to formally introduce matter in apposition or to precede an extended explanation. Note that a dash might be substituted for the colon. (See D48 for the use of commas with appositives. See H12 for the use of capitals after a colon.)

All the difficulty is due to just one little man: *James Nelson.*

The headings of the report are these: *the cause of the flood in Fremont County, the damage done by the flood, and the help given to the farmers by the Red Cross.*

I have been trained in three skills: *double-entry bookkeeping, typing, and shorthand.*

The next question that came up for discussion was this: *Are the requirements for membership strict enough?*

Everything was in good shape: *the paper stacked, the pencils sharpened, the chairs placed.*

Democracy presupposes two conditions: *that the majority of the people be informed and intelligent, and that the electors use their power fully and honestly.*

We all know the steady progress of the morning: *a sleepy cup of coffee, a glance at the headlines, a dull ride to work.*

She felt as you would expect: *worried, frightened, perplexed.*

D84 Use a colon to introduce a quotation of more than one sentence. (A comma is sufficient if such a quotation is short.)

Boswell wrote of Oliver Goldsmith:

> Goldsmith's incessant desire of being conspicuous in company was the occasion of his sometimes appearing to such disadvantage as one should hardly have supposed possible in a man of his genius. . . . One evening, in a circle of wits, he found fault with me for talking of Johnson as entitled to the honor of unquestionable superiority. "Sir," said he, "you are for making a monarchy of what should be a republic."

D85 A colon may be used before a short quotation (one sentence, for example) whenever the quotation is felt to be formally or emphatically introduced.

The commander comments: "Your directions are clear and must be carried out fully and immediately."

In his last letter—and note this carefully—he says: "The governor will hear no more talk whatever about a parole for Tompkins."

D86 Use a colon to introduce a clause that summarizes what has gone before. (A dash is also common in this use. See D93.)

You are to appear at the Vendome at precisely four o'clock; you are to select a table near the door; you are to leave at precisely four-fifteen: *these things you must do exactly and without fail.*

A shred of wet, muddy tweed coat; a scrap of paper torn from a railroad timetable; a hat carefully placed on the head of the stone Audubon in the park: *that was all we had to go on.*

D87 Use a colon to introduce items that are indented like paragraphs, provided that the introductory statement could stand as a sentence by itself. If the introductory statement is incomplete, use a dash.

These things should be kept in mind:

We are not obliged to repress our intelligence and try to persuade ourselves that an evil person is a saint.

On the other hand, we are obliged to make every effort to give the benefit of any reasonable doubt when we are assessing an individual's character.

We must not decide for ourselves that a person is certainly destined for heaven or hell.

If it will help, we may divide the whole problem into these three topics for discussion:

The usefulness of an electronics club.

The difficulties of founding an electronics club.

The usefulness weighed against the difficulties.

To tabulate our reasons for our action in this particular case, Milton was admitted because—

She has the draftsmanship we need.

She is a worker.

She can work with others.

The charges made against her by Mosser were accompanied by not one solid bit of evidence.

D88 Use a colon to separate items that contain semicolons.

Trains leave in the morning at seven, eight, and nine from the Euston Station; at seven, eight-fifteen, and ten from the Paddington Station: in the afternoon at one, two, and three from the Euston Station; at twelve-ten, one, three, and four-thirty from the Paddington Station.

D89 Use a colon to divide hours from minutes when time is written in figures.

10:20 A.M.   1:07 P.M.   5:00 P.M.

D90 Use a colon after the salutation of a formal letter.

Dear Miss Smithers: Very Reverend and
Gentlemen: dear Monsignor:
Dear Sir: Dear Mrs. Thorn:

D91 Use a colon to divide psalm or chapter from verse when these numbers are indicated by figures alone.

Ps. 32:1 [meaning Psalm 32, verse 1]

II Cor. 5:1 [meaning the Second Epistle to the Corinthians, Chapter 5, verse 1]

The dash

D92 Use dashes to show that a sentence is broken up, interrupted, unfinished, or suddenly changed.[27]

Tell me—tell me the truth—are you my sister?

I came upstairs and entered the room to find—

When I think how your life has been spent—how old did you say you were?

---

[27] See D23 for the use of ellipsis points to show that a sentence trails off with words left unsaid. See also D20.

D93 Use a dash before that part of a sentence which summarizes what has gone before.[28]

Mr. Micawber warned that a person will be worried and unhappy who, making ten pounds a week, spends fifteen; who buys clothes and flowers and theater tickets heedlessly; who spends tomorrow's salary today—*who, in short, lives beyond his income.*

D94 Dashes may be used for emphasis instead of commas to set off a parenthetical expression, and they are preferred if the construction of the parenthetical expression does not fit the rest of the sentence or itself contains punctuation.[29]

A woman named Ida Runn—*what a name*—is waiting to see you.

Didn't Joe Cain—*he went to law school after college, you remember*—become a noted attorney in New York?

D95 If a parenthetical remark is a direct question or an exclamation, you may put a question mark or exclamation point before the final dash.

Joe Cain—he went to law school after college, *don't you remember?*—became a noted attorney in New York.

The second boy—*plucky little fellow!*—was not to be intimidated by Mr. Robble's rumbling and grumbling.

D96 A dash may be used instead of a comma after a substantive appositive that stands at the beginning of a sentence. A dash should be used if the appositive is itself punctuated or long.

A person of conviction—that is what we need.

Food, clothing, shelter—these are the material needs of human beings.

---

[28] A colon may be used in the same way but is somewhat more formal. See D86.

[29] See D105 for the use of parentheses with parenthetical expressions.

Reading slowly for a full understanding and enjoyment of what is said — this is what should be aimed at.

D97 Dashes may be used to set off nonrestrictive appositives within the sentence more emphatically than commas do. They should be used if the appositives contain their own punctuation, or if they are long, or if they would otherwise be misread.

The first letter of the alphabet — *a* — was all that Marko learned in the first eight weeks.

Tod's brothers — *Jake, Harry, and Al* — are all as pleasant as he.

The plot of the play — *the story of a mortgage, a sick father, a beautiful daughter, and a villain* — is trite, unblushing melodrama; but the actors enjoy themselves.

Everything — *whatever he earned as wages and whatever came to him as tips* — went anonymously to the people he had wronged.

When you admit what I say — *that some kind of discipline in speaking and acting is necessary for every growing boy and girl* — then we can make plans together.

One thing — *hard workers* — is what we need for success.

D98 A dash may be used before an appositive at the end of a sentence. (A dash is more emphatic than a comma but less formal than a colon. See D48, D83.)

One thing I do not like — *spinach.*

A friend of mine telephoned me today, a woman I haven't spoken to for ten years — *Anita Sanchez.*

D99 Use dashes to set off an appositive introduced by *namely, for example, that is,* and so on, within the sentence.[30]

One city — *namely, Brooklyn* — was not represented.

A salad of some kind — *for example, a tossed salad* — would be better with the steak.

---

[30] Parentheses may also be used here.

D100 Use a dash before *namely, for example, that is,* and so on, to introduce an appositive at the end of a sentence.[31]

Sammy paid the same fee—*namely, five dollars.*

D101 Do not use dashes to set off an expression containing only figures.

[Wrong:] The year of the crash—1929—made no change in Paulinus.
[Right:] The year of the crash, 1929, made no change in Paulinus.
[Right:] The year of the crash (1929) made no change in Paulinus.

D102 Dashes may be used to set off nonrestrictive modifiers more emphatically than commas do, especially if the modifiers contain their own punctuation.

Mr. Pierce is as pleasant a man as you would care to meet—*in his own odd way.*

Agnes answered with a giggle—*which infuriated me, startled Higgins, and made Cleo guffaw*—but did not offer any useful information.

D103 Use a dash instead of a colon to introduce items that are indented like paragraphs when the introductory statement could not stand by itself as a complete sentence.[32]

To tabulate the reasons for our action in this particular case, Milton was admitted because—
She has the skills we need.
She is a worker.
She can work with others.
The charges made against her by Mosser were accompanied by not one solid bit of evidence.

D104 Use dashes sparingly. Their too-frequent use results in restless and childish writing.

---

[31] A semicolon may also be used here. See D82.
[32] Do not apply this rule to outlines. See N76-81.

Parentheses and brackets

D105 Use parentheses to enclose a parenthetical remark, something that has only a comparatively remote connection in thought, or when the parenthetical expression already contains a dash, or when one or more independent sentences are parenthetical.

Enclosed please find my check for twelve dollars ($12).[33]

The author confuses James Mill (1773-1836) with his son, John Stuart Mill (1806-73).

One of the earliest detective stories (Collins's *The Moonstone)* is better constructed than many later examples.

The hero of my story (I write this for your private information) was not always an honest person.

If the phrase is short (say, four or five words), the comma may be omitted.

The figures (78, 76, and 75 — Roland adds 74, but no one else agrees with her) turned up 180 times in four hours.

Feuerbach tore the paper to shreds. (As we have said, he loves drama.) Then he burst into tears.

D106 Parentheses may be used to enclose a nonrestrictive appositive;[34] they should be used when the appositive contains a dash.

The social studies (history, geography, and civics) are taught in all elementary schools.

We were offered some milk (which was fresh) and some wine (which was sour); there was no solid food in the inn.

Jonathan Crespy (a friend — and a loyal friend, I may say) reluctantly admitted that Julius should go.

---

[33] Use figures in parentheses only when extreme clarity or business style demands repetition. See D109.

[34] For the use of commas and dashes with nonrestrictive appositives, see D48 and D97.

D107 Place in parentheses letters or figures used to mark the divisions of an enumeration in a sentence, a paragraph, or other continuous text.[35]

I maintain (1) that Watson did not come to London; (2) that, even if he had come, he could not have met Holmes; and (3) that Watson's letter to Holmes was actually written by Vance.

There were two possibilities: *(a)* to go home and *(b)* to fight.

D108 Do not use periods with the figures or letters described in D107.

D109 In business letters and commercial and technical documents, figures are sometimes given in parentheses after written numbers.

Send me twenty-five (25) pairs of basketball shorts and a dozen (12) handballs.

Enclosed is my check for twelve dollars ($12).

D110 When a sentence in parentheses interrupts another sentence, do not capitalize the first word of the sentence in parentheses nor end it with a period.

Though I have often been tempted to quit (such thoughts surely come to everyone), the example of More's fortitude has always given me courage to go on.	Here the sentence in parentheses interrupts another sentence. No capital and no period.
They say he was a wealthy man. (That was in 1960, of course, when a dollar bought more than it buys now.) Whether or not he was is beside the point.	Here the sentence in parentheses does *not* interrupt another sentence.

---

[35] Do not apply this rule to outlines. See N80.

D111 If a period, comma, semicolon, or dash is needed at the end of a parenthesis that interrupts a sentence, place the mark outside the parentheses.

Karen did not know (or so she said).

Here she gave her strange, though accurate (and handsomely delivered), account of the disaster.

Tilton was born the year of the flood (1961); he doesn't remember much about it.

D112 If a colon, question mark, or exclamation point belongs only to the parenthesis, place the mark inside the parentheses and end the sentence with another mark.

(Helen:) There is something you are forgetting!
Karen did not know (or did she?).
Yates absconded with my fishing tackle (the scoundrel!).

D113 If a colon, question mark, or exclamation point belongs only to the rest of the sentence or to both the parenthesis and the rest of the sentence, place the mark outside the parentheses.

Perón mentions three *ladrones* (robbers): Gonzales, Trega, and the nameless butcher.

Would you care to join us (in other words, will you take the dare)?

Chesterton said the most startling thing (on page 7)!

D114 Enclose independent parenthetical sentences in parentheses. They are punctuated and capitalized just like other sentences. The end punctuation, of course, is placed inside the parentheses.

I had just met the man. (Oldenburg insists I met him a year earlier. Oldenburg, however, remembers things more or less as he pleases.) We had been introduced at the club's annual dinner by Clesi, a mutual friend.

Staub took the floor. (It has never been explained how the chair happened to recognize him; no alert presiding officer would have done so.) He began a speech that ran three days and nights.

Staub took the floor. (Why did the chair recognize him? That has never been satisfactorily explained.) He began a speech that lasted three days and nights.

D115 Use brackets [ ] to enclose a remark that is inserted into a quotation.

"So they [that is, Christian and Hopeful] were forced to go, because he [Giant Despair] was stronger than they. They had also but little to say, for they knew themselves in a fault. The giant, therefore, drove them before him, and put them into his castle [Doubting Castle], into a very dark dungeon."

—JOHN BUNYAN, *THE PILGRIM'S PROGRESS*

D116 Use brackets to enclose parenthetical material within a parenthesis.

You will find this passage in Albert the Great's commentary on the Gospel of St. Luke (in Albert the Great's collected works [in Latin], edited by Borgnet [Paris: Vives, 1890-99], Vol. XXII).

Quotation marks

D117 Put a direct quotation in double quotation marks.

"I have no intention of budging," she said.

She answered, "I have no intention of budging."

"I have no intention of budging" she answered, "until you have given me your promise."

"Is "A penny saved is a penny earned" as old an adage as "If wishes were horses, beggars would ride"?[36]

When I say "The urn is a vase," I simply state a fact.

His example is the sentence "Man is an animal."[36]

---

[36] Do not use a comma before a quotation of this kind if the quotation is restrictive. Use a comma if the quotation is nonrestrictive; for example, *Butler quoted a sentence, "Man is an animal," as his only reply.*

What is the meaning of the metaphor "Fame is a spur"?

Some people do not accept such principles as "Whatever is moved is moved by another." [37]

D118 Put in single quotation marks a quotation within a quotation.

"We must remember," said the orator, "the immortal words of a great patriot, 'Give me liberty or give me death!'"

D119 Do not use quotation marks if words are directed by a person to himself or are merely unexpressed thoughts (but capitalize the first word). The words may be italicized.

I thought to myself, They did not expect me.

No doubt you have said to yourself, Why am I here?

Jill said to herself, Here we go again!

They were thinking, We will have to pay.

Why not send it on? he said to himself.

The children were thinking, They're going to stop us.

She will accept my essay topic if I develop a satisfactory outline, I thought to myself.

D120 Do not put in quotation marks an indirect quotation that does not use another's exact words. You may put in double quotation marks an indirect quotation that uses another's exact words if you want it unmistakable that you are quoting. (An indirect quotation is introduced by the conjunctions *whether, if,* or *that* either expressed or implied.)

The editor said my article was too long.
Elaine commented that cigarettes are injurious to one's health.
Elaine commented that "cigarettes are injurious to one's health."

---

[37] Do not use a comma before the quotation when it is preceded by *as.*

(In sentences like the previous example, it is usually better to avoid *that* and express the idea as a direct quotation.)

D121 In literary writing (such as fiction), put all sentences belonging to a single uninterrupted quotation in one set of quotation marks. (But see D123.)

> Trafford replied: "I don't think you understand my position. I am not here to defraud you people. But I cannot return your money just now without defrauding others."

> Erin warned me: "Don't you dare pass this time, partner. I made a demand bid, and you have to answer. I said two spades, and Eil said three clubs. Come on, you have to say something."

> "Mickey and I want to go duck hunting in Scheller's slough today. May I go, and may I take Dad's shotgun, and may I stay out until five?" Richard asked.

D122 In literary writing (such as fiction), when a continuous quotation falls into paragraphs, place quotation marks at the beginning of each paragraph, but at the end of only the last. (But see D123.)

> "I was ten years old at the time," began Joe Manning. "My brother and I lived in a shanty near the docks. I say 'lived,' but really we only slept there; we lived in the streets. We ate when and where we could; we got money anyhow; and we made friends of vicious boys and girls as abandoned as we.
> "Then one day I was taken to the hospital badly hurt. Mrs. Parkham saw me there, adopted me, and took me West to live. My whole life was changed. I never heard from my brother, never saw him again.
> "All that happened twenty years ago. How can you expect me to recognize this murderer as my brother? It's some kind of trick to get money out of Mrs. Parkham."

D123 In professional and technical writing (such as reports and theses) do not use quotation marks with a quotation of four lines (or forty words) or more. Instead, indent the quotation five spaces (with an additional five spaces for the opening line of any paragraph).[38]

Now that we have seen some of the principles of description, we can profit by analyzing the following paragraphs from Dickens's *Pickwick Papers*:

> It was a long room, with crimson-covered benches, and wax candles in glass chandeliers. The musicians were securely confined in an elevated den, and quadrilles were being systematically got through by two or three sets of dancers. Two card tables were made up in the adjoining card room, and two pairs of old ladies, and a corresponding number of stout gentlemen, were executing whist therein.
>
> The finale concluded, the dancers promenaded the room, and Mr. Tupman and his companion stationed themselves in a corner to observe the company.

D124 In dialogue, use a new paragraph and a new set of quotation marks every time the speaker changes.

> "It seems to me," said Dr. Nichols, "that you ought to sell the farm and buy yourself a college education. You want an education, don't you?"
>
> "Yes, sir," I said; "but would the sale fetch enough money to pay all my expenses?"
>
> "Why, yes, I should think so. As a matter of fact, I myself am prepared to offer you forty thousand for the place. That's perhaps a bit more than you would get if you put it on the market. But we are good friends, and the property is worth it.

---

[38] These longer quotations may be single or double spaced, according to the style requirements of the paper. Note that some research-paper formats indent block quotations ten spaces. With regard to the opening line of a paragraph in a block quotation, different style sheets for research writing have their distinctive ways of handling indentation. See Section N on the research paper.

Will you sell it to me?"

"No, sir," I said, "I wouldn't sell it to you unless you were the last person who wanted it."

"Why, my boy, you surprise and embarrass me. Why wouldn't you sell it to me?"

"Because you just front for a big syndicate that buys up farms, works the land to death with the same money crop for about ten years, and then moves on, leaving dead dust and Johnson grass. I'll sell my land to someone who respects the good earth and wants a home."

D125 Capitalize the first word of a directly quoted sentence when it appears within another sentence.

Cecil replied, "My mother is a very determined person."

"My mother," replied Cecil, "is a very determined person." [*Is* is not the first word of the directly quoted sentence.]

Then, "Don't you worry," she whispered. "For an old woman I'm feeling very fit indeed. Why, I've many a song in me yet and many a quarrel, too."

Is "A penny saved is a penny earned" as old an adage as "If wishes were horses, beggars would ride"?

D126 Do not capitalize the first word of a directly quoted sentence fragment unless the fragment begins the sentence in which it stands.

Margaret won't speak to "those common Kellys," as she calls them.

He is always talking about "roughing it," by which he means putting up at a luxury cabin not more than ten miles from some interesting town.

"My mother," replied Cecil, "is a very determined person." [Note that *is* is not capitalized, since it is the first word of only a fragment, not of a sentence.]

She said, "For an old woman I'm feeling very fit indeed." But her "very fit" sounded unconvincing, spoken as it was in a rather feeble voice.

"Crazy as a loon," he called me.

"If wishes were horses," we could overtake Selwyn.

D127 Put periods and commas inside the second quotation mark.[39]

As usual, the newspapers denounced the strikers as "rough-necks," "hoodlums," and "traitors."

"It seems," said the traveler, "that there is nobody here."

Packer replied glumly, "All he said to me was, 'No, I won't.'"

No, you're thinking of the "Johnson Rag," not the "Tiger Rag."

D128 Put colons and semicolons outside the second quotation mark.

These were included under "necessary expenses": theater tickets, four new novels, and a foot-long taxi bill.

Curtiss said, "I don't think so"; but it was obvious that he *did* think so.

D129 Put question marks and exclamation points (a) inside the second quotation mark if they belong to the quoted matter or to both the quoted matter and the rest of the sentence; (b) outside, if they belong to the rest of the sentence only.

Pilate asked, "What is truth?"	These marks belong to the quoted matter only; hence, inside the quotation marks.
I thought of the famous cry, "They shall not pass!"	
Who asked "What is truth?"	These marks belong to both the quoted matter and the rest of the sentence; hence, inside.
How stupid of you to keep shouting, "Police!"	

---

[39] The system here given of writing quotation marks with other marks of punctuation is common in the United States. British usage is different.

Who wrote "Miniver Cheevy"?	These marks belong to the rest of the sentence only; hence, outside.
Yet these men, thieves and murderers, prate of "decency"!	

D130 If a direct quotation is broken by an expression like *he said*, and if the part before the break would ordinarily be followed by a semicolon, use a comma instead and put the semicolon after the *he said* expression.

"That was thoughtless—incredibly so," he said; "but I forgive you."

D131 Put in quotation marks (but do not italicize) the title of something that is mentioned as part of a larger work.[40]

"Hamlet" in *The Seven Greatest Tragedies*	"Hamlet" would ordinarily be italicized, since it is a play. But here it is put in quotation marks as part of a larger work that is also named.

Italics may be used if one title is not inside the other.

Marquand's *The Late George Apley* in *A Marquand Reader*	*The Late George Apley* is italicized since it is ordinarily published as a book by itself.

D132 Put in quotation marks (but do not italicize) the title of an article, short story, essay, chapter; or of a poem, musical work, or story that is not long enough to make a book by itself—whether or not these are mentioned as part of a larger work.[41]

"Ode to a Nightingale" in *The Oxford Book of English Verse*
"Ode to a Nightingale"
"On Leisure" from *Essays in Idleness*
"On Leisure"

---

[40] For italics with titles of books, see D144. For a title within a title, see D145. For research-paper norms, see N113, N119, N139.

[41] For italics with titles of longer literary and musical works, see D144-45.

> "Summertime" from *Porgy and Bess*
> "Summertime"
> "White Christmas"

D133 Use quotation marks for regular radio and television programs. (Lengthy television specials and movies may be put in italics. See D144.)

> "Invitation to Learning" [radio program]
> "Meet the Press" [television show]
> *Star Wars* [motion picture]

D134 Do not put in quotation marks (or italicize either) the titles of charters, acts, statutes, reports, and so on, or of alliances and treaties.

> Act of Supremacy
> Emancipation Proclamation
> Articles of Confederation
> Stamp Act
> Declaration of Independence
> Treaty of Versailles

D135 Do not put in quotation marks (or italicize either) —

A. The names of the Bible or of its books, divisions, parts, or versions or the names of revered works of other religions.

the Bible	the New Jerusalem Bible
the Book of Psalms	the Septuagint
the Synoptic Gospels	the Koran
the Reims-Douay Version	the Talmud

B. The titles of prayers.

the Lord's Prayer	the Shema
the Hail Mary	the Shahada

C. The titles of the Liturgy of the Hours, Roman Missal,

Book of Common Prayer, or the parts of these and similar books.

the Liturgy of the Hours	the Book of Common Prayer
the Divine Office	Morning Prayer
the Roman Missal	Eucharistic Prayer
the Proper	the Common

D. The names of creeds, confessions of faith, and catechisms.

the Apostles' Creed	the Baltimore Catechism
the Augsburg Confession	the Thirty-nine Articles

D136 Put in quotation marks words that need setting off for clearness.

"I said—incorrectly—that my brother and I 'lived' in a shanty near the docks."

"Ngaio Marsh" is not the name of an African swamp but of a woman detective-story writer.

What a gap there is between "ought" and "is"!

D137 Words followed by their definition or explanation are frequently put in quotation marks or italics.

"At your service" signifies that the speaker is ready to obey orders.

Geometer means a person skilled in geometry.

Harris tweed is a kind of cloth, so named because it was originally made in Harris, in the Hebrides.

D138 An occasional technical word or term, which can be misunderstood by the reader or which is unknown to him, may be put in quotation marks the first time that it occurs in a work.

The money was borrowed from the bank by an "entrepreneur."

D139 An expression on a different language level from that of the rest of the composition (for example, a slang expression in a rather formal context) may be put in quotation marks. (If you find yourself using this rule a great deal in the course of a composition, then you are probably changing language levels too often, or the language level is not what you think it is.)

> The man had no residence, no employment, no prospect of it, and no desire for any of these things. He was a "bum."

D140 It is usually bad taste to put in quotation marks a word that is used ironically or given a forced meaning. It is all right to do so, however, when there is a real chance that intelligent readers might otherwise be misled.

> For Brutus is an honorable man.
>
> Not: For Brutus is an "honorable" man.

> I have had quite enough of your remarkable "hospitality," Henrietta.

D141 Single quotation marks are properly used to enclose a quotation within a quotation (see D118). Other uses are uncommon. Single quotation marks are sometimes used, for example, to differentiate a term from other similar terms or to emphasize a word or expression (but double quotation marks or italics are commonly used in these situations; see D136, D137).

D142 Use brackets [ ] to enclose a remark that is inserted into a quotation.

> "So they [that is, Christian and Hopeful] were forced to go, because he [Giant Despair] was stronger than they. They had also but little to say, for they knew themselves in a fault. The giant, therefore, drove them before him, and put them into his castle [Doubting Castle], into a very dark dungeon."
>
> —JOHN BUNYAN, *THE PILGRIM'S PROGRESS*

Italics

D143 To indicate in manuscript that a word is italicized, draw a line under it. In typing use italic type or underscore the word.

D144 Although the titles of books, pamphlets, plays, and motion pictures are sometimes put in quotation marks, preferred usage calls for italics. (Use quotation marks for regular radio and television programs.)

> Thackeray's *Vanity Fair* [book]
> Lord's *I Can Do Anything* [pamphlet]
> Shakespeare's *Julius Caesar* [play]
> *Star Wars* [motion picutre]
> Milton's *Paradise Lost* [a long poem,
>   often printed as a book]
> "Invitation to Learning" [radio program]
> "Meet the Press" [television show]

D145 The title of a book may contain within itself a second title, the title of another book. There are two ways of handling the second title: either (a) put it in roman type or (b) italicize it and put it within double quotation marks. (See also D131.)

> *Dickens's* Pickwick Papers *as History*
> *Dickens's "Pickwick Papers" as History*

D146 Although the titles of papal bulls, encyclicals, *motu proprio's*, and apostolic constitutions are sometimes put in quotation marks, preferred usage calls for italics.

> *Apostolicae Curae* [bull]
> *Rerum Novarum* [encyclical]

D147 Do not italicize (or put in quotation marks either) the titles of directories, manuals, and similar works.

> Blue Book   Corporation Manual
> City Directory   Social Register

D148 Do not italicize (or put in quotation marks either) the titles of charters, acts, statutes, reports, and so on, or of alliances and treaties.

> Act of Supremacy
> Emancipation Proclamation
> Articles of Confederation
> Declaration of Independence
> Stamp Act
> Treaty of Versailles

D149 Do not italicize (or put in quotation marks either) —

A. The names of the Bible, its books, divisions, parts, or versions or the names of revered books of other religions.

> the Bible   the New Jerusalem Bible
> the Book of Psalms   the Septuagint
> the Synoptic Gospels   the Koran
> the Reims-Douay Version   the Talmud

B. The titles of prayers.

> the Lord's Prayer   the Shema
> the Hail Mary   the Shahada

C. The titles of the Liturgy of the Hours, Roman Missal, Book of Common Prayer, or the parts of these and similar books.

> the Liturgy of the Hours   the Book of Common
>   Prayer
> the Divine Office   Morning Prayer
> the Roman Missal   Eucharistic Prayer
> the Proper   the Common

D. The names of creeds, confessions of faith, and catechisms.

> the Apostles' Creed   the Baltimore Catechism
> the Augsburg Confession   the Thirty-nine Articles

D150 Italicize the titles of magazines and newspapers. (The initial article is capitalized and italicized if it is part of the official title.)

> the latest issue of *Newsweek*
> a copy of *U.S. News and World Report*
> the *Reader's Digest*
> *The New York Times*
> the *Christian Science Monitor*
> the *Reno Examiner*
> *The Boston Globe*

Sometimes the name of the city in which a newspaper is published is not italicized or is omitted.

> the New York *Daily News*
> *The Courier-Journal* (Louisville)

D151 Italicize the titles of works of art such as paintings, statues, and lengthy musical works, including operas and ballets.

> Raphael's *Sistine Madonna* [painting]
> Praxiteles' *Hermes* [statue]
> Beethoven's *Emperor Concerto* [lengthy musical work]
> Gilbert and Sullivan's *Iolanthe* [opera]
> *Oklahoma!* [musical comedy]
> *Swan Lake* [ballet]

D152 Italicize the names of ships, aircraft, spacecraft, and trains (but do not italicize or capitalize the initial article). Capitalize but do not italicize HMS, USS, etc., preceding the names of ships.

> the *Queen Elizabeth* [ship]
> the *China Clipper* [airplane]
> the *Zephyr* [train]
> the USS *Skate* [submarine]
> the *Apollo II* [spaceship]

D153 Do not italicize the name of a steamship line, airline, or railroad.

> the Cunard Line
> United Airlines
> Union Pacific Railroad

D154 Italicize foreign words and phrases not yet adopted into English.

> *dolce far niente*   *Mimosa pudica*
> *en famille*   *mutatis mutandis*
> *mal de mer*   *weltanschauung*

D155 Italicize a word used only as a word, a letter used only as a letter, and a figure (number) used only as a figure.

> Jimmy, spell *measles.*
> Write *ought to be* where you have *is.*
> Both *grammar* and *glamour,* curiously enough, came originally from the same word.
> Your *o*s and *a*s look too much alike.
> Use a capital *S* there.
> All the *8*s on this page are in the wrong type.

A word may be italicized to make its function clearer in a sentence.

> There is a good reason for a *no* in this situation.

D156 Do not italicize (or put in quotation marks either) letters used for names.

> The house was sold by A to her brother, B.
> Mayor L— will give the main address.
> Who is the mysterious Mrs. X?

D157 Use italics for emphasis very sparingly.

> Menge has *not* been retaken.

The apostrophe

D158 Use *'s* to form the possessive of singular nouns (except those in D160-61).[42]

Edison's inventions	James's coat
Byrd's discoveries	woman's shoes
Dickens's novels	fox's brush
Keats's sonnets	cow's horns

D159 Use *'s* to form the possessive of names that end in silent *s* or *x*.

Descartes's philosophy	Des Moines's population
Charlevoix's discoveries	Illinois's capitol

Phrases like those above are regularly recast to avoid apparent awkwardness:

the philosophy of Descartes	the Des Moines population
the discoveries of Charlevoix	the Illinois capitol

D160 Use the apostrophe (') alone to form the possessive singular of the following:

A. Certain expressions using the word *sake*: *for acquaintance' sake, for appearance' sake, for conscience' sake, for goodness' sake,* and so on.

B. Classical and mythological names ending in *s* or *es*, like *Alcibiades (Alcibiades'), Socrates (Socrates'), Xerxes (Xerxes'), Achilles (Achilles'), Mars (Mars').*

C. Certain biblical names ending in *s* or *es*: *Jesus (Jesus'), Moses (Moses').*

---

[42] There are other, equally common systems of showing possession. The one used in this book, however, has the advantage of simplicity, which seems to outweigh the disadvantage of an occasional awkward expression like *Dickens's novels.* Morever, this system more accurately reflects spoken English in words like boss's, duchess's. For the possessive case, see C183-84.

D161 In general, use the apostrophe (') alone with singular nouns to avoid awkward pronounciation (for example, three successive *s* or *z* sounds).

> *Jesus'* words   *Moses'* leadership   *Texas'* senator

(These expressions are frequently replaced by *words of Jesus, leadership of Moses, Texas senator* or *senator from Texas.*)

D162 Use *'s* to form the possessive of plural nouns that do not end in *s*.

alumnae's card party	men's shoes
alumni's wishes	oxen's yoke
children's clothing	women's gloves

D163 Use only the apostrophe (') to form the possessive of plural nouns that end in *s*.

Davises' fence	boys' caps
Joneses' front yard	cows' horns
Smiths' garage	foxes' brushes

D164 Add the apostrophe or *'s* to the last word of compound words in the possessive. (Compound words follow D158-63 according as the last word of the compound is singular or plural, ends in *s* or not.)

> your daughter-in-law's success
> the herdsmen's cries
> the emperor of Japan's palace
> the master of ceremonies' jokes

D165 Add the apostrophe or *'s* to the last word of titles in the possessive case (except those in D167).

> Pope John Paul II's encyclicals
> the district attorney's office
> Henry VIII's wives
> the Standard Oil Company's tankers
> the Lord Mayor of London's cat
> the Guild of Goldsmiths' annual exhibit

D166 Use *'s* to form the possessive of abbreviations.

> NBC's *Meet the Press*
> Joshua Miller, Sr.'s, will
> Daniel A. Lord, S.J.'s, pageants

D167 Some titles in the possessive case are "frozen"; that is, they omit the apostrophe or *'s.*[43]

> | | |
> |---|---|
> | Bankers Association | St. Marys, Kansas |
> | Diners Club | Teachers College |
> | Governors Island | Veterans Administration |

D168 If two or more nouns possess something together (joint possession), add the apostrophe or *'s* to the last only.

> Abercrombie and Fitch's clothing for men
> Gilbert and Sullivan's operas
> Beaumont and Fletcher's plays
> the juniors and seniors' poor-relief work

D169 If two or more nouns possess something separately, add the apostrophe or *'s* to each.

> Tom's, Dick's, and Harry's overcoats
> Wordsworth's and Shelley's poetry

D170 Use an apostrophe or *'s* to form the possessive case of those indefinite and reciprocal pronouns that have a possessive case (except *who, which, what,* and their compounds).

> | | |
> |---|---|
> | another's idea | someone's umbrella |
> | others' ideas | somebody else's watch |
> | anyone's guess | each other's clothes |
> | nobody's business | one another's eyes |

---

[43] This usage is more common when *by* or *for* is understood rather than *of.* Compare *teachers college* and *teachers' salaries.* In some instances one element functions as an adjective rather than as a noun: *United States citizen.*

D171 Do not use an apostrophe with the personal, interrogative, relative, and possessive pronouns or adjectives.

mine	ours	yours	his
hers	its	theirs	whose

D172 Use an apostrophe in a contracted word to indicate the omission of a letter or letters.

can't [*not* ca'nt]	ev'ry
doesn't [*not* does'nt]	he's
don't [*not* do'nt]	I'm
isn't [*not* is'nt]	o'
it's [*for* it is]	o'clock
who's [*for* who is]	th'

D173 In the number of a year, the first two numerals are sometimes replaced by an apostrophe.

the spirit of '76	the class of '48
vintage of '02	the events of '65
depression of '32	the Panic of '93

D174 Use either an unitalicized *s* or an unitalicized *'s* to form the plural of titles of books and magazines, foreign words, letters, figures, and words used as words.

Bring your *King Lear*s and *Commonweal*s to class.
Bring your *King Lear*'s and *Commonweal*'s to class.

The various *esse*s come to the same thing.
The various *esse*'s come to the same thing.

Mind your *p*s and *q*s.
Mind your *p*'s and *q*'s.

Your *7*s look just like your *9*s.
Your *7*'s look just like your *9*'s.

*I*s and *me*s are too prominent in your talk.
I's and *me*'s are too prominent in your talk.

D175 Use *'s* to form the plural of a word that would otherwise be unclear.

Here's my list of do's and don'ts.

D176 Use *'s* to form the plural of capital letters in abbreviation with periods.

All the candidates have M.A.'s.

But the plural of capital letters and the plural of abbreviations in capital letters without periods are formed by adding *s* alone.

The youngster has been well schooled in the three Rs.
This is a meeting of VIPs.

D177 Except for the cases in D174-75, do not use the apostrophe to form the plural of a word.

books   *snouts*

two ~~book's~~ on the table   long, pointed ~~snout's~~

D178 Do not use an apostrophe for which you cannot give a rule or solid precedent.

The hyphen

D179 When two nouns not ordinarily used in combination are used as one word, connect them with a hyphen.[44]

Father Abram Ryan was the *poet-priest* of the South.
He is the only *philosopher-statesman* in Washington.
Some modern painters might be classified as *artist-salespersons*.

D180 Ordinarily hyphenate a compound modifier preceding a noun.[45] (But see D181.)

burnt-red geraniums	loud-talking people
do-as-I-please manner	saber-toothed tiger
door-to-door canvass	self-winding watch
fun-loving children	so-called geniuses
ill-timed remark	well-phrased sentences
leather-covered book	world-without-end problems

---

[44] For compound nouns written as two words (without a hyphen), see I 9.
[45] Note the difference in meaning between *red and white roses* (two kinds of roses) and *red-and-white roses* (one kind).

D181 Do not hyphen (a) compound proper adjectives or (b) compound proper nouns or well-established compound common nouns that are used as adjectives.[46]

East Indian spices	New Orleans restaurants
Wiliam and Mary teams	North American forests
Lake District scenery	Old English ballads
foreign aid plan	high school play

D182 Do not hyphenate the adverb *very* or an adverb ending in *ly* and the adjective or adverb it modifies.

She was a *very happy* person.

Randy's *tightly swollen* eye resulted from faking to the right instead of to the left.

Mrs. Grenery is always *stylishly dressed.*

Mike's *badly swollen* hand pained him a great deal.

This factory was *extraordinarily well* planned.

D183 Ordinarily do not use a hyphen when compound words used as an adjective follow the noun they modify.[47]

[Preceding:] They made *long-range* plans.
[Following:] Their plans were *long range.*

[Preceding:] She was a *law-abiding* citizen.
[Following:] As a citizen, she was *law abiding.*

[Preceding:] This is a *well-chosen* adverb.
[Following:] This adverb is *well chosen.*

---

[46] For greater clarity, a hyphen should be used with a compound common modifier if that word is both preceded by another modifier and followed by a noun; for example, a comprehensive *foreign-aid* program, a remarkable *high-school* play.

[47] For the sake of clarity, the hyphen is often retained when compound words used as an adjective follow the verb *be;* for example, "Our guest *is soft-spoken.*"

D184 Use a hyphen after *re* and some other prefixes to prevent confusion.[48]

Mr. Antonescu *re-covered* the stolen chair.
Christianity could partly *re-create* the Garden of Eden.
The school plans to *de-emphasize* its football program.

D185 Use a hyphen after the prefixes *self, ex* (meaning "former"), and in some instances *anti,* and after prefixes before words beginning with a capital letter.[49]

self-inflicted	anti-inflation
ex-senator	un-Christian

D186 Use a hyphen between words when it will help to keep the reader from falsely combining them with other words.

Dr. Cox is president of the *insane-hospital* board.
Twelve *foot-soldiers* walked up the path.

D187 When a modifier is used before a compound noun written as two words, join the noun with a hyphen.

drop curtain	worn drop-curtain
dry rot	pervasive dry-rot
butt hinges	two butt-hinges

D188 When several words combine with the same final element to form compound words, hyphens follow each of the initial elements.

The policy will be changed from sixty- to ninety-day coverage.

D189 Hyphenate compound numbers from twenty-one to ninety-nine.

I'll be *twenty-one* next Tuesday.

---

[48] See I 19.
[49] See I 18.

D190 Hyphenate a fraction when it is used as an adjective or adverb.

> Can I get lumber in *one-half* and *two-thirds* lengths?
> The gas tank is *three-fourths* full.

D191 Do not hyphenate a fraction when it is used as a noun. (If, however, the fraction contains a compound number from twenty-one to ninety-nine, that number must be hyphenated according to D189.)

> Crumbock lost *one half* of his savings.
> *Two thirds* of the distance remains.
> I was airsick for *three fourths* of the trip.
> *Five thirty-seconds* is not very much of an error.
> This bottle contains almost *twelve twenty-sevenths* of the acid.
> Why, *twenty-one thirty-seconds* is more than half!

D192 No general rules can be given here for hyphenating ordinary compound words, because usage varies so widely. Consult a current dictionary.

D193 Whenever you have doubts about a hyphen and these rules or a dictionary cannot help you, do not use the hyphen.

Division of words

E1 The following rules apply chiefly to matter that is hand-written or typed (on a typewriter or on a word processor), rather than to printed matter which, in some instances, may follow more liberal norms.

E2 Do not divide a word at the end of a line when it is at all possible and reasonable to avoid making such a division. Such divisions, though necessary in some cases, decreases readability.

E3   Use a dictionary in order to be sure what the syllables of a word are.

E4   If there seems to be no way to avoid dividing a word at the end of a line, be sure to make the division between syllables only.

> *fruit-*
> Autumn is the season of ~~frui~~
> *fulness*
> ~~tfulness.~~

> *imag-*
> His sickness is only an ~~ima~~
> *inary*
> ~~ginary~~ ailment.

E5   If a word begins with a prefix, make the division after the prefix.

> *in-*
> Casey was said to be an ~~intrac~~
> *tractable*
> ~~table~~ young rebel.

E6   Do not divide (a) one-syllable words (like *golf, thought,* and *praised)* or (b) words of five letters or less (like *inner, mania,* and *rival).*

E7   Do not divide a word after one letter.

> It seems that we live in ~~e~~
> *eventful*
> ~~ventful~~ days.

E8   Do not carry only two letters of a divided word to the next line.

> *violently*
> Mark has protested ~~violent~~
> ~~ly~~ to the instructor.

E9 Divide hyphenated compound words at the hyphen (in other words, avoid two hyphens).

[Wrong:]	We visited a pov- erty-stricken area.
[Right:]	We visited a poverty- stricken area.

E10 Divide a solid compound word between the elements of the compound.

book-
  case
	master-
	  piece

E11 Give consideration to pronunciation in dividing a word (to assist the reader and to avoid awkwardness).

[Poor:]	[Better:]

ambi-
  tious
	am-
	  bitious

super-
  ior
	su-
	  perior

E12 As far as possible, do not divide the syllables of a proper noun or adjective.

Here is an issue of *National ~~Geo-~~*
Geographic
~~graphic.~~

E13 Do not divide abbreviations,[1] acronyms, contractions, or numerals.

E14 As far as possible, do not end more than five lines on a page in hyphens.

E15 As far as possible, do not end more than two consecutive lines in hyphens.

E16 Do not divide the last word on a page.

---

[1] An abbreviation like AFL-CIO may be divided after the hyphen.

Abbreviations

F1 Abbreviate these Latin words or write them out in the equivalent English: *id est (i.e.); exempli gratia (e.g.); et cetera (etc.); et alibi, et alii (et al.); ibidem (ibid.); videlicet (viz.).* (In text it is preferable to write *that is* in place of *i.e.; for example* in place of *e.g.; and so forth* or *and so on* in place of *etc.; and elsewhere* or *and others* in place of *et al.;* and *namely* in place of *viz.*)[1]

[Right:] We found paper, kindling, *etc.,* all laid ready for a fire.
[Better:] We found paper, kindling, *and so forth,* all laid ready for a fire.

F2 Abbreviate eras of time and A.M. (*or* a.m.) and P.M. (*or* p.m.)[2] when these are accompanied by figures.[3]

There is not a scrap of evidence before 10 B.C.
There is not a scrap of evidence until ten years before Christ.

In A.D. 1300[4] the university was still rather small.

Anno Domini thirteen hundred dawned on a university that was still rather small.

The masking stops at 6:00 P.M.
The masking stops at six in the evening.

---

[1] For a list of abbreviations, see N72. For ZIP code abbreviations, see S62.

[2] Printed matter uses small capitals for the abbreviations A.M. and P.M. When this is impractical, either capitals or lowercase letters may be used. The abbreviations A.D. and B.C. may be set in small or regular capitals.

[3] Put in figures the hours of the day if A.M. or P.M. is used, except at the beginning of a sentence. Spell out the time of day when A.M. or P.M. is not used. See G8.

[4] Although A.D. is now commonly placed after the date, careful writers still place A.D. before, unless the date is a century expressed in words.

In some scholarly works C.E. and B.C.E. ("common era" and "before the common era") are used in place of A.D. and B.C.

F3 Except in technical lists (where abbreviation is optional), do not abbreviate but spell out the names of the months and of the days of the week.

Tuesday, February

There is going to be a class night on ~~Tues., Feb.~~ 9.

F4 Except in technical lists, gazetteers, and other reference works or the headings and addresses of letters (where abbreviation is optional), spell out geographical elements like *fort, island, mount, river, west.*

Fort Lauderdale	*Port* Arthur
Pelee *Island*	Indian *River*
Mount Vernon	*West* Palm Beach

F5 Names of countries are not abbreviated. An exception is made for the Union of Soviet Socialist Republics, usually abbreviated U.S.S.R.[5]

F6 Abbreviate these titles always and only when they precede proper names: *Mr., Messrs.; Mrs., Mmes.; Dr.* (doctor*), Drs.* (doctors*).*[6]

That must be *Mr.* Clark in the closet.

See here, *mister*, that's airline property.

I can guarantee that *Drs.* Pell and Nive will find something wrong with you.

I'm sorry, but the *doctors* are both ill.

F7 Do not abbreviate personal titles that are followed only by the surname (or equivalent).

General Powell	*Brother* Sebian
Senator Kennedy	*Sister* Teresa

---

[5] In informal writing U.S.A. and U.S. (as an adjective but not as a noun) are acceptable abbreviations.

[6] Strictly speaking, *Ms.* is not an abbreviation (it is a coinage, not a shortened form). For its plural forms, see S26.

F8 Personal titles may be abbreviated if the full name is given.

Maj. Gen. Robert A. Moses *Asst. Prof.* Jeremiah Tindale
Sen. Edward Kennedy *Br.* John Sebian

F9 Abbreviate *reverend* and *honorable* only in the addresses and headings of letters, and not even then if they are preceded by *the.*

Rev. Francis X. Clements
St. Ignatius Rectory
502 Seward Avenue
Clifton, North Carolina

We were harangued by the *Honorable* Cyrus R. Schumacher.

The Reverend Francis X. Clements
St. Ignatius Rectory
502 Seward Avenue
Clifton, North Carolina

F10 Except in technical lists, do not abbreviate first and last names but only middle names, unless the person himself uses initials.[7]

Charles
Mr. Chas. Dyke

William
Wm. Colgrave

George
Geo. O. Pickton

Julia
J. R. Connaught

She signs her name *J. V.* Train.
The register is signed *M.* Moresby Mult.

F11 Abbreviate *junior, senior,* academic degrees, the names of religious orders, and like designations when they are used after a person's name, and set them off by commas.

Does anybody here know an Andrew Johnson, *Jr.?*
Lieutenant Lee Smayda, *USN,* has been reassigned.

---

[7] The initials in a personal name are followed by a period and a space.

James B. Fall, *Ph.D.*,[8] held us in his drowsy spell for four hours.
Father Patrick Donovan, *O.S.B.*,[8] blessed the new fire engine.

F12 The abbreviations, *Sr., Jr., III,* and *IV* follow a complete name (not a family name alone).[9] In informal writing it is acceptable to use these terms with a person's given name; for example, *Bill, Jr.*

Robert F. Cudahy, *Sr.*, spoke at the convention.
Joseph Fitzwiller *III* is vacationing in Bermuda.
Do you have Carl Agostino, *Jr.*'s phone number?

F13 Except in technical lists and references, do not abbreviate units of measurement, courses of instruction, and labels for divisions of written works.

That fence is four *feet* [not *ft.*] high.
She is taking a course in English *literature* [not *lit.*].
Read *Chapter* [not *Ch.*] 5 for tomorrow.

F14 Except in technical lists and references or the headings and addresses of letters (where abbreviation is common), do not abbreviate but spell out such words as *street, boulevard, avenue, page, chapter, company, manufacturing, brothers, consolidated, limited, incorporated, building, university,* and *railroad.*

The first shift at Able Seal *Manufacturing Company* comprises about five hundred workers.

The clubroom, a two-by-four affair on Wellston *Street,* could hold a typewriter and an upright hand press.

They work at Widgets *Incorporated* on Utopia *Boulevard.*

In *Chapter 2, page 23,* there is an unsupported statement about the company's financial stability.

---

[8] In informal writing and in alphabetical lists, periods and spaces are regularly omitted from abbreviations designating religious orders and academic degrees.

[9] A comma precedes and follows *Jr.* and *Sr.* within a sentence, but no commas are used with *III* or *IV.*

F15 Most abbreviations in all-capital letters do not use periods. Among these are the names of states; the titles of government agencies, service organizations, labor unions, athletic associations; the call letters of broadcasting stations; standard time zones; and those abbreviations like CARE, NATO, and UNESCO that are pronounced like words (acronyms).[10]

NJ	USMC	EST
FBI	CIO	NASA
ABC	NCAA	IOC
SEATO	GAO	CIA
KABL	WNBC-TV	NAACP

F16 Use a period after abbreviations in lowercase letters that might otherwise be construed as words in themselves.

c.o.d.	fig.	no.

F17 With expressions of foreign origin, use a period in abbreviations having lowercase letters that represent words. (Notice that there is no space after an internal period.)

a.m.	e.g.	i.e.

Periods are regularly omitted with other lowercase abbreviations representing several words.

ips	mph	rpm

F18 In general, with abbreviations of two or more words that consist of more than single letters, use a period and a space after each element in the abbreviation.

Maj. Gen.	S. Dak.	op. cit.

---

[10] Latin abbreviations in capitals retain periods (for example, N.B., Q.E.D., R.I.P.). For an extensive list of abbreviations, see Ralph DeSola, *Abbreviations Dictionary,* 8th edition, Boca Raton, Florida: CRC Press, 1992.

Academic abbreviations, however, are written with periods but no internal spaces.[11]

Ph.D.   Ed.D.   LL.B.

F19 In technical or scientific writing, on business forms, and in lists and tables, ordinarily abbreviate units of measurement without periods.[12]

F20 Use no comma after the period of an abbreviation unless a comma is required for clarity or by one of the rules of punctuation listed elsewhere in this book.

[Wrong:] I have a 7:00 P.M., class.
[Right:] I have a 7:00 P.M. class.[13]

[Wrong:] In A.D., 64 Nero fiddled while Rome burned.
[Right:] In A.D. 64 Nero fiddled while Rome burned.

If the schedule says P.M., P.M. is what it means.	Here the comma is required for clarity.
Planes leave at 7:00 P.M., at 11:00 P.M., and at 1:00 A.M.	Here the commas are required by D32.
Pencils, sketching pads, binoculars, etc., will have to be provided by the bird watchers themselves.	*Etc.* is generally considered to be parenthetical, and so the comma is required by D54. See also D32.

F21 Except in the cases provided for in these rules and a few others for which you can find good authority, do not use abbreviations. If the use of technical abbreviations and acronyms is appropriate in particular cases, they should be defined the first time they are used.

F22 For the use of abbreviations in documentation and footnotes, see N102-13, N116-19, N131-39.

---

[11] Professional designations such as CPA (certified public accountant) are usually written without periods when they stand alone but with periods when they accompany academic degrees; for example, *Jonathan Calafano, M.A., C.P.A.*

[12] In formal writing, units of measurement are spelled out. See F 13.

[13] Printed matter uses small capitals for the abbreviations A.M. and P.M. When this is impractical, either capitals or lowercase letters may be used.

G

Numbers

G1 Always spell out numbers at the beginning of a sentence.

Nineteen eighty-three
~~1983~~ was not a bad year for wheat.

Thirteen
~~13~~ people were injured when the bus overturned.

G2 When it would be awkward to spell out a number at the beginning of a sentence, recast the sentence.

Instead of—
Four million, two hundred and forty-six thousand, five hundred and forty-two dollars was the company's gross in the first five years of operation.

Write this—
In the first five years of operation, the company grossed $4,246,542.

G3 In general, spell out all numbers expressed in only one or two words, provided they are not affected by some other rule in this section.[1]

He was in the hospital *three* months and *seventeen* days.
With bones and feathers, this is about a *five*-pound chicken.
In *sixty-eight* cities, *ten thousand* people gave *two* dollars each.
At *forty-fifty* the *three* golf clubs were a bargain.

Some important distinctions regarding this rule are identified in G4, 8, 10, 12, 14, 15, 16, 17-23.

---

[1] See D189 for the use of hyphens in writing numbers.

G4 Following the norm in G3, spell out numbers from 2,100 to 9,900[2] when they are expressed only in hundreds.[3]

[Wrong:] The auditorium held *two thousand one hundred people.*
[Right:] The auditorium held *twenty-one hundred people.*
[Right if intended to be read as *two thousand one hundred:*] The auditorium held 2,100 people.

[Wrong:] The auditorium held *twenty-three hundred and forty* people.
[Right:] The auditorium held 2,340 people.

G5 In text, spell out numbers of sessions of Congress, military bodies, and political divisions and subdivisions when such numbers are under 101.[3]

> Eightieth Congress, second session
> Seventeenth Division
> 162nd Infantry
> Ninth Congressional District, Fifty-second Ward

G6 Spell out the ages of persons and things (except in the cases treated in G12).

> a woman aged fifty-two
> a nine-year-old shrub

G7 Spell out the names of particular centuries, decades and hundreds.[3]

Display was typical of the *eighties;* the *nineties* were not so lavish. The *eighteen-hundreds* were years of savage economic warfare. She is a connoisseur of *seventeenth century* Italian art.

Acceptable but less formal–
In the 1970's (*not* '70's) she was a rebel without a cause.

---

[2] Use commas with numbers of four digits or more (3,450; 4,500,000). Do not use commas with years under five digits (1492), page numbers, radio-frequency designations, serial numbers, telephone numbers, addresses, ZIP codes, and degrees of temperature.
[3] See D189 for the use of hyphens in writing numbers.

G8 Put in figures the time of day if A.M. or P.M.[4] is used; otherwise spell out the time of day.

> 6:00 P.M.   11:45 A.M.

We adjourned at *ten o'clock* [*but* at 10:00 P.M. *or* at 10 P.M.].
We will meet at *three o'clock* [*not* 3 o'clock].

The time of day is usually written in words. (If the time is emphasized, use figures with A.M. and P.M.)

G9 Spell out sums in cents up to one hundred (except for the cases treated in G12).

> four cents   ninety-eight cents

G10 To avoid encumbering a text with a series of spelled-out numbers, use figures.

He bet on lottery numbers 66, 32, 45, and 8.

G11 In formal style (e.g., wedding invitations) spell out all numbers; in technical and business style (e.g., office memos) use figures.

G12 In technical, statistical, and business writing—where it is important that the reader be able to work with figures—put dimensions, degrees, distances, weights, measures, sums of money, and the like, in figures even though they could be expressed in one or two words. (But do not put these numbers in figures if they begin a sentence. See G1. Also see G22.)

> Decimals and percentages: .05 of an inch, 7 per cent
> Dimensions: 8 by 11 inches, 3 by 5 by 9 feet
> Degrees: 70° F., 30° C.
> Distances: 15 miles, 9 yards, 2 inches
> Weights: 3 tons, 15 pounds, 5 ounces
> Measures: 5 gallons, 2 pints, 50 bushels, 1 peck
> Sums of money: $5.00, $43.85, $.85, 85¢
> Ages: 18 years, 1 month, and 3 days

---

[4] Printed matter uses small capitals for the abbreviations of A.M. and P.M. When this is impractical, either capitals or lowercase letters may be used.

G13 In general, put in figures numbers expressed in more than two words, provided they are not affected by some other rule in this section.

1,556 hospitals	101 airplanes
1,250,000 people	514 pennies
123 times	28,634,878 tons
422 ships	134 countries

D
E
F
G

G14 Uneven large numbers over one million may be expressed in mixed form.

3¼ million	4.5 billion

G15 Put years and dates in figures except for the case in G1 and except when, in text, the day precedes the month or the month is omitted.[5]

1990	June 3
March 1, 1990[6]	April 1

Nineteen eighty-three was not a bad year for wheat.

The *fifth* of May is a day of much celebration in Mexico, for on the *fifth* the revolution is commemorated.

We expect him to arrive on August 5 in time for the celebration.[7]

G16 Put in figures (roman or arabic as required) the page numbers, chapter numbers, and other divisions of books.

page 39	column 4	Volume III
pp. 39-72	line 18	Vol. 3
Chapter V	scene 1	Book I
Chap. 5	verse 3	No. 16

---

[5] See D189 for the use of hyphens in writing numbers.

[6] In many foreign countries and in military texts, a cardinal number precedes the month; for example, 1 March 1990.

[7] Do not use *-nd*, *-rd*, *-st*, or *-th* with the day when it is given in figures. (Such numbers are, however, pronounced as ordinals.)

G17 Spell out numbers 1 through 10 when they are used as street names.

Second Avenue   *Ninth* Street

G18 In addresses (where space is limited and instant recognition is important), put in figures numbers over 10 that are used as street names.

> 30th Street
> 134 West 12th Street
> [But to avoid a confusing sequence of numbers:]
> 134 Twelfth Street

G19 Put in figures room and house numbers (except for the case in G1).

> Room 14
> 15 Rosalind Drive
> 3648 Fifth Avenue

G20 Figures are frequently used to express scores, votes, and so on.

> 5-to-3 victory
> majority of only 200 votes

G21 Put in figures the numbers in abbreviated measurements (except for the case in G1).

> 75 m.p.h.   700 ft/sec
> 8 mi.   2 ft., 9 in.
> 5 lb. bag   30%

G22 If similar numbers come under conflicting rules in the same sentence or in neighboring sentences, write them all in figures or spell them all out according to G1, G23, and G24, if you can do so without awkwardness.

G23 When similar-type numbers that could be expressed in two words or less are clustered together, it is preferable to put them in figures.

Of the 35 students in my twelfth-grade class, 20 are girls and 15 are boys.

G24 If some of the numbers would have to be expressed in more than two words, put them all in figures.[8]

[Wrong:] The number of accidents recorded in the three-year period were *fifty-five, seventy-three,* and 108, respectively.
[Wrong:] The number of accidents recorded in the three-year period were *fifty-five, seventy-three,* and *one hundred and eight,* respectively.
[Right:] The number of accidents recorded in the three-year period were 55, 73, and 108, respectively. [Note that *three* of "three-year" is not affected because it is not, according to the sense of the sentence, a number similar to the others.][8]

G25 For greater readability, separate numbers that stand together within a sentence.

[Poor:] The total shipment of eggs was 950, 105 of which were broken.
[Better:] Of the 950 eggs in the shipment, 105 were broken.

G26 For the sake of clarity in certain expressions, use a combination of figures and spelled-out numbers.

She ordered thirty 20-page pamphlets.

G27 In hyphenating figures, omit hundreds from the second unless the first ends in two zeros or the hundreds change.

pp. 27-29

7640-95 [*not* 7640-7695]
1009-11 [*not* 1009-10011]
pp. 223-26 [*not* pp. 223-226]

But—
1900-1914 [because of the two zeros]
487-504 [because of the changing hundreds]

---

[8] See G22, G26.

In another and simplified method, the second number includes only the changed part of the first number: 4–15, 61–2, 83–112, 1003–6, 486–513, 12542–619.

G28 In hyphenating figures, if the second-last figure of the first number is zero, do not repeat it in the second number.

pp. 1207-9 [*not* 1207-09]

G29 In hyphenating dates before Christ, repeat the hundreds, since the numbers diminish rather than increase.

494-426 B.C. [*not* 494-26]

Capitals

Line and sentence capitals

H1 Capitalize the first word of a sentence.

They say he was a wealthy man. (*That* was in 1960, of course, when a dollar bought more than it buys now.)

H2 When a sentence in parentheses interrupts another sentence, do not capitalize the first word of the sentence in parentheses nor end it with a period.

Though I have often been tempted to quit (*such* thoughts surely come to every person), the example of More's fortitude in spite of his circumstances gives me courage.

In this example the sentence in parentheses interrupts another sentence.

They say he was a wealthy man. (*That* was in 1960, of course, when a dollar bought more than it buys now.)

In this example the sentence in parentheses does not interrupt another sentence.

H3 Within a sentence you may capitalize, if you like, the first word of a question that is put in the form of a direct question but is not quoted.[1] The capital makes the question rather formal and emphatic.

> The crucial question is, *Will* this help you to reach your goal?
> Ms. Ford's invariable morning question was, *did* you sleep well?
> He was always the first to ask, *when* are we going home?

H4 If words are directed by a person to himself or are merely unspoken thoughts, capitalize the first word. (You may italicize the words, but do not use quotation marks.)

> I thought to myself, Where is all this going to end?
> She sometimes asked herself, Why am I here?
> *It's all over now*, he said to himself.

H5 Capitalize the first word of a directly quoted sentence, even when it appears within another sentence.[2]

> Cecil replied, "*My* mother is a very determined person."

> "*My* mother," replied Cecil, "is a very determined person."
> [*Is* is not the first word of the directly quoted sentence.]

> Then, "*Don't* you worry," she whispered. "*For* an old woman I'm feeling very fit indeed. *Why*, I've many a song in me yet, and many a quarrel too."

---

[1] A direct question is a question expressed in the words of the speaker; for example, "Where is the platypus?" An indirect question gives the sense of the speaker's question without quotation; for example, "She asked where the platypus was." Indirect questions are frequently introduced by *whether* and by *if* in the sense of *whether*.

[2] A direct quotation is a quotation in the speaker's or writer's own words that is not introduced by the conjunctions *whether*, *if*, or *that* either expressed or implied.

H6 Capitalize the first word of a direct quotation only if the quotation is complete in itself, formally introduced, and not closely (grammatically) tied with what precedes it.

Shakespeare wrote, "*We* are such stuff as dreams are made of."

Caesar was warned to "*beware* the Ides of March."

We would always leave Aunt Millie's with "*come* again" ringing in our ears.

H7 Do not capitalize the first word of a directly quoted sentence fragment, unless the fragment begins the sentence in which it stands.[3]

Margaret won't speak to "*those* common Kellys," as she calls them.

"*My* mother," replied Cecil, "*is* a very determined person." [Note that *is* is not capitalized, since it is not the first word of a sentence but of a fragment.]

She said, "For an old woman I'm feeling very fit indeed." But her "*very* fit" sounded unconvincing, spoken as it was in a rather feeble voice.

"*Crazy* as a loon," he called me.

"*If* wishes were horses," we could overtake Selwyn.

---

[3] Do not confuse a sentence fragment or half-sentence with an interrupted sentence or elliptical sentence. In the following, the quoted sentence is an interrupted sentence, not a sentence fragment, and hence is capitalized.

Margot was stopped just as she began to say, "Then you mean that the ghost isn't—"

In the following, the quoted portion is an elliptical sentence, not a sentence fragment, and hence is capitalized.

Shelley turned around and said very carefully, very deliberately, "Not a chance."

H8 Do not capitalize the first word of an indirect quotation.[4]

Elaine commented that *cigarettes* are injurious to one's health.

The editor said *my* article was too long.

Jamie questioned whether *most* students really do care about their classmates.

H9 Ordinarily capitalize the first word of each line of poetry.[5]

> Being your slave, what should I do but tend
> Upon the hours and times of your desire?
> I have no precious time at all to spend,
> Nor services to do, till you require.
>
> —WILLIAM SHAKESPEARE

H10 Do not capitalize a line of poetry that simply runs over from the preceding line for lack of room.

> The cloud shadows of midnight possess their
>   own repose,
> For the weary winds are silent, or the moon
>   is in the deep;
> Some respite to its turbulence unresting ocean
>   knows;
> Whatever moves or toils or grieves hath its
>   appointed sleep.
>
> —PERCY BYSSHE SHELLEY

---

[4] See D120. An indirect quotation is a quotation introduced by the conjunctions *whether, if,* or *that* either expressed or implied.

[5] In some modern poetry this rule (as well as many others) does not apply. If you quote such poetry, follow copy exactly.

> I am afraid, dear friend,
> that something trivial will come
>   of men
>   with dollars.
>
> —MICHEL CHAMBRE

See H10.

H11 When the beginning of a line of poetry is omitted, do not capitalize the first word.

> . . . hast thou golden slumbers?
>   O sweet content!
> . . . is thy mind perplexed?
>   O punishment!

—Thomas Dekker

H12 Ordinarily capitalize the first word after a colon when the colon introduces a complete sentence (see D83-87).[6] Regularly capitalize the first word after a colon when the colon introduces a formal statement, a quotation, or material of more than one sentence.

My advice to you is this: *Stay* in bed Monday and Tuesday, and stay in the house at least until noon Saturday.

They asked me the same old tiresome question over and over again: *Where* were you, and with whom, last Thursday afternoon?

This is the problem we must talk over: *The* woman is old and getting feeble, has no money, cannot stay any longer at her niece's, and has gotten into trouble at the police station.

In his last letter—and note this carefully—he says: "The governor will hear no more talk whatever of a parole for Tompkins."

Boswell wrote of Oliver Goldsmith: "His incessant desire of being conspicuous in company was the occasion of his sometimes appearing to such disadvantage as one should hardly have supposed possible in a man of his genius."

He presented only two bits of information: (1) the pool had been completed; (2) it had been completed under budget.

Manu's objection was disappointing: not only was it petty, but it was also ill-timed.

---

[6] There is really no consistent general practice in using capitals after a colon in cases like this. To use them is more conservative.

H13 Do not capitalize the first word after a colon when the colon introduces merely a word, phrase, or clause—unless you want strong emphasis.

All the difficulty is due to just one little person: the boss.

My faults are these: temper, inexperience, and awkwardness.

There is only one thing I want: to sit down and take these shoes off.

Democracy presupposes two conditions: that the majority of the people be informed and intelligent, and that the electors use their power fully and honestly.

Verdict: Not guilty.

H14 Capitalize the first word of each line in the heading and address of a letter.

The Narrows	The Shorthorn
Pawhasset, New York	Arlington State College
February 15, 1990	Arlington, Texas
The Roberts Family	The Debate Team
326 Westwood	Elspeth High School
Campo, CA 92006	Wotan, NV 89301

H15 Capitalize the first word in the salutation of a letter. Do not capitalize *dear* unless it is the first word.

Dear Sirs:	Reverend and dear Father:
Dear Aunt Marie,	My dear Aunt Jane:
Dear Sir or Madam:	Gentlemen:

H16 Capitalize only the first word in the complimentary close.

Yours truly,	Sincerely yours,
Very truly yours,	Yours sincerely,
Your friend,	Very sincerely yours,

H17   When a title is set in two or more lines (for example, on a title page or at the beginning of an essay), capitalize the first word of each line.[7]

Marius
The King's Henchman

A Short Dissertation
On Buying Pigs in a Poke

Proper nouns and adjectives

H18   In general, capitalize proper nouns—the particular names of particular persons, places, and things.

May I have an appointment with Mr. *Anthony Powers*, please?

Let's stop off at *Niagara Falls*.

The lobby of the *Statler Hotel* will be a good place to meet.

Wasn't *Man o' War* one of the greatest race horses?

On June 15, 1215, the king signed the *Magna Charta*, or *Great Charter*.

H19   In general, capitalize proper adjectives; that is, adjectives derived from proper nouns. (See H21.)

American	North Korean
Christian	Olympian
Napoleonic	South American

H20   Do not capitalize prefixes such as *ante, anti, ex, inter, non, post, pre, semi, un* when they are used with hyphens to join proper nouns or adjectives.

pre-Islamic	pro-British
non-Jewish	anti-Bolshevik

---

[7] For the capitalization of others words in titles, see H126.

Is it *un-American* [adjective] to want God in the schools?
For a *non-Catholic* [noun] she shows a remarkable knowledge of
the liturgy.

H21 Do not capitalize words derived from proper nouns but
no longer depending on them for their meaning.

apache [Parisian gangster], from Apache Indian
artesian well, from Artesium in ancient France
babel of opinion, from the Tower of Babel
bedlam [uproar, confusion], from Bedlam [Bethlehem] Hospi-
    tal for lunatics
china [porcelain ware], from China
gothic type, from Gothic
italic type, from Italic, pertaining to ancient Italy
macadam [a road finishing], from John L. McAdam, Scots en-
    gineer
mulligan stew, from Mulligan
pasteurize, from Pasteur
quisling, from Vidkun Quisling
roman type, from Roman
venetian blinds, from Venetian, pertaining to Venice
watt [volt-ampere], from James Watt, Scots inventor
champagne, from California and elsewhere [but *Champagne*,
    from France]

If you tear another *jersey*, you'll have to play in an overcoat.

The *bedlam* at Bedlam could never have been more wildly noisy
than dinnertime at Miss Willick's school.

Religious terms

H22 In general, capitalize a religious term only if there is
good authority for it or if it is necessary in order to
avoid ambiguity. The trend is toward less capitalization.

Religious books, prayers

H23 Capitalize the word *Bible* and its synonyms, and the titles of the sacred writings of all religions.[8] (Do not use italics or quotation marks.)

the Bhagavad-Gita	Mishna
the Bible	the New Jerusalem Bible
the Book of Life	Rig-Veda
the Holy Bible	the Scriptures
Holy Writ	the Talmud
the Koran	Tao-te Ching

H24 Do not capitalize words derived from those in the preceding rule.

biblical	scriptural
koranic	talmudic
mishnaic	vedic

H25 Capitalize all texts, versions, and revisions of the Bible and all canons (that is, lists of inspired books).[9] (Do not use italics or quotation marks.)

the King James Version	the Revised Standard
the New American Bible	Version
the New International	the Roman Catholic Canon
Version	the Septuagint
the New Jerusalem Bible	the Vulgate

H26 Capitalize all parts and books of the Bible.[9] (Do not use italics or quotation marks.)

the Acts of the Apostles	the New Testament
the Apocalypse	the Old Testament
the Book of Psalms	the Pentateuch
Deuteronomy	Proverbs

---

[8] Do not capitalize *the* or short conjunctions, articles, and short prepositions within such names or titles. See H126-29.

[9] Do not capitalize initial *the* or short conjunctions, articles, and short prepositions within such names or titles. See H126-29.

the Epistles   the Psalms

Genesis   the Psalter

the Letter to Philemon the Synoptic Gospels

H27 Capitalize the nouns *gospel* and *gospels* when they refer to one or more of the first four books of the New Testament, but not otherwise. (Do not use italics or quotation marks.)

Everyone should read the Gospels and know them.
This passage is from the Gospel according to St. John.
Preach the *gospel* to every creature.
"Oh," he said, "big business has its own *gospel.*"

H28 Do not capitalize the adjective *gospel.*

Millions of people have never heard the *gospel* message.
Business executives should act upon *gospel* principles.
I'm telling you the *gospel* truth.

H29 Capitalize the titles of Christ's and others' discourses that are known by names equivalent to the titles of literary works.[10] (Do not use italics or quotation marks.)

the Discourse at the Last Supper

the Eight Beatitudes

the Sermon on the Mount

the Magnificat

The Sermon on the Mount and the Discourse at the Last Supper were addressed to different audiences.

But—
Our Lord gave a *discourse* at the Last Supper.
There are *eight beatitudes.*

---

[10] Do not capitalize initial *the* or short conjunctions, articles, and short prepositions within such names or titles. See H126-29.

H30 Capitalize the titles of Christ's parables.[11] (Do not use italics or quotation marks.)

the Faithful Steward   the Ten Virgins
the Five Talents   the Unjust Steward
the Good Samaritan   the Unmerciful Servant

The Prodigal Son is one of the greatest of all short stories.

The *prodigal son* [the person, not the parable, here] asked for less than his father gave him.

H31 Capitalize the titles of prayers.[11] (Do not use italics or quotation marks.)

Ave Maria   Lord's Prayer
Benedictus   Magnificat
Creed   Memorare
Glory Be to the Father   Pater Noster
Hail Mary   Shahada
Litany of the Saints   Shema

We always recited the Memorare to ask for good weather on picnics and holidays.

Say the Glory Be to the Father at the end of each decade of the Rosary.

Let *glory be to the Father,* not to me, for this day's work. [Not the title of a prayer here.]

H32 Do not capitalize descriptive names of real or imaginary biblical characters.

The *good thief* was saved.
Repent as the *prodigal son* did.
The *faithful steward* was commended.
The *good samaritan* should be the model of all who wish to be good neighbors.

---

[11] Do not capitalize initial *the* or short conjunctions, articles, and short prepositions within such names or titles. See H126-29.

H33 Capitalize the titles *Liturgy of the Hours, Missal (Roman), Book of Common Prayer,* and the parts of these and similar books.[12]

Liturgy of the Hours	Book of Common Prayer
the Divine Office	Morning Prayer
Roman Missal	Eucharistic Prayer
the Proper	the Common

H34 Capitalize the names of all creeds, confessions of faith, catechisms.[12] (Do not use italics or quotation marks.)

the American Catechism	the Nicene Creed
the Apostles' Creed	the Thirty-nine Articles
the Augsburg Confession	the Westminster Confession

Names of God

H35 Capitalize the names of God.

Allah	Logos
the Almighty	Lord
Brahma	Messias [Messiah]
Christ	the Most High
the Divine Persons	the Omnipotent
Father	Paraclete
First Person (of the Trinity)	Savior
God	Second Person (of the Trinity)
God-Man	the Supreme Being
the Holy One	Third Person (of the Trinity)
Holy Spirit	Trinity
Jehovah	the Word
Jesus	Yahweh

---

[12] Do not capitalize initial *the* or short conjunctions, articles, and short prepositions within such names or titles. See H126-29.

H36 Capitalize the following names whenever they are used as proper names of God—wherever they are substitute names, that is.[13]

Advocate	the Lord of Lords
Comforter	Maker
the Creator	Master
the Good Shepherd	the Prince of Peace
the Infant Jesus	the Redeemer
the King of Heaven	Savior
the King of Kings	the Son
the Lamb of God	the Son of God
Lord	the Son of Man

Adore your *Maker.*
Simeon was glad because he had seen his *Redeemer* and *Savior.*

H37 Do not capitalize names such as those in H36 when they are used simply as descriptive predicates or appositives.

God is our *maker.*
[But:] Adore your Maker.

Christ is the *son* of Mary.
[But:] The Son of God is Jesus Christ.

All nations have longed for a *redeemer,* a *savior.*
[But:] Simeon was glad because he had seen his *Redeemer* and *Savior.*

Christ came into the world as an *infant.*
[But:] The Magi adored the *Infant.*

Our Lord proved himself the *master* of his enemies.
[But:] "Peace!" cried Martha, "The *Master* is coming."

Christ, the *good shepherd,* searched for the lost sheep.
[But:] Teach us, *Good Shepherd,* to be kind.

Jesus is the *lord* of the world.

---

[13] Do not capitalize initial *the* or short conjunctions, articles, and short prepositions within such names or titles. See H126-29.

[But:] You can heal me, *Lord,* if you will.

Christ, as *lord of lords* and *king of kings,* has all power.
[But:] Jesus, *King of Kings,* have mercy on me!

Jesus is the *bread of angels.*
[But:] O *Bread of Angels,* be our strength!

The Holy Spirit is our *comforter.*
[But:] Courage comes from the grace of the *Comforter.*

God is the one true *sanctifier* of souls.
[But:] Pray that the *Sanctifier* may give light to people's minds.

H38   Do not capitalize adjectives accompanying the names of God (unless the adjectives combine with the name to form a descriptive substitute name—an epithet, that is).[14]

all-wise Creator	loving Savior
almighty God	merciful Father
eternal Father	our Lord
Father almighty	our Savior

H39   Capitalize adjectives and adverbs in descriptive substitute names of God (in epithets for God, that is) whenever such names would lose their meaning if the adjective or adverb were left out.

the First Cause	the Most High
Immutable One	the Only Begotten

Such reasoning brings one back to the *First Cause.*
It is the *Only Begotten* who is altogether pleasing to his Father.

H40   Capitalize *divinity, providence,* and *deity* when they are used as names of God.

May the *Divinity* guide your steps!
Christ proved his *divinity* by his miracles.

Place your hope in *Providence.*

---

[14] See H39.

God's *providence* directs all things.

All people must worship the *Deity*.
The ancient Egyptians had their *deities*.

H41   Do not capitalize *name, holy name, fatherhood*, or *sonship*.

Judge with mercy, in the *name* of God!
Show reverence for the *holy name*.
The thought of God's *fatherhood* will comfort you.
Christ was conscious of his divine *sonship*.

H42   Capitalize *body* or *blood* only when it is a synonym for the Eucharist.

Every second day Eric received the *Body* of Christ.
Catholics genuflect to the most precious *Body* and *Blood*.

The *body* of Christ in the tomb could be adored.
Christ gave his *blood* for us.

H43   Capitalize *heart* only in the name *Sacred Heart* or when it is used as an abbreviation for the name. Do not capitalize the words for any other part of Christ's body.

The *Sacred Heart* is our refuge and our hope.
His *Heart* is our refuge and our hope.

Jesus was meek and humble of *heart*.
They pierced his *hands* and his *feet;* they counted all his *bones*.

H44   Do not capitalize *humanity, hypostatic union, mystical union, cross*.

We shall meditate on Christ's *humanity*.

What is meant by the *hypostatic union?*

Some saints have been granted the unusual grace of *mystical union* with God.

In the *cross* of Christ is our salvation.

H45 Do not capitalize pronouns and possessive adjectives referring to God unless such capitals are necessary to avoid ambiguity.[15]

Christ went *himself* to raise *his* friend Lazarus from the dead.

The Father and I are one, and *we* will keep *our* faithful safe from the world.

The Lord told Jeremiah to warn *His* people.

H46 Although other pronouns and possessive adjectives referring to God are capitalized by some writers, *it, one, who, whose, whom, that* are not capitalized unless the reference to God would otherwise be obscure.

Our hope is in Christ, *who* redeemed us.

[If there is no other indication that *who* refers to God:] I know *Who* has care of me.

H47 Do not capitalize *god* when it refers to a false deity, or *gods, goddess*, and *goddesses*.

The Romans built a temple to Mars, the *god* of war.
Juno was queen of all the *gods* and *goddesses*.

Names of the Blessed Virgin

H48 Capitalize the names of the Blessed Virgin; but do not capitalize *blessed* when it is preceded by another adjective and *and*, or by an adverb.

Blessed Virgin	our Lady
Blessed Virgin Mary	our Queen
Immaculate Conception	Queen
Lady	Virgin
Mother of Mercy	Virgin Mary

Let us pray to the *glorious and blessed* Virgin.
Let us pray to the *ever-blessed* Virgin.

---

[15] See H46.

H49 Do not capitalize *virgin* when it is not used as a proper name or part of a proper name.

Mary was a *virgin* and the mother of Jesus.

H50 Capitalize the following names of the Blessed Virgin (and all such names as are found in the Litany of Loretto) whenever they are used as proper names—whenever they are descriptive substitute names (that is, epithets).

Mother of Christ	Refuge of Sinners
Immaculate Heart	Help of Christians

H51 Do not capitalize the names in H50 when they are used as simple descriptive predicates or appositives.

Mary, *the mother of Christ,* was also asked to the wedding.
[But:] O *Mother of Christ,* be my mother!

Mary has always been the *refuge of sinners.*
[But:] Let us pray to the *Refuge of Sinners.*

H52 Do not capitalize adjectives accompanying the names of the Blessed Virgin.[16]

What an ugly statue of *our* Lady!

Mary, *immaculate* and *holy,* never knew sin.

St. Bernard wrote many sermons in praise of his *gracious* and *loving* Queen.

H53 Capitalize *mother* when it is a substitute for the proper name of the Blessed Virgin, not otherwise.

Then, *Mother,* pray for me.
The book was dedicated to the *Mother* of God.
Jesus had a human *mother* but not a human father.
Christ's *Mother* is our *mother* also.

---

[16] This rule does not apply to blessed, for which see H48.
    There are a few "frozen" titles like *Our Lady of Good Counsel, Our Lady of Lourdes, Our Lady of Mercy,* in which the *our* is considered part of the title and is capitalized. Make use of this exception.

Holy Family, events of the Redemption

H54 Capitalize *Holy Family.*

Quickly the *Holy Family* fled into Egypt.

H55 Do not capitalize the names of events and states of being in the life of our Lord and the Blessed Virgin except for the following, which long usage has decided should be capitalized.

the Advent [of Christ]	the Last Supper
the Ascension	the Nativity
the Assumption	the Passion
the Crucifixion	Pentecost
the Immaculate Conception	the Resurrection
the Incarnation	the Sermon on the Mount
the Last Judgment	the Visitation

The *flight* into Egypt took place during that part of our Lord's life of which we know almost nothing.

The *public life* of Christ lasted a scant three years.

Our *redemption* was accomplished with the death of the Redeemer.

The *descent* of the Holy Spirit was followed by the first general manifestation of the new Church to the world.

At the *circumcision* Jesus received his name.

Christ endured a *passion* all the more horrible because he was utterly innocent.

Surely, after the *Passion* Christ knows our sufferings very well.

Mary's *Immaculate Conception* sheds glory on us too when we are in the state of grace.

Note 1. Many terms similar to the ones listed in the columns above are not capitalized. When in doubt, consult the most recent edition of a good dictionary.

Note 2. Of course, when names not ordinarily capitalized fall under some other rule, they are capitalized. For example, *scourging at the pillar* is capitalized when it is used as the name of a mystery of the rosary; *circumcision* is capitalized when it is used as the name of a feast.

H56 When two or more of the names indicated in H55 are used together in the same sentence and one is not capitalized, do not capitalize the others.

It is surprising how many people confuse the *virgin birth* with the *immaculate conception.*

We read of the *passion, death,* and *resurrection* of Christ.

H57 Capitalize *redemption* when it is preceded by *the* and refers to the entire series of events constituting our redemption by Christ.

The second volume treats of *the Redemption.*
We should be grateful to God for our *redemption.*

Angels, Holy Souls, devils

H58 Capitalize *angel, archangel,* and *guardian angel* only when they are used as titles in direct address in place of proper names, or as titles followed by proper names. Do not capitalize the classes of angels, like *seraphim* or *principalities.*

O *Archangel* Michael, defend us from evil!
Help and protect me, *Guardian Angel.*

Pray to your *guardian angel* every day.
I always think of the *seraphim* as bigger than the *cherubim.*

H59 Do not capitalize *holy souls, poor souls,* or *souls in purgatory.*

November is the month of the *holy souls.*
O *holy souls,* pray for us!
Mass will be said tomorrow morning for the *souls in purgatory.*

H60   Capitalize all synonyms for *Satan* except *devil.*[17]

the Archfiend	His Satanic Majesty
Beelzebub	Lucifer
the Evil One	the Prince of Darkness

The *devil* goes about like a roaring lion.

Heaven, hell, purgatory

H61   Capitalize *Gehenna, Hades, Elysian Fields, Garden of Eden, Pearly Gates,* and *Tartarus,*[17] but not *Abraham's bosom, beatific vision, heaven, hell, purgatory, nether regions,* and *nirvana.*

Christ sometimes spoke of *hell* as *Gehenna.*

If we cannot be perfectly happy in *heaven* without football, then we shall have football in *heaven.*

H62   Capitalize *paradise* only when it is used as a synonym for *Garden of Eden.*

God talked familiarly with Adam in *Paradise.*
Everyone's hope is to reach *paradise* some day.

H63   Do not capitalize *kingdom of God* or *kingdom of heaven.*

There will be neither tears nor pain nor death in the *kingdom of heaven.*

Churches, church members, church

H64   Capitalize the names of all religions and their adherents.[18]

Anglican Church	Islam
Anglicans	Muslim
Baptists	Lutheran Church
Buddhism	Lutherans

---

[17] Do not capitalize initial *the* or short conjunctions, articles, and short prepositions within such names or titles. See H126-29.

[18] Do not capitalize initial *the* or short conjunctions, articles, and short prepositions within such names or titles. See H126-29.

Buddhists	Protestantism
Catholicism	Protestants
Catholics	Roman Catholic Church

H65 Capitalize *church* as part of the formal name of a building and when it appears as part of the title of a universal, national, regional, or denominational religious organization or body.[19]

> On the corner is the First Baptist *Church.*
> She is a member of the Roman Catholic *Church.*

H66 Capitalize synonyms for the Church or its collective membership such as *Holy Mother (the) Church, Mystical Body of Christ,* and *People of God.*[20] Do not capitalize a merely descriptive expression such as *our holy mother, the Church.*

> Such are the teachings of *Holy Mother Church.*

> All her children are the constant concern of *our holy mother, the Church.*

> We are members of the *Mystical Body of Christ.*

> The prayers of the *People of God* are efficacious.

H67 Do not capitalize *church* standing alone when it indicates a building, when it is used as an adjective, or when it refers to more than one religious denomination. And do not capitalize *church* when it is used as part of the description, rather than as part of the proper name, of a building.

> There seems to be a *church* on every corner.
> It is *church* law that parishioners must help support their pastor.
> The question of *church* and state is much argued.

---

[19] When *church* designates a particular religious organization or body and stands alone, it is not capitalized.

[20] Usage is divided on capitalizing *mystical body* and *people of God.* Since, however, these expressions are sometimes construed in a popular or nontechnical sense, capitalization seems appropriate to distinguish their use as theological concepts.

That is the Baptist *church*.	Here *church* is part of a description rather than part of a proper name.
On the corner is the First Baptist *Church*.	Here *church* is part of a proper, particular, name.

Mass, the sacraments

H68 Capitalize *Liturgy of the Word, Liturgy of the Eucharist,* and *Mass* (even when used as an adjective) along with its parts.[21]

Canon	Postcommunion
Consecration	Proper

He is one of the readers for the *Liturgy of the Word.*
The congregation stands during the reading of the *Gospel.*
The storm struck while the priest was at the *Offertory.*
No one put away the *Mass* vestments.

[Many in the secular press do not capitalize *Mass.*]

H69 Except for H68, do not capitalize *liturgy.*

The *liturgy* has undergone many changes in recent years.

H70 Do not capitalize adjectives modifying *Mass.*

requiem Mass	solemn high Mass

H71 Do not capitalize *sacrament* or the names of the sacraments (except the Eucharist, for which see H72).

Ted has received the *sacrament of baptism,* but he has never received *confirmation.*

I have received the *anointing of the sick* three times.

Who instituted *penance*; that is, the *sacrament of reconciliation?*

My uncle returned to the *sacraments.*

---

[21] Do not capitalize inital *the* or short conjunctions, articles, and short prepositions within such names or titles. See H126-29.

H72   Capitalize the names of the Holy Eucharist and the Eucharistic Sacrifice.[22]

Blessed Eucharist	Liturgy of the Eucharist
Blessed Sacrament	Real Presence
Communion	sacrament of the Eucharist
Eucharist	sacrifice of the Mass
Holy Communion	Viaticum

H73   Do not capitalize adjectives and adverbs modifying the terms listed in H72.

Every night there will be devotions in honor of the *most adorable* Sacrament of the Altar.

H74   Do not capitalize *host, sacred host, sacred species, transubstantiation.*

The priest elevated the *sacred host.*
Vandals scattered the *sacred species* all over the sanctuary.

Services, Devotions, Objects, Symbols

H75   Capitalize the following church services and devotions (but not *service* and *devotion*).[22]

Benediction [of the Blessed Sacrament]
First Friday devotions
Holy Hour
Novena of Grace [of the Sorrowful Mother,
    of the Sacred Heart, *and so on*]
Stations of the Cross
Way of the Cross

There will be rosary and *Benediction* this evening.
The priest raised his hand in benediction (blessing).

---

[22] Do not capitalize inital *the* or short conjunctions, articles, and short prepositions within such names or titles. See H126-29.

H76 Do not capitalize the following words except when they appear as part of the names in H75 or come under some other rule.

benediction	retreat
blessing	rosary
day of recollection	seder
exposition	thanksgiving
grace	triduum
litany	veneration
morning prayer	worship service
novena	

The priest raised his hand in *benediction* [blessing].

There will be a *sermon* and *prayers,* followed by *exposition* and *veneration* of the relic.

This *novena* is the Novena of Grace.

There will be *rosary* and Benediction at 8:15 P.M.

After the *litany* the clergy and the laity marched in procession around the church.

H77 Capitalize the titles of the mysteries of the rosary: *the Carrying of the Cross, the Crowning of the Blessed Virgin Mary, the Crowning with Thorns, the Crucifixion, the Descent of the Holy Spirit,* and so on.[23]

The fourth glorious mystery is the *Assumption of the Blessed Virgin Mary into Heaven.*

H78 Do not capitalize objects or symbols of religious significance.

chalice	mezuzah
cross	rosary
holy water	sanctuary

---

[23] Do not capitalize inital *the* or short conjunctions, articles, and short prepositions within such names or titles. See H126-29.

Classes and orders of people in the Church

H79 Do not capitalize the names of classes of people such as *patriarchs, prophets, doctors* and *fathers of the Church, apostles,* and *disciples.*

> The greatest of the *prophets* was John the Baptist.
> St. Robert Bellarmine is a *doctor of the Church.*
> Give me the name of the earliest church *father.*
> The *apostles* were simple, not stupid, men.
> Christ's grace produced Peter, the *apostle.*
> There were all sorts of men among the *disciples.*
> Name three famous *patriarchs* of Constantinople.

H80 Capitalize the names of religious orders and the names by which their members are known.[24]

Brothers of Mary	Benedictines
Christian Brothers	Cistercians
Daughters of Divine Charity	Dominicans
Institute of Charity	Franciscans
Order of Preachers	Jesuits
Sisters of Charity	Marianists
Sisters of Notre Dame	Oblates
Sisters of St. Joseph	Trappists

H81 Do not capitalize *congregation, order,* and so on, unless they are used as part of an official title.

> The Jesuit *order* [the Society of Jesus] considers the foreign missions one of its primary works.

> The *Order of Preachers* was founded by St. Dominic.

> This *congregation* numbers more than two thousand religious.

> The *Congregation of the Missions,* whose members are known as Vincentians, has three parishes in our town.

---

[24] Do not capitalize initial *the* or short conjunctions, articles, and short prepositions within such names or titles. See H126-29.

Three *religious* were caught in the rain, and you should have seen what happened to those white things they wear.

She joined the *Religious of the Missions* and was sent to New York, and there she spent the rest of her life.

H82 Do not capitalize such words as *priest, monk, nun,* and so on, when they are used as common nouns; that is, not as a title or part of a title.

abbot	deacon	patriarch
archbishop	dean	pope
archimandrite	evangelist	priest
ayatollah	friar	prior
bishop	guru	rabbi
bonze	imam	rector
canon	minister	religious
cardinal	monk	sadhu
catechumen	mother superior	scholastic
chaplain	novice	theologian
cleric	nun	vicar
curate	pastor	

What is the difference between an *archbishop* and a *bishop?*
A *deacon,* unlike a *priest,* may not say Mass.
The *ministers* for the liturgy will vest in the east sacristy.

Apostolic See, Papacy

H83 Capitalize *Apostolic See, Holy See,* and *Chair of Peter,* meaning the supreme governing authority of the Catholic Church.

All Catholics must obey the *Apostolic See.*

The last two popes in the *Chair of Peter* understood Africa fairly well.

H84 Do not capitalize *papacy.*

The system of government in the Roman Catholic Church is known as the *papacy.*

Personal titles

H85 Capitalize all religious, civil, military, and social titles that are followed by a proper name.

Pope John Paul II
His Holiness, Pope
  John XXIII
Archibishop Runcie
Patriarch Demetrius
His Eminence, Cardinal
  Bernardin of Chicago
Cardinal O'Connor
Bishop Manning
Admiral Nimitz
Alderman Porter Smith
Ambassador John J. Archer
Captain Smollet
Chairman Kelly
Chief Justice Warren Burger
Commissioner Walker
Dame Edith Sitwell
Director George Lucas
Mr. Rollins
Mrs. James B. Sellen
Reverend Alan Mays

Monsignor Fleckler
Canon Appleby
Mother Marie
Sister Mary Helen
Pastor Hartman
Prince Philip
Rabbi Lebowitz
Father Thomas Reid
Brother Jonathan
General Heath
Governor Herman Long
Judge J. Robert Regan
Lieutenant Seldon
  Wadsworth
Mayor James G. Fogarty
President Clinton
Professor Walter Briggs
Ms. Helen McIntyre
Master John Smithers
Senator Glenn
Sir George Bottomley

At this point *Bishop* Manning rose in protest.

The *Abbot* Marmion would hardly agree with *Miss* Kelly.

I believe the last speaker was *Ambassador* John J. Archer.

General Chennault urged that Chiang Kai-shek's forces be allowed to attack the Chinese on the mainland.

The lady in question is a *Mrs.* James B. Sellen.

Last evening *Rabbi* Rosenblum and *Pastor* Hartman moderated an interesting discussion on the Dead Sea Scrolls.

H86 Do not capitalize words that serve primarily as job descriptions rather than as formal titles[25] even when these are followed by a proper name.

His brief encounter with *halfback* Steiner left him crippled for life.

As usual, there was some disagreement between *architect* Riley and *treasurer* J. Charles Lambert.

H87 Do not capitalize formal titles[25] (or occupational descriptions) before appositives.

His brief encounter with the *halfback,* Steiner, left him crippled for life.

As usual, there was some disagreement between the *architect,* Riley, and the *treasurer,* J. Charles Lambert.

Do you prefer the *poet* Wordsworth or the *poet* Longfellow?

The French president, Mitterand, spoke to reporters.

H88 Except for those mentioned in H89, capitalize titles that are used in direct address. (Such titles are a substitute for a proper name and serve to identify the person who is being addressed.)

Please, *Mr. Secretary,* will you read the minutes of the last meeting?
Welcome, *Senator,* to our banquet.
Your position, *Judge,* is perfectly clear.
Will *Your Excellency* please sign this?
Be so kind, *Your Eminence,* as to sit over here.

H89 Do not capitalize *sir, madam,* and broad general terms (like *gentlemen, ladies,* and *children*) that can be applied to wide classes of persons, except when they are followed by a proper name or are used as part of the salutation of a letter.

---

[25] A formal title indicates a significant range of authority, professional activity, or academic prominence and is so linked to the individual that it is regarded as part of the person's name (*President* Bush, *Archbishop* Romero). Other so-called titles are really job descriptions (*astronaut* John Glenn, *auctioneer* Fred Smith).

Yes, *sir*, you'll find him in.
No, *madam*; the boat has sailed.
Listen carefully, *gentlemen*, to this hypocrite.
But, *lady*, that's the only hat I own!
See here, my dear *child*, that's my nose!

Dear Sirs:	Gentlemen:
Dear Madam:	Dear Editors:

H90 Do not capitalize *mister, master,* and *miss* when they are not followed by a proper name; nor terms of address used opprobriously, like *nitwit, slowpoke,* or *stupid.*

You don't know the half of it, *mister.*

Indeed, *master,* the third camel does have an irresponsible expression on its face.

You'll find flat silver on the third floor, *miss.*

Hurry up, *slowpoke!*

H91 In general, do not capitalize a title not followed by a proper name unless it is in direct address or is affected by another of the rules of capitals.[26]

The *pope* spoke on the radio today.
The *cardinal* asked the *pope* what to do.
John XXIII was elected *pope* on October 28, 1958.
Henry IV, *king* of England, had not yet been heard from.
I'm sorry, but the *governor* will not see you.
Should the *president* carry his complaint to Congress?
Was Fred Vinson ever *chief justice* of the United States?
Cardinal O'Connor, *archbishop* of New York, hurried to Rome.

---

[26] Titles of the highest political or religious rank may be capitalized if they refer to a specific individual even though they are not followed by that person's name; for example, the *President* (of one's own country), the *Pope.*

H92 Always capitalize *father* (a priest) and *brother* and *sister* (religious),[27] whether or not they are used in direct address or before a proper name.[28]

> Father David Reid   Brother Jonathan   Sister Mary Helen

> I have two *Sisters* and a *Brother* in my class.
> Bucky has an uncle who is an Oblate *Father*.

H93 Capitalize such titles as *His Holiness, His Eminence, His Excellency,* and *His Honor* even when they are used without the person's name.

> You have just heard a broadcast by *His Holiness*.
> I wasn't able to see *His Eminence*.
> I wasn't able to see *His Eminence,* the cardinal.
> Gentlemen, *His Honor* is detained.
> Gentlemen, *His Honor,* the mayor, is detained.
> Have you met *His Excellency,* the British ambassador?

H94 Capitalize all epithets and nicknames.[29]

Apostle of the Gentiles	Lone Eagle
Billy the Kid	Maid of Orleans
Charles the Bold	Panhandle
the Emancipator	Richard the Lion-Hearted
Father of His Country	St. Leo the Great
the Holy Father	Sunshine State
Iron Chancellor	the Swedish Nightingale
Land of the Rising Sun	Twin Cities
Ivan the Terrible	Wild West
Leo XIII, the Pope	William the Silent
of Labor	the Wizard of Menlo
	Park

---

[27] Capitalizing these religous titles frequently helps to obviate confusion with the same terms when they indicate blood relationship.

[28] For abbreviations of such titles, see F7-8.

[29] Do not capitalize inital *the* or short conjunctions, articles, and short prepositions within such names or titles. See H126-29.

H95 Capitalize *honorable* and *reverend* when they are used as titles; and always use them with a given name or initials as well as a surname. They should not be used with a surname alone.

> the Honorable J. L. Byrne
> the Reverend Aloysius Benton
> Rev. James McIntyre[30]

H96 If an unhyphenated compound title is to be capitalized, capitalize all the words in it (except, of course, conjunctions, articles, and prepositions).[31]

> Secretary of State Baker
> Field Marshall Dahlings
> Lieutenant Commander Hayes
> Foreign Minister Wilson
> Rear Admiral Budde

H97 Capitalize only the first word of a hyphenated compound title before a proper name, but do not capitalize *ex* and *pro*.

> President-elect Clinton
> ex-President Carter
> pro-American Franz Lederhosen

H98 Capitalize *Jr., Sr.*, and all other abbreviations of titles following a name.

> Samuel Thompson, Sr.   Fletcher Stanton, Ph.D.[32]
> Samuel Thompson, Jr.   Lowell Winship, O.P.[32]
> Albert Livingston, Esq.   Mary Lauer, D.D.S. [32]

---

[30] *Honorable* and *reverend* may be abbreviated in informal writing. For such abbreviations within the heading and address of a letter, see F9.

[31] See H127.

[32] In informal writing and in alphabetical lists, periods are frequently omitted from abbreviations designating academic degrees or religious orders. See F11, F15.

H99 Capitalize *father, mother, brother, sister, uncle, aunt, cousin,* and other kinship names when they are used in direct address or as a substitute for a person's name or as part of a person's name.

In direct address or as a substitute for a person's name—
You can't make *Mother* [that is, Mary or Mrs. Wilkes] rest.
That's *Dad's* [that is, James's or Mr. Wilkes's] umbrella.
See here, *Aunt* [that is, Agatha or Miss Wilkes], I love the girl.
Stay out of *Sister's* [that is, Betty's] room.
Is that *Junior* [that is, Harold or Harold Martin, Jr.] sitting there in the car?

As part of a person's name—
His family calls him *Brother* George.
Here come *Aunt* Mary and *Uncle* Julian.
Is it true that *Cousin* John married in Kalupa?
This is *Mother* O'Meara, my wife's mother.

H100 Do not capitalize kinship names when they are used as common nouns; that is, not in direct address or as a substitute for a person's name or as part of a person's name.

Tell Walter's *father* to come to the phone.
Your *mother* certainly looks young.
A *sister* should not give away a *brother's* secrets.
The *uncle* is a director of some railroad or other.

H101 Sometimes you will have a kinship name that has a possessive in front of it and a person's name after it. In such cases capitalize the kinship name if you want to use it as a title, as part of the person's name; do not capitalize it if it simply means "uncle [or cousin, and so on] whose name is such-and-such." (In most instances, a kinship name preceded by a modifier is not capitalized.)

You've met my *Grandfather* Monty, Gene; well, this is my *Grandfather* Ryan.

I've never gotten a kind word from my *grandfather* Monty [that is, from my grandfather whose name is Monty].

Our own dear *Cousin* Elbert has lentigo.
Our own dear *cousin* Elbert has lentigo [that is, cousin whose name is Elbert].

This will introduce my *Uncle* Henry, who wants to sell you a casket.
This will introduce my *uncle* Henry, who wants to sell you a casket [that is, uncle whose name is Henry].

My *sister* Nancy is a writer [that is, sister whose name is Nancy].
My *brother* Joe paints [that is, brother whose name is Joe].

Your *grandmother*, Sarah Green, and I are good friends [that is, grandmother, whose name is Sarah Green].

My *aunt*, Mrs. Willoughby Patterne, has trouble with poltergeists [that is, aunt, whose name is Mrs. Willoughby Patterne].

Your *uncle*, Commodore Squash, is seasick [that is, uncle, whose name is Commodore Squash].

Places, divisions, directions, buildings

H102 Capitalize the names of political and administrative divisions.[33]

Alaska	the Northwest Territories
the Archdiocese of Boston	the Philippines
Baton Rouge	the Republic [United States]
the British Empire	Sioux City
City of Chicago	the State of New Mexico
Diocese of Lafayette	Tenth Congressional District
the Dominion of Canada	the Twelth Precinct
Fourth Ward	the United Kingdom
the Helenburg Deanery	United States of America
Louisiana	Vatican City
the Netherlands	Warren Township

[33] Do not capitalize initial *the* or short conjunctions, articles, and short prepositions within such names or titles. See H126-29.

I live in *Sioux* City.
The *Clayton County* sheriff took office yesterday.

H103 Capitalize the names of sections of states, cities, towns, and so on.[34]

Beacon Hill	Jackson Square
the Delta	the Left Bank
Fourth Ward	the Loop
the Gold Coast	the Seventh Precinct

We had a typical *Vieux Carré* meal.
Chicago also has a *Gold Coast.*

H104 Capitalize the names of streets, avenues, boulevards, and so on.

Commercial Alley	Portland Place
Gracie Square	Regent Court
Highway 61	Sheridan Road
Lindell Boulevard	Sherman Parkway
Minnesota Avenue	Twelfth Street
Natchez Trace	U.S. Route 61

Are trucks allowed on the *Lincoln Highway?*
Harry is a *Park Row* cowboy.

H105 Capitalize geographical names.

Adirondack Mountains	Gulf of Mexico
Aleutians	Gulf Stream
Alton Lake	Isle of Man
Arctic Zone	Japanese Currents
Atlantic Coast	Lake Erie
Bad Lands	Marquette State Park
Cumberland Gap	Mississippi River
Death Valley	Mount Hood
English Channel	Pacific Ocean

---

[34] Do not capitalize initial *the* or short conjunctions, articles, and short prepositions within such names or titles. See H126-29.

the Equator	Pikes Peak
Fly Creek	Rocky Mountain
Gonzaro Pass	National Park
Grand Canyon	Torrid Zone

The *Japanese Currents* warm California, don't they?
Yes, Cap really was a *Mississippi River* pilot.

H106 Do not capitalize *kingdom, empire, state, diocese, parish,*[35] *city, county, town, precinct, street, avenue, square, coast, stream, zone, island, mountain, lake, river, park, creek,* and like words unless they are used as part of a proper or official name.

Britain has liquidated her *empire.*
Our *ward* has suddenly gone Republican.
Tyrrell Street is really a broad *avenue.*
These *islands* cannot be the Aleutians.
This jagged, ugly *peak* is unlike anything in the Adirondacks.
Which is the largest of the three *lakes,* Lake Michigan?

The *State* of Illinois is prosecuting the murderers.
The *State* is prosecuting the murderers.
This is the Badger *State.*
The *state* of Idaho grows apples and other fruits.
Our *state* is not large, but it is progressive.
Totalitarianism believes in an all-powerful *state.*

Make your check payable to the *City* of St. Louis.
Make your check payable to the *City.*
Not many *cities* have grown as rapidly as the *city* of Houston.

Cleveland is in Cuyahoga *County.*
The *county* of Westchester is in New York.

We belong to Sacred Heart *Parish.*[35]
The *parish* has a very active theater group.

---

[35] Usage is divided in capitalizing *parish.*

H107 Capitalize the nouns *north, south, east, west,* and their noun combinations and derivatives only when they refer to a region of the nation or of the world, but not when they refer to direction.[36]

The civilization of the *East* is older than that of the *West.*

The *South* is the nation's winter playground.

The temperament of the typical *Northerner* is different from that of the typical *Southerner.*

Out of the *Middle West* comes food for the world.

We traveled *southwest* from the ranch.

To the *north* lay the mountains; to the *west,* the sea.

Most of us up-state North Dakotans do not realize that more than ninety per cent of the wheat used to make spaghetti is raised to the *south* of us, in the region below Grand Forks.

H108 Capitalize the adjectives and adverbs *north, south, east, west,* and their combinations and derivatives only when they are part of an established name for a definite region or refer to distinctive social, cultural, or political aspects of a region. Do not capitalize them when they refer to direction or to the points of the compass.[37]

But *Eastern* civilization is older than *Western.*
She spent a year in *Southeast* Asia.
She spent a year in *southeastern* Asia.
He has a fondness for *Southern* cooking.
Springfield lies a few miles to the *east.*
I like the *northwest* section of the country.
The wind is *southerly.*
Drive *east* until you reach Cumberland Gap.

---

[36] See H108.
[37] See H107.

H109 Capitalize the names of bridges, buildings, churches, chapels, clubs, libraries, and monuments.[38]

Hell Gate Bridge	St. Francis Xavier Church
Grand Central Station	Rogers Memorial Chapel
Humboldt Building	Racquet Club
Municipal Auditorium	Newberry Library
Museum of Modern Art	Lincoln Memorial
Yacht Club	Beth-El Temple

H110 Do not capitalize words like *bridge, building, church, library, monument,* unless they are part of a proper name.[39]

There should be a *bridge* near Southport.
Alice fell asleep in the *chapel.*

Countries, governments, and international organizations

H111 Capitalize the names of countries, governments, and international organizations.

United States
Organization of Petroleum Exporting Countries
Zimbabwe
British Commonwealth
European Economic Community
Republic of South Africa
North Atlantic Treaty Organization
Organization of American States
United Nations

H112 Do not capitalize *commonwealth, confederation,* and so on, unless they are used as part of a proper name or as a synonym for a proper name.

Queen Elizabeth made an official tour of the *Commonwealth.*
Britain's *commonwealth* is loosely held together.

---

[38] Do not capitalize initial *the* or short conjunctions, articles, and short prepositions within such names or titles. See 126-29.

[39] For capitalizing these terms as shortened titles, see H148.

H113 Capitalize *Republic, Nation, and Union,* when they are a synonym for *United States.* Otherwise do not capitalize them.

Since 1787 the *Republic,* like other nations, has had its scoundrels in high office.

In this great *republic* of ours each of us has a share.

H114 Do not capitalize *federal government* or *government.*

The *federal government* exercises control over interstate commerce.

There is adequate housing for *government* workers.

The *government* of the United States cannot be sued except under certain restrictions.

The United States *government* has its own printing office.

The *government* of the state has decided that rural areas wil have to suffer.

H115 Capitalize the names of political parties and their adherents (but not the word party).[40]

Democratic party	Democrats
Labor party	Laborites
Republican party	Republicans

Many a *Republican* holds the principles of the *Democratic party.* Markoe is a *Labor party* hack.

H116 Capitalize such words as *democrat* and *republican* when they refer to the Democratic and Republican parties, but not when they are used in their general meaning.[41]

There's really not much difference between *Democratic* and *Republican* aims and promises in this election.

The king banished Lamberti because of his *republican* principles.

Fuller could be called an eighteenth-century *democrat.*

[40] See H116.
[41] See H115.

H117 Capitalize the names of all national, state, county, municipal, and town assemblies, departments, bureaus, commissions, offices, courts, and so on.[42]

Allen County Traffic Bureau	Hewesport Board of Aldermen
Bureau of Standards	House [of Representatives]
Cabinet	House of Commons
Circuit Cout of Appeals	House of Lords
Civil Service Commission	Office of Education
Commons	Ohio House of Representatives
Congress	
Department of Public Works	Parliament
Farm Labor Board	Senate
Federal Bureau of Investigation	Senate Finance Committee
	State Department of Health
Foreign Office	Supreme Court

John Wesley Snyder was secretary of the *Treasury* in 1949.
Hiss had worked in the *Department of State* at the time.
You want to talk to the chairman of the *Board of Health*, a Dr. Gleason.

Organizations, institutions, schools

H118 Capitalize the names of organizations, associations, foundations, societies, companies, railroads and banks.[42]

American Legion	Rockefeller Foundation
Bay Shore Traction	Society for the Prevention of Cruelty to Animals
Camera Club	
Chicago Community Trust	Sock and Buskin
Eastman Kodak Company	Station WEW
First National Bank	Steuben Glass
Knights of Columbus	Union Pacific Railroad

[42] Do not capitalize initial *the* or short conjunctions, articles, and short prepositions within such names or titles. See H126-29.

National Association for the Advancement of Colored People	United Way Volunteers of America Woods School Fathers' Club

Herrick is going to be nominated for the *National Honor Society*.
I remember hearing that Toolen is a *General Mills* vice-president.

H119 Capitalize the names of educational institutions and of their schools and departments.[43]

Loyola University	Temple Hall
Pennsylvania State Teachers College	Ladue Grammar School
	Public School No. 8
Eden Seminary	Century Business School
Harvard Medical School	Miss Drane's Secretarial
Howe Military School	School
St. Benedict Academy	Department of Philosophy
Woodward High School	of Fordham University

Gonzaga High School refuses to recognize any of my credits in home economics.

The *Wilson High* glee club—it has a resounding name that I've forgotten—is not very good.

My aunt, Helen Merkle, is head of the *Latin Department* at *Marlin*.

H120 Do not capitalize *freshman, sophomore, junior,* or *senior.*

I'm a *freshman* at Parkham.
The *sophomore* class is having a meeting today.
The *juniors* are giving a dance for the *seniors.*
On you, *seniors*, depends the spirit of the student body.

H121 Do not capitalize words like *club, assembly, bureau, commission, association, foundation, corporation, company, railroad, bank, university, college, department,* or *school,* unless they are part of a proper name.[44]

---

[43] Do not capitalize initial *the* or short conjunctions, articles, and short prepositions within such names or titles. See H126-29.

Put your money in the *bank*—any *bank,* even Stillson's Bank of Commerce.

The *university* is going to finish the stadium next spring.

The Wilson High glee *club*—it has a resounding name that I've forgotten—is not very good.

A *commission* was set up to investigate the shock effects of fresh air on city dwellers who go to the country too suddenly.

What's the name of that *college* in Moorhead?

Military groups

H122 Do not capitalize the nouns *army* or *navy* unless they refer to the United States Army or Navy.[45]

The *Army* has worn a variety of uniforms since Washington's day [meaning the United States Army].

The *Navy* is sometimes almost absurdly jealous of its traditions [meaning the United States Navy].

A career in the *army* was all that Russia could offer him then.

The Brazilian *army* was represented in the council by General Longino Finkler.

H123 Do not capitalize the adjectives *army* and *navy* when used without *United* States, and ordinarily do not capitalize *naval.*

We spent the first three weeks in an *army* barracks in Hawaii, doing nothing but twiddling our thumbs and waiting.

Some years ago *navy* officers were rather vehement in protesting unification of the armed forces.

United Staes *naval* power has increased sharply since 1949.

---

[44] For capitalizing these terms as shortened titles, see H148.
[45] See H123-24.

He was a member of the Naval Reserve for ten years.

An unidentified *United States Army* spokesperson was credited with starting the rumor.

United States Navy personnel reported to the consulate.

H124 Capitalize the names of military divisions, regiments, companies and so on.

This is a memorial to the dead of the *Rainbow Division.*

There is no word from *Company F.*

Jarkie had his share of experiences in the *Medical Corps.*

The *Marine Corps* does not have enough marines to chance an engagement of that scope.

Under orders, the *Eighth Army* held off for three days.[46]

The Royal Scots Fusiliers held the high ground near Aberdeen.

A task force from the Seventh Fleet entered the Persian Gulf.

The Afrika Korps was under the command of the Desert Fox, Field Marshal Erwin Rommel.

H125 Do not capitalize words like *division, regiment, company* when they are not part of a proper name.

Three *divisions* were strung along the Rhine.

The *cavalry,* as a matter of fact, hasn't ridden horses in years.

Just how much air power could accomplish without *infantry* is something we do not intend to find out just now.

The Thirty-third Infantry *Division* outflanked the enemy and quickly cut off the only escape route.

---

[46] *Army* is capitalized because it is part of the proper name of a military unit.

Titles of works and events

Publications, works of art

H126 Capitalize the first word in the titles of books, magazines, newspapers, essays, articles, poems, plays, motion pictures, paintings, and so on. Capitalize all words within the titles except conjunctions, articles, and prepositions (C-A-P).[47]

> *The Life of Dr. Samuel Johnson* [book]
> "On the Extinction of the Venetian Republic, 1802" [poem]
> *Washington Crossing the Delaware* [painting]

H127 Do not capitalize conjunctions, articles, or prepositions (C-A-P) within titles, unless a conjunction or preposition is five or more letters long.

> The article was entitled "Ups *and* Downs of *an* Elevator Operator."

> Sidney H. Coleman was then the executive vice president of the Society *for the* Prevention *of* Cruelty *to* Animals.

> I have returned *Costume Throughout the Ages* to the library.

H128 Capitalize a conjunction, article, or preposition when it occurs after a colon within the title.

> *Receding Frontiers: An Interpretation* is the title of his dissertation.

> Please send me a microfilm copy of Rudge's "Polynesian Days: In a Yawl Through the Islands."

---

[47] For the capitalization of the initial *the, a,* or *an* with such titles, see H128 and H159. For the capitalization of a conjunction, article, or preposition within a title, see H127-28. For the capitalization of a final conjunction, article, or preposition, see H129.

See also H131-32.

For italics with such titles, see D144-51. For quotation marks with such titles, see D131-135.

H129　Capitalize a conjunction, article, or preposition when it occurs as the last word in a title.

> *Either Get Out—Or*
> "Various Meanings of *The*"
> *Truths to Live By*

H130　In text, do not capitalize initial *the* in the titles of newspapers and magazines.

> This is the December 16 issue of the *Saturday Evening Post.*
> The story was carried by the *Times-Picayune.*

H131　If a hyphen occurs in the title of a book, poem, and so on, capitalize the word following the hyphen only if that word is ordinarily a noun or proper adjective.

> *Nineteenth-Century Science* [noun]
> "Some Thrills of Deep-Sea Fishing" [noun]
> "This Year's All-American Team" [proper adjective]

H132　If a hyphen occurs in the title of a book, poem, and so on, do not capitalize the word following the hyphen if it is a common adjective or if the hyphen merely joins a prefix like *ultra, co,* or *self* to the following word.

"Thirty-second Street's New Look"	*Second* is a common adjective.
The Case of the Dark-green Shade	*Green* is a common adjective.
Lives of Little-known Saints	*Known* is a common adjective or participle.
"What is Co-management?"	*Co* is a mere prefix.
The Ultra-ambitious Oyster	*Ultra* is a mere prefix here.
How to Be Self-reliant	*Self* is a mere prefix here.

H133　Capitalize the title of a book series. (Do not use italics or quotation marks.)

> She bought a copy of G. K. Chesterton's *Robert Browning* in the English Men of Letters series.

H134 Capitalize the titles of directories, manuals, and similar works. (Do not use italics or quotation marks.)

Blue Book	Corporation Manual
City Directory	Social Register

Events and eras

H135 Capitalize the names of historical events and eras.

American Revolution	World War II
French Revolution	Boxer Rebellion
Great Depression	Bronze Age
Industrial Revolution	Dark Ages
the Flood	Middle Ages
Reconstruction (U.S.A.)	Elizabethan Age
Reformation	Christian Era
Renaissance	Norman Conquest
Reign of Terror	Atomic Age

but:

gold rush	Dreyfus affair
civil rights movement	cold war

H136 Ordinarily do not capitalize *day, era, period, epoch,* and *century* in the names of H135 unless they begin the title or are capitalized in a dictionary. (See also H146.)

Colonial days	Revolutionary period
Pliocene epoch	Victorian era

H137 Capitalize the names of expositions, fairs, festivals, and so on,[48] but not the names of events that have only a very local and minor interest.

Drake Relays	amateur night
Great Lakes Exposition	Mothers' Club card party
Humboldt County Fair	our annual strawberry
Olympic Games	festival
	the turkey raffle

---

[48] Do not capitalize initial *the* or short conjunctions, articles, and short prepositions within such names or titles. See H126-29.

Charters, acts, alliances, treaties

H138 Capitalize the titles of charters, acts, statutes, reports, and so on.[49] (Do not use italics or quotation marks.)

Act of Supremacy	Declaration of
Atlantic Charter	Independence
Constitution [of the	Magna Charta
United States]	Monroe Doctrine
Atomic Energy Act	Stamp Act
Marshall Plan	

H139 Capitalize the titles of alliances and treaties.[49] (Do not use italics or quotation marks.)

Articles of Confederation	Quadruple Alliance
Treaty of Versailles	North Atlantic Treaty
Organization of	Organization
American States	SALT Treaty

Languages, peoples, academic courses

H140 Capitalize the names of languages, peoples, races, and tribes, whether in noun or adjective form.[50]

Latin	Spanish	Bushmen
French	Caucasian	Iroquois
English	Indian	Mohawk
Spartan	Negro	Scandinavian

Howard thinks it incredible that the ancient *Romans* communicated in *Latin*.

I should like to take *Spanish* 3.
They used to converse in the *Greek* language—*Attic*, of course.

A *Frenchman*, Lauras, told me that *Russian* is the most euphonious of languages.

---

[49] Do not capitalize initial *the* or short conjunctions, articles, and short prepositions within such names or titles. See H126-29.
[50] See H141-42.

Crane studied *Romance* languages at Oxford.

As a child Sheila learned the *Cherokee* dialect—or is it a language?

There is good *Italian* cooking to be had here.

H141 Do not capitalize general terms that can be applied to several races or peoples.[51]

blacks	half-breed	redskin
gypsy	mulatto	whites
aborigine	quadroon	colored

There will be no segregation of *whites* from Negroes in heaven.
In Memphis there are Irish *gypsies* known as the Travelers.
In those days the *white man* was not very welcome in Japan.

H142 Do not capitalize *language, people, race, tribe,* and so on.[52]

Why not take a *language*?
Up there the Indians speak their own Taos *dialect.*
What's the origin of the French *language*?
The American *people* will stand for it.
These songs were produced by the Negro *race.*
Several *tribes* made up the Iroquois *nation.*

H143 Do not capitalize such words as *history, mathematics, chemistry, physics, religion,* and *algebra* unless they are used with a number to designate a specific course.

This year I'm taking *history* and *geometry,* but not Latin or *physics.*

I'm taking *History* 6 and *Chemistry* 1.

I used to think *religion* a dull subject, but *Religion* 4 has begun to interest me.

Marie did not do well in *algebra,* but she took an instant liking to *geometry.*

---

[51] See H140.
[52] See H140-41.

314

Days, months, seasons, festivals

H144 Capitalize the names of the days of the week, the months of the year, holidays, holydays, and ecclesiastical seasons, feast days, and fast days.[53] (Do not use italics or quotation marks.)

Tuesday	Easter
January	Pentecost
Fourth of July	Advent
the Fourth	Feast of St. Agnes
Halloween	Ascension Thursday
Labor Day	Passover
Presidents' Day	Christmas
Rosh Hashana	Ash Wednesday
Thanksgiving	Day of Atonement
All Saints' Day	New Year's Eve

H145 Do not capitalize *day* when the name of a holyday or holiday makes sense without it.

Ed Buono's birthday is on Christmas *day*.	*Day* is not necessary.
Labor *Day* signals the end of summer.	*Day* is necessary.
New Year's *Day* is her favorite holiday.	*Day* is necessary to distinguish this holiday from New Year's *Eve*.

H146 Do not capitalize *day, week, month, year, century, era, epoch, aeon, period, age,* and so on, when they are not used as part of a title.[54]

Bills flood in with the mail every *day* of the *week*.

There have been many revolutions during the *month* of July.

---

[53] Do not capitalize initial *the* or short conjunctions, articles, and short prepositions within such names or titles. See H126-29.
See H145-46.

[54] Quite often these terms are not capitalized even when they are part of a title. See H136 and H145.

Terence spouts glibly about the eighteenth *century* but says nothing of the present *year.*

Our *era* is quite properly called the Christian Era.

Beowulf is not an *epoch;* it's an epic.

During that *period* of the Stone Age, I imagine, dress design was sharply limited by the materials available.

In an *age* when everyone runs with the herd, Monica is quite content to please God and, incidentally, herself.

H147 Do not capitalize *spring, summer, winter, autumn,* and *fall* unless they are personified.

Mrs. Williams and the children go to Maine in the late *spring,* stay all *summer,* and return in the *fall.*

We must get ready for Old Man *Winter.*

Miscellaneous capitals

H148 Capitalize names that are clearly short forms of titles that must be capitalized.[55]

The best place in the world to live is the *States* [the United States].

The *Street* [Wall Street] was in panic.

The *Terror* [the Reign of Terror] lasted from about March 1793 to July 1794.

The *Republic* was born in 1776.

At first he lived near Riverside Drive and then, later, on the *Drive* itself.

The *High School* [St. Benet's High School] cordially welcomes Your Excellency.

---

[55] The context frequently determines whether the expression is *clearly* a short form of the title. If there is some suspicion that the expression is a mere common-noun designation, do not capitalize it; for example, "The *high school* has bought a multiple-unit public address system."

H149 With the exception of those listed in H150, capitalize any word or its abbreviation that is followed by a numeral or a letter.

Act III	Lesson 7
Answer 10	List A
Appendix V	Number (No.) 7
Article II	Part IV
Book I	Question 6
Chapter V (5)	Room 16 (Room B)
Chart XVI	Rule 18
Exercise 19	Volume III (Vol. 3)

H150 Do not capitalize the following minor subdivisions. (See H149.)

page 39	footnote 7
pp. 39-51	letter b
column 4	stanza 3
paragraph *a*	verse 3
line 18	v. 2
note 7	scene 2

H151 Capitalize the special adjective in a trade name, but not the common name it modifies. (If the common noun is part of the copyrighted name, it is capitalized.)

Blue Label tomatoes	Zenith television
Cafe du Monde coffee	Stetson hats
Camel cigarettes	Sunrise bacon
Ivory soap	Wrigley's Doublemint gum

H152 Capitalize (and italicize) the names of ships, aircraft, spacecraft, trains, and so on, but do not capitalize the initial article.[56]

the *Queen Elizabeth II* [ship]
the *China Clipper* [airplane]
the *Zephyr* [train]
the *Discovery* [spaceship]

---

[56] For italics with titles, see D152.

H153 Capitalize *I* and *O*.[57]

> *I* came, *I* saw, *I* conquered.
> Hear me, *O* my friends!

H154 Do not capitalize *yes, no, oh, good-bye, good morning, amen,* and so on, unless they begin a sentence.[58]

> *Oh,* Marsha has a most pleasant way of saying *yes.*
> A gentleman can always say *no* courteously.
> I said *good-bye* without regret.
> Janice always added a smile to her *good morning.*
> To that prayer we add a hearty *amen.*
> In a faltering voice Grandpa answered, *"Yes."*

H155 Capitalize and italicize *whereas* and *resolved* in resolutions, and capitalize the first word following them.

> *Whereas,* The fourth day of . . .
> *Resolved* [or, *Be it resolved*], That the members . . .

H156 You may capitalize words for which special, usually humorous, emphasis is wanted. (Use this capitalization only very rarely.)

> He looked with the greatest disdain upon the *Common Herd.*
> She fell into theosophy on her way to the *Higher Things* in life.

H157 Capitalize words that are personified.

> Man in the Moon   the Reaper

> We must get ready for *Old Man River.*

> With surprising speed, *Nature* completed another masterpiece.

> Then *Spring*—with her gentle showers and warm sun—arrived.

---

[57] *O* (nowadays reserved for direct address in rather poetic language) is always capitalized and never followed by a comma. *Oh* is not capitalized and is usually followed by a comma.

[58] For the use of italics with such words, see D155.

> . . . bring with thee
> Jest and youthful Jollity,
>
> . . . .
>
> Sport that wrinkled Care derides
> And Laughter holding both his sides.
>
> —JOHN MILTON

H158 Capitalize the names of the heavenly bodies and the signs of the zodiac, but not *sun* and *moon.*

Big Dipper	Saturn
Milky Way	sun
moon	Taurus

It is impossible to see the *Southern Cross* from here.
A circle with a dot in the center is the symbol for the *sun.*

H159 In general, do not capitalize *the, a,* or *an* when it precedes a title or proper name (except for the cases in H126-29, H160-62). The article is not ordinarily regarded as part of the title or name. (The word *the* at the beginning of the title of an institution or an organization is capitalized only if it is part of the official corporate name of the institution or organization and that name is called for.)

In *the* Bible are *the* Old Testament and *the* New Testament.

The funeral service was based on *the* Anglican Book of Common Prayer.

Josefina works for *the* Department of Commerce.

It was dark when they reached *the* Cumberland Gap.

Today, *the* Fourth of July, is a great holiday.

Where is *the* First National Bank?

Side by side on my desk are *the* American College Dictionary and *the* Concise Oxford Dictionary.

The book was copyrighted by *The* University of Chicago.

H160 Capitalize *the* when it is the first word in the heading or address of a letter.

H161 Capitalize *the* in a certain few place names. (They will be found in a dictionary or gazetteer.)

While in the Netherlands we made a trip to *The Hague.*
East of Portland is the city of *The Dalles.*

H162 Capitalize *the* (as well as any demonstrative) preceding a noun when they form a kind of proper name or title.

For Siger of Brabant, Aristotle is *The* Philosopher.
They call me *The* Worm.
To June's parents, he was *That* Actor.

Spelling

In general[1]

I1 Practically every rule of spelling has exceptions. But the following rules hold often enough to make them useful.

I2 When in doubt about the spelling of a word, consult a dictionary. Only the dictionary habit ensures correctness.

I3 American usage, in some instances, is different from British usage. British usage is best for Britons, American usage for Americans.

American usage	*British usage*
center	centre
theater	theatre
sepulcher	sepulchre

[1] For proper spelling and punctuation of the possessive case of nouns and pronouns, see D158-71.

analyze	analyse
apologize	apologise
dramatize	dramatise
behavior	behaviour
humor	humour
labor	labour
judgment	judgement
mold	mould
offense	offence

The Plural of Nouns [2]

14 Form the plural of most nouns by adding *s*. [3]

alley—alleys	chair—chairs
baboon—baboons	crowd—crowds

15 When the singular of a noun ends in *ch, sh, s, x,* or *z,* add *es* to form the plural.

bench—benches	glass—glasses
church—churches	hoax—hoaxes
crash—crashes	fox—foxes
rush—rushes	quiz—quizzes [4]
genius—geniuses	whiz—whizzes [4]

16 When the singular of a noun ends in *y* preceded by a consonant, change *y* to *i* and add *es*. [5]

ally—allies	library—libraries
army—armies	mercy—mercies
lady—ladies	sky—skies

---

[2] For the plural of pronouns, see A29-30, A32, A38, A56. For the plural of verbs, see A65-66.

[3] Some few words form the plural by adding *'s*. See D174-75.

[4] Nouns ending in *z* frequently double the *z* in forming the plural.

[5] A consonant can be defined as a letter of the alphabet that is not *a, e, i, o,* or *u*. (More technically, it is a letter that cannot be named unless a vowel is pronounced with it; for example, *t* cannot be named without an *e* sound.) *U* preceded by *q* is considered a consonant; thus the plural of *colloquy* is not *colloquys* but *colloquies*.

¶7 When the singular of a noun ends in *y* preceded by a vowel, add *s*.[6]

alley—alleys	monkey—monkeys
alloy—alloys	play—plays
essay—essays	tray—trays
key—keys	valley—valleys

¶8 When a compound noun is written as one word, form the plural of the last word.

bathhouse—bathhouses   teaspoonful—teaspoonfuls

¶9 When a compound noun is written as two words, add the plural form to the noun portion or to the more significant word.

player piano—player pianos
snake dance—snake dances
major general—major generals
consul general—consuls general
sergeant major—sergeants major
maid of honor—maids of honor

¶10 Generally, when a compound noun is written with hyphens, form the plural of the first word. The rule, however, does not hold where it would make for awkwardness or absurdity of pronunciation or meaning.

sister-in-law—sisters-in-law
passer-by—passers-by
man-of-war—men-of-war
But—
good-for-nothing—good-for-nothings
two-year-old—two-year-olds
shut-in—shut-ins
face-off—face-offs
forget-me-not—forget-me-nots

---

[6] The vowels are *a, e, i, o, u* (and, in some words, *y*). They are letters that can be sounded without the help of another letter.

111 Some nouns have the same form in the singular and in the plural.

deer—deer	sheep—sheep
moose—moose	species—species
series—series	swine—swine

112 For the plural of nouns not covered by the rules, see a dictionary. The following is a list of some that may give you trouble:

A. Words ending in *o*:

cameo—cameos	radio—radios
curio—curios	rodeo—rodeos
auto—autos	piano—pianos[7]
dynamo—dynamos	solo—solos[7]
memo—memos	soprano—sopranos[7]
bronco—broncos[8]	poncho—ponchos[8]
gaucho—gauchos[8]	sombrero—sombreros[8]
echo—echoes	tomato—tomatoes
hero—heroes	tornado—tornadoes
potato—potatoes	veto—vetoes
banjo—banjos, banjoes	hobo—hobos, hoboes
cargo—cargos, cargoes	motto—mottos, mottoes
halo—halos, haloes	volcano—volcanos,
mosquito—mosquitoes,	volcanoes
mosquitos	zero—zeros, zeroes

B. Words that still keep a foreign ending:

addendum—addenda	datum—data
alumna—alumnae[9]	ellipsis—ellipses
alumnus—alumni[10]	erratum—errata
analysis—analyses	focus—foci

---

[7] Musical terms of Italian origin add *s*.
[8] Words of Spanish origin usually add *s*.
[9] Pronounced "alum-knee."
[10] Pronounced "alum-nye."

antithesis—antitheses   hypothesis—hypotheses
axis—axes   index—indices, indexes
appendix—appendixes,   medium—media
   appendices   oasis—oases
bacillus—bacilli   ovum—ova
bacterium—bacteria   parenthesis—parentheses
beau—beaux, beaus   phylum—phyla
candelabrum—candelabra   radius—radii
chateau—chateaux,   stratum—strata
   chateaus   synopsis—synopses
ciborium—ciboria   tableau—tableaux,
crisis—crises   tableaus
curriculum—curricula,   terminus—termini
   curriculums   thesis—theses

C. Words that end in *f, fe,* or *ff*:

belief—beliefs   handkerchief—handker-
brief—briefs   chiefs
chief—chiefs   proof—proofs
cliff—cliffs   reef—reefs
fife—fifes   roof—roofs
grief—griefs   tariff—tariffs

calf—calves   loaf—loaves
elf—elves   self—selves
half—halves   sheaf—sheaves
knife—knives   thief—thieves
leaf—leaves   wife—wives
life—lives   wolf—wolves

dwarf—dwarfs, dwarves   scarf—scarfs, scarves
hoof—hoofs, hooves   wharf—wharfs, wharves

D. *Child, ox,* and words that change the root:

child—children   man—men
foot—feet   mouse—mice
gentleman—gentlemen   ox—oxen
goose—geese   tooth—teeth
louse—lice   woman—women

ie and ei

113 When spelling words with *ie* and *ei* in them, make use of the rhyme—

I before *e*[11]
Except after *c*
Or when sounded like *a*
As in *neighbor* and *weigh.*

After letters other than c:

achieve	brief	grief	siege
apiece	chief	niece	sieve
belief	field	relieve	thief
believe	fierce	shield	yield

[Some exceptions:] *caffeine, codeine, either, leisure, neither, protein, seize, seizure*

After c:

ceiling	conceive	perceive
conceited	deceive	receive

When sounded like a:

deign	neighbor	their
feign	reign	veil
freight	rein	vein
heinous	sleigh	weigh
inveigh	surveillance	weight

Ceed, cede, and sede

114 Memorize the spelling of these verbs:

Ceed:

exceed	proceed	succeed

---

[11] The rule applies only to the sound of long *e* (as in *knee*). Thus, for example, words with *ie* or *ei* pronounced as long or short *i* are beyond the scope of the rule [*Fahrenheit, gneiss, height, seismic, sleight, stein, counterfeit, financier, foreign, foreigner, forfeit, sovereign, sovereignty, surfeit, weird,* etc.].

Cede:

accede	intercede	recede
cede	precede	secede
concede		

Sede:

supersede

Prefixes

I15   A prefix is one or more syllables or a word added at the beginning of a word or root to change (or occasionally to intensify) its meaning.

admit	readmit [admit again]
lead	mislead
national	international
educated	self-educated
flammable	inflammable
iterate	reiterate

I16   When adding a prefix to a word or root, do not double letters or drop letters.

antisocial	discharge	readmit
belabor	misshapen	re-enter
bemoan	misstate	reinforce
coerce	mistake	uncertain
coherent	occur	underrate
debase	overrun	unnatural
demonstrate	oversee	withhold
disable	prelection	withstand

[Exception:] *all: already, although, altogether, always*

I17   The final consonant of some prefixes changes to match the first letter of the next element.

ad—> <u>app</u>rehension, <u>att</u>end
com—> <u>coll</u>ect, <u>corr</u>elation
in—> <u>ill</u>egal, <u>irr</u>esponsible
ob—> <u>occ</u>ur, <u>off</u>er
sub—> <u>suff</u>er, <u>sugg</u>est

118 Use a hyphen after the prefixes *self, ex* (meaning "former"), and in some instances *anti,* and after prefixes before words beginning with a capital letter.[12]

self-made	anti-hero
ex-governor	un-American

119 Use a hyphen after some prefixes to prevent confusion.[13]

co-op	re-collect [*vs.* recollect]
de-emphasize	re-create [*vs.* recreate]
de-ice	re-lease [*vs.* release]

Suffixes

120 A suffix is a syllable or several syllables added at the end of a word or root to change its meaning or give it grammatical function.

cold	colder [more cold]
sudden	suddeness

121 When adding a suffix to a word ending in a single consonant, double the final consonant of the word only if all of the following points are verified:

A. The word is accented on the last syllable.[14]

bag[15]	begin

B. The final consonant is preceded by a single vowel.

bag	begin

---

[12] See D185.

[13] See D184.

[14] The accent must not shift off the final syllable of the original word. For example, the final consonant in *prefer* does not double in *preference* because the accent shifts. Other common words that shift the accent are *confer, conference; defer, deference; infer, inference.*

[15] One-syllable words, of course, are accented on the last (the only) syllable.

C. The suffix begins with a vowel.

abet—abetted	occur—occurred
bag—baggage	patrol—patrolling
begin—beginning	plan—planned
big—biggest	rebel—rebelled
clan—clannish	refer—referred
concur—concurred	regret—regretting
deter—deterred	run—running
dispel—dispelled	sad—saddening
get—getting	sit—sitting
grab—grabbing	transfer—transferred
impel—impelled	wed—wedding
infer—inferred	wit—witty

[Some exceptions:] *chagrined, formatting, gaseous*

122   When adding a suffix to a word that ends in a double consonant, keep the double consonant.

add—added	full—fullness
address—addresses	[*also* fulness]
butt—butted	odd—oddly
dull—dullness	puff—puffy
[*also* dulness]	shrill—shrilly
ebb—ebbing	stiff—stiffness
embarrass—embarrass-	will—willful
ment	[*also* wilful]

123   Keep final *l* before a suffix beginning with *l*.

accidental—accidentally	occasional—occasionally
cool—coolly	soul—soulless
final—finally	usual—usually

124   Except for the cases in 121, American usage does not double final *l* before a suffix that begins with a vowel.

equal—equaled	travel—traveled

125 Keep *n* before the suffix *ness.*

> barren—barrenness   sudden—suddenness

126 Keep silent *e* before a suffix that begins with a consonant.

> docile—docilely   manage—management
> hate—hateful   pale—paleness

[Some exceptions:] *abridgment, acknowledgment, argument, duly, judgment, truly, wholly.*

127 Keep silent *e* if it both—

A. Follows soft *c* or soft *g.*

> peace   advantage

B. Precedes the suffix *able* or *ous.*

> peaceable   advantageous
>
> change—changeable   marriage—marriageable
> courage—courageous   notice—noticeable
> enforce—enforceable   outrage—outrageous
> manage—manageable   service—serviceable

128 Change final *ie* to *y* before the suffix *ing.*

> die—dying   lie—lying   tie—tying

129 In all cases not covered by 127-28, omit silent final *e* before a suffix that begins with a vowel.

> argue—arguing   hope—hoping
> arrive—arriving   please—pleasant
> desire—desirable   plume—plumage
> force—forcible   purple—purplish
> give—given   true—truer
> guide—guidance   type—typing

[Some exceptions:] *dyeing* (tinting with dye), *hoeing, singeing* (burning slightly, as feathers), *tingeing* (staining)

I 30   If a word ends in *y* preceded by a consonant, change the *y* to *i* (unless the suffix begins with *i*; for example, *cry—crying*).

anarchy—anarchical	fly—flier [*also* flyer]
body—bodily	hardy—hardiness
bounty—bountiful	mercy—merciless
busy—busier	sly—slily [*better* slyly]
cry—cried	study—studious
dry—drily [*better* dryly]	try—tried
duty—dutiful	whinny—whinnied

[Exceptions:] Words formed from one-syllable adjectives like *dry, shy, sly, spry, and wry: dryness, shyly, shyness, slyly, slyness, spryly, spryness, wryly, wryness*

I 3I   If a word ends in *y* preceded by a vowel, keep the *y* before the suffix.

allay—allayed	gay—gayety [*better* gaiety]
annoy—annoyance	gay—gayly [*better* gaily]
buy—buying	joy—joyful
coy—coyer	obey—obeying

[Some exceptions:] *day—daily, lay—laid, lay—lain, pay—paid, say—said, slay—slain*

I 32   Add *k* to final *c* before the suffixes *ing, ed, er,* and *y* (so that *c* will not be pronounced as *s*).

frolic—frolicking, frolicked, frolicker, frolicky
picnic—picnicking, picnicked, picnicker
mimic—mimicking, mimicked
panic—panicking, panicked, panicky
traffic—trafficking, trafficked

I 33   Words ending in the sound *ize* are generally, in American usage, spelt *ize*. (In general, the British spelling for such words is *ise*.)

Americanize	galvanize
apologize	harmonize
baptize	homogenize

canonize	modernize
catechize	organize
characterize	pasteurize
civilize	pulverize
criticize	recognize
devitalize	specialize
dramatize	sympathize

[Common exceptions:] *advertise, advise, chastise, comprise, compromise, despise, devise, disguise, enterprise, exercise, improvise, revise, supervise, surprise; analyze*

Study advice

134 Own and make use of a good college dictionary of the English language. Since the language is constantly changing and growing and since practically every rule of spelling has exceptions, a good current dictionary is an indispensable guide for the serious writer.[16]

135 The following procedures are helpful for improving spelling:

1. Learn the spelling rules in I4-33.

2. Memorize the correct spelling of troublesome words.

3. Make use of mnemonic devices. For example, the opposite of "all wrong" is "all right" (not "alright").

4. When you have difficulty spelling a word,

—look at the word carefully, letter by letter, and say it out loud. Listen to the pronunciation of the word as you say it. Form a picture of the word in your mind.

—close your eyes and spell the word.

—study the word by syllables. Write the word syllable

---

[16] A dictionary is necessary, for example, to check the spelling of words ending in *-ance, -ence, -ant, -ent,* since there are no adequate rules for such words.

by syllable. (Check a dictionary if you are not sure of the syllables in the word.)

—say the word out loud syllable by syllable. (Incorrect pronunciation of the word can lead to incorrect spelling.)

—write the word again from memory. Check the spelling.

5. Keep a list of the words that you misspell. If you find that you are misspelling the same word frequently, write the word slowly and carefully several times until you are sure that you are spelling it correctly. Underline the parts of the word that cause you trouble.

6. Always proofread what you have written to see if any words are misspelled.

Spelling list

I 36 On the following pages is a list of commonly misspelled words. A systematic review of these words will help you reduce your spelling errors. Study only a small group of words at a time, following the procedures listed in I 35.

A	abbreviate	aerial	applies
	absence	affects [modifies]	appreciate
	absorption	aggravate	approach
	abundance	aggressive	appropriate
	academy	aisle	approval
	accelerator	allege	approximate
	acceptable	allotted	arctic
	acceptance	all right	argument
	accessible	almost	around
	accidentally	already	arouse
	accommodate	altar [structure]	arrangement
	accompany	alter [change]	arrival
	accumulate	altogether	article
	accuracy	amateur	ascension
	ache	among	ascertain

achievement   amount   assassination
acknowledgment   analysis   assess
acquaintance   analyze   assured
acquire   ancient   athletic
across   annual   attacked
addressed   anonymous   attempt
adequate   answer   attendance
admissible   apology   attention
admittance   apparatus   available
adolescent   apparent   authority
advantageous   appearance   auxiliary
advisable   appetite   awful
advice   applicant   awkward

B   bachelor   beggar   bookkeeper
baggage   beginning   boundary
balance   behavior   bouquet
balloon   belief   breathe
banana   believable   brilliant
barbarous   beneficial   Britain
basically   benefited   bulletin
beautiful   bicycle   buoy
becoming   biscuit   business
before   blasphemy   busy

C   caffeine   clothes   conscious
calendar   cloths   considerably
camouflage   coarse   consistent
campaign   colonel   conspicuous
canceled   colossal   contemptible
cancellation   column   continuous
candidate   commission   controlled
capacity   committed   controversy
career   committee   convenience
caricature   comparative   convenient
carrying   compelled   coolly
cashier   competent   cordially
catastrophe   competition   corroborate
category   complacence   cough

celebrate	complexion	counsel
cellar	comprehensible	counterfeit
cemetery	conceit	courageous
census	conceivable	course
certain	concern	courteous
challenge	concession	courtesy
changeable	concurred	criticism
characteristic	condemn	criticize
chief	connoisseur	cruelty
choose	conquer	cupboard
chosen	conscience	curiosity
circumstances	conscientious	cylinder

D

dealt	desert	disappear
deceive	desirable	disappoint
decide	despair	disastrous
decision	desperate	disciple
defendant	dessert [food]	discipline
defensible	destroy	discrepancy
deficient	determine	disease
definite	detrimental	dissatisfied
delinquent	develop	divide
demolition	development	doesn't
dependent	difference	dominance
descendant	dilemma	drought
describe	dining	dyeing [coloring]
description	diploma	dying

E

early	enterprise	exception
easily	entertain	excerpt
economical	enthusiasm	excitement
ecstasy	envelop [verb]	exercise
effects	envelope [noun]	exhausted
efficiency	environment	exhibit
efficient	equipment	exhilaration
eighth	equipped	existence
eligible	erroneous	expense
eliminate	especially	experience
embarrass	etc.	explanation

eminent
emphasize
encyclopedia
endeavor
enough

etiquette
evidently
exaggerate
exceedingly
excellent

extemporaneous
extension
extraordinary
extremely
exuberant

F Fahrenheit
fallacy
familiar
fascinate
feasible
February
feminine
fictitious
field
fierce

fiery
finally
financial
flexible
flies
fluorescent
forcible
forehead
foreign
forfeit

formally
formerly
forty
fourth
forward
freight
friend
fulfill
fundamental
further

G gaiety
galloped
gauged
generally
genius
gentlemen
genuine
ghost

glimpse
gnarled
gossiped
government
gouged
governor
grammar
grateful

grievance
grocery
guarantee
guard
guess
guardian
guidance
gullible

H handkerchief
handsome
half
handled
haphazard
happiness

harass
having
hectic
height
heroes
hindrance

hoping
hospital
humorous
hurriedly
hygiene
hypocrisy

I idiosyncrasy
illegible
illiterate
imaginary
imagination
immigrant
immediately

independent
indispensable
individual
influential
ingenious
initial
initiative

interested
interfere
interference
interpret
interrupt
invisible
involvement

	imminent	inquiry	irrelevant
	impossible	instance	irresistible
	inaugurate	integrate	issuing
	incidentally	intellectual	it's [contraction]
	inconvenience	intelligence	its [possessive]
	independence	intercede	itself
J	jealous	jeopardize	judgment
K	keenness	khaki	knack
	kerosene	kindergarten	knowledgeable
L	laboratory	liable	livelihood
	laid	library	lonely
	later	license	loneliness
	latter	licorice	loose
	led	lieutenant	lose
	legitimate	lightning	losing
	leisure	likely	luxurious
	length	liquor	lying
M	magazine	mediocre	misspell
	magnificence	melancholy	morale
	maintenance	mere	mortgage
	manageable	messenger	mosquito
	maneuver	metaphor	mourning
	marriageable	mileage	movable
	material	miniature	municipal
	mathematics	minimum	murmur
	meadow	minute	muscle
	meant	miscellaneous	mutual
	medicine	mischievous	mysterious
N	naive	neither	noisily
	naturally	nevertheless	noticeable
	necessary	nickel	nowadays
	negotiate	niece	nucleus
	Negroes	ninety	nuisance
	neighbor	ninth	nutritious
O	obedience	occurred	opportunity
	obligatory	occurrence	opposite

oblige
obsess
obstacle
occasion
occasionally
occur

o'clock
omission
omitted
operate
opinion
opponent

oppression
optimism
optimistic
original
originate
outrageous

P pageant
paid
pamphlet
panicked
parallel
paralysis
parliament
partial
particularly
pastime
peaceable
peasant
peculiar
perceive
perceptible
perform
performance
perhaps
permanent
permissible
perseverance
persistent
personally

personnel
perspiration
persuade
phenomenon
philosophy
physical
physician
picnicking
piece
planned
playwright
pleasant
pleasure
pneumonia
poison
politician
portrayed
possession
possible
practically
practice
precede
precious

preference
preferred
prejudice
preliminary
presumptuous
prestige
prevalent
principal
principles
privilege
probably
procedure
proceed
profession
professor
prominent
propaganda
propagate
prophecy [noun]
prophesy [verb]
psychology
pursue
pursuit

Q quandary
quantity
quarrel

questionnaire
quiet
quite

quitting
quiz
quizzes

R radical
realize
really
rebellion
recede

recurrence
reference
referred
regrettable
rehearsal

repellent
repetition
replies
representative
resource

receipt	relevant	responsibility
receive	relief	restaurant
recently	relieve	reveal
reciprocate	religious	rhyme
recognize	reminisce	rhythm
recommendation	remittance	ridiculous

S

sacrifice	similar	stretch
safety	simultaneous	strictly
salary	sincerely	studying
satisfactory	skeptical	substantial
scarcely	society	subtle
scenery	solemn	subtlety
schedule	sophomore	succeed
science	source	success
scissors	souvenir	sufficient
secretary	sovereign	suggestion
seize	spaghetti	summary
sense	speak	summed
sensible	special	superfluous
sentence	species	superintendent
separate	specifically	supersede
sergeant	specimen	superstitious
serial	speech	suppose
several	sponsor	suppress
severely	stationary [fixed]	surely
shepherd	stationery [paper]	surgeon
shining	statistics	surprise
shriek	stopped	suspicion
siege	straight	syllable
sieve	strength	sympathy
significant	strenuous	synonym

T

taboo	they're	tragedy
tailor	thief	transferred
tariff	thorough	treasure
tattoo	though	tremendous
technique	thought	tried
temperament	through	tries

	temperature	tier	triumph
	temporary	together	trouble
	tenant	tolerance	truly
	tendency	tomorrow	Tuesday
	their	too	twelfth
	theoretical	toward	typical
	therefore	traffic	tyranny
U	unanimous	unnecessary	useful
	undoubtedly	unscrupulous	using
	unfortunately	until	usually
	unique	usage	utterance
V	vaccine	vegetables	view
	vacuum	vehement	vigorous
	valleys	vehicle	village
	valuable	veil	villain
	varieties	vengeance	vinegar
	various	versatile	visible
	vaudeville	vessel	voluminous
W	waiver [re- nouncement]	welfare	wield
		whether	women
	wallop	whisper	woolen
	warrant	whistle	worrying
	weapon	whole	writer
	weather	wholly	writhe
	Wednesday	who's [con- traction]	writing
	weight		written
	weird	whose [possessive]	
Y	yacht	yoke [link]	your [possessive]
	yield	yolk [egg]	you're [contrac- tion]
Z	zealous	zenith	zephyr

Diagraming

In general

J1 A diagram of a sentence is a picture that shows the interrelation of the words, phrases, and clauses. Diagrams are a good way to analyze the structure of a sentence. They will frequently, though by no means always, reveal the grammatical flaw in a bad sentence; and they will untangle a complicated sentence so that one can see, for example, whether *who* or *whom* is required.[1]

Diagraming simple sentences

Subject noun and predicate verb

J2 Diagram a subject noun or pronoun and a predicate verb like this:

MODEL

subject noun | predicate verb

People are singing.

people | are singing

---

[1] Traditional, structural, and transformational grammars, quite naturally, have distinctive methods of diagraming. This book presents traditional grammar and diagraming.

Traditional diagrams are often referred to as Reed-Kellog diagrams after Alonzo Reed and Brainerd Kellogg who brought these diagrams to their familiar form in *Higher Lessons in English* (four editions: 1877, 1885, 1896, 1909). The same system is presented in Susan E. Harman and Homer C. House, *Descriptive English Grammar,* 2nd edition, 1950. A comprehensive and responsible modification of traditional diagraming can be found in Raymond W. Pence and Donald W. Emery, *A Grammar of Present-day English,* 1963.

J3 Diagram a compound subject like this:

MODEL

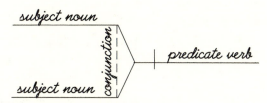

Josephina and *Angela* disappeared.

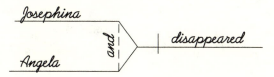

Either *Bill* or *John*, hardly *Kenneth*, will do.

The diagram stresses the connective force of *hardly*.

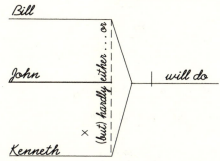

Either *Bill* or *John*, hardly *Kenneth*, will do.

The diagram stresses the adverbial force of *hardly*. (Compound elliptical sentence.)

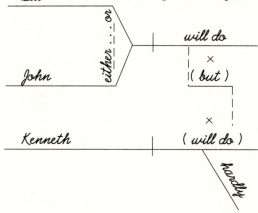

I, not *you*, am responsible.

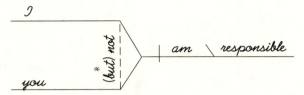

My *friend* and *neighbor*, Kittredge, is celebrating.

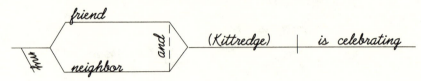

Raisins, *peanuts*, and *jelly* will mix.

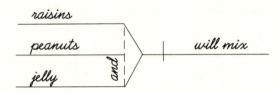

J4 Diagram a compound predicate like this:

Fairbanks *turned* and *ran*.

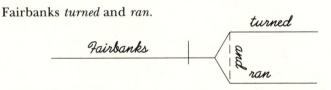

Fairbanks not only *turned* and *ran* but also *screamed*.

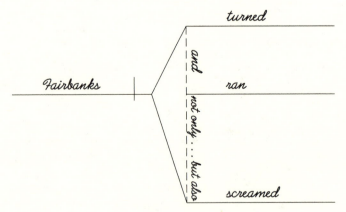

Fairbanks and Schlegel *turned* and *ran*.

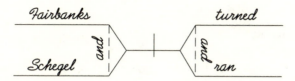

Expletive

J5   An expletive:

MODEL

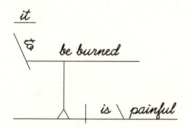

It is painful to be burned.

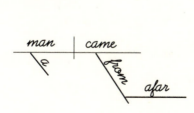

There came a man from afar.

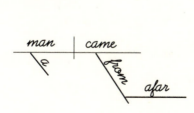

343

Direct objects

J6   A direct object:

MODEL

| subject noun | predicate verb | direct object |

Hilary is playing *golf.*

| *Hilary* | *is playing* | *golf* |

Mirabel likes *parades* and *pageants.*

J7   Two direct objects (not a compound direct object):

MODEL

| subject noun | predicate verb | first object | second object |

Mr. Claudel teaches *Adrian algebra.*

| *Mr. Claudel* | *teaches* | *Adrian* | *algebra* |

Hear *me* my *lessons.*

| (*you*) | *hear* | *me* | *lessons* |

Indirect objects

J8   An indirect object:

MODEL

344

Joe brought *Mother* flowers.

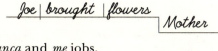

Dad got *Blanca* and *me* jobs.

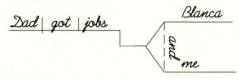

Complements

J9 A predicate noun, pronoun, or adjective:

MODEL

This is *milk*.

This is *milky*.

This | is \ milky

Raeburn is getting *tired* and *angry*.

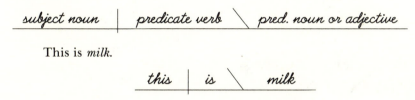

Pitkin was named and was elected *president*.

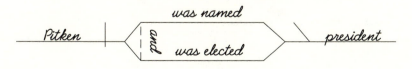

J10 An objective complement:

MODEL

$$\text{subject noun} \mid \text{predicate verb} \mid \text{dir. object} \diagup \text{obj. complement}$$

Boykin appointed Fleisch *administrator*.

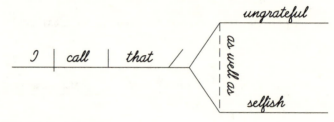

I call that *ungrateful* as well as *selfish*.

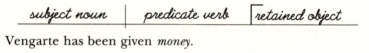

Retained objects

J11 A retained object:

MODEL

$$\text{subject noun} \mid \text{predicate verb} \mid \overline{\text{retained object}}$$

Vengarte has been given *money*.

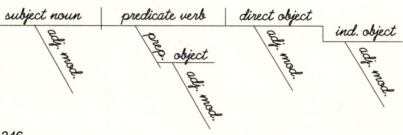

Modifying adjective

J12 A modifying adjective:

MODEL

$$\text{subject noun} \mid \text{predicate verb} \mid \text{direct object} \quad \text{ind. object}$$

At *the morning* inspection *the* major gave *only* me *a second* glance.

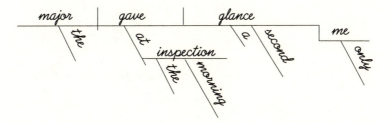

Whimpering and *barking,* the dog circled the porcupine.

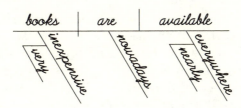

Adverbs and adverbial nouns

J13   An adverb:

MODEL

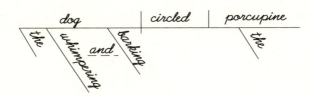

Very inexpensive books are *nowadays nearly everywhere* available.

Hats get *more* and *more* absurd.

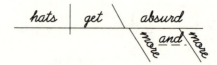

Friedel, groping *blindly* and *awkwardly, finally* found the light cord.

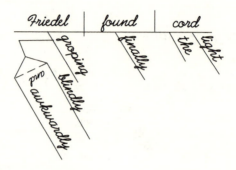

J14 An adverbial noun:

Dougherty went *home yester-day morning.*

Home, yesterday, and *morning* are adverbial nouns.

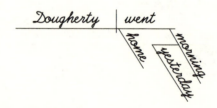

Phrases in general

J15 The subject noun or pronoun of a verbal is set off from the verbal by the same perpendicular line, extended a little below the horizontal line, that is used to set off a subject noun or pronoun from a predicate verb (J2). The direct and indirect objects, predicate complements, retained objects, and objective complements of verbals are diagramed just like those of predicate verbs (J6-11).

Noun phrases

J16   Prepositional noun phrases are not very common; but, when they occur, diagram them like this:

Over the fence is out.

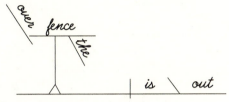

The smoke is coming from *under the house.*

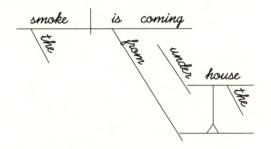

J17   A gerund noun phrase:

MODEL

Calling your enemy names is futile.

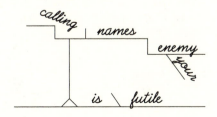

Arguing with Linda is *fighting the wind.*

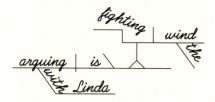

MODEL

Becoming a man takes more than growing up.

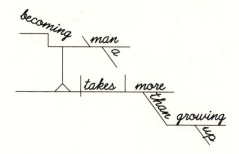

MODEL

There is no doubt about *her being elected.*

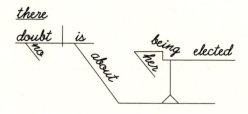

Your snubbing me and playing deaf only make me persistent.

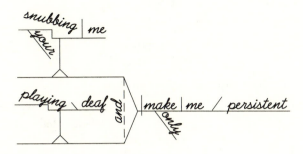

J18 An infinitive noun phrase:

MODEL

We asked the waiter *to bring Laury a bib*.

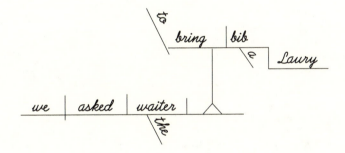

To object is reasonable this time.

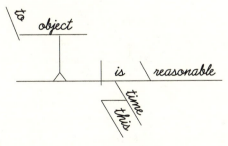

The girls are *to dress as natives.*

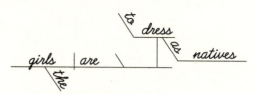

Someone ought *to tie the bell on.*

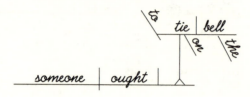

MODEL

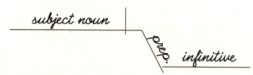

We know *him to be a reader.*

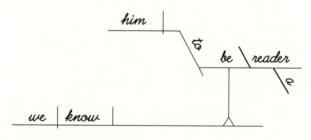

For her to object is unusual.

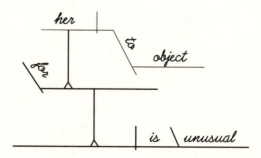

Your brother seems *to be restless.*

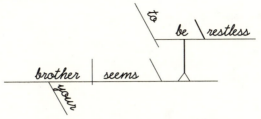

It is useless *to whine, to plead, or to argue with me.*

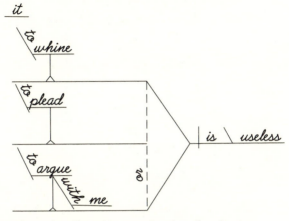

Prepositional adjective and adverb phrases

J19 A prepositional adjective phrase:

MODEL

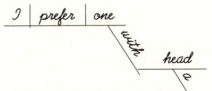

I prefer one *with a head.*

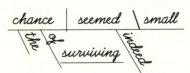

The chance *of surviving* seemed small indeed.

J20 A prepositional adverb phrase:

We swam daily *near the mouth.*

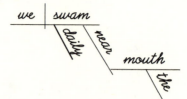

Gene plunged forward, sinking *to his knees.*

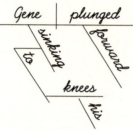

Who's afraid *of a striped kitten?*

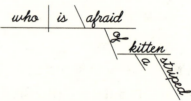

Infinitive adjective and adverb phrases

J21 An infinitive adjective phrase:

You appear *to be troubled.*

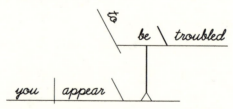

The will *to win* can be important.

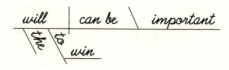

J22 An infinitive adverb phrase:

Put the pot on the stove *to boil.*

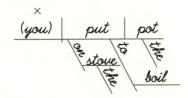

Is everyone ready *to return* to the surface?

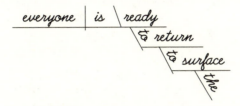

Afraid *to destroy the map,* I dropped it out the window.

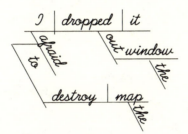

The beggar was too surprised *to say thanks or speak at all.*

Participial adjective phrases

J23   A participial adjective phrase:

MODEL

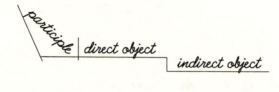

Having given me another sly look, Mr. Snipe departed.

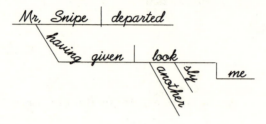

MODEL

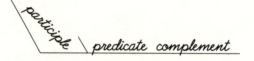

I noticed hundreds of people *standing idle.*

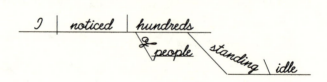

Quarak, *screeching a warning and beckoning wildly*, swung away to the treetops.

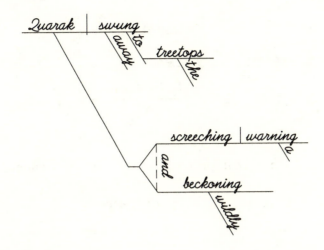

Appositives

J24 Place appositive nouns after and next to the head word in the diagram and enclose them in parentheses.

MODEL

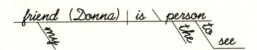

My friend *Donna* is the person to see.

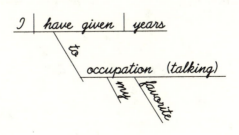

I have given years to my favorite occupation, *talking*.

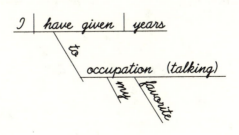

The manager's nephews— *Clem, Lem,* and young *Bartholomew*— have good jobs.

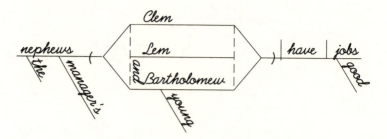

The regional sport, *racing jack rabbits,* is strenuous.

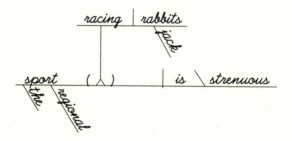

Andirons, or *firedogs,* sat in the center of the huge fireplace.

Or merely stresses the appositive and helps the rhythm.

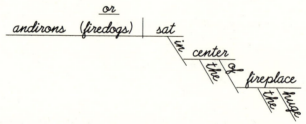

Another fact—namely, your *absence*—is against you.

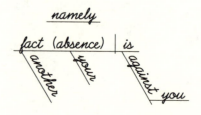

Modifying possessives

J25   Possessives are often adjectives. When they are so, diagram them like adjectives.

Calvin's doctrine is frightening.

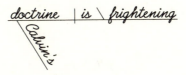

Independent Elements

J26   Since independent elements have no grammatical connection with the rest of the sentence, they are diagramed by themselves, above or below the sentence or clause in which they appear.

J27   Independent words, phrases, or clauses are diagramed just like other words, phrases, or clauses.

J28   A nominative absolute:

MODELS

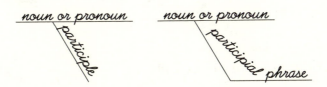

The battle won, the tanks retired.

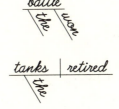

I'm glad, *no one needing the house,* to let you stay in it.

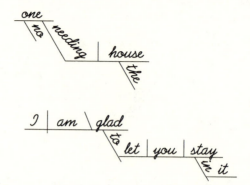

His mouth open in astonishment, the actor stood stock-still.

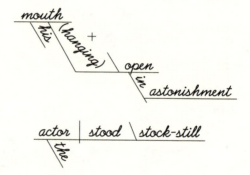

J29   A noun in direct address:

Ms. Froebes, have you anything to say?

Gentlemen, be seated.

J30 An exclamatory word:

Golly, I like the looks of the cowboy riding Terror!

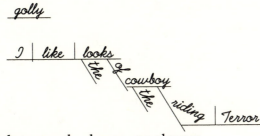

J31 An absolute word, phrase, or clause:

Fetch me the candle snuffer, *please.*

Granting your facts, have you a solution?

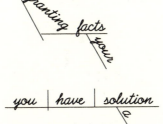

By the way, has anyone found a license plate with an automobile attached?

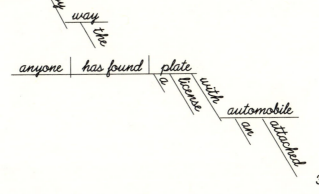

361

We all, *to be sure*, need mercy.

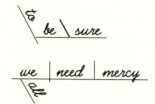

Who *do you suppose* ate the icing?

Consider *do you suppose* in this case to be merely thrown into the sentence. If it were not, it would be the independent clause with the *who* clause as its object.

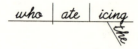

This is the person whom *I imagine* we were to avoid.

Complex sentence.

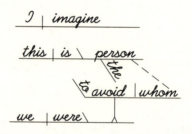

Among the rocks we found abalones; *that is*, ear shells.

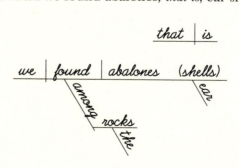

Helmer was a hero; *that is to say*, he did not let his fear rule him.   Compound sentence.

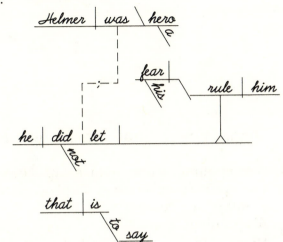

Fergen was a hobo or, *shall we say*, a gentleman of the road.

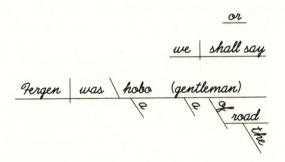

Words Omitted

J32 In diagraming, replace an omitted word or group of words. Enclose it in parentheses, and put an x above it.

Bring me no more reports.

You are not so sensitive as I.   Complex sentence.

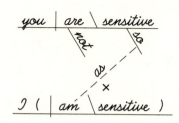

Diagraming compound sentences

J33   A compound sentence is made up of two or more clauses that could stand alone as simple sentences. So the diagraming of a compound sentence adds nothing to the diagraming of a simple sentence (J2-32) except the showing of connection between the clauses.

J34   When *and, or, nor, but, for, so,* or *yet* is omitted between the clauses of a compound sentence, put a semicolon between them in the diagram, like this:

Everybody talks about the weather; nobody does anything about it.

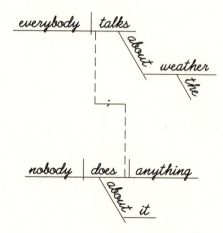

Everybody talks about the weather; still [conjunctive adverb], nobody does anything about it.

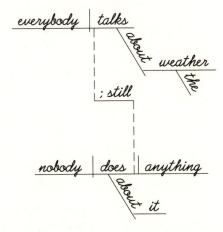

J35 When *and, or, nor, but, for, so,* or *yet* is used between the clauses of a compound sentence, diagram the sentence like this:

Everybody talks about the weather, *but* nobody does anything about it.

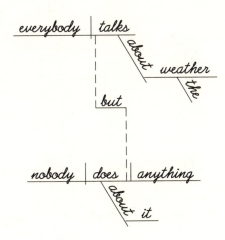

Everybody talks about the weather, *but* still nobody does anything about it.

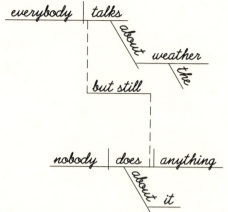

The Kenwig family was not proud, *but* the neighbors ought to know about Morleena's French lessons; *so* she was told to mention them very humbly.

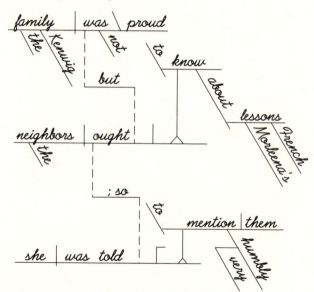

Diagraming complex sentences

Noun Clauses

J36   Put a noun clause on a stilt.

MODEL

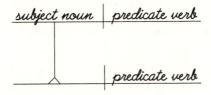

Sentences with subject noun clauses—

Whoever buys this car buys trash.

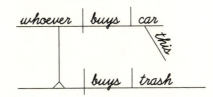

It was foretold in the Old Testament *that the Messiah would be born in Bethlehem.*

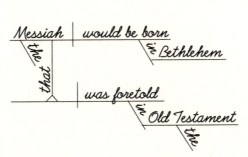

Where you have been and *what you bought there* are nobody's business.

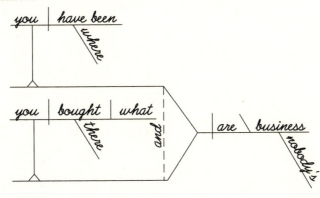

Sentences with object noun clauses—

Tell me *whether you will return in time.*

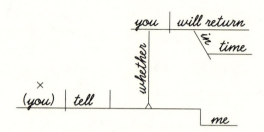

It is a question of *how we can raise the money* and *when we can have the hall.*

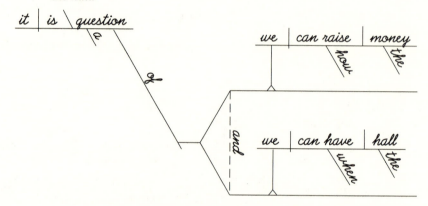

Ted, knowing only *what was required,* did not make a good record at college.

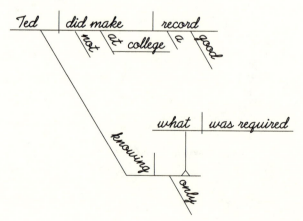

We had an argument about *whose snapshot should be submitted.*

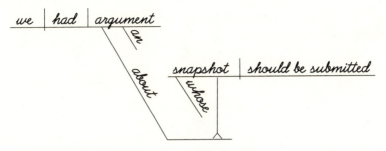

Sentences with noun-clause complements—

Holiness is *what we are striving for.*

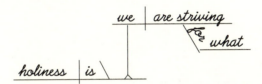

Rose discovered Mullen to be *what she least expected*—intelligent.

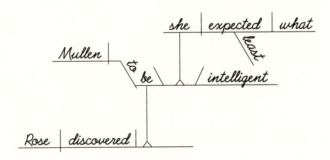

The question is, *who has the chipmunk.*

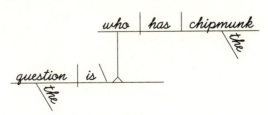

Sentences with noun-clause appositives—

Don's excuse, *that he had a flat tire,* sounded a bit thin.

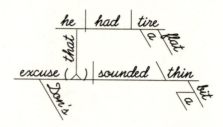

Everything—*whatever he earned* and *whatever came to him as tips*—he gave to his mother.

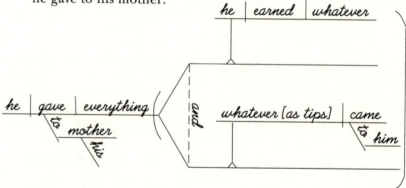

My Protestant friend is deterred by one difficulty, namely, *how can confession be necessary and good?*

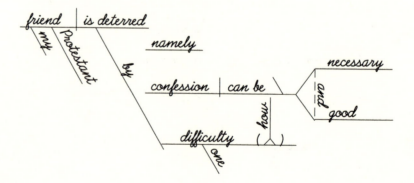

Adjective Clauses

J37 Draw a dotted line from the relative word in the adjective clause to the antecedent in the other clause. (Do not put the relative word on the dotted line.)

The Battle of Lepanto, *which Chesterton made the subject of this poem,* saved Europe from the Turks.

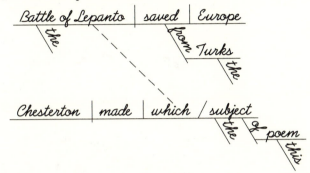

The sultan put his army through tactics *that would check the enemy's latest move.*

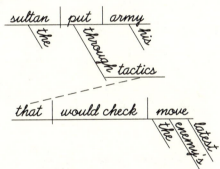

Conrad, *whose novel you just read,* died in 1924.

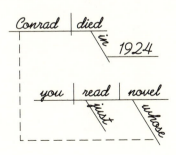

Holt told us the reason *why the fan belt had broken.*

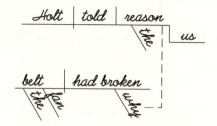

Tina is a person *who we know will work for us.*

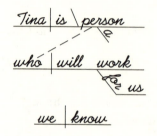

This is the lacquer *that we were waiting for* and *that arrived too late for use on our biggest contract.*

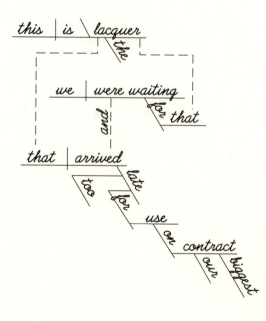

Alfredo is the uncle of Jake, *who is the cousin of Dunbar, who in turn is my uncle.*

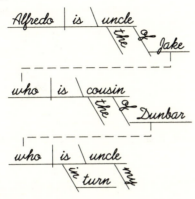

J38   On those rather rare occasions when a whole clause rather than an individual word or phrase is the antecedent of an adjective clause, draw the dotted line from the relative word in the adjective clause to the line under the predicate verb of the other clause.

Margaret threw away my pipe with the broken stem, *which annoyed me very much.*

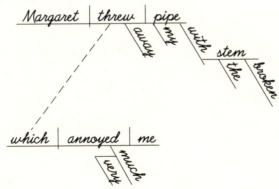

Adverb clauses

J39   Draw a dotted line from the predicate verb of the adverb clause to the word that the adverb clause modifies. On this dotted line, write the subordinating conjunction.

The latch was on *when I tried the door.*

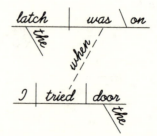

Charles behaved so badly *that we had to put him into a padded cell.*

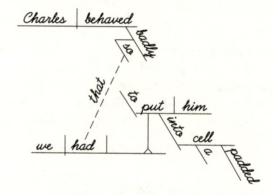

A diamond is harder *than any other precious stone.*

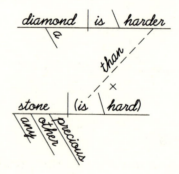

He sometimes acts *as though he were demented.*

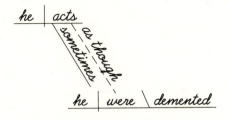

Had I the right, I would abolish advertising.

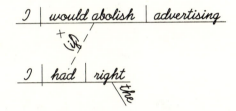

When one is tired and longs for rest, he can find repose at Slumphaven — *if he can pay for it.*

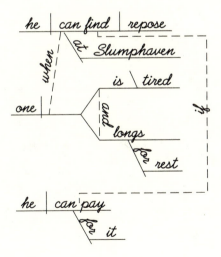

Where a million people blacken the sand like bees swarming thick on a limb and *where every one of the million is in motion,* there I lie and try to get a sun tan.

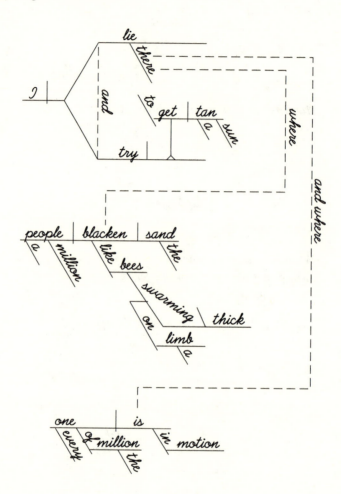

When Jason and I arrived at school and *then I remembered my books at home, seven miles away,* then I got a little upset—like a volcano.

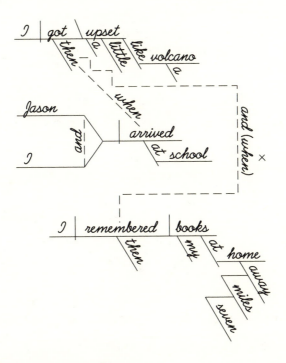

MIxed Dependent Clauses

J40 It often happens that you will find a noun and an adjective, a noun and an adverb, or all three kinds of clauses together in one sentence. When this happens, diagram each kind according to its own form and rules. (Diagrams such as those in J40-41 are really virtuoso stunts, included in this book chiefly to convince the skeptical that complicated sentences can be diagramed. They are not, as a matter of fact, very useful, since their very complication makes them difficult to follow and the relationships the diagrams are meant to point up become obscure. Ordinarily one has little need to diagram more than one or two clauses at a time.)

The fact *that Renard was a journalist with whom I had become acquainted while I was taking a vacation in Santa Fe* was written down in my report.

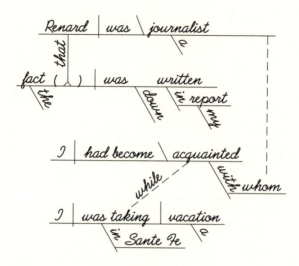

Diagraming compound-complex sentences

J41   A compound-complex sentence:

Rosita waited patiently for news; but, when they returned, the girls had nothing to report about Miggy.

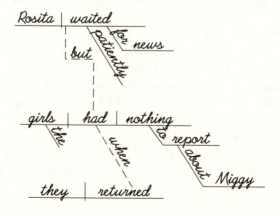

While Rome burned, Nero fiddled and his courtiers laughed.

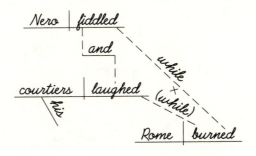

Vittorio fairly jigged with irritation when the bagpipes struck up, but McTavish seemed to enjoy the music.

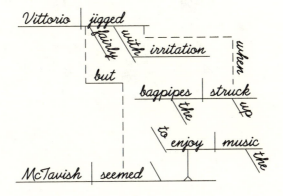

Magellan was killed in the Philippines; nevertheless, his companions, eager to prove that the world is round, continued their westward journey until their ships at length cast anchor off the coast of Spain.

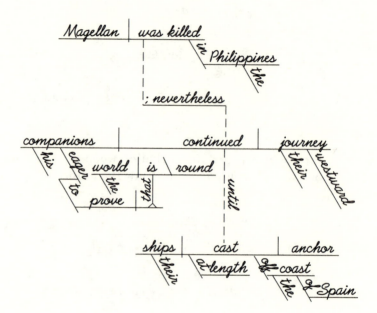

Among the pioneers in the modern French school of music was Cesar Franck, the greatest and most famous composer that Belgium has produced; in fact, musicians so esteemed him that they made a cult of him and his music even before he died.

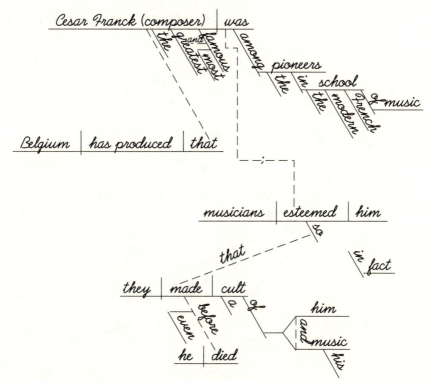

Diagraming direct quotations

J42 If a direct quotation is a half-sentence that can be considered part of the sentence or clause in which it stands, diagram it as part of the sentence or clause.

Mrs. Moulton shouted loudly that she was "plenty peeved!"

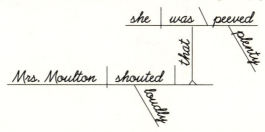

J43   If a direct quotation is not a half-sentence but a sentence, diagram it as you would any other sentence. Diagram the *he/she said* portion of the sentence independently of the quotation.

"My people" said the chief, "do not wish to fight your people."

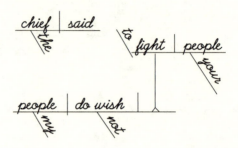

"Give us back our self-respect," shouted Tomanski, teetering on a rickety old chair, but maintaining his position above the crowd.

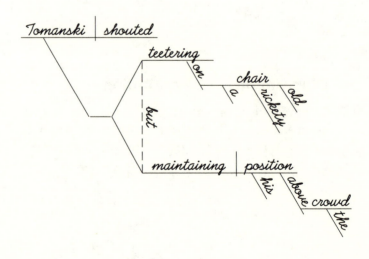

The sentence — structure and diction

Unity in the sentence[1]

K1 Unity means oneness. In composition, unity requires that there be only one main thought and that all the other thoughts and words in a sentence, paragraph, or essay directly or indirectly reinforce the one main thought.

K2 Put into separate sentences ideas that are not plainly related. (Be careful, however, to avoid a choppy style.)

Franklin D. Roosevelt had infantile paralysis and was president when the base at Pearl Harbor was attacked.	There is no relationship between the paralysis and the attack. So put the two ideas into separate sentences.

Franklin D. Roosevelt had infantile paralysis.
Franklin D. Roosevelt was president when the base at Pearl Harbor was attacked.

At the banquet of the Good Neighbor Club the toasts were in Spanish, the rest of the evening being spent in dancing.	There is no relationship between the toasts and the dancing. These two ideas should, therefore, be handled in two separate sentences.

At the banquet of the Good Neighbor Club, the toasts were in Spanish. Once the toasts were over, there was dancing the rest of the evening.

---

[1] For the definition of a sentence and for sentences according to use and structure, see B1-18.

K3 If the sentence does not become unwieldy or cluttered, put into it all ideas that are closely related.

On the second floor, above the chapel, is the library. It contains about a hundred thousand books. It also subscribes to and circulates most of the current periodicals.

Let us suppose that the writer wants to say that there is a large library on the second floor. All of that can be put into one sentence with considerable gain in unity of impression. Below, the fragments are knit together into one clear and unified statement of the facts.

On the second floor, above the chapel, is a library that houses about a hundred thousand books and nearly all the current periodicals.

K4 Do not write rambling, talkative sentences that include too many details.

When the wheezy old Ford had gasped its way up the dirt road of Mohawk Mound and then, with clanks and jolts, had tottered down the other side, through the cool dawn, into the valley through which the Saco Creek flowed, we piled together, beneath a big white oak where the Ford was left, our tent, duffel bags, cooking equipment, radio, fishing rods, and baskets, preparatory to taking a mile-and-a-half hike through thick, thorny underbrush to our camp site on the creek where we were to fish for a long weekend.

Although this sentence is talking about a lot of pleasant things of interest to everyone, the reader learns to hate it before it closes. It contains too many details. It rambles. It becomes a maze, a labyrinth. See how clear it becomes in the next example, where it is broken up into three sentences.

Through the cool dawn the wheezy old Ford gasped its way up the dirt road of Mohawk Mound and then, with clanks and jolts, tottered down the other side into the valley where flowed the Saco Creek. Beneath a big white oak, under which the Ford was left, we piled together our tent, duffel bags, cooking equipment, radio, fishing rods, and baskets. Our camp site on the Creek, where we were to spend a long weekend fishing, was a mile and a half away through thick, thorny underbrush.

K5 Do not write tag-at-the-end sentences.

Summer is the time when the outdoors is most inviting, at least in good weather.	Just when the reader thinks he has the thought clear, the sentence reverses itself a little and confuses him. Give the reader the qualifying *at least* phrase early in the sentence where he is conditioned to expect it.

Summer—at least in good weather—is the time when the outdoors is most inviting.

K6 Write concise sentences. Do this by eliminating needless words and—where it is possible without loss of effectiveness—by reducing clauses to phrases and phrases to words.

[Wordy:] When they were twenty miles into the desert, they thought they saw, on the rise in front of them, a UFO.

[Concise:] Twenty miles into the desert, they thought they saw, on the rise ahead, a UFO.

K7 Save the independent clause of a sentence for the main idea; and do not put two ideas into two independent clauses unless the ideas are of equal or very nearly equal importance.

I entered the room, and Forhan was still sitting and staring at nothing.	Suppose that what Forhan was doing is the one main idea. Turn the first independent

385

clause into something subordinate; say, a dependent modifying clause. That will make the independent clause, *sitting and staring at nothing,* stand out clearly.

When I entered the room, Forhan was still sitting and staring at nothing.

They had not shown much interest in the elephant when he was merely ravaging their homes, but it was different now that he was going to be shot.	The author wants to contrast the crowd's attitude toward the elephant earlier and now. An effective way to do this is to put each idea into an independent clause.

— GEORGE ORWELL,
"SHOOTING AN ELEPHANT"

Coherence in the sentence

K8   Coherence requires that, for the sake of clarity, ideas and words follow one another in an orderly manner and that the connections between parts be made clear.

K9   If there is a reasonable chance that the relationship between ideas and words may be mistaken, the sentence, paragraph, or essay is incoherent.

K10 Coherence in the sentence means that the parts of a sentence—words, phrases, and clauses—are rightly put together.

K11 The principal enemies of coherence in the sentence are dangling, misplaced, and squinting modifiers; unparallel structure for parallel ideas; faulty connectives and connections; and illogical expressions.

Modifiers

K12 Place modifying words, phrases, and clauses as near as you reasonably can to the words which they modify; and do not make use of dangling, misplaced, or squinting modifiers.[2]

[Dangling modifier:] *To sing well,* the diaphragm should be extended.
[Right:] *To sing well,* you must extend your diaphragm.

[Misplaced modifier:] *Orange and crimson,* the poet gazed long at the sunset.
[Right:] The poet gazed long at the *orange and crimson* sunset.

[Squinting modifier:] Pat was notified *on the following day* to register for her classes.
[Right:] *On the following day* Pat was notified to register for her classes.
[Also right, but with different meaning:] Pat was notified to register for her classes *on the following day.*

Parallel Structures

K13 Where you can do so without forcing or awkwardness, express like ideas in like words and like constructions.

Here are like ideas, but they are expressed in unlike words:

Just as Suarez High School is distinguished for its dramatics, so the students of Aquinas High School have become prominent in debating.	Suarez High School
	the students of Aquinas High School
	is distinguished for its dramatics
	have become prominent in debating

---

[2] See C312-20. For adverbs within split infinitives, see C387.

387

Parallel ideas are given parallel expression:

Just as Suarez high School is distinguished for dramatics, so Aquinas High School is distinguished for debating.	Suarez High School Aquinas High School is distinguished for dramatics is distinguished for debating

Just as the students of Suarez High School have become distinguished for dramatics, so the students of Aquinas High School have become distinguished for debating.	the students . . . School the students . . . School have become distinguished for dramatics have become distinguished for debating

K14 Keep sentence parts parallel when they are joined by *and, or, nor, but,* and other coordinating conjunctions.

He was notified that he was needed by the Army and to report for duty.	This sentence is incoherent. For no reason *and* is made to connect a dependent clause with an infinitive phrase. See how much cleaner an impression the sentence makes below where *and* connects two dependent noun clauses.

He was notified that he was needed by the Army and that he should report for duty.

Lupita rode her bicycle not only through the neighborhood but also rode across the bridge.	This sentence is incoherent. *Not only . . . but also* is made to connect *through the neighborhood* and *rode*—a phrase and a predicate verb that are unlike not only in construction but also in thought. The sentence is more coherent below, where the conjunction connects two phrases and ideas that are somewhat alike.

Lupita rode her bicycle not only through the neighborhood but also across the bridge.

For Denis, who had to regain his inn without attracting notice, there was real danger as well as merely feeling uncomfortable in the walk; and he went warily and with boldness at once, and at every corner pausing to make an observation.

This sentence is incoherent and, as a result, somewhat unclear. *As well as* connects the noun *danger* with the gerund phrase *feeling uncomfortable*. It is all right to connect a noun with a noun phrase when there is no noun ready to hand that will carry the thought. But here there is a noun ready to hand, and the reader is vaguely aware of the fact. Again, *and* is made to connect the adverb *warily* with the prepositional phrase *with boldness*. It is not a blunder to connect an adverb with an adverb phrase; but see how the sentence gains in sharp clarity below where two adverbs are used. Lastly, *and* is made to connect the predicate verb *went* with the participle *pausing*; and that is an out-and-out blunder that makes the sentence unpleasant and, to some degree, confusing.

For Denis, who had to regain his inn without attracting notice, there was real danger as well as mere discomfort in the walk; and he went warily and boldly at once, and at every corner paused to make an observation.

—Robert Louis Stevenson,
"The Sire de Malétroit's Door," *New Arabian nights*

389

K15 Do not use *and, or, nor, but,* and other coordinating conjunctions between sentence parts that are not parallel in thought.

I was punished for breaking silence and a cup.	True, *silence* and *cup* are both nouns. But the meaning of *break silence* and the meaning of *break a cup* are so divergent that they should not be connected as they are here. The sentence had better be rephrased as below. (This sort of expression, however, is sometimes justified rhetorically. The figure of speech is called "zeugma.")

I was punished for talking at the wrong time and for breaking a cup.

A man, tall and with a key, came up the stairs and let us in.	*Tall* is an adjective and *with a key* is an adjective phrase, but their meaning is so divergent that they should not be connected as they are here. The sentence had better be rephrased as below.

A tall man came up the stairs and let us in with his key.

Between the silver ribbon of morning and the green glittering ribbon of sea, the boat touched Harwich and let loose a swarm of folk like flies, among whom the man we must follow and who wore a beard was by no means conspicuous—nor wished to be.	[*Whom*] *we must follow* and *who wore a beard* are both adjective clauses, but their meaning is so divergent that they should not be connected as they are here. The connection is not natural. *Bearded man we must follow* would solve the difficulty nicely; or the beard could be saved for a completely separate sentence, as below.

Between the silver ribbon of morning and the green glittering ribbon of sea, the boat touched Harwich and let loose a swarm of folk like flies, among whom the man we must follow was by no means conspicuous — nor wished to be. . . . His lean face was dark . . . and ended in a curt, black beard that looked Spanish and suggested an Elizabethan ruff.

—G. K. Chesterton,
"The Blue Cross," *The Innocence of Father Brown*

K16 Do not shift the subject focus needlessly.

Bravely the little boy spoke to the maid; but, instead of getting a reply, she slammed the door in his face.

The subject focus in the first clause is the boy; in the second it is the maid (*she*). The sentence can be made to read much more smoothly (and, incidentally, the misplaced phrase can be avoided) if the subjects are kept the same.

Bravely the little boy spoke to the maid; but, instead of getting a reply, he saw the door slammed in his face.

He was the sort of man whom anybody could lead on a string to the North Pole; it was not surprising that an actor like Flambeau, dressed as another priest, could lead him to Hampstead Heath.

—G. K. Chesterton,
"The Blue Cross," *The Innocence of Father Brown*

Here the subject focus changes frequently, but with good enough cause. Very awkward constructions and weak passives would result if the subject stayed the same. The sentence is coherent, the subjects are not confusing.

K17 Do not shift voice needlessly.

Killian brought us food and medicines; but, best of all, we were given news of the rescue sleds by him.

The change to passive voice (*were given*) is scarcely necessary or helpful; and the sentence reads very much more

391

smoothly (much more coherently) below, where the active voice is used in both clauses of the sentence and the idea of the first subject is retained throughout.

Killian brought us food and medicines; but, best of all, he gave us news of the rescue sleds.

K18 Do not shift person or number needlessly.

Well, I like history because people interest me; and certainly history provides you with people of every imaginable type and class.	The shift from *I* and *me* to *you* is unnecessary, troublesome, and incoherent. The sentence is a good deal smoother and clearer when it is rewritten in the ways shown below.

[Good:] Well, I like history because people interest me; and certainly history provides me with people of every imaginable type and class.

[Even better:] Well, I like history because I like to analyze people; and in history I certainly find people of every imaginable type and class.

One went in, not as into most shops, in the mood of: "Please serve me, and let me go!" but restfully, as you enter a church; and, sitting on the single wooden chair, waited—for there was never anybody there.	*You* distracts. The sentence is more coherent below.

One went in, not as into most shops, in the mood of: "Please serve me, and let me go!" but restfully, as one enters a church; and, sitting on the single wooden chair, waited—for there was never anybody there.

—JOHN GALSWORTHY,
"QUALITY," *THE INN OF TRANQUILITY*

K19 Do not shift present and past time needlessly.

When at last I find him, Vladinov is very happy to see me, assures me that he can get papers for me and can smuggle me across the border without attracting notice, but wanted more money than he had already been paid.	The writer is using the "vivid present" which is quite all right—a good device if not overworked. But the shift to the past in *wanted* is unnecessary, jarring, distracting—incoherent. Say *wants more money than he has . . .*
He caught hold of a springy young sapling and to it he fastens his hunting knife, with the blade pointing down the trail; with a bit of wild grapevine he tied back the sapling.	The shift to the present in *fastens* is needless and distracting. Richard Connell's sentence, below, is very much better.

He caught hold of a springy young sapling and to it he fastened his hunting knife, with the blade pointing down the trail; with a bit of wild grapevine he tied back the sapling.

—RICHARD CONNELL,
"THE MOST DANGEROUS GAME"

Connectives and Connections

K20 Use connectives that express your meaning precisely.

Andrew is slow, and he leads his class.	*And* hardly expresses the writer's idea plainly; and so there is a chance that the reader may be puzzled or annoyed.
Andrew is slow, but he leads his class.	*But* makes good sense and rules out misunderstanding.
Andrew is slow, and yet he leads his class.	*And yet* makes good sense and rules out misunderstanding.

I always felt a deep sympathy for the students, though I knew only their names; yet none of them was without trials and humiliations.	A faulty connective, *yet*, makes nonsense of an otherwise sensible sentence.
I always felt a deep sympathy for the students, though I knew only their names; for none of them was without trials and humiliations.	*For* makes the last clause the reason for the sympathy and pulls the meaning of the sentence together—makes the sentence coherent.
On the brown face of Velvet Pants there was not the slightest trace of fear, as he was smiling a slight, amused smile.	The meaning of *as* is not clear. Does it mean *while*? Does it perhaps mean *because*? As a matter of fact, neither *while* nor *because* makes perfect sense here. The meaning intended is much clearer in the sentence below.

On the brown face of Velvet Pants there was not the slightest trace of fear; indeed, he was smiling a slight, amused smile.

—RICHARD CONNELL, "THE UNFAMILIAR"

K21 Occasionally *and* can be used without obscurity in the sense of *and yet* or *but*. For example, if a father said to his son, "I never heard of anyone your age camping out alone," the son might reply with perfect clarity, "Joe Bergen is only twelve, and he camps out alone." Ordinarily, however, *and* is not an adequate substitute for *and yet* or *but*.

[Wrong:] The charming old woman spent hours in the gift shop, looking at countless items and checking prices, and she did not purchase a single item.

[Right:] The charming old woman spent hours in the gift shop, looking at countless items and checking prices, and yet she did not purchase a single item.

K22 Do not omit a word that is important to the clear and easy expression of your thought.[3]

They sell crabs at the Fulton Fish Market.	In this sentence *they* does not mean "people in general." It should be either given an antecedent, replaced by a noun, or eliminated altogether as in the construction below.

Crabs are sold at the Fulton Fish Market.

Hurried radio calls were sent out to all state police officers to stop the maroon convertible, but they were too late.	Which were too late, the calls or the police officers? *They* does not say which. The point is of no great consequence in this sentence; yet such little obscurities mark the incoherent—and unread—writer.

Hurried radio calls were sent out to all state policemen to stop the maroon convertible, but the calls were too late.

The elder Legruy seemed eager to get rid but not to pay for my services.	The sense is clear; but an important word has been annoyingly omitted.

The elder Legruy seemed eager to get rid of my services but not to pay for them.

My friend Mrs. Lummy has more fascinating ailments, like rushes of blood to the elbow, than anybody I know.	The sentence is absurd. Since Mrs. Lummy is "my friend" I must know her; yet the sentence says that I do not, since she has more ailments than "anybody I know."

My friend Mrs. Lummy has more fascinating ailments, like rushes of blood to the elbow, than anybody else I know.

---

[3] See C225-28, C262, C287-88, C290-91, C295, C297, C300, C322-23.

K23   Subordinate conjunction *that* is regularly omitted when such omission is not a cause for misreading the sentence or for weakening its effectiveness. The longer the sentence, the more likely *that* should be retained.

She said (that) she was sorry.	*That* may be omitted in this sentence without any loss in meaning or effectiveness.
Mary Ann saw Jimmy, her boyfriend since grade school, would not make the team.	Only upon completion of the sentence does the reader realize that *Jimmy* is not the direct object of *saw* but is rather the subject of the noun clause. In other words, Mary Ann did not *see* Jimmy. Such a misinterpretation could be avoided by inserting *that* before *Jimmy.*

Logical phrasing

K24   Phrase your sentences thoughtfully and logically so that they make sense and can have only one meaning.

Make yourself comfortable until half-past ten, when the moderator will begin his talk.	Grammatically this sentence is quite all right; nonetheless it is incoherent, thoughtlessly phrased. For it may mean simply that one should wait until the speech begins, or it may imply that once the speech begins all comfort will be at an end. As phrased below, the sentence does not insult the moderator.

Since the moderator's talk does not begin until half-past ten, you may as well make yourself comfortable while you are waiting.

The fireplace, which had not yet been lighted, made the room seem colder.

The fact that the fireplace held no fire is pushed into a subordinate nonrestrictive clause. This focuses attention on the independent clause—*the fireplace made the room seem colder.* That idea seems illogical. The sentence below would not puzzle the reader even for a moment.

The cold, black, fireless hearth only made the room seem colder.

The garret windows were opened, and pails were emptied, and there goes a new suit of clothes!

The writer of this became so carried away that he omitted a step or two from his narrative—a step or two that the reader would like to have; namely, that the clothes are on a person in the street below. In the sentence below, Macaulay writes a more coherent, if less lively, sentence.

The garret windows were opened, and pails were emptied, with little regard to those who were passing below.

—THOMAS BABINGTON MACAULEY, *HISTORY OF ENGLAND FROM THE ACCESSION OF JAMES II*

K25 Do not use *first* when no other items follow.

K26 In enumerating items use *first, second, third, fourth,* and so on. You may also use *firstly, secondly, thirdly, fourthly*; but not *first, secondly, thirdly, fourthly.*

K27 Do not use *finally* when other items follow.

K28 Do not use *therefore, consequently,* and so on, when what follows is not even in a wide sense a conclusion from what preceded it. Say *and now* or something of the sort.

Therefore, in conclusion let me say that it has been a pleasure to address such an intelligent and attentive audience.	*Therefore* is wrong here unless the speaker has been arguing to prove that he has enjoyed speaking to this audience— which is hardly likely. *And now* would be much better.

Emphasis in the sentence

K29 Emphasis means relative stress. In writing, emphasis requires that more important thoughts be made to stand out from less important thoughts. Your writing is properly emphatic when your reader knows, without thinking the matter over, which thoughts you consider most important, which less, and which least important.

K30 Regularly use the active voice. Although there is a legitimate use for the passive, the active is more direct and vigorous. Moreover, the passive adds unnecessary words, slows down the writing, and obscures the main actor in the sentence.

[Poor:] You will always be remembered that way by me.
[Good:] I will always remember you that way.
[Proper passive:] Their car was sideswiped by a runaway truck.

K31 Ordinarily put statements in positive form. Although there is a proper use for negative statements, the positive is more direct and usually more meaningful.

[Weak:] If you want to live, don't drive so fast.
[Better:] If you want to live, drive slower.
[Appropriate negative:] Despite everything you say, he is not reliable.

Double negatives should be used sparingly, and then only for effect.

[Poor:] She is not an unlikely candidate.
[Better:] She is a possible candidate.
[Appropriate double negative used by a young scion receiving his inheritance:] This is not an unhappy moment!

K32 Save the independent clause of a sentence for the main idea; and do not put two ideas into two independent clauses unless the ideas are of equal or very nearly equal importance.

I entered the room, and Forhan was still sitting and staring at nothing.

Suppose that what Forhan was doing is the one main idea. Turn the first independent clause into something subordinate; say, a dependent clause for proper emphasis.

When I entered the room, Forhan was still sitting and staring at nothing.

[Wrong:] The computer malfunctioned, and he was very upset.
[Right:] Because the computer malfunctioned, he was very upset.

[Wrong:] Although you should understand that your comments will be counterproductive, you have every reason to criticize.
[Right:] Although you have every reason to criticize, you should understand that your comments will be counterproductive.

[Wrong:] When my new life began, I decided to cooperate with others.
[Right:] When I decided to cooperate with others, my new life began.

One day I believe that he [Shakespeare] would have written it [prose] as well as Dryden, and the next day I begin to fear that he would have produced something as bad as Swinburne. He had the ear, but he lacked the logical sense.

Within each of these two sentences, the ideas are parallel. The author does well to balance them in independent clauses.

—H. L. Mencken,
"The Poet and his Art"

K33   Put emphasis in a sentence by arranging a series in the order of climax: important idea, more important idea, most important idea.

Willard is highly accomplished: he can dance, play Mozart well on the piano, and wiggle his ears.

Unless the writer is striving for humor, this sentence is weak, unemphatic. The sentence below is emphatic—it distributes stress properly, arranging Willard's accomplishments in some sort of ascending scale.

Willard is highly accomplished: he can wiggle his ears, dance, and play Mozart well on the piano.

I came, I saw, I conquered.

This sentence of Julius Caesar's is so handsomely emphatic that, though worn out by frequent quotation and parody, it remains an excellent example of climax.

[Poor:] Simon Legree was blackhearted, cruel, and rude.
[Better:] Simon Legree was rude, cruel, and blackhearted.

K34 Place the main idea in an independent clause at the end of the sentence. (Of course, doing this consistently would result in a monotonous style.)

Looking at the long line to the ticket window and then at his watch, *Jeff reluctantly turned for home.*

When all the books had been shelved and the room restored to order, *Francine locked the library door.*

K35 Use only those words that add to the clarity of the sentence. Conversely, omit needless words.

[Unemphatic:] In a manner of speaking and, indeed, to put the thing plainly and as briefly as possible, the pie is truly and undeniably delicious, Mrs. Crane.

[Emphatic:] Mrs. Crane, the pie is delicious.

[Less emphatic:] Sunlight is poured out even on those who are wicked.

[More emphatic:] The sun shines even on the wicked.

[Emphatic, for every word works:] Especially was he beloved by the pretty girls along the Connecticut, whose favor he used to court by presents of the best smoking tobacco in his stock, knowing well that the country lasses of New England are generally great performers on pipes.

—NATHANIEL HAWTHORNE,
"MR. HIGGINBOTHAM'S CATASTROPHE," *TWICE-TOLD TALES*

Dog bit boy.	This is clear and emphatic enough, but it is unpleasantly curt. The mind dislikes waste, but it does not like poverty of expression. *The dog bit the boy* is much better.

K36   Occasionally, but not regularly, give emphasis to an idea by saying in so many words that it is important.[4]

I have a skillet and a bass to fry in it.	This sentence is clear. It may be made even clearer and more pleasant by the addition of *what is more important.*

I have a skillet and, what is more important, a bass to fry in it.

The house has a tall, narrow stone face pierced only by a door at street level and two eyelike windows under the roof with bars on them.	If the writer intends to make the bars on the windows an important part of his story, he had better emphasize them with two or three underscoring words, as below.

The house had a tall, narrow stone face pierced only by a door at street level and two eyelike windows under the roof with—remarkable fact—bars on them.

K37   Occasionally, but not regularly, give emphasis to a word or an expression by taking it out of its usual place in a sentence or clause and placing it at the beginning or at the end.[5] Take care to do this without awkwardness or loss of clarity.

Go I must and will; stay I cannot.	The usual order of such a sentence is *I must and will go; I cannot stay.* Place *go* and *stay* at the beginning of their clauses and you call attention to them, emphasize them.
To forgive the injury is easy; to forget it may be beyond my power.	Emphasis and sharp contrast are gained by putting *forgive* and *forget* at the beginning of their clauses.

---

[4] See K41.
[5] See K38 and K41.

I am a reasonable person, but this I will not tolerate.

The usual order of such a sentence is *I am a reasonable person, but I will not tolerate this.* Putting the object pronoun *this* before the subject pronoun gives it prominence and emphasis.

Relentlessly the dentist drilled into Blake's tooth.

The usual order is *The dentist drilled relentlessly into Blake's tooth.* Putting *relentlessly* first gives it great prominence and strong emphasis.

Boundless and constant is the mercy of God.

The usual order: *The mercy of God is boundless and constant.*

An excellent athlete and a good scholar is Jonathan.

The usual order: *Jonathan is an excellent athlete and a good scholar.*

There had quietly entered the room a tall, poised, handsome woman—Lady Hitchcock.

The usual order: *A tall, poised, handsome woman, Lady Hitchcock, had quietly entered the room.* Placing the name last gives it prominence.

K38 There is a strong literary flavor about many inverted sentence orders.[6] In very natural, informal, conversational, or matter-of-fact writing, be careful to use only those that do not sound grand—too big for the subject matter, the mood of the piece, or the audience.

K39 Emphasize thoughts by repeating them; but do this only sparingly.

Kroner was hated throughout the ship, hated by the captain, hated by the second mate, and hated especially by

In this sentence, *hated* receives great stress by being repeated four times.

---

[6] See K37.

the crew that he disciplined and worked without mercy.

"You are behaving ridiculously, quite ridiculously," he said with quiet venom.	The repetition implies that the speaker thinks the matter over and still reaches the same verdict. This lends force.
It's useless, useless, I tell you; it's completely useless.	Here the repetition of *useless* makes a very heavy sentence, with a note of despair.
First in war, first in peace, and first in the hearts of his countrymen, he was second to none in the humble and endearing scenes of private life . . .	These are the famous opening words of Henry Lee's funeral oration in honor of George Washington. Here emphasis is achieved by the repetition of the words *first in* three times.
Alone, alone, all, all alone, Alone on a wide, wide sea!	These two lines—an elliptical sentence from "The Ancient Mariner"—contain a multiple repetition.

K40 Particularly after a number of long sentences, a short sentence can be effective in providing variety, emphasis, and (occasionally) finality.

To "come along" meant that he would change his ways and consent to be the husband she had traveled so far to find. It was he who, unforgivably, taught her that there are people in the world for whom "coming along" is a perpetual process, people who are destined never to arrive. For ten years he came along, but when he left her he was the same man she had married. He had not changed at all.

—James Baldwin,
Go Tell It on the Mountain

K41 The devices described in K36-37 and K39 should not be used in sentence after sentence. Ordinarily give your reader time to forget that you have used them before you use them again.

Suspense sentences

K42 Suspense could be defined as a state in which a person does not yet know, but wants to know, and feels that he will get to know. Its effect is to sharpen the importance, the appeal, the impact of the thing that one wants to know.

K43 Occasionally write a rather long sentence in which you do not release the predicate verb or (in the case of a complex sentence) the independent clause until the end or nearly the end of the sentence.

Under the brilliant lights of the marquee, huddling out of the rain after the play and waiting for his Cadillac to draw up to the curb, the fabulous Mr. Endacre was shot and killed.

Notice that you could not place a period at any point in this sentence until after the word *shot*, which occurs near the end. This is a suspense sentence. Compare it with the following sentence, which could be stopped very soon after it is begun and which consequently does not arouse much suspense in the reader.

The fabulous Mr. Endacre was shot and killed under the brilliant lights of the marquee, huddling out of the rain after the play and waiting for his Cadillac to draw up to the curb.

There is no suspense in this sentence. The important information is released in the first six or seven words, before the reader's expectation and desire to know have been aroused. As a result, *the fabulous Mr. Endacre was shot and killed* does not here receive the prominence it does in the previous sentence.

405

K44   A periodic sentence is a very long suspense sentence, usually rather grand and emotional in tone and ordinarily about something important.

> To bring under one yoke, after the manner of old Rome, a hundred discordant peoples; to maintain each of them in its own privileges within its legitimate range of action; to allow them severally the indulgence of national feelings, and the stimulus of rival interests; and yet withal to blend them into one great social establishment, and to pledge them to the perpetuity of the one imperial power; —this is an achievement which carries with it the unequivocal token of genius in the race which effects it.
>
> —JOHN HENRY NEWMAN, *THE IDEA OF A UNIVERSITY*

K45   A semisuspense sentence is a sentence that employs a suspense structure for a good part of the sentence and then adds further remarks. Semisuspense sentences are very useful.

Near the mouth of the stream, at the foot of the cliff on Mount Durion, Jud the Trapper held his strange school, where Jason spent ten years learning to wrestle, to box, to hunt, to play the fiddle, and to make the great pharmacy of the woods yield him its medicines to cure his hurts.	Suspense construction is used down through *strange school.*

K46   To get suspense in the structure of a sentence—

A. Begin with modifiers—adjectives, adverbs, adjective and adverb phrases and clauses—or noun clauses.

On the twelfth day of the search, near the head of the lake, in a kind of hollow well screened from the shore by a growth of spruce, the	Adjective and adverb phrases.

McAllisters found the remains of a fire, and a message, still clear, scrawled in the dirt.

Whenever I find myself growing grim about the mouth; whenever it is a damp, drizzly November in my soul; whenever I find myself involuntarily pausing before coffin warehouses and bringing up the rear of every funeral I meet; and especially whenever my temper gets such an upper hand of me that it requires a strong moral principle to prevent me from deliberately stepping into the street and methodically knocking people's hats off—then I account it high time to get to sea as soon as I can.

—HERMAN MELVILLE, ADAPTED FROM *MOBY DICK*

If skillfully written, dependent clauses (adverb, adjective, and noun) can hold off the point of a sentence quite awhile. It is possible to pile up a good number of them before releasing the independent clause. Some of the independent clauses themselves can be rather long, provided that they remain clear. In this selection the adverbial *whenever* clauses and the other dependent clauses that they contain postpone the release of the independent clause until considerable suspense has been built up.

B. Begin with an accumulation of subject nouns (and noun phrases or clauses) with or without modifiers.

The chair facing the door, the kettle steaming on the stove, the cups and silver laid ready, the bread with two slices already cut and lying at the end of the loaf, the newspaper on the table— everything in the room seemed to be waiting, waiting—but not for me.

That a child of five should be lecturing their guest on geopolitics, that one of the adults of the family should be cutting out little dolls of paper and putting them to sleep with songs, that the ice cream should be kept in the oven, the car on the porch, the chickens in the master bedroom, and the guest of honor in the garage didn't seem at all strange to the strange McSwivverns.

C. Begin with nominative absolutes.

The greatest prudes often being the greatest hypocrites and Fowler clearly being a great prude, it is little wonder that he gave everyone about him the devil of an itch to prick the outer bubble of his pietism and disclose his fraud.

D. Begin with direct objects.

The England that he loved so much, the England that had hunted him and tried its best to break his body on the rack, the England where a handful of Catholics stood firm in the sea of scorn and danger that lapped them round, the England that was home—that England Father Gerard would never see again.

E. Put modifiers or appositives between the subject noun and the predicate verb.

And this corrupt politician, petty, in love with the dollar, faithless to every trust that has ever been given him, is now to decide what shall be law and what shall not?

A woman, a stranger to me but very affable, really charming, who said she was an old friend of yours from your days at Wallace High, borrowed your car.

K47 A loose sentence is the opposite of a suspense sentence. It is a sentence of some length that could be stopped by a period a good deal before its end. (There are border-line sentences which might be described as either loose or suspense sentences.)

The fabulous Mr. Endacre was shot / and killed / under the brilliant lights of the marquee, / huddling out of the rain / after the play / and waiting for his Cadillac / to draw up to the curb.	The sentence at left could be stopped by a period at any of the points indicated by the division lines. It is clearly a loose sentence.
Whenever there is time, I stop at Mrs. Welker's / on my way home / to exchange news /	This is predominantly a loose sentence, but the adverbial clause lends just enough sus-

K

with her / and to find out how her arthritis is treating her.

pense to make it a troublesome borderline case.

K48 A loose sentence is not inferior to a suspense sentence and may be every bit as soundly and as artfully constructed. The loose sentence is the backbone of most writing. (But see K49.)

K49 Avoid a series of loose sentences. Such writing becomes monotonous. Solutions include interjecting an occasional short and simple sentence, a suspense or periodic sentence, or a compound sentence with clauses joined by a semicolon.

Sentence development

K50 Two qualities, chiefly, make a style adult: clearness and variety. Provided one's thought is clear, one's writing will also be clear if it has unity, coherence, and emphasis (see K1-39). The following rules will help toward variety.

K51 Put variety into your writing by carefully mixing sentence patterns. Do not always write sentences of the same length and kind. Study K40-48, K52-61.

Combining sentences

K52 When sentences or independent clauses fall into a monotonous pattern because of uniform length and structure, the pattern can often be broken by combining some of the sentences or independent clauses according to the rules that follow.

K53 When two or more dull sentences or clauses have predicates that are identical or nearly identical in thought, combine them into one sentence or clause by using a compound subject.

The Williamses have people over from the city every weekend. The Carbanks have

None of the sentences at left is bad in itself. But the first four work the same pattern

people over too. But Dad says we come to Florida to get away from people. Mother agrees with him. It's all very difficult for a nineteen-year-old daughter who must see men if she is to marry one some day.

to death for no reason. They are all short and choppy in rhythm. The brevity and choppiness do not echo the thought or serve any other purpose. In the next version below, a compound subject combines the first two sentences nicely and breaks up the monotony. (The second and third sentences also could easily be combined if it seemed desirable.)

The Williamses and the Carbanks have people over from the city every weekend. But Dad says we come to Florida to get away from people. Mother agrees with him. It's all very difficult for a nineteen-year-old daughter who must see men if she is to marry one some day.

K54 When two or more dull sentences or clauses have subjects that are identical or nearly identical in thought, combine them into one sentence or clause by using a compound predicate.

Fowler was hesitant. He was indecisive. He was afraid to talk in public. But he was very intelligent. Clark was aggressive. He always knew what he wanted. He loved an audience. But he was not precisely a thinker. The two men were born partners.

There is no reason for releasing the thought to readers in these driblets or for wearying them with so many sentences of the same length. By combining predicates, in the version below, the writer produces a pleasant arrangement of two long sentences and one short one.

Fowler was hesitant, indecisive, afraid to talk in public, but very intelligent. Clark was aggressive, always knew what he wanted, loved an audience, but was not precisely a thinker. The two men were born partners.

K55 When one dull sentence explains a noun or pronoun in another dull sentence, turn the explanatory sentence into an appositive. (Use the same technique with dull independent clauses.)

Everyone else was happy. Everyone else had friends. But nobody noticed Benito. He was a hungry dreamer and a jailbird.

These sentences are so nearly uniform that monotony develops by the end of the passage. Turn the last sentence into an appositive.

Everyone else was happy. Everyone else had friends. But nobody noticed Benito—hungry dreamer and jailbird.

The boss of any business worries a lot. He feels it his duty to worry. No one can help him. But I heard a strange rumor today. There is a new machine to do his worrying for him.

An appositive noun clause can break the monotonous pattern at left.

The boss of any business worries a lot. He feels it his duty to worry. No one can help him. But today I heard the strange rumor that there is a new machine to do his worrying for him.

K56 Combine two or more dull sentences or independent clauses by means of the expletive[7] construction.

[Monotonous:] You have made up your mind. This is obvious. You are going to sing. No one can stop you. But the band will not play.

[Better:] It is obvious that you have made up your mind to sing. No one can stop you. But the band will not play.

---

[7] The expletives are the words *it* and *there* standing in place of the real subject. See A129.

K57 Combine two or more dull sentences or independent clauses by turning the less important into a nominative absolute.[8]

[Monotonous:] The Ferrari skidded up to the barrier. Its horn was blaring, and its tires were screaming. The driver jumped out.

[Better:] Horn blaring and tires screaming, the Ferrari skidded up to the barrier. The driver jumped out.

K58 Do not put the more important of two thoughts in a nominative absolute. The nominative absolute is a humble frame suitable only to secondary thoughts.

K59 It takes a trained eye and ear to discriminate between an awkward nominative absolute and one that is at home in its sentence. So (a) use nominative absolutes sparingly; (b) read your sentences aloud to detect awkward sound or rhythm; and (c) note, when you read good authors, how they use nominative absolutes effectively.

K60 If one of a series of dull sentences or independent clauses tells when, where, how, or why, turn it into an adverb, an adverb phrase, or an adverb clause.[9]

[Monotonous:] One moment we were all standing around the skunk. It happened suddenly. The skunk was alone.

[Better:] One moment we were all standing around the skunk. Suddenly the skunk was alone.

[Monotonous:] The infantry had a difficult time. They crawled through Huertgen's mud and mines. They crawled for endless, slow, and costly miles.

[Better:] The infantry had a difficult time. For endless, slow, and costly miles, they crawled through Huertgen's mud and mines.

---

[8] See K58-59.

[9] Subordinate only secondary thoughts in this way. Unity and emphasis require that, as far as possible, the independent clause or the subject noun and predicate verb of a simple sentence be reserved for the more important idea.

[Monotonous:] Tucker was timid, and he was reluctant. Somehow he got himself up on the stage.

[Better:] Though Tucker was timid and reluctant, he somehow got himself up on the stage.

K61   Sometimes one or more of a series of dull sentences or independent clauses can be turned into an adjective, an adjective phrase, or an adjective clause.[10]

[Monotonous:] Toward the northeast, at daybreak, loomed Gibraltar. It was large. It was grand and gray.

There could be a reason in some contexts for breaking up the thought into such tiny fragments; for example, humor. But ordinarily such a pattern is irritating.

[Better:] Toward the northeast, at daybreak, loomed Gibraltar, large, grand, and gray.

[Monotonous:] This is an account of Mrs. Wendell Morgan. She is an elderly woman. She is known familiarly to all of lower Howard Avenue. She is of frowzy appearance, vague manner, and undiscerning look.

[Better:] This is an account of Mrs. Wendell Morgan. Elderly, of frowzy appearance, vague manner, and undiscerning look, she is known familiarly to all of lower Howard Avenue.

[Monotonous:] In my henhouse are two jumpy hens. At the slightest disturbance they panic the rest of the flock. Last night this proved fortunate. It saved my hens.

[Better:] In my henhouse are two jumpy hens that, at the slightest disturbance, panic the rest of the flock. Last night this proved fortunate. It saved my hens.

K62   In order to avoid monotony, develop the main ideas of sentences in a variety of ways—by enumeration, by giving

---

[10] Subordinate only secondary thoughts in this way. Unity and emphasis require that, as far as possible, the independent clause or the subject noun and predicate verb of a simple sentence be reserved for the more important idea.

circumstances, by comparison and contrast, by giving causes and effects, by giving examples, and by repetition. Study K63-74.

Enumeration in the sentence

K63   Develop a sentence thought by dividing an idea in the subject or predicate into its parts.

[Thought:] Irving Berlin wrote some enduring popular music.

| [Development:] Irving Berlin, master of melody and creator of pleasing rhythms, wrote some enduring popular music. | The idea in the subject, Irving Berlin, is divided into parts, broken up into several notions that come to mind when one says "Irving Berlin." |

[Thought:] Irving Berlin wrote some enduring popular music.

| [Development:] Irving Berlin wrote some enduring popular music: "God Bless America," "White Christmas," and "Easter Parade." | An idea in the predicate, enduring popular music, is divided into parts, into a list of titles—broken up into what comes to mind when one says "enduring popular music." |

[Thought:] I shan't easily forget that time aboard the *Nanette*.

| [Development:] I shan't easily forget that time aboard the *Nanette*, when we ran for a glorious week before a spanking breeze, when the days where gold and blue and white, when the stars at night lay in the sky like diamonds bedded lightly in soot, and when, in shocking contrast, I lived in constant, nauseating terror of Captain Twilliger's great, hard fists. | An idea in the predicate, "that time," is divided into parts, sliced into the several concrete, individual things that made up the time spent aboard the *Nanette*. |

Circumstances in the sentence

K64 Develop a sentence thought by giving the circumstances related to it—by answering the question *when, where, how, or why is this?*

[Thought:] Be ready to come in the morning.

[Development:] Be ready to come in the morning, whenever you get the signal from Carlita.	The adverb clause answers the question *When in the morning?*

[Thought:] I'm afraid Tarky doesn't like me.

[Development:] I'm afraid Tarky doesn't like me, for I caught him in my closet putting ants and a caramel into the pocket of my jeans.	The independent clause introduced by *for* answers the questions *Why am I afraid?*

Comparison and contrast in the sentence

K65 Comparison consists in bringing out points of similarity between two or more things.

K66 Contrast consists in bringing out points of dissimilarity between two or more things.

K67 A contrast may be made only between things in which there are also some points of similarity obvious to the reader. It would be silly to say "Joe is not like the letter *r*," since the reader does not expect Joe to be like the letter *r*. But it is quite all right to say "Joe is not like Jim" because the reader knows that Joe is like Jim in many ways.

K68 In nontechnical talk the word *comparison* is frequently used to include contrast and to mean the showing of points of dissimilarity as well as similarity between two or more things.

K69   Develop a sentence thought by using comparison, contrast, or both.

[Thought:] Hugh Bright is a flashy dresser.

[Development:] Hugh Bright is a flashy dresser, who, with his green hats, lemon ties, purple shirts, and fancy oxfords, looks like something out of a technicolor nightmare.	Hugh Bright is compared to something out of a technicolor nightmare.

[Thought:] Joe Frazer was a fighter, not a boxer.

[Development:] Joe Frazer was a fighter, not a boxer, who asked only to stand toe-to-toe and slug—unlike Mohammed Ali, who, by footwork, by strategy, and by tactical retreat, gained time to study and to wear down his adversary.	Joe Frazer is contrasted with Mohammed Ali.

[Thought:] The ricksha is an oriental vehicle.

[Development:] The ricksha is an oriental vehicle that resembles a wheelchair, though, unlike a wheelchair, it has shafts like a carriage, with a man instead of a horse between them.	The ricksha is both compared to, and contrasted with, first a wheel chair and then a horse-drawn carriage.

Cause and effect in the sentence

K70   Develop a sentence thought by stating some of the causes of, or reasons for, the truth or event in the sentence.

[Thought:] The place was called Township—a confusing name.

[Development:] The place was called Township—a confusing name—not because anyone thought the word useful or musical, but because an Alvin J. Township, lumber-

The original thought is developed by dismissing one reason for the rather odd name and giving another.

man, had built most of its public buildings out of his profits and had desired to stamp his generosity with his trademark.

K71 Develop a sentence thought by stating some of the effects or consequences of the truth or event in the sentence.

[Thought:] A great tree on the bank suddenly tottered and crashed to earth.

[Development:] A great tree on the bank suddenly tottered and crashed to earth, shattering the night quiet, with the result that Mack, startled, lurched heavily away from the noise, overbalancing the canoe and sending us, our clothes, provisions, guns, and the tent into the black, icy river.

The effects of the crash—the shattering of the quiet, the tipping of the canoe, the loss of the baggage, and the icy plunge—are used to build a very nice sentence.

Examples in the sentence

K72 Develop a sentence thought by giving particular instances or concrete examples of the general or abstract truth in the sentence.

[Thought:] People are always eager to blind themselves to what is unpleasant.

[Development:] People are always eager to blind themselves to what is unpleasant; for example, after World War II, Americans put on

The general notion *people* is made particular and concrete by the example of Americans in the development, and the eagerness to blind themselves

417

rose-colored glasses to look at Russia and cried, "What a friendly democracy she is."

to unpleasant things is reduced to a particular example of what Americans did once World War II was safely concluded.

K73 It is not always necessary to use an expression like *for example* or *for instance* when developing a thought by giving examples.

Repetition in the sentence

K74 Develop a sentence topic by repeating an idea in the subject or predicate in different words and with greater clarity or force.

[Thought:] Paul Adams was no sycophant.

[Development:] Paul Adams was no sycophant, not the sort to trail behind campus playboys, waiting his chance to pat them on the back, nor the sort to flatter their feeble wit with loud guffaws.

An idea in the predicate, sycophant, is repeated in a descriptive definition that to most readers will be clearer than the word itself.

Selecting words and phrases

The right word

K75 Use the right word or expression. This general rule is made practical in the following particular rules.

K76 Use words and expressions clear to the intended audience.

It is my pleasant privilege to announce that on the imminent anniversary of the signing of that document by which our great nation threw off the yoke of a tyrannical mother country there will be a great

This speech, bad writing in itself, is hopelessly worded if it is intended for pupils in the fifth grade. But they could understand the version below without any difficulty.

pyrotechnical display in the vicinity of Moore's Wharf on Back Bay about eight-thirty in the evening. Billets admitting you to this extravaganza go at the ridiculously low tariff of fifty cents each. But before I enter into commerce with you for the sale of these admissions to volcanic wonders, I must have the solemn pledge of this assembly of splendid little potential citizens of our commonwealth that not one of you will attempt to break through the cordon surrounding those who will activate the instruments of the display, but that you will all content yourselves with the role of spectator. Ladies and gentlemen, will you gage me your honor for that?

I'm happy to tell you that on the Fourth of July there will be a big fireworks display near Moore's Wharf on Back Bay about 8:30 P.M. Tickets to see the fireworks cost only fifty cents. But before I sell you any tickets, all of you must promise that you will not try to go beyond the lines and get close to those who will be shooting off the fireworks, but will stand and watch where you are supposed to. Do you promise?

K77 When you cannot tell, except in a general way, who your audience will be, keep K78-90.

K78 Ordinarily use words currently in common use. (This requires a good deal of reading and listening; otherwise you will not know what words are in common use.)

[Doubtful:] It is a parlous journey to cross this sea.
[Better:] It is a perilous journey to cross this sea.

[Doubtful:] He was perforce working two jobs to support his family.
[Better:]He was by necessity working two jobs to support his family.

K79 Ordinarily, when you use an uncommon word, make sure that other words around it can carry the main sense without it.

You will learn to add color and life to your essays, sparkle and verve.

Even if *verve* is not understood, the other words make the main meaning of the sentence clear.

K80   Unless you have good reason for using them, avoid foreign words and phrases and those words that good dictionaries label "archaic," "obsolete," "rare," "especially British," "dialect," and so on.[11]

K81   There is good reason to use the words and phrases discussed in K80 if you cannot express the thought adequately or accurately without them. Do not use them to show off.

K82   Use words or expressions suitable to the kind of composition you are writing: words which convey the mood and atmosphere you wish to create and which are proper to your particular purpose and for your particular readers.[12]

K83   Without good reason, do not change language levels.

A. Formal Level. Formal diction uses language familiar to an educated audience and manifests learning and precision. In formal language one would use *purchase* rather than *get, intelligent* rather than *smart, demonstrate* rather than *show.*

1. Technical language is a type of formal language frequently found in official documents or reports in specialized fields. Some typical vocabulary: *divestiture* (economics), *file menu* (computer technology), *flagellum* (biology), *hypostasis* (medicine).

2. Gobbledygook, formal language gone awry, is inflated bureaucratic language. It tends to be abstract, indirect, pompous, verbose. It uses such expressions as *terminate* rather than *end, at this point in time* rather than *now, vertical-transportation-corps member* rather than *elevator operator, energetic disassembly* rather than *explosion.*

---

[11] See K81. For the use of slang, see K88-89.
[12] See K84-94 and M33.

B. Informal Level. This is the language of ordinary conversation. *Get* and *smart* are examples of informal words. This level of language also includes colloquialisms, regionalisms, and slang.

1. Colloquialisms include contractions *(isn't)*, clipped forms *(pro* for *professional)*, combined verb forms *(check it out)*, and generally loose or imprecise expressions like *sort of, funny* (strange).

2. Regionalisms are words and expressions peculiar to a particular geographic area. A *paper bag* is a *paper sack* in eastern states. *Kerosene* is *coal oil* in eastern Pennsylvania and Virginia. In the South *string beans* are *snap bean*s and *to carry* is *to tote.*

3. Slang words are very informal language. Some examples are *wheels* for *car, bummer* for *bad experience,* and *bucks* fo*r money.*

C. Nonstandard level. These words fall below all levels of acceptable English. They are usually ungrammatical; for example, *hisself, nowheres.*

K84   In formal compositions[13] ordinarily avoid colloquial words and expressions; that is, words marked "colloquial" in the dictionary or expressions characteristic only of rather informal conversation. Also avoid contractions.

We the people of the United States, in order to fix up the rather sloppy union we have	The style of the paragraphs at left would be ill suited to the Constitution of the

---

[13] Formal compositions are those that, by reason of the subject matter, the occasion, the audience, or something of the kind, should be somewhat impersonal and rather dignified. Such are term papers; constitutions of organizations; speeches on formal occasions (valedictories, for example); impersonal reports, essays, and so on; ordinary business letters; letters to officials; letters of congratulations, acceptance, or condolence written to other than intimate friends.

had up to now, to make sure that everybody gets what's coming to him, that nobody gets funny at home, that we United States, of which they are a parody.

won't be a pushover for a foreign enemy, that people get their big needs taken care of, and that we and our kids have a generous slice of freedom, do here set up this Constitution of the United States.

Section 1. When it comes to making laws, well, we'll just let Congress handle that.

Ladies and gentlemen, *we cannot* [not *can't*] finance essential services without an increase in taxes.

K85   It is not contrary to the principle of K84 to include in formal compositions direct quotations which contain colloquialisms, provided, of course, that the quotations further your purpose.

K86   In informal compositions, use colloquial words and expressions where they best achieve your purpose— best carry the meaning, best establish the right mood and atmosphere, characterize a person or express an idea economically and vividly.[14]

The fact is, Jack was making a general nuisance of himself. So much so that Sheriff Bannock Burns, an advocate of stern and, always, singular justice, began picking vigilantes. Sheriff Burns had been around quite awhile. He was observant and pretty tolerant for a lawman. He had to be.

This quotation from a high school student's composition uses colloquialisms to advantage, for it indirectly produces the atmosphere proper to a western by means of typically informal language.

---

[14] Good English varies according to the occasion in the same way that clothing varies according to the occasion. Just as formal wear is appropriate for a prom but not for a soccer game, so shorts and tee shirt are fine for softball but not for a wedding.

He knew the countryside well. He knew when somebody's yearlings got into the wrong corral, or why a local was suddenly—and unexplainedly—well to do.

K87   Great care is needed in the selection of colloquialisms. They must not clash with the rest of the composition, with the mood, with the occasion, and so on. For example, the colloquial *ain't* might mar a good newspaper account of a basketball game, whereas the colloquial *swell* might be quite in order.

K88   Even in informal compositions use slang only sparingly and judiciously; when, that is, nothing else will accomplish your purpose as well.[15]

K89   Most new slang gets old quickly, and much of it dies altogether in a rather short time. Accordingly it is a good idea, generally, to avoid new slang fads even when they seem to serve your purpose. There are, moreover, degrees of respectability in slang.

K90   Ordinarily do not use a big word or a sonorous, high-sounding expression where a little word or an unpretentious expression will say the same thing as clearly, movingly, and economically.

[Ordinarily poor:] Decapitate the miscreant.
[Ordinarily better:] Cut the scoundrel's head off.

K91   Avoid exclusive gender words whenever it is appropriate to do so, provided there is no resultant awkwardness or loss of meaning.

[Gender oriented:] A person should always try to do *his* best.
[Better:] Individuals should always try to do *their* best.

[Gender oriented:] They had to *man* the pumps all night.
[Better:] They had to *work* the pumps all night.

---

[15] Slang is very informal language that is characteristically more metaphorical and short-lived than ordinary language. See K83.

[Gender oriented:] Elizabeth Barrett Browning is an outstanding *poetess.*

[Preferred:] Elizabeth Barrett Browning is an outstanding *poet.*

K92 Use the accurate word or expression.[16]

For example, do not say "The scene was gorgeous," if there was nothing magnificent or resplendently beautiful about it. Content yourself with something like "The countryside was very pretty." Do not say "Then a marvelous thing happened," if the reader is going to discover that you really should have said "Then a surprising thing happened."

K93 The accuracy required by K92 is literary, not scientific. Scientific accuracy is ordinarily out of place except in scientific writing.

[Poor:] Tomlin was of average size, weighing about 160 pounds, standing 5 feet 10, and having a waistline of 32 inches.

[Better:] Tomlin was of average size, reasonably tall and slender, but not remarkably so.

K94 Choose words with appropriate connotation for your purpose.

The denotation of a word is its dictionary meaning. The connotation of a word is all the associations and emotional baggage the word brings with it. *Red,* for example, may have various connotations: warmth, danger, socialism. A word's connotation becomes clear from context.

The *red* glow of the fire was comforting.
His hand was swollen and flaming *red.*

That *gang* is constantly in trouble with the police.
Our *gang* always had great times together.

We were eagerly awaiting an *old-fashioned* barbecue.
There are few activities more discouraging than preparing a festive dinner on an *old-fashioned* stove.

---

[16] See K93.

The connotations of words can change the slant of an entire passage. Notice the differing implications in these pairs of italicized words:

> *diplomatic* or *evasive* procedure
> *high-spirited* or *roughneck* activity
> *backward* or *undeveloped* country
> *orderly* or *fussy* person
> *smell* or *scent* of clothes
> *departure* or *deviation* from custom

The concrete and the particular word

K95 A concrete word or expression presents persons and things as they really are through a direct appeal to one or more of the five senses. An abstract word or expression presents persons and things stripped down to a bare idea, without sense appeal.

Abstract	*Concrete*
God created *life.*	God created *you.*
Age complains.	An *elderly spinster* complains.
Paul wanted *wealth.*	Paul wanted *a big bank balance, an estate, a fleet of Cadillacs, and a yacht.*
Justice must prevail.	Ward Riley must get back his stolen money.
Improvement results from practice.	With a lot of practice, you can correct that slice.
Misfortune struck her down.	Judy lost her job, her apartment, and her savings.
A lengthy period of inclement weather set in.	It rained for a week.
Life has its ironies.	The guard was shot by a police officer.

K96   A particular word or expression calls to mind only one idea—or, at least, fewer ideas than a more general word or expression would. A general word or expression is one that could call to mind a number of ideas.

General	*Particular*
The man brought home a dog.	*Uncle Henry* brought home a dog.
People are waiting for you down in the drawing room.	*Janet and the electrician* are waiting for you down in the drawing room.
Stalin was *ruthless*.	To get his way, Stalin *starved two million people*.
A *dog* makes a good and faithful companion.	An *Airedale* makes a good and faithful companion.
The *noise* startled her.	The *gunshot* startled her.

K97   Make liberal use of concrete and particular words and expressions.[17]

K98   Concrete and particular expressions are not better than abstract or general ones for every purpose. The latter, while less vivid, have their important uses. Use abstract or general terms—

A. To save words.

B. For precise statements of principle or definition.

C. To phrase brief, clear topic statements that will be made more concrete or particular in the development.

---

[17] See K98. Some words, while they are not actually abstract, have what has been called "the smell of abstraction." Technically, the italicized words in these sentences are both concrete: "*God* has been good to me"; "*The Deity* has been good to me." But *the Deity* brings with it a faint air of the abstract word *deity* (without the article) and hence lacks the vividness of the word *God*.

D. In summaries of matter that has been or will be treated concretely and particularly.

E. To avoid loading a paragraph with too much detail.

F. To relieve too much concreteness and particularity.

The manner of telling

In general

K99 The ordinary way to tell a thing is to say it straight out. Most of your writing should be like that. To go in for too many expressions is to weaken your style and rob it of sincerity. On the other hand, although people admire what is solid and plain, they do not like too much of it. It is therefore necessary to vary plain talk with the little turns that bring pleasure if they are not used awkwardly or too often.

Here's this nice healthy kid, comfortable with his peers and parents, as unconcerned about his looks as a bulldog, his awareness focused completely outside himself. Then, literally overnight, these subversive distilleries in his body start shooting out all kinds of magic potions—like a werewolf at full moon. His limbs elongate and go gangly and ungovernable; his face gets fuzzy and knobby; and a lot of vulpine urges start whispering in hitherto unsuspected cellars of his soul. Heaven gets blasted to hell. He's always been able to get his arms and legs to do what he wanted them to do; his voice never played such humiliating tricks on him; and other parts of his body seem to have willfully independent minds of their own, too. If the boy's parents think they've spawned an alien changeling, how do they think the boy himself feels?

—WILLIAM O'MALLEY, S.J.,
"FATHERING AN ADOLESCENT BOY"

Figures of speech

K100   A figure of speech is a change from the ordinary manner of expression, a change used for effect.

K101   A simile is a comparison between things that are in general unlike, using *like, as,* or other comparative words. More briefly, a simile is an express comparison between unlike things.[18]

Thérèse has large, dark eyes.	This is a plain statement.
Thérèse's eyes are like the night itself, large and dark and full of soft mystery.	This is a simile. Eyes are compared to night in some points in which they are alike. Eyes on the whole are very unlike night (in fact the two differ entirely in nature, which is usually the case with the terms of a simile). The comparison is made with a comparative word—*like.*

K102   A simile may be short or long.

For example, many of Christ's parables are long similes; some, for instance, that begin, "The kingdom of heaven is like . . ."

K103   A simile may be negative.

Tracy could no more have written this note than a snake can cross its legs.

To put the matter gently and to avoid bruising your feelings—in my opinion this daub of yours resembles a painting about as much as a ten-watt bulb resembles a sunset.

The idea dawned on him very slowly, certainly not like a flash of light.

---

[18] The comparison must be made between things that are in general unlike, or there is no figure of speech. For example, "Mary is as tall as Katherine" is not a figure of speech but an ordinary comparison.

K104 The comparison in a simile should be better known to the reader, easier to see, or more appealing to the imagination than a plain statement of the thought.

He was as timid as a rabbit during the hunting season.	This is a good simile. It is probably more vivid and less vague than the plain statement of the fact that "He was timid."
Her eyes were like chrysolite.	Too few people know what chrysolite looks like. Unless written for mineralogists, this simile is of little value.

K105 Similes are often awkward or too obvious. In such cases, use a metaphor.

[Awkward simile:] We could not hear above the wind, which was like a wild orchestra.

[Better:] We could not hear above the wild symphony of the wind.

K106 A metaphor is a comparison between things that are in general unlike, without the use of *as, like,* or other comparative words. More briefly, a metaphor is an implied comparison between unlike things.[19]

The night is in Thérèse's eyes, large and dark and full of soft mystery.[20]

You see, Michael's trouble is that he is a turtle. Whenever he sees the shadow of something that might be unpleasant, he quickly withdraws into his shell and holds himself close in nervous tension until pretty certain that the danger is past. In that way, it is true, he escapes a lot of the annoyances that

---

[19] Like the simile (K104), the metaphor should be better known, easier to see, or more appealing to the imagination than a plain statement.
[20] Compare this with the example of a simile under K101.

plague other people; but he has more fears. Worst of all, he misses so much of the life he might enjoy if only he stuck his neck out a little more frequently. And it is ironic that, despite all his efforts to protect himself from harsh realities, he is almost fated to share the doom of turtles: to be stepped on, crushed, or tossed into the soup. For even turtles cannot protect themselves from big things. They can only take what is in store for them—take it like turtles. It's a pity that Michael is not less of a turtle and more of a man.

K107 Although similes and metaphors are at bottom the same, not every simile can readily be turned into a metaphor.

K108 Personification is a particular kind of metaphor. It is a figure of speech that gives the qualities or actions of persons to abstractions and other things that are not persons.

History is not kind to conservative people.	History is treated as a person, since only persons can be kind in the strict sense.

Fear lived with us in that house. It stared at us from the mirror in the morning. It gripped our throats when we tried to eat. It sat by our beds and caressed us with icy fingers when we tried to sleep.

K109 Balance or parallelism is a rhetorical figure of speech used regularly to highlight similar ideas. Ordinarily use like structures for like thoughts.[21]

Let every nation know, whether it wishes us well or ill, that we shall pay any price, bear any burden, meet any hardship, support any friend, oppose any foe to assure the survival and success of liberty.

—JOHN F. KENNEDY,
"INAUGURAL ADDRESS"

---

[21] See K13-19.

430

K110 When parallel structure becomes lengthy, it is often advisable to break it in order to avoid monotony. The break is usually, though not always, most effective if placed near the end.

> Cissie was upstairs on the sleeping porch, and she heard nothing. David was drying dishes with Kathy in the kitchen, and they heard nothing. Mother was ironing in the basement, and she heard nothing. Aunt Sylvia was listening to a television show; and [break] whatever she heard, it was certainly not the howl of a jaguar.

K111 Antithesis is a particular form of balance or parallelism. It is a figure of speech in which opposed ideas are balanced and placed next to each other or in parallel positions.

> That isn't the truth; it's a lie.

> You seem so wise, and yet how foolish you are.

> Brake inspection may cost you one hour; an accident may cost you one life.

> We thought him honest; he is deceitful. We thought him wise; he is only shrewd. We thought his own people esteemed him; they despise him. We thought he loved us; he hates us.

K112 Antithesis is usually a very forceful, very striking figure. Do not use too much of it.

K113 Climax is a rhetorical figure of speech in which thoughts are arranged in ascending order of importance, interest, or effectiveness for a particular audience. Sentences, paragraphs, and entire compositions can be arranged in climactic order; so also words.[22]

> I came, I saw, I conquered.

> Think what you want, say what you want, but do what I tell you.

---

[22]See K33, L28-29, and M76.

K114 Anticlimax is a rhetorical figure of speech in which, for purposes of humor or scorn, climax is observed up to the end of a series of thoughts which appear to be building to something important and then some unimportant idea is mentioned in the last, most important position.

If you want to understand Daglesby's influence in the school, you must remember that he is no ordinary man made up, like you and me, of a soul, two arms, two legs, and so forth. You must realize that he belongs to a race apart, to the golden boys who represent the best that America can produce. You must weigh the fact that he is one of the demigods, a little larger than life and the dream come true of every man in the country. You must learn to accept this tremendous truth—he is a successful football player.

> Here thou, great Anna, whom three realms obey,
> Dost sometimes counsel take—and sometimes tea.[23]

—ALEXANDER POPE,
"THE RAPE OF THE LOCK," iii, 8

K115 Irony is a figure of speech in which one thing is said while obviously the opposite is meant.

[Said to a man riding an ancient, spiritless hack, incapable of more than a painful walk:] Think you'll be able to bust that bronc?

K116 Irony may be gentle or cutting. When it is cutting, it is called sarcasm.

[Said to a bouncy partner at a dance:] I like to dance with you; but then when I was a little girl, I liked to seesaw, too.

[Said of England's most bloody executioner:] Gentle Topcliff!

---

[23] "Anna" is Queen Anne of England, reigning when this poem was written. *Tea* is pronounced *tay*.

K117 Apostrophe is a figure of speech in which an absent or dead person or a personified thing is directly addressed by the speaker.

What, Washington, would you say now of "foreign entanglements" if you could see the world as it is today?

Ambition, you have been a cruel mistress to me. I will serve you no longer.

K118 Substitution[24] is a figure of speech in which, because they suggest each other in some way or are otherwise closely associated—

A. The maker or source is used for the thing made.

Along with many another illustrious, godly author, *Thomas Aquinas* was burned when Elstra made a bonfire of "subversive" books.	Thomas Aquinas, the writer or maker of the books, is substituted for the books.

B. The thing made is used for the maker or source.

Capital has learned to sit down and talk with *labor*.	Capital, the thing, is substituted for the people who possess it. Labor, the thing, is substituted for the people who perform it.

C. The sign is used for the thing signified.

I'm afraid we will have to punish those *sullen looks*.	Unless he is unreasonable, the speaker does not wish to punish the looks, which are only a sign, but the person who wears them or the attitude that they signify.

---

[24] "Substitution" is a name used in this book to replace *metonymy* and *synecdoche*. Metonymy is a figure of speech in which a word is used for another which it suggests or which is closely associated with it. Synecdoche is a figure of speech in which the part is put for the whole or the whole for the part.

D. The container is used for the thing contained.

Who steals my *purse* steals trash.	Iago does not mean the container—the purse itself—but the thing in the purse—money.

E. A part is used for the whole.

We sailed for Barcelona in a good *bottom.*	Part of the ship, bottom, is used for the whole ship.
Drought gripped the land. Not a *green ear* stood on any *stalk* in all that country.	The species, ears of corn, is used for the general classification, vegetation.

F. The whole is used for a part.

The *nation* went to the polls that day to vote for war or peace.	The whole nation is used for those who actually voted.
This *animal* builds great cities like London.	The general classification, animal, is used for the particular species, human being.

K119 Hyperbole is a figure of speech in which the writer exaggerates, not in order to deceive, but to emphasize a point, create humor, or achieve some similar effect.

An *endless* stream of wharf rats poured over the side the moment the ship docked at Suez.

K120 Paradox is a figure of speech in which, to jolt the reader into a new realization, the writer states a seeming contradiction that will later be explained or that will yield sense on second thought.

He who loses his life for My sake will save it.

K121 Onomatopoeia is a figure of speech in which words are used whose sound suggests their sense.

There broke on our ears the *clang of cymbals* and the *strident, brassy blasts* of *haughty trumpets.*

K122 Do not strive for onomatopoeia unless you have good reason to think your audience or reader will be in the mood for it. It falls very flat when the context or the reader is not ready for it.

K123 Alliteration is a figure of speech in which the same sound is repeated noticeably at the beginning of words placed close together.[25]

> *Full fathom five thy father lies.*

K124 Of all the figures of speech, alliteration should be used the most sparingly. Only reading aloud can teach a writer to use it well.

K125 Make sure that every figure of speech is consistent with itself and consistent with the thoughts around it.

> [Badly mixed figures:] Ladies and gentlemen, I smell a rat; I see it in the air, and I will nip it in the bud!

K126 To avoid hackneyed, worn-out writing—

A. Work out your own original figures to express your own thoughts.

B. When unable to produce an adequate original figure or when the context deserves only a trite, dull figure, do not call attention to the one you have borrowed or emphasize it in any way.[26]

K127 Clichés are trite expressions. Once fresh and vivid, they became overworked precisely because they were so good. Although such expressions are acceptable in informal speech, they should be avoided in formal writing. Some examples are *add insult to injury, crazy as a loon, quick as a flash, wax eloquent, white as a sheet, beat a dead horse, flat as a pancake.*

---

[25] When the repetition of a sound is not exclusively at the beginning of words, it is called *assonance* (for vowel sounds) or *consonance* (for consonant sounds).

[26] See K128.

K128 A great many figures of speech have become so common that they have passed beyond triteness into the very idiom of the language; for example, *in the long run, right-hand man.* There is no prohibition against these common figures, unless you use a great number of them too close together.

K129 If you use figures of speech merely as ornaments, something added to a composition to "pretty up" your work, you will fall into what is called, without compliment, "fine writing." Follow K130-33.

K130 Rethink every thought that you write down. Make sure that it is now your own.

K131 It often helps to write the first draft of a composition in the form of a letter to someone you know or at least to someone real, and then afterwards to remove the paraphernalia of the letter.

K132 When writing the second draft of a composition, ask yourself constantly of each sentence, each figure—

A. Does this directly or indirectly help the meaning of the main thought of the composition?

B. Does it help the central mood or atmosphere?

C. Does it fit the audience for which I intend the composition?

D. Does it fit the real or pretended writer?

K133 Probe your mind and feelings until you find out why you like or dislike this or that passage in your own or in others' work and until you know whether your own reasons are good or bad. Reading a passage out loud often reveals its strengths and weaknesses. Read slowly and try to visualize what you are reading.

Color in writing

K134 Open your eyes to the colorful glory of the world, to its variety and shading.

[Good, but wanting in color:] When she had been warped away from the dock, she flung out her great sails before the following gale, heeled a little under the impact, and then stood smartly down the bay. I tell you it made my heart stand still to look at her.

[With color:] When she had been warped away from the dock, she flung out her great crimson sails, quartered with gold crosses, before the following gale. Her black hull heeled a little under the impact, and then she stood smartly down the bay in the filtered-yellow afterrain. I tell you it made my heart stand still to look at her.

K135 In describing color, appeal to something the reader is certain to know well. But see K136.

[Good:] His hair was brownish-red.
[Probably clearer:] His name, like his hair, was "Rusty."

[Good:] They used an ugly rough-finish brown tile in the shower room.
[Probably clearer:] They used an ugly rough-finish milk-chocolate tile in the shower room.

[Good:] Over her white shirt and dark slacks she wore a bright red jacket.
[Probably clearer:] Over her white shirt and dark slacks she wore a neon-red jacket.

K136 Often it is not important that a reader get a definite notion of the color of an object. Do not slow your writing and bore your reader by going in for precision where precision is not necessary. Even if the detail is incisive and original, have the courage to omit it in favor of focus and pace.

Suggestion

K137 Do not always make things so plain for your readers that there is nothing for them to do but passively nod their heads. Use suggestion now and then.[27]

K138 Suggestion is supplying the reader with sufficient, and only sufficient, information for him to make out the thought correctly and easily by himself.

[Plain statement:] Thompson is a coward.
[Suggestion:] Oh, Thompson talks a good fight.

[Plain statement:] The prisoner died at three o'clock.
[Suggestion:] By three o'clock the prisoner's soul, at least, had escaped its cell.

[Plain statement:] It looks as though the senator has been accumulating wealth unethically.
[Suggestion:] I'm afraid there's jam on the senator's fingers.

[Plain statement:] Hazel was a mediocre writer.
[Suggestion:] Hazel made the columns of the *New Yorker* once, when a critic recommended her novel to insomniacs.

[Plain statement:] Pearson sobbed out his plea. The judge was not impressed. She merely smiled thinly.
[Suggestion:] Pearson sobbed out his plea. The judge smiled thinly.

Rhythm

K139 Read your writing aloud to yourself. Then revise your sentences according to the verdict of your ears.[28]

Examples of good prose rhythm

But little do people perceive what solitude is: for a crowd is not company, and faces are but a gallery of pictures, and talk but a tinkling symbol where there is no love.

---

[27] For the use of suggestion in narratives, see R53-54.
[28] Balance and antithesis (K109-12), climax (K113), anticlimax (K114), and alliteration (K123-24) are involved in rhythm.

Far away rang the cry of Judith to the watchmen on the city walls: Open the gates! God is on our side. Open the gates! His power yet lives in Israel.

—BOOK OF JUDITH, 13:13

In the common experience of misery, in the common sorrow of great catastrophes, in humiliation and distress, under the blows of the executioner or the bombs of total war, in concentration camps, in the hovels of starving people in great cities, in any common necessity, the doors of solitude open and man recognizes man.

—JACQUES MARITAIN, *RANSOMING THE TIME*

In addition to rhythm, the following passage illustrates a subtle and effective use of sound (alliteration, assonance, consonance).

Yes, the newspapers were right: snow was general all over Ireland. It was falling on every part of the dark central plain, on the treeless hills, falling softly upon the Bog of Allen and, farther westward, softly falling into the dark mutinous Shannon waves. It was falling, too, upon every part of the lonely church yard on the hill where Michael Furey lay buried. It lay thickly drifted on the crooked crosses and headstones, on the spears of the little gate, on the barren thorns. His soul swooned slowly as he heard the snow falling faintly through the universe and faintly falling, like the descent of their lasted end, upon all the living and the dead.

—JAMES JOYCE, "THE DEAD"

Sentence structure and diction checklist

K140 As a final step, check your sentence structure and diction against the following standards:

1. unified sentences K2-4

2. concise sentences, no wordiness K6, K35

3. main idea in independent clause K7, K32

4. proper coordination and subordination K32

5. parallel structure for parallel or contrasting ideas K11-15, K109-112

6. proper placement of modifiers K12

7. appropriate connectives K20

8. necessary words K22-23

9. logical phrasing K24-28

10. positive statements K31

11. active voice K30

12. no needless shifts in subject or in verb voice or tense K16-17, K19

13. no needless shifts in person or number K18

14. effective arrangement of words and ideas K33-34, K37-38, K113-14

15. variety of sentence length K40, K43-49

16. variety of sentence structure K43-49, K52-62

17. appropriate thought development K63-74

18. precise word meanings K92-93, K95-98

19. restricted use of gender words K91

20. appropriate language for audience and occasion K76-90

21. vivid language K95-97, K125-26, also figures of speech

22. fresh figures of speech (tropes) K100-108, K115-21, K125-29

23. connotation, suggestion K94, K137-38

24. color K134-36

25. sounds of words K121-24

26. rhythmic sentences K139

27. revision K130-33

L

The paragraph

In general

L1 A paragraph is a sentence or a group of sentences separated by indention or by a similar device from other sentences in the same piece of writing.[1]

This is a paragraph. The first line is, as you see, indented, set back a little from the left-hand margin formed by the other lines. It is the technical essential of a paragraph that it be set off by indentation or by some other device from the rest of the piece of writing. But, as other rules will indicate, a paragraph ordinarily corresponds to a unit of thought. In fact, the reason for the indentation and, consequently, for the paragraphing is to set off one unit of thought from another. Thus the reader is prevented from mixing up things that should be kept separate, and the mind is given little rests between units.

L2 In continuous composition, a good paragraph is a group of sentences that all develop a single topic thought (although occasionally a paragraph will consist of only one sentence by itself).

Write your name and address in the upper right-hand corner of the page. Below your name and centered on the page, write the title of your story. Skip several line spaces and then indent for the first paragraph. Leave margins of one inch at the sides and the bottom of the page.

The topic thought of the paragraph: *Here is the format your paper must follow.*

---

[1] For paragraphs in dialogue see D124.

> And now let us leave the format of the paper for a moment and consider the content.

> This is a one-sentence paragraph, used as a bridge between parts of the composition.

L3 Occasionally a paragraph is complete in itself, and there results a one-paragraph composition like the ones to be found in some newspaper editorials or in the writings of some columnists. A paragraph however, is generally a part—a new side or phase, a step forward: in brief, a division or a subdivision—of a larger composition.

L4 Except in the block form of typed letters, in outlines, in printed displays, and in certain kinds of technical writing, the first line of every paragraph should be indented; that is, the first line should be set in a little from the left-hand margin.[2] When indention is not used, paragraphs are indicated in some other way, usually by the insertion of extra space between them.

L5 The first line of a handwritten paragraph should be indented one-half inch or slightly more; the first line of a typewritten paragraph, from three to eight (usually five) characters.[3]

L6 The first lines of all paragraphs in the same composition should be indented uniformly.

> The first indented paragraph will govern the indentation of those that follow.

> This paragraph, as you see, is indented uniformly with the one immediately above. So with any others in the same composition.

---

[2] In some printed styles the first paragraph is not indented, since there is no preceding paragraph from which it needs to be set off.

[3] For indentation in handwritten personal letters, see the model in S80. For indentation in typed business letters, see S10. For paragraph indentation in research papers, see models in N114 (MLA), N123 (APA), N140 (University of Chicago).

Unity in the paragraph

L7 Unity means oneness. In composition, unity requires that there be only one main thought and that all the other thoughts and words in a sentence, paragraph, or composition directly or indirectly reinforce the one main thought.

L8 The topic thought of a paragraph is the one clear, rather brief thought that answers the question *What is the paragraph about?*

It is presumptuous for a writer to think that everything has fallen into place with the first draft. Perhaps ideas need to be more clearly expressed or better arranged. Quite possibly a word here or there needs to be changed. Sentence style, transition words, correct grammar are other important considerations. Of the hundreds of decisions a writer has made in the first draft, certainly some of them can be improved by reviewing and revising.

The topic thought of the paragraph: *Revision is necessary.*

L9 Put one, and only one, topic thought into each paragraph.

It was Miss Murdstone who was arrived, and a gloomy-looking lady she was; dark, like her brother, whom she greatly resembled in face and voice, and with very heavy eyebrows, nearly meeting over her large nose . . . . She

As it is given here, this paragraph has two topic thought: (1) *Miss Murdstone was an unpleasant-appearing woman.* (2) *Murdstone was an unpleasant name.* When a paragraph is given to each topic thought, as in the second version

443

brought with her two uncompromising hard black boxes, with her initials on the lids in hard brass nails. When she paid the coachman she took her money out of a hard steel purse, and she kept the purse in a very gaol of a bag which hung upon her arm by a heavy chain and shut up like a bite. I had never, at that time, seen such a metallic lady altogether as Miss Murdstone was. Murdstone—I thought this an odd name, one that sounded dark and forbidding. It was not a familiar English name, and I have never heard it since. It filled me with fear and made me, beforehand, uneasy about meeting its bearer.

below, each paragraph gains in unity of impression.

It was Miss Murdstone who was arrived, and a gloomy-looking lady she was; dark, like her brother, whom she greatly resembled in face and voice, and with very heavy eyebrows, nearly meeting over her large nose . . . . She brought with her two uncompromising hard black boxes, with her initials on the lids in hard brass nails. When she paid the coachman she took her money out of a hard steel purse, and she kept the purse in a very gaol of a bag which hung upon her arm by a heavy chain and shut up like a bite. I had never, at that time, seen such a metallic lady altogether as Miss Murdstone was.

Murdstone—I thought this an odd name, one that sounded dark and forbidding. It was not a familiar English name, and I have never heard it since. It filled me with fear and made me, beforehand, uneasy about meeting its bearer.

—Adapted from Charles Dickens,
The Personal History of David Copperfield

L10   Make each sentence of a paragraph develop the topic thought either directly or indirectly.

Mr. Claudius had a very elaborate funeral. There were great banks of flowers. I myself have never cared much for flowers at a funeral. At funerals they seem to raise a cloying sweetness that infects

This is not a good paragraph. The topic thought, not fully expressed in any one sentence, is: Mr. Claudius's grand funeral did not fit him. But the third and fourth sentences do not develop this

the good clean air. There were a great many mourners, enough to fill the great church. The music was of the finest, for the uncertain singers of the parish had made way for surer, grander voices hired for the occasion. The cortege was piloted to the cemetery by a whole platoon of motorcycle policemen. It all seemed singularly inappropriate to the character of Mr. Claudius, who had tried so hard all his life for plainness and simplicity, only to have pomp thrust upon him at the very end.

topic thought either directly or indirectly. They should be put into another paragraph, if they are worth keeping, or dropped entirely. At the very least they should be put in parentheses—but only if they are very much worth keeping—to show that they interrupt the progress of the paragraph and are an aside, a digression.

It was not until my second week in the city that I developed the first unmistakable symptoms of the New York willies. I always felt an ineluctable guilt when I was just taking it easy in New York when all those grand museums, libraries, plays, concerts, and that whole vast infinitude of cultural opportunities beckoned me with promises of enrichment. I began to have trouble sleeping and felt as if I should be reading the complete works of Proust or learning a foreign language or rolling out my own pasta or taking a course at the New School on the history of film. The city always stimulated some long-dormant gland of self-improvement when I crossed her rivers. I would never feel good enough for New York, but I would always feel better if I was at least taking steps to measure up to her eminent standards.

The topic thought, *In my second week I began to develop symptoms of the New York willies,* is developed directly by the third sentence: *I began to have trouble sleeping. . . .* The other sentences develop the thought indirectly.

—Pat Conroy, *The Prince of Tides*

L11   If the paragraph does not become unwieldy or cluttered, put into it all the ideas that develop one topic thought.

My first glimpse of Europe was the shore of Spain.

Since we got into the Mediterranean, we have been becalmed for some days within easy view of it. All along are fine mountains, brown all day, and with a bloom on them at sunset like that of a ripe plum.

Here and there at their feet little white towns are sprinkled along the edge of the water, like the grains of rice dropped by the princess in the story. Sometimes we see larger buildings on the mountain slopes, probably convents.

I sit and wonder whether the farther peaks may not be the Sierra Morena (the rusty saw) of Don Quixote. I resolve that they shall be, and am content. Surely latitude and longitude never showed me any particular respect, that I should be over-scrupulous with them.

The false stop after each paragraph here makes the reader think that the writer has done with the topic thought. The reader is consequently thrown off to find the writer taking it up again and again. The treatment in the passage below is much clearer.

My first glimpse of Europe was the shore of Spain. Since we got into the Mediterranean, we have been becalmed for some days within easy view of it. All along are fine mountains, brown all day, and with a bloom on them at sunset like that of a ripe plum. Here and there at their feet little white towns are sprinkled along the edge of the water, like the grains of rice dropped by the princess in the story. Sometimes we see larger buildings on the mountain slopes, probably convents. I sit and wonder whether the farther peaks may not be the Sierra Morena (the rusty saw) of Don Quixote. I resolve that they shall be, and am content. Surely latitude and longitude never showed me any particular respect, that I should be over-scrupulous with them.

—James Russell Lowell, *Fireside Travels*

L12 A topic sentence is the topic thought of a paragraph expressed in one sentence of the paragraph itself. (The topic thought may use up the whole sentence or it may take up only part of it.)

> *If our goal is educational and economic equity and parity—and it is— then we need affirmative action to catch up.* We are behind as a result of discrimination and denial of opportunity. There is one white attorney for every 680 whites, but only one black attorney for every 4,000 blacks; one white physician for every 659 whites, but only one black physician for every 5,000 blacks; and one white dentist for every 1,900 whites, but only one black dentist for every 8,400 blacks. Less than 1 percent of all engineers—or of all practicing chemists—is black. Cruel and uncompassionate injustice created gaps like these. We need creative justice and compassion to help us close them.
>
> —JESSE JACKSON,
> "WHY BLACKS NEED AFFIRMATIVE ACTION"

While every paragraph has a topic thought, not all paragraphs have a topic sentence.

> He stood trembling and whimpering and biting at his finger. His eyes widened suddenly on sight of a hot cinder from his bucket eating through a stack of shirts. The red ring in the material widened and deepened and little curls of smoke rose from them. Terry plunged his way through the mass of garments to a shelf near the lavatory where a bucket of water was stored and grabbed it down and flung it! If was empty, the bottom rotted out! The boy became hopelessly confused at that moment and, as he whirled about looking for respite, the shirts closed on him like the tentacles of a soft octopus. He threw his hands up to knock them off, backing up as he did, and his feet slipped over the edge of the elevator shaft. Terry plunged down screaming but it went unheard, for the noon whistle drowned it.

This paragraph does not have a topic sentence, but it does have a topic thought: *This is how Terry Devlin died.*

> —LEON URIS, *TRINITY*

447

L13 Ordinarily express the topic thought of a paragraph in a topic sentence—unless, that is, doing so would hurt the paragraph. (For example, a topic sentence would be a mistake if it would give away too soon the secret that is creating suspense in a story.)

L14 Ordinarily put the topic sentence at the beginning of a paragraph; occasionally—for, say, suspense or variety—put it at the end.

Beyond all words and petitions the effective protest was boycott, known as Non-Importation. Already set in motion in response to the Sugar Act, a program to cut off imports of English goods was now formally adopted by groups of merchants in Boston, New York and Philadelphia. The call swept through the colonies on winds of enthusiasm. Women brought their spinning wheels into the minister's parlor or to the courthouse to compete in the number of skeins they could turn out for homespun to replace English cloth. Flax was spun for shirts "fine enough for the best gentlemen in America." By the end of the year, imports were £305,000 less than the year before out of a total of some £2 million.

The topic sentence is the first sentence in the paragraph. As such it provides a limiting and unifying frame for the particular statements that follow. This topic sentence could not be placed as effectively anywhere else in the paragraph.

—Barbara W. Tuchman, *The March of Folly*

Ten minutes later, *Chicago* was on a heading of zero-eight-one, steaming at fifteen knots. Deep, but in relatively warm water from the ocean current that begins in the Gulf of Mexico and runs all the way to the Barents Sea, she enjoyed sonar conditions that made detection by a surface ship nearly impossible. The water pressure prevented cavitation noises. Her engines could drive the

Here the topic sentence is placed last in the paragraph with good effect. It rounds off the ideas of the paragraph like a little summary.

submarine at this speed with only a fraction of her total rated power, obviating the need for reactor pumps. The reactor's cooling water circulated on natural convection currents, which eliminated the major source of radiated noise. *Chicago was completely in her element, a noiseless shadow moving through black water.*

—Tom Clancy, *Red Storm Rising*

L15 In some paragraphs the topic sentence is understood, not expressed; the paragraphs cannot be expected to have a topic sentence. That is true of dialogue paragraphs and many descriptive paragraphs. It is true also of many narrative paragraphs where the topic sentence would often have to be something like *Here is what happened in the next ten minutes.*[4]

Topic sentence and controlling idea

L16 The majority of descriptive and narrative paragraphs do not have topic sentences. On the other hand, most argumentative and expository paragraphs do have topic sentences. Since these latter paragraph forms are widely used, it is important to discuss the topic sentence.

L17 A topic sentence is the topic thought of a paragraph expressed in one sentence of a paragraph. A topic sentence almost always makes a paragraph clearer than it would be without one. It keeps both writer and reader on track.

L18 A topic sentence should express a judgment. "That car costs $10,000" is not a satisfactory topic sentence because it merely states a fact. It contains no idea that can be developed. "This car is worth every cent of $10,000" is a satisfactory topic sentence because it expresses a judgment and, therefore, can be developed.

[4] See the second example in L12.

L19 Because a topic sentence is a useful guide for achieving unity in the paragraph, it is frequently placed first in the paragraph. (A topic sentence may appear elsewhere in the paragraph or be omitted. See L12, L15.)

L20 Every topic sentence has a controlling idea. This controlling idea limits the subject matter to be discussed in the paragraph and may be expressed in a word, phrase, or clause.

Consider the topic sentence "Hang gliding is a thrilling hobby." *Hang gliding* is the subject matter of the paragraph. Since the topic of hang gliding is too extensive to be treated in one paragraph, the subject matter must be narrowed. This limitation is expressed in the controlling idea. Here *thrilling hobby* limits and controls the subject matter. In the following topic sentences, the controlling idea is expressed in italics:

Leonard Bernstein was a *musical genius.*
Television has *not lived up to its potential.*
Our major concern now is *whether she is qualified.*

Coherence in the paragraph

L21 Coherence requires that, for the sake of clarity, ideas and words follow one another in an orderly manner and that the connections between parts be made clear.

L22 Coherence in the paragraph means that the sentences of the paragraph are rightly put together and properly connected with each other.

L23 When you are moving from sentence to sentence, keep the same voice, person, number, and time, and the same subject, unless the thought requires a change.

[Poor:] Al was driving too fast when he sees the exit. The car bounces over the curbing as he desperately turned onto the ramp.

{Improved:] Al was driving too fast when he saw the exit. Desperately he turned onto the ramp, bouncing the car over the curbing.

Connectives and connections

L24 Connectives within a paragraph include transition words or phrases, pronouns, the same word or phrase repeated, and synonyms. Typical transition words and phrases include—

[addition:] *and, also, again, in addition, furthermore, moreover*
[similarity:] *also, likewise, similarly, in like manner, in the same way*
[emphasis:] *certainly, clearly, indeed, in fact, in other words*
[example:] *for example, for instance*
[contrast:] *but, yet, however, nevertheless, on the contrary, on the other hand*
[concession:] *although, granted, though, even though*
[result:] *consequently, therefore, thus*
[conclusion:] *finally, in conclusion*

L25 Establish clear connections where they are needed between sentences, and make sure that connectives are used with precision. (See also C228.)

The rifle seemed to be in good condition. The bore was pitted with rust.

One could speak these two sentences and, by bearing down heavily on *seemed*, make the meaning of the paragraph clear. But when one puts them in writing something is needed to bridge the gap between them. The two versions of the sentence given below will be clearer to readers.

At first the rifle seemed to be in good condition. However, the bore was pitted with rust.

At first alerts readers for the change of thought in the second sentence; then *however* makes certain that they will not miss it.

At first glance the rifle seemed to be in good condition. On closer inspection its

This is even clearer. *At first glance* and *on closer inspection* make the relationship of the

bore proved to be pitted with rust.

The demonstrators marched their way up to the capitol slowly, chanting slogans and singing rousing songs. The way was long and the wind strong, but all of them kept up the steady pace and chanted and sang as though they had breath to spare. In the meantime, two elderly women strode firmly along, carrying a heavy banner.

two sentences altogether unmistakable.

The writer does well to put a connective phrase at the beginning of the last sentence. One is needed, since there is a shift from the main body of the marchers to the women at its end. But *in the meantime* does not express the relationship as precisely as the connective below. The women could be in another part of the state.

The demonstrators marched their way up to the capitol slowly, chanting slogans and singing rousing songs. The way was long and the wind strong, but all of them kept up the steady pace and chanted and sang as though they had breath to spare. At the end of the procession, two elderly women strode firmly along, carrying a heavy banner.

Hepner and Wolfram thrust aside the two retainers who guarded the door, strode into the center of the hall, and, standing back to back between the two rows of tables, smilingly faced the chieftains and lords, who had half risen from the benches and half stretched tentative fingers toward swords and knives. Then casually, quietly, he said, "My comrade and I will lop the first hand that touches a hilt."

The paragraph reads clearly enough until the fourth word (*he*) of the second sentence. Then the reader would like to know whether Hepner or Wolfram is doing the talking. The version below corrects this problem.

Hepner and Wolfram thrust aside the two retainers who guarded the door, strode into the center of the hall, and, standing back to back between the two rows of tables, smilingly faced the chieftains and lords, who had half risen from the benches and half stretched tentative fingers toward swords and knives. Then casually, quietly, Hepner said, "My comrade and I will lop the first hand that touches a hilt."

Time order

L26   When relating a series of events, put first what happened first, second what happened second, and so on.[5]

[Serra and Portolá were right in thinking that their countrymen were at hand.] The approaching Indians brought them the good tidings that San Diego was but a two-days' journey even for Portolá's tired men and still more tired beasts. The next day they were met by ten soldiers whom the *comandante,* Rivera y Moncada, had sent to escort them to their destination. The colonization of California had begun. The Indians had said that both ships were in port, that the first land expedition had arrived long since, and that there were many friars on the spot. Cheered and heartened, the company pushed on over a country so broken and rock-strewn that Serra—always a truth-teller—feared his heart would stop beating from sheer fright. It was the next day that the ten soldiers mentioned above met them. Under their guidance they encamped for the last night on level ground by running water, and in the morning, July 1st, 1769, they reached a gentle

The time sequence of the paragraph at left is badly scrambled. Do not be surprised that it sounds as if it makes sense and yet confuses badly. See how much clearer, more pleasant, more interesting it is in the paragraph next below, where the events follow the order of time.

---

[5] Sometimes there is good reason for not following the order of time when relating a series of events. For example, it is permissible, for purposes of interest, to start with an important event and then go back to the events that led up to it. What is required is that you keep to the order of time unless you are certain that even without it your writing will still be clear and effective.

eminence from which they could see the ships riding at anchor, and the Spanish flag flying in the breeze, Portolá's soldiers fired a salute which was answered joyously from land and
sea. The sacred expedition of Galvez had entered the promised
land.

[Serra and Portolá were right in thinking that their countrymen were at hand.] The approaching Indians brought them
the good tidings that San Diego was but a two-days' journey
even for Portolá's tired men and still more tired beasts. They
said that both ships were in port, that the first land expedition
had arrived long since, and that there were many friars on the
spot. Cheered and heartened, the company pushed on over a
country so broken and rock-strewn that Serra—always a truth-
teller—feared his heart would stop beating from sheer fright.
The next day they were met by ten soldiers whom the *comandante,*
Rivera y Moncada, had sent to escort them to their destination.
Under their guidance they encamped for the last night on level
ground by running water, and in the morning, July 1st, 1769,
they reached a gentle eminence from which they could see the
ships riding at anchor, and the Spanish flag flying in the breeze.
Portolá's soldiers fired a salute which was answered joyously
from land and sea. The sacred expedition of Galvez had entered
the promised land. The colonization of California had begun.

—AGNES REPPLIER, *JUNIPERO SERRA*

Space Order

L27   In the treatment of things that can be located spatially,
the reader's mind likes to follow the habits of one's
eyes. The eye generally moves from one thing to another consecutively and does not skip about, unless it is
excited or restless or not really interested in seeing. Do
not confuse and annoy your reader by jumping from
place to place. Proceed in orderly fashion; for example,
from left to right or from top to bottom.

One sock drooped about the heel of her left sneaker; the other sock was not visible,	This paragraph is annoyingly disordered. It is clear enough, for the subject being describ-

having no doubt slipped under the arch of her foot and bunched there uncomfortably. Her nose was a mere indication, a reminder of what a nose is ordinarily like. A great rip in the seat of her jeans caused her some understandable concern; and this rip she was at pains to hold together with her unoccupied right hand, with a pathetic pretense of not noticing what she was doing, in the hope that no one else would notice either. The top of one shoe had torn away from the rubber sole and now presented the parody of an open mouth disclosing a thick brown tongue—her grimy big toe. In her left arm she cradled a shaggy, dispirited, dry-nosed small dog—of a black that was partly brown

ed is not difficult; but the reader's mind is made to return over and over again to a part of the girl's body (or to the dog) which should have been finished with once and for all. The mind's eye is jerked from shoe to nose to jeans to shoe to dog to eyes to torso to dog to shoes to dog. If this sort of thing continued for any length of time, any reader would soon weary of the effort to follow the writer. In the reorganization given in the paragraph below, the writer selects a natural, coherent order (just one of several possible orders) and proceeds from bottom to top without any annoying and confusing twists, turns, and returns.

L

and a white that was gray. Her eyes were the eyes of a girl of nine years old, which is to say that they were beautiful—as yet unglazed by the hardness and the fixity that comes with looking out always for the big opportunity. She wore no jacket despite the bite of the air. Occasionally the dog would squirm and attempt to lick her face. There were no strings in her shoes. One of the dog's hind legs was splinted and bandaged, and that rather expertly.

The top of one stringless sneaker had torn away from the sole and now presented the parody of an open mouth disclosing a thick brown tongue—the girl's grimy big toe. One sock drooped about the heel of her left shoe; the other sock was not visible, having no doubt slipped under the arch of her foot and bunched there uncomfortably. A great rip in the seat of her jeans caused her some understandable concern; and this rip she was at pains to hold together with her unoccupied right hand, with a pathetic pretense of not noticing what she was doing, in the hope that no one else would notice either. In her left arm she cradled a shaggy, dispirited, dry-nosed small dog—of a black that was partly brown and a white that was gray. One of the dog's hind legs was splinted and bandaged, and that rather expertly. Occasionally the dog would squirm and attempt to lick the girl's face. The girl wore no jacket despite the bite of the air. Her nose was a mere indication, a reminder of what a nose is ordinarily like. Her eyes were the eyes of a girl of nine years old, which is to say that they were beautiful—as yet unglazed by the hardness and the fixity that comes with looking out always for the big opportunity.

The sand-hills here run down to the sea, and end in two spits of rock jutting out opposite each other, till you lose sight of them in the water. One is called the North Spit and one the South. Between the two, shifting backward and forward at certain seasons of the year, lies the most horrible quicksand on the shores of Yorkshire. At the

Collins, the author of this passage, follows an easy order of place. He takes the reader's eye out along two parallel hills that can both be seen at once, to the quicksand between them, and out to the barrier that hems in the sand and walls out the sea.

turn of the tide something goes on in the unknown deeps below, which sets the whole face of the quicksand quivering and trembling in a manner most remarkable to see, and which has given to it, among the people in our parts, the name of the Shivering Sand. A great bank, half a mile out, nigh the mouth of the bay, breaks the force of the main ocean coming in from the offing. Winter and summer, when the tide flows over the quicksand, the sea seems to leave the waves behind it on the bank, and rolls its waters in smoothly with a heave, and covers the sand in silence. A lonesome and horrid retreat I can tell you! No boat ventures into this bay. No children from our fishing-village, called Cobb's Hole, ever come here to play. The very birds of the air, as it seems to me, give the Shivering Sand a wide berth.

—WILKIE COLLINS, *THE MOONSTONE*

Order of interest or importance

L28 In a paragraph in which neither events nor localized things are discussed, it is impossible to use the order of time or place. In such a paragraph it is good to use the order of interest or importance.

L29 After the topic sentence, if there is one, begin with the least interesting or important idea, go on to a more interesting or important idea, and so on, and end with the most interesting or important idea.

It was perfectly clear to me what I ought to do. I ought to walk up to within, say, twenty-five yards of the elephant and test his behavior. If he charged, I could shoot; if he took no notice of me, it would be safe to leave him until the mahout came back. But also I knew that I was going to do no such thing. I was a poor shot with a rifle and the ground was soft mud into which one would sink at every step. If the elephant charged and I missed him, I should have about as much chance as a toad under a steam-roller. But even then I was not thinking particularly of my own skin, only of the watchful yellow faces behind. For at that moment, with the crowd watching me, I was not

The topic thought of this paragraph is that Orwell knew he had to shoot the rogue elephant. His intention here is not primarily to put a series of events before the reader; thus he cannot use the order of time. He has no series of items that can be located in space for the reader; thus he cannot use the order of place. He does have a series of steps in his reasoning to decide to shoot the elephant to put before the reader, and he quite properly elects to give them in the order of importance. He gives the least important first: he ought to test the animal by approaching it and then to shoot it or to wait for its keeper. Then he gives a more important thought: he

457

afraid in the ordinary sense, as I would have been alone. A white man mustn't be frightened in front of "natives"; and so, in general, he isn't frightened. The sole thought in my mind was that if anything went wrong those two thousand Burmans would see me pursued, caught, tramped and reduced to a grinning corpse like that Indian up the hill. And if that happened, it was quite probable that some of was a poor shot, the ground was unfirm, and he would probably be trampled. He saves for last his most important reason: it would not be acceptable for a white colonialist to be laughed at by the "natives." The mind of the reader receives a clear impression from this order. There is a progression, a progression that makes sense.

them would laugh. That would never do. There was only one alternative. I shoved the cartridges into the magazine and lay down on the road to get a better aim.

—GEORGE ORWELL, "SHOOTING AN ELEPHANT"

L30 When you are in control of the order, as in a story, you can frequently make two or more of the orders of time, of place, and of importance or interest coincide, with consequent gain in clarity and interest.

The new foreman of the road gang, Black Scott, was a stupid and cruel man. As the weeks of June passed, the road gang, fed to the teeth with his tyrannical way and vile tongue, grew lazier and lazier: the men loitered long at the water barrel, spent half hours cleaning their shovels and picks, continually rested what they claimed were strained backs and blistered hands, and often spent the day lying "sick" in their bunks. At mealtime, when Black Scott was with them, they said nothing, only asking for food in a mutter or with a sneer. After meals and at night, they gathered in little groups and cursed the food, the job, the weather—and especially Black Scott and his cruel, domineering ways. Thus passed June and July, the men simmering in a surly rage; and by the end of August hatred had rotted their hearts and evil taken full possession of their minds. Black Scott was in danger of his life.

L31 Most of the time it is quite justifiable to subordinate the order of time or the order of place to the order of interest or importance in those paragraphs where the various orders are combined. But do not use an order or combination of orders that is not clear.

L32 There are other orders of paragraph development; for example, the order of general to specific or specific to general (which in simplest terms means putting the topic sentence first or last respectively, with details in the body of the paragraph). Any order may be used that will be clear and easy.

Emphasis in the paragraph

L33 Emphasis means relative stress. In writing, emphasis requires that more important thoughts be made to stand out from less important thoughts. Your writing is properly emphatic when your reader knows, without thinking the matter over, which thoughts you consider most important, which less, and which least important.

L34 Ordinarily place an important idea at the beginning or the end of a paragraph.

[The spring of 1846] was a busy season in the city of St. Louis. Not only were emigrants from every part of the country preparing for the journey to Oregon and California, but an unusual number of traders were making ready their wagons and outfits for Santa Fé. Many of the emigrants, especially those bound for California, were persons of wealth and standing. The hotels were crowded, and the gunsmiths and saddlers were kept constantly at work in providing arms and equipment for the different parties of travelers. Steamboats were leaving the levee and passing up the Missouri, crowded with passengers on their way to the frontier.

In the first sentence of this paragraph, Parkman puts the important thought of the whole paragraph.

—FRANCIS PARKMAN, JR., THE OREGON TRAIL

459

[Topic thought:] Only a good person has an awareness of good and evil.

[Development:] One last point. Remember that, as I said, the right direction leads not only to peace but to knowledge. When a person is getting better he understands more clearly the evil that is in him. When a person is getting worse, he understands his own badness less and less. A moderately bad person knows he is not very good: a thoroughly bad person thinks he is all right. This is common sense, really. You understand sleep when you are awake, not while you are sleeping. You can see mistakes in arithmetic when your mind is working properly: while you are making them you cannot see them. You can understand the nature of drunkenness when you are sober, not when you are drunk. Good people know about both good and evil: bad people do not know about either.

The second and third sentences of the paragraph introduce the topic thought, but its clearest and most succinct expression is in the last sentence.

—Adapted from C. S. Lewis, *Mere Christianity*

L35 Put a series of ideas within a paragraph in the order of climax—least important or interesting, more important or interesting, still more important or interesting, most important or interesting.[6]

Warren Hastings was born on December 6, 1732. His mother died a few days later, and he was left dependent upon his impoverished grandfather. The child was early

In this paragraph Macauley describes the young Warren Hastings. Macaulay's chief interest in him is his ambition to be "Hastings of Daylesford"—his determination to

---

[6] When applying this principle to a paragraph that begins with a topic sentence, use the order of climax in the sentences that follow the topic sentence—insofar as it is reasonable to do so.

sent to the village school, where he learned his letters at the same desk as the sons of the peasants; nor did anything in his clothes or training indicate that his life was to be widely different from that of the farm boys with whom he studied and played. But no cloud could overcast the dawn of Hastings' genius and ambition. The farm boys noticed, and long remembered, how eagerly young

become a wealthy and important man. Consequently Macaulay first writes a few sentences about Hastings's birth and early training, and then gives the greater part of the paragraph to discussing Hastings's ambition. This interest, this importance, not only comes last in the paragraph but is given by far the greater detail.

Hastings took to books. The daily sight of the lands that his ancestors had possessed and that had passed into the hands of strangers, filled his young brain with wild fancies and projects. He loved to hear stories of the wealth and greatness of his ancestors, of their splendid estates, their loyalty to the government, and their valor. One bright summer day, Hastings, then just seven years old, lay on the bank of the stream that flows through the old domain of the Hastings family. There and then, as he told the tale seventy years later, there rose in his mind the scheme that, through all the turns of his eventful career, was never abandoned. He would recover the lands that had belonged to his ancestors. He would be Hastings of Daylesford. This purpose, formed in boyhood and poverty, grew stronger as his mind developed and as his fortunes improved. He pursued his purpose with that calm but indomitable force of will that was the most striking peculiarity of his character. When, under a tropical sun, he ruled fifty millions of Asiatics, his hopes, amidst all the cares of war, finance, and legislation, still pointed to Daylesford. And when his long public life, so singularly checkered with good and evil, with glory and blame, had at length closed forever, it was to Daylesford he retired to die.

—Adapted from Thomas Babington Macauley,
"Warren Hastings"

[Topic thought:] Chemical spraying set up a chain reaction of destruction.

[Development:] But with the "improvement" instituted by the Forest Service, the willows went the way of the sagebrush, killed by the same impartial spray. When Justice Douglas visited the area in 1959, the year of the spraying, he was shocked to see the shriveled and dying willows—the "vast, incredible damage." What would become of the moose? Of the beavers and the little world they had constructed? A year later he returned to read the answers in the devastated landscape. The moose were gone and so were the beaver. Their principal dam had gone out for want of attention by its skilled architects, and the lake had drained away. None of the large trout were left. None could live in the tiny creek that remained, threading its way through a bare, hot land where no shade remained. The living world was shattered.

In this paragraph a series of consequences listed in chronological order builds to the last sentence.

—RACHEL CARSON, *SILENT SPRING*

L36　Occasionally emphasize an important idea by repeating it within a paragraph. Ordinarily repeat it in somewhat different words; rarely in the very same words.

Finally, oppressed by the clatter, the blaring of the orchestra, the tinkle of insincere conversation, Fleurin made his way across the dance floor, through the French doors that opened on the lawn, across the lawn, to the sea wall. Peace, he thought— I must find peace. Not the peace of emptiness, for that is only silence. I must have the peace of fullness, and that means love. There can be no

The repetition of the words *love* and *peace*, and of the ideas of emptiness, fullness, and so on in this paragraph seems justified and effective. For somehow the repetition conveys a bit of Fleurin's desperate hunger for a meaning and a purpose in life. The paragraph below, which does not use repetition, loses in clarity and effect.

peace without love. When I love the things that fill, not the things that empty, then I will have peace.

Finally, oppressed by the clatter, the blaring of the orchestra, the tinkle of insincere conversation, Fleurin made his way across the dance floor, through the French doors that opened on the lawn, across the lawn, to the sea wall. Peace, he thought—I must find something to quiet my mind. But I don't want emptiness. I want fullness. That means I want love. There can be no real tranquillity unless the heart has fastened on something. But if I love the things that enrich a person, not the things that beggar him, then I may find satisfaction.

After my experience of civil protest and a night in jail for crossing the white line marking the boundary of the nuclear site in Beatty, Nevada, I felt more and more convinced of two points: that it is sometimes necessary to break the law publicly and that one should be prepared to go to jail as a consequence. In response to the judge I explained that our act of civil disobedience was required by an overwhelming necessity to call to public attention the huge and terrible disorder which lies beneath the smooth and ordinary rules and arrangements of our society. For what appears on the surface to be a normal way of life includes within it the preparation of the means for annihilation, and only an act which deliberately and publicly breaks the rules can adequately sound the alarm at what lies beneath it. Gandhi went to jail repeatedly; Thoreau and Bertrand Russell went to jail, as did British ladies demanding votes for women,

This paragraph uses one of the most emphatic repetition devices there are. A thought is stated at the beginning. Then, after the point has been developed, the same thought is repeated—sometimes in the very same words; sometimes, as here, in slightly different words—at the end of the paragraph. The placement gives the same thought the benefit of the two most striking positions in the paragraph. What is more, it forges the paragraph together into one compact, sharp blade of thought that can hardly fail to penetrate the mind and leave an impression there.

L

some of whom got their teeth knocked out there in the course of being force-fed. So have a legion of less famous men and women been imprisoned for working for national independence, religious toleration, desegregation, and the ending of some war thought evil. To assert the ultimate value of persons in a world of national and international purposes, I am convinced that one must be willing to take personal action and personal risks—to break the law publicly, in a nonviolent manner and with a moral purpose, may well mean going to jail.

—Adapted from Lisa Peattie,
"One Night in the Beatty Lockup"

L37   Occasionally put the idea that you wish to emphasize into a very brief sentence, and all the other ideas into rather long sentences. Place the brief sentence at the beginning or, often better, at the end of the paragraph. The difference in the length of the sentences will call attention sharply to the idea in the short one.

The torrential rain made an infernal racket on the dry palmettos that roofed the fragile half-shelter—roofed it so imperfectly, however, that little cascades of cold water often found the neck of a man's poncho and ran down his back, drenching him and leaving him shivering. What water missed the neck of one's poncho dripped, or ran, or somehow found its way to the ground, and there joined with the soft earth to make first soupy gumbo and then a muddy lake most uncomfortable to sit in—and, of course, it was either sit in the muddy lake or stand up on the broken leg. All in all, Felito felt miserable.

All in all, Felito felt miserable gains considerable emphasis because it is a short sentence coming after two very long ones. Notice that the paragraph next below, which ends with a long sentence, fails to make so sharp an impression, even though it is a good paragraph.

The torrential rain made an infernal racket on the dry

Poor Felito felt very miserable is smothered a bit in this ver-

palmettos that roofed the
fragile half-shelter—roofed it
so imperfectly, however, that
little cascades of cold water
sion, though not so badly that
the thought is obscured.

often found the neck of a man's poncho and ran down his
back, drenching him and leaving him shivering. What water
missed the neck of one's poncho dripped, or ran, or somehow
found its way to the ground, and there joined with the soft
earth to make first a soupy gumbo and then a muddy lake most
uncomfortable to sit in—and, of course, it was either sit in the
muddy lake or stand up on the broken leg. With all of these
things to contend with and no means of contending with them
except patience, poor Felito felt very miserable indeed and
longed for some change, almost any change, in his circumstances.

Paragraph development

L38 Every paragraph must develop the topic thought (and
topic sentence, if there is one). This is accomplished
through a series of supporting statements. Some of
these statements are likely to be more important than
others, but all of them must in some way explain the
topic thought.

L39 Sentences in the body of a paragraph that directly support the topic thought (or topic sentence) are called
major support statements. Many paragraphs have no
further explanation or proof.

[Topic sentence:] Carolina Bello is an accomplished musician.
    A. She plays piano, cello, and harp.
    B. She received a special grant to study abroad.
    C. She has given numerous recitals.

L40 Any sentence in the body of the paragraph containing
information, examples, or other material that clarifies
or explains a major support statement is called a minor
support statement. The arabic-numbered sentences in
the model outline below are support statements.

[Topic sentence:] Mike Franz was a remarkable high school athlete.

    A. He played outstanding varsity baseball for three years.
       1. He rarely made an error.
       2. He batted over .300 each year.

    B. He was an all-city defensive end on the football team in junior and senior years.
       1. He started in every game.
       2. He averaged two sacks per game.

L41 Put variety into paragraphs by developing the topic thoughts in different ways. Common methods of development are details, division and classification, circumstances, comparison and contrast, cause and effect, examples, repetition, definition, analogy, and combinations of these methods.

Details in the paragraph

L42 Develop a topic thought by enumerating important details (factual material) that support the controlling idea.[7]

[Topic thought:] The gorgeous spectacle brought gasps of admiration.

[Development:] So gorgeous was the spectacle on the May morning of 1910 when nine kings rode in the funeral of Edward VII of England that the crowd, waiting in hushed and black-clad awe, could not keep back gasps of admiration. In scarlet and blue and green and purple, three by three the sovereigns rode through the palace gates, with plumed helmets, gold braid, crimson sashes, and jeweled orders flashing in the sun. After them came five heirs apparent, forty more imperial or royal highnesses, seven

The paragraph supplies a series of details to support the topic sentence.

---

[7]For the notion of controlling idea, see L20.

queens—four dowager and three regnant—and a scattering of special ambassadors from uncrowned countries. Together they represented seventy nations in the greatest assemblage of royalty and rank ever gathered in one place. The muffled tongue of Big Ben tolled nine by the clock as the cortege left the palace, but on history's clock it was sunset, and the sun of the old world was setting in a dying blaze of splendor never to be seen again.

—Barbara Tuchman, *The Guns of August*

[Topic thought:] Other people, wide awake, passed to and fro.

[Development:] While he lay sound asleep in the shade, other people were wide awake, and passed to and fro, afoot, on horseback, and in all sorts of vehicles, along the sunny road by his bed-chamber [beneath the trees]. Some looked neither to the right hand nor the left, and knew not that he was there; some merely glanced that way, without admitting the slumberer among their busy thoughts; some laughed to see how soundly he slept; and several, whose hearts were brimming full of scorn, ejected their venomous superfluity on David Swan. A middle-aged widow, when nobody else was near, thrust her head a little way into the recess, and vowed that the young fellow looked charming in his sleep. A temperance lecturer saw him, and wrought poor David into the texture of his evening discourse, as an awful instance of dead drunkenness by the roadside. But censure, praise, merriment, scorn, and indifference were all one, or rather all nothing, to David Swan.

The idea in the subject (other people) is divided into appropriate detail: some who looked, some who merely glanced, some who laughed, several whose hearts were brimming, a middle-aged widow, a temperance lecturer. The last sentence neatly summarizes the entire enumeration.

—Nathaniel Hawthorne, "David Swan"

Division and classification in the paragraph

L43 Develop a topic thought by breaking down an idea, object, or process into its parts (division) and then arranging these divisions in some sensible pattern (classification).

[Topic thought:] There are three New Yorks.

[Development:] There are roughly three New Yorks. There is, first, the New York of the man or woman who was born here, who takes the city for granted and accepts its size and its turbulence as natural and inevitable. Second,

The first part of the paragraph divides and classifies three New Yorks. The latter part of the paragraph provides a fuller description of the third type.

there is the New York of the commuter—the city that is devoured by locusts each day and spat out each night. Third, there is the New York of the person who was born somewhere else and came to New York in quest of something. Of these three trembling cities the greatest is the last—the city of final destination, the city that is a goal. It is this third city that accounts for New York's high-strung disposition, its poetical deportment, its dedication to the arts, and its incomparable achievements. Commuters give the city its tidal restlessness; natives give it solidity and continuity, but the settlers give it passion. And whether it is a farmer arriving from Italy to set up a small grocery store in a slum, or a young girl arriving from a small town in Mississippi to escape the indignity of being observed by neighbors, or a boy arriving from the Corn Belt with a manuscript in his suitcase and a pain in his heart, it makes no difference: each embraces New York with the fresh eyes of an adventurer, each generates heat and light to dwarf the Consolidated Edison Company.

—E. B. WHITE,
HERE IS NEW YORK

Circumstances in the paragraph

L44 Develop a topic thought by giving the circumstances related to it—by answering the question *When, where, how,* or *why is this?*

[Topic thought:] The landing on HMS *Invincible* was different (and more difficult).

[Development:] The landing on the HMS *Invincible* was different from the COD's arrival on the *Kennedy*. The ride became rocky as Parker descended through the clouds, and it occurred to Ryan that they were on the leading edge of the same storm he'd endured the night before. The canopy was coated with rain, and he heard the impact of thousands of raindrops on the airframe—or was it hail? Watching the instruments, he saw that Parker leveled out at a thousand feet, while they were still in the clouds, then descended more slowly, breaking into the clear at a hundred feet. The *Invincible* was scarcely half the *Kennedy's* size. He watched her bobbing actively on the fifteen-foot seas. Parker used the same technique as before. He hovered briefly on the carrier's port side, then slid to the right, dropping the fighter twenty feet onto a painted circle. The landing was hard, but Ryan was able to see it coming. The canopy came up at once.

The circumstances that made landing different center on the weather and on the ship; namely, leading edge of the storm, rain (or hail), smaller and bobbing *Invincible*, hard landing.

—Tom Clancy,
The Hunt for Red October

[Topic thought:] Various conditions accelerate the conversion of nitrogen and hydrogen into ammonia.

[Development:] Under various conditions the rate of reaction between nitrogen and hydrogen to form ammonia can be accelerated. One way to speed up the reaction

The paragraph states conditions or circumstances for increasing the rate of chemical reaction.

469

is to increase pressure. Another procedure is to raise the temperature of the chemicals. A third way to accelerate the reaction is to introduce a catalyst. Obviously, the introduction of all three methods to optimum levels provides for the greatest increase in rate.

Comparison and contrast in the paragraph

L45 Develop a topic thought by using comparison, contrast, or both.[8]

[Topic thought:] Anton looked out of place among the many sophisticates on the beach terrace.

[Development:] Imagine a cur, an ordinary mangy dog from the streets, with melancholy, affectionate eyes, half fearful, half trusting. Imagine such a dog thrust among the trained, poised, petted, combed, curled, and perfumed canine aristocrats at a dog	The writer gives the reader a double comparison. Anton is like a cur and the cocktail sophisticates are like canine aristocrats. The two groups are also contrasted with each other.

show—but himself utterly unaware of any differences. If the other dogs make him seem the more ragged and smelly, he makes them seem the more pretentious and silly. Such was Anton, funny little man, among the sleek sophisticates gathered for cocktails at five on the terrace at the beach.

[Topic thought:] Florida and California oranges are very different from each other.

[Development:] An orange grown in Florida usually has a thin and tightly fitting skin,	The author develops this contrast paragraph through a series of alternating state-

---

[8] Comparison consists in bringing out points of similarity between two or more things; contrast brings out dissimilarities. In a nontechnical sense the term *comparison* is frequently used to include points of dissimilarity. See K65-68.

and it is also heavy with juice. Californians say that if you want to eat a Florida orange you have to get into a bathtub first. California oranges are light in weight and have thick skins that break easily and come off in hunks. The flesh inside is marvelously sweet, and the segments almost separate themselves. In Florida, it is said that you can run over a California orange with a ten-ton truck and not even wet the pavement. The differences from which these hyperboles arise will prevail in the two states even if the type of orange is the same. In arid climates, like California's, oranges develop a thick albedo, which is the white part of the skin. Florida is one of the two or three most rained-upon states in the United States. California uses the Colorado River and similarly impressive sources to irrigate its oranges, but of course irrigation can only do so much. The annual difference in rainfall between Florida and California orange-growing areas is one million one hundred and forty thousand gallons per acre. For years, California was the leading orange state, but Florida surpassed California in 1942, and grows three times as many oranges now. California oranges, for their part, can safely be called three times as beautiful.

—JOHN MCPHEE, *ORANGES*

A comparison or contrast can be implicit—that is, one part is given, and the other part is left for the reader to supply.

[Topic thought:] Elise Deniquet is a difficult, unpleasant person.

[Development:] Right now Elise Deniquet is purring, for everything is to her liking. She can sit quiet and sleek in a chair by the fire and look at you with drowsy eyes, for all the world as though cream were the limit of her ments about Florida and California oranges.

Although the word *cat* is never mentioned, Elise Deniquet is obviously compared to a *cat* (there is an implied metaphor); and the writer appeals to our knowledge of cats in attempting to tell us what Elise is like.

L

ambition. But she can suddenly hiss and spit and terrify one who treads unwarily on her special interests. And, as all her friends know well, her claws are real.

Cause and effect in the paragraph

L46   Develop a topic thought by stating some of the causes of, or reasons for, the truth or event it relates.

[Topic thought:] Rice farming is a cooperative effort.

[Development:] In the farmlands of Southeast Asia it is typical to see clusters of thatched houses surrounded by extensive rice paddies. This pattern did not emerge by chance, but rather by necessity. The cultivation of rice requires the construction and maintenance of an irrigation system—something beyond the capability of a single family. Even more importantly, the planting and harvesting of rice cannot be done efficiently without the cooperation of at least two dozen people. Simply put, a single family cannot produce enough rice for its own needs, but a cluster of families working together can produce a surplus.

The paragraph gives reasons why people work cooperatively in the rice fields.

L47   Develop a topic thought by stating some of the effects or consequences of the truth or event it relates.

[Topic thought:] Japan is a nation that is living by its wits, discipline, and hard work.

[Development:] Japan is a nation that, lacking natural resources, must live by its wits, by social discipline, and by plain hard work. It is not surprising, therefore, to discover that during the last twenty years Japan has quietly been establishing a new, higher set of educational standards for the world. On a whole raft of international tests of achievement in science and math, Japanese

The effect, or result, of Japanese intelligence, discipline, and work is stated in the second sentence: an outstanding education. The remaining sentences provide supporting evidence.

students outperform all others. Japan's newspaper readership level is the world's highest. A considerably larger percentage of Japanese (90 percent) than American (75 percent) or Europeans (mostly below 50 percent) finish the twelfth grade, and a greater proportion of males complete university B.A. degrees in Japan than in other countries. Japanese children attend school about fifty more days each year than American students, which means that, by high-school graduation, they have been in school somewhere between three and four more years than their American counterparts.

—Thomas P. Rohlen,
"Japanese Education—If They Can Do It, Should We?"

Examples in the paragraph

L48 Develop a topic thought by giving particular instances or concrete examples of the general or abstract truth that it relates.

[Topic thought:] I realize that there are vast regions of writing where "I" isn't allowed.

[Development:] I realize that there are vast regions of writing where "I" isn't allowed. Newspapers don't want "I" in their news stories; many magazines don't want it in their articles; businesses and institutions don't want it in the reports they send so profusely into the American home; colleges don't want "I" in their term papers or dissertations; and English teachers discourage any first-person pronoun except the literary "we" ("We see in Melville's symbolic use of the white whale. . . "). Many of those prohibitions are valid. Newspaper articles should consist of news, reported objectively. I also sympathize with teachers who don't want to give students an easy escape into opinion— "I think Hamlet was stupid"—before the students have grappled with the discipline of assessing a work on its merits and on external sources. "I" can be a self-indulgence and a cop-out.

The topic statement is developed by various examples. Supporting argument is then given for two examples.

—William Zinsser, *On Writing Well*

Repetition in the paragraph

L49   Develop a topic thought by repeating an idea in the subject or predicate in different words and with greater clarity or force.

[Topic thought:] Let the disaffected students get out.

[Development:] Let the disaffected students get out. Let them take themselves to other schools; let them find a school with the atmosphere and the background for sophisticates. Let them stop complaining about student counselors of their own choosing, stop indulging their talent for hypocritical criticism, stop murdering their fellow students with words, stop leaving organizations and activities to run themselves. In brief, let these parasites decamp and carry to appropriate surroundings their genius for elegant worthlessness.

The second sentence repeats and enlarges on the first sentence. The third sentence enlarges upon the notion of *disaffected* in a parallel and repetitive form. The fourth sentence summarizes the paragraph.

Repetition is regularly used in conjunction with other forms of paragraph development. Properly employed, it is an effective method for clarifying or emphasizing an idea.

Definition in the paragraph

L50   Occasionally develop a paragraph by definition. A paragraph of definition sets down the basic qualities of the subject as given by an independent source or as interpreted by the author.

[Topic thought:] Let us define plot.

[Development:] Let us define plot. We have defined story as a narrative of events arranged in their time-sequence. A plot is also a narrative of events, the emphasis falling on causality.

This paragraph is developed by definition. *Plot* is defined in itself and also in contrast to the definition of *story*.

"The king died and then the queen died," is a story. "The king died, and then the queen died of grief," is a plot. The time-sequence is preserved, but the sense of causality overshadows it. Or again: "The queen died, no one knew why, until it was discovered that it was through grief at the death of the king." This is a plot with a mystery in it, a form capable of high development. It suspends the time-sequence, it moves as far away from the story as its limitations will allow. Consider the death of the queen. If it is in a story we say "and then?" If it is in a plot we ask "why?" That is the fundamental difference between these two aspects of the novel. A plot cannot be told to a gaping audience of cave men or to a tyrannical sultan or to their modern descendant the movie-public. They can only be kept awake by "and then—and then—" They can only supply curiosity. But a plot demands intelligence and memory also.

—E. M. FORSTER, *ASPECTS OF THE NOVEL*

Analogy in the paragraph

L51   In suitable situations develop a paragraph by analogy. An analogy is a detailed comparison built on the assumption that if two things are alike in some particulars they will be alike in others. Although legitimate analogies are not easily constructed, they can be an effective occasional means of paragraph development.

[Topic thought:] Ants are much like human beings.

[Development:] Ants are much like human beings. The queen, drone, and worker ants have specific roles in society. In some colonies nurses, soldiers, builders, and food gatherers provide medical care, protection, shelter, and food respectively. Ants constantly exchange information. They farm and even raise livestock. They fight devastating battles and use chemical sprays to confuse the enemy. Like human beings they accomplish great feats of engineering and construction. But this is where the analogy ends.

The analogy—the detailed comparison between ants and human beings—is obvious.

[Topic thought:] Good writing style is lean style.

[Development:] The good style is the lean style. Like a good distance runner, it hasn't an ounce of excess fat anywhere on it. And like the good distance runner, it moves without excess motion. Its arms don't flail out in all directions; they swing easily at the sides in a beautiful economy of effort. A good style has the same grace and beauty in its motion as a good athlete because there's nothing wasted. Everything is there for a purpose.

In this analogy the notion of good writing style is made clearer by a comparison to a good distance runner.

—LAURENCE PERRINE,
"FIFTEEN WAYS TO WRITE FIVE HUNDRED WORDS"

Combination of methods in the paragraph

L52 Paragraphs are frequently developed by a combination of two or more methods.

[Topic thought:] The fish rose to the bait.

[Development:]The fish rose to the bait. When he reached office, Echo McWilliams found pacing up and down the corridor in front of the closed door, an apprehensive little man with a darting eye, who introduced himself as David Ubelini, attorney at law. By nine o'clock, two other nervous and unhappy characters had presented themselves as the brothers Selvaggio, and expressed a readiness to talk—in return for a one-third cut of the reward money and a promise of immunity. At three o'clock in the afternoon, just one hour before his deadline, another quondam associate of Nick the Barber, anxious to pay off an old grudge, had supplied Echo with the last bit of information he needed; and so at three-thirty he set out for his meeting with Mr. District Attorney.

The subject of the topic thought (fish) is divided into David Ubelini, the brothers Selvaggio, and another quondam associate. At the same time, the whole topic thought is developed by telling when and how the fish rose to the bait.

The essay

The formal essay

M1 An essay is a group of paragraphs developing a central thought.[1]

    A. A formal essay is impersonal, objective, often in the third person, and usually expository or argumentative.

    B. An informal essay is personal, conversational, frequently in the first person, often combining exposition with description and narration.

Selecting a topic

M2 Select an interesting topic. If a topic does not interest you, it is unlikely that you will interest your readers. (If the general topic is assigned, try to find an aspect that interests you.)

M3 Gather ideas on the topic. You can do this by brainstorming or by clustering.

    A. *Brainstorming*. List ideas as they occur, without regard for order. Selectivity and organization come later.

> movies
> expensive (for customer)
> sex
> violence

---

[1] An essay may be only one paragraph. There are one-paragraph essays from Francis Bacon to today's in-class essay answers. The concern here, however, is with a typically structured essay.

comedies
noisy audience
popcorn on seats, floor
expensive to produce
vs. videocassettes
movie stars
new theaters
better sound
large screen
reruns
advertising
cable movies

When the list is finished, group those items that are suitable for an essay.

B. *Clustering.* Begin with the topic word and let the mind work freely by association. Link words by means of circles and arrows.

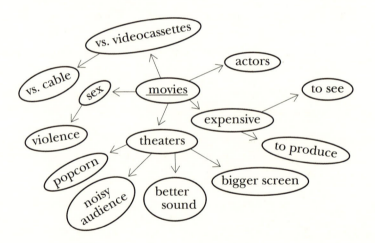

Clustering is the beginning of structure. Related groups emerge, any one of which might become the subject area of an essay.

M4 If you are unable to develop a brainstorming list or a cluster, either select a different topic or prime the imagination with questions.

A. Concept, term, idea	How is it defined? What is it similar to or related to? What are its applications? Is it valuable? Why or why not? Does it need to be modified or changed?
B. Object	What are its physical characteristics (size, shape, color)? What are its origins? How do its parts interrelate? How does it function? What are its uses? How is it similar to other objects? Of what importance is it?
C. Person	What are the person's physical characteristics? What other characteristics (attitudes, interests, and so on) are distinctive? What is the person's occupation? Ambitions? Accomplishments?
D. Event, action	What happened? What were its causes? What were it's consequences? What were the expenses? Who was involved? To what can it be compared?

M5 Continue to limit a topic until you can express the central idea for an essay in one sentence.

[Topic thought:] Theater attendance is becoming less attractive to average movie-goers.

The thesis statement

M6   The topic idea of an essay is expressed in a thesis statement (just as the topic idea of a paragraph is expressed in a topic sentence).[2]

M7   The thesis statement is developed in the body paragraphs of the essay (just as a topic sentence of a paragraph is developed through major and minor support statements in the paragraph).

M8   A good thesis statement has certain characteristics.

A. It narrows the general topic to the precise subject matter of the essay.

[Poor:] Diets are harmful.
[Good:] Crash diets are harmful.

[Poor:] Financial investments are risky.
[Good:] Investment in junk bonds is risky.

B. It affirms or denies (predicates) something specific about the subject and usually conveys the writer's opinion and purpose.

[Poor:] My city is great.
[Not very good:] My city provides many cultural offerings.
[Good:] My city has an outstanding art museum.

[Poor:] Paris is an unusual city.
[Good:] Paris is a romantic city.
[Good:] Paris is a cosmopolitan city.

---

[2] A question may serve as a thesis statement. Even with a question, however, there is an implicit statement that guides the essay. For example, a writer might pose the question "Is capital punishment an effective deterrent to crime?" He uses the question rather than a statement to arouse interest and encourage discussion. Implicit in the question, however, is one of three statements: (1) Capital punishment is an effective deterrent to crime, (2) Capital punishment is not an effective deterrent to crime, (3) There are valid arguments for and against capital punishment as an effective deterrent to crime.

C. It expresses only one main idea. If there are two ideas, one is subordinate.[3]

> [Not very good:] TV coverage of an athletic event is entertaining, but actual presence at the event is more exciting. [Good:] Although TV coverage of an athletic event is entertaining, actual presence at the event is more exciting.

D. It is so limited that every major point in it can be treated in the space of an essay.

E. It may suggest the type of development to be used in the essay.

> [Statement suggesting enumeration of different kinds of audience:] TV commercials are directed to specific audiences.

M9 Essays have a basic structure:

Introduction: usually one paragraph with a thesis statement.

Body: usually multiple paragraphs developing the thesis statement.

Conclusion: usually one paragraph providing a sense of completeness.

The introduction

M10 An introduction has a two-fold purpose: to create interest and to present the essay topic. This purpose is usually accomplished in an introductory paragraph.

M11 To arouse interest, a writer may first have to put the

---

[3] If there are coordinate ideas in the thesis statement, they are usually developed equally in the essay. Thus, a compound thesis statement usually compounds the writing task. A non-professional writer should write and develop a thesis statement with only one central idea.

audience in a receptive mood ("Yes, there is a reason why this dropout is talking on education") or to settle doubts about bringing up a particular subject ("Yes, drugs should be discussed at this meeting").

M12 Create interest with one or several techniques.[4]

A. Stress a topic's importance.

> . . . If we don't solve this problem soon, our lakes and rivers will be hopelessly polluted . . .

B. Ask a series of questions.

> . . . Are we doomed to follow in the footsteps of our predecessors? Do we really want to change? If we do want to change, do we really have a choice?

C. Make a provocative or startling statement.

> . . . This country's priorities are clear. We now spend more money each year on pet food than we do on baby food . . .

D. Use a quotation.

> . . . "Television is a medium of entertainment, which permits millions of people to listen to the same joke at the same time, and yet remain lonesome." (T. S. Eliot)

E. Use a brief incident or anecdote.

> . . . Two brothers were unable to settle their dispute on the division of the estate left by their father, and so they took their problem to a judge. After hearing their arguments, the judge ruled: "Let one brother divide the estate, and let the other brother have first choice." In a similar vein . . .

F. Descend logically from general statements to par-

---

[4] An introductory paragraph may give the divisions of the essay. However, this type of introduction is best reserved for lengthy, complicated essays and for research papers.

ticular statements, ending with the thesis statement.

> According to the scriptural account, the patriarch Abraham took on the duties of parenting at the ripe young age of one hundred. Many fathers would testify to the rigors of parenting at any age. So too would many high school teachers. Anyone who has been associated with the high school scene knows its rigors only too well. The physical requirements pale beside the sheer psychic drainage that alertness to the demands of young minds and vigilance over adolescent friskiness take. But Julian Maline, eighty years young, in the patriarchal tradition, still finds satisfaction in midwifing the birth of Gallic understanding in the minds of his first-year French students each day of the school year.

M13 Ordinarily place the thesis statement at the end of the introduction.[5]

M14 It is sometimes easier to write the introduction last. If it is written first, reread it when the essay is finished to see if it fits. Change what is inappropriate.

The conclusion

M15 Not every essay needs a concluding paragraph. Often one is added to eliminate abruptness and to give a sense of completeness. Sometimes the organizational pattern or the length and complexity of the essay calls for one.

M16 If there is a concluding paragraph, it should contain a paraphrase of the thesis statement. Beyond this requirement the writer is free to complete the conclusion in any of a variety of ways.

---

[5] The position of the thesis statement is arbitrary. It may appear anywhere in the introduction, in the conclusion, or merely be implied. Apprentice writers are encouraged to place it last in the introduction and thus provide a clear focus for writing the body paragraphs.

M17 The conclusion, however, is not the place to introduce a substantial body of new material. By its position, the concluding paragraph of an essay is very emphatic. Do not squander the opportunity to reinforce your ideas and to satisfy your audience.

M18 Consider the following techniques in writing a conclusion:

A. Use the "echo" technique (sometimes referred to as a "circular closing") and bring back from the introduction or body of the essay some significant symbol, figure of speech, key word or phrase.

> . . . And so, Shaw's comment notwithstanding, youth is not wasted on the young. It is . . .

B. End with a memorable quotation or an authoritative statement.

> . . . Adlai Stevenson reminds us, "Patriotism is not a short and frenzied outburst of emotion but the tranquil and steady dedication of a lifetime" . . .

C. Finish on a rousing note and reinforce the persuasiveness of the whole essay.

> . . . Carry yourselves, then, like the American soldiers that you are, and fear nothing but yourselves. Remember that America depends upon your courage, that she has no defense but you, that she entrusts herself to you . . .

D. Lower the audience from an emotional state to a calmer one.

> . . . So died, violently, a man who hated violence. Life has its ironies, doesn't it? And hardly a man dies without some little irony at the end to make a cynic mock—and a good person smile with understanding of the divine humor and the divine unexpectedness in things . . .

M

E. Begin with a paraphrase of the thesis statement and then widen out to more general statements.

> TV advertising has become less informative and more entertaining in recent years. This change simply reflects the general preference of our society. We do like to be entertained. Unfortunately we are coming to that moment when we will need to remind ourselves that important decisions in life should be based on information and reason, not on entertainment value.

F. Summarize the main points of the essay. (Use this method only if the essay is long or complicated. You may use it, for example, to conclude a research paper.)

Development of the body paragraphs

M19 Some of the more serviceable ways of developing the main ideas of the essay are by enumeration of details and facts, division and classification, circumstances, comparison and contrast, causes and effects, examples, and repetition.

Details and facts

M20 Development by enumerating relevant details or facts:

> [Thesis statement:][6] Joan Quanis is well qualified to be a member of the school board.
> [Paragraph:] A life-long resident of the community, she knows its needs.
> [Paragraph:] She is familiar with the public school system both as former student and teacher.
> [Paragraph:] A mother with young children, she is interested in improving the system.
> [Paragraph:] She has served on various educational committees.
> [Paragraph:] She is a dedicated worker.

---

[6] Only skeletal development of the essay is given here.

Division and classification

M21   Development by dividing a topic into its parts:

[Thesis statement:][7] Distinctive types of propulsion are used in airplanes today.

[Paragraph:] Small planes and older ones are propeller driven.

[Paragraph:] Most commercial planes today are jet propelled.

[Paragraph:] The turbo-prop combines features of propeller and jet propulsion.

[Paragraph:] The helicopter uses horizontally mounted rotary blades.

Circumstances

M22   Development by giving circumstances:

[Thesis statement:] Rear Admiral Jesse B. Oldendorf annihilated Nishimura's fleet.

It is not often that a classic textbook problem in naval warfare comes to life in actual battle, but it certainly did happen once in modern times. During World War II Rear Admiral Jesse B. Oldendorf annihilated Nishimura's fleet.	Introduction
The action took place on October 25-26, 1944, soon after MacArthur's return to the Philippines, at a time when a breakthrough by Nishimura would have jeopardized our chances of winning the war in the Pacific.	When?

---

[7] Only skeletal development of the essay is given here.

Oldendorf's fleet was plugging the gap between Surigao Strait and the part of Leyte Gulf where American landing operations were proceeding under the protection of a number of inadequate old warships.

Where?

Nishimura, who might have skirted Surigao Strait and, going around on the outside of the islands, bottled up the whole American operation in Leyte Gulf and blasted it at will, chose rather to string out his fleet single file in the long narrow alley of Surigao. He lacked anything worthy the name of reconnaissance and did not suspect that the Americans lay athwart the end of the strait. Thus it happened that he steamed straight up the center of Oldendorf's battle line and created the T-formation in which the perpendicular is subject to murderous cross fire.

How?

Because of the annihilation that followed, the Pacific war went to the Americans; and the tacticians will have something to talk about for years to come.

Conclusion

M

Comparison and contrast

M23 Development by using comparison, contrast, or both:

[Thesis statement:][8] Although similar in some ways, New Orleans and San Francisco have certain distinctive characteristics.

[Paragraph of comparison:] Both are major cities located near a body of water.

[Paragraph of contrast:] New Orleans is located on open, level ground; San Francisco is situated in a confined and hilly area.

[Paragraph of comparison:] Both cities have a cosmopolitan population, with residents and visitors from many countries.

[Paragraph of comparison:] Both cities have excellent restaurants and a great variety of places to visit and things to see.

[Paragraph of contrast:] New Orleans has its French Quarter; San Francisco has its Chinatown.

[Paragraph of contrast:] New Orleans has a unique cultural heritage, predominantly French; San Francisco does not have such a cultural heritage despite its Spanish origin.

M24 In M23 the topic is developed in a series of comparisons and contrasts. Another form of development is one long comparison or contrast running through several or all the body paragraphs.[9]

Cause and effect

M25 Development by stating some of the causes of, or reasons for, a particular truth or event:

[Thesis statement:][10] Brown, Lovett, and Driscoll do look a little weary this morning.

[Paragraph:] It seems that they attended the game last night in Driscoll's Model-A Ford—not a restful equipage.

[Paragraph:] Moreover, on the way home, the Ford began to disintegrate.

---

[8] Only skeletal development of the essay is given here.

[9] If a comparison is precise and extended, it is an analogy.

[10] For this and the following essay topics, only skeletal development is given.

[Paragraph:] The boys left it and walked seven stumbling dark miles to a farm, where they rented a horse.

[Paragraph:] The horse, a spavined hack not up to pulling automobiles, soon collapsed and had to be put on top of the car to rest.

[Paragraph:] The boys pushed the car and the horse the remaining five miles to Houston.

[Paragraph:] In Houston they were arrested for trucking livestock without a license.

[Paragraph:] At 6:00 A.M. Driscoll's father bailed them out—just in time to get ready for school.

M26 Development by stating the effects or consequences of a particular truth or event:

[Thesis statement:] The city was smothered under twenty-five inches of snow.

[Paragraph:] Traffic was strangled.

[Paragraph:] A fearful fire hazard was created (fire engines were snowed up in their garages).

[Paragraph:] Normal city life was in great part paralyzed.

[Paragraph:] The removal of the snow cost the city $232,170 for each inch of snow, or about $6,000,000 altogether.

[Paragraph:] But, of course, there were many who squeezed some fun out of the queer state of affairs.

Examples

M27 Development by giving relevant concrete examples:

[Thesis statement:] Unable to prove everything, people live by faith.

[Paragraph:] It is only by faith in the testimony of witnesses that many of us know that there actually was a George Washington, president of the United States.

[Paragraph:] We should all starve to death or go slowly mad if we did not believe that our restaurants and cooks use salt for seasoning, and not arsenic, when they say they use salt.

[Paragraph:] One who buys or sells stocks would be reduced

to gibbering paralysis if he did not believe the quotations that come to him over the wires or in the newspapers.

[Paragraph:] Even the ordinary affairs of everyday life would become a nightmare if one did not accept on faith much of what others tell him.

[Conclusion:] If we believe so much and act—rationally indeed—upon that belief, then let us not preen ourselves on having a "scientific" mind that must have a demonstration of everything.

Repetition

M28 Development by repeating an idea with greater clarity or from a different angle.

[Thesis statement:] We must love what is good or else we will be unhappy.

[Paragraph:] To love evil is to be unhappy.

[Paragraph:] All human joy worthy of the name is founded in loving what is good.

[Paragraph:] If we do not love what is good, we really do not love anything, including ourselves.

[Paragraph:] If we do not love what is good, the universe is a shrieking nightmare or a cold waste.

[Conclusion:] Do not be dismayed; for to love what is good is to love and to get—now or later—everything that can satisfy and thrill the human heart.

M29 Repetition must be used with care, for useless repetition bores readers.

Combination of methods

M30 Combinations of two or more of the methods explained in M20-29 are commonly used to develop sentences, paragraphs, or essays. A single method can be monotonous.

[Thesis statement:] Things began to change when Mr. Smoothy arrived at Tecky Mills.

Development by giving circumstances

[Paragraph (when?):] He turned up right after the union at Tecky Mills had negotiated a fair contract with the management.

[Paragraph (how?):] He slipped right in without a stir at the router that old Jim Cabo had vacated when he was pensioned and retired.

Development by enumeration

[Paragraph:] "Mr. Smoothy" was a quiet fellow, rather well-mannered, whose real name was Joel Tollern.

[Paragraph:] He made friends easily.

Development by repetition

[Paragraph:] Yes; one day "Mr. Smoothy" drifted into Tecky Mills. [This paragraph, is used to produce an atmosphere of suspense and slight foreboding, as well as to refocus the reader's attention.]

Development by giving effects

[Paragraph:] The atmosphere of the Mills began to change.

[Paragraph:] The men began to change.

[Paragraph:] Things began to happen to the work—annoying things, dangerous things.

Development by comparison

[Paragraph:] It was as though a kind of corruption had begun to stir and bubble in the Mills.

Development by giving causes

[Paragraph:] Why had "Mr. Smoothy" come?

In the following example a series of causes and effects, circumstances, and so on are combined with narration.

It must not be understood that Joe was more of a coward than most boys. He could take a reasonable amount of physical punishment with a reasonable amount of suppressed whimpering. Joe's difficulty was pride.

Until the time that he was ten, he had lived in a rural area where he got his schooling at home and had the companionship of only two or three boys. He had learned to hunt, but not to shoot baskets. He had learned to plow a field, but not to field a ball. At the age of ten he came to live in the city and found that he was an ignoramus in all the sciences at which city boys excel. He could have learned them even then, but he was too proud. Pride kept him from courting the laughs and jeers that greet the late beginner. He pretended that he did not care for sports and spent his time watching the others and joining them only in those diversions at which they were no less green than he.

He had a glib and entertaining tongue; he was generous enough not only with possessions but with praise; and so he never lacked companions, friends, invitations. Indeed, whole days might pass during which he would account himself happy; but then would come one of those embarrassing incidents that he had learned to dread.

There was the time, for instance, when the coach, a kindly man with no knowledge of Joe's frame of mind, had tried to shame him, in front of a number of the school heroes, into going out for baseball. The coach was not entirely to be blamed. To the casual observer Joe did look like a ballplayer, and the technique of shaming a boy is not altogether bad pedagogy in some circumstances.

There were other embarrassing moments, too, when, for example, he had to pretend not to see a football that bounced his way, lest he should betray his girlish awkwardness in throwing it back to the players. Little by little he had learned a trick that absorbed the scorn of schoolmates and turned their jibes to friendly raillery. The trick was to anticipate the laugh against himself, to play for it, and thus turn an embarrassing situation into an amusing one. If he could not avoid returning a ball, he shouted: "Watch out! Here comes my spit ball." He would make elaborate show of spitting delicately on his finger tips. "It's illegal, but it's tricky. You'd better back up!" His wild and feeble peg would be greeted with mild merriment; and the impression would circulate that he could really do much better if he were not such a clown [and so on].

Writing the rough draft

M31 When you determine your thesis statement, you should also determine your purpose in writing. Do you wish to entertain? explain? persuade? Your purpose will affect selection and presentation of material.

M32 Next, consider your audience. Is the audience your peers? your instructor? some special group? Remember that audience affects word choice, sentence style, examples, and organization of ideas.

[Addressed, properly, to fifth grade students:] Before I sell you any tickets, all of you must promise that you will not try to go beyond the lines and get close to those who will be shooting off the fireworks.

[Addressed, improperly, to fifth-grade students:] Before I enter into commerce with you for the sale of these admissions to volcanic wonders, I must have the solemn pledge of this assembly of splendid citizens of our commonweatlh that not one of you will attempt to break through the cordon surrounding those who will activate the instruments of display.

M33 Subject matter, purpose, audience, and the writer's temporarily assumed speaker role regularly interact upon one another as well as upon the writing process itself. For example, the writer assumes a specific attitude (speaker role) toward an audience for the purpose of effectively presenting selected subject matter; from another prospective subject matter, audience, and purpose affect the speaker voice or role.

Writing Process

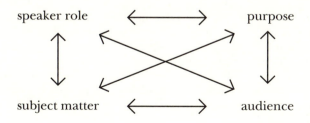

M34   Construct a tentative outline. After all, you should have a general sense of direction when you begin to write. Understand, however, that you are not committing yourself irrevocably to the items and sequence of this outline. You will probably modify the outline as you write.[11]

Thesis statement: Theater attendance is becoming less attractive to average movie-goers.

   I.   Theater attendance
      A. Inconvenient
      B. Expensive
      C. Confining
      D. Noisy
  II.   Cable movies
      A. Inexpensive
      B. Informal
 III.   Videocassette movies
      A. Convenient
      B. Inexpensive
      C. Informal

M35   As you write, follow the outline.

M36   Define terms as necessary for readers to have a clear understanding of the essay.[12]

M37   Write without interruption. Don't stop to consult a dictionary or a thesaurus. At this point flow of ideas is more important than correctness of phrase.

M38   Leave wide margins and ample space between lines for corrections and insertions.[13]

---

[11] Your instructor may want a detailed outline turned in with the essay. If so, write it when you write the final draft. For the format of various types of outlines, see N75-80.

[12] For a discussion of definition and its various forms, see Section O.

[13] Even if you use a word processor, it is good to run off a hard copy of your first draft, take a fresh look at what you have written, and make any additional changes on paper before returning to the word processor for another draft.

M39 Should a mental block develop, either reread what you have written and gather impetus to continue or take a break.

Revising the essay

Unity

M40 Unity means oneness. Unity in a composition requires that there be only one main thought and that all other thoughts and words in a sentence, paragraph, or essay directly or indirectly reinforce the main thought.

M41 A unified essay ordinarily develops one idea and maintains a consistent attitude toward that idea.[14]

M42 Every sentence should develop its topic sentence and every paragraph should develop the thesis statement.

M43 It is not necessary that every paragraph develop the thesis statement *directly*. Paragraph A, for example, may develop the thesis statement, and paragraph B and C may develop paragraph A. But do not carry such indirect development to the point where the reader loses the trail.

M44 At this point, it is helpful to write a full sentence outline based on the rough draft. Such an outline will immediately show up any inadequacies in the essay.[15]

M45 Check the outline on the following points:

A. Does every major division support the thesis statement?

B. Do all major divisions add up to neither more nor less than the thesis statement?

---

[14] In some instances a writer may develop both sides of an issue and encourage readers to make a decision.

[15] For the format of various types of outlines, see N75–80.

C. Do the subdivisions below each statement support that statement?

D. Does the group of subdivisions below a statement add up to neither more nor less than the statement itself?

Thesis:

I.

II.

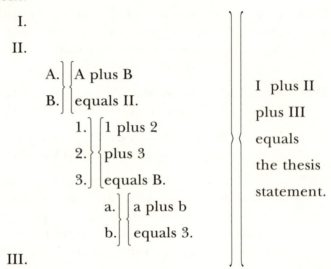

A. A plus B
B. equals II.

1. 1 plus 2
2. plus 3
3. equals B.

a. a plus b
b. equals 3.

I plus II

plus III

equals

the thesis

statement.

III.

M46 If the essay or any of the paragraphs is underdeveloped, see M20-30 on methods of development.

M47 The introduction should be related to the essay topic and lead naturally to it.

Coherence

M48 Coherence is the principle of composition which requires that, for the sake of clarity, ideas and words follow one another in an orderly manner and that the connections between parts be made clear.

M49 Coherence means that the words, sentences, paragraphs, and divisions of the essay are rightly put together and properly connected.

M50 Arrange the main and subordinate parts of an essay in one of the following or similar orders:

A. *The order of time.* First tell what happened first; second, tell what happened after that; third, tell what happened after that; and so on. (This order is particularly useful in narratives.)

Like an iceberg that had calved off a glacier, the great bulk of the north side of the volcano remained afloat in a molten sea. It was a mountain in itself, and, moreover, it moved. It was landscape on the loose, an incongruous itinerant alp, its summit high above the lava plain, its heading north by northwest. The mobile mountain had a nine-acre base and a sharp peak. It weighed two million tons. People looking up from almost any street in town could see its silhouette filling the sky—today in one place, tomorrow, in another. Someone named it Flakkarinn. And no one ever called it anything else. Flakkarinn the Wanderer.

The pressure wave that was created when Flakkarinn came off the volcano moved through the lava for a number of days and squeezed from the periphery new freshets of red rock. Some of this was in the lobe that stopped at the harbor wall. Flakkarinn, sliding downhill, also made bow waves in the molten lava through which it plowed. And as it went along it dug a kind of trough. Lava filled in behind it. Where Flakkarinn broke the crust of the earlier flow, fresh streams of molten material poured forth. People climbed up and rode on Flakkarinn. It shook as it travelled. In its first two weeks, it went half a mile.

— John McPhee, *The Control of Nature*

B. *The order of place.* Start at the bottom and go to the top, or start at the top and go to the bottom, or start at the right and go to the left, and so on; or start at one end and go to the other, and so on. (This order is particularly useful in descriptions.)

I was told to look for Mr. Forous on Salinas Street.
Salinas Street is a long, dirty, festering wound running through the south flank of Claymore from the river to the open prairie west of town.

At the river end it presents a pair of saloons, like gatehouses, on either side of the street. Dives they are, and look it; but they are the soundest edifices on the whole street and do not prepare one for the incredible squalor beyond.

After the saloons come two rows of hovels, gaping slack-jawed at each other across the wide, pitted, trash-strewn thoroughfare. "Hovels" has too grand a sound to describe the unbelievable jungle of drunken, staggering, slouching structures thrown together with wire, packing cases, sections of rusted metal culvert, cardboard, and old license plates nailed to overlap in pathetic parody of shingles and clapboard. These are the homes of the "Salinas Street Slush-Eaters," as the rest of Claymore cynically calls them—these foul and rickety nightmares that do not shelter the inmates from so much as a curious glance.

After several hundred yards of these, on the north side of the street there is a little clearing in the center of which rises—but not very high—Father Andreas's church: a shed, roofed with tin, open on three sides, and floored with dirt except for the platform under the "sanctuary" [and so on].

C. *The order of interest or importance.* Start with the least important or interesting thought and move by degrees to the most interesting or important.

[*Time*'s chief reporter, Jack Skow, had no success gathering information on J. D. Salinger from his sister, Doris.] There were other rebuffs of this nature—Peter de Vries told the magazine's reporter, "No, I don't want to hear your questions. If you asked me how to spell his name, I wouldn't feel free to tell you. If there are gaps in your story, they're gaps Salinger *wants* in the story."

Salinger wanted gaps in his story. For the *Time* sleuths this could mean only one thing, Salinger had Something to Hide. To judge from the narrative that can be pieced together from *Time*'s archive (a bulging folder of notes, telexes, memos, and dispatches), it was not long before a distinct line of investigation started to emerge: that the key to Salinger's reclusiveness, or furtiveness, could be fathomed by decoding his two most celebrated stories—"A Perfect Day for Bananafish" and "For Esme—with Love and Squalor." The stories had two things in common: a hero whose nerves had been badly damaged in the war and a little girl heroine who for a moment seems to offer him salvation. "Bananafish" was thought to be the more significant of the two because it inaugurates Salinger's weird obsession with the family Glass.

"Why did Seymour kill himself?" *Time* wondered. If the story was based on Salinger's own life, then two lines of questioning had to be pursued. First, who and where was Salinger's first wife? Was she the Muriel of "Bananafish" and of "Raise High the Roof Beam, Carpenters"? Second, who and where was Sybil, the little girl Seymour/Salinger befriends on the beach in Florida? *Time* operatives were dispatched across the land with orders to locate the real-life counterparts of Muriel and Sybil.

—IAN HAMILTON, *IN SEARCH OF J. D. SALINGER*

D. *The logical order.* Follow a series of causes and effects, circumstances and results, and so on.

As young women, whether students or not, we're still in the stage most valued by male-dominant cultures: we have our full potential as workers, wives, sex partners, and child bearers.

That means we haven't yet experienced the life events that are most radicalizing for women: entering the paid-labor force and discovering how women are treated there; marrying and finding out that it is not yet an equal partnership; having children and discovering who is responsible for them and who is not; and aging, still a greater penalty for women than for men.

Furthermore, new ambitions nourished by the rebirth of feminism may make young women feel and behave a little like a classical immigrant group. We are determined to prove ourselves, to achieve academic excellence, and to prepare for interesting and successful careers. More noses are kept to the grindstones in an effort to demonstrate new-found abilities, and perhaps to allay suspicions that women still have to have more and better credentials than men. This doesn't leave much time for activism. Indeed, we may not yet know that it is necessary.

In addition, the very progress into previously all-male careers that may be revolutionary for women is seen as conservative and conformist by outside critics. Assuming male radicalism to be the measure of change, they interpret any concern with careers as evidence of "campus conservatism." In fact, "dropping out" may be a departure for men, but "dropping in" is a new thing for women. Progress lies in the direction we have not been.

Like most groups of newly arrived or awakened, our faith in education and paper degrees also has yet to be shaken. For instance, the percentage of women enrolled in colleges and universities has been increasing at the same time that the percentage of men has been decreasing. Among students entering college in 1978, women *outnumbered* men for the first time. This hope of excelling at the existing game is probably reinforced by the greater cultural pressure on females to be "good girls" and observe somebody else's rules.

—GLORIA STEINEM,
"WHY YOUNG WOMEN ARE MORE CONSERVATIVE"

E. *The psychological order.* Follow the order that will make your matter more interesting, easier to understand, or more acceptable to a particular audience. The following speech from Shakespeare's *Julius Caesar* is a classic example of the use of crowd psychology.

ANTONY: Friends, Romans, countrymen, lend me your ears;
I come to bury Caesar, not to praise him.
The evil that men do lives after them;
The good is oft interred with their bones.
So let it be with Caesar. The noble Brutus
Hath told you Caesar was ambitious:

At the beginning of this speech the crowd is hostile to Antony and the dead Caesar. Antony does not dare to give them his thesis right at the beginning, does not dare to say that Caesar was a great and just ruler and that he has been foully murdered. He would never get a hearing. He therefore begins most modestly. He carefully balances every item of praise of

If it were so, it was a grievous
fault;
And grievously hath Caesar
answer'd it.
Here, under leave of Brutus
and the rest
(For Brutus is an honourable
man;
So are they all, all honourable
men,)
Come I to speak in Caesar's
funeral.
He was my friend, faithful and
just to me:
But Brutus says he was ambi-
tious;
And Brutus is an honourable
man.
He hath brought many cap-
tives home to Rome,
Whose ransoms did the gen-
eral coffers fill:
Did this in Caesar seem am-
bitious?
When that the poor have
cried, Caesar hath wept:
Ambition should be made of
sterner stuff:
Yet Brutus says he was ambi-
tious;
And Brutus is an honourable
man.
You all did see that on the
Lupercal
I thrice presented him a kingly
crown,
Which he did thrice refuse:
was this ambition?

Caesar with the charge of
ambition brought against
him. He mentions traits of
character that the crowd can
accept without feeling dis-
loyal to Brutus. Then he
skillfully begins to set before
them more sentimental facts,
leading their emotions inch
by inch, then foot by foot,
then yard by yard away from
the convictions that Brutus
has planted in them a scant
few minutes before. When he
has got them weeping with
him, he shocks them with the
sudden sight of Caesar's
shredded body. Then (near
the end of the speech, not
given here) he caps everything with what he has saved
till the last—the poorest argument against ambition, but
the argument that will mean
most to the crowd—the fact
that Caesar has left a little
money to every Roman citizen
and has willed his private estates as public parks. The
money and the parks buy the
mob for Antony, and he sets
it to burning down Rome and
lynching his enemies. Had he
proceeded in any other way,
he would soon have lost his
hearing and possibly his head.
He used a psychological order, adapted to his audience.

M

Yet Brutus says he was ambitious;
And, sure, he is an honourable man.
I speak not to disprove what Brutus spoke,
But here I am to speak what I do know.
You all did love him once, not without cause;
What cause withholds you, then, to mourn for him?
O judgment, thou art fled to brutish beasts,
And men have lost their reason!—Bear with me;
My heart is in the coffin there with Caesar,
And I must pause till it come back to me.

FIRST CITIZEN: Methinks there is much reason in his sayings.

SECOND CITIZEN: If thou consider rightly of the matter, Caesar
    has had great wrong.

THIRD CITIZEN: Has he, masters?
I fear there will a worse come in his place.

FOURTH CITIZEN: Mark'd ye his words? He would not take the
    crown;
Therefore 'tis certain he was not ambitious.

FIRST CITIZEN: If it be found so, some will dear abide it.

SECOND CITIZEN: Poor soul! his eyes are red as fire with weeping.

THIRD CITIZEN: There's not a nobler man in Rome than Antony.

FOURTH CITIZEN: Now mark him, he begins again to speak.

ANTONY: But yesterday, the word of Caesar might
Have stood against the world; now, lies he there,
And none so poor to do him reverence.
O masters! if I were dispos'd to stir
Your hearts and minds to mutiny and rage,
I should do Brutus wrong, and Cassius wrong,
Who, you all know, are honourable men:
I will not do them wrong; I rather choose
To wrong the dead, to wrong myself, and you,
Than I will wrong such honourable men,
But here's a parchment with the seal of Caesar,
I found it in his closet; 'tis his will:
Let but the commons hear this testament,
(Which, pardon me, I do not mean to read,)
And they would go and kiss dead Caesar's wounds,
And dip their napkins in his sacred blood;
Yea, beg a hair of him for memory,

And, dying, mention it within their wills,
Bequeathing it, as a rich legacy,
Unto their issue.

FOURTH CITIZEN: We'll hear the will: read it, Mark Antony.

CITIZENS: The will, the will! we will hear Caesar's will.

ANTONY: Have patience, gentle friends, I must not read it;
It is not meet you know how Caesar loved you.
You are not wood, you are not stones, but men;
And, being men, hearing the will of Caesar,
It will inflame you, it will make you mad:
'Tis good you know not that you are his heirs;
For if you should, O, what would come of it!

FOURTH CITIZEN: Read the will; we'll hear it, Antony;
You shall read us the will; Caesar's will.

ANTONY: Will you be patient? Will you stay a while?
I have o'ershot myself to tell you of it;
I fear I wrong the honourable men,
Whose daggers have stabb'd Caesar; I do fear it.

FOURTH CITIZEN: They were traitors: honourable men!

CITIZENS: The will! The testament!

SECOND CITIZEN: They were villains, murderers! The will! Read
the will!

ANTONY: You will compel me, then, to read the will?
Then make a ring about the corse of Caesar,
And let me show you him that made the will.
Shall I descend? and will you give me leave?

CITIZENS: Come down.

SECOND CITIZEN: Descend. [*Antony comes down.*]

THIRD CITIZEN: You shall have leave.

FOURTH CITIZEN: A ring; stand round.

FIRST CITIZEN: Stand from the hearse, stand from the body.

SECOND CITIZEN: Room for Antony, most noble Antony!

ANTONY: Nay, press not so upon me; stand far off.

CITIZENS: Stand back! Room! Bear back!

ANTONY: If you have tears, prepare to shed them now.
You all do know this mantle: I remember
The first time ever Caesar put it on;
'Twas on a summer's evening, in his tent,
That day he overcame the Nervii—

Look, in this place, ran Cassius' dagger through:
See what a rent the envious Casca made:
Through this the well-beloved Brutus stabb'd;
And, as he pluck'd his cursed steel away,
Mark how the blood of Caesar follow'd it,
As rushing out of doors, to be resolv'd
If Brutus so unkindly knock'd, or no;
For Brutus, as you know, was Caesar's angel:
Judge, O you gods, how dearly Caesar lov'd him!
This was the most unkindest cut of all;
For when the noble Caesar saw him stab,
Ingratitude, more strong than traitors' arms,
Quite vanquish'd him: then burst his mighty heart;
And, in his mantle muffling up his face,
Even at the base of Pompey's statue,
Which all the while ran blood, great Caesar fell.
O, what a fall was there, my countrymen!
Then I, and you, and all of us fell down,
Whilst bloody treason flourish'd over us.
O, now you weep; and, I perceive, you feel
The dint of pity; these are gracious drops.
Kind souls, what, weep you when you but behold
Our Caesar's vesture wounded? Look you here,
Here is himself, marr'd, as you see, with traitors.
First Citizen: O piteous spectacle!
Second Citizen: O noble Caesar!
Third Citizen: O woeful day!
Fourth Citizen: O traitors, villains!
First Citizen: O most bloody sight!
Second Citizen: We will be revenged: revenge—about—seek—
    burn—fire—kill—slay—let not a traitor live [and so on].

—William Shakespeare,
Julius Caesar, Act III, scene 2

M

M51 It happens often enough that one of the other orders listed in M50 is also the best psychological order for a certain audience under certain circumstances.

M52 Do not use the psychological order as an excuse to throw away all order. Make sure that you yourself have a plan that you can explain on demand and then take care that readers always know where they are, what is happening, and can see the connections between the parts of the essay.

M53 Supply the reader with all the information necessary for an easy following of the thought.

> . . . Elaine had a good job and put aside a little money as she went. With her savings and money from a few small investments, she hoped some day to move out of the ghetto and buy a modest house in the suburbs.
>
> *When the economy turned sour and she was forced to take a cut in pay,* her outlook on life changed dramatically. The house of her dreams was no longer a possibility. Now she spent her time planning how to cut expenses . . .

> . . . The aspect of the experiment he [Gorbachev] was promoting fixed the factory's total wage bill for the next five years, while at the same time demanding higher production. The reform had the Thatcherite effect of giving workers an incentive to reduce their numbers and thus leave the remainder a bigger share of the same cake. His main job was to reassure the redundant that there would be retraining and new jobs guaranteed—and his success has taken him into the ranks of the *Nomenklatura.*
>
> The *Nomenklatura* is the key to understanding the way the Communist party exercises control. It is simply two lists. The first, the *osnovnaya,* is the list of jobs in key political and economic management positions throughout the country to which

The information in the second paragraph (in this case, a definition) is essential to a clear understanding of the third paragraph.

M

the party holds the monopoly of appointment. There are roughly 600,000 of these jobs and they represent the commanding heights of Soviet life. The second list is the *uchetnaya*, a catalogue of rather fewer than a million names of those who are judged suitable to fill a *Nomenklatura* vacancy as it occurs. It is a gigantic system of patronage, similar to the practice by which vicarage appointments in the Church of England used to be in the gift of the local aristocracy, and with obvious parallels to the network of political and civil service patronage controlled by a modern British prime minister or American president. Like the old-school-tie network, at an individual level it is based on personal loyalty and acquaintance. Brezhnev looked after the group of managers he had come to know when he ran the industrial city of Dnepropretrovsk, and Gorbachev is now promoting the people he grew to trust in his home region of Stavropol and Krasnodar.

One of the more interesting features of Gorbachev's career in Stavropol was the cautious way in which he began to erode the traditional power of the *Nomenklatura* system, by introducing the principle of elections. Not all the *Nomenklatura* lists are controlled from Moscow. The central committee of the party at the Moscow headquarters on Staraya Ploshadz has about 50,000 jobs on its list, which include key posts in ministries . . .

—Martin Walker, *The Waking Giant*

M54 Supply necessary information when or before the reader needs it. Do not use devices like *I forgot to tell you* or *it should have been mentioned earlier that* . . .

This is incoherent	*This is coherent*
Terrence McFarlane looked at the people around him. There were about thirty of them altogether, most of them dozing, lulled by the	Terrence McFarlane looked at the people around him. There were about thirty of them altogether, most of them dozing, lulled by the

rhythmic sway as well as by the want of fresh air. McFarlane could stare at them without seeming impolite. Like everybody else over twenty-five, he enjoyed looking at people and trying to guess what sort they were and what had made them like that.

That sailor, for instance, had an interesting face. Even in sleep, which usually relaxes a man's features, the sailor looked hard. He was the youngest person on the bus and yet the bitterest-looking of the lot.

rhythmic sway of the bus as well as by the want of fresh air. McFarlane could stare at them without seeming impolite. Like everybody else over twenty-five, he enjoyed looking at people and trying to guess what sort they were and what had made them like that.

That sailor, for instance, had an interesting face. Even in sleep, which usually relaxes a man's features, the sailor looked hard. He was the youngest person on the bus and yet the bitterest-looking of the lot.

M55 To supply missing connections, to make vague ones more definite, and to smooth out abrupt transitions, use bridge words, phrases, sentences, and paragraphs.

M56 Some common bridge words are *this, that; but, still, yet, however; then, next, first (second* or *secondly, third* or *thirdly,* and so on); *while, finally, meanwhile, afterward;* and *so, therefore, consequently.*

M57 *Meanwhile* and similar connectives are very helpful in holding the reader on the track when the writer is keeping two or more series of events going at once.

M58 Do not use *so* when a mere time connection or no connection at all exists between parts.

... told both of us to dress for dinner since she was having

At

guests. ~~So at~~ eight o'clock the guests began to arrive [and so on].

Well,
. . . that finishes everything I have to say. ~~So~~ it has been fun chatting with you by mail [and so on].

M59 When using *this, that, he,* and other pronouns as bridge words, take care that it is always clear just what each one's antecedent is. When this is not clear, drop the pronoun in favor of some other word or phrase whose reference is not vague.

Preston took his place at my left, Henri at my right, and Piggot directly in front of me.

Piggot
~~He~~ snarled at me: "Dirty little sneak! What are you doing in a school with decent fellows?"

The boulder-strewn roads that wound over the ugly mountains were very hard on the jeeps, rattling them into junk heaps in two months or less. The altitude, also, seemed to affect the operation of the sturdy little cars. But perhaps the Greeks, with no touch at all for mechanical things and no skill in driving, caused more damage and breakdowns than the terrain and the altitude together.

These difficulties
~~This~~ finally made Major Shellabarger decide to call a conference of the American observers and General Karapopoloumenos's staff.

M60 Some common bridge phrases are *this* and *that* plus a noun, *on the other hand, on the contrary, after that, in the second place, in the last part, in the next part, in the meantime, as a consequence,* and *as a result.*

Murca, we discovered, was fond of a noisome cheese that he had brought with him in considerable quantity.

This peculiarity did not endear him to the others [and so on].

M61 A bridge sentence may be used at the beginning of a paragraph to link it with the preceding paragraph.

. . . seventy-five percent of these people eat no breakfast and wear no shoes, even in winter. There is no doctor, no nurse. People who are sick recover or die without help.

The province lies in a narrow strip of land between two mountain ranges. One would imagine that such a situation would be conducive to . . .

The transition from the sad plight of the people to the geography of the province is so abrupt as to be distracting. A bridge sentence would help.

. . . seventy-five percent of these people eat no breakfast and wear no shoes, even in winter. There is no doctor, no nurse. People who are sick recover or die without help.

One of the causes of all the misery we have been relating is the geography of the place. The province lies in a narrow strip of land between two mountain ranges. One would imagine that such a situation would be conducive to . . .

M62 A bridge sentence may be used at the end of a paragraph to link it with the next paragraph.

. . . within the same month Alphonse had lost his girlfriend and his part-time job. He had also failed three subjects and was on academic probation.

It seems that Alphonse had saved his money and had recently bought a car. One day . . .

The transition from Alphonse's troubles to the purchase of a car is abrupt and confusing. A bridge sentence would help.

. . . within the same month Alphonse had lost his girlfriend and his part-time job. He had also failed three subjects and was on academic probation. But this wasn't the end of his troubles.

It seems that Alphonse had saved his money and had recently bought a car. One day . . .

M63 Bridge paragraphs are used to close gaps between sections of an essay.

> . . . that the student who has neglected philosophy, theology, history, languages, and art for courses that bear more directly on physics, will find himself well educated for research in physics but not for life.
>
>   The liberally educated person *may* not be as well equipped for getting a particular job . . .

> *If the first part of the essay is discussing undergraduate specialization and the second part is discussing liberal education, then the jump is too abrupt. The reader needs a good formal warning that a major change of direction is taking place. A bridge word, phrase, or sentence would not mark the change emphatically enough for a major division; so the writer had better use a bridge paragraph:*

> . . . that the student who has neglected philosophy, theology, history, languages, and art for courses that bear more directly on physics, will find himself well educated for research in physics but not for life.
>
>   You see, then, the advantages and disadvantages of undergraduate specialization. What about a liberal arts course of studies? Has it anything better to offer? We shall try to answer that question now in the second half of this discussion.
>
>   The liberally educated person *may* not be as well equipped for getting a particular job, but . . .

M64 Do not use bridge words, phrases, sentences, or paragraphs where they are not needed to make clear the connection and relationship between the parts of the essay. Unnecessary transitional expressions slow pace and inflate a text.

M65 Unless there is a reason to change, keep to the same grammatical subject within a paragraph.

> The rise of English is a remarkable story. When Julius Caesar landed in Britain nearly two thousand years ago, English did not exist. Five hundred years later, *Englisc*, incomprehensible to modern ears, was probably spoken by as few people as

currently speak Cherokee—and with about as little influence. Nearly a thousand years later, at the end of the sixteenth century, when William Shakespeare was in his prime, English was the native speech of between five and seven million Englishmen and it was, in the words of a contemporary, "of small reatch, it stretcheth no further than this iland of ours, naie not there over all".

Four hundred years later, the contrast is extraordinary. Between 1600 and the present, in armies, navies, companies and expeditions, the speakers of English—including Scots, Irish, Welsh, American and many more—travelled into every corner of the globe, carrying their language and culture with them. Today, English is used by at least 750 million people, and barely half of these speak it as a mother tongue. Some estimates have put that figure closer to one billion. Whatever the total, English at the end of the twentieth century is more widely scattered, more widely spoken and written, than any other language has ever been. It has become *the* language of the planet, the first truly global language.

—Robert McCrum, William Cran, Robert MacNeil,
The Story of English

M66 Enhance coherence by the use of pronouns, synonyms, and the repetition of key words.

M67 Reading an essay out loud is an effective way to spot weaknesses in coherence.

Emphasis

M68 Emphasis means relative stress. In writing, emphasis is the principle which requires that more important ideas be made to stand out from less important ideas. Writing is properly emphatic when readers know, without thinking the matter over, which ideas are most important, which less, and which least important.

M69 Make clear the relative importance of ideas in an essay. You will accomplish this by observing the rules that follow.

M70   Give the most important ideas the most space, the less important ideas less space, and so on.

M71   An important idea is sometimes so persuasive and so easy to understand in itself that to give it fuller treatment than less important ideas would be to blow it up with empty verbiage. When this happens, ignore M70 and use some other emphasis device.

M72   The introduction and conclusion should be short in comparison with the body of the essay. For example, in a five-paragraph essay the introduction and conclusion together should be one-third or less of the entire essay. In a lengthy essay, the proportion would be even less.

M73   Put important ideas in emphatic positions. See M74-75.

M74   The most emphatic position in an essay is ordinarily near the end. It is, therefore, a good place to (a) restate the thesis statement, (b) summarize the main points of the essay, (c) use the most telling argument or most striking presentation, (d) introduce the most interesting incident, or (e) release readers from mounting suspense by telling them what you want them to remember.

M75   The second most emphatic position in an essay is ordinarily near the beginning. Consequently, use the opening paragraph to introduce the topic and to interest the audience in its development.

M76   After the introduction, start with the least important or interesting thought and move by degrees to the most interesting or important.

Meltdown is a vague word, too loosely used during the Chernobyl crisis, but the worst case of a meltdown had already been avoided when the chain reaction stopped. The new fear was of something rather different: the glowing-hot reactor core burning its way through the floor of the power station and into the earth. And every extra ton of the vital shielding the helicopters were dropping was helping to press the reactor core down through its floor. Below that floor lay the water table, ominously close to the surface. At the very least, the sinking reactor would contaminate the ground water of the Dnieper valley, with awesome consequences for the vital granary of the Ukraine, for the city of Kiev and, eventually, for the Black Sea itself.

But even before that happened, the likelihood was that the reactor would instantly vaporise any pockets of water it reached, creating a kind of steam bomb, able to explode the reactor and its 5000-ton burden of irradiated sand. They would be blasted into the air in a cloud of radiation that would have made the first plume seem like so much air-freshener.

There was no single solution to this threat. A series of remedial measures had to be taken simultaneously. The first priority was to cool the reactor, because the insulation effect of the sand had started to increase the core temperature, which could eventually have made the core go critical again. The cooling was done through a complex system of tubes feeding liquid nitrogen, which were pushed into place by radio-controlled robots, at least three of them supplied from West Germany.

Beneath the reactor, teams of miners were boring a series of tunnels. There were tunnels to pump out the ground water, and tunnels driven directly underneath the reactor to pump in cement and molten lead. The lead was intended to stop radiation seeping into the water table, and the cement was a giant barrier to slow, and eventually stop the sinking reactor. At the same time huge screens of lead [and so on].

— MARTIN WALKER, *THE WAKING GIANT*

M77 Sometimes clarity or some other important consideration makes it inadvisable to follow M73-76. For example, there are circumstances in which it is good to have a very unemphatic, gentle opening that promises very little. In such cases, use some other emphatic device.

M78 Get emphasis for an idea by contrasting its treatment with the treatment of the other ideas around it.

M79 Rarely, use visual devices like the setting off of a single brief statement in a paragraph by itself.

It was obvious that a single extra division would turn the tide for us. We were doing well. We were holding Klavic's army longer than anybody had thought we could.

A single extra division would have given our left flank the strength it needed to advance. We all knew that that extra division, under Aubrey Tarleton, had been ordered up since the night before. We were all waiting tensely for it, hour after hour. But Tarleton never came.

It was Tarleton's unexplainable absence that finally broke [and so on].

The sentence *But Tarleton never came* receives some emphasis in the first version as the last sentence in its paragraph, but more in the second as a paragraph by itself.

It was obvious that a single extra division would turn the tide for us. We were doing well. We were holding Klavic's army longer than anybody had thought we could.

A single extra division would have given our left flank the strength it needed to advance. We all knew that that extra division, under Aubrey Tarleton, had been ordered up since the night before. We were all waiting tensely for it, hour after hour.

But Tarleton never came.

It was Tarleton's unexplainable absence that finally broke [and so on].

M80 Some writers overwork the visual-contrast trick of M79. It is an obvious form of emphasis, and readers do not like obvious tricks. So never use visual contrast to the point where readers may come to notice what you are doing.

M81 Occasionally emphasize a thought by changes in rhythm, sound, sentence structure, and so on.

Laugh! Laugh loud! Be brittle and staccato. What you do, do quickly. Move along. Do, do, do. Never think. Achieve; win things; acquire things; fight for things; hold on to things. Never look at yourself. You won't like what you see. It will disturb you. Just get things for yourself. Pad yourself around with them. Insulate yourself against biting winds. And drink; above all, drink. Drink the sharp sting out of life. Soften the blinding light of life by looking at it through the bottom of a bottle.

Notice that in the first paragraph nearly all the sentences are brief and that the only two long sentences are loose sentences. Many of the words—for example, *brittle, do, think, fight*—have a sharp sound. The second paragraph is a long periodic sentence, containing a good many mouth-filling words of long, full, liquid, sonorous, or softened sound—for example, *overwhelm, drown, hush, rolls, flows, intones.*

But a quiet voice, a voice welling up in serenity to engulf the world's madness, to overwhelm it and drown it and hush it forever, a voice whose tide rolls out and laps the shores of eternity, a voice that flows some day into every heart, a voice raised in Galilee intones: "Thou fool, this night do they require thy soul of thee."

M82 Occasionally emphasize an idea by repeating it in the course of an essay. Sometimes, in very oratorical and emphatic essays, an idea may be repeated several times in exactly the same words. But usually the repetition must be dressed up a bit if it is to please and not seem too naked a device.

Drivers of automobiles do not think enough.

At a time when safety councils, police, and automobile clubs use all kinds of publicity—posters, advertisements, markers—to make streets and highways safe, drivers of automobiles never seem to realize that they are being alerted, never seem to question what they do behind the wheel of a car.

Recently a national magazine published photographs of automobile accidents, cars smashed and wrenched into junk, bloody and battered bodies lying on the highway. All of the accidents were due to some foolishness on the part of the drivers, who were going too fast or neglected warning signs or passed other cars when they should not have.

Readers of the magazine were appalled—and rightly—at what they saw; but how many of them asked whether they did not themselves often drive just as foolishly? They did not stop to think.

Before every major holiday the newspapers, with frightening accuracy, will foretell the number of automobile accidents that will occur on that holiday. Readers are shocked, deplore all this carelessness (which other people, of course, are guilty of), and no doubt murmur, "Something ought to be done." But they are never led to examine what they do as drivers themselves, whether they drive too fast, ignore traffic regulations, or take needless chances.

Drivers of automobiles do not think enough.

M83 Occasionally get emphasis by stating that a thought is important, interesting, or something of the kind.

> And now we come to the most practical solution that I have to offer, an idea that I am sure is worth all my other suggestions put together. . .

M84 Of all the ways of getting emphasis, this by express statement (M83) is the most annoying when it is abused. The writer who abuses it is somewhat like the wit who ruins jokes by always saying, "I want to tell you a story that will simply slay you. You'll die laughing." Keep in mind the principles in M85-86.

M85 Do not say that an idea is important, interesting, or anything of the kind unless you are sure that it is; and do not say that an idea is *more* important, interesting and so on, than it actually is.

> [An insult to the intelligence of reader or listener:] And now to the question that all America is asking: What cigarette guarantees the safest smoking enjoyment?

M86 Even if you have several very important or interesting points, do not *state* that more than one or two of them are important or interesting. Use other emphasis devices for the rest.

Essay revision checklist

M87 As a final check on an essay, consider the following questions:

1. Does the essay discuss all major components of the thesis statement?

2. Are difficult or ambiguous terms defined?

3. Do all the body paragraphs support the thesis either directly or indirectly?

4. Do the sentences in each paragraph support the topic sentence of that paragraph?

5. Are there adequate details, reasons, examples, and so on, to support each major idea?

6. Is the overall organizational pattern appropriate to the subject matter, purpose, and audience?

7. Are ideas presented in a systematic way?

8. Are important ideas properly emphasized?

9. Are the relationships between supporting statements and thesis clearly presented?

10. Is there any irrelevant material?

11. Are there effective transitions between ideas and paragraphs?

12. Is the tone of the essay appropriate for the topic, audience, and role of the writer?

13. Is the introduction interesting, informative, and clearly related to the subject matter of the essay?

14. Does the conclusion supply a sense of completeness?

15. In general, does the essay have clarity, economy, and accuracy?

16. Is the title brief, informative, and engaging?

(For a checklist on sentence structure and diction, see K140.)

Preparing the final copy[16]

M88 Use standard 8 1/2 by 11 inch paper. Do not use erasable or "onionskin" paper; such paper smudges easily and is difficult to read. Write or type on only one side of a page.

M89 If the paper is handwritten, write legibly in blue or black ink. If the paper is typed, avoid unusual type fonts.

M90 Observe proper margins.

A. In general, leave a one-inch margin on all sides of the page. If the paper is to be bound, leave a one and one-half inch margin on the left. In typing do not justify the right-hand margin.

B. The spacing at the top of the first page depends on what style manual is used.[17]

M91 Double-space typed papers. Handwritten papers may be single spaced if the lines are at least one-half inch apart.

---

[16] For special directives in preparing the final copy on a word processor, see T22-31.

[17] For directives and models on format and documentation, see N114 (MLA), N123 (APA), N140 (University of Chicago).

M92 Pages are ordinarily numbered in the upper right corner, just inside the right margin. The exact location depends on what style manual is used.[18]

M93 Follow instructor's directions on the position of the essay title, your name, course, and date.

M94 An essay title, like an introduction, should inform and pique interest. It should also be brief.

> [Poor:] Fast Food
> [Improved:] Fast Food and the Nutritional Requirements of Americans
> [Better:] How Nutritional Is Fast Food?

M95 If an essay has a clever or humorous title, the reader has a right to expect a clever or humorous essay. Make sure that title and essay match.

M96 The use of a title page and the position of a title depend on the style manual used.[19] Some instructors may have their own requirements.

M97 The title is ordinarily typed in capital and lowercase letters and not italicized (not underlined). Some styles require all-capital letters.[20]

M98 Proofreading is necessary. It helps to read the paper out loud.

M99 Corrections should not be visible. Computers and most electronic typewriters facilitate such corrections. A handwritten paper or one typed on a conventional typewriter requires a good ink eraser or correction fluid or tape.

---

[18] For directives and models on format and documentations, see N114 (MLA), N123 (APA), N140 (University of Chicago).

[19] For directives and models on format and documentation, see N114 (MLA), N123 (APA), N140 (University of Chicago).

[20] For the University of Chicago style, see N140.

M100 Model formal essay:

A Sense of Commitment—Do We Need It?

A long-time business associate pulls out of an important real-estate project after years of planning. A couple are divorced following fifteen years of marriage. A nun leaves her religious order. Such occurrences are increasing in frequency and lead to one unavoidable conclusion: permanent commitment is not what it used to be. Indeed, after a rather uniform history, the attitude toward permanent commitment is now changing to the point that one of life's traditional values is threatened.

The notion of a permanent, unbreakable commitment has a long history. According to the Bible God and Abraham made a covenant, a commitment to last forever. One of the glories of the Roman Empire was a legal system built on the premise that contracts were permanent. Into the last century a handshake between an employer and employee would seal a contract that might last a lifetime. Until relatively recent times the web of human society was held together by the fact that a promise made could only be broken if a person or group or state was willing to suffer the consequences of a sinful or criminal act.

Today we take it for granted that individuals will ignore promises, disregard treaties, break vows, violate contracts. This country has the highest divorce rate in the world. Athletes renegotiate for a higher salary in the middle of their contract if they have had an especially good season (they would not think of renegotiating for a lower salary after a bad season!). In the middle of a three-year contract workers strike for higher wages. Those who break a contract usually argue that conditions have changed, and therefore their contract is no longer binding.

Certainly the accelerating changes in society—many of them brought on by the advances in science—have affected the practice of commitment. Science has opened up new and enticing fields of human endeavor and provided better communication and transportation, thus fueling individual desire and mobility. With the increasing number of opportunities, the individual's greater awareness and mobility, and companies' changing needs, it is not surprising that serial careerism is

M

becoming an apt description for employment. These changes in the work place have had a subtle effect on commitment in other areas of life such as marriage and religion.

Another reason for the decline in commitment is the growing appetite for immediate gratification. This appetite has been nourished by a consumer economy and whetted by the advertising media. Taking into account only the television medium, sociologists estimate that the average American in the first twenty years of his life will see approximately one million commercials at the rate of about one thousand each week. Whether touting new cars or toothpaste, these ads implicitly guarantee their owner immediate satisfaction. Subconsciously Americans have transferred this dangerous message to other areas of life. If something does not give them satisfaction, they will commit themselves to something else—at least for a while.

Obviously not everything deserves the same degree of commitment. One is not committed to planting petunias in the back yard every year for the rest of one's life. On the other hand, a person does make serious commitments to God, spouse, society. The unfortunate situation today is that some people treat a garden and a spouse the same way. In doing so they have lost an important distinction; in effect, they have lost a sense of permanent commitment.

Permanent commitment embodies important values for both the individual and society. First of all, commitment gives a certain stability and focus to a person's life. No individual can be really happy without a purpose; permanent commitment provides that purpose. Secondly, commitment relieves a person from petty, internal struggles along with a host of encumbering decisions. In effect, permanent commitment is liberating because an individual with a long-term commitment, such as teaching, politics, or raising a family, surrenders small selfish interests in favor of an over-all objective. Other concerns are judged in relation to it, thus simplifying life. Thirdly, commitment creates a whole new future; it opens realities that are closed to those who make no such commitment. For example, a couple committed to the permanency of marriage will work their way through rocky shoals to deeper waters inaccessible to the uncommitted. In other words, committed people find creative answers and survive countless crises; uncommitted people go down before any and every contrary wind. In addition to personal value, commitment is obviously important to society. Without it, business projects would collapse, international cooperation would become impossible, and even governments would fall. It is commitment, after all, that keeps society from chaos.

Do we need a sense of commitment? Clearly, yes. In our changing world, some values are disappearing. For our own sake and that of society, permanent commitment must not be one of them.

Critical essay

M101 A critical essay explains and evaluates. It can be on any topic in any area—from philosophy or politics to a painting or a play. Most student assignments require analysis or evaluation of some literary or non-literary work such as a novel, short story, poem, nonfiction work, or movie.

M102 Writing a critical essay requires familiarity with the genre, or category, to which a work belongs. Information on particular genres is available in any good library.

M103 Some knowledge of the author or artist is usually helpful, since biographical details can lead to better understanding of a work. Biographical material is available in the reference section of a library.

M104 Four basic critical questions guide analysis of a literary or artistic work:

What is the author trying to communicate?

What means or techniques does the author use?

How well does the author use these means or techniques?

Is the message worth communicating?

Not all of these questions need to be answered in one essay, but they show the scope of criticism.

M105 Understand what kind of critical paper you are writing. Are you analyzing a work and interpreting its meaning? Are you also evaluating it?

analyze—> carefully consider the different elements of a work[21]

interpret—> determine what the work means

evaluate—> judge the effectiveness of the work

Reading and preparing to write

M106 First read the work for enjoyment. Although you may jot down ideas or questions as you read, do not stop to write lengthy notes.

M107 Reflect on what you have read. Try to understand the author's purpose and method; you cannot criticize a work until you know the author's purpose. Formulate significant questions or define areas that interest you. To understand and appreciate a text (especially a poem), read it over slowly and out loud several times.

M108 In analyzing nonfiction prose, consider these basic questions:

What is the central idea?

What is the author's purpose?

Is the author objective?

Is the presentation logical?

Does the author present adequate supporting evidence?

For what audience is the author writing?

---

[21] It is not possible to analyze all aspects of a work in one essay. Select one aspect of the work for analysis; for example, theme, plot, character, setting, or genre.

Is the subject worth treating?

Is the style clear and effective?

M109 In analyzing a work of fiction, consider these basic questions:

How are the characters presented?

What motivates the characters?

What are the major conflicts?

What is the theme?

Of what importance is the setting (time and place)?

Are the structure and pace effective?

What is the point of view and how does it affect the story?

What is the tone of the story and how does it reveal the author's intentions?

Are there any significant images or symbols?

M110 In analyzing a poem, consider these basic questions:

What is the purpose or theme of the poem?

What are the most important images?

What are the figures of speech and how effective are they?

How do sound and rhythm contribute to the meaning and total effect of the poem?

M111 If ideas do not come readily to mind, try brainstorming or clustering as described in M3.

M112 Select a worthwhile and manageable topic. A topic should not be so obvious or trite as to be uninteresting nor so comprehensive or complex as to be beyond the scope of an essay.

[Poor:] The different poetic worlds of Emily Dickinson and Walt Whitman.

[Poor:] The importance of computers in the design and production of automobiles and other products.

M113 Write a tentative thesis statement that is both specific and arguable. In other words, take a stand on a well-defined point. "Martha is realistically portrayed" is too general a thesis statement for a short paper. On the other hand, "Martha's pride prevents fulfillment of her need to be loved" is appropriate.

M114 Reread the work slowly, analytically. Keep the written thesis statement in front of you. As you read, look for supporting material. Take notes.

M115 When you have finished reading, make any necessary adjustments in the thesis statement.

M116 If necessary, check secondary sources for additional insights, support, or background.[22]

Writing the rough draft

M117 Arrange your notes in some logical order and write a tentative topic outline.[23]

M118 Working from the outline and notes, write a rough draft with as little interruption as possible. Maintaining a flow of ideas is important.

M119 The full title and author of the work under discussion should be mentioned at the beginning of the essay. Do not begin, "In this story . . ."

M120 If readers are familiar with the work, there is no need for a summary. If readers are not familiar with the work, summarize only what is necessary for understanding the analysis. If you are analyzing a poem, type the entire poem (unless it is very long) so that readers can refer to it.

---

[22] The primary source is the work under discussion. Secondary sources are biographies, commentaries, and other materials that shed light on the primary source. See N55-56.

[23] For examples of topic outlines, see M34 and N76.

M121 In a formal essay avoid personal intrusions like "it seems to me" and "in my opinion."[24] If a judgment is warranted by the facts, why say it is true because it seems so to you? Moreover, the introduction of first-person comments distracts from the real subject. If a judgment is only possible or probable, say so in third person; for example, "it is probably true that . . . "

M122 As necessary, define terms for audience understanding.[25]

M123 Support every major point in the essay with evidence. An unsupported assertion has little value. Moreover, unsupported statements weaken the entire paper and adversely affect the reader's overall confidence in the writer.

M124 Quotations from the work can enliven and support a thesis, but they should be brief and to the point. Long quotations are rarely effective and give the impression that the writer is padding the essay.

M125 It is sometimes helpful to use secondary sources for support or explanation.[26]

M126 If you are able to do so, enrich the essay with comparisons to similar works or to other works by the same author.

M127 If you include a value judgment, avoid subjective comments like "This is the best book I have ever read" or "I did not like this story." Instead, offer a specific, objective statement like "This book will appeal to mystery lovers" or "Lengthy passages of scientific information will prevent some readers from enjoying this book."

---

[24] Informal essays are frequently written in the first person. In such essays expressions like "it seems to me" and "in my opinion" are not out of place.

[25] For discussion of definition and its various forms, see Section O.

[26] If you use secondary sources to support your presentation, you must acknowledge them in your essay. For proper in-text reference format, see N101-109 (MLA), N116-18 (APA), N125-37 (University of Chicago).

Revising and writing the final copy

M128 Review the essay to detect any needless repetitions or gaps in organization.

M129 Make certain that you have not wandered from the point through needless summaries or irrelevant historical or biographical material.

M130 Check to see that you have adequate supporting evidence from the work itself.

M131 Incorporate short quotations in the text and identify them by providing the speaker's name or the situation.

> Mr. Dimmesdale makes another "vain show of expiation" as he stands upon the scaffold.

> Hester's experience taught her a great deal about truth and falsehood. She had committed herself to the truth—except when that truth might adversely affect the life and reputation of Arthur Dimmesdale. Then, as she said, she "consented to a deception. But a lie is never good, even though death threaten on the other side."

M132 Check verb tenses for consistency. Events in a story are best related in present tense, whereas events in an author's life are properly related in past tense.

> In preparation for writing *The Grapes of Wrath*, Steinbeck joined some migrant workers and traveled with them to California. His experiences were similar to those the Joads experience as they leave Oklahoma and seek employment in California.

M133 Verify that sources used in the essay are properly documented.[27]

M134 For an essay-revision checklist, see M87. For a sentence structure and diction checklist, see K140.

---

[27] On plagiarism, see N71. On quotations, see N92-94. On in-text reference format, see N101-109 (MLA), N116-18 (APA), N125-37 (University of Chicago).

M135 In preparing the final copy, include a bibliography page if you have used research material.[28] Follow any special directives.

M136 For guidelines for the final copy, see M88-99.

M137 Model critical essay:

The Ultimate Self-Deception of Dorian Gray

It may be a cliché to say that something is "as sure as sin," but the simile underlies a reality that few can ignore. Evil is an unavoidable fact of the human condition, and throughout history people have struggled to account for its presence and to explain its essence. Oscar Wilde, in his novel *The Picture of Dorian Gray*, explores the dimensions of evil as they impact upon his main character. For Wilde evil is best understood as a person's deliberate choice of illusion in preference to reality.

In the novel a youthful and innocent Dorian Gray is confronted with his newly painted portrait. He makes a wish—that he might always remain as youthful looking as he does in the painting. "If it were I who was to be always young, and the picture that was to grow old! For that—for that— I would give everything!" With such a wish he expresses a desire to separate himself from the inscrutable process of changing, aging, and moving towards death. He wishes to have the hands of time stopped and, perhaps, to evade the call of eternity. For reasons the novelist never makes quite clear, Dorian's wish is granted. He remains looking ever young; but his portrait, the mirror of his real self, bears every mark of age and sin.

With this fundamental decision to escape the limits of human existence, Dorian begins to exhibit a chain of behaviors with a common link: evading that which is real for that which is illusory. The first example of this misdirection surfaces in his relationship with Sybil Vane. Dorian has fallen in love with the beautiful young actress. On stage she epitomizes for him all

----

[28] For bibliography format, see N113 (MLA), N119 (APA), N139 (University of Chicago).

that is exquisite and meaningful. Her roles are marvelous expressions of life's challenges and achievements. Enthusiastically Dorian says to his friend, "Harry! Why didn't you tell me that the only thing worth loving is an actress?" Unfortunately Sybil plummets in his esteem when, no longer playing a role, she reveals her human imperfection. Compounding his original choice of the unreal one more time, Dorian rejects the ingenuous young girl. In so doing he cruelly tramples on her sensitivities. Crushed, she takes her own life, and Dorian wreaks further debasement upon himself.

Life moves on for Dorian, and he continues to live the unreal. In his various adventures he consistently chooses what is not true. He falls into a reverie with Roman Catholicism, but what he finds attractive is its liturgical trappings, not its spiritual essence. He comes to prefer the dreams that he can engender by trips into the drug world on the docks over the reality of everyday existence. He turns his back on philanthropy and embraces philandering.

Dorian, of course, pays a price for his sinful choices. His body retains the beauty and vigor of youth, but he is tortured by the image of his depravity daily etched deeper upon his portrait. Although he has recurring impulses to reform his life, he sinks into despair of such a possibility. He is haunted by the fear that others will see the emptiness and ugliness of his inner self. When Basil Hallward pleads with Dorian to see once more that portrait which he had painted of him, the wish is granted. Dorian unveils the ugliness that his life has become and which the canvas so starkly reveals. Basil can only recoil in horror. "My God! If it is true," he exclaims, "and this is what you have done with your life, why, you must be worse even than those who talk against you fancy you to be!" Again Dorian chooses illusion. He plunges a knife into the neck of his former friend—as if somehow in murdering Basil Hallward he could silence his own conscience.

Dorian's final sin comes from the fairy-tale belief that he can erase a lifetime of misdeeds by destroying the canvas upon which they have been painted. Dorian would seek self-forgiveness rather than bend his knee to that One alone who can give

it. As he slashes his portrait, he destroys all that is really genuine about himself. When he does that, he inevitably forfeits life
itself.

The Picture of Dorian Gray has remained an enduring classic.
For both the Victorian and the contemporary reader, it is a
clear reminder of the critical importance to examine life realistically. Man is not life's author, and wish as he might that he
could devise its plot, he cannot. The earthly wayfarer will either
embrace reality and have the possibility for good, or he will
sink into fantasy and perish in illusion.

—JAMES A. TOMAN

The review

M138 A review is a brief discussion of a current work such as
a book, movie, play, or musical performance. Typically
shorter than a critical essay with greater emphasis on
narrative summary and less concern with detailed
analysis, a review (in the popular sense) emphasizes
information with the purpose of helping readers decide whether they want to read or see the work under
discussion. The following book review appeared in *Time*
magazine.

Foucault's Pendulum
by Umberto Eco

A man named Casaubon hides after closing time in a Paris
museum called the Conservatoire des Arts et Métiers. Nearby,
an enormous pendulum swings silently in the gathering darkness, mute testimony, as a 19th century French scientist named
Foucalt first demonstrated, to the rotation of the earth. Casaubon
is here because he suspects something terrible will happen
before dawn. If he is correct, then he and two friends, playful
inventors of a plot to rule the world, do not have long to live.
In their machinations, have he and his coconspirators acciden-
tally stumbled across some dangerous truth? Or, perhaps worse,
have their own words created forces that will try to destroy
them?

From this spooky, arresting premise, Umberto Eco has launched a novel that is even more intricate and absorbing than his international best seller *The Name of the Rose* (1983). Unlike its predecessor, *Foucault's Pendulum* does not restrict its range of interests to monastic, medieval arcana. This time Eco's framework is vast—capacious enough to embrace reams of ancient, abstruse writings and a host of contemporary references or allusions. The latter include the Yellow Submarine, *Casablanca,* Tom and Jerry, Lina Wertmuller, Barbara Cartland, Stephen King, Superman, *Raiders of the Lost Ark,* Flash Gordon, the Pink Panther, Minnie Mouse and *Hellzapoppin.* What do all of these things have to do with one another? Eco's teasing answer: maybe everything, maybe nothing at all.

Readers will have to take sides here, or struggle to find a compromise somewhere in the middle ground. For beneath its endlessly diverting surface, Eco's novel constitutes a litmus test for ways of looking at history and the world. Casaubon, the narrator, recalls himself as a younger man, when he was willing to take facts at face value, to be what he calls incredulous. He recognizes and scorns another manner of thinking: "If two things don't fit, but you believe both of them, thinking that somewhere, hidden, there must be a third thing that connects them, that's credulity." But then, as a graduate student in Milan, he writes a doctoral thesis on the Knights of the Temple, a medieval order of warrior-monks formed in the 12th century and suppressed by the Pope in the 14th, who have vanished into a spiraling legend. Francis Bacon was a secret Templar, according to some spuriously authoritative sources; so according to others, were Columbus, Mozart, and Hitler.

At first, Casaubon laughs at such lunacies. His merriment is shared by Belbo and Diotallevi, editors at a Milanese publishing house. Given his expertise, Casaubon is hired as a consultant to advise on the endless stream of Templar manuscripts that flood the editorial offices. Eventually, these three scoffers find an amusing way to waste their time. Using Belbo's new word processor, they concoct "the Plan," a plausible scenario revealing a Templar plot to unleash unimaginable powers from the center of the earth in order to rule the world.

Of course, this experiment gets out of hand. Casaubon, no longer incredulous, finds himself questioning all facets of reality, "asking them to tell me not their superficial story but another, deeper story." At this point, the narrator is hooked, as will be anyone who has heeded him thus far. True believers, skeptics, those waffling in between: all are in for a scarifying shock of recognition.

— Paul Gray

The essay examination

M139 Writing an in-class essay involves much the same process as writing an out-of-class essay. Time, however, is more restricted for the essay examination. Because of this restraint, your essay will probably be shorter and less polished than you would like. Nevertheless, it will be judged on logic and completeness, clarity of expression, and mechanical correctness. It is important, therefore, to marshal your knowledge and skills for this kind of assignment.

Preparing for the essay examination

M140 Prepare by reviewing the matter for the examination. Read your notes and textbook, isolate and review important concepts, memorize basic facts.

Some essay examinations are not based on class matter, but rather test ability to analyze and interpret unfamiliar material. For such examinations it is important to review basic patterns of analysis and interpretation.

M141 Come prepared; bring pen and paper. Don't be a last-minute borrower.

Planning the essay answer

M142 Read each essay question carefully. Various questions may call for longer or shorter answers. Given a choice, select questions you can best answer.

M143 Allot time to each question. Determine how much of that time should be given to planning the answer.

M144 Read the first selected question again—carefully. The most embarrassing error (and a not uncommon one) is to write a "perfect" answer to an unasked question.

M145 Examine key words in the essay question: command words, subject words, limitation words. See M146-47.

M146 Command words must be carefully interpreted.

A. *Analyze*—to break into parts as an aid to understanding

(Any systematic development is satisfactory here.)

B. *Compare/contrast*—to compare means to show similarities and differences; to contrast means to show differences (See K68.)

(The block method or an item vs. item method is effective. See M23, M24.)

C. *Criticize*—to judge, to point out both good and bad points

(Present one side and then the other.)

D. *Describe*—to give a word picture, without judgment, of someone or something

(The answer is best arranged chronologically or spatially.)

E. *Discuss*—to give a full response, treating a subject from all sides

(Because of the scope and complexity of this type of question, careful thought must be given to its development.)

F. *Evaluate*—to judge, to assess the value or significance of something, usually by pointing out both good and bad elements

(Present one side and then the other.)

G. *Explain*—to make clear, clarify, usually by giving causes and effects

(A logical step-by-step organization is appropriate here.)

H. *Interpret*—to clarify, to explain the significance of something

(Any logical, systematic development may be used.)

I. *Prove*—to give evidence, to convince

J. *Relate*—to show similarities or connections; *relate* also means to tell a story.

(In the first sense, any systematic organization is satisfactory; in the second sense, the best order is chronological.)

K. *Review*—to survey, to reexamine

(A logical or chronological development is appropriate here.)

The importance of command words is obvious when you consider that each essay question below, answered correctly, would result in a different answer.

Evaluate the atomic orbital theory. (Judge strengths and weaknesses.)

Review the atomic orbital theory. (Present historical or logical sequence.)

Analyze the atomic orbital theory. (Break into parts and examine.)

M147 Other key words indicate the subject matter and the limitation of the subject matter.

Discuss Swift's persona in "A Modest Proposal."
command   limitation   subject matter

Analyze the arrangement of the elements in the Periodic Table
command   subject matter

on the basis of energy levels.
           limitation

Compare Catholic and Lutheran teaching on the Eucharist.
command   limitation   subject matter

Criticize Corregio's use of foreshortening.
command   limitation   subject matter

If you identify the command word, the subject matter, and the limitation, you will most probably address the right issues.

M148 Brainstorm for ideas. When you finish your list, cross off and group ideas, working toward an outline.

M149 Develop a thesis statement. If you rephrase the three basic terms in the essay question (command term, subject, limitation) into a thesis statement, you will be answering the right question.

[Question:] Explain the function of the intercalary chapters in Steinbeck's *The Grapes of Wrath.*
[Thesis statement:] The intercalary chapters in Steinbeck's *The Grapes of Wrath* enhance the themes of the novel.

[Question:] Review the possible motives for Stalin's role in the development of the Nazi-Soviet Pact of 1939.
[Thesis statement:] The possible motives for Stalin's role in the development of the Nazi-Soviet Pact of 1939 include the defense of Russia, the need to buy time, and the return of Russian lands.

[Question:] Analyze Aristotle's notion of the tragic hero.
[Thesis statement:] Aristotle's notion of the tragic hero has three basic components: a noble person, a flaw, and an inevitable downfall.

M150 If there is time, draw up a working outline. Each major division will represent a paragraph in your answer. Fill in as many subdivisions as possible; these will be the details, examples, and so on, for the paragraphs.

M

Writing the essay answer

M151 Write the thesis statement as a one-sentence introductory paragraph.

M152 Write the body of the essay, following your outline point by point.

A. Begin each paragraph with a clear topic sentence.

B. Use transitions to show the progression of your thought.

C. As you proceed, make certain that each point is adequately developed with facts, examples, quotations.

D. Avoid vague statements and unsupported generalities.

M153 Ordinarily write in third person. Avoid expressions like "I think" or "it seems to me."

M154 Skip lines if the paper is narrow lined. Wide spacing makes it easier for you to insert small corrections and certainly makes it easier for the examiner to read the essay. Legibility and format do make a difference.

M155 Ordinarily there is no need to write a conclusion. On the other hand, if the essay development has been complex or the essay is not tightly unified, a concluding paragraph of one or two sentences can be useful. The conclusion may include a paraphrase of the thesis statement.

M156 Leave enough time to reread your essay. In particular, check the following points:

—clearly worded thesis statement

—topic sentences that develop the thesis

—each major point adequately developed

—effective transitions between ideas

—no irrelevant material

—no awkward phrasing

—no omitted words

—correct spelling, punctuation

—legibility

M157 Do not hesitate to make corrections or changes, but be neat and legible. Box in new material and use arrows to indicate proper location.

M158 If a question calls for a one-paragraph answer, follow the general essay-answer procedure described in M139-56. A one-paragraph answer is a miniature essay with a topic sentence in place of a thesis statement and support sentences in place of topic sentences.

M159 Model essay question and answer:

QUESTION:
      Review the major reasons for Napoleon's defeat in Russia in 1812.

ANSWER:
      Four main causes led to Napoleon's military defeat in Russia in the year 1812.
      The first major cause was his brother Jerome's delay at the outset of the march into Russia. Jerome, who commanded three corps totaling 70,000 men on Napoleon's right flank, was to march and close a trap on the Russian army commanded by Barclay (130,000 men) and Bagration (43,000). Jerome delayed on his march. Napoleon with 220,000 men, marched uselessly for days and then watched as Barclay and Bagration slipped through the still open trap. Because of Jerome's delay, the Russian army escaped to conduct a fighting retreat.
      Another important cause was the weather. In June it was fiercely hot and too early for crops to be ripe. The heat led to exhaustion of soldiers and horses, and the shortage of ripe grain and food led to hunger and disease. After the first five weeks on the march, Napoleon's army had lost 100,000

men—one fourth of the main force—and one third of its horses. Colic had broken out among the horses, both the cavalry mounts and the draught horses pulling the cannon and supply wagons. In the early winter, cold weather was the enemy. It froze men and horses at night as they rested and sometimes even as they stood on guard duty. The land, denuded by war, was now covered with snow and stiff with frost. The occasional few days' thaw of the new winter only reduced the land to impassable mud. Marching, supply, order of men and wagons became impossible.

A third significant cause was the vast distances of Russia. After the first five weeks of marching and fighting the Russian rear guard, the Grand Army had covered two hundred miles. In France or the Germanies this was a long distance. In Russia it was nothing at all. It was barely half way to Moscow. Over these great distances there were no roads in Russia to speak of. The Grand Army marched and skirmished all those miles over open, flat fields with the horses dragging the wagons and cannon as best they could.

Finally, the lack of discipline in the French army was a major cause of defeat. This factor is often overlooked. The French Grand Army was two-thirds German, Austrian, Polish, and Italian. These men were not especially enthusiastic for the French Revolution. They were often its victims, not its benefi- ciaries. They obeyed reluctantly and slowly; the glory of the Emperor and his French officers meant nothing to them. The Czar's soldiers, on the other hand, were totally Russian, de- fending their homeland and accustomed to accepting orders from their officers, all of whom were nobles who had run the country forever as far as the soldiers were concerned.

As the Grand Army began its march into Russia in June of 1812, these four causes were in place and would ultimately be the major factors in Napoleon's defeat.

Research Paper

In general

N1 The research paper is a lengthy, documented expository or argumentative essay.[1]

N2 Exposition is that form of writing or talking whose purpose is to explain or inform.[2] Typical examples of exposition are textbooks, histories, most essays, and some research papers.[3]

N3 Argumentation[4] is that form of writing or talking whose purpose is to convince another of the truth of some statement.[5] Examples of argumentation are some research papers, an occasional political speech, and lawyers' closing statements to juries.

N4 Writing a research paper is a complex undertaking. It is important, therefore, to proceed in a systematic way.

Step 1. Understanding the assignment

Step 2. Selecting a topic

Step 3. Finding sources

---

[1] A research paper differs from a short expository essay in its length, its manner of using source materials, and its formalized documentation. It may also be more formal in style.

[2] Almost always, the four forms of discourse (exposition, narration, description, and argument) are mingled in a composition of any length at all. Thus it happens that an exposition may contain narration, and so on.

[3] For a discussion of the short expository theme, see M1-100.

[4] For a discussion of argumentation, see P1-91.

[5] Argumentation makes use of exposition, description, and narration, but for its own purpose.

Step 4. Formulating a thesis statement and writing a topic outline

Step 5. Reading and taking notes

Step 6. Writing a detailed outline

Step 7. Writing and revising the rough draft

Step 8. Preparing the final copy

Step 1. Understanding the assignment

N5 There are two basic kinds of research papers. Know which kind you are expected to write.

A. A report is an organized compilation of material on a particular topic. It surveys available information on a specific subject, then selects, arranges, and presents this information with proper documentation.

B. An evaluation not only presents information but also analyzes it and often argues to a thesis. In other words, it arrives at conclusions through critical analysis and frequently argues to a position. An evaluation paper may emphasize analysis or argumentation.

N6 Know the required length of the paper (the number of pages or words).

N7 Know the final due date and what is to be turned in at that time. For example, are note cards and an outline due with the paper?

Step 2. Selecting a topic

N8 The subject need not, and ordinarily will not, be new. The treatment may well be. There are very few new subjects under the sun, but the approaches to any given subject are practically limitless.

N9 Choose some subject that you would enjoy learning something about. The alternative spells drudgery.

N10   Keep your readers in mind when you choose your subject. Will they be interested? Interested or not, will they benefit from being told something about this subject? Will your instructor accept a treatment of this subject from you?

N11   The topic should be worthwhile. Trivial topics (e.g., "The Design and Production of Hairpins") are not worth the effort that a research paper requires.

N12   The topic should be suitable for research. "The Excitement of Hang Gliding" may be an appropriate topic for a short essay, but it does not lend itself to extensive research and documentation.

N13   Avoid subjective topics (for example, "The Greater Sensibility of the Middle Class"). Such topics reflect personal opinion and cannot be adequately supported from reputable published sources.

N14   Choose a topic with sufficient material available. If you find only two or three sources on your topic, expand or change the topic.

N15   Avoid topics that are too technical (for example, "The Importance of Surface Tension During the Chemical Pulping of Wood"). Such topics demand both specialized knowledge on the part of the writer and scholarly sources that may not be readily available.

N16   The topic should be neither too broad nor too limited. "Italian Involvement in World War II" is obviously too broad a topic for a research paper (that subject calls for a book). On the other hand, "The Effectiveness of Eskimo Headgear" is too specialized and limited. Your topic has the right scope if you are able to handle every significant point in the course of your paper—no more and no less.

[Too broad:] Roman Engineering
[Still too broad:] Roman Aquaducts
[Satisfactory:] Construction of the Appian Aquaduct
[Too limited:] The Stone Used in the Appian Aquaduct

N17 For an overview of your topic, read a general article in an encyclopedia. Such reading should confirm you in your interest and will enlighten you on the scope of your topic so that you can begin to limit your topic more precisely. Some general encyclopedias are—

> *Collier's Encyclopedia*
> *Compton's Encyclopedia and Fact Index*
> *The Encyclopaedia Britannica*
> *The Encyclopedia Americana*

Step 3. Finding sources

N18 You can begin to gather sources by checking the bibliographies (lists of books and articles) which follow encyclopedia articles, by checking subject entries in the library card or computer catalog, and by looking for bibliographies and references in individual books on your subject. To proceed beyond this point in your research, you need to become familiar with the library and its resources.

Reference works

N19 The reference section of a library provides basic information and extensive source material for your research. The following types of books—some of a general nature, others limited to specific disciplines—are located there.

abstracts (summaries of selected articles)

almanacs (lists, charts, statistics)

atlases (maps, often with tables and charts)

bibliographies (lists of books and/or articles in particular fields)

biographical dictionaries and indexes

dictionaries (definitions of words in a given language)

encyclopedias (articles on specific topics)

gazeteers (geographical dictionaries)

handbooks (definitions, short articles in a particular field)

indexes (lists of articles–sometimes books–in various fields)

yearbooks (annual publications bringing larger ones up to date)

N20 The use of abstracts can reduce research time. By reading these summaries of articles, you can readily determine whether the articles themselves will be helpful in your research. A few of these reference works are listed here.

> *Abstracts in Anthropology*
> *Biological Abstracts*
> *Chemical Abstracts*
> *Historical Abstracts*
> *Language and Language Behavior Abstracts*
> *Physics Abstracts*
> *Psychological Abstracts*
> *Religious and Theological Abstracts*
> *Science Abstracts*
> *Sociological Abstracts*

N21 Bibliographies and indexes are particularly useful in finding sources on a research topic.

N22 A bibliography is a customized list of books, articles, and other materials on particular subjects. There are various types of bibliographies.

> A. A bibliography of bibliographies lists bibliographies according to subject area. If you cannot locate a bibliography on your topic, consult one of the following:
>
> *Bibliographic Index: A Cumulative Bibliography of Bibliographies,* 1938-present.
>
> *Subject Guide to Books in Print*
>
> *World Bibliography of Bibliographies.* 2 vols.
>
> *A World Bibliography of Bibliographies and of Bibliographical Catalogues, Calendars, Abstracts, Digests, Indexes, and the Like.* 5 vols.
>
> B. A selective bibliography lists the best-known or most important works in particular fields.

543

C. An annotated bibliography provides brief explanations or comments on the works cited. This is a particularly useful type of bibliography.

D. An annual bibliography lists the works published in particular fields for a given year.

N23 Indexes may be used to locate periodical articles, chapters in books, pamphlets, songs, speeches, poems, and editorials. Because indexes catalog articles from periodicals, they are essential in researching any current topic. Some important indexes are listed below.[6]

Reader's Guide to Periodical Literature. This guide has been published since 1900 and is updated semi-monthly. It lists (by author, title, and subject) articles published each year in more than one hundred popular magazines.

The New York Times Index (1913–). This index provides a record of current events. Articles with short summaries are listed alphabetically by subject.

Essay and General Literature Index (1900–). Updated semi-annually, this index lists thousands of articles that appear in books (rather than in periodicals) and that might not appear in other bibliographies and indexes.

Monthly Catalog of United States Government Publications.

Citation Indexes. These indexes are published in the humanities, the sciences, and the social sciences and list all articles published in a given year that mention a particular article.[7] Seeing which articles are most influential can be useful in research.

Journal Abstracts. In addition to bibliographic information, abstracts provide a brief summary of each article.

Poole's Index to Periodical Literature (1802-81, 1882-1906). This is a subject index to nineteenth century periodicals.

---

[6] Other indexes are described under "Microfilm Indexes," N36.

[7] The three citation indexes are *Art & Humanities Citation Index, Science Citation Index,* and *Social Sciences Citation Index.*

Biography Index (1946–). This is a subject index to articles and sections of books that are essentially biographical.

Books in Print. This series has been published annually since 1873. Books are indexed by author, title, and subject.

Book Review Digest. Published annually, this series contains selected excerpts from reviews at the time the books were published.

Book Review Index (1965–). This index covers 230 journals and lists books that have one or more reviews.

Cumulative Book Index (1898–) Published monthly, this index lists and briefly describes recently published books.

N24 One of the keys to finding sources for your topic is having the right subject headings. Looking for sources under the wrong heading is a sure way to frustration. For example, the subject "butlers" can be effectively researched only under "domestics" or "manservants." Helpful guides for finding subject headings are the two-volume *Library of Congress Subject Headings* and, for the Dewey system, *Sears's List of Subject Headings.*

N25 In researching your topic, identify the kind of information you need and then consult the proper sources. If you cannot find what you need, consult a librarian.

general information on the topic–> encyclopedias

definitions of terms related to the topic–> dictionaries, specialized handbooks

research sources related to the topic–> bibliographies

biographical information –> biographical dictionaries, encyclopedias

statistical information–> yearbooks, almanacs, handbooks

articles–> indexes to periodical literature

additional books–> subject heading in the card catalog, bibliographies at end of sources already obtained

N26 Browsing in the reference section of the library can be rewarding if you have the Dewey or Library of Congress number for your general topic (see N39, N40). In this way you can begin your research immediately with the resources at hand. (At some point, of course, you should check the catalogs for other sources.)

N27 Reference materials are available on a wide range of subject areas. You will find encyclopedias, handbooks, bibliographies, indexes, and databases[8] in most fields, including the following:

Art
Biological Sciences
Business
Chemistry and Chemical Engineering
Computer Science
Economics
Ecology
Education
Electronics
Ethnic Studies
Film, TV
Geography
Geology
Health and Physical Education
History
Journalism and Mass Communications
Language and Literature
Foreign Languages
Mathematics
Medieval Studies
Music
Mythology, Folklore
Philosophy
Physics
Political Science
Psychology

---

[8] Databases are electronic catalogs accessed by computer.

Religion
Sociology and Social Work
Speech
Women's Studies

N28 Typical research areas with a few of their encyclopedias,
bibliographies, indexes, and databases are listed below.

Art

Britannica Encyclopedia of American Art. Chicago: Encyclopaedia
  Britannica, 1973.
Encyclopedia of Painting. Ed. Bernard S. Myers. 4th ed. New
  York: Crown, 1979.
Encyclopedia of World Art. 15 vols. New York: McGraw-Hill, 1959-
  68. Supplements 1983, 1987.
Oxford Companion to Twentieth Century Art. Ed. Harold Osborne.
  Oxford: Oxford University Press, 1981.

Arntzen, Etta, and Robert Rainwater. *Guide to the Literature of
  Art History.* Chicago: American Library Assoc., 1981.
Art Index. New York: Wilson, 1929–present.
*Art Research Methods and Resources: A Guide to Finding Art Informa-
  tion.* Ed. L. S. Jones. 3rd ed. Dubuque: Kendall/Hunt, 1990.
Arts in America: A Bibliography. Ed. Bernard Karpel. 4 vols. Wash-
  ington, D.C.: Smithsonian Institution, 1980.
Bibliographic Guide to Art and Architecture. Boston: Hall, 1977–
  1990. New York: New York Public Library, 1991–present.
Index to Art Periodicals. Chicago: Hall, 1970. Supplement 1974.

ARCHITECTURE DATABASE (RILA)
ART BIBLIOGRAPHIES MODERN
ART INDEX (WILSONLINE)

Film, TV

Broadcast Television: A Research Guide. Ed. F. C. Schreibman. Los
  Angeles: AFI Education Services, 1983.
The Complete Encyclopedia of Television Programs, 1949-1972. 2nd
  rev. ed. New York: A. S. Barnes, 1981.
Halliwell, Leslie. *Halliwell's Film Guide.* New York: Harper, 1994.

Halliwell's Filmgoers's and Video Viewer's Companion. Ed. Leslie
   Halliwell. 9th ed. New York: HarperCollins, 1990.
International Encyclopedia of the Film. Ed. Roger Manvell. New
   York: Crown, 1972.
New York Times Encyclopedia of Film. 13 vols. Ed. Gene Brown.
   New York: Garland, 1992.
The Oxford Companion to Film. Ed. Liz-Anne Bawden. New York:
   Oxford University Press, 1976.

Armour, Robert A. *Film: A Reference Guide.* Westport, CT:
   Greenwood Press, 1980.
Film Literature Index. Albany, New York: Filmdex, 1973–present.
International Index to Film Periodicals. New York: Bowker, 1972–
   present.
Manchel, Frank. *Film Study: An Analytical Bibliography.* 4 vols.
   Rutherford, New Jersey: Farleigh Dickinson University Press,
   1990.
McCavitt, William E. *Radio and Television: A Selected Annotated
   Bibliography.* Metuchen, New Jersey: Scarecrow, 1978. Supple-
   ments to 1982.

ARTS AND HUMANITIES SEARCH
HUMANITIES INDEX
MAGILL'S SURVEY OF CINEMA (COMPUSERVE, DIALOG)

History, political science

Encyclopedia of American History. Ed. Rischard B. Morris. 6th ed.
   New York: Harper, 1982.
Encyclopedia of American Political History. Ed. Jack P. Greene. 3
   vols. New York: Scribner's, 1984.
Encyclopedia of Colonial and Revolutionary America. New York:
   Facts on File, 1989.
An Encyclopedia of World History: Ancient, Medieval and Modern.
   5th ed. Boston: Houghton Mifflin, 1973.
Martin, Michael R. et al. *An Encyclopedia of Latin-American His-
   tory.* Rev. ed. Westport, CT: Greenwood, 1981.
New Cambridge Modern History. 14 vols. London: Cambridge
   University Press, 1957-79.

America: History and Life: Abstracts, Citations, Bibliographies, and Indexes. Santa Barbara: Clio Press, 1964–present.

Bibliography of English History. Oxford: Clarendon, 1928–present.

Breisach, Ernst. *Historiography: Ancient, Medieval, and Modern.* Chicago: University of Chicago Press, 1983.

Harvard Guide to American History. Ed. Frank Friedel. Rev. ed. 2 vols. Cambridge: Belknap, 1974.

Historical Abstracts. Santa Barbara: Clio Press, 1955–present.

Historigraphy: An Annotated Bibliography of Journal Articles, Books, and Dissertations. Ed. Susan B. Kinnell. 2 vols. Lakeville, CT: Clio, 1987.

International Bibliography of Historical Sciences. New Providence, NJ: Bowker-Saur, 1930–present.

International Bibliography of Political Science. Chicago: Aldine, 1953–present.

Political Science: A Bibliographical Guide to the Literature. 1974.

Roach John P. C. *A Bibliography of Modern History.* New York: Cambridge University Press, 1968.

AMERICA: HISTORY AND LIFE (COMPUSERVE, DIALOG)

HISTORICAL ABSTRACTS

PAIS INTTERNATIONAL (BRS, COMPUSERVE, DIALOG)

SOCIOLOGICAL ABSTRACTS (BRS, DIALOG)

Literature

Benet's Reader's Encyclopedia. Ed. George Perkins. New York: Harper & Row, 1991.

McGraw-Hill Encyclopedia of World Drama. Ed. Stanley Hochman. 5 vols. New York: McGraw Hill, 1983.

The New Guide to Modern World Literature. Martin Seymour-Smith. Rev. Ed. London: Macmillan Ltd., 1985.

The Oxford Companion to American Literature. Ed. James D. Hart. 5th ed. New York: Oxford University Press, 1983.

The Oxford Companion to Classical Literature. Ed. M. C. Howatson. 2nd ed. New York: Oxford University Press, 1989.

Oxford Companion to the Theater. Ed. Phyllis Hartnell. 4th ed. New York: Oxford University Press, 1983.

The Science Fiction Encyclopedia. Ed. Peter Nicholls. Garden City, New York: Doubleday, 1979.

Abstracts of English Studies. Boulder: University of Colorado, 1958–present.

Bibliographical Guide to the Study of the Literature of the U.S.A. 5th rev. and enl. ed. Eds. Clarence Gohdes and Sanford Marowitz. Durham, NC: Duke University Press, 1989.

Contemporary Authors: A Bibliographical Guide to Current Writers in Fiction, General Nonfiction, Poetry, Journalism, Drama, Motion Pictures, Television, and Other Fields. Eds. Frances Locher and Ann Evory. Detroit: Gale, 1967–present.

Humanities Index. New York: Wilson, 1974–present.

MLA International Bibliography of Books and Articles on the Modern Languages and Literatures. New York: Modern Language Association, 1921–present.

New Cambridge Bibliography of English Literature. 5 vols. London: Cambridge University Press, 1966-77.

Science Fiction and Fantasy Research Index. Ed. Hal W. Hall. San Bernardino: Borgo Press, 1993.

Shorter Cambridge Bibliography. New York: Cambridge University Press, 1981.

LLBA (LINGUISTICS AND LANGUAGE BEHAVIOR ABSTRACTS)
MLA BIBLIOGRAPHY

Music

International Cyclopedia of Music and Musicians. Ed Oscar Thompson. 11th ed. New York: Dodd, Mead, 1985.

Kinkle, Roger D. *The Complete Encyclopedia of Popular Music and Jazz 1900-1950.* 4 vols. New Rochelle, NY: Arlington, 1974.

Moore, Frank L. *Crowell's Handbook of World Opera.* Westport, CT: Greenwood, 1974.

New College Encyclopedia of Music. Eds. J. A. Westrup and F. L. Harrison. Rev. by Conrad Wilson. NY: Norton, 1981.

The New Grove Dictionary of Music and Musicians. Ed. Stanley Sadie. 20 vols. London: Macmillan, 1980.

Stambler, Irwin. *Encyclopedia of Pop, Rock, and Soul.* New York,

St. Martin's, 1977.

Bibliographic Guide to Music. Boston: Hall, 1980–present.
Music Article Guide. Philadelphia: Information Services, Inc. 1966–present.
Music Index: The Key to Current Musical Periodical Literature. Warren, MI: Harmonic Park Pr., 1950–present.
Music Reference and Research Materials: An Annotated Bibliography. Ed. V. Duckles. 4th ed. Boston: Schirmer, 1988.

RILM (REPERTOIRE INTERNATIONAL DE LITTERATURE DE MUSI-CALE) ABSTRACTS
ARTS & HUMANITIES SEARCH

Philosophy, religion

The New Catholic Encyclopedia. 15 vols. 1967. Palatine, IL: Publishers Guild, 1981. 4 supp. vols. 1972–1995.
The Concise Encyclopedia of Western Philosophy and Philosophers. Ed. James O. Urmson. 3rd. ed. New York: Routledge, 1990.
Copleston, Frederick. *A History of Philosophy.* 9 vols. Garden City, NY: Doubleday, 1985.
Encyclopedia of Bioethics. 2 vols. Ed. Warren Reich. New York: Macmillan, 1982.
Encyclopedia of Philosophy. Ed. Paul Edwards. 4 vols. New York: Free Press, 1973.
The Encyclopedia of Religion. Ed. Mircea Eliade. 16 vols. New York: Macmillan, 1986.
The New Standard Jewish Encyclopedia. Ed. Geoffrey Wigoder. New York: Facts on File, 1992.

Philosopher's Index. Bowling Green, OH: Bowling Green University Press, 1967–present.
Reference Works for Theological Research: An Annotated Selective Bibliographical Guide. Ed. Robert Kepple. 2nd ed. Washington: UP of America, 1981.
Religion Index One: Periodicals. Chicago: American Theological Library Assoc., 1949–present.
Religions: A Select, Classified Bibliography. Ed. J. F. Mitros. New York: Learned, 1973.

N

Research Guide to Philosophy. Ed. T. N. Tice and T. P. Slavens. Chicago: American Library Assoc., 1983.

Research Guide to Religious Studies. Eds. F. Wilson and T. P. Slavens. Chicago: American Library Assoc., 1982.

PHILOSOPHER'S INDEX

RELIGION INDEX

Science

The Encyclopedia of the Biological Sciences. Ed. Peter Gray. New York: Van Nostrand Reinhold, 1981.

Encyclopedia of Chemistry. Eds. Clifford A. Hampel and Gessner G. Hawley. 4th ed. New York: Van Nostrand Reinhold, 1984.

Encyclopedia of Computer Science and Technology. Eds. Jack Belzer, et al. 21 vols. New York: Dekker, 1975-90.

Encyclopedia of Physics. 3rd ed. New York: Van Nostrand, 1990.

The New Larousse Encyclopedia of Animal Life. New York: Larousse, 1980.

The McGraw-Hill Encyclopedia of Science and Technology. 6th ed. 20 vols. New York: McGraw, 1987.

Ocean World Encyclopedia. Ed. Donald Groves. New York : McGraw-Hill, 1980.

Van Nostrand's Scientific Encyclopedia. Ed. Douglas M. Considine. 7th ed. 2 vols. New York: Van Nostrand Reinhold, 1988.

Applied Science and Technology Index: New York: Wilson, 1958–present.

Bibliography and Index of Geology. Boulder, CO: Geological Society of America, 1933–present.

Biological and Agricultural Index. New York: Wilson, 1964–present. (From 1948 to 1962 this work was called *Agricultural Index.*)

Current Physics Index. New York: American Institute of Physics, 1975–present.

General Science Index: New York: Wilson, 1978–present.

Science and Engineering Literature. Eds. H. R. Malinowsky. 3rd ed. Littleton, CO: Libraries Unlimited, 1980.

Solid State Physics Literature Guides, New York: Plenum, 1972–present.

CHEMSEARCH

SCISEARCH

GENERAL SCIENCE INDEX (COMPUSERVE, WILSONDISC)

Social sciences

Encyclopedia of Psychology. Ed. Raymond J. Corsini. 4 vols. New York: Wiley, 1984.

Encyclopedia of Social Work. 2 vols. Silver Springs, MD: National Association of Social Workers, 1987.

International Encyclopedia of Psychiatry, Psychology, Psychoanalysis, and Neurology. New York: Aesculapius, 1983.

International Encyclopedia of the Social Sciences. 18 vols. New York: Macmillan, 1968; Free Press, 1979.

International Bibliography of the Social Sciences. Chicago: Aldine, 1951–present

Reference Sources in Social Work: An Annotated Bibliography. Ed. James H. Conrad. Metuchen, New Jersey: Scarecrow, 1982.

Social Science Reference Sources. Ed. Tze-chung Li. Westport, CT: Greenwood. 1980.

Social Sciences Index: New York: Wilson, 1974–present.

Sociological Abstracts. LaJolla, CA : Sociological Abstracts Inc., 1953–present.

Sources of Information in the Social Sciences. Ed. William Webb. 3rd ed. Chicago: American Library Assoc., 1986.

FAMILY RESOURCES

SOCIAL SCISEARCH (BRS)

SOCIAL SCIENCE INDEX (COMPUSERVE)

N29 If you cannot locate reference sources for your topic, do not hesitate to ask a librarian for help. The following books are also useful:

Books for College Libraries. 3rd ed. 6 vols. Chicago: American Library Association, 1988.

Cheney, Francis Neel, and Wiley J. Williams. *Fundamental Reference Sources.* Chicago: American Library Assn., 1980.

Clarke, Jack A., ed. *The Reader's Adviser.* 6 vols. New York: R. R. Bowker Company, 1988.

Harris, Sherwood, ed. *Where to Look It Up.* New York: Prentice Hall, 1991.

Katz, William. *Your Library: A Reference Guide.* 2nd ed. New York: Holt, Rinehart & Winston, 1984.

Lang, Jovian P., ed. *Reference Sources for Small and Medium-sized Libraries.* 5th ed. Chicago: American Library Association, 1992.

Marcaccio, Kathleen V., ed. *Computer-readable Databases.* 7th ed. New York: Gale, 1991. Available online as *Database of Databases* (DIALOG file 230).

McCormick, Mona. *The New York Times Guide to Reference Materials.* Rev. ed. New York: New American Library, 1986.

Sheehy, Eugene P. *Guide to Reference Books.* 10th ed. Chicago: American Library Assn., 1986. Supplement 1992.

Stevens, Rolland, and Joan M. Walton. *Reference Work in the Public Library.* Littleton, CO: Libraries Unlimited, 1983.

Walford, A. J. *Guide to Reference Materials.* London: Library Association. Vol. 1, 6th ed., *Science & Technology,* 1993. Vols. 2 and 3, 3rd ed. *Social & Historical Sciences, Philosophy and Religion and Generalities, Languages, the Arts and Literature,* 1975.

In addition, check again the sources mentioned in N22-23.

Computer search

N30   Various bibliographies and indexes are now listed in databases. (Databases are electronic catalogs accessed by computer.) Many colleges subscribe to information services that provide access to hundreds of databases. Two typical information services are–

BRS (Bibliographical Retrieval Services), Information Technologies, Latham, New York

Dialog Information Services, Palo Alto, California

There are also print database directories; for example,

Directory of Online Databases, Detroit: Gale.

Omni Online Database Directory, New York: Macmillan Publishing Company.

N31   Some computer searches are free and can be conducted by the researcher following simple directions. Other searches are conducted by trained personnel. There is a charge for many searches according to the time involved and the extent of the printout.

N32   Computer searches are very thorough and may yield more information than is needed. It is important to narrow the search so that time and money are not wasted generating information that cannot be used.

N33   For better efficiency, work with library personnel on the following steps:

A. Consider the scope of the various databases. Make sure that your topic is included in the database that you select and that all the important sources are indexed in it.

B. Having chosen a database, be careful to select the right descriptors. Descriptors are key words that allow the computer to call up books and articles containing those key words. If the key words are too general, hundreds or thousands of entries may be called up at a waste of both time and money. Selecting a combination of key words is the best way to narrow a search.

[Topic:] Teaching Science in the Middle School
[Descriptor too general:] Teaching Science
[Descriptor too general:] Middle School
[Descriptor narrowed:] Teaching Science AND Middle School

A list of key words and phrases accompanies each database; some of these are printed, some can be called up on a viewing terminal. In addition, various information services publish a thesaurus that lists descriptors. A typical guide is *Thesaurus of ERIC Descriptors.*

N34   Once the key words have been entered, the computer will indicate the number of available citations. At this point you may either close the search (and make a printout) or narrow the search.

N35   When you have completed the search, select the format
you want for the printout. The simplest format is the
typical bibliographical entry with title, author, and
publication information. The fullest format also includes an abstract, reprint costs, and other key words.

Microfilm indexes

N36   A number of indexes are available on microfilm.[9] Microfilm is 35mm. film wound on a reel and threaded
through a reader that magnifies the print. Some important microfilm indexes are–

> *The Business Index.* This index covers 375 magazines, journals,
> and similar publications.
> *Legal Resource Index.* This index covers 680 journals, six law
> newspapers, and relevant law materials from the Library of
> Congress collection.
> *The Magazine Index.* This index is more extensive than the
> *Reader's Guide to Periodical Literature.*
> *The National Newspaper Index.* This index covers three papers:
> *The New York Times*, the *Christian Science Monitor*, and *The Wall
> Street Journal.*

N37   If the research materials you need are not available in
your library, ask the librarian about an interlibrary loan.
Libraries usually belong to one of the large resource
networks that make such loans easy. Two of these systems
are Online Computer Library Center Inc. (OCLC) and
Research Libraries Information Network (RLIN).

Library classification systems

N38   In order to find library books and other materials relevant to your topic, you should become familiar with
the two library classification systems: the Dewey Decimal system and the Library of Congress system.

---

[9] Microform, which reduces printed materials to small bits of film, has
two principal forms: microfiche and microfilm. Microfiche is a flat 4 x 6
sheet of film that holds an average of ninety-eight pages per sheet. A
reader is used to magnify images. Many magazine articles are available on
microfiche. Microfilm is described in the text above.

N39 The Dewey Decimal system divides books into numbered classes.[10]

000 GENERALITIES
010 Bibliography
020 Library & information sciences
030 General encyclopedic works
040
050 General serial publications
060 General organizations & museology
070 Journalism, publishing, newspapers
080 General collections
090 Manuscripts & book rarities

100 PHILOSOPHY & RELATED DISCIPLINES
110 Metaphysics
120 Epistemology, causation, humankind
130 Paranormal phenomena & arts
140 Specific philosophical viewpoints
150 Psychology
160 Logic
170 Ethics (moral philosophy)
180 Ancient, medieval, Oriental
190 Modern Western philosophy

200 RELIGION
210 Natural religion
220 Bible
230 Christian theology
240 Christian moral & devotional
250 Local church & religious orders
260 Social & ecclesiastical theology
270 History & geography of church
280 Christian denominations & sects
290 Other & comparative religions

300 SOCIAL SCIENCES
310 Statistics
320 Political science
330 Economics
340 Law
350 Public administration
360 Social problems & services
370 Education
380 Commerce (Trade)
390 Customs, etiquette, folklore

400 LANGUAGE
410 Linguistics
420 English & Anglo-Saxon languages
430 Germanic languages, German
440 Romance languages, French
450 Italian, Romanian, Rhaeto-Romanic
460 Spanish & Portuguese languages
470 Italic languages, Latin
480 Hellenic, Classical Greek
490 Other languages

500 PURE SCIENCES
510 Mathematics
520 Astronomy & allied sciences
530 Physics
540 Chemistry & allied sciences
550 Science of earth & other worlds
560 Paleontology, Paleozoology
570 Life sciences
580 Botanical sciences
590 Zoological sciences

600 TECHNOLOGY (APPLIED SCIENCES)
610 Medical sciences, Medicine
620 Engineering & allied operations
630 Agriculture & related technologies
640 Home economics & family living
650 Management & auxiliary services
660 Chemical & related technologies
670 Manufactures
680 Manufacture of specific uses
690 Buildings

700 ARTS
710 Civic & landscape art
720 Architecture
730 Plastic arts, Sculpture
740 Drawing, decorative & minor arts
750 Painting & paintings
760 Graphic arts, Prints
770 Photography & photographs
780 Music
790 Recreational & performing arts

800 LITERATURE (BELLES-LETTRES)
810 American literature in English
820 English & Anglo-Saxon literatures
830 Literatures of Germanic languages
840 Literatures of Romance languages
850 Italian, Romanian, Rhaeto-Romanic
860 Spanish & Portuguese literatures
870 Italic literatures, Latin
880 Hellenic literatures, Greek
890 Literature of other languages

900 GENERAL GEOGRAPHY & HISTORY
910 General geography, Travel
920 General biography & genealogy
930 General history of ancient world
940 General history of Europe
950 General history of Asia
960 General history of Africa
970 General history of North America
980 General history of South America
990 General history of other areas

---

[10] In smaller libraries fiction works are often cataloged separately.

N40   The Library of Congress system (used by larger libraries) divides books into lettered classes.[11]

A GENERAL WORKS
AC Collections
AE Encyclopedias (General)
AG Dictionaries and other general
    reference books
AI Indexes (General)
AN Newspapers
AP Periodicals (General)
AS Societies, Academies
AY Yearbooks (General)
AZ History of scholarship and learning
B PHILOSOPHY, PSYCHOLOGY
    AND RELIGION
B Collections
BC Logic
BD Speculative philosophy
BF Psychology
BH Esthetics
BJ Ethics
BL Religions
BS Bible and Exegesis
C HISTORY—AUXILIARY SCIENCES
CB History of Civilization (General)
CJ Numismatics
CT Biography
D HISTORY : GENERAL & OLD WORLD
D General
DA Great Britain
DC France
DD Germany
DE Greco-Roman World
DF Greece
DG Italy
DK Soviet Union
DS Asia
DT Africa
DU Oceania
E AMERICA (GENERAL)
    & UNITED STATES
F UNITED STATES (LOCAL) & AMERICA
    (EXCEPT THE UNITED STATES)
G GEOGRAPHY, ANTHROPOLGY,
    RECREATION
G Geography (General)
GA Mathematical Geography
GB Physical Geography
GC Oceanography
GR Folklore
GT Manners and Customs
GV Recreation, Leisure
H SOCIAL SCIENCES (GENERAL)
HA Statistics
HB–HJ Economics (General)
HE Transportation and Communication
HF Commerce
HM–HX Sociology

J POLITICAL SCIENCE
J Documents
JA General Works
JC Political theory
JF Constitutional history & administration
JK United States
JX International Law
K LAW
L EDUCATION
LA History of Education
LB Theory and practice of education
LC Special aspects of education
LD United States
M MUSIC
N FINE ARTS
P LANGUAGE AND LITERATURE
P Philology and Linguistics (General)
PA Classical Languages and Literature
PB–PH Modern European Language
PC Romance languages
PD Germanic (Teutonic) languages
PE English
PJ–PL Oriental languages & literatures
PM American Indian, Artificial languages
PN Literary history and civilization
PO Romance literatures
PR English literature
PS American literature
PT Germanic literatures
PZ Juvenile belles lettres
Q SCIENCE
QA Mathematics
QB Astronomy
QC Physics
QD Chemistry
QE Geology
QH Natural history, Biology
QK Botany
QL Zoology
QM Human anatomy
QP Physiology
QR Microbiology
R MEDICINE
S AGRICULTURE (General)
SB Plant culture (General)
SD Forestry
SF Animal culture
SK Hunting
T TECHNOLOGY (General)
TA–TH Engineering and construction
TK Electrical engineering. Electronics.
    Nuclear engineering
TR Photography
TT Handicrafts. Arts and crafts
U MILITARY SCIENCE
V NAVAL SCIENCE
Z LIBRARY SCIENCE

[11] Because of space limitations the divisions here are necessarily incomplete.

Library Catalogs

N41 The library catalog lists all the materials that are in the library's collection and indicates where they can be found. Many libraries have on-line catalogs (computerized listings) which provide the same information as the traditional card catalogs. [12]

N42 Card catalogs are customarily divided in one of two ways:

A. A divided catalog has one catalog for authors and titles and another catalog for subjects. [13]

B. A dictionary catalog has authors, titles, and subjects in one alphabetical list.

N43 A single book has at least three cards–one each for author, title, and subject. There may be additional cards for other subject headings, cards for editor, joint author, and so on.

N44 The most complete information is on the main entry card (usually the author card). There you will find the call number of the book, the author's name, the title of the book, the publisher, and the place and date of publication.

N45 There are two library classification systems: Dewey (used in smaller libraries) and the Library of Congress systems.

---

[12] On-line catalogs have certain advantages over card catalogs. For instance, the reader can combine searches for an author and a key word in the title. A search can also be made on one key word in a title. Many on-line catalogs say if the book is currently in or out of the library. Because on-line catalogs can be so easily updated, they are usually current.

[13] Checking the subject cards related to your topic is one way of gathering sources. One particular advantage of this method is that you know these sources are available in the library.

N46   Typical Dewey cards look like this:

Comeback   Title Card

362.4   Bowe, Frank
B 674   Comeback: six remarkable people who triumphed over disability.
        Foreward by William Glasser.   Harper & Row ©1981

PHYSICALLY HANDICAPPED--BIOGRAPHY   Subject Card

362.4   Bowe, Frank
B 674   Comeback: six remarkable people who triumphed over disability.
        Foreward by William Glasser.   Harper & Row ©1981

        Bowe, Frank   1 Author Card
362.4   Comeback: six remarkable people who triumphed over disability.   2
B 674   Foreward by William Glasser.   Harper & Row ©1981   3
           172p   4
           Offers portraits of six remarkable people who overcame severe   5
           physical handicaps in unusual and effective ways. Bibliog   6
           1 Physically handicapped--Biography   7
           1 T   8
        ISBN 0-06-010489-9   9

N

1. This is the last and first name of the author.

2. This number is the Dewey subject classification number. It tells you what section of the library the book is in. It and the number on the next line constitute the call number. The title and subtitle of the book follow the call number.

3. The Cutter number is the author number. This number tells you exactly where the book can be found in that section. The remainder of the line provides bibliographical information–special forward, publisher, copyright date.

4. This is the number of pages in the book.

5. Lines 5 and 6 provide a brief description of the book's contents.

6. "Bibliog" means that the book contains a list of titles related to the present topic.

7. This is technically called a *tracing*. It indicates that the library catalog has a card for the book under this subject heading.

8. This is another tracing. The library catalog also has a card for this book under its title.

9. The abbreviation stands for International Standard Book Number (often used in purchasing).

N

N47   Typical Library of Congress cards look like this:

	Design and analysis of experiments	Title Card
QA	Montgomery, Douglas C.	
279	Design and analysis of experiments	
.M66	Douglas C. Montgomery 2nd ed. New York: Wiley, 1984	

	Experimental design	Subject Card
QA	Montgomery, Douglas C.	
279	Design and analysis of experiments	
.M66	Douglas C. Montgomery 2nd ed. New York: Wiley, 1984	

QA	Montgomery, Douglas C.	1 Author Card
279	Design and analysis of experiments	2
.M66	Douglas C. Montgomery. 2nd ed.	3
	New York: Wiley, 1984.	4
	xvi, 538p. ill., 24cm	5
	Bibliography: p. 499-504.	6
	Includes index.	7
	ISBN 0-471-86812-4	8
	1. Experimental design I. Title	9

N

1. The letters are the first part of the call number for the book and indicate the section of the library where the book is shelved. Since this is the author card, the author's name also appears here, last name first.

2. The numbers are the second part of the call number and establish more precisely the location of the book. The title of the book is also given.

3. The letter and number, often referred to as the Cutter number, are the author and work designation. The author's name follows, then the edition of the book.

4. The line lists the city, publishing company, and the date of publication.

5. This is the first of three lines providing detailed information on the book. This line states that there is an introduction of sixteen pages, the text runs 538 pages, the text is illustrated, and the book size (height) is twenty-four centimeters.

6. The book has a bibliography on pages 499-504.

7. The book has an index.

8. The line gives the International Standard Book Number (often used for purchasing).

9. Any subject headings under which the book is also cataloged are listed in arabic numerals. Other tracings, such as title, are listed in roman numerals.

Limiting and evaluating sources

N48 Write down the author, title, and call number of the books and periodicals you are interested in. (If the catalog is for several university libraries, also write down the name of the library.) If the library has open stacks, you can look for your titles and browse at the same time. In this way you may discover additional titles.

N49   As you find your sources, look them over to see if they really are what you need for your paper. Examine the following (all of which apply to books, some also to articles):

A. *Table of contents.* Chapter headings indicate subject-matter divisions.

B. *Preface.* This gives the author's purpose and plan.

C. *Introduction.* It usually gives a brief overview of the subject.

D. *Index.* It shows what terms are covered and how well they are covered.

E. *Bibliography and footnotes or endnotes.* These give an indication of the level of scholarship and may even provide additional sources for your paper.

F. *Author.* If the author is an established scholar in the field, there is an additional reason for using the source.

G. *Publication date.* If all other considerations are equal, the more recent publication should be better because it has the advantage of building on the information and scholarship of earlier works.

Step 4. Formulating a thesis statement and writing a topic outline

N50   Once you have read a few general articles in reference works and gathered various source materials, you should write a simple thesis statement.[14] You may very well modify it during the course of your reading; but it simply makes good sense to limit, from the beginning, the scope of your research and curtail excessive reading and notetaking.

N51   Writing out the thesis statement exposes any weaknesses in it. Moreover, a written statement lying on your desk

---

[14] For another discussion of thesis statement, see M6-8.

564

before your eyes is a constant reminder of what the research paper is supposed to be about and keeps you from straying off into useless digressions.

N52   If it is at all possible to do–and it almost always is–state your thesis statement in a single, uncomplicated declarative sentence. The briefer and less complicated the thesis statement, the easier it is to develop it coherently. A question is not satisfactory because it does not indicate and limit development. A compound sentence is not satisfactory because it presents two ideas to be developed and does not provide a sharp focus.

N53   In writing a thesis statement, observe these norms:

1. Limit the general subject sharply.

   [Poor:] The study of marine life is worthwhile.

   The general subject "study of marine life" needs to be narrowed. As written, the thesis statement is more appropriate for a book than for a research paper.

2. State something specific about the subject matter.

   [Poor:] Kelp is an interesting plant.

   The predication of kelp as "an interesting plant" is vague and too general.

3. Avoid extravagant and superlative terms when writing the thesis statement.

   [Poor:] Kelp is an incredible plant.

   It would be difficult to prove that this plant is "incredible." Even if you proved it, most readers would be skeptical.

4. Make the thesis statement as definite as you reasonably can.

   [Satisfactory:] Kelp is a useful marine plant.

At the beginning of the research process, this thesis statement is satisfactory. As research continues, however, the word "useful" should be made more specific.

N54 Next, write a working outline. Since you have done some reading on your topic, you should be able to set up tentatively the major divisions of your paper (the roman numeral divisions). You may change or modify these as you take notes.

> Thesis: Kelp is a useful marine plant.
>   I. Important definitions
> II. Support and protection for marine life
> III. Energy source
> IV. Food

You will develop the subdivisions of the outline as you read and take notes.

Step 5. Reading and taking notes

N55 There are two basic kinds of source material: primary and secondary sources.

A. Primary sources are original documents such as literary works, speeches, letters, eye-witness accounts.

B. Secondary sources are commentaries on original works. Each type of material has its advantages. Primary sources provide immediacy and accuracy. Secondary sources usually provide analysis, synthesis, or interpretation. You will probably have occasion to use both kinds of sources in your research.

N56 Exercise care in evaluating secondary sources, whether they are books or articles. Distinguish opinion from bias and uninformed opinion from well-informed opinion. You will probably find that critics do not agree. In such cases, you should read one secondary source against another and refer to the primary source before coming to any conclusions. Such comparative reading should lead you to a balanced view and may well provide new insights.

N57   Before you begin to do any serious reading from a book, check the table of contents and the index for sections pertinent to your subject and then read just those sections. If the source is an article, read the introduction to help determine what parts of the article you should read.

N58   Read sources with specific questions in mind. Skim the material until you come to relevant passages; then read carefully and take notes.

N59   Begin to read according to the divisions in your outline. (There is no need, however, to cover the points in order.) Read the most promising sources first. Take notes on material that appears useful.

N60   As you read, regularly work back and forth between note cards and outline. Otherwise you may amass more information than you need on some points and not enough on others. If you regularly arrange the note cards according to your outline, you can tell instantly that you should stop or continue research in certain areas.

N61   As you take notes, make any adjustments in your topic outline and fill in subpoints. Insert these changes and additions into your written outline. Do not work from memory.

Types of notes

N62   As you begin to take notes from a source, the first card you complete is a bibliography card (source card). Write down all the information that you will need for the final bibliography for your paper: author, title, city, publisher, date. For the sake of accuracy, copy this information from the source itself, not from a card catalog or a bibliographical index. It is also useful to number and annotate cards. If you are using sources from several libraries, include the name of the library for possible future reference.

James H. Otto and Albert Towle.
<u>Modern Biology</u>. New York: Holt,
Rinehart and Winston, 1985.

– useful discussion on kelp.

574
08m

N63 Write notes on cards (preferably 4 x 6) with only one idea to a card. In this way you will be able to insert, rearrange, or discard cards and material as you continue with your research.[15]

N64 There are four basic kinds of notes: quotation, paraphrase, summary, and outline. Each has its special uses.

N65 Use a direct quotation for information that is particularly important or that is especially well phrased. Be sure to use quotation marks and to insert three ellipsis points to indicate any omission from the original.[16] You must, of course, acknowledge the source in your paper.

N66 Use a paraphrase[17] to record information that you consider important but that you put in your own words. If you borrow any distinctive phraseology from the author, these words must be put in quotation marks. Even if you do not quote any of the author's distinctive phraseology, you are copying the author's ideas; consequently you must acknowledge the source in your paper.

---

[15] Ultimately you should have cards on all the critical points of the outline.

[16] For the varying uses of ellipsis points with quoted matter, see D21-23.

[17] A paraphrase is a rewording of the original in approximately the same number of words.

N67 Use a summary note to express the main idea of a passage. This procedure is more difficult than it appears. First, read the original, noticing any headings and key concepts. Incorporate these into your summary. Next, reread both the passage and the summary to see that you have distilled the essence of the original. Summaries of specialized knowledge (as opposed to common knowledge[18]) need documentation in your paper.

N68 Use an outline note if only facts are taken from a source. If the information is common knowledge,[18] it does not need documentation in your paper.

```
 3                          kelp structure


 Thallophyte plants consist of
     a) rootlike holdfast
     b) stemlike stipe
        (Some stipe have epidermis,
        cortex, medulla)
     c) leaflike blade

 Keeton, p. 968
```

N69 A combination note with either paraphrase or summary and quotation is particularly useful since this is the kind of writing you will use in the final paper.

---

[18]Common knowledge is that information shared by people generally or by specialists in a particular field. A fact or opinion available in only one or two sources is not common knowledge.

```
5                              Elk kelp/Growth

Elk kelp that begins growing in the
spring grows at a faster rate than
kelp starting later in the season.
Although it is not as luxuriant as
giant kelp, it "nonetheless grows as
much as 25 feet in a year's time, one
of the world's fastest growing plants."

Earle, p. 426
```

N70 In addition to the actual note, every note card must have a content label and a source reference. In the model card in N69, "Elk kelp/Growth" is the content label and "Earle, p. 426" is the source reference. The content label facilitates the arrangement of cards according to the points in the outline. The source reference makes possible proper documentation in your paper. It is also useful to number the cards. This procedure can save time in working with the outline and in indicating quotations and references in the text.

Plagiarism

N71 In taking notes, you should understand that you are to acknowledge all borrowed material, whether it is in the author's own words or not. Simply put, an author has a right to both his or her ideas and language. If you use either, you must give proper documentation. If you fail to do so, you are guilty of plagiarism.

You do not, of course, document material that is common knowledge. For example, the date of assassination of John F. Kennedy or the number of elements in the Periodic Table should not be documented. Such information may not be instantly on the tip of your tongue, but it is considered common knowledge as far as documentation is concerned. In addition, common knowledge in specific fields need not be documented. For example, the general plan of Chaucer's *Canterbury Tales* is common knowledge in a specific field.

Compare the original passage below with the plagiarized version that follows it.

> The brown algae are almost exclusively marine, the few freshwater species being quite rare. Many of the plants called seaweeds are members of this division. They are most common along rocky coasts of the cooler parts of the oceans, where they normally grow attached to the bottom in the littoral (intertidal) and upper sublittoral zones. They may be seen in great abundance covering the rocks exposed at low tide along the New England coast.
>
> (Keeton, *Biological Science*, pp. 965-6)

```
    Almost all brown algae are found in
ocean waters. They are especially common
where the water is cool and the coast is
rocky.  There they grow attached to the
bottom in the intertidal zones.  They ap-
pear, for example, in great abundance cov-
ering the rocks at low tide along much of
the New England coast.
```

N

The second sentence in the researcher's version above may be considered common knowledge in a specialized field. The other sentences, however, are examples of plagiarism. For the most part the research writer takes the author's ideas and paraphrases them. Such use of another's ideas without proper attribution is plagiarism. In addition, the research writer occasionally uses the very words of the original author. Compare, for instance, the last sentence in each of the versions above. The last sentence might well be considered common knowledge; however, since the research writer uses the author's own words, it is a form of plagiarism.

Even if readers do not notice the plagiarism, the lack of a reference citing a source weakens the research and the authority of the paper.

Abbreviations in research work

N72 You should become familiar with the various abbreviations used in research. Although some of the ones listed below have fallen into disuse, you will undoubtedly encounter them in reading older works. In your own writing confine abbreviations to notes and bibliography.

app.	appendix
art.	article
b.	born
B.C.E.	before the common era
bk.	book
c.	copyright
c., ca.	*circa*, about, approximately
C.E.	common era
cf.	*confer*, compare
ch., chap.	chapter
col.	column
comp.	compiler, compiled by
d.	died
div.	division
e.g.	*exempli gratia*, for example
ed.	edition, edited by, editor
et al.	*et alii*, and others
et seq.	*et sequens*, and the following
etc.	*et cetera*, and so on
ex.	example
fig.	figure
f. (ff.)	*folio*, on the following page (on the following pages)
f.r. (fr.)	*folio recto*, on the front of the page
f.v. (fv.)	*folio verso*, on the back of the page
fl.	*floruit*, flourished (used when a person's birth and death dates are not known)

fr.	from
front.	frontispiece
fwd.	forward
ibid.	*ibidem*, in the same place
i.e.	*id est*, that is
id.	*idem*, the same
inf., infra	below
l. (ll.)	line (lines)
loc. cit.	*loco citato*, in the place cited
ms. (mss.)/ MS (MSS)	manuscript (manuscripts)
n.	*natus*, born
n. (nn.)	note (notes)
N.B.	*nota bene*, mark well
n.d.	no date
n.p.	no place; no publisher
no. (nos.)	number (numbers)
n.s., ns	new series
obs.	obsolete
op.	*opus* (work)
op. cit.	*opere citato*, in the work cited
o.s., os	old series, original series
p. (pp.)	page, (pages)
par.	paragraph
pass./ passim	here and there
pl.	plate, plural
pt. (pts.)	part (parts)
qtd.	quoted
q.v.	*quod vide*, which see
rev.	revised, revision
rpt.	reprint, reprinted by
sc.	scene
sc.	*scilicet*, namely
sec. (secs.)	section (sections)
ser.	series
[sic]	so, thus; read as it stands
st.	stanza
supp.	supplement

N

sup., supra	above
s.v.	*sub verbo, sub voce,* under the word (in reference to listings)
trans.	translated by, translator, translation
ts. (tss.)	typescript (typescripts)
ut sup.	*ut supra,* as above
v. (vv.)	verse (verses)
v., vs.	*versus,* against
v.	*vide,* see
v.s.	*vide supra,* see above
var.	variant
viz.	*videlicet,* namely
vol. (vols.)	volume (volumes)

Step 6. Writing a detailed outline

N73   An outline is a sketch showing the thesis statement and the main points of its development.[19]

N74   The outline is not merely a helpful adjunct to the writing of expository themes; it is also a useful form of exposition in its own right. It is sometimes the clearest way to initially present a difficult subject to your readers, since it gives them an uncomplicated, over-all view. It also offers a convenient set of hooks on which to hang an extempore talk. Lastly, an outline can be a help to study. When, for example, you have to put great masses of matter into your head to pass an examination, you would do well to outline the material, to organize it into a unified whole, and then to study the outline.

N75   There are three basic types of outlines: the topic outline, the sentence outline, and the combination outline.

---

[19] In this book *outline* is a technical term reserved for exposition. The outline sketch of a narrative from which the final form is written is called a plan or plot, and the sketch of an argument or persuasive speech is called a brief. (In popular speech *outline* is often used for all three of these forms and even for summaries and condensations.)

N76 A topic outline is a list of the points to be discussed, arranged to show their equal or unequal importance and expressed (with the exception of the thesis statement) in words or phrases. Here is a partial topic outline constructed of nouns and noun phrases:

Thesis: The acid-rain phenomenon is causing damage to natural and constructed environments.

   I. Acid rain
      A. sulfuric acid
      B. Nitric acid
  II. Soil and vegetation
      A. Soil
      B. Crop yield
      C. Tree growth
 III. Water and aquatic life
      A. Water quality
      B. Fish population
         1. Gills
         2. Spawning
      C. Plant life

N77 A topic outline is succinct but fails, through lack of completeness, to make clear statements and show relationships. A topic outline makes a good working outline for an essay. The final outline, however, is better expressed in a sentence or a combination form as explained below.

N78 A sentence outline is composed of complete sentences arranged to show the relative importance of ideas. These sentences, perhaps with some embellishment, may very well be used in the essay itself. Here is a partial sentence outline:

Thesis: The acid-rain phenomenon is causing damage to natural and constructed environments.

   I. Acid rain has two major components.

   A. Sulfuric acid, resulting from the emission of sulfur dioxide into the air from burning coal, is a major component of acid rain.

   B. Nitric acid, resulting from the emission of nitrogen oxides into the air from vehicular exhaust, is another major component of acid rain.

II. Acid rain has harmful effects on soil and vegetation.

   A. Acid rain lowers the pH (hydrogen power) in the soil.

   B. Crop yield is reduced because of the low fertility of the soil.

   C. Tree growth is reduced because of the low fertility of the soil.

III. In recent years acidified lakes and streams have sharply accelerated the decline of fish population and aquatic plant life.

   A. The water quality of lakes and streams is made toxic by acid rain.

   B. Fish have difficulty surviving in acidified lakes and streams.

      1. Fish are placed under heavy stress because their gills are unable to obtain sufficient oxygen from the water.

      2. Most species of fish are unable to spawn in acidic water.

   C. The variety and vitality of plant life are under attack in acidified lakes and streams.

N79 A combination outline has formal elements of both the topic and the sentence outline. Main divisions are written as sentences, subdivisions are written as words or phrases. Here is a partial combination outline using sentences along with nouns and noun phrases:

Thesis: The acid-rain phenomenon is causing damage
to natural and constructed environments.

  I. Acid rain has two major components.
  - A. Sulfuric acid
  - B. Nitric acid

 II. Acid rain has harmful effects on soil and vege-
tation.
  - A. Soil
  - B. Crop yield
  - C. Tree growth

III. In recent years acidified lakes and streams
have sharply accelerated the decline of fish
population and aquatic plant life.
  - A. Water quality
  - B. Fish population
    - 1. gills
    - 2. Spawning
  - C. Plant life

N80 The divisions of an outline are regularly labeled in the
following order:

       I.

         A.

         B.

            1.

            2.

               a.

               b.

                  (1)

                  (2)

                     (a)

                     (b)

                        i.

                        ii.

     II.

        A.

        B.

           1.

           2.

N

N81 Note the following points about formal outlines:

1. Ordinarily the introduction and the conclusion are not part of the outline.

2. Put a period after all numbers or letters not followed by a mark of parenthesis.

3. Double space between the number or letter (with its period or parenthesis) and the entry that follows.

4. Begin each entry with a capital letter.

5. Do not use a period after an entry unless it is a complete sentence.

6. Do not use a single subhead under any head. (When anything is divided, there will necessarily be at least two resulting subdivisions.)

7. If it is not possible to come up with two subheads, combine the single subhead with its head.

Wrong	*Right*
I. The panic	I. The panic, July 1742
A. July 1742	II. The rebellion
II. The rebellion	

8. The heads in each series marked with the same kind of letter or figure should be of equal or nearly equal importance. For example, Head II should be equal to or nearly equal to Head I; Head B under Head I should be equal to or nearly equal to Head A, but not equal to Head I; and so on.

9. When possible, express like heads in parallel form. Such parallelism aids the mind in recognizing ideas of comparable importance.

10. Whenever you can easily carry parallelism beyond the first word of any entry, do so. At the same time do not cling to parallel form at the expense of clarity or efficiency.

N82 The heads and subheads of the outline may in some cases coincide with the topic sentences of paragraphs written from the outline. But there need not be one paragraph or only one paragraph for each head or subhead of the outline.

N83 Do not hesitate to alter the outline while you are writing the essay, but show the alterations on paper. Do not work without a written outline.

Step 7. Writing and revising the rough draft

N84 As you read and took notes, you should have made any necessary adjustments in your outline. Now arrange your cards in the order of your outline.

   A. Do you have cards on every significant point in the outline? If not, you should do further research.

   B. Are there cards that do not fit into the outline? You must expect that there will be some material that you cannot use. Have the courage to discard it.

N85 In writing the introduction give the divisions of the paper, state the specific issues that will be addressed, or give the general procedure that will be followed in developing the thesis. The introduction should conclude with the thesis statement.

N86 Follow the outline as you write, using your note cards wherever appropriate. Individual paragraphs may correspond to entries in your outline.

N87 As far as possible, write without interruption. You should, at least, complete a major division of the paper in one sitting. Don't stop to research some technicality or to check on word choice or spelling. Such matters can be taken care of later. If questions arise, write notes in the margin for future investigation and continue to write. Do, however, make every effort to be clear and logical. Use transitional words and phrases between ideas.

N88 Space the lines of the rough draft very widely and leave abundant margins at the top, bottom, and sides for corrections and insertions. If you are using lined paper, it is usually a good idea to skip every other line. It can be helpful to begin each paragraph on a separate page. Double-space a typed rough draft.[20] A crowded and messy rough draft can treble your work and lead to disorganized writing.

N89 The paragraphs and sections of the research paper can be developed in a variety of ways: details and facts, division and classification, circumstances, comparison and contrast, cause and effect, example, and so on. (See M19-30.) If you are having difficulty developing an idea, consider in turn each of these options.

N90 Make good use of your source material (note cards). If you do, you will probably have a variety of quotations, summaries, and paraphrases in the essay; and sources will be properly integrated into the text.

N91 Incorporate short quotations into the running text. Use long quotations sparingly. These latter tend to weaken emphasis and often show a lack of assimilation on the part of the researcher.

N92 In copying a direct quotation, you must indicate any deviation from the original. If words are omitted, ellipsis points should be inserted.[21] If words are explained, brackets should be placed around the explanation. If a word is misspelled in the original, you should reproduce the error and indicate after it that it is not your error by adding *sic* (thus) in brackets.

N

---

[20] Even if you use a word processor, you should double space. The best way to revise is to print a hard copy, write in changes, and then return to the computer for the final copy. For advice in writing and revising with a word processor, see T12-21.

[21] For the varying uses of ellipsis points with quoted matter, see D21-23.

"The EPA [Environmental Protection Agency] 'Sewergate' scandal focused American attention on a uniquely modern problem: disposing of hazardous waste . . . more than 280 million meter [sic] tons a year."

N93 A direct quotation of more than four lines (or more than forty words) is set off in block form. In writing the rough draft, you may choose simply to write a reference number to the note card that contains the quotation or scotch-tape the card in place and continue to write without actually copying the quotation.

N94 Whenever you use a source other than a direct quotation, you must take care to indicate in the text the beginning and the end of the source material. The end is clearly indicated by a number, author, or page reference. The beginning may be effectively indicated by expressions like "According to Hanna . . . " or "Researchers have concluded . . . " By these and other means the reader will be able to tell where the reference material begins.

N95 With every card you use, insert the source (author with page number or note card number) into your text. Attempting to confirm documentation later is an annoying waste of time. Moreover, failing to note sources at this time can easily lead to accidental plagiarism (which, to an instructor, may readily appear to be deliberate plagiarism).

N96 The conclusion to the research paper should include a paraphrase of the thesis statement. If the paper is lengthy or complex, it should also briefly summarize the main points of the paper. Other types of conclusion are discussed in M18.

N97 When you finish the rough draft, put the essay aside for a day or two before revising it. The time interval will allow you to come to the essay with a fresh perspective.

N98   Reread and revise the rough draft.[22] As you do so, consider the following questions:

1. Does the introduction effectively state the purpose of the paper?

2. Are essential terms defined?[23]

3. Are all the major divisions of the outline adequately developed?

4. Is each paragraph adequately developed with supporting statements?

5. Does the sequencing in the outline need to be changed?

6. Are there gaps or repetitions in the sequence of the ideas?

7. Are there any parts of the paper that are irrelevant and should be deleted?

8. Is there need for more documentation at certain points? (Every major and critical point should be documented.)

9. Are sources integrated into the text?

10. Are transitions smooth and effective?

11. Are additional transitional words and phrases needed?

12. Is there variety of sentence length and structure?

13. Are verb tenses consistent?

14. Are words used precisely?

15. Are there any usage or punctuation problems?

16. Is the conclusion effective?

N

---

[22] For a discussion of essay form and structure, see M10-87. For a discussion of sentence style and word choice, see K1-140.

[23] For a discussion of definition, see O3-27.

Step 8. Preparing the final copy

N99   There are various styles of documentation and format for the research paper. Use whichever guide you prefer or are assigned–and use it consistently. Do not mix styles.

This handbook discusses MLA documentation (N100-N114), APA documentation (N115-N123), the University of Chicago footnote-style documentation (N124-N140 and provides some information on additional styles of documentation (N141-N146).

MLA documentation and format

N100   The author-page system of documentation set down in the *MLA Handbook for Writers of Research Papers* is used widely in the humanities. Three parts to this style of documentation are of particular concern here: parenthetical references in the text, explanatory notes, and list of works cited.

N101   The in-text reference regularly gives the author's last name and the page reference. There are two basic ways of doing this:

1. Cite the author's last name and the appropriate page number(s) in parentheses after the reference.

   "One of the most difficult things to explain to Courts is that writers don't necessarily approve of their characters' behaviour" (Mortimer 182).[24]

2. Use the author's last name in the text and place the page number(s) in parentheses after the reference.

   Mortimer commented, "One of the most difficult things to explain to Courts is that writers don't necessarily approve of their characters' behaviour" (182).

---

[24]When you do not have access to a printed source and use a database with distinctive or no pagination, identify either the paragraph (e.g., Smith, par. 20) or the page (e.g., Smith 7 of 10 — meaning page 7 of 10). Either method distinguishes the source as a database and provides usable information.

If you are referring to the entire work rather than to specific pages, give the author's last name and omit any parenthetical page references.

Obviously these in-text references are adequate only if further information is given in the Works Cited list at the end of the paper.

Works Cited

Mortimer, John.   <u>Clinging to the Wreckage</u>. New York: Penguin, 1982.

N102 If the source has two authors, give the last name of each. If the source has three authors, give either the last name of each or merely the last name of the first author followed by *et al.* (and others). If there are four or more authors, give the last name of the first author followed by *et al.* (and others).

"The nominal bare infinitive clause (without *to*) is severely limited in its functions. It may be the subject complement or (rarely) subject in a pseudo-cleft sentence" (Quirk et al. 1067).

Works Cited

Quirk, Randolph, et al. <u>A Comprehensive Grammar of the English Language</u>. New York: Longman, 1985.

N103 If there is no identifiable author of the book or article, cite a shortened version of the title (or the entire title if it is short) in place of the author's name. If you shorten the title, be sure to begin with the word by which the title is alphabetized in the list of Works Cited.

N104 If your paper cites two or more titles by the same author, add a shortened title to any in-text references. There are two convenient ways of doing this.

1. "Indeed, we may go this far: The television commercial is not at all about the character of products to be consumed" (Postman, <u>Amusing</u>, 128).
2. Postman reflects in <u>The Disappearance of Childhood</u> that "electric media find it impossible to withhold any secrets.

Without secrets, of course, there can be no such thing as childhood" (80).

N105 If you are quoting from a secondary source, use the following form. (It is, of course, preferable to find and quote the primary source.)

Walter Ong points out that in oral cultures both proverbs and sayings are very important: "They are incessant. They form the substance of thought itself. Thought in any extended form is impossible without them, for it consists in them" (qtd. in Postman 19).

N106 Since novels, plays, and poems are available in many editions, you should provide additional information to help the reader find the passage in question. Type a semicolon after the page number and then add other information such as the part, section, or chapter (pt., sec., ch.) of the work.

"He stumbled over the threshold and fell forward into the room—with a roar of pain, as his shapeless, swollen arm struck against something" (Undset 831; bk. 3, pt. 2, ch.4).

Works Cited

Undset, Sigrid. <u>Kristen Lavransdatter</u>. New York: Knopf, 1955.

N107 For verse plays and poems, omit page numbers and cite instead the part or act (with scene) and line number(s). Use arabic numerals for acts and scenes (*Macbeth* 3.2.1-15) unless your instructor specifies roman numerals (*Macbeth* III. ii. 1-15).

N108 If there is an omission at the end of a quoted sentence, the parenthetical reference goes outside the ellipsis points but inside the final period.

"Oratory is no longer, as it was in classical times, or in the eighteenth century, considered an art. Most politicians' speeches are merely shrill assertions of their opponents' errors . . . " (Mortimer 188).

N109 If a quotation is set off in block form, begin the parenthetical reference at the third space after the final period. (See N114.)

585

Mortimer gradually became aware of the gulf between law and literature:

> One of the most difficult things to explain to Courts is that writers don't necessarily approve of their characters' behaviour. Because Shakespeare wrote *Othello* and *Macbeth* it doesn't mean that he approved of wife murder and the stabbing of house guests. (182)

N110 In-text references to tables and figures should be direct (for example, "See Table 5.") Place tables and figures as close as possible to the text they illustrate. A table is regularly labeled "Table" (at the left margin), given an arabic numeral, and captioned. The source of the table and any notes appear below the table. Various types of figures are labeled "Figure" (or "Fig."), given an arabic numeral, and a title or caption. All of this is placed below the figure, beginning at the left margin.

N111 Explanatory notes are used for two purposes:

1. to provide additional information on some point in the text,[25]

2. to list additional sources related to the text.

[Text:] Write without interruption. Leave wide margins and ample space between lines for later corrections and insertions.[1] If at some point you develop a mental block, either stop and take a break or go back and reread what you have written, gathering impetus to continue.

Notes

[1] Even if you use a word processor, it is good to run off a hard copy of your first draft, take a fresh look at what you have written, and make any additional changes on paper before returning to the word processor for another draft.

[Text:] Direct speech gives a person's actual spoken or written words.[2]

---

[25] Ordinarily such information should be incorporated into the text or be omitted.

Notes
　²For a discussion of direct speech, see Quirk et al. (1021-24).

Notice that sources cited in the type of note immediately above are documented in Works Cited like any parenthetical reference.

Works Cited
Quirk, Randolph, et al. <u>A Comprehensive Grammar of the English Language</u>. New York: Longman, 1985.

N112 Regarding notes, follow these guidelines:

The in-text superscript number for a note is placed immediately after a word or punctuation mark (usually at the end of a sentence).

A corresponding superscript number (followed by a space) is placed before the actual note.

Although the actual note may be placed at the bottom of the page (footnote), MLA style recommends a separately numbered page (endnotes) immediately following the text and before Works Cited. Type *Notes* centered one inch from the top of the page, double space, indent five spaces from the left margin, type the matching superscript number, skip one space, and type the note. If the note carries over onto a second or third line, begin typing at the left margin and double space.

N113 In preparing the list of Works Cited, follow these guidelines:

1. The Works Cited page follows immediately after the last page of the essay. (If there is an endnotes page, it is placed before the Works Cited page.)

2. If you are required to list all the relevant sources that you read and not merely the ones that you used in the essay, then title this page Works Consulted.

3. Center the title Works Cited one inch from the top edge; double space to the first entry.

4. Begin the first line of an entry at the left margin. Successive lines of an entry are indented five spaces.

5. Double space within and between entries.

6. Arrange entries alphabetically by author (last name first). If there is no identifiable author, put the title of the work first (but do not list according to an initial article.

7. If there is more than one author of a work, invert the first author's name only (last name first).

8. In a succession of works by the same author, arrange them alphabetically (but not by any initial articles). Instead of repeating the author's name for a second work, type three hyphens and a period.

9. Double space after divisional periods within an entry (not, for example, after the period following a middle initial).

10. You need not underline the spaces between words in a title; it is, however, easier to do so.

11. If you are citing a title that includes the title of a work that would ordinarily be underlined, neither underline the shorter (interior) title nor put it in quotation marks.

<u>Dickens's</u> Pickwick Papers <u>as History</u>

12. If you are citing a title that includes the title of a work that would ordinarily be in quotation marks (poem, essay, short story), retain the quotation marks and underline the entire title.

Woodson, Thomas, ed. <u>Twentieth Century Interpretations of "The Fall of the House of Usher."</u> Englewood Cliffs, NJ: Prentice, 1969.

13. In citing a periodical give the pages for the complete article; for example, 8-11. If an article is not printed on consecutive pages (if, in other words, there is interven-

ing material), write the first page number and a plus sign; for example, 12+.

14. In general, use arabic numbers. Roman numerals are used for personal titles (Louis XIV) and the preliminary pages of a book (ii-xiv).

15. In general, use lowercase abbreviations; for example, vol. (volume), trans. (named translator), ed. (editor). However, when these abbreviations follow a period, they should be capitalized.

> The Encyclopedia of the Biological Sciences. Ed. Peter Gray.
>   New York: Van Nostrand, 1981.

When there is more than one name in a publishing company's title, use only the first name.

Harcourt (for Harcourt Brace Jovanovich, Inc.)
McGraw (for McGraw-Hill, Inc.)

Works cited: sample entries

Book by one author

Mortimer, John. Clinging to the Wreckage: A Part of Life.
   New York: Penguin, 1982.

Two or more books by the same author

Postman, Neil. Amusing Ourselves to Death: Public
   Discourse in the Age of Show Business. New York:
   Penguin, 1985.
— . The Disappearance of Childhood. New York:
   Delacorte, 1982.

Book by two or three authors

Williams, Frederick, Ronald E. Rice, and Everett M. Rogers.
   Research Methods and the New Media. New York:
   Free Press, 1988.

Book by four or more authors

Quirk, Randolph, et al. <u>A Comprehensive Grammar of the
    English Language</u>. New York: Longman, 1985.

   or

Quirk, Randolph, Sidney Greenbaum, Geoffrey Leech, and
    Jan Svartvik. <u>A Comprehensive Grammar of the
    English Language</u>. New York: Longman, 1985.

Book by a corporate author

American Psychological Association. <u>Diagnostic and
    Statistical Manual of Mental Disorders</u>. 3rd rev. ed.
    Washington: APA, 1987.

Book, no author or editor

<u>Scribner Desk Dictionary of American History</u>. New York:
    Scribner's, 1984.

Book with an editor

Samson, Jim, ed. <u>Chopin Studies</u>. New York: Cambridge
    UP, 1988.

Multivolume work

Leonard, Thomas, Cynthia Crippen, and Marc Aronson.
    <u>Day by Day: the Seventies</u>. 2 vols. New York: Facts on
    File, 1988.

Edition other than the first

Zinsser, William. <u>On Writing Well</u>. 3rd ed. New York:
    Harper, 1985.

Work included in a larger work

Baldwin, James. "Sonny's Blues." <u>American Short Story
    Masterpieces</u>. Eds. Raymond Carver and Tom Jenks.
    New York: Delacorte, 1987.

N

Signed article in a reference book

Hackenbroch, Yvonne. "Filagree Work." Encyclopedia
Americana. 1986 ed.

Unsigned article in a reference book

"Paine, Thomas." Webster's American Biographies. 3rd ed.
1979.

Article in a journal with continuous pagination

Moloney, Raymond. "African Christology." Theological
Studies 48 (1987): 505-15.

Article in a journal with separate pagination

Noonan, Guy Francis. "The Alcoholic's Reentry after
Treatment." Human Development 9.3 (1988): 19-23.

Article in a magazine

Traub, James. "Shake Them Bones." New Yorker 13 Mar.
1995: 48+.

Signed Article in a Newspaper

Canby, Vincent. "Japan's Best Movies Aren't a Leading
Export." New York Times 20 Nov. 1988, sec. 2: 1.

(On Mondays through Fridays the sections in *The New
York Times* are labeled A, B, C, D.)

Unsigned article in a newspaper

"Fewer testing positive for drugs." Plain Dealer [Cleveland]
30 June 1995, final ed.: Cl.

(Note that all months are abbreviated except May, June,
July.)

Book review

Jackson, Wallace. "A Figurative Quest." Rev. of The
Linguistic Moment: From Wordsworth to Stevens by
J. Hillis Miller. Kenyon Review, Summer 1986: 120-25.

Government document

United States Dept. of Labor, Bur. of Labor Stat. <u>Occupational Outlook Handbook</u>. 1988-89 ed. Bulletin 2300. Washington: GPO, 1988.

Film, television

<u>The Last Emperor</u>. Dir. Bernardo Bertolucci. With John Lone and Peter O'Toole. Columbia, 1987.

"Can You Still Get Polio?" <u>Nova</u>. Prod. Nancy Porter. PBS. WGBH, Boston. 5 Apr. 1988.

Interview

Dubas, Bohdan. Personal interview. 12 Feb. 1994.

Guiliano, John. Interview. "Life After Death in El Salvador." <u>America</u> 4 Dec. 1993: 12+.

Electronic publications

Documentation of material accessed by computer has similarities to documentation of ordinary printed matter.

Portable Databases

After the name of the author and the usual publication data, continue with the title of the database (underlined), publication medium (e.g., CD-ROM), the name of the vendor (if relevant), and conclude with the electronic publication date.

Angier, Natalie. "Chemists Learn Why Vegetables Are Good for You." <u>New York Times</u> 13 Apr. 1993, late ed.: C1. <u>New York Times Ondisc</u>. CD-ROM. UMI-Proquest. Oct. 1993.

Online Databases

If there is also a print source for the material, list the author and the usual publication data and continue with the title of the database (underlined), the publication medium (Online), the name of the computer service, and the date of access. If there is no print source, list in order the following when they are available: name of author, title of accessed material, date of material, title of database (underlined), publication medium (Online), name of computer network or service, date of access.

"Middle Ages." <u>Academic American Encyclopedia</u>. Online. Prodigy. Dec. 1994.

MLA guidelines and model

N114 In typing the MLA-style research paper, observe the following guidelines.

1. Use standard type on 8 1/2 x 11 inch white paper of good quality. Type on only one side of a page.

2. If an outline is required, it precedes the essay.

3. There is no title page. List all identification information at the top left corner of the first page.

4. Maintain a one-inch margin on all four sides of a page.

5. Beginning with the first page of the essay, all pages are numbered consecutively in the upper right-hand corner.

6. Hyphenation of words at the ends of lines is discouraged.

7. The entire paper (essay, long quotations, reference pages) is double-spaced.

8. Quotations of more than four lines are indented ten letter spaces (1 inch) from the left margin and none from the right. The first lines of any subsequent paragraphs within the quotation are indented an additional three spaces. Block quotations are not set off in quotation marks.

9. Poetry quotations of more than three lines are treated like block prose quotations. Shorter poetry quotations that do not require special emphasis are incorporated into the text with quotation marks and a virgule (/) to separate any lines.

10. All references are typed in alphabetical order on a separate page titled "Works Cited."

Explanatory notes to model on facing page

- There is no title page.

- There is a one-inch margin on all sides.

- All typing is double-spaced.

-A- Pages are numbered consecutively, each number typed just inside the right margin and below the one-half inch top margin. The author's last name appears before the page number. (As an alternative, the author's name and page number may be typed one line lower and thus be one double space above the the left-hand matter.)

-B- At the upper left, double-spaced (just inside the top and left one-inch margins) is the author's name, the instructor's name, the course designation, and the date. (If a title page is required, this information goes there instead.)

- If an outline is required, it is placed before the first page of the essay, and the information that appears here in the upper left appears instead in the corresponding location on the outline page. (For different types of outlines, see N75-79.)

- If an outline and a title page are both required, the author's name, etc., appear centered on the title page and not on the outline. (Sample title pages appear with the APA and University of Chicago models in N123, N140.)

-C- The title is centered and appears, double-spaced, below the introductory information and double-spaced above the text. The title is not underlined nor set off in quotation marks and is not typed in all capital letters.

-D- The first line of each paragraph is indented five letter spaces (one-half inch).

-A-   Herberger 1

-B-   Mark A. Herberger

Professor Schoen

English 115

May 2, 1990

-C-   Hardy Kelp: Protector and Supplier

-D-   The ocean is one of the last geographic frontiers

on planet earth. Its depths hold a treasure yet to be

mined. As the needs of the human race grow, it is only

a matter of time before this frontier covering three-

fourths of the planet is methodically explored. In addi-

tion to providing an understanding of the marine ecosys-

tem, such exploration will almost certainly lead to dis-

coveries immediately useful to the world's population.

Scientists already know, for example, that the ocean

is a rich source of chemicals and food. Because of its

potential in these areas, kelp is currently undergoing

serious scientific investigation. One of the hardiest,

least understood marine algae, kelp provides protection

for many species of marine life and is a valuable source

for the future production of natural gas and food.

-D-   Kelp is a brown algae, <u>Phylum phaeophyte</u>, which is

not common in the Atlantic but is abundant in cooler

coastal waters of the Pacific in the Western Hemisphere

from Cape Horn to the Arctic. The largest species of

N

Explanatory notes to model on facing page

-A-   The author's last name and the page number are typed below the one-half inch top margin and just inside the right one-inch margin. (As an alternative, the author's name and page number may be typed one line lower and thus be one double space above the text.)

-B-   There is a one-inch margin on all sides.

-C-   When only the author's name or the title of the work and the page number appear in parenthetical documentation, there is no punctuation between them.

-D-   Paragraphs are indented five spaces.

-E-   Since this second quotation is more than four typed lines, it is indented ten letter spaces (1 inch) from the left margin and typed double-spaced without quotation marks. The first line of the quotation is not indented more than the other lines even though, in the original, this line begins a paragraph. (In a quotation of two or more paragraphs, the first line of each subsequent paragraph is indented an additional three spaces. In such cases the first line of the first paragraph is indented only if it begins a paragraph.)

-F-   The author's name does not appear at the end of this particular quotation because it is in the text above the quotation. An abbreviated title, however, does appear with the page number because there are two sources by the same author cited in this paper.

-G-   In a block quotation the parenthetical reference begins at the third space after the end punctuation.

-A-   Herberger 2

-B-   seaweed is found off the coast of North America, from

-C-   Mexico's Baja Peninsula to Canada (Prescott 78-79).

-D-   Although most kelp is anywhere from a few inches to

      three or four feet in length, the kelp off North America

      grows up to two hundred or three hundred feet. "To reach

      such size in its brief lifetime, giant kelp grows faster

      than any other plant in the world--two feet and more in

-C-   a single day" (North 253). Through photosynthesis,

      nutrients from the water and energy from the sun

      nourish the kelp's incredible growth.

-D-   Kelp and other seaweeds grow at varying depths ac-

      cording to water conditions, reports researcher Sylvia

      Earle:

-E-   In clear tropical seas I have found seaweeds

                       living at depths greater than 600 feet, but

                       in less transparent temperate waters most

                       plants grow within 150 feet of the surface.

                       In the environs of Catalina the giant kelp

                       is common in depths to about 60 feet. Below

                       that, plant life becomes increasingly

                       sparse, except for occasional stands of the

                       bizarre-looking elk kelp and other deep-

-F-G-   water species. ("Undersea" 414)

Explanatory notes to model on facing page

— There is a one-inch margin on all sides.

-A- The author's last name and the page number appear below the one-half inch top margin and immediately inside the right one-inch margin. (As an alternative, the author's name and page number may be typed one line lower and thus be one double space above the heading.)

-B- The heading is typed in uppercase and lowercase letters and centered one inch below the top edge.

-C- There is one blank line between the heading and the first entry.

-D- The first line of an entry begins at the left margin. Successive lines of an entry are indented five letter spaces (one-half inch).

-E- Entries are double-spaced and arranged alphabetically, using the letter-by-letter system. Notice this sequence:

> Descartes, Rene
> De Sica, Vittoria
> Saint-Exupery, Antoine de
> St. Denis, Ruth

-F- There is a double space after divisional periods within an entry.

— For the format of particular types of entries, see examples on the facing page and in N113. There are, for instance, careful distinctions to be made in documenting references to a journal (such as *Oceans*) and to a magazine (such as *Science*).

-A-   Herberger 12

-B-C-   Works Cited

-D-   Abbott, Isabella A., and George J. Hollenberg.   <u>Marine</u>

-E-   <u>Algae of California</u>. Stanford, CA: Stanford UP, 1976.

-F-   Chapman, A. R. O. <u>Biology of Sesaweeds: Levels of</u>

       <u>Organization</u>. Baltimore: University Park Press, 1979.

       Dayton, P. K., and M. J. Tegner. "Catastrophic Storms,

           El Nino, and Patch Stability in a S. California

           Kelp Community." <u>Science</u> 20 Apr. 1984: 283-85.

       Earle, Sylvia A. "Tomorrow's Oceans." <u>Oceans</u> 16.2

           (1983): 9-13.

       ---. "Undersea World of a Kelp Forest." <u>National Geo-</u>

           <u>graphic</u> 158 (1980): 411-26.

       Fryer, Lee, and Dick Simmons. <u>Food Power from the Sea:</u>

           <u>The Seaweed Story</u>. New York: Mason/Charter, 1977.

       North, Wheeler J. "Sequoias of the Sea." <u>National</u>

           <u>Geographic</u> 142 (1972): 251-69.

       Prescott, G. W. <u>The Algae: A Review</u>. Boston: Houghton,

           1968.

       "The Secret Life of Seaweed." <u>Oceans</u> 19.4 (1986): 72.

       Strivastava, L. M., ed. <u>Synthetic and Degradative</u>

           <u>Processes in Marine Macrophytes</u>. Berlin: Walter

           de Gruyter, 1982.

APA documentation and format

N115 The name-year, or author-date, system of documentation set down in the *Publication Manual of the American Psychological Association* is used widely in the social and physical sciences. There are three parts to this style of documentation that are of concern here: parenthetical references in the text, a reference page following the text, and notes.

N116 The in-text reference regularly gives the author's last name, the year of publication, and the page. Typical situations are illustrated below.

1. If the author's name does not appear in the text, place the author's last name, the year of publication, and the page in parentheses at the end of the reference.

   Oratory is dead. Where one might hope to find it—namely, in politics and the law—there is only loud accusation and dull repetition of facts (Mortimer, 1982, p. 188).

2. If the author's name appears in the text, simply provide the date and the page in parentheses.

   Mortimer (1982) observed that courts find it difficult to believe that an author does not condone his characters' actions (p. 182).

3. If the author's name and the date are given in text, add only the page reference in parentheses.

   In 1982 Mortimer commented, "One of the most difficult things to explain to Courts is that writers don't necessarily approve of their characters' behaviour" (p. 182).

4. If the reference is to an entire work (rather than to a part), use only the author's last name and the year of publication.

   Postman (1985) has some disturbing things to say about public discourse in the age of television.

5. If a work has two authors, give both last names. If the work has three or more authors, give all their last names in the first reference but only the first author's last name followed by *et al.* in subsequent references.

First reference:

"The nominal bare infinitive clause (without *to*) is severely limited in its functions. It may be the subject complement (or rarely) subject in a pseudo-cleft sentence" (Quirk, Greenbaum, Leech, & Svartvik, 1985, p. 1067).

Note that in the running text the *and* linking the last two authors' names is spelled out. In parenthetical references an ampersand (&) is used in such cases.

Subsequent references:

According to Quirk et al. (1985) backshift is optional in certain time-reference cases (p. 1027).

6. If you cite two or more sources by the same author and they are not published in the same year, the publication date is enough to distinguish one source from the other. If you cite two or more works by the same author and they are published in the same year, arrange the titles alphabetically, designating them *a*, *b*, and so on.

These letter designations also appear in the list of references that follow the essay.

Asimov, I. (1983a). <u>The measure of the universe</u>. New York: Harper & Row.
Asimov, I. (1983b). <u>The roving mind</u>. Buffalo, NY: Prometheus Books.

7. If two or more authors have the same last name, include their initials in all citations.

8. If a work has no identifiable author, cite the first two or three words of the title instead. (Do not use quotation marks for the title of an article or chapter; underline the title of a book.)

N

9. When you do not have access to the original source but use a database with its different pagination, cite either the paragraph (e.g., par. 20) or the page (e.g., 7/10—meaning page 7 of 10). Either method distinguishes the source as a database and provides usable information.

Obviously these in-text references are adequate only if further information is given in the Reference list at the end of the paper.

References

Mortimer, John. (1982). <u>Clinging to the Wreckage</u>. New York: Penguin.

N117 If there is an omission at the end of the quoted sentence, the parenthetical reference goes outside the ellipsis points but inside the final period.

"Oratory is no longer, as it was in classical time, or in the eighteenth century, considered an art. Most politicians' speeches are merely shrill assertions of their opponents' errors..." (Mortimer, 1982, p. 188).

N118 If a quotation is set off in block form (indented five spaces), place the parenthetical reference after the final period.

Mortimer (1982) gradually became aware of the gulf between law and literature:

> One of the most difficult things to explain to Courts is that writers don't necessarily approve of their characters' behaviour. Because Shakespeare wrote *Othello* and *Macbeth* it doesn't mean that he approved of wife murder and the stabbing of house guests. (p. 182)

N119 The reference list at the end of an essay documents the sources used in the essay. In preparing the reference page, observe the following guidelines:

1. The reference page is placed after the essay.

2. Center the title "References" at the top of the page, double space, and begin the first entry. (See model in N123 for exact position.)

3. If you are required to list all the relevant works that you read and not merely the ones that you used in the essay, then title the references page "Bibliography."

4. Begin the first line of an entry at the left margin. Successive lines of an entry are indented consistently three to five spaces.

5. Skip one space after commas and semicolons. Skip two spaces after a colon except in ratios, two-part titles, and between city and publisher in a reference list (one space). Skip two spaces after end punctuation of a sentence and between separate parts of a reference citation. Skip one space after the initials in a person's name and none after *internal* periods in an abbreviation.

6. In submitting a paper for publication, double space within and between entries. In submitting a final copy to an instructor, you may single space *within* entries and double space *between* entries.

7. Arrange entries alphabetically by author (last name first). If there is no identifiable author, put the title of the work first (positioned alphabetically by the first significant word in the title).

8. Put the last name first for all authors in an entry. Use initials for their first and middle names.

9. When there is more than one author of a work, name them all. Use an ampersand (&) before the name of the last author.

10. In a succession of works by the same author, repeat the author's name for each entry. Arrange the works in order of the year of publication. If there are two or more works in the same year, arrange them alphabetically according to title, designating them *a*, *b*, and so on. (See the example under No. 6 in N116.)

11. Place the publication date in parentheses after the author's name and follow that with a period.

12. Place the title of the work after the year of publication.

13. In the title of any book or article, capitalize only the first word of the title and of any subtitle, the first word after a colon, and all proper names (in noun or adjective form).

14. Underline book titles; do not put article titles in quotation marks.

15. In the reference page do not use quotation marks to set off the title of an essay or the chapter of a book. Do use quotation marks for such titles in the text of the essay.

16. Underline and use uppercase and lowercase letters for the titles of periodicals.

17. Underline the spaces between words in titles that are italicized.

18. In periodical references, use arabic numerals for the volume number and underline it. Do not use *vol.* before the number.

19. Use arabic, not roman, numerals whenever possible.

20. Use *p.* or *pp.* in page-number references to newspapers and magazines. Omit *p.* or *pp.* in references to journal articles.

21. In giving the name of the publisher, omit unnecessary terms such as *Publishers, Co.,* or *Inc.*

References: sample entries[26]

Book by one author

Mortimer, John. (1982). <u>Clinging to the wreckage</u>. New York: Penguin.

Two or more books by the same author

Postman, Neil. (1982). <u>The disappearance of childhood</u>. New York: Delacorte.

Postman, Neil. (1985). <u>Amusing ourselves to death: Public discourse in the age of show business</u>. New York: Penguin.

Book by more than one author

Williams, F., Rice, R. E., & Rogers, E. M. (1988). <u>Research methods and the new media</u>. New York: Free Press.

Book by a corporate author

American Psychiatric Association. (1987). <u>Diagnostic and statistical manual of mental disorders</u> (3rd rev. ed.). Washington, DC: Author.

[When the author and the publisher are identical, use *Author* as the name of the publisher.]

N

Book, no author or editor

<u>Scribner desk dictionary of American history</u>. (1984). New York: Scribner's.

Book with an editor

Samson, J. (Ed.). (1988). <u>Chopin studies</u>. New York: Cambridge University Press.

---

[26] Since APA style is used primarily for the social and physical sciences, some of the model titles in this section appear out of place. They have been used, however, so that a direct comparison may be made with the other styles described in this handbook (notably MLA and *Manual for Writers*) where these same titles are appropriately used.

Multivolume work

Leonard, T., Crippen, C., & Aronson, M. (1988). <u>Day by day: The seventies</u> (2 vols.). New York: Facts on File Publications.

Edition other than the first

Zinsser, W. (1985). <u>On writing well</u> (3rd ed.). New York: Harper and Row.

Work included in a larger work

Baldwin, J. (1987). Sonny's blues. In R. Carver and T. Jenks (Eds.), <u>American short story masterpieces</u>. New York: Delacorte.

Signed article in a reference work

Hackenbroch, Y. (1986). Filigree work. In <u>Encyclopedia Americana</u>. Danbury, CT: Grolier.

Unsigned article in a reference work

Semiconductors. (1989). <u>Van Nostrand's Scientific Encyclopedia</u>. New York: Van Nostrand.

Article in a journal with continuous pagination

Moloney, R. (1987). African christology. <u>Theological Studies</u>, <u>48</u>, 505-15.

Article in a journal with separate pagination

Noonan, G. F. (1988). The alcoholic's reentry after treatment. <u>Human Development</u>, <u>9</u>(3), 19-23.

Article in a magazine

McGuigan, C. (1988, November 28). The Dada of invention. <u>Newsweek</u>, 86.

Signed article in a newspaper

Canby, V. (1988, November 20). Japan's best movies aren't a leading export. <u>New York Times</u>, sec. 2, p. 1.

Unsigned article in a newspaper

Older America has its say. (1988, November 29). Detroit
    Free Press, p. B3.

Book review

Jackson, W. (1986). A figurative quest [Review of The linguistic
    moment: From Wordsworth to Stevens]. Kenyon Review,
    8(3), 120-25.

Government document

Department of Labor, Bureau of Labor Statistics. (1988).
    Occupational outlook handbook (1988-89 ed., Bulletin
    2300). Washington, DC: U. S. Government Printing Office.

Film, television

Thomas, J. (Producer), & Bertolucci, B. (Director). (1987).
    The last emperor [Film]. Burbank, CA: Columbia.

Porter, N. (Producer). (1988). Can you still get polio?
    [Television]. Nova. Boston: WGBH.

Electronic publications

If print and electronic forms of the source material are
the same, a reference to the printed form is currently
preferred. If print and electronic forms are not the
same and you used the electronic form, pattern your
bibliography entry after the following examples.

Meyer, A. S., & Bock, K. (1992). The tip-of-the-tongue
phenomenon: Blocking or partial activation? [On-line].
Memory & Cognition, 20, 715-726. Abstract from: DIALOG
File: PsycINFO Item: 80-16351

Meyer, A. S., & Bock, K. (1992). The tip-of-the-tongue
phenomenon: Blocking or partial activation? [CD-ROM}.
Memory & Cognition, 20, 715-726. Abstract from:
SilverPlatter File: PsycLIT Item: 80-16351

Miller, M. E. (1993). The Interactive Tester (Version 4.0)
[Computer software]. Westminster, CA: Psytek Services.

In all entries the date should indicate the year of publication or, if the material is regularly updated, the most recent date. If the source has no date, give the complete date of your search (e.g., 1995, July 11).

Interview

Toolan, David S. (1993, December 4. [Interview with John Guiliano, social worker in El Salvador]. <u>America</u>, 12–14, 20–22.

Personal interviews are not included in the bibliography because they do not represent recoverable data. Cite them in the text only. Here is one acceptable format: "Bohdan Dubas (telephone interview, Feruary 4, 1994) provided useful information on . . . "

N120 Four types of notes may appear in APA documented papers submitted for publication: author identification, copyright permission, table, and content. Of these four types, table and content notes are found in final copies of student papers.

N121 Author identification notes are typed double-spaced on a separate page with "Author Notes" capitalized and centered at the top. The first line of each paragraph is indented five spaces. For copyright permission notes, their necessity and format, see the *Publication Manual of the American Psychological Association*.

N122 In a manuscript submitted for publication, figures, tables, and footnotes are placed after the manuscript on separate pages and appropriately titled. In student research papers such material is frequently incorporated into the text. In student papers a short table appears on the same page with the corresponding text. A long table or figure that takes no more than one page is placed immediately after the page on which the table or figure is first mentioned. (Longer tables, proofs, etc. are placed in an appendix.) Table captions and figure notes are typed below the table or figure. Type "Table" (or "Figure") followed by an arabic number. Number tables and figures consecutively in the order in which they are numbered in the text.

Content footnotes in a final copy of a student paper may be typed at the bottom of the appropriate pages or on a separate page titled "Footnotes" at the end of the essay. Notes may be single-spaced (double-spaced between notes). Indent the first line of each note five spaces (succeeding lines begin at the left margin). Number the footnotes to correspond with their numbers in the text. Use superscript arabic numerals both in the text and at the beginning of the footnote with no intervening space between number and text. Keep such footnotes at a minimum.

APA guidelines and model

N123 In typing the APA-style research paper, observe the following guidelines:[27]

1. Use standard type on 8 1/2 x 11 inch white paper of good quality. Type on only one side of a page.

2. Use a title page. (See model following these guidelines.)

3. Headings are used throughout the manuscript to establish the importance of each topic and, in effect, serve as a partial outline. Topics of equal importance have the same level of heading. Do not use a heading for the introduction.

4. The introductory material for a dissertation regularly includes a table of contents and an abstract. This material, along with the manuscript headings, obviates the need for any outline. An outline is frequently required for a shorter paper (for example,

N

---

[27] Additional details on format for APA-documented student papers are left to the writer or the instructor, since the *APA Publication Manual* is concerned almost exclusively with the submission of manuscripts to an editorial staff prior to publication.

an essay or an underclass research paper). The outline follows the title page and precedes the essay.[28]

5. When submitting a manuscript for publication, maintain a one and one-half inch margin on all sides of every page. In student papers maintain uniform margins of at least one inch at the top, bottom and right on every page. The left margin may be increased up to one and one-half inches to allow for binding. The top margin of the first page (and the first page of any chapter or section) may be wider than the other margins.

6. In a manuscript submitted for publication, every page is counted and numbered. In a student final copy every page is counted but not every page (for example, a figure page) is numbered. Type page numbers in the upper right-hand corner immediately inside the right margin and double-spaced below the short title. As an alternative, the title (followed by five spaces) and the page number may be placed on the same line.

7. In submitting a manuscript for publication, type the first two or three words from the title uniformly one inch or one and one-half inches below the top edge. This procedure is also frequently required of student papers.

8. When submitting a manuscript for publication, do not hyphenate words at the end of a line (editors will take care of such matters). In preparing a final student copy (for example, essay, research paper), you may hyphenate words at the end of a line.

9. When submitting a manuscript for publication, double-space throughout. In a final copy of a student paper, generally double-space; but you may

---

[28] For a discussion of outlines, see N73-83.

single-space table titles and headings, figure captions, long quotations (more than forty words), and *within* references and footnotes (double-space *between* references and footnotes).

10. Quotations of more than forty words are indented five spaces from the left margin, with no additional indentation for the first line if it begins a paragraph. The first line of any subsequent paragraphs within the quotation are indented an additional five spaces. The quotation may be single-spaced in a final copy (not in a manuscript copy). Do not use quotation marks.

11. All sources used in the paper are documented in alphabetical order on a separate page titled "References."

12. In scientific papers, headings (Method, Experiment, Results, and so on) are used to indicate different sections. (There is, however, no heading for the introduction.) Major headings are centered; minor headings are flush left and underlined—all double-spaced below and above contiguous material.

Some additional directives accompany the following model.

N

N.B. Upon completion of a paper, check the points on submitting a final copy in N148 at the end of the research-paper section. If you are using a word processor, check T22-30 before running off a final copy.

Explanatory notes to model on facing page

-A- At the upper right just inside the selected one to one and one-half inch top and right margins are a shortened form of the title and (double-spaced below it) the page number. As an alternative the title (followed by five spaces) and the page number may be placed on the same line.

-B- The title, located in the top half of the page, is centered and typed in uppercase and lowercase letters. If the title runs to more than one line, it is double-spaced. The title is not underlined nor set off in quotation marks.

-C- The author's name is centered and double-spaced below the title. (If the paper is prepared for publication, the institution's name is centered one double-space below the author's name.)

-D- APA style does not provide complete title-page instructions for student papers. For such papers it is helpful (and probably necessary) to include the course designation, the instructor's name, and the submission date. These may be placed near the bottom of the page.

-A-   Kelp

                                                                  1

-B-   Hardy Kelp: Protector and Supplier

-C-   Mark A. Herberger

                              Biology 103

-D-   Professor Schoen

                          March 10, 1990

Explanatory notes to model on facing page

— There are uniform margins of at least one inch at the top, bottom, and right of the page. The left margin may be increased up to one and one-half inches to allow for binding.

-**A**- At the upper right immediately inside the top and right margins are a shortened title and (double-spaced below it) the page number. As an alternative the title (followed by five spaces) and the page number may be placed on the same line.

— Introductory material for a thesis or a dissertation usually includes an abstract and a table of contents on separate pages. Each title is centered and double-spaced (or more) below the page number. The abstract and the table of contents begin double spaced (or more) below their respective titles. This manual illustrates only the abstract.

-**B**- The title "Abstract" is centered and double-spaced (or more) below the page number.

-**C**- The abstract begins double-spaced (or more) below the title. It consists of one paragraph and varies in length from 75 to 150 words, depending on the complexity of the subject. The paragraph is double-spaced without first-line indentation.

-A-   Kelp

                                                        2

-B-   Abstract

-C- Kelp is one of the hardiest of marine algae with
an incredible growth rate and near indestructi-
bility.   It provides protection for extensive
animal and plant life (750 species) and is a
valuable source for the future production of
natural gas. Kelp is also a source of food for
animals and humans and is used in the production
of algin (as an additive in foods, paints, cosmetics, pharmaceuticals) and chemicals.

N

Explanatory notes to model on facing page

— Some undergraduate instructors may want an outline in place of an abstract. The model here is one acceptable form.

— There are uniform margins of at least one inch at the top, bottom, and right of the page. The left margin may be increased up to one and one-half inches to allow for binding.

-A- At the upper right immediately inside the top and right margins are a shortened title and (double-spaced below it) the page number. As an alternative the title (followed by five spaces) and the page number may be placed on the same line.

-B- The title "Outline" is centered and double spaced (or more) below the page number.

-C- The outline begins double-spaced or more below the title.

-D- The outline is double-spaced.

The outline on the facing page is a combination outline. For a discussion of the different types of outlines, see N75-79.

N.B. An outline that is more than one page continues on the second line below the page number.

-A-   Kelp

                                                    2

-B-   Outline

-C-   Thesis: One of the hardiest and least understood of all

-D-   marine algae, kelp provides protection for many

               species of marine life and is a valuable source

               for the future production of natural gas and

               food.

          I. Kelp has the most potential for growth of any

               marine algae and is hardy enough to come back

               from near total destruction.

             A. Range

             B. Incredible growth rate

             C. Advanced cell tissues

             D. Survivability

                 1. Sea urchins

                 2. Storms

                 3. Season

         II. Kelp supports and protects many varieties

               of marine life both animal and plant.

             A. Support for 750 species

             B. Egg hatcheries

             C. Protection for marine life

                 1. Elk kelp

                 2. Small fish schools

Explanatory notes to model on facing page

— There are uniform margins of at least one inch at the top, bottom, and right of the page. The left margin may be increased up to one and one-half inches to allow for binding.

-A- The shortened title and the page number (double-spaced below) are placed immediately inside the top and right margins. As an alternative the title (followed by five spaces) and the page number may be placed on the same line.

-B- The title of the paper is centered, double-spaced (or more) below the page number.

-C- The essay begins double-spaced (or more) below the title.

-D- The first line of a paragraph is indented five spaces.

-E- The essay is double-spaced.

— In scientific papers, headings (Method, Experiment, Results, and so on) are used to indicate different sections. (There is, however, no heading for the introduction.) Major headings are centered; minor headings are flush left and underlined—all double-spaced below and above contiguous material. Consult *Publication Manual of the American Psychological Association* for detailed information.

-A-   Kelp

                                                        4

-B-   Hardy Kelp: Protector and Supplier

-C-D-   The ocean is one of the last geographic frontiers on

-E-   planet earth. Its depths hold a treasure trove yet to be

        mined. As the needs of the human race grow, it is only a

        matter of time before this great frontier covering three

        fourths of the planet is methodically explored. In addi-

        tion to providing an understanding of the marine ecosys-

        tem, such exploration will almost certainly lead to dis-

        coveries immediately useful to the world's population.

        Scientists already know, for example, that the ocean is a

        rich source of chemicals and food. Because of its poten-

        tial in these areas, kelp is currently undergoing serious

        scientific investigation. One of the hardiest and least

        understood of all marine algae, kelp provides protection

        for many species of marine life and is a valuable source

        for the future production of natural gas and food.

-D-   Kelp is a brown algae, <u>Phylum phaeophyte</u>, which

        is not common in the Atlantic but is abundant in

        cooler coastal waters of the Pacific in the Western

        Hemsphere from Cape Horn to the Arctic. The largest

        species of this seaweed is found off the coast of

N

Explanatory notes to model on facing page

— There are uniform margins of at least one inch at the top, bottom, and right of the page. The left margin may be increased up to one and one-half inches to allow for binding.

-A- The shortened title and the page number (double-spaced below) are placed immediately inside the top and right margins. As an alternative the title (followed by five spaces) and the page number may be placed on the same line.

-B- There is one blank line between the page number and the text.

-C- The in-text reference gives the author's last name, the year of publication, and the page.

-D- The first line of a paragraph is indented five spaces.

-E- Since this second quotation is more than forty words, it is indented five spaces from the left margin. The first line is not indented more than the other lines of the quotation even though, in the original, this particular line begins a paragraph. (If a quotation is more than one paragraph, the first line of each succeeding paragraph is indented an additional five spaces.)

-F- Block quotations may be single-spaced. There are no quotation marks.

-G- The author's name and the year do not appear at the end of this particular quotation because they are in the text above the quotation. There is one blank space before the parenthesis.

N

-A-   Kelp

-B-   5

-C- North America, from Mexico's Baja Peninsula to
Canada (Prescott, 1968, pp. 78-79). Although most kelp
is anywhere from a few inches to three or four feet in
length, the kelp off North America grows up to two
hundred or three hundred feet long. "To reach such
size in its brief lifetime, giant kelp grows faster
than any other plant in the world—two feet and more in

-C- a single day" (North, 1972, p. 253). Through the process
of photosynthesis, nutrients from the water and energy
from the sun nourish the kelp's incredible growth. The
plant gets these nutrients for its remarkable growth
through the main body of the thallus.

-D-   Kelp and other seaweeds grow at varying depths
according to water conditions, reports researcher
Sylvia Earle (1980):

-E-F-   In clear tropical seas I have found seaweeds
          living at depths greater than 600 feet, but in
          less transparent temperate waters most plants
          grow within 150 feet of the surface. In the envi-
          rons of Catalina the giant kelp is common in
          depths to about 60 feet. Below that, plant life
          becomes increasingly sparse, except for occa-
          sional stands of the bizarre-looking elk kelp and

-G-   other deep-water species. (p.414)

Explanatory notes to model on facing page

—   There are uniform margins of at least one inch at the top, bottom, and right of the page. The left margin may be increased up to one and one-half inches to allow for binding.

-A- The shortened title and the page number (double-spaced below) are placed immediately inside the top and right margins. As an alternative the title (followed by five spaces) and the page number may be placed on the same line.

-B- There is one blank line between the page number and the heading "References." The heading is typed in uppercase and lowercase letters and centered.

-C- There is one blank line between the title and the first entry.

-D- The first line of each entry begins at the left margin. The second and succeeding lines of an entry are indented consistently three to five spaces. There is a double space after divisional periods within an entry.

-E- Entries may be single-spaced (but double-spaced between entries).

—   For the format of different types of entries, see the examples on the facing page and N119.

N

-A-   Kelp

                                                              12

-B-C-   References

-D-   Abbott, I. A., & Hollenberg, G. J. (1976).   Marine algae

-E-   of California. Stanford, CA: Stanford University Press.

        Chapman, A. R. O. (1979).   Biology of seaweeds: Levels of

           organization. Baltimore: University Park Press.

        Dayton, P. K., & Tegner, M. J. (1984, April 20).

           Catastrophic storms, El Nino, and patch stability in

           a S. California kelp community. Science, 283-85.

        Earle, S. A. (1980).   Undersea world of a kelp forest.

           National Geographic 158, 411-26.

        Earle, S. A. (1983).   Tomorrow's oceans. Oceans, 16(2),

           9-13.

        Fryer, L., & Simmons, D. (1977).   Food power from the sea:

           The seaweed story. New York: Mason/Charter.

        North, W. J. (1972).   Sequoias of the sea. National

           Geographic 142, 251-69.

        Prescott, G. W. (1968).   The algae: A review.   Boston:

           Houghton Mifflin.

        The secret life of seaweed. (1986). Oceans, 19(4), 72.

        Strivastava, L. M. (Ed.).   (1982).   Synthetic and

           degradative processes in marine macrophytes. Berlin:

           Walter de Gruyter.

Footnote style documentation and format

N124 The footnote system set down in *A Manual for Writers of Term Papers, Theses, and Dissertations* (based on *The Chicago Manual of Style*) is widely used in the fine arts and in some fields in the humanities. Two parts of this style of documentation are of concern here: notes (reference notes and content notes) and bibliography.

N125 In this system arabic superscript numbers placed after references in the text correspond to numbers and notes at the bottom of pages where the references occur. (A long footnote may be carried over to the next page.) Footnotes are arranged in numerical order.

N126 The superscript numbers in the text are placed at the end of the reference (without any intervening space) rather than after an author's name used to introduce the passage.

N127 Text and footnotes are separated by a line of twenty spaces (made by striking the underline key) beginning at the left-hand margin on the first line beneath the text. Footnotes begin two spaces below this line.

N128 The first line of each footnote is indented the same number of spaces as the paragraphs in the text (consistently six, seven, or eight spaces). The arabic superscript number is placed immediately before the note (with no intervening space).

N129 Footnotes are single-spaced, but double-spaced *between* notes.

N130 The first time a work is referenced in a note, the entry should contain complete information. For a book this means author's full name, the title of the work, any editor, translator, edition other than the first, the specific reference (volume, if any, and page number), and publication data.

Postman clearly sets down his objectives:

> I will try to demonstrate by concrete example that television's way of knowing is uncompromisingly hostile to typography's way of knowing; that television's conversations promote incoherence and triviality; that the phrase "serious television" is a contradiction in terms; and that television speaks in only one persistent voice—the voice of entertainment.[1]

---

[1] Neil Postman, <u>Amusing Ourselves to Death: Public Discourse in the Age of Show Business</u> (New York: Penguin, 1984), 80.

N131 The first time a journal or periodical is referenced in a note, the entry should contain complete information: author's full name, title of article, name of periodical, volume number or issue, publication date in parentheses, and page number(s).

[2] Eric Valli and Diane Summers, "Honey Hunters of Nepal," <u>National Geographic</u> 174 (November 1988): 662.

Even though magazines of general interest may have volume numbers, they are better identified by date alone. The date, in effect, takes the place of the volume number.

[3] Cathleen McGuigan, "The Dada of Invention," <u>Newsweek</u>, 28 November 1988, 86.

Material accessed by computer is treated like ordinary printed matter but concludes with additional information: the name of the service, the name of the vendor providing the service, the accession or identifying numbers within the service, and the page reference. (If the material is revised, include the most recent date.) Because of certain ambiguities created by database pagination, it is necessary to cite either the paragraph (e.g., par. 20) or the page (e.g., p. 7 of 10).

[1] Rosabel Flax, <u>Guidelines for Teaching Mathematics K-12</u> (Topeka: Kansas State Department of Education, 1979) [database on-line]; available from DIALOG, ERIC, ED 178312, par. 7.

N132 Subsequent references to a work are made in shortened form.

1. When references to the same work (book or periodical) follow one another without an intervening reference, *Ibid.* ("in the same place") is used to repeat as much of the preceding reference as possible. If the two references have even the page reference in common, *Ibid.* suffices for the second reference. If the two references are the same except for the page number, *Ibid.* plus the page number suffices for the second reference.

> ⁴John Mortimer, <u>Clinging to the Wreckage</u> (New York: Penguin, 1982), 182.
> ⁵Ibid., 188.

(Notice that *Ibid.* is not underlined.)

2. A subsequent reference to a work that is not immediately preceding is made in one of two ways:

Cite the author's last name, the title of the work (frequently in shortened form), and the page reference.

> ⁶Mortimer, <u>Clinging</u>, 189.

Cite the author's last name and the page reference. Include the title (frequently shortened) of the work only when two or more works by the same author are cited.

> ⁷Asimov, <u>Roving</u>, 58.
> ⁸ Isaac Asimov, <u>The Measure of the Universe</u> (New York: Harper & Row, 1983), 89.
> ⁹Asimov, <u>Roving</u>, 95.

N133 If there is no identifiable author, begin with the title instead. (Use quotation marks for the title of an article or chapter; underline the title of a book.)

N134 If a work has two or three authors, give the full names of all authors in normal order. (Separate the names of three or more authors with commas, the last comma before *and*).

If a work has more than three authors, cite in the note (but not in the bibliography) the full name of the first author followed by *et al.* or *and others*. Whichever expression you choose "et al." or "and others," use it consistently throughout the paper.

N135 If you are quoting from a secondary source (not the primary one), use the following form.

[Text:] Walter Ong points out that in oral cultures both proverbs and sayings are very important: "They are incessant. They form the substance of thought itself. Thought in any extended form is impossible without them, for it consists in them."[10]

---

[10] Walter Ong, <u>Orality and Literacy</u> (New York: Methuen, 1982), 35, quoted in Neil Postman, <u>Amusing Ourselves to Death: Public Discourse in the Age of Show Business</u> (New York: Penguin, 1985), 19.

N136 For plays and long poems, omit the page numbers and cite instead the part or act (with scene) and line number(s). Use arabic numerals for acts and scenes (*Macbeth* 3.2.1-15) unless your instructor specifies roman numerals (*Macbeth* III.ii.1-15).

N137 Refer to page(s) by number alone. The abbreviations "p." and "pp." precede numbers only where their absence might cause confusion.

N138 All text references to tables and figures should be made by number (for example, "See Table 5."). Tables and figures should be placed as close as possible to the first reference in the text. Type "Table" plus an arabic number and any title. Skip three lines and insert the table. Skip three lines below the table and resume with the text. Figure labels and legends are regularly placed below the figure or illustration. Sometimes a table or a figure occupies an entire page in the text. Sometimes, because of their size, tables (and figures) are placed in an appendix.

N139 In preparing the list or Works Cited, follow these guidelines:

1. The Works Cited page is placed after the essay. (If there is a notes page, it is placed before the Works Cited page.)

2. Other titles for this page are "Selected Bibliography" and "Sources Consulted."

3. Center "Works Cited" two inches from the top of the page, skip three lines, and begin the first entry.

4. Begin the first line of an entry at the left margin. Successive lines of an entry are indented five spaces.

5. Single-space within entries; skip one line between entries.

6. Double space after divisional periods within an entry (not, for example, after the period following an author's middle initial).

7. Arrange entries alphabetically by author (last name first).

8. If there is more than one author of a work, invert the first author's name only.

9. If there is no identifiable author, put the title of the work first (positioned alphabetically by the first significant word in the title).

10. If there is a succession of works by the same author, arrange them alphabetically by title (but not by any initial articles) or chronologically by date. Instead of repeating the author's name, type eight underscores and a period.

11. The underlining of titles of books, periodicals, and so on, is optional in the bibliography; the style, however, should be consistent. (Such underlining is, of course, required elsewhere in the paper.)

12. In citing a title that includes the title of another book, underline the entire title and set off the interior title in quotation marks.

13. When the title of a book occurs within a title that is set off in quotation marks, the book title is underlined.

14. In general, use arabic numerals. Use roman numerals for the introductory pages of a work if the work itself does so.

15. Refer to page(s) by number alone. The abbreviations "p." and "pp." precede page numbers only if their absence might cause confusion.

16. Do not use shortened forms for the names of publishing companies.

Bibliography: sample entries

Book by one author

Mortimer, John. <u>Clinging to the Wreckage</u>. New York: Penguin, 1982.

Two or more books by the same author

Postman, Neil. <u>Amusing Ourselves to Death: Public Discourse in the Age of Show Business</u>. New York: Penguin, 1985.

————. <u>The Disappearance of Childhood</u>. New York: Delacorte, 1982.

Book by more than one author

Williams, Frederick, Ronald E. Rice, and Everett M. Rogers. <u>Research Methods and the New Media</u>. New York: Free Press, 1988.

Book by a corporate author

American Psychological Association. <u>Diagnostics and Statistical Manual of Mental Disorders</u>. 3rd rev. ed.
Wasington: American Psychological Association, 1987.

Book, no author or editor

<u>Scribner Desk Dictionary of American History</u>. New York:
Scribner's, 1984.

Book with an editor

Samson, Jim, ed. <u>Chopin Studies</u>. New York: Cambridge
University Press, 1988.

Multivolume work

Leonard, Thomas, Cynthia Crippen, and Marc Aronson. <u>Day
by Day: the Seventies</u>. 2 vols. New York: Facts on File
Publications, 1988.

Edition other than the first

Zinsser, William. <u>On Writing Well</u>. 3rd ed. New York: Harper
& Row, 1985.

Work included in a larger work

Baldwin, James. "Sonny's Blues." Story in <u>American Short Story
Masterpieces</u>, eds. Raymond Carver and Tom Jenks.
New York: Delacorte, 1987.

Signed article in a reference work

Cayne, Bernard S., and David T. Holland, eds. <u>Encyclopedia
Americana</u>. Danbury, CT: Grolier Incorporated, 1986.
S.v. "Filigree Work," by Yvonne Hackenbroch.

(The abbreviation *s.v.* stands for the Latin *sub verbo* or
sub voce and means "under the word.")

Unsigned article in a reference work

<u>Webster's American Biographies</u>, 1979 ed. S.v. "Paine, Thomas."

Article in a journal with continuous pagination

Moloney, Raymond. "African Christology." <u>Theological Studies</u> 48 (September 1987): 505-15.

Article in a journal with separate pagination

Noonan, Guy Francis. "The Alcoholic's Reentry after Treatment." <u>Human Development</u> 9 (Summer 1988): 19-23.

Article in a magazine

McGuigan, Cathleen. "The Dada of Invention." <u>Newsweek</u>, 28 November 1988, 86.

Signed article in a newspaper

Canby, Vincent. "Japan's Best Movies Aren't a Leading Export." <u>New York Times</u>, 20 November 1988, sec. 2, p. 1.

Unsigned article in a newspaper

"Older America Has Its Say." <u>Detroit Free Press</u>, 29 November 1988, sec. B, p. 3.

Book review

Jackson, Wallace. Review of <u>The Linguistic Moment: From Wordsworth to Stevens</u>, by J. Hillis Miller. In <u>Kenyon Review</u>, n.s. 8 (Summer 1986): 120-25.

(The abbreviation *n.s.* means "new series.")

Government document

U. S. Department of Labor. Bureau of Labor Statistics. <u>Occupational Outlook Handbook</u>. 1988-89 ed. Bulletin 2300. Washington, D.C.: GPO, 1988.

For citations of government publications, use any one of the following styles consistently:

> Washington, D.C.: U.S. Government Printing Office, 1988.
> Washington, D.C.: Government Printing Office, 1988.
> Washington, D.C.: GPO, 1988.
> Washington, 1988.

Film, television

Thomas, Jeremy (producer) and Bernardo Bertolucci (director). The Last Emperor. With John Lone and Peter O'Toole. Columbia, 1987. Film.

Porter, Nancy (producer). "Can You Still Get Polio?" Nova series. PBS. Boston: WGBH. 5 April 1988.

(In these two examples the title of the production may be placed first and the producer second.)

Electronic publications

Material accessed by computer is treated like ordinary printed matter but concludes with additional information: the name of the service, the name of the vendor providing the service, the accession or identifying numbers within the service. If the material is revised, include the most recent date.

Flax, Rosabel. Guidelines for Teaching mathematics K-12. Topeka: Kansas Department of Education, 1979. Database on-line. Available from DIALOG, ERIC, ED 178312.

"Middle Ages." Academic American Encyclopedia. Database on-line. Available from Prodigy. Accessed 26 March 1994.

If there is no print source, list in order the following when they are available: name of author, title of accessed material, date of material, title of database, name of computer network or service, and date of access (e.g., 14 July 1995).

Interview

Dubas, Bohdan, accountant. Interview by author, 12 February 1994.

(Technically an interview must be preserved in some retrievable form to be included in a bibliography.)

Guiliano, John. "Life After Death in El Salvador: Interview by David S. Toolan." <u>America</u>, 4 December 1993. 12.

Footnote style-documentation and model

N140 In typing the footnote-style research paper, observe the following guidelines:

1. Use standard type on 8 1/2 x 11 inch white paper of good quality. Type on only one side of a page.

2. Prepare a title page. In addition, the front matter (preliminary material) may include a preface, table of contents, lists of tables and illustrations, and an abstract.

3. An underclass term paper may require only a title page and an outline before the text.[29]

4. Maintain a one-inch margin on all four sides of each page. (The bottom margin may be shortened to add one line of text and thus avoid beginning the next page with a very short line.)

5. For the front matter, number pages in roman centered at the bottom of the page (seventh line from the edge). Begin with "ii" since the title page— although not numbered—is counted. Number the remaining parts of the paper in arabic numbers centered at the top of the page (on the seventh line from the edge) except on pages that have a major heading. On those pages place the number at the bottom of the page, centered on the seventh line above the edge. (An alternate method of pagination for the text and end matter is to number pages inside the upper-right margins—except for the first page of any division in the paper, where the numbers are centered below the text.)

---

[29] For a discussion of outlines, see N73-83.

6. For a discussion of headings and subheadings, their forms and uses, see *A Manual for Writers of Term Papers, Theses, and Dissertations.*

7. Do not justify the right-hand margin. Follow a reliable dictionary in dividing words at the ends of lines.

8. The paper should be double-spaced, except for block quotations, notes, captions, legends, and long headings, which are single-spaced.

9. Indent paragraphs six to eight spaces. Whatever indentation you choose, be consistent.

10. A quotation that runs to four or more lines of text should be indented four spaces from the left margin and single-spaced. The first lines of any paragraphs in the original are indicated in a block quotation by an indentation of an additional four spaces.

11. Quotations of two or more lines of poetry are centered on the page and single- or double-spaced in imitation of the original. If the lines of the poem are too long to be centered, they should be indented four spaces with the runover lines indented an additional four spaces.

12. Text and footnotes are separated by a line of twenty spaces (made with the underline key) beginning at the left margin on the first line below the text. The footnote begins two lines below this line (in other words, one line is skipped). The first line of each footnote is indented the same number of spaces as the first line of paragraphs in the text (consistently six, seven, or eight spaces). Each footnote begins with a superscript arabic number immediately before (i.e., no intervening space) the first word of the footnote.

13. Footnotes on a page of less than full text are typed in the usual manner immediately below the text (not at the bottom of the page).

14. All references used in the paper are documented in alphabetical order on a separate page titled either "Selected Bibiliography," "Works Cited," or "Sources Consulted."

Some additional directives accompany the following model.

N.B. Upon completion of a paper, check the points on submitting a final copy in N148 at the end of the research-paper section. If you are using a word processor, check T22-30 before running off a final copy.

N

Explanatory notes to model on facing page

—   All entries on the title page are typed in capitals and centered. (A bound paper will require a greater left margin.)

-A-   The school or college name is typed at least one inch from the top edge.

A-B-C There is one inch or more between each of the top three entries.

A'-B'-C' Space A' is equal to or greater than space A. Space B and B' are equal. Space C and C' are equal.

-D-   There are two blank lines in space D.

-E-   These lines are double spaced.

—   The title page is counted as p.1, but it is not numbered.

N

-A-

BRENNER COLLEGE

-B-

HARDY KELP: PRESERVER AND SUPPLIER

-C-

-E-

PAPER SUBMITTED IN PARTIAL FULFILLMENT

OF THE REQUIREMENTS FOR THE COURSE

IN FRESHMAN COMPOSITION

-D-

DEPARTMENT OF ENGLISH

-C'-

-E-

BY

MARK A. HERBERGER

-B'-

-E-

CELINA, KENTUCKY

MARCH 1990

-A'-

N

Explanatory notes to model on facing page

—   Preliminary pages (such as table of contents, abstract, preface, acknowledgements, lists of illustrations, lists .of tables) have their headings in capitals either one or two inches from the top edge with page number in roman centered one inch from the bottom of the page. For detailed directives on the format of such pages, see *A Manual for Writers of Term Papers, Theses, and Dissertions.*

-A-   If an outline is required, the heading is centered in capitals two inches from the top edge, and the page number is centered in roman one inch from the bottom page.

-B-   The outline begins on the third line below the heading and is double spaced.

—   There is a margin of at least one inch on all four sides of the page. A greater margin is permissible on the left to allow for binding.

—   The outline on the facing page is a combination outline. For information on the different types of outlines, see N75-79.

-A-   OUTLINE

-B-   Thesis: One of the hardiest and least understood of

                all marine algae, kelp provides protection

                for many species of marine life and is a

                valuable source for the future production of

                natural gas and food.

        I.   Kelp has the most potential for growth of

             any marine algae and is hardy enough to

             come back from near total destruction.

             A.   Range

             B.   Incredible growth rate

             C.   Advanced cell tissues

             D.   Survivability

                  1.   Sea urchins

                  2.   Storms

                  3.   Seasons

        II. Kelp supports and protects many varieties

             of marine life both animal and plant.

             A.   Support for 750 species

             B.   Egg hatcheries

             C.   Protection for marine life

                  1.   Elk kelp

-A-   ii

Explanatory notes to model on facing page

—   There is a margin of at least one inch on all four sides. A greater margin is permissible on the left to allow for binding.

-A-   The outline continues below a top margin of one inch.

-B-   The outline is double-spaced.

-C-   The page number is centered in roman one inch from the bottom of the page.

N

-A-   2. Small fish schools

                 3. Sea otters

-B-   III. Kelp demonstrates great potential as an

              energy source.

              A. Production of natural gas

              B. Successful test farms

        IV. Kelp is a source of food and food additives.

              A. Use as fodder

              B. Potential food source for humans

              C. Production of algin

                   1. Use in foods

                   2. Use in other products

                        a. Paints

                        b. Cosmetics

                        c. Pharmaceuticals

              D. Production of chemicals

-C-   iii

N

Explanatory notes to model on facing page

—   As a rule, general headings (CHAPTER 2, and so on) are typed two inches from the top edge (on the thirteenth line), are centered, and typed entirely in capitals.

-A-   Double-spaced below the general heading, the title is centered and typed all in capitals. If there is no general heading, the title is typed in its place (centered and in capitals on the thirteenth line from the top edge).

If the title requires more than forty-eight spaces, it is set in inverted pyramid form in double-spaced lines.

-B-   There are two blank lines between the title and first line of the text.

-C-   The first lines of paragraphs are indented uniformly either six, seven, or eight spaces. The essay is double-spaced.

-D-   There is a margin of one inch on all sides. (A wider margin is permitted on the left if the paper is to be bound, and a narrower margin is permitted on the bottom to avoid carrying over a short final line of a paragraph to the next page.)

-E-   A line of twenty spaces (made with the underline key) is typed on the line below the text. Footnotes, single-spaced, begin on the second line below that line. The first line of a footnote is indented the same number of spaces as the first line of a paragraph. There is no space between the superscript and the first word of the footnote.

-F-   The page number is centered on the seventh line from the bottom edge. There is one blank line between the page number and the last line of the footnote.

642

-A-
-B-   HARDY KELP: PROTECTOR AND SUPPLIER
-C-
-D-   The ocean is one of the last geographic frontiers

on planet earth. As the needs of the human race grow it

is only a matter of time before this great frontier is

methodically explored. In addition to providing an under-

standing of the marine ecosystem, such exploration will

almost certainly lead to discoveries immediately useful to

the world's population. Scientists already know, for ex-

ample, that the ocean is a rich source of chemicals and

food. Because of its potential in these areas, kelp is

currently undergoing serious scientific investigation.

One of the hardiest and least understood of all marine

algae, kelp provides protection for many species of marine

life and is a valuable source for the future produc-

tion of natural gas and food.

-C-   Kelp is a brown algae, <u>Phylum phaeophyte</u>, which

is not common in the Atlantic but is abundant in cooler

coastal waters of the Pacific in the Western Hemisphere

from Cape Horn to the Arctic. The largest species of this

seaweed is found off the coast of North America, from

Mexico's Baja Penninsula to Canada.[1] Although most kelp is

-E-   [1]G. W. Prescott, <u>The Algae: A Review</u> (Boston:
Houghton Mifflin, 1968), 77-78.

-F-   4

N

Explanatory notes to model on facing page

-A- The page number is centered on the seventh line below the top edge. (An alternate location for the page number is on the same line but immediately inside the right one-inch margin.)

-B- The text begins on the ninth line from the top edge.

-C- There is a margin of one inch on all sides. (A wider margin is permitted on the left if the paper is to be bound, and a narrower margin is permitted on the bottom to avoid carrying over a short final line of a paragraph to the next page.)

-D- The first lines of paragraphs are indented uniformly either six, seven, or eight spaces.

-E- The block quotation is indented four spaces from the left margin and single-spaced. Since the first line of this particular quotation begins a paragraph in the original, it is indented an additional four spaces.

-F- A line of twenty spaces (made with the underline key) is typed on the line below the text. Footnotes begin two lines below that line. The first line of a footnote is indented the same number of spaces as the first line of a paragraph. There is no space between the superscript and the first word of the footnote.

-G- Footnotes are single-spaced with a double space between footnotes.

-A-   5

-B-C- anywhere from a few inches to three or four feet in length,

the kelp off North America grows up to two hundred or

three hundred feet. "To reach such size in its brief life-

time, giant kelp grows faster than any other plant in the

world—two feet and more in a single day."[2] Through the

process of photosynthesis, nutrients from the water and

energy from the sun nourish the kelp's incredible growth.

Although mature strands begin to die after four or five

months, new fronds continually replace them; thus kelp

grows unabated. The plant has a holdfast which attaches

itself to anything stationary. But the holdfast does not

draw nutrients from the soil; rather the plant gets the

nutrients for its incredible growth through the main

body of the thallus.

-D-   Kelp and other seaweeds grow at varying depths accord-

ing to water conditions, reports researcher Sylvia Earle:

-E-   In clear tropical seas I have found seaweeds
living at depths greater than 600 feet, but in less
temperate waters most plants grow within 150 feet of
the surface. In the environs of Catalina the giant
kelp is common in depths to about 60 feet. Below
that plant life becomes increasingly sparse, except
for occasional stands of the bizarre-looking elk kelp
and other deep-water species.[3]

-F-   [2]Wheeler J. North, "Sequoias of the Sea," <u>National
Geographic</u> 142 (August 1972): 254.

-G-   [3]Sylvia A. Earle, "Undersea World of a Kelp Forest," <u>National Geographic</u> 158 (September 1980): 414.

Explanatory notes to model on facing page

-A-   The heading is typed all in capitals and centered two inches from the top edge (on the thirteenth line).

-B-   There are two blank lines between the heading and the first entry.

-C-   There is a one-inch margin on all sides. Double space after divisional periods within an entry (not, for example, after the period following a middle initial).

-D-   Entries are single-spaced with one blank line between entries. The second and succeeding lines of an entry are indented five spaces.

-E-   Since this page has a heading, the page number appears centered at the bottom of the page, one inch above the edge, and double-spaced below the last entry on a full page.

—   For the format of different types of entries, see the examples on the facing page and N139. There are, for instance, careful distinctions to be made in documenting references to a journal (such as *Oceans)* and to a magazine (such as *Science)*.

-A-
-B-
-C-

-D-

WORKS CITED

Abbott, Isabella A., and George J. Hollenberg. <u>Marine Algae of California</u>. Stanford, CA: Stanford University Press, 1976.

Chapman, A. R. O. <u>Biology of Seaweeds: Levels of Organization</u>. Baltimore: University Park Press, 1979.

Dayton, P. K., and M. J. Tegner. "Catastrophic Storms, El Nino, and Patch Stability in a S. California Kelp Community," <u>Science</u>, 20 April 1984: 283-85.

Earle, Sylvia A. "Tomorrow's Oceans," <u>Oceans</u>, 16 (March-April 1983): 9-13.

_____. "Undersea World of a Kelp Forest," <u>National Geographic</u> 158 (September 1980): 411-26.

Fryer, Lee, and Dick Simmons. <u>Food Power from the Sea: The Seaweed Story</u>. New York: Mason/Charter, 1977.

North, Wheeler J. "Sequoias of the Sea," <u>National Geographic</u> 142 (August 1972): 251-69.

Prescott, G. W. <u>The Algae: A Review</u>. Boston: Houghton Mifflin, 1968.

"The Secret Life of Seaweed." <u>Oceans</u>, 19 (July-August 1986): 72.

Strivastava, L. M., ed. <u>Synthetic and Degradative Processes in Marine Microphytes</u>. Berlin: Walter de Gruyter & Co., 1982.

N

-E-   12

Other styles of documentation and format

N141 The number-reference documentation and format for the research paper is frequently used in the fields of science and technology. In this system a number (in parentheses, in brackets, or slightly above the line of type) appears in the text wherever an outside source is used. These numbers correspond to a numbered list of works cited on a page at the end of the paper. These references may be arranged in the order of their appearance in the paper or they may be arranged alphabetically (in which case the numbers do not appear in consecutive order in the text). This list of works is usually titled "References" or "References and Notes."

N142 The content and arrangement of notes are distinctive characteristics of the number-reference style of documentation.

[Text:] We must be extremely cautious in discussing animal behavior in terms of human behavior (1).

References and Notes

1. Keeton, W. T. <u>Biological Science</u>, Norton, New York, 1980.

In some disciplines if the references are not arranged alphabetically, the author's name is typed in the normal order (for example, W. T. Keeton). Notice that the publisher precedes the city of publication and that a page reference is not required. In-text page references may be required for paraphrases and direct quotations.

N143 There are numerous variations of periodical documentation in the number-reference system. One typical form is given here.

References and Notes

2. Noonan, G. F. "The alcoholic's reentry after treatment," <u>Human Development</u>, <u>9</u>, 3 (Fall 1988), 19-23.

Notice that only the first word of the article title is capitalized and that the volume number is underlined.

Either the complete pagination of the article or the first page number is included.

N144 In typing the number-reference style of research paper, observe the following guidelines:

1. Use standard type on 8 1/2 x 11 inch white paper of good quality.

2. Type on only one side of a page.

3. Use a title page.

4. Maintain a one-inch margin on all sides of a page.

5. Double-space the entire paper.

6. Number all pages (beginning with the title page) in the upper-right corner.

7. Type your last name to the left of the page number on every page.

8. An abstract or an outline comes between the title page and the essay.

9. Do not hyphenate words at the ends of lines.

10. Type all references on a separate page titled "References" or "References and Notes."

N145 There are other styles of documentation used in specialized fields. A few of these style manuals are listed here.

CBE Style Manual Committee. *CBE Style Manual: A Guide for Authors, Editors, and Publishers in the Biological Sciences.* 5th ed., rev. Bethesda, MD: Council of Biology Editors, 1983.

American Chemical Society. *Handbook for Authors of Papers in American Chemical Society Publications.* Washington: American Chemical Society, 1978.

Cochran, Wendell, Peter Fenner, and Mary Hill, eds. *Geowriting: A Guide to Writing, Editing, and Printing in Earth Science.* Alexandria, VA: American Geological Institute, 1984.

N

American Mathematical Society. *A Manual for Authors of Mathematical Papers.* 7th ed. Providence, RI: American Mathematical Society, 1980.

Iverson, Cheryl, et al. *American Medical Association Manual of Style.* 8th ed. Baltimore: Williams & Wilkins, 1989.

N146 By examining scholarly journals in a particular field, you can discover the type of documentation they follow. These journals also include information on documentation for those who wish to submit manuscripts for publication.

N147 Departments in most colleges and universities follow a particular style of documentation. Know which style you are expected to follow.

Final copy checklist

N148 Before submitting the final copy of your research paper, check the following points:

1. Have you consistently used the proper style of documentation?

2. Have you proofread the paper and made all necessary corrections?

3. Are all corrections done carefully so that they are barely detectable?

4. Is an abstract, outline, and so on, required with the paper?

5. If a title page is required, have you used the proper format?

6. Are pages assembled in the right order? (For example, if there is a notes page, it should be placed before the bibliography.)

7. Are note cards or a rough draft due with the paper?

8. Is the paper to be bound, stapled in one corner, or paper-clipped?

N

O

Definition

In general

O1 Definition is the explanation of the meaning of a word or phrase.

O2 A good definition explains a word in terms that are better understood by the reader than the word to be defined.

> [Not a good definition for most readers:] *Mallophaga* are an order or suborder of ametabolous insects with mandibulate mouth, valvate labium, shovel-shaped head, and flat body.

> [A better definition for most readers:] *Mallophaga* are bird lice.

O3 The need for definition depends upon the word and the situation in which it is used. Do not, for example, define *osteomyelitis* for physicians. On the other hand, do define it briefly (as an infection of bone marrow or bone structures) for a general audience. But do not waste time and insult readers by defining common words in conventional use.

O4 The type of definition depends on the situation in which the word is used. For example, the scientific definition of *mallophaga* in O2 is precisely suited to the zoologist. On the other hand, the second definition is appropriate in an article on maintaining an aviary and addressed to the general public.

O5 Definitions occur frequently at the beginning of an essay, since concepts under discussion need to be clarified early. This is particularly true of argumentation and research papers.

O
P

Types of definition

O6   Two of the most common and useful forms of definition are synonym and logical definition.

Definition by synonym[1]

O7   A synonym is a word that has the same or nearly the
same meaning as another word in the same language.

O8   Define a word by giving a synonym that is better known
to the reader.

> An apothecary is a druggist.
> He complained of vertigo; that is, dizziness.

O9   Find the most exact synonym you can.

> [Not very good:] A condor is a bird.
> [Better:] A condor is a vulture.

> [Not very good:] A buccaneer is a robber.
> [Better:] A buccaneer is a pirate.

> [Not very good:] A dwelling is a building.
> [Better:] A dwelling is a house.

O10   Keep parallelism between the word to be defined and
its definition.

> [Wrong:] *Chanting* [gerund] means "to sing" [infinitive].
> [Right:] *Chanting* [gerund] means "singing" [gerund].

> [Wrong:] *Oaf* [noun] means "stupid" [adjective].
> [Right:] *Oaf* [noun] means "blockhead" [noun].

> [Wrong:] Rapture [abstract noun] means "a mystic" [concrete
> noun].
> [Right:] Rapture [abstract noun] means "ecstasy" [abstract
> noun].

O11   Verbal parallelism must sometimes yield to parallelism
of thought. For example, if a noun, like *narration*, has

---

[1] This is also called definition by substitution or appositive.

an action sense, then it may be defined by a gerund: "*Narration* is 'telling.'" In a context where a participle has a descriptive rather than an action sense, it may be defined by an adjective: "*Enervated* means 'weak'" instead of "*Enervated* means 'weakened.'"

O12 Advantages of definition by synonym: (a) It is often the easiest method of definition for the writer—and often the easiest for the reader, since a synonym is brief, easy to remember, and does not clutter the mind with details. (b) It is often the more informal way of defining a term; it defines adequately without halting the easy flow of the composition.

He was an apothecary—one of those chemists who fill physicians' prescriptions and sell drugs, medicines, and allied chemical preparations—but he earned many a guinea on real estate deals undertaken for the great lords of his day.

This is rather formal. The full definition between the dashes tends to halt the easy flow of the writing.

He was an apothecary—a druggist—but he earned many a guinea on real estate deals undertaken for the lords of his day.

This is informal. The synonym between the dashes slows the reader scarcely at all.

O13 There are disadvantages to definition by synonym: (a) Definition by synonym is often very inexact. (b) Moreover, synonyms often do not supply very much information. If, therefore, you need greater exactness or more information than can be supplied by a synonym, use a logical definition instead.[2]

---

[2] See O14-22.

For example, to define a chair as a seat does not say exactly what a chair is; for a sofa or a bench is also a seat, and yet it is not a chair. Again, to say that a condor is a vulture does not offer a great deal of information. There are vultures that are not condors, and condors have a number of interesting characteristics that such a definition omits. If the reader did not know what a condor is and if condors played a considerable part in the theme, he might have reason to wish for a fuller definition.

Logical definition

O14   In a logical (formal) definition, a word is defined by giving (a) its general class (*genus*) and (b) the characteristics that make it different from the other things of that class (*specific differences*).

Word to be defined	Class	Distinguishing characteristics
chair	seat	with a back, for one person
exposition	that form of writing or talking	that has for its purpose explaining or informing
child	female or male human being	in the period before puberty
brittleness	quality of material substances	that renders them easily broken or snapped
creeps	moves along	with the body prone and close to the ground, or slowly or stealthily or timidly

spasmodically	in a manner	that is fitful, lacks continuity, or is intermittent
monotonous	occurring	without change or variety

O15   Do not give the widest, but the narrowest, general class the reader may be expected to know. (The wider the general class the greater number of differentiating characteristics required to limit the word.)

For example, in defining the noun *wrench*, do not say that it is an "object" (a material thing) or a "device" (a mechanical contrivance). The narrowest meaningful class is "tool" (an implement held in the hand). A wrench is a tool for holding and turning nuts, bolts, pipes, and so on.

O16   Do not use the pronoun *one* as the general class.

[Too vague:] A rifle is one that has grooves in the barrel to rotate the bullet.
[Better:] A rifle is a shoulder firearm that has grooves in the barrel to rotate the bullet.
[Correct, since here *one* clearly means "a person" and is not vague:] An emperor is one who rules an empire. A renegade is one who deserts to the enemy.

O17   Keep parallelism in your definitions.

[Not parallel:] "brittle": that quality of material substances that renders them easily broken or snapped
[Parallel:] "brittle": possessing that quality of material substances that renders them easily broken or snapped

[Not parallel:] Boasting is when one talks about actions or ability with too much pride.
[Parallel:] Boasting is talking about actions or ability with too much pride.

[Not parallel:] A church is where people worship publicly.
[Parallel:] A church is a building set apart for public worship.

O
P

O18   Except for the cases in O19-20, do not repeat, in the definition, the word to be defined.

[Wrong:] An anthology is an anthology of poems or other literary compositions.
[Right:] An anthology is a collection of poems or other literary compositions.

[Wrong:] "healthful": conducive to health
[Right:] "healthful": conducive to the well-being and vigor of the body

O19   When the term to be defined is made up of two words, one of which is already well known to the reader, it is quite usual and correct to repeat the well-known word in the definition.

For example, readers may ordinarily be presumed to know what a rifle is; so this definition of an automatic rifle is in order: "An automatic rifle is a rifle whose recoil rejects the used shells, replaces them with new bullets, and fires the new bullets as long as the trigger is held in firing position."

O20   When the purpose of a definition is to show that the unknown word is merely a variation of a known word or a word built from a well-known root, repetition is quite all right.

"terrible": inspiring terror
"informal": not formal

O21   In definitions avoid words that carry connotation or emotion. Definitions should be free of judgment or bias.

[Unbiased:] "franglais": French marked by a considerable number of borrowings from English
[Biased:] "franglais": French marked by a considerable number of intrusions from English

[Unbiased:] "mannerism": a peculiarity in behavior, speech, and so on, that has become a habit
[Biased:] "mannerism": a queer way of behaving, speaking, and so on, that has become a habit

O
P

O22 In defining terms, select both essential and distinguishing characteristics. For instance, although the number of players on a football team is an essential characteristic, it is not enough to distinguish football from soccer. The type of ball, the way the ball is moved, and the scoring do distinguish the two sports.

O23 Over and above the general class and the necessary distinguishing characteristics, add other characteristics and information as you like or the matter requires. Non-essential characteristics are properly used to add color; they function as description, not as definition.

For example, you need not content yourself with this definition: "Mrs. Paul Durfee is a housewife and a mother." You may add, for example, that she is a widow, that she is thirty-seven years old, and that she has three children—as you like and as the matter requires. In this connection, note that a definition need not be confined to a single sentence. Moreover, it may be so interwoven with other matter that the writer defines only obliquely, while directly discussing something else; for example, see the examples under O12.

Negative definition

O24 A negative definition is ordinarily not satisfactory because it merely states what something is not. In most cases it would take a long list of negatives to eliminate all pretenders to a particular definition. At the same time, a negative definition in conjunction with a positive definition can be effective.

O
P

Thinking it over, I decided that a jerk is basically a person without insight. He is not necessarily a fool or a dope, because some extremely clever persons can be jerks. In fact, it has little to do with intelligence as we commonly think of it; it is, rather, a kind of subtle but persuasive aroma emanating from the inner part of the personality.

I know a college president who can be described only as a jerk. He is not an unintelligent man, nor unlearned, nor even unschooled in the social amenities. Yet he is a jerk *cum laude,* because of a fatal flaw in his nature—he is totally incapable of looking into the mirror of his soul and shuddering at what he sees there.

A jerk, then, is a man (or woman) who is utterly unable to see himself as he appears to others. He has no grace, he is tactless without meaning to be, he is a bore even to his best friends, he is an egotist without charm. All of us are egotists to some extent, but most of us—unlike the jerk—are perfectly and horribly aware of it when we make asses of ourselves. The jerk never knows.

—SIDNEY J. HARRIS, *Last Things First*

Paired or field definition

O25 Sometimes a word or concept is so closely related to another that the two are best defined in relation to each other. In effect, the words share a field of meaning. In this sense, hook and eye fasteners, line positions on a football team (center, guard, tackle, end), or ranks in the army (second lieutenant, first lieutenant, captain, major, lieutenant colonel, and so on) are conveniently defined in pairs or groups.

Stipulative definition

O26 In a stipulative definition a word is defined in a particular way for the purpose at hand. It may be that a certain word has several meanings and the writer is concerned with only one of them; it may be that a recently discovered phenomenon or the extension of a new term has yet to be precisely defined. In these and other cases, the writer says, or stipulates, that a word means such-and-so for the purpose of the present discussion. *Liberal* and *hyperspace* are examples of words that may be so defined.

Extended definition

O27 An abstract term or a complex logical definition can be clarified through extended definition. This kind of definition may include a formal definition but amplifies it by analogy, description, example, comparison, contrast, or some other type of explanation.

What is play—and what is it not? Let us consult language, and then return to children.

The sunlight playing on the waves qualifies for the attribute "playful" because it faithfully remains within the rules of the game. It does not really interfere with the chemical world of the waves. It insists only on an intermingling of appearances. These patterns change with effortless rapidity and with a repetitiveness which promises pleasing phenomena within a predictable range without ever creating the same configuration twice.

When man plays he must intermingle with things and people in a similarly uninvolved and light fashion. He must do something which he has chosen to do without being compelled by urgent interests or impelled by strong passion; he must feel entertained and free of any fear or hope of serious consequences. He is on vacation from social and economic reality— or, as is most commonly emphasized: *he does not work.* It is this opposition to work which gives play a number of connotations. One of these is "mere fun"—whether it is hard to do or not. As Mark Twain commented, "constructing artificial flowers . . . is work, while climbing the Mont Blanc is only amusement." In Puritan times and places, however, mere fun always connoted sin; the Quakers warned that you must "gather the flowers of pleasure in the fields of duty." Men of equally Puritan mind could permit play only because they believed that to find "relief from moral activity is in itself a moral necessity." Poets, however, place the emphasis elsewhere: "Man is perfectly human only when he plays," said Schiller. Thus play is a borderline phenomenon to a number of human activities and, in its own playful way, it tries to elude definition.

O
P

It is true that even the most strenuous and dangerous play is by definition not work; it does not produce commodities. Where it does, it "goes professional." But this fact, from the start, makes the comparison of adult and child's play somewhat senseless; for the adult is a commodity-producing and commodity-exchanging being, whereas the child is only preparing to become one. To the working adult, play is re-creation. It permits a periodical stepping out from those forms of defined limitations which are his social reality.

[And so on.]

—ERIK H. ERIKSON, *CHILDHOOD AND SOCIETY*

O28 An extended definition may constitute an entire essay. Such an essay may include the various methods of development as mentioned in O27 or may simply amplify one method. An outline for an essay based on logical definition might look like this:

Thesis: Term defined
    I. General class
   II. Essential distinguishing characteristics
      A. Essential characteristic 1
      B. Essential characteristic 2
      C. Essential characteristic 3
  III. Other characteristics
      A. Characteristic 1
      B. Characteristic 2

O
P

Argument

In general

P1 Argument seeks to convince another of the truth of some statement.[1]

P2 Argument uses exposition, description, and narration—but for its own purpose.

Planning the argument

The thesis

P3 The simple statement of an argument is called a thesis or proposition.

P4 A *truth* thesis states that a thing is or is not so.

God exists.
Americans do not love money.
Felicity Frisbie was a victim of circumstances.

P5 An *action* thesis states that something should or should not be done.

Congress should not adjourn before passing the Lytton Bill.
You should vote for Ed Roberts for secretary of the association.

O
P

P6 Write out the thesis.

---

[1] Persuasion is that form of talking or writing whose purpose is to make others feel or do what you want them to. Argument addresses itself to the intellect; persuasion, to the feelings or to the will. Ordinarily you must persuade your hearers as well as convince them; and hence, except in philosophy and mathematics classes, pure argument—an appeal to the intellect only—is seldom used. A mixture of argument and persuasion is the usual thing. For this reason the two are treated together in this book.

P7 If it is at all possible to do so—and it almost always is— state the thesis in a single, uncomplicated declarative sentence.[2] If you cannot express the thesis in this way, you probably do not have a clear grasp of the problem.

P8 The thesis must be debatable. "Silver tarnishes easily" is not a debatable proposition. It is simply a statement of fact. On the other hand, "Offshore oil drilling should be prohibited" is debatable. Reasonable people can find evidence to support or attack this proposition.

P9 Avoid extravagant and superlative terms when stating the thesis.[3]

[Poor:] Government policy on housing for the poor is ridiculous.
[Improved:] Government policy on housing for the poor is inadequate.

P10 Make the thesis as definite as possible.[3]

[Poor:] Diets are harmful.
[Good:] Crash diets are harmful.

[Poor:] Financial investments are risky.
[Good:] Investment in junk bonds is risky.

P11 Make sure that the thesis states only certain truths as certain.

For example, unless something is certain, say, "It is probable that fifty percent of all Americans suffer from self-induced ailments." If something is not even probable, but merely possible, say so.

O
P

---

[2] For further treatment see M6-8 and N52-53. The rules and examples that are given there for thesis statements apply to argumentative propositions as well.

[3] For further treatment see M8 and N53. The rules and examples that are given there for thesis statements apply to argumentative propositions as well.

P12 Make sure that the thesis does not commit you to prove more than you have to prove, more than you should, or more than you can.

For example, if your purpose were simply to clear a friend of charges of incompetence in office, you would do badly to state this thesis, "Jack White has performed the duties of treasurer in a competent manner and is, in fact, the most able member of this organization." If you fail to prove that he is the most able man, that failure may reflect on your proof of his competence, when you might with ease have carried the point of his competence alone.

P13 Make the thesis as clear and concise as possible. If either you or your audience is vague about what is to be proved or what is to be done, you will probably lose their support. If the thesis rambles, it will be difficult for you or them to keep it in mind.

The brief

P14 Write an outline of the argument.

P15 The outline of an argument is called a brief. Since it has a different purpose from that of the outline of an expository essay or the plot of a narrative, it also has a different form.[4]

P16 Always write a brief in complete sentences only.

P17 A brief has three principal parts: introduction, proof, and conclusion.

P18 The introduction[5] has a number of functions:

A. It states the thesis.

B. It defines any terms that have more than one meaning or that might not be understood.[6]

---

[4] See the example under P21.
[5] See the example under P21.
[6] See P50-52.

C. It gives any explanation or background necessary to the understanding of the argument.

D. It states the issues.

P19 The issues are the major points on which the truth or falsity of the thesis hangs. It is of the greatest importance that both the writer and the audience understand what the issues are. Confusion often conquers truth when the issues are not stated clearly and when the opposition is permitted to evade them.

P20 The proof once again states each issue, following it with the word *because* and reasons.

P21 The conclusion recapitulates the issues as briefly as possible and restates the thesis.

    I.   Introduction
        A. *Thesis.*—H. B. Stenson is guilty of plagiarism.
        B. *Definition.*—"Plagiarism" is the passing off as one's own the stolen writing of another.
        C. *Explanation.*—The victim of the plagiarism is Talbot Sparks.
        D. *Issues.*—I will prove my case by establishing the following issues:
           1. The two stories are identical.
           2. Sparks's story was written three months before Stenson's.
           3. Stenson had access to Sparks's story.
           4. Stenson made use of Sparks's story.
    II. Proof
        A. The two stories are identical, *because*—
           1. Mr. Judson, authorized by this court, has pronounced them so.
           2. Your own eyes will prove them so.
        B. Sparks's story was written three months before Stenson's, *because*—
           1. Three reliable witnesses testify that they read Sparks's story before July 3, 1989.

O
P

        2. Stenson's own admission and the testimony of a reliable witness show that his story was not written before October 7, 1989.

    C. Stenson had access to Sparks's story, *because* Sparks had given it to him for two days to criticize.

    D. Stenson made use of Sparks's story, *because*—

        1. There is no other reasonable explanation of the fact that the stories are identical.

        2. Stenson admitted to a reliable witness that he had copied the story.

III. Conclusion

Since the stories are identical, since Sparks's story was written before Stenson's, since Stenson had access to Sparks's story, and since Stenson made use of Sparks's story, therefore H. B. Stenson is guilty of plagiarism.

P22 If you are going to use the brief as the outline for a written presentation, you need not write out the conclusion as shown in P21, since the matter it contains is already stated in the issues. But if you are going to use it for making an extempore talk, then you should write out the conclusion; for there will be no time to leaf back through pages looking for the issues and the thesis.

Evidence

P23 Arguments consist of assertions supported by evidence. Assertions without evidence do not establish anything.

P24 In determining the validity of evidence, it is important to distinguish between fact, opinion, belief, and prejudice.

A. A fact is a verifiable statement that something happened or is true.

Our football team had a losing season.
Housing costs are rising.

B. An opinion is a judgment based on facts.

Based on the fact of increasing air traffic, a person may form the opinion that extensive government regulation is required. Working from the same fact, another person may judge that only one thing is needed: training and hiring of additional air-traffic controllers.

C. A belief is a conviction that something is true, based on one's values, cultural background, and so on. Consequently, beliefs—unlike opinions—are not radically affected by facts and are essentially unarguable. However, if the speaker and audience share certain beliefs, the speaker's task is rendered easier.

She believes that God punishes the wicked.

D. A prejudice is an opinion or judgment formed before the facts are known. Unlike a belief, a prejudice can be argued against by the presentation of facts.

Teenagers are disrespectful.

This statement can be countered by showing that some teenagers are respectful and some adults are disrespectful (thus teenagers should not be singled out).

P25 In gathering evidence, keep in mind the following:

A. Evidence should be gathered from more than one source. A wide base gives better support for the thesis. Moreover, it is possible that any one source may be inaccurate or biased, whereas multiple sources all concurring on a given point provide reasonable certainty.

B. Not everything in print is true. Even the most reputable sources occasionally lapse into error. Independent confirmation is necessary for all essential or suspect information.

O
P

C. Fact and opinion must be carefully distinguished. A fact can be verified, whereas an opinion—although based on evidence—is open to debate.

[Fact:] The price of computers has dropped substantially in recent years.
[Opinion:] Computers are the most important invention of the twentieth century.

Methods of reasoning

P26 Inductive reasoning proceeds from specific bits of information to general statements based on that information. The validity of any general statement is founded on the assumption that what is true of various particulars (objects, people, etc.) is true for all members of that class. The more evidence accumulated, the more likely that the generalization is valid. By its very nature induction does not provide certainty.[7]

After walking and driving around a neighborhood over a period of months, a person concludes that most of the kids in the area have bicycles.

A scientist runs hundreds of experiments and concludes to a general statement based on the assembled data.[8]

P27 The validity of the inductive process is safeguarded by observance of these criteria:

—sufficient examples to support a generalization

—typical (not exceptional) and varied examples

—evidence from reliable sources

—evidence that is relevant to the generalization

—generalization limited to the evidence

O
P

[7] If two few instances are used, the result is a hasty generalization. See P76.

[8] The scientific method proceeds by induction.

P28 Deductive reasoning proceeds from a generalization to a particular application. The validity of the deduction depends on the truth of the generalization. See P29.

P29 The basic form of deduction is the syllogism. It argues from a general statement (major premise) to a particular conclusion.

[Major premise:] Diamonds are expensive.
[Minor premise:] This stone is a diamond.
[Conclusion:] This stone is expensive.

If the premises are valid, the conclusion follows with certainty. It is important, therefore, to have reliable premises.[9]

Sometimes a premise can be overstated and invalidate the conclusion.

[Overstated premise:] Bus drivers are always courteous.
[Modified premise:] Bus drivers are usually courteous.

Frequently a deductive argument is based on an unstated premise.

Ms. Hodges has taught logic for ten years, so she should know a good deal about the subject.
[Unstated premise:] Anyone who has taught logic for ten years knows a good deal about the subject.

Some of the errors resulting from the improper construction of a syllogism are discussed under Fallacies, P58–P83.

O
P

---

[9] Syllogisms must have a distributed middle term, namely a term that appears in both the major and minor premise (but not in the conclusion) and is distributed in subject and predicate. In the syllogism below the conclusion is invalid because the middle term is not distributed.
All students want to succeed.
Lupita wants to succeed.
Therefore Lupita is a student.

P30 Induction and deduction are often found together. Through a process of induction, a generalization is arrived at; then the generalization is used as the major premise in a syllogism leading to a particular conclusion.

After sampling many green apples, you conclude that all green apples are very firm and tart. With this general statement as the major premise in a syllogism, you deduce that the green apple you are about to eat is also very firm and tart.

Types of arguments

P31 Argue from accepted or established general truths or principles.

I believe that all of us hold to the principle that one may not do evil to accomplish good. It is true that Nevvers is slowly strangling decency and freedom in the city and the county. It is true, also, that it has proved impossible to pry him loose with any legitimate wedge. It is temptingly true that he has now been delivered into our hands and that, if I tell only one little lie on the witness stand tomorrow morning, I can send him to rot in jail where he belongs and assure the election of an honest person. But if I did so, I would forsake one of the precious principles that should separate people like us from people like Nevvers. I will not fight evil with evil. I will not become what I hate. And you will not ask me to.

P32 Appeal to an accepted authority. An authority is a person whose views on a subject are generally acceptable because of his known and proved knowledge of the matter and because of his integrity.

You may call upon the authority of a doctor to prove a point in surgery or internal medicine; you may call on the views of Planck to prove a point in physics; you may call upon the authority of an engineer to prove a point in bridge building; you may call on the authority of a coach to prove a statement about the athletic ability of a member of his team or about changes that should be made in the rules of a game; and so on.

P33 When appealing to an accepted authority, remember—

A. A person who is an authority in one field is not automatically an authority in another. For example, the fact that Einstein is an authority in physics does not make him an authority in art. Nor is an athlete an authority on nutrition or beer, especially when he is paid to endorse the product.

B. When the declarations of authorities conflict, the argument from authority must be dropped or must be bolstered by other arguments to prove the superiority of the authority you have selected. Authority is not a matter of majority rule, and so sometimes a single authority may outweigh a host of others.

C. Whatever your audience may think, the value of an authority's statement is conditioned by that person's fallibility. Psychiatrists, for example, are sometimes called as expert witnesses on both sides in a trial.

D. When all the authorities agree, the strength and effectiveness of your argument is, naturally, increased and reinforced immeasurably.

P34 Argue from a cause to an effect. Causes produce effects; so, if you can show that the cause of a thing exists, you will prove that the effect exists or will exist. However, if such an argument is to give a certain conclusion, there must be a necessary connection between the cause and the effect; that is, the cause must be such that the effect can flow only from it. If there is not a necessary connection between the cause and the effect, the conclusion will vary in value from mere possibility to high probability.

O
P

For three and a half years, as you well know from your study of the weather reports, no rain has fallen in this region, which was once covered with rich farms.

[Certain conclusion because of necessary connections:] This means, as you can well understand, that no crops have been grown on this land, that cattle have died of thirst, and that human beings cannot support life here any longer.

670

P35 Argue from effect to cause.

For example, if you came upon a skyscraper in the wilderness, you would at once conclude that either human beings or some higher agency had been at work; that is, from the effect you would correctly and with certitude conclude to the cause.

P36 Argue from the evidence of circumstances. Circumstantial evidence, more often than not, affords only probability of high or low degree.

For example, if a man is seen to enter a bar and, two hours later, to stagger away from it, bawling a song at the top of his voice in the public street, one might conclude with some justice that these circumstances—the bar, the staggering, the loud singing—point to a bout of drinking. On the other hand, a person seen reeling down the street might be a victim of epilepsy or diabetes.

P37 Argue from specific instances.

A. An inductive argument must be founded on the examination of a great number of particular cases under a wide range of circumstances. Such an examination, however, can rarely be related to an audience in detail. It usually has to be summarized in a sentence or so.

After various surveys of private citizens, local businesses, and city officials, it is clear that our city wants to restrain its population growth.

B. In some instances it suffices to supply one example.

I strongly urge you not to buy Rigomort theater seats for your auditoriums. I sat in, or rather thrust myself into, one of them the other day and found myself embraced with alarming and acutely uncomfortable pressure by the

The invasive arm bracket and the protruding screws may or may not be typical of all Rigomort theater seats, but the narrowness of the seat is. In this respect all seats of the same model may be fairly judged by this one.

arms of the thing. When I tried to stand up to let a patron of the theater pass in front of me, one of the arm brackets tore away the pocket of my coat; and screws protruding from the bottom of the seat clawed a vicious rip in my trousers. Yet I am of average size.

P38   Argue from common experience.

People want to park their cars close to the building where they work for several reasons. First of all, it is convenient and saves time. Secondly, it means less walking through inclement weather. Consequently, putting a mall between this office building and the proposed parking lot is not a good idea.

P39   Argue from analogy. The argument from analogy means that if two things are alike in some particulars, then they will be alike in others.

It is reasonable to argue that, after two years in prison, Herman would not want a job that confines him to a small windowless room eight hours a day and requires him to punch out a predetermined number of gaskets for an uncompromising employer.

P40   Use the argument from analogy with caution, for it can readily lead to false conclusions. It is best used as merely persuasive proof; and, of course, it should not be proposed to an audience as conclusive by itself.

P41   Argue from the statements of reliable witnesses (identified in P42). People are not natural liars; consequently their statements that a thing is so (their testimony) is excellent proof.

P42   With regard to a witness, the audience must grant you, or you must prove, these four points:

1. that there is nothing to show that the witness is given to lying. (If possible, show that the witness has a reputation for telling the truth, or better, is a person of outstanding integrity.)

O
P

2. that the witness has no reason for lying in this particular case (that is, that it would be of no advantage for this person to lie).

3. that the witness has enough understanding to repeat accurately what he or she saw or heard.

4. that the witness was careful and attentive in watching or listening.

P43 First-hand (eyewitness) testimony is the more readily convincing; but second-hand testimony, coming through several witnesses in turn, is quite good, provided it fulfills the four conditions of P42.

Writing the argument[10]

P44 In general, argument makes use of everything available

---

[10] In presenting an oral argument, pay particular attention to these points:

1. Ordinarily you should use the opening moments of your argument to catch your audience's interest and make them like you.
    A. Amuse them.
    B. Compliment them. Be sincere and specific. Insincerity, whether detected or not, degrades the speaker; and it is often detected. General compliments do not impress.
    C. Concede something that they hold and that they do not expect you to grant.
    D. Use a modest, straightforward tone where they might expect sarcasm, reproach, or invective.
2. Except when you have good reason to be impersonal—as, for instance, when you are trying to give the impression that you are merely presenting truth, not attempting to persuade anyone to anything—
    A. Use direct address (the second person), but judiciously.
    B. Use direct questions, but sparingly.
3. In a closely reasoned argument that is rather complicated, it is usually good, near the end, to recapitulate the issues and the thesis so as to leave with the audience as clear a notion as possible of what you have accomplished. The treatment, however, need not be dry.

O
P

from the other three forms of writing. An argument fleshes the skinny bones of its brief with exposition, description, and narration.

P45   In writing an effective paper, it is important to know the audience. Their cultural, educational, and political background will influence the selection of arguments, examples, and other supporting evidence.[11]

P46   General knowledge is rarely convincing. You will probably have to do research to gather evidence in support of your position.

P47   An action thesis (P5) requires an appeal to the emotions. People are convinced by logic, but they are not ordinarily persuaded to action without an emotional appeal. Vivid examples and rhetorical questions are two common ways of motivating an audience to action.

Introduction

P48   The introduction of an argumentative essay states the problem and often indicates a solution. Quotations, anecdotes, and other devices may be used to arouse interest and to lead to the central issue.[12]

P49   The problem and any solution must be carefully worded. They must be definite, clear, and free of the vagueness that comes with loosely constructed generalities. The solution must be limited and defensible.[13]

[Too general:] Any coach with a losing record should be fired. [Specific:] Unless there is an unusual conjunction of extenuating circumstances (difficult schedule, lack of talented players, inadequate practice facilities), a coach with a losing record for three consecutive years should be fired.

---

[11] Always keep in mind the relationship between subject matter, audience, purpose, and speaker role. See M33.

[12] See M10-13 on the introduction of an essay.

[13] On wording a thesis, see P7-13.

Body of the essay

P50 Essential terms must be defined at the beginning of the paper. If basic terms are unclear, the development of the argument will be unclear. Moreover, the argument may be prolonged unnecessarily because opposing sides misundertand terms that have not been adequately defined.[14] An argument that Brand X is superior to Brand Y must begin with a clear definition of "superior."

P51 Occasionally a term must be changed to allow clearer definition of the issue. For instance, words like *justice, success, right,* and *wrong* are abstract and sometimes difficult to define.

[Poor:] United States involvement in the Middle East is right. [Better:] United States involvement in the Middle East protects American interests there.

P52 Two of the most common and useful types of definitions are synonym and logical definition. See O7-23.

P53 Various forms of development may be used including cause and effect, comparison and contrast, examples, and statistics. For the various forms of essay development, see M19-30.

P54 Argumentation relies on a variety of sources—from facts to statistics to expert opinion. These sources, whether used in direct quotation or used simply for content, must be acknowledged either in the text or by way of footnote and sometimes also in a bibliography.[15] Writers who fail to acknowledge sources are guilty of two serious errors: (1) they are not providing the support needed for their arguments, (2) they are guilty of plagiarism.

O
P

---

[14] For a discusssion of definition, see Section O.
[15] For various types of documentation, see N101-113 (MLA), N116-19 (APA), N125-39 (University of Chicago).

P55 Among the basic structures for an argumentative essay are the following:

Strategy 1

1. Present the first main point and supporting evidence.

2. Present the second main point and supporting evidence.

3. Present the third main point and supporting evidence.

4. Present the fourth main point and supporting evidence.

And so on.

It is best to arrange these points in the order of climax—from least to most important.

Strategy 2

1. Summarize the arguments against your position as honestly as you can. In doing this you show familiarity with the issues and project objectivity. You also provide a background against which to set your arguments.

2. Make a clear transition and present your arguments as in Strategy 1.

Strategy 3

1. Admit, or concede, that your opponent is correct (or partially correct) in some claim or claims. This shows that you are fair and will probably present your own claims fairly.

2. Make a clear transition and present your arguments as in Strategy 1.

Strategy 4

Present and respond to each of the opponent's claims. Conclude with your own position.

1. Claim #1
   Response

2. Claim #2
   Response

3. Claim #3
   Response

4. Claim #4
   Response

Summary of your position.

Conclusion

P56 The conclusion should recapitulate the basic points in the argument and restate the thesis. A graphic example or a striking quotation can be effective. Do not overstate the thesis, but do combine logic and emotion to bring the argument to a satisfying conclusion.

P57 Use the following checklist as a guide to revision.

1. Is the thesis stated with precision?

2. Are all essential terms clearly defined?

3. Is there adequate evidence to support each argument?

4. Are the various arguments presented in the most effective sequence?

5. Have any steps been omitted from any argument?

6. Have all sides of the issue been considered?

7. Are there any irrelevant arguments or extraneous material?

O
P

8. Has any evidence been misused in support of an argument?

9. Do all generalizations have adequate factual support?

10. Are comparisons valid?

11. Are all authorities reliable and unbiased?

12. Have major opposition arguments been countered?

13. Are sources documented?

14. Does the conclusion summarize the argument and restate the thesis?

For a checklist on essay development, see M87.

For a checklist on sentence structure and diction, see K140.

Fallacies

P58   A reasoning process that is not logical is called a fallacy. Sometimes fallacies are used deliberately, but more often they are the result of faulty reasoning. You should know the common fallacies so that you may avoid them in your own work and detect them when you are refuting the arguments of others.

Mistaking the question (*ignoratio elenchi*)

P59   Mistaking the question is arguing for or against something other than the thesis, motion, or resolution actually proposed for discussion.

[This speaker, supposed to be arguing the question "Team sports build character," has mistaken the question for "Group activities build character":] Working on the school paper or yearbook not only develops intellectual skills such as writing and design layout but also helps to build character through shared responsibility, cooperation, and compromise . . .

P60 To refute an argument that mistakes the question, call the attention of your opponent and the audience to the mistake and restate the actual question.

Bob has argued eloquently and at some length on the personal-enrichment qualities of certain co-curricular activities. I, for one, find his arguments convincing. Unfortunately, he did not address the issue before us this evening; namely, team sports build character. Let us put aside Bob's comments for another time and concern ourselves now with the announced topic.

Begging the question (*petitio principii*)

P61 Begging the question is taking for granted what you ought to be proving. It is an evasion of the issue. In effect, you are asking your audience to accept your ideas from the beginning, without proof.

The top building priority for this school should be a new library. Certainly all of us want this institution to be foremost in academics. To achieve this, it needs an outstanding repository of knowledge available to all the students. In other words, the school needs a new library.

P62 The common refutation of an argument that begs the question is to show your opponent and the audience that he has not proved, but merely stated, the question.

Thank you for presenting the issue of building a new library. At the same time, let the record show that although the issue was raised, there has thus far been no evidence to show the inadequacy of the present library and the need for a new one.

O
P

Vicious circle

P63 A vicious circle is proving *A* by *B* and *B* by *A*.

The problem now is that we need more money to advertise our product in order to get it before the public eye. The solution is, of course, greater sales. With greater sales we will have more money for advertising.

P64 An effective way of refuting a vicious circle is to strip it of verbiage and present it in all its naked illogic.

> Joe, you have just proved that the money for advertising will come from sales and that sales will provide money for advertising. No, Joe. You might as well say that B comes after A because A comes before B. The basic problem still stands: we need money for advertising.

False causality (*post hoc, ergo propter hoc*)

P65 False causality is assuming that, since one thing happens after another, it is therefore caused by that other.

> I will never drink milk again. Last night, just before I went to bed, I drank a glass of milk. Then this morning, when I tried to get up, I found that I had a bursting head and that my stomach was one great ache.

P66 A simple question will often refute false causality.

> Could nothing else have made you feel ill? Do you think that you should conclude that milk was the culprit without looking for a more likely suspect?

False assumption

P67 False assumption is taking something to be true that is not true and building an argument on it.

> The ABC Company is not a suitable contractor for this project. The company has been involved in shoddy construction work for the city for the last ten years. The repair and reconstruction costs are all documented . . .
>
> [But arguing against the ABC Company for the contract under consideration is pointless, since the company did not enter a bid.]

Be careful to check for unsound and hidden assumptions in others' arguments and in your own.

For example, the assumption behind "Don't argue with teachers; you will never win" is "Teachers are not fair."

P68 False assumption is such a bad blunder that the best refutation, ordinarily, is simply to call attention to it. Occasionally, however, it is necessary to be severe about it, lest the audience be misled.

False appeal to common knowledge

P69 False appeal to common knowledge or consent is using a phrase like *as everybody knows* or *only a fool would deny that,* when the point in question is not a matter of common knowledge or consent and may even be untrue.

> I don't have to take time out to prove to people as enlightened as you that American-style democracy is the only good form of government. Only power-mad rulers and benighted Europeans, long accustomed to the surrender of their freedom of thought, would dare to offer any rebuttal.

P70 False appeal to common knowledge or consent is one of the more vicious fallacies when used deliberately, for it plays upon that snobbishness in people.

P71 The refutation of false appeal to common knowledge or consent is (a) to point out that you, at least, do not know or do not consent to the statement of your opponent, and (b) to cite people of excellent knowledge and authority who disagree with it or deny it.

Argument by unfair implication

P72 Argument by unfair implication is the stating of a fact or a truth but using it to imply something that does not follow from it.

> The other day I was talking to a medical student, and a rather bright one. I asked him whether he knew what St. Anthony's fire was and what its cause was. He said he didn't know; he couldn't answer my

> The implication in this argument is that if a presumably bright medical student cannot answer a question then the training given in our medical schools is poor.

O
P

question at all. A fine medical school he goes to! What kind of doctor is this country turning out?

P73   The refutation of argument by unfair implication is to examine your opponent's statement and the conclusion drawn from it, and to show that the implied connection between the two does not exist.

Mr. Glenn seems to feel that if a medical student does not know the answer to a question the education is defective. I think Mr. Glenn is being quite unfair to the student and to the medical school. (I am acquainted with both.) First of all, the term "St. Anthony's fire" is one not commonly encountered as a synonym for erysipelas or ergotism. And neither of those things can our medical student be expected to know much about at this stage of training.

Ambiguity of terms

P74   Ambiguity of terms, or equivocation, is an illogical shifting of the meaning of words.

Bernice argues that we must be conservative in our use of natural resources in the manufacture of our product. But this company cannot afford to be conservative and still be competitive.

P75   The refutation of an argument based on ambiguous terms is to redefine the terms.

Alan, you are using "conservative" is two different senses. Yes, we should conserve our natural resources. No, this company cannot afford to be unprogressive.

Defective induction

P76   Defective induction, or hasty generalization, is an argument based on too few instances or on an examination made unscientifically, without controls or sufficient variation of circumstances.

Sheep, my friends, are all white. I know. I have two sheep, and they are both white.

P77 The refutation of defective induction is either to show that too few instances have been examined or that the examination was unscientific, or else to bring up a fact that refutes the induction, according to the old dictum "An argument cannot batter down a fact" (*contra factum non valet illatio*).

The gentleman who spoke just before me proved, or seemed to prove, that all sheep are white. I should hesitate to attack his conclusion were it not that I happen to have a sheep with me— a sheep that is black. Bill, will you please bring in that sheep?

False Analogy

P78 False analogy is arguing that, because two things are alike in some particulars, they will therefore certainly be alike in others.

For example, in a certain television commercial, the salesperson dips two sponges in water, one coated with a water-resistant material. The uncoated sponge becomes soft. Then he says that the same thing happens to whiskers that have been cleared of water-resistant film by his product. He often concludes with remarks implying that he has proved that his product softens whiskers.

P79 The refutation of false analogy is to point out the differences between the two things that are compared and to show how these must be taken into consideration no less than the similarities.

Either-or fallacy

P80 An either-or fallacy is a false dilemma that reduces a complicated issue to only two sides.

Either the tax levy is passed, or hundreds of people will lose their jobs.

Reductive fallacy

P81 The reductive fallacy occurs when a simple cause is given for a complex effect.

The Roman Empire collapsed because it was overextended. Heart attacks are caused by stress.

Non sequitur

P82 A non sequitur ("it does not follow") occurs when there is no logical relationship between two or more ideas or when a conclusion does not follow from its premises.

There would be a dramatic decrease in the number of traffic accidents if there were better driver education courses.

Ad hominem

P83 An ad hominem ("against the person") argument attacks the person, ignoring the issue under consideration.[16] This technique is similar to that of "red herring" because it distracts from the main issue.[17]

How can you take her advice on nursing homes seriously? She is a known gambler and a professed spiritualist.

Occasionally a person's character should be questioned. For example, a witness who has been guilty of lying and dishonesty in the past or someone posing as an expert should be challenged. In such cases "attacking the person" is not a fallacy.

Propaganda techniques

P84 In addition to the common fallacies, there are unfair techniques used by propagandists to persuade without

---

[16] The smear technique is an extended form of the *ad hominem* argument. It is sometimes used in political campaigns but often backfires when voters recognize the tactic.

[17] For "red herring" see P86.

evidence. You should be alert to these techniques and avoid them in your own writing.

Stereotype

P85 A stereotype is an overslimplified characterization of a person or group. It frequently makes a general statement from two few instances.

Fat people are jovial.
He is a typical politician—glib and dishonest.

Red herring

P86 The expression *red herring* has its origin in smoked herring with a reddish color used to provide a false scent and lead hunting dogs down the wrong trail. As an argumentative technique it is used to distract from the real issue.

[Statement:] There should be a 25 mph speed limit on our residential streets.
[Red Herring:] Driving on our residential streets will be safe if we keep the kids from using them as playgrounds.

Misuse of authority

P87 The misuse-of-authority tactic uses unqualified or biased authorities to endorse a product or a position.

A singer endorses a soft drink.
A scientist defends the safety of her latest invention.

Transfer

P88 The transfer technique uses association rather than logic as a basis for a conclusion. The speaker tries to associate himself (or others) with persons or ideas that are respected, thereby winning approval.[18] A person may claim, for example, to be a patriot or a friend of the president.

---

[18] When it is used negatively, transfer is a form of "name calling."

Card stacking

P89 In card stacking only evidence supporting an argument
is selected. Contrary evidence is discarded. This technique
is particularly dangerous because the evidence presented
is accurate; it is just that the picture is incomplete.

> The economic scene in town is encouraging. Over 150 hourly
> workers were recalled last month.
> [Nothing is said about the plant that closed and the company
> that filed for bankruptcy.]

Statistics can easily mislead unless they are carefully interpreted and prudently used.

Misrepresentation

P90 Misrepresentation distorts an opponent's view with the
intention of setting up an extreme position that can be
easily attacked.[19]

> [Statement:] As a mother with five children, I am constantly on
> the go—cooking for them, transporting them, caring for their
> aches and pains . . .
> [Misrepresentation:] It seems to me that Mrs. Smith ought to
> love her children; then she would not think of herself as being
> overworked.

Bandwagon

P91 The bandwagon technique works on people's latent
desire to belong (to "jump on the bandwagon") and to
go with a winner.

> Buy Crunchy cereal—everybody's favorite.
> Buy a Corsair, winner of five stock-car races this year.

---

[19] In a similar vein, the "straw man" device stuffs and sets up a dummy
issue with considerable detail.

686

Q

Description

In general

Q1 Description is that form of writing or talking whose purpose is the creating of pictures, sounds, smells, and touch sensations in the imagination of the reader.[1]

Q2 Description is often combined with exposition, argumentation, and especially narration.[2] It may be used to describe a product, to enhance an example, to give vividness and immediacy to a story. In general, description is used to strengthen an impression or emphasize a point.

Q3 Pure description is description for its own sake and is nowadays seldom found except in travelogues, books discussing works of art, and so on.

Q4 Running description is description used more or less incidentally to dress, enliven, or enrich narration, exposition, or argument. The description may be long (several paragraphs) or very short (just a word or two).

The viewpoint

Q5 A viewpoint is the actual or imaginary position from which a writer or speaker sees what he or she is describing.

Q
R

---

[1] For matters not treated in this section but involving description, see K100-139 (figures of speech) and R46-52 (description in narration).

[2] Unlike expository paragraphs, many descriptive paragraphs do not have a topic sentence. They do, however, have a general focus; for example, the exterior of the old mansion, the dowdy appearance of Aunt Mame.

Q6 Select a physical viewpoint (for example, one corner of a room or the stern of a boat) and describe only what can be seen from it.

Q7 Follow Q6 with regard to mental viewpoint or attitude of mind. For example, the appearance and character of a man are likely to seem very different to one who loves him, to one who hates him, to his employer, to his dog, to a guard, to a person he has injured, and to a person to whom he has loaned money.

Q8 When there is need, change the viewpoint.

Q9 When you think that your reader might otherwise be confused, indicate that the viewpoint is changing.

From where we stood at the edge of the woods in front of it, we saw that the house was set in a clearing in the firs, halfway up the hillside, giving it an air of privacy and rest. It was a large three-story frame building. Through exposure to the elements, its weatherboarding had achieved that shade

From where we stood at the edge of the woods in front of it states explicitly what the first viewpoint is; the two expressions inside and at the rear of the house give unmistakable notification of a change in the writer's viewpoint.

known in Dallas as Lambert green, which makes houses look old, cool, and substantial. The front supported twin gables, each with its dormer window, one at either end of the gray slate roof. Tall chimneys rose above the ridge of the roof. Although there was nothing in the sum total that an architect would care to sign his name to, the house presented an agreeable, quiet welcome when first we came upon it in the clearing.

Inside, we were to discover, it was a pleasant-enough house if one intended to stay only the summer. The rooms were large and cool, the furniture plain but comfortable. The kitchen, an old-fashioned affair, was full of shining copperware hung on a rack above the table and on hooks about the walls.

At the rear of the house was a kind of patio with a little pool in the center, a place that invited me to set up my equipment at once and get to work.

Q10 Unless there is very good reason for not doing so,[3] finish with one viewpoint before going on to the next. Do not jump back and forth from one viewpoint to another.

Q11 There is occasionally—not often—good reason for jumping back and forth from one viewpoint to another. If you do move back and forth, maintain parallel structure to help the reader.

[In this passage, the writer wants sharp contrast. He has taken care, however, that there is no confusion:] I can explain the discrepancy, Your Excellency. Hale was in the hollow. I was on the hill. Hale saw only the cloud of dust that hung above the desert; I saw the flash of the sun on red tunics and gold braid. Hale heard only the faint sounds of a wagon caravan; I heard the staccato mutter of Spanish orders and Spanish replies. Hale smelled only the still air of the hollow; my nose was offended by the reek of the corpses jolting along in the last wagon. When I add that Hale had strictest orders not to leave the hollow in any contingency, it must be clear that this court-martial is doing him the gravest injustice, especially now that he is dead and can offer no defense.

The basic image

Q12 In descriptions of some length or complication, ordinarily begin with the basic image.[4]

Q13 In visual description, the basic image usually consists of the general size, shape, and color of the object.

It was a large white house, modeled on Mount Vernon and set in a great sweep of lawn.

He was a great, dark brute of a man, with a huge torso balanced on absurdly inadequate-looking legs.

Q
R

---

[3] See Q11.
[4] See Q13-19.

Q14 Often enough, the size, the shape, or the color is omitted from the basic image when one or another of them is of no significance to the description.

He was a great brute of a man, with a huge torso balanced on absurdly inadequate-looking legs.

Q15 In auditory description, the basic image usually consists of a general classification of the sound that is heard.

As we turned the corner, our ears were assailed by a loud roar compounded of many noises, all fierce and frightening.

I noticed at first that it was a kind of light tapping, a sound I had never heard before, yet somehow familiar.

Q16 In tactile description, the basic image usually consists of a general classification of the touch involved.

I felt something wet and sticky, and wondered for a moment whether I had put my hand into one of the still-warm pots on the stove.

Maria felt the dry, ropelike thing stir and writhe in her grip.

Q17 In olfactory description, the basic image usually consists of a general classification of the smell as strong or faint, pleasant or disagreeable, and so on.

It was a pungent, disagreeable odor that seemed to envelop the whole quarter of town where the stockyards lay.

Q18 In the description of things that are not experienced by the external senses (for instance, a mood or a person's character), the basic "image" is usually a general classification of the thing as good, bad, timid, dull, weary, hopeless, uneasy, cheerful, or something of the kind.

Von Tolen wasn't at all what you would expect a Prussian general to be. He was a nervous little mouse of a man, quite afraid of the world.

Q
R

I can describe the feeling only as a special sort of uneasiness, a pleasantly unpleasant expectation that something exciting was going to happen.

Q19 Occasionally it is quite reasonable to begin even a long or complicated description with something other than the fundamental image of the object.

What I noticed first was an eyebrow—a most imperious eyebrow, raised above a cold blue eye. When finally I was able to detach my attention from the eyebrow, I found that the eye was contemplating me steadily over a frond of one of those potted plants that some hotel managers still use to underscore the general ugliness of lobbies.

In this passage the writer has decided to make capital of one feature of his character—an eyebrow. He intends to harp on that eyebrow from time to time in the course of his story and so begins his description with it.

Filling in the picture

Q20 Once you have the basic image, set down the most striking features of the object and then fill in a few minor details, if they are necessary to the description or will enrich it.

[Basic image:] One's first impression of Mr. Starrett was of a tall, dark, very slender man—with teeth. [Most striking feature:] These teeth were not crooked, did not protrude, lacked none of their rightful number. All of them were Mr. Starrett's own. Indeed, they were such unexceptionable teeth that it is a wonder that they were the first thing about him that one noticed. One noticed them because they were always, always visible, gleaming and resplendent, between lips fixed in a perpetual, mocking smile—a smile quite without common mirth but full of relish for some secret joke that Mr. Starrett found in everything he looked upon. The smile disappeared only when he gazed into a mirror. He seemed to find no joke there, and so the teeth retreated for the moment to well-earned privacy and concealment.

[Minor details:] The man behind the teeth appeared pleasant enough. His hair was black with flecks of gray, his eyes blue and clear. His handshake was firm, his manner cordial. If it had not been for his smile, one would have been interested in making his acquaintance.

Q21 Be selective in the use of detail. In general, if details do not further an over-all purpose, they should be omitted.

The black Porsche careened down the street, sideswiping first a blue Honda Accord and then a red Ford Tempo. Swerving wildly, it narrowly missed a rusting and already damaged streetlight and then sped on past Markham's Department Store where mannikins dressed in bright and elegant spring fashions stared back impassively. In a sudden finale the Porsche impaled itself on a city fire hydrant, sending a geyser of water into the night air.

The excessive detail in this paragraph is distracting. The simpler version below is more effective.

The black Porsche careened down the deserted street, sideswiping two cars and narrowly missing a streetlight. It continued on past the frozen stares of mannikins in Markham's Department Store and, in a sudden finale, came to rest on a fire hydrant, sending a geyser of water into the night air.

Q22 Avoid clichés and overworked images.[5]

She turned white as a sheet and stared into space.
A sixth sense tells me that this is just the tip of the iceberg.

Q23 Avoid extravagant or exaggerated description.

The bonbon was a savory delight beyond compare, fitting ambrosia for the gods.

Aunt Mabel was built like a truck.

---

[5] See K127.

Q24 Occasionally, especially for reasons of emphasis, it is best to save the most striking detail until the last.

> The town was just as I had remembered it: the one dusty-yellow street with a line of stores on each side, gap-toothed with vacant lots; the church and the courthouse facing each other near the middle of town; and the water trough, dry for years, in front of the post office. There was one difference. The place was deserted.

Q25 Ordinarily arrange descriptive details in some kind of order or sequence. Such an arrangement assists the reader. The most commonly used orders in description are place and interest or importance.[6]

A. *The order of place.* Start at the bottom and go to the top, or start at the top and go to the bottom, or start at the right and go to the left, and so on; or start at one end and go to the other, and so on.

> The two bedraggled men stood at the edge of the forest. To their left the woods fell away to rocky terrain. Straight before them in gently rising undulations rose a series of apparently endless hills. To their right a faint path beckoned to a picturesque valley in the distance. Their decision was easy.

B. *The order of interest or importance.* Start with the least important or interesting thought and move by degrees to the most interesting or important, or reverse the order and move from most to least interesting or important.

> The rowboat wallowed, half-filled with rainwater. Held in by the gunwales, a life-preserver floated near one of the seats. A small tin can, inadequate in such a situation, lay in a watery grave in the stern.

Q
R

---

[6] These and other sequences are discussed in M50.

Brief sketches

Q26 Often the full technique—basic image, striking details, and minor details—slows the composition objectionably. When this happens, do a brief sketch, selecting one or two striking or fundamental features of the object and letting them suggest the rest.

> Brown entered a room that was *all glitter and gleam, from the chandeliers to the men's shirt fronts and the women's jewelry.* He hurried in the wake of his *frenzied* hostess from group to group, murmuring in response to introductions and moving on before he could make sure of a single name or face. Finally he was deposited near the refreshments with a trio that Mrs. Daggers seemed to think he might complement: *an empty-headed socialite occupied in saying nothing and sweeping the room with a selective eye, a handsome man who looked like an executive* and who turned out to be an executive's secretary, and Miss Dutreil. He would hardly have noted Miss Dutreil, *fortyish, mousy, and dowdy*, if she had not said a remarkable thing.

R

Narrative Writing

In general

R1 A narrative relates a series of events.

R2 Some narrative writing simply entertains; for example, certain stories or anecdotes. Other narrative writing has a further purpose; for example, to make a statement about life, to show change through experience, to compare or contrast events. Narration often combines with the other forms of discourse (that is, with description, exposition, argumentation) to arouse interest or to illustrate a point.

R3 A narrative may be true (as in histories, biographies, and autobiographies) or fictional (as in short stories and novels).

The narrative composition

R4 A narrative composition is a composition whose purpose is the relating of a series of events.

Choosing a subject[1]

R5 If the subject is not new, at least the treatment should be.

R6 When the subject of a narrative has not been assigned or has not suggested itself naturally, jotting down answers to these questions may stimulate the imagination:

1. What happened to me during the first eight years of my life that impressed me or others as especially interesting, strange, humorous, puzzling, difficult, or splendid? What happened during the second eight years? And so on.

2. What problem, interest, amusing thing, hope, fear, fascination has occupied my mind a good deal lately?

3. What have I read, heard, or seen that stirred, delighted, unnerved, or amused me or that made me think?

4. What do I dislike heartily?

5. What do I like particularly?

6. What have I discovered about living that is different from what people have told me it is or should be?

---

[1] Some material in R5-13 applies more to nonfiction than to fiction narratives.

7. What is there worth remarking about my dog or cat, my enemy, my friend, my father, my mother, or someone or something else that plays a large part in my life?

8. What would I like to do with my life?

9. What would I care to change in the world at large or in my world?

10. What is that unusual life, so different from my own, that attracts me, even though the possibility of my living it is remote or nonexistent?

R7 Once you have a central idea for a narrative, start thinking around the subject. Do some free writing; that is, start writing down the fragmentary ideas that occur to you.

[Central idea:] Pirates.

[Free writing:] I like pirates. I like pirates?

Why? Costumes? Life they lead? I wouldn't want to be a pirate in real life. Stinking ships. Why do I like pirates? Ah, because they did brave deeds gracefully.

I'll bet they seldom did. Or very few of them. My whole idea is based on Francis Drake, Rafael Sabatini, Hornblower stories, and Hollywood pirates.

I could play a pirate in Hollywood. Fun. Well, I could be an extra, anyway. Wear a cutlass and swing it. Imagine playing a pirate-extra in Hollywood and then having to come home each day to ordinary life.

Could do that. Have character play pirate-extra, then come home to drab, lonely life. Decides he will live like pirate. Turns home into ship. Builds crow's-nest atop chimney. Makes dog walk the plank. Gets into trouble with neighbors for running Jolly Roger on television aerial and striding up and down on front porch with patch over one eye, hailing passing pedestrians with "Ship ahoy!" County-asylum people arrive.

Other techniques for exploring a topic are brainstorming and clustering. Brainstorming generates a list of words and phrases without any particular order and may include snippets of conversation, objects in a scene, and so on. Clustering produces related groups of words, often graphically linked by circles and arrows. See M3 for examples.

The topic idea

R8 When you have a subject and have thought about it, select a topic idea. In other words, decide what you want to say about life or people through the story.

R9 The kind of treatment the narrative is to get (humorous, acid, sympathetic, and so on) will depend to some extent on the selection of a topic idea. On it will depend what you are going to stress: action, character, atmosphere, and so on.

Five ridiculous things happened when John Curlew tried to play pirate.[2]	This narrative stresses events. In the development character will probably turn out to be secondary.
John Curlew was born out of time, as he discovered when he tried to play pirate.	This stresses character. In the development events will probably turn out to be secondary, though not unimportant.
There is no room for fools like Mr. J. Curlew, pirate, in this modern world.	This is unsympathetic—even acid. The emphasis will probably be on character.
Playing pirate, Mr. Curlew found himself beset by a world hostile to simple delight.	This is sympathetic to the main character—even sentimental. The treatment may be rather whimsical.
Against the drabness of a suburban neighborhood, John Curlew flashed madly for a moment, then was abruptly extinguished.	This stresses atmosphere, impressions, emotional reactions, and that sort of thing.

---

[2] The topic statements given here are all based on the free writing that illustrates R7.

R10 Write out the topic idea. Writing it out often exposes weaknesses in it. A written statement, moreover, lying on the desk before your eyes, is a constant reminder of what the narrative is about and may prevent useless digressions.

> Life had not been kind to Darrell Britts.
> My trip to Italy was very rewarding.
> In a world of conformists imaginative people seem eccentric.

R11 If it is at all possible to do so, write the topic idea in a single declarative sentence.

>   A. A single sentence—because the briefer and less complicated the topic statement, the easier it is to develop it coherently.
>
>   B. A declarative sentence—because questions do not indicate and limit development. There are innumerable developments possible if the topic is "How did Denton beat Plainville?" But the two chief parts of the narrative are already plain if the topic is "Denton beat Plainville by using the 'I' formation and concentrating on Joe Jacoby."
>
>   C. A complete sentence—because half-sentences and very elliptical sentences cause the same trouble that questions do.

R12 Limit the range of ideas sharply when stating the topic idea, or you will find yourself writing an endless narrative.

R13 Make the topic idea as definite as you reasonably can.

> [Vague, leading to uncertain planning and development:] It required several things to bring Dan McKay to terms.
> [Definite, leading to clear-cut planning and development:] It required three censures to force Dan McKay to resign.

The plan or plot[3]

R14 The plan or plot is the arrangement of events in a narrative. (Without a plan, a story rambles.) The outline of a narrative is called a plan when it is the skeleton of a straight narrative (R58) and a plot when it is the skeleton of plot narrative (R59).

R15 The arrangement of events can be chronological, predominantly chronological with flashbacks, or episodic with events grouped but not necessarily in sequential order.

R16 Once you have written down the topic idea, write a plan or a plot.

> A. List and number the main events of your narrative in the order in which you wish to present them.
>
> B. Under each of these main events, list circumstances that contribute notably to it.
>
> C. Do not go into detail.
>
> D. To avoid complications use the vivid present whenever you can. (In developing the plot or plan into a full narrative, ordinarily use the past.)

Plan of a narrative letter

Topic idea— I am quite all right after being lost for a night.

1. I meet Eileen and make a date with her.[4]
   This happens in front of the church, on Sunday.
   I bring the boys from my camp to church.

2. I set out Monday evening in a canoe for Eileen's camp.
   It is two miles away directly across the lake.
   From there we are to use her car to drive to town for a movie.

---

[3] This and the following sections apply both to fiction and nonfiction narratives.

[4] This and the following sentences may be written as phrases; for example, "meet Eileen," "make date."

3. I am taken from my course by a bonfire.
    I think it is directly in front of Camp Moony.
    It is either to the east or to the west of Moony.
    It is deserted.

4. Lost now, I paddle in one direction for a while.
    There is nothing by which to take a bearing.

5. I enter an inlet.
    The night is so dark that I cannot see anything but the shore that I am keeping on my right.
    As a result, I enter inlet after inlet, without knowing that I am doing so.

6. I discover that I am hopelessly lost.

7. I decide to tie up for the night.
    The night is long, but I have cigarettes; the night is cold, but I have a jacket.

8. At dawn, I find my way to Eileen's camp.
    She has aroused both camps.
    A search for me is on.

9. There are no bad aftereffects to the misadventure.

Letter developed from the above plan

> Camp Woogwooly
> Oskwog, Maine
> July 10, 1991

Dear Mom,

Now that you are hearing from me in person, you will have to believe that I am quite all right. I am glad that Mr. Twiller's telegram reached you in time to keep you from making a useless trip up here. It was silly of Joe to alarm you with his telephone call. Of course, I'd like to see you; but I know that you would hardly welcome the expense of an unnecessary trip, especially now that things are not going well with Dad.

Here is the correct version of what happened, Joe's hysterical account notwithstanding. (Joe loves drama; you should know that.)

On Sundays, I round up the boys in the camp and take them to church. Last Sunday—that was July 7— I met Eileen Kirsch just as we were going into the church. I had had no idea that she was up in this neck of the woods; and as you can imagine, I was quite surprised and delighted to see her. It turns out that she is a counselor at a girls' camp near here, a much ritzier place than ours, situated just across the lake from us. Well, we made a date for the following night. Both of us welcomed the prospect of one night away from the brats. (I like the kids in my cabin; they're fun and as interesting as ants under glass. They can teach me at least as much as I can teach them. On the whole, they're well-behaved, too; so I really can't complain. But once in a while I want to get away from their treble squeak. They sound like mice on a hot griddle.)

On Monday, then, I set out in one of our canoes for Eileen's camp, Moonetonkwonk. (These pseudoaboriginal names!) Eileen has a car up here with her, and we intended to use it to drive into town for a show. The movie and a drugstore are all that Oskwog has to offer in the way of night life—which is monotonous but convenient for my wallet. Now, the camp lies just across the lake, not more than two miles from us. I should have been able to hit it swimming blindfold under water. And I *would* have hit it, had I not been seduced from my course by the flickering of a bonfire.

Moony, I thought is the only place hereabout that would build a bonfire; so that must be Moony.

I steered for the fire and was right upon it before I realized that it must be a good distance either to the east or to the west of Moony, since there was no sign of a camp. There wasn't so much as a star overhead; and, looking back across the lake, I found I couldn't see even the glimmer of a lamp at Woogwooly from which to take a bearing. I realize now that a little hill to the west must have come between me and the lights in the boys' cabins.

For a minute or so I sat staring across the bow at the bonfire. It was utterly deserted. The girls must have set it earlier and gone off and left it—bad woodcraft, even for a girls' camp. (To be quite frank, they're usually much more careful about that sort of thing than we are.)

Well, I thought, there's nothing to do but to try the east or the west; and, since I don't know where the camp is, I'll go on in the direction in which the canoe is drifting. So, not alarmed but merely anxious not to be very late for my date, I struck out into the darkness ahead, keeping the shore on my right.

The night was really very dark; otherwise I would have noticed that I was leaving the lake and entering an inlet. As I know now, the inlet opened into other inlets and sloughs. By keeping a shoreline always on my right, I found my way—without realizing what was happening—from one pass to another, until I was trapped in a labyrinth of small waterways. It was not until, after some time, I had decided that I had gone east far enough, and had reversed my course, that I discovered what had happened to me. Almost immediately I was confronted by a shoreline that should not have been lying across my bow. For a moment I was confused, then I understood the situation. I paddled a bit longer to see if I could find a way out; but every five minutes or so brought me up against banks or shore that were unfamiliar, until it was painfully clear that I no longer knew north from nougat. It seemed foolish to spend the night threshing about in a maze; so I tied the canoe to a willow, put on my jacket and pulled the collar up about my ears, and spent the night smoking cigarettes and sleeping. To be quite candid, I did a good deal more sleeping than smoking. The bottom of the canoe was not altogether uncomfortable; there was plenty of room to stretch out; there was a cushion for my head.

At dawn I found my way, without much difficulty now that I could see, to Moonetonkwonk to let Eileen know what had happened. It was then that I found out that she had become alarmed, had phoned our camp, alarmed Joe, and started that torchlight boatsearch on the lake that he told you about. I'm afraid the brats very much enjoyed looking for my body.

So there's the whole thing. You will want to know if I was cold. Not very. The nights up here, even in July, are not warm; but I had my jacket. Was I frightened? Yes, but not very much. Were there any aftereffects? Well, I was hungry from doing a lot of paddling I had not expected to do.

With love,
PETER

Two series of events

R17 Ordinarily keep two or more distinct series of events in separate narratives. It sometimes happens, however, that two series of events that come together at one or two points must be kept going in the same narrative.

R18 Draw a two-column plan or plot, one column for each series of events. Encircle and connect those events in which the two series converge.

Wyck series	*Alfredo series*
1. General Wyck and General Alfredo plan to converge on Templi. Alfredo from east, Wyck from southwest. Rendezvous set for 8:00 A.M. the next day.	1. General Wyck and General Alfredo plan to converge on Templi. Alfredo from east, Wyck from southwest. Rendezvous set for 8:00 A.M. the next day.
2. Wyck makes better time than he had expected. Roads in better shape than reported. No mechanical trouble in motorized units.	2. A bridge halts Alfredo for four hours. Patrols had mistakenly reported it safe. It must be shored up.
3. At 3:00 P.M. of first day, Wyck meets and overcomes resistance. Ambush by small party causes delay of one hour.	3. Unmapped Fascist mine field delays Alfredo another three hours. Several casualties.
4. Nonetheless Wyck manages to arrive at rendezvous on time.	4. Alfredo arrives at Templi at 3:00 P.M. of second day, seven hours late for rendezvous. Hears no firing. No sound of Wyck.

Q
R

5. At 8:00 A.M. sharp, Wyck attacks Templi.
     Meets full resistance. No diversion from the east.

6. After five hours he retires.
     Four-fifths of his troops are casualties.

7. At safe distance he sits down to wait for word of Alfredo.

8. Alfredo meets Wyck.

9. They decide to combine forces and attack again from southwest.

10. They are routed.

11. Wyck is killed.

5. Decides not to attack but to make contact with Wyck.
     Circles wide to south-west.

6. Alfredo meets Wyck.

7. They decide to combine forces and attack again from southwest.

8. They are routed.

9. Alfredo leads remnant of forces back to Alva.
     Two-thirds casualties.

10. Alfredo thinks it would have been better to halve forces after making con-tact and follow original plan.

Narrative developed from the plan above

The loss of Templi did not receive much publicity during the war, presumably for reasons of security. After the war, as far as I have been able to discover, it received no attention what-ever. Yet it is a rather interesting episode in the fierce battle for the Micarno region.

Two identical forces—each a mixture of Italian and American infantry complemented by American tanks and other motorized units, one under the command of Brigadier Gen-eral Maurice L. Wyck of the United States Army, the other under General Almiral Alfredo of the friendly Italian forces fighting with the Americans in Italy—planned to converge on the little but strategic town of Templi for a concerted attack at eight the following morning.

Wyck was to attack from the southwest, Alfredo from the east—the only other approach offering good cover.

Their divergent routes were about equal in length, so the

two forces set out for Templi at the same time.

From the time that he left Alva, Wyck's progress was much more rapid than he had expected it to be. For once, reconnaissance had been wrong in the right way; the roads turned out to be in much better condition than reports had indicated. Moreover, the motorized units proceeded without the mechanical breakdowns so usual that commanding officers come to consider them inevitable—breakdowns that can snarl traffic for hours on narrow byways.

At 3:00 P.M., however, Wyck did run into trouble. A small party of Fascists fighting for the Germans—less than fifty— held up the advance for a little less than an hour with four machine guns, two of which swept the road where it passed through a narrow defile. They were finally cleared out without the loss of one American or allied soldier; and Wyck proceeded on his way, still well ahead of schedule.

The roads continued good; and so Wyck arrived at the southwestern approach to Templi well before his time, deployed his forces, and entered battle at precisely 8:00 A.M.

Within an hour it was apparent that he was meeting the full resistance of Templi. No one was creating a diversion at the eastern end of the little town. Hard pressed for a decision, Wyck fanned his men out in a quarter circle in the southwest and did what he could with what he had.

Where was Alfredo? Shortly after setting out from Alva, he had run into a serious annoyance. A bridge, the only crossing of the Laruna within miles, lay in his path. Whether through mistake or carelessness, patrols had reported the bridge to be in good shape. Alfredo discovered that it practically required rebuilding before it could sustain his vehicular traffic. Quite understandably loath to abandon his motor units, he spent four precious hours shoring up the supports with timbers and laying steel mats across its rotted, sagging floor.

Hardly had he crossed the bridge and once more achieved a good forward pace, when the head of his column tripped the first of the mines that Fascists had laid both across the road and a good distance to either side of it. Progress was agonizingly slow as his men cautiously picked their way, not without casualties, through the mine fields. To hurry the men would have

Q
R

been to murder a good number of them. His tension and irritation mounting as the precious moments fled by, Alfredo finally had to resign himself to arriving at least seven hours late for his rendezvous.

Meanwhile, at Templi, Wyck's unsupported troops were getting a very bad worst of it. By one o'clock four fifths of his men were casualties. He then made a decision that he would have made hours before had he not momently expected the arrival of Alfredo in the east. He withdrew to a safe distance and sat down to wait for word of Alfredo.

Some two hours after Wyck's withdrawal, Alfredo arrived at the eastern approach to Templi. There was, of course, no sight or sound of Wyck, since firing had ceased a good deal earlier. At this juncture, Alfredo proceeded more wisely than had Wyck. He determined to make contact with the latter before attacking the town. Consequently, he circled widely to the southwest until he came upon Wyck with the remaining fifth of his forces.

At the conference that ensued, three possible plans lay before the generals: to give up Templi as lost; to combine forces and attack at one point; to divide their combined forces in two and proceed on the original plan of simultaneous attacks from the east and southwest.

It is a credit to their valor—though perhaps not to their military acumen—that they never seriously considered their first plan. They chose the second. But now, with the element of surprise gone and their total troops reduced almost by half, the attempt ended in a complete rout of the Americans and their allies and in the death of Wyck, who was killed in his command car. Alfredo limped back to Alva with only one third of the men who had set out from there two days or so before.

Assessing the defeat afterward, Alfredo said that he was now convinced that he and Wyck had made the wrong decision, that it would have been better to halve forces and follow the original plan of simultaneous attacks from two approaches.

Be that as it may, it is clear even to the layman that the battle of Templi was fought with a shocking disregard for elementary communications between separated groups. Had Alfredo been able to warn Wyck that he would be seven hours late in reaching the town, Wyck would have been able to hold his attack. Military men whom I quizzed about the affair were inclined, almost to a man, to shrug their shoulders and remark that not even in World War II were communications always what they should have been. In the case of Templi, that fact spelled disaster.

R19 When treating two separate series of events in the same narrative—[5]

A. Change from one series to the other only when necessary.

B. But do not let one series go unmentioned so long that the reader may forget about it.

C. Announce the changes from one series to another by expressions like *meanwhile, on the other side of the river,* and so on.[6]

Introducing and concluding a narrative [7]

R20 When suspense is not an important factor at the beginning of a story, ordinarily introduce a narrative in one of these ways:

A. By stating the topic idea in palatable fashion.

> [Topic idea:] I have found a friend.
> [Introduction containing topic idea:] We use a lot of words carelessly, and one of them is *loneliness.* Until I came to live alone for five years under the cold eyes of the Tarrana Indians, I had no idea what it meant. And that is why the next sentence has enormous significance for me. Today I have found a friend.

B. By answering the questions *who, what, when, where, how,* and *why*—or as many of them as are useful.

> After trailing Saulter High School for three quarters, the South High School Marauders managed to salvage a 7-6

---

[5] See an example of this kind of composition under R18.

[6] For a treatment of bridge expressions, see M54-64.

[7] For general notions about introductions and conclusions, see M10-12 and M18.

victory in the last three minutes of play this afternoon at Barry Stadium. Ten thousand prep-football fans watched the thrilling close of the game, as the Marauders uncorked everything they had in a desperate and successful effort to keep the league championship trophy for another year.

R21 When initial impact is important, begin a story in one of the following ways (sometimes continuing with one of the introductions of R20).[8]

A. Start the story with an incident.

Petrie had been watching for an hour, but nothing had happened in the tall gray house across the street. No matter; he had at his disposal all the hours that he would need, and he was determined to spend them in patience. He had come to the end of a long quest, and his quarry was in the gray house across the street. It would be silly, he thought, to let himself become impatient now after having been patient for so very many years. But he had to own to a certain excitement now that the end had come. He could not afford that excitement. His finger must be steady on the trigger. No slips.

Quite suddenly, without warning, the blank face of the gray house took on expression. The front door was opening. It did not open wide. Someone, standing in the shadow of the hall beyond the door, was looking out carefully before venturing onto the porch. *But he can't see me*, thought Petrie, and the corners of his mouth rose in the faintest parody of a smile.

Now the person, apparently having discovered nothing to suggest retreat, stepped out on the porch. When the morning sunlight fell full across his face, Petrie gazed at it in disbelief and dismay. The wrong man! And yet he knew for certain that there had been only one man in the house. Then his eyes narrowed. No. Of course. The fellow had simply shaved off the beard. This was his man.

The man took a packet of cigarettes from his pocket, fished in it for a moment very deliberately, turning his head

---

[8] See R22-23.

meanwhile to take in the whole length of the street, and finally put a cigarette in his mouth. His hand went back to his pocket for a match.

Petrie fired. The man crumpled to the floor of the porch, kicked grotesquely for a moment, and then lay still.

[The methods of R27 Start here:] It was a long road that led Petrie to the window across the street from the tall gray house where a man now lay dead on the porch. It began in Harely, Connecticut, where Petrie—Hale Petrie, quite respectable then before things had begun to happen to him, and a man who had never thought of killing—had worked at the only drugstore in the village and dreamed of marrying Cally Ralls [and so on].

B. Start the story with a conversation.

"It is too bad, isn't it," sighed Letitia, "that whenever a really eligible man finds his way by accident to Bancroft, he is bagged by the Daltons before he can get to know any of the rest of us charming people."

"Eligible?" inquired Alice Train, as sharp and angular a woman as Letitia was round and placid.

"Eligible for Helen and Esther, of course." Letitia's candor was by turns amusing or disconcerting. "You do know, my dear—let's not pretend that you don't; we've known and liked each other too long for that—that I have two daughters who are of no earthly use to me and whom I should like to marry off to two pleasant, guileless, unsuspecting, well-to-do men."

"Why guileless and unsuspecting, Mamma?" asked Esther, stepping inopportunely from the house to the terrace where Letitia and Alice were sitting in the sun.

"You weren't supposed to hear that, my love," sighed Letitia.

"But I did hear it. So you might as well tell me. Why guileless and unsuspecting?"

"Well, then, my sweet—because someone not guileless and unsuspecting might discover, before he married you, that you, my dove, are a shrew; and that your sister, for all

Q
R

her appearance of cheerful vigor, has the backbone of an oyster and the same colorful personality."

[The methods of R20 start here:] Meanwhile, at the other end of town, the eligible young man most recently bagged by the Daltons was just waking from a prolonged rest in the comfortable bed in the best Dalton guest room. He was Herbert Q. Waterman—and looked it, right down to the Q. He understood very well that in Bancroft he was a catch, and he intended to do nothing to dispel that notion. The fact that his total wealth [and so on].

R22 Not every story should begin briskly, and so an incident or a conversation is not to be used in every case. Gauge the mood of your narrative.

R23 You must not keep the reader waiting too long before you use one or both of the introductions of R20. So keep the opening incident or conversation short. How short depends on the length of the story. A reader does not mind waiting as much as a chapter or two in a long novel; but in a rather short story—say, five hundred words—the reader ordinarily does not care to wait beyond a few paragraphs.

R24 Ordinarily conclude a straight narrative[9] in one of the following ways or by any combination of two or more of them:

A. By giving a variation of the introduction.

[Introduction:] We use a lot of words carelessly, and one of them is *loneliness*. Until I came to live alone for five years under the cold eyes of the Tarrana Indians, I had no idea what it meant. And that is why the next sentence has enormous significance for me. Today I have found a friend.

[Conclusion:] And so I have a friend. Xuatl has all the filthy customs and manners of his people. When he grins at me with his filed teeth, he looks more like hunger than benevolence. But he has offered me a precious gift. He is sincere; he is good. I need his friendship; and he, poor man, has need of what I can give him.

---

[9] See R58.

B. By pointing a moral, a lesson, or a conclusion, from the events related in the theme.

> His has been what many an unthinking person would call a full life. Yet, when he came to die, he could not look back on a single act that would bring him comfort in his last conscious moment, ease his passage into eternity, or give him something to say to his judge. Now he must stand mute before God—he mute, who had so many frivolous things to say as he wasted away his precious years entertaining his pathetic little coterie.

C. By recapitulating the main events of the narrative.

> This is my story. It differs strikingly from the wild tales circulated by my adversaries. I was in France working on the *Herald* at the time they claim I was in Moscow. From France I went to China to cover the peasant uprising. From China I returned to California, where I have lived in retirement and silence until this moment, when the FBI has permitted me to speak and set the record straight.

D. By speculating about subsequent events.

> There you have the situation at the present time. No one would care to risk his reputation on a flat statement of what tomorrow will bring. But I am willing to hazard a guess, if it will be accepted as a guess and nothing more: Within thirty-six hours Paneast-Falton will sit down with union officials to write a new contract that will involve considerable compromise on both sides.

E. By an observation not closely, yet not too remotely, connected with the events of the narrative.

> As the roar of that holocaust died and the gruesome work of separating bodies from the debris began, a boy who could hardly have been more than seventeen years old looked at me and said, "Golly, what a show!" He seemed pleased. I can only hope that he was hysterical.

Paragraphing narratives

R25   Many a narrative paragraph cannot be said in any strict sense to have a topic sentence.[10] You will therefore need the following rules and suggestions.

R26   In general, when you are not dealing with topic sentences, group in paragraphs those events and thoughts that go together naturally.

R27   Start a new paragraph when the focus shifts to another character or set of characters.

> By half past ten, though Elise had left, it seemed that the bickering would go on all night. Groot, as usual, spoke right on without listening to anyone else. Aunt Tib made querulous little side remarks that sounded like the piping of a frightened bird above the storm. Peleas and Melisance added to the din by barking through the windows at the sort of thing that dogs see and bark at in the night.
>
> [Focus shifts; so a new paragraph:] William, in the meantime, had said nothing. It is not my quarrel, he thought, and any attempt to get into it will be resented as an intrusion.

R28   Start a new paragraph when there is a shift in mood or atmosphere.

> The little girl's face was, to be sure, a picture of woe. If she had been the sort to cry, she would have been crying; and somehow it pierced the heart of the bystanders the more deeply that she was not crying. The whole thing was the more poignant because we did not know her language and could not help her at all.
>
> [Mood shifts; so a new paragraph:] Quite without prelude to prepare us for the change, all shadows fled from her face and were replaced by a smile so warm and a glance so bright that one felt as one does when a fire is lighted in a cold and lonely cabin in the wilderness.

R29   Start a new paragraph when events take a turn from the line that they have been pursuing.

---

[10] See L8-13 and L15.

It was an ordeal for which they were not prepared, that trek through the desert. For days without end, it seemed, they made their way through all but intolerable heat and then at night sat or lay half frozen as close as they could get to the fire.

[Events take a turn; so a new paragraph:] About the seventh day Stebbins made a proposal that was to render life easier for a time but was eventually to lead them into disaster. He suggested that they sleep by day inside and underneath the wagons and travel by night.

R30 Start a new paragraph when there is a lapse of time.

He bade farewell several times to Miss Lindsey, started out the wrong door, found the right one, hooked his sleeve on its knob, disentangled himself, tripped over his own feet, and finally took his departure.

[Lapse of time; so a new paragraph:] Fifteen minutes later he was back again to retrieve his hat, which Miss Lindsey handed him without a word. She was quite afraid to speak.

R31 Start a new paragraph when there is a break in the action.

Hurtling down the slope, it crashed from boulder to boulder with harsh rending and pounding noises, and finally disappeared over the brink. After several moments there came from below the faint sound of a splash. Then all was still.

[Break in the action; so a new paragraph:] We looked at one another stunned.

R32 Start a new paragraph when there is a change of setting.

Altogether it was an unlovely forest whose great trees lifted their arms above us not so much, it seemed, in benediction as in a gesture of menace and oppression.

[Change of setting; so a new paragraph:] At length we emerged from the woods onto the plain. Here an immense prospect lay before us, apparently bounded only by the horizon and rolling away in gentle swells to the west.

R33 Start a new paragraph when there is a change from one series of events to another.

Q
R

Hard pressed for a decision, Wyck fanned his men out in a quarter circle in the southwest and did what he could with what he had.

[Change from one series of events to another; so a new paragraph:] Where was Alfredo? Shortly after setting out from Alva, he had run into a serious annoyance. A bridge [and so on].

R34 Start a new paragraph when there is a change in speaker.[11]

"It seems to me," said Aunt Jane, "That your daughter made a wise decision in going away to college."

"Yes, " I said, "but she would be a comfort to her sick father if she were home."

R35 Rarely, use visual devices like the setting off of a single brief statement in a paragraph by itself.[12]

It was obvious that a single extra division would turn the tide for us. We were doing well. We were holding Klavic's army longer than anybody had thought we could.

A single extra division would have given our left flank the strength it needed to advance. We all knew that that extra division, under Aubrey Tarleton, had been ordered up since the night before. We were all waiting tensely for it, hour after hour.

But Tarleton never came.

Narrative pace and sequence

R36 Dramatic narrative relates events as if they were happening, with considerable detail. Use dramatic narrative for important parts of a story.

R37 Summary narrative condenses information, leaving out most details. Use summary narrative for relatively unimportant parts of a story.

R38 A good narrative has proper pace to maintain audience interest. The pace is rarely constant, sometimes slowing

---

[11] See D124.

[12] Some popular modern writers overwork the visual contrast trick.

down to supply important information or to bring a scene to life (dramatic narrative), sometimes speeding up and providing a mere summary of relatively unimportant material (summary narrative).

R39 Ordinarily put events in chronological order. Use flashback and unusual time sequences only if they contribute to interest in the narrative and do not confuse the reader.[13]

From the time that he left Alva, Wyck's progress was much more rapid than he had expected it to be. For once, reconnaissance had been wrong in the right way; the roads turned out to be in much better condition than reports had indicated. Moreover, the motorized units proceeded without the mechanical breakdowns so usual that commanding officers come to consider them inevitable–breakdowns that can snarl traffic for hours on narrow byways.

At 3:00 P.M., however, Wyck did run into trouble. A small party of Fascists fighting for the Germans—less than fifty—held up the advance for a little less than an hour with four machine guns, two of which swept the road where it passed through a narrow defile. They were finally cleared out without the loss of one American or allied soldier; and Wyck proceeded on his way, still well ahead of schedule.

The roads continued good; and so Wyck arrived at the southwestern approach to Templi well before his time, deployed his forces, and entered battle at precisely 8:00 A.M. the next day.

Within an hour it was apparent that he was meeting the full resistance of Templi. No one was creating a diversion at the eastern end of the little town. Hard pressed for a decision, Wyck fanned his men out in a quarter circle in the southwest and did what he could with what he had [and so on].

R40 Supply the reader with all information needed for an easy following of the thought.

---

[13] See R59.

One fine day in late March, when it looked as if spring had decided to stay, Mark Hokins cut himself a generous slice from the flitch that hung in his smokehouse, took a loaf of bread from the box in the kitchen cupboard, filled a bottle with water, and set out at a good pace across the valley towards the mountains and the village of Little Rawlings.

What makes the passage at the left incoherent is the omission of one little bit of information that is important to the good order of the composition. In the revision below, the missing information is supplied at the beginning of the second paragraph.

The supplies would hardly have been adequate for anyone else. But Hokins had taught himself to do with little—had even taught himself to enjoy doing with little. Looking at his tall leanness and the set of his jaw, you sensed immediately that this man was an ascetic, keeping himself in training against a day to come.

One fine day in Late March, when it looked as if spring had decided to stay, Mark Hokins cut himself a generous slice from the flitch that hung in his smokehouse, took a loaf of bread from the box in the kitchen cupboard, filled a bottle with water, and set out at a good pace across the valley toward the mountains and the village of Little Rawlings.

Since Little Rawlings was three days of good walking away, the supplies would hardly have been adequate for anyone else. But Hokins had taught himself to do with little—had even taught himself to enjoy doing with little. Looking at his tall leanness and the set of his jaw, you sensed immediately that this man was an ascetic keeping himself in training against a day to come.

R41 Do not change the verb tenses without reason. Avoid, for example, slipping carelessly from present to past tense or from past to present tense.[14]

R42 Ordinarily maintain a consistent point of view. The narrative points of view are first person (*I, we*) and third person (*he, she, they*).[15]

---

[14] For the verb tenses and their uses, see, C116-44.

[15] The various distinctions in point of view (*omniscient, concealed, limited,* and so on), properly discussed in fiction writing, are beyond the scope of this section.

Emphasis in narratives

R43 Start with the least important or interesting thought and move by degrees to the most interesting or important.

As a matter of fact, it was rather a full day. I spent several hours getting the dummy for the *Colombiere Clarion* ready for the printer and another forty minutes working out that silly exercise in emphasis for English class tomorrow.

I spent another three hours doing something rather interesting: watching the men at D'Astignac Studios painting a backdrop for the school's production of *Everyman*. I found it amazing that they could work so quickly. Watching them slap paint on—mostly with ten-inch brushes—you would imagine that the result was going to look like something my manic-depressive little sister thinks up out of her water-color kit. On the contrary, they achieved a perfect copy of Laury's design and got it on a canvas twenty by forty feet in less than three hours.

But the thing that will make it a day to remember was something that happened down at the printer's. I was helping Mr. Shelton lay out our copy according to the dummy, when a rather fat, bald, tired-looking man came out of the office and walked over to the shop table where we were working. When he picked up a sheaf of *Clarion* copy and started reading through it, I felt rather annoyed that he hadn't asked anybody's permission. But I didn't say anything. He took advantage of a pause in the discussion I was having with Shelton to ask very curtly, "Who wrote this thing on the prize debates at Colombiere?"

"I did," I said without looking up.

"You, eh?"

"Uh-huh."

"Well, son, when you finish high school and college, if you're still fool enough to like newspaper work, come down and get a job from me."

"Yes?" I said; "and who are you, mister?"

"Priestly, " he answered; "R. C. Priestly, city editor, Wichita *Herald*. Darned good paper, and an excellent city editor."

R44   Occasionally emphasize a thought by introducing it
with an abrupt change of mood or atmosphere.

It was a mournful evening. Sheila sat in the window seat, staring out into the night. There was not enough light in the room behind her to make reflections on the panes, and so she could see out quite well; and what she saw was melancholy enough: a few giant cypresses starting up, stark and bare and grotesque, out of the black water of the swamp and gesticulating in silhouette against the faintly luminous sky. They shuddered a little when the wind came raging at them and howled on past the house and the window from which Sheila was looking out. Once she thought she saw something move in the dark water under the cypresses, but she could not be sure.

"Blow me for an empty bag," cried a voice behind her. "Here's a good room with a fine fire laid. Let's make port and drop anchor in here, Jackie—if, of course, the young lady over there in the window doesn't mind sharing this snuggery with us. The pretty young lady, I should say, Jackie; for the girl is pretty, though you're too young to notice—or are you, lad?" Sheila turned to find a great stout man and a boy in his teens standing in the doorway, both with their mouths open—the man's because he was talking and the boy's because he was gawking.

The man and the boy are given importance, and their entrance is pointed up sharply by the abrupt change of mood and atmosphere between the first and second paragraphs.

R45   Occasionally emphasize an important idea by putting it
in a short sentence at the end of a paragraph.

It was half-way through the morning, and he had not breakfasted; the slight litter of other breakfasts stood about on the table to remind him of his hunger; and adding a poached egg to his order, he proceeded musingly to shake some white sugar into

He had put salt in it gathers a great deal of emphasis from the contrast between its length and that of most of the sentences that have gone before. In fact, the sentence gains such emphasis that the reader would feel cheated if the salt turned out to be un-

his coffee, thinking all the time about Flambeau. He remembered how Flambeau had escaped, once by a pair of nail scissors, and once by a house on fire; once by having to pay for an unstamped letter, important to the story. (It turns out to be important; for it is one of a trail of clues left by Flambeau's victim for the detective to follow, and it leads to Flambeau's capture.) and once by getting people to look through a telescope at a comet that might destroy the world. He thought his detective brain as good as the criminal's, which was true. But he fully realized the disadvantage. "The criminal is the creative artist; the detective only the critic," he said with a sour smile, and lifted his coffee cup to his lips slowly, and put it down very quickly. He had put salt in it.

—G. K. Chesterton, "The Blue Cross"

Description in narratives

R46 Narratives that neglect the help of description are bare, colorless, dead. They are suitable only for reports in which dryness is at a premium. Ordinarily it is not enough to relate what people do, say, or think; you must often tell how they do, say, or think it.

R47 To make a narrative vivid, give dramatic details of bodily action.[16]

> [Without details:] Jack gave an utterly inadequate answer.
> [With details:] Jack flushed to the roots of his hair. He dropped his gaze to the floor, ran his finger around the edge of his collar, coughed once or twice, and finally stammered out an utterly inadequate answer.

R48 To make a narrative vivid, give dramatic details of sense perception. In other words, tell concretely and specifically what the character sees, hears, feels with the sense of touch, and—if it will help—what the character smells and tastes. Do not exhaust one sense and then go on to

---

[16] See R52.

the next. Mingle sensations in the same way in which one experiences them in real life. Combine this method with R47.[17]

[Without details:] With a great effort Hawkins jumped, caught the top of the wall, and pulled himself up.

[With details:] Hawkins leaped mightily for the top of the wall. His upflung right hand slapped smartly on the ledge and found a grip. The gulp of air that had been burning his lungs rushed through his lips in a tearing gasp. Dangling from a wrist already aching and beginning to swell, he cautiously brought his other hand up and rubbed in the loose cement at the top of the wall for a grip. He stayed there a moment, his head hanging back and his face turned upward, the sweat running into his eyes and turning greasy and chill. Finally his toes found a crevice. Summoning his strength in a second effort that ran like fire down his arms and cut like a knife through his toes, he pulled himself to where he could get one leg over the wall, and then the rest of his body to the ledge. For a moment he lay there, his face in the dusty, crumbling cement still warm from the sun that had gone down hours before. The salt sweat ran into his mouth, lessening the dryness but not the thirst.

R49   To make a narrative vivid, give dramatic details of emotional reactions. In other words, tell in some detail what the character feels.[18]

I was no sooner certain of my opponent's death than I began to feel sick, faint, and *terrified*. The hot blood was running over my back and chest. The dirk, where it had pinned my shoulder to the mast, seemed to burn like a hot iron; *yet it was not so much these real sufferings that distressed me, for these, it seemed to me, I could bear without a murmur; it was the horror I had upon my mind of falling down from the crosstrees into that still green water beside the body of the coxswain.*

I clung with both hands till my nails ached, and I shut my eyes as if to cover up the peril. Gradually my mind came back

---

[17] See R52.
[18] See R52.

again, my pulses quieted down to a more natural time, and I was once more in possession of myself.[19]

—Robert Louis Stevenson, *Treasure Island*

R50 To make a narrative vivid, give dramatic details of a character's thoughts and speech. In other words, a passage can often be improved by telling not only what a character does, senses, and feels, but also what a character thinks or says, or both—quoting thought and speech either directly or indirectly.[20]

[Without details:] The boys went down to the pawn shop and pawned the guitar.

[With details:] The boys went down to the pawn shop and pawned the guitar. Geez! thought George, fifty dollars; now I can afford to take Susie to the dance. But since he knew how Tracy felt about giving up their only musical instrument, he kept the elation out of his face and merely muttered, "Well, that's that. Let's get out of here."

R51 Direct quotation (the speaker's own words) is usually more vivid than indirect quotations *(he said that, they asked whether)* and therefore better in climaxes. But either sort becomes obvious and monotonous if it is used almost exclusively.

R52 How much detail[21] you should use depends upon the importance to the story of what you are describing. Do not detain the reader with a detailed treatment of unimportant matters.

Nervously she waited for the bus. Crowds of people pushed by, hurrying to trains and cars, hurrying to get into a traffic jam somewhere else. A few small shops were still open

This paragraph includes irrelevant details that slow the pace and muddy the line of development. The version below is clear and to the point.

---

[19] The italics in this passage are the editor's.
[20] See R51-52.
[21] See R46-50, Q21.

with the fading hope of attracting some buyers on their way home. She was late and knew that Bill would be worrying about her. It was all that salesperson's fault. If he hadn't confused her order and then doubly confused the billing, she would be home by now.

Nervously she waited for the bus. She was late and knew that Bill would be worrying about her. It was all that salesperson's fault. If he hadn't confused her order and then doubly confused the billing, she would be home by now.

Suggestion in narratives

R53 When you are certain that the reader will not miss your meaning and when dramatic narrative is appropriate, suggest character, mood, atmosphere, or incident rather than state it plainly.

[Plain statement:] It was on Tuesday of that week that I first met Mr. Helmuth. He turned out to be a mean old man. If that were all, it would be enough. But he turned out to be dangerous as well.

[Suggestion:] It was on the Tuesday of that week that I first met Mr. Helmuth. I had strayed through a breach in the wall where a freshet had dislodged some of the loosely laid stones and effected a rough gate. I found the estate on the other side very beautiful but in pitiful disrepair. The grass needed cutting; the flower beds were choked with weeds and dotted with blooms dead on their stalks; and the house that I could glimpse through the elms and evergreens could have done with a coat of paint. I came upon Mr. Helmuth very suddenly, as I turned the corner of an untrimmed hedge much higher than a man. He had obviously seen me before I caught sight of him, for he showed no surprise.

"You're trespassin'," he said.

"I know it." I managed a laugh, but it was embarrassed and apologetic. "I hoped you wouldn't mind. You're Mr. Helmuth, aren't you? It was time to pay you a call anyway, since we're going to be neighbors."

"I'm Helmuth. I take it you're Fax. Well, Mr. Fax, I ain't much given to payin' or receivin' calls. You're trespassin'." His pale watery eyes looked resolutely over my shoulder. The weathered, loose skin of his face was crisscrossed with cracks like a piece of old leather. Some twenty years before, when he had been fifty, he must have been a great hulking man. But now he was stooped; all muscle tissue and fat seemed to have melted from his frame; for wherever skin was visible—at his face, his neck, his forearms and hands—it hung loose, mottled, and heavy-veined, with scarcely anything between it and the bones to give it contour.

"I apologize, sir," I said, since he was technically in the right, "for trespassing. But now that I'm here, perhaps you'll let me look around your beautiful place. I especially envy you your elms."

He drew a revolver from the pocket of his trousers, flicked open the breech and turned it toward me. "What do you see?" he asked, his lip lifting slightly over one yellow fang.

"Why," I stammered, looking at the six brassy heads in the chambers, "why, a revolver, a loaded revolver."

He flipped the breech closed with his finger and pointed the gun at me. "Get goin'."

"What?"

He shot at the ground near my feet. "Get goin'."

R54 Suggestion is useful for putting the reader in the mood for what is going to happen and for intensifying the feeling of suspense.

Ta-da-*dum*. The drumbeat fades into an interval of silence, broken only by the sound of shuffling feet. Ta-da-*dum* —then the shuffle of feet. Ta-da-*dum* —then the shuffle of feet. It is a dead march, or at least a march of the dead. Over the heads of the long column slowly streaming through the dusk, the angry heavens thrust out long menacing fingers of cloud, their edges smeared with blood by the dying sun. Round about them in the valley, the breeze sighs, rouses itself to a sobbing wail, to a scream and dies. Along the narrow clay road, the poplars stand at attention, somber and inscrutable, as the doomed march forward to the beat of the dead march. The faces of the men are white and drawn. They know what awaits them. They feel that it is inevitable, and they march like a hypnotized battalion to meet what they cannot escape.

Climax

R55   In narratives in which the order of events is under your control and particularly in plot narratives,[22] place your most interesting or most important event at, or very near, the end.

R56   Perhaps the easiest way to make sure that your plot narrative[23] will have climax is to plan it backwards from the most interesting or important event.

R57   As far as the circumstances of the composition permit, follow the general rules of emphasis in M74-77.

Straight narrative and plot narrative

R58   Straight narrative records a series of events without introducing complications and solutions. It is the form of narrative found in most news accounts in newspapers, in most history books, and so on. It may be lively or quiet, factual or fictional.

R59   Plot narrative deliberately introduces complications and obstacles that the characters in the story must overcome if they are to meet success, happiness, and so on. Without complications, there is no plot. Plot narrative is usually fictional—though not always. It always makes use of suspense and climax.[24] It usually stresses cause and effect in human beings.

Q
R

---

[22] See R59.
[23] See R59.
[24] See R55–57.

Letters, résumés, and memos

Business letters[1]

S1 Business letters are used to request information, apply for a job, order a product, make complaints, provide a formal record, take care of financial and consumer matters, and so on.

Content

S2 Although various kinds of business letters have distinctive subject matter and format, they do have certain elements in common: brevity, directness, and accuracy. See S3-5.

S3 Good business letters are brief.

A. Ordinarily a business letter should be kept to one page or less.

B. The main point should be made quickly, without chattiness. Many businesses receive hundreds of letters each day. Better service results if the writer's needs are immediately clear.

C. The letter should be confined to one easily digested topic. If there are several scarcely related topics, it is better to send several letters. This makes for brevity and easy reading, and permits the routing of different matters to different departments.

D. Long compliments at the beginning or end of a business letter usually defeat their purpose by making

---

[1] A good manual on business letters and memos is William A. Sabin, *The Gregg Reference Manual,* 6th edition, New York: McGraw-Hill Book Company, 1990.

the reader impatient. A short complimentary paragraph, provided that there is really something to say, is in order. But such bromides as *with every good wish* or *we hope that this finds you in good health* are out of place.

S4 Good business letters are direct and clear.

A. Jargon is out of place in a business letter: *yours of the 7th inst. to hand; in reference to the matters that we have had under discussion, let me say that* ; and so on. Although such language is deeply imbedded in much business correspondence, careful writers avoid it.

B. Pomposity, ornament, gush, breeziness, long and involved sentences, and passive voice are out of place.

[Poor:] It is certainly hoped that our merchandise will meet with your complete satisfaction.
[Better:] I hope you will like the samples.

C. A straightforward *I* is better than *the writer*, a passive form, or *we*. *We*, however, is in order when the writer is expressing notions that clearly pertain to the organization rather than to the individual; for example, *we do not publish comic books.*

D. Technical terms are appropriate only if there is good reason for using them and there is assurance that the reader will understand them.

S5 Good business letters are accurate.

A. They supply all necessary information.

B. They state definite qualities, quantities, order numbers, catalog numbers, catalog descriptions, dates, academic grades, places, names, ages, addresses, and so on.

C. They acknowledge any previous related letter from the correspondent and give its date accurately. (The correspondent may want to look up the copy in his file.)

s

726

Form

S6 Good quality white unruled paper, 8 1/2 x 11 inches, is the standard paper for a business letter. Only one side of each sheet is used.

S7 It is proper to use a black typewriter ribbon or blue, black, or blue-black ink.

S8 Letters should be clean—free of smudges, visible erasures, mistakes, crossouts, corrections, creases, tears, and strike-overs. A messy letter makes a poor impression and may adversely affect the recipient's response.

S9 Letters are single-spaced. Whatever business style is used, the letter should be centered on the stationery so that the margins are balanced all around it.

S10 Business letters have their special conventions. A writer who does not follow them gives the impression that he or she is uninformed or careless. In either case such a letter may alienate the recipient and result in a lack of attention to the letter's contents.

Business letters regularly use one of the following styles:

A. *Block style.* Lines begin at the left margin. The only exceptions are display quotations, tables, and similar material. See model in S11.

B. *Modified block style*—standard format. The dateline, the complimentary close, and the writer identification begin at the center of the page.[2] Other lines begin at the left margin. This is the most commonly used style. See model in S12.

C. *Modified block style*—with indented paragraphs. This style is the same as described in B above except that

---

[2]The dateline, complimentary close, and writer identification may be positioned elsewhere as long as they begin in the same vertical line. They may be moved, for example, to the right so that the longest line ends at the right margin.

the first line of each body paragraph is indented five spaces. See model in S13.

D. *Simplified style.* All lines begin at the left margin (as in block style). The salutation is omitted in favor of an all-capital subject line. The complimentary close is omitted, and the writer's identification is typed in all-capitals on one line.[3] See model in S14.

The next four pages illustrate the basic styles of business letters described above.

S

---

[3] With the elimination of the salutation, the simplified style avoids one annoying problem: addressing a person of unknown name or sex. With this style such awkward salutations as "Dear Sir or Madam," "To Whom It May Concern," and "Dear Business Manager" are eliminated.

S11   Block-style business letter:

```
IBM          International Business Machines Corporation
             US Marketing & Services, 900 King Street, Rye Brook, New York, 10573
```

                                      (2 spaces)
August 12, 1990
                                      (1 space)
CONFIDENTIAL
                                      (1 space)
Robert J. Fornes
1726 New Hampshire Ave., NW
Washington, DC   20009
                                      (1 space)
Dear Mr. Fornes:
                                      (1 space)
Subject: Severance Pay
                                      (1 space)
....
....
....
....
                                      (1 space)
....
....
....
....
                                      (1 space)
Sincerely,

                                      (3 spaces)

Arthur G. Hartman
Personnel Manager

bc

S

S12 Modified block-style business letter—standard format:

MULTIMEDIA CORPORATION

100 SOUTH WACKER DRIVE / CHICAGO, IL 60606-2174
TELEPHONE 312/871-5050

(2 spaces)

September 8, 1990

(4 spaces)

Carl J. Wagner
3400 W. Michigan Street
Milwaukee, WI 53208-3898

(1 space)

Dear Mr. Wagner:

(1 space)

....
....
....
....

(1 space)

....
....
....
....
....

(1 space)

        Sincerely yours,

(1 space)

        Multimedia Corporation

(3 spaces)

        Mrs. Jane Ruddy, Manager
        Education Media Division

(1 space)

ml
Enclosure

S13 Modified block-style business letter—indented paragraphs:

(The following is an example of a personal business letter written from home on blank stationery.)

(11 spaces)

3601 Lindell Blvd.
St. Louis, MO 63108
November 20, 1990

(4 spaces)

Irwin International, Inc.
2101 Commonwealth Blvd.
Ann Arbor, MI 48105
            (1 space)
Attention: Accounting Department
            (1 space)
Gentlemen:

            (1 space)
      ....
....
....
....
....

            (1 space)
      ....
....
....
....
....

            (1 space)
            Sincerely,

            (3 spaces)

            Peter J. Catanzaro
            (1 space)
P.S. ....
....

S14   Simplified-style business letter:

AMICON INDUSTRIES, INC. 470 Schrock Rd./Unit E • Columbus, Ohio 43229 • (614) 436-0924

(3 spaces)

October 5, 1990

(4 spaces)

Michael C. Bickerstaff
Loyola Academy
Wilmette, Il 60091-1089

(2 spaces)

RECONDITIONING NAUTILUS FITNESS EQUIPMENT

(2 spaces)

....
....
....
....
....

(1 space)

....
....
....
....
....

(4 spaces)

FRANK C. SCHWARTZ — AREA SALES REPRESENTATIVE

(1 space)

kb
cc James J. Fennessy

S

Margins

S15   Margins depend to some extent on the length of the letter and the size of the stationery. The general principle is that the letter should be centered on the page. On 8 1/2 x 11 inch stationery, a short letter should have two-inch side margins, a medium letter one and one-half inch side margins, a long letter (most of one page or more) one-inch side margins.

Letterhead or return address[4] and dateline

S16   The top margin on the first page of a letter depends on the type of stationery and the length of the letter.

A. Printed stationery. The dateline (first typed element) is placed on the third line below the printed letterhead or on the twelfth line from the top edge.[5] If the letter is short, the dateline may be placed as low as the nineteenth line from the top edge.[6] See also S21.

B. Unprinted stationery. If the letter is written on behalf of an organization, a double-spaced centered letterhead is typed beginning on the seventh line from the top edge. The date is typed three spaces below the letterhead.[7] If the letter is written as a personal business letter (for an individual, not for an organization), a single-spaced return address is typed beginning one and one-half to two inches (ninth to twelfth lines) from the top edge. The return address begins at the middle of the page in modified block style (it may also be positioned so that the longest

---

[4] The letterhead or return address is included with the letter so that the person who receives the letter may be able to answer even if the envelope is misplaced.

[5] Do not abbreviate the month.

[6] An alternative is to place the dateline on the third line below the letterhead and leave additional space between the dateline and the inside address.

[7] Do not abbreviate the month.

line ends at the right margin); it begins at the left margin in other styles.[8]

C. Continuation pages. The second and succeeding pages of a letter should be on plain paper of the same quality as the first page. The top margin is six lines (one inch). The name of the addressee is typed beginning on the seventh line at the left margin. The letter continues on the third line below the heading. Either of the following styles may be used.

Wesson and Pierce, Accountant
Page 2
January 20, 1990

or

Wesson and Pierce, Accountants   2   January 20, 1990

(This style uses the full width of the typing area.)

S17 The final page of a letter should contain at least two lines of the final paragraph plus the complimentary close, signature lines, and closing notations.

S18 The bottom margin on any full page should be at least one inch (six lines).

S19 A short letter may be lengthened by increasing the side margins, lowering the dateline, leaving more space between the dateline and the inside address, leaving four to six lines for the signature, leaving extra lines before and between reference initials, enclosure notations, and postscripts.

S20 A long letter may be shortened by single-spacing a typewritten letterhead, raising the date, leaving fewer lines between the date and the inside address, leaving only two blank lines for a signature, raising reference initials one line.

---

[8] The writer's name is not included in the return address since it appears at the end of the letter.

S21 With letterhead stationery (printed or typed), the date is placed on the third line below the letterhead. The dateline may be centered on the page or positioned so that it ends at the right margin or placed attractively and appropriately in relation to the letterhead. In block and simplified styles, the date starts at the left margin.

S22 If a letter is personal or confidential, the appropriate notation is placed on the second line below the date, beginning at the left margin (See S11). The notation should be entirely in capitals or underscored in a capital and small letters.

PERSONAL *or* <u>Personal</u>
CONFIDENTIAL *or* <u>Confidential</u>

S23 The inside address ordinarily appears on the fifth line below the date or on the third line below any special notation below the date.

S24 The inside address is identical with the address on the envelope. Including it with the letter ensures that it will reach the right desk even if the envelope is misplaced.

A. Letter addressed to an individual:

Ms. Mary FitzGerald
3441 North Ashland Ave.
Chicago, Illinois 60657

Mrs. Louella Boerger
1225 Flaire Dr., Apt. 225
Toledo, OH 43615

B. Letter addressed to an organization:

Advertising Manager
PCW Communications, Inc.
501 Second Street
San Francisco, CA 98107

Mr. Raymond C. Varhola
National Sales Manager
Mirus Corporation
4301 Great American Pkwy.
Santa Clara, California 95054

Whenever possible, a letter should be addressed to a specific individual in the organization and include that person's job title and department. Letters addressed impersonally to a title or an organization will eventually find their way to the right desk, but they lack the impact of a letter written to an individual.

Attention line

S25 When a letter is addressed to a company, an attention line is frequently used to route the letter to a particular person or department. The attention line indicates that the letter deals with a business matter (rather than with a personal matter) and may be handled, if necessary, by another person than the one addressed.[9] The word *attention* should not be abbreviated. Any of the forms below is acceptable.[10]

Market Engineering Corp.
1675 Larimer St.
Denver, CO 80202
    (1 line space)
Attention: Mr. Carlos Mertz
    (1 line space)
Ladies and Gentlemen:
	Market Engineering Corp.
	1675 Larimer Street
	Denver, CO 80202
	    (1 line space)
	ATTENTION: Mr. Carlos Mertz
	    (1 line space)
	Gentlemen:

Iris Graphics, Inc.
Attention: Jon E. Carter
6 Crosby Drive
Beford, MA 01730
    (1 line space)
Ladies and Gentlemen:
	Iris Graphics, Inc.
	ATTENTION: JON E. CARTER
	6 Crosby Dr.
	Beford, MA 01730
	    (1 line space)
	Gentlemen:

Salutation

S26 The salutation is typed at the left margin, beginning on the second line below the inside address or on the second line below an attention line placed below the

S

---

[9] When possible, omit the attention line and address the letter directly to an individual by name or by title.

[10] There are two letter spaces following the colon after "Attention." Notice that the salutation agrees with the inside address, not with the name in the attention line.

address. The salutation is followed by a colon.[11] Common forms of salutation are listed here. Additional forms of salutation are listed under S64.

To one person—name, gender, and courtesy title known:

Dear Mrs. Hearns: Dear Mr. Wilhelms:
Dear Ms. Goebel: Dear Miss Dowling:

To one person—name known, gender unknown:

Dear Gene Miller: Dear V. C. Boufford:

To one person—name unknown, gender known:

Dear Sir: Sir: [more formal]
Dear Madam: Madam: [more formal]

To one person—name unknown, gender unknown:

Dear Sir or Madam: Sir or Madam: [more formal]
Dear Madam or Sir: Madam or Sir: [more formal]

To one woman—courtesy title unknown:

Dear Ms. Stetz: Dear Marilyn Stetz:

To two or more men:

Dear Mr. Harris and Mr. Prochaska:
Dear Messrs. Harris and Prochaska:

To two or more women:

Dear Mrs. Kuback, Ms. Lowell, and Miss Harmon:
Dear Mrs. Quinlan and Mrs. Fletcher:
Dear Mesdames Quinlan and Fletcher:
Dear Ms. Kysela and Ms. Griesmer:
Dear Mses. [*or* Mss.] Kysela and Griesmer:
Dear Miss Stanner and Miss Konya:
Dear Misses Stanner and Konya:

---

[11] There is no punctuation after the salutation if open punctuation is used. A comma follows the salutation of a social-business letter.

To several persons

> Dear Mrs. Farone, Ms. Gabor, Mr. Zachlin, and Miss Barton:
> Dear Colleagues [Friends, Neighbors, and so on]:

To an organization composed entirely of men

> Gentlemen:

To an organization composed entirely of women

> Ladies: *or* Mesdames:

To an organization composed of men and women

> Ladies and Gentlemen:

S27 Avoid the salutations *Dear Sirs* and *Gentlemen* unless you are writing to an all-male organization. Avoid the salutation *To Whom It May Concern* unless you are writing a letter for general distribution to individuals unknown to you.

S28 If you are on a first-name basis with the person to whom you are writing, you should still use the person's full name and title on the inside address. You may, however, use the first name (followed by a comma) in the salutation.

Subject line

S29 When a subject line is used, it functions as a content title for the body of the letter.

S30 In simplified letter style the subject line takes the place of the salutation. In this style the subject line—in capitals—begins at the left margin on the third line below the inside address. See S14.

S31 In other letter styles the subject line (with a line skipped above and below it) appears between the salutation and the body of the letter. The subject line may be typed beginning at the left margin or be indented to correspond to the indentation of the first line of the paragraph or be centered on the page. It may be typed in capitals or in capitals and small letters. Sometimes the subject line is

s

underscored for special emphasis. The word *Subject:* or *Re:* may be used as an introduction. See S11.

Body

S32 The body of the letter is single-spaced with double-spacing between paragraphs.

S33 Quoted material of four or more typed lines is indented five spaces from each side margin with a line skipped above and below the quotation.

S34 Tables are centered within the left and right margins and indented at least five spaces from each margin, if possible.

S35 Items of a list are single-spaced with one line skipped above and below the list. If any one item requires more than one line, a blank line is inserted between all items. Items are typed either the full width of the letter or are indented five spaces from each margin.

Complimentary close

S36 The complimentary close is typed on the second line below the last line of the letter. It begins at the left margin in block style and at the center of the page in modified block style. It is omitted in simplified style.

S37 Only the first word of a complimentary close is capitalized. A comma follows the complimentary close. (There is, however, no punctuation after the complimentary close in open punctuation style.)

S38 Common complimentary closes are *Sincerely, Sincerely yours, Yours truly.* Formal letters to high government officials, diplomats, and members of the clergy might close with *Respectfully yours.*

Company name and signature lines

S39 A company name may be used after the complimentary close. If it is used, the name is typed all in capitals on the second line directly below the complimentary close. See S40.

S40 The writer's name is typed on the fourth line below the company name (if the company name is used). Otherwise the writer's name is typed on the fourth line below the complimentary close.[12]

Sincerely,

   (one line space)

VARGO AND WESSON, INC.

   (three line spaces for name)

Michael X. Stewart

Michael X. Stewart
Assistant Manager
Credit Department

Sincerely yours,

   (one line space)

DATEMASTER, INC.

   (three line spaces for name)

Anthony B. Cordelli

Anthony B. Cordelli
Vice President

S41 The typed name and the handwritten signature are ordinarily identical.[13] If signed photocopies are sent, the original should not be signed before copies are made. A photocopied signature does not look authentic. (Copies may be signed or unsigned.)

S42 Unless a woman is called by a special title, she should include a courtesy title (*Miss, Mrs., Ms.*) with her signature. Such a procedure saves the respondent from guessing at the proper form of address. The courtesy title may appear either in the handwritten signature or in the typed signature. In the handwritten signature, the title is enclosed in parentheses.

Sincerely,

   (three line spaces for name)

Martha O. Winkler

Mrs. Martha O. Winkler

Sincerely yours,

   (three line spaces for name)

(Ms.) Sarah G. Novotny

Sarah G. Novotny

s

---

[12] In simplified style the writer's name and title are typed all in capitals on the fifth line below the body of the letter, beginning at the left margin. See S14.

[13] In a social-business letter the full name is typed, but the first name alone may be signed.

S43 In general, special titles should appear after a person's name, not before it.

Constance B. Pavlick, Ph.D. [*not* Dr. Constance B. Pavlick]
Eunice Ditzel, M.D. [*not* Dr. Eunice Ditzel]

Francis X. Cassidy
Lieutenant Commander, USN

Walter D. Spillman
Dean of Students

S44 When a title cannot properly be placed after a person's name, it is placed before.

Rev. Robert J. Lab

Reference initials

S45 Reference initials are typed on the second line below the final signature line. These initials are used to identify the following:

A. The typist completing the letter:

    mjh   mh   MJH

B. The writer of the letter (first set of initials) and the typist:

    RTB:mjh   RTB:MJH   rtb/mh   RB/mjh

Enclosure notation

S46 If one or more items are sent in the envelope with the letter, an enclosure notation is typed on the first or second line below the immediately preceding entry (reference initials or signature line), beginning at the left margin. The following styles are commonly used.

Enclosure	2 Enclosures
Enc.	Enclosures (2)

Enclosures:
  1. Invoice #546
  2. Check for $200
	Check enclosed

S

S47   If material is sent separately, a special notation is typed on the line below the enclosure notation (if any). The following styles are used.

Separate cover (1)   Separate mailing 1

Under separate cover: In separate mailing:
    1. Catalog   Annual report
    2. Annual report

Copy notation

S48   When copies of a letter are sent to other individuals, a copy notation is added at the left margin on the first or second line below the previous entry (that is, below the enclosure notation, the reference initials, or the signature lines). If several individuals are to receive copies, the names are listed alphabetically or according to the rank of the individuals. Skip one space after *cc* and two after *cc:* before a person's name.

cc Virginia Niehaus
   Wilma Kurman
   Carlos Ramirez

Other styles are sometimes used.

CC Mrs. Reddy   cc: J. Hammond
    Mr. Baddour   A. Tischer

copy to maintenance

S49   If it is necessary to send a copy of a letter to someone without the addressee's knowledge, a blind copy notation (*bcc*) is used on the copy but not on the original.

S50   When there are enclosures with a letter that is sent to several people, it is preferable to indicate who receives the enclosures.

cc Ed Heintschel (with enclosures)
   Jenny Laska (without enclosures)

s

Postscript

S51 A postscript may be used to give special emphasis to an idea or to state an afterthought. The postscript is blocked or indented to match the body paragraphs and appears on the second line below the copy notation (or whatever is last). It is typed with or without *PS:*, *PS.*, or *P.S.* (There are two spaces after the punctuation and before the postscript.)

> P.S. Despite the accident (or perhaps because of it) George is already planning next summer's fishing trip to Canada.

S52 A second postscript is introduced by *PPS:*, *PPS.*, or *P.S.* (or by no abbreviation at all if none was used for the first postscript) and typed as a separate paragraph.

Addressing envelopes

S53 Addresses on an envelope are in block style and single-spaced. They may be typed entirely in capitals.

S54 The second-last line of an address contains a street address or a post-office box number.

S55 The last line of an address contains the name of the city and state and the ZIP code. The name of the state may be spelled out or be typed as a two-letter abbreviation.[14] The ZIP code may be placed either one or two spaces after the state.

S56 With a large envelope (business, No. 10), the address begins on the fourteenth line from the top and about four inches from the left edge (seven spaces left of center).

S57 With a small envelope or a postcard, the address begins on the twelfth line from the top and about three inches from the left edge (seven spaces left of center).

s

---

[14] For a list of abbreviations of states, see S62.

S58 With a window envelope the address should be positioned so that there is at least a one-eighth inch clearance between the four sides of the block address and the edges of the window frame.

S59 If there is a printed return address on the envelope, the writer's name is typed on the line above the return address. The exact position of the name depends on the style of the return address (block left or centered).

S60 A typed return address begins on line three from the top and approximately one-half inch from the left edge.

```
Mark R. French
1216 Elmwood Rd.
Rocky River, OH 44116
```

```
                    Mr. Calvin P. Winick
                    Palmer Video Corp.
                    1767 Morris Avenue
                    Union, NJ   07083
```

S61 A notation such as *Personal* or *Please Forward* is typed with the first letter of each main word capitalized and the notation underscored or with all letters in capitals on the third line below the return address and aligned left with the return address.[15]

---

[15] If an attention line is used in the letter (S25), it should also appear on the envelope. *Attention:* or *ATTENTION:* may be positioned exactly as the personal notation in S61, followed by the person's name; or it may be included within the block address, immediately below the name of the addressee, in which case it may begin with an abbreviation (usually ATTN or Attn.).

```
B. L. Corna
Hanns Ebensten Travel, Inc.
513 Fleming Street
Key West, FL  33040

Personal

                    Mrs.  Amelia  J.Wenzel
                    2813  West  88th  Street
                    Indianapolis,  IN    46268
```

S62   In the address of a letter, the name of the state or of the United States territory may be spelled out or typed as a two-letter abbreviation. In other situations the standard abbreviations listed below are commonly used.[16]

Ala.	AL	Kans	KS	Ohio	OH
Alaska	AK	Ky.	KY	Okla.	OK
Amer. Samoa	AS	La.	LA	Oreg.	OR
Ariz.	AZ	Maine	ME	Pa.	PA
Ark.	AR	Md.	MD	P.R.	PR
Calif.	CA	Mass.	MA	R.I.	RI
C.Z.	CZ	Mich.	MI	S.C.	SC
Colo.	CO	Minn.	MN	S. Dak.[17]	SD
Conn.	CT	Miss.	MS	Tenn.	TN
Del.	DE	Mo.	MO	Tex.	TX
D.C.	DC	Mont.	MT	Utah	UT
Fla.	FL	Nebr.	NE	Vt.	VT
Ga.	GA	Nev.	NV	Va.	VA
Guam	GU	N.H.	NH	V.I.	VI
Hawaii	HI	N.J.	NJ	Wash.	WA
Idaho	ID	N. Mex.[17]	NM	W. Va.[17]	WV
Ill.	IL	N.Y.	NY	Wis.	WI
Ind.	IN	N.C.	NC	Wyo.	WY
Iowa	IA	N. Dak.[17]	ND		

[16] The standard abbreviations are commonly used in lists, bibliographies, indexes, and so on.

[17] A geographic abbreviation composed of more than single initials has a space after an internal period.

Folding and inserting letters

S63   The type of fold depends on the size of the stationery and the size of the envelope.

A. Standard 8 1/2 x 11 inch stationery and a business envelope (No. 10):

Turn up the bottom third of the page and make a crease. Turn down the top of the page to within 3/8 inch of the first crease. Then make a second crease. Insert the letter into the envelope second crease first with the short fold to the back of the envelope.

B. Standard 8 1/2 x 11 inch stationery and a small envelope:

Turn up the bottom of the page to within 3/8 inch of the top edge and make a crease. Bring the right edge a little less than one third of the way to the left and make a crease. Bring the left edge to within 3/8 inch of the right crease and make another crease. Insert the left crease into the envelope first with the short final fold to the back of the envelope.

C. Monarch (7 1/4" x 10 1/2") stationery with appropriate No. 7 envelope:

Follow the procedure under *A* .

D. Baronial (5 1/2" x 8 1/2") stationery with a No. 6 3/4 envelope:

If the stationery is 5 1/2 inch width, follow the procedure under *A* .

If the stationery is 8 1/2 inch width, bring the right edge a little less than one third of the way to the left and make a crease. Bring the left edge to within 3/8 inch of the right crease and make another crease. Insert the left crease into the envelope first with the short final fold to the back of the envelope.

Forms of address

S64 The forms listed below are the correct ones for addressing letters to government officials, diplomats, clergy and religious, education officials, professional people, military personnel, individuals, couples, and organizations. (Wherever *Ms.* is used, *Mrs.* or *Miss* may be substituted.)

GOVERNMENT OFFICIALS

president, U.S.

The President	Mr./Madam President:
The White House	Dear Mr./Madam President:
Washington, DC 20500	

former president, U.S.

The Honorable Lee A. Roe	Dear Mr./Ms. Roe:
(local address)	

vice president, U.S.

The Vice President	Dear Mr./Madam Vice President:
United States Senate	
Washington, DC 20510	

or

The Honorable Lee A. Roe
Vice President of the United States
Washington, DC 20510

cabinet member

The Honorable Lee A. Roe	Sir:
Secretary of (department)	Dear Mr./Madam Secretary:
Washington, DC (ZIP code)	

or

The Secretary of (department)
Washington, DC (ZIP code)

S

U.S. senator

The Honorable Lee A. Roe   Dear Senator Roe:
United States Senate
Washington, DC 20510

or

The Honorable Lee A. Roe
United States Senate
(local address)

U.S. representative

The Honorable Lee A. Roe   Sir:
House of Representatives   Dear Representative Roe:
Washington, DC 20515   Dear Mr./Ms. Roe:

or

The Honorable Lee A. Roe
Representative in Congress
(local address)

chief justice, U.S. supreme court

The Chief Justice of the   Sir:
     United States   Dear Mr./Madam Chief Justice:
Washington, DC 20543   Madam:

or

The Chief Justice
The Supreme Court
Washington, DC 20543

associate justice, U.S. supreme court

Mr./Madam Justice Roe   Sir/Madam:
The Supreme Court   Dear Mr./Madam Justice Roe:
Washington, DC 20543   Dear Mr./Ms. Justice:

judge (federal, state, local court)

The Honorable Lee A. Roe   Dear Judge Roe:
Judge of the Court of
     (name of court)
(local address)

governor

The Honorable Lee A. Roe
Governor of (state)
(state capital, state, ZIP code)

Sir/Madam:
Dear Governor Roe:

state senator

The Honorable Lee A. Roe
The State Senate
(state capital, state, ZIP code)

Sir/Madam:
Dear Senator Roe:

state representative or assembly member

The Honorable Lee A. Roe
House of Representatives
  (*or* The State Assembly)
(state capital, state, ZIP code)

Sir/Madam:
Dear Mr./Ms. Roe:

mayor

The Honorable Lee A. Roe
Mayor of (city)
(city, state, ZIP code)

Sir/Madam:
Dear Mayor Roe:
Dear Mr./Ms. Mayor:

or

The Mayor of the City of (city)
(city, state, ZIP code)

district attorney

The Honorable Lee A. Roe
District Attorney
(address)

Dear District Attorney Roe:
Dear Mr./Ms. Roe:

DIPLOMATS

secretary general, United Nations

His/Her Excellency Lee A. Roe
Secretary of the United Nations
United Nations Plaza
New York, NY 10017

Excellency:
Dear Mr./Madam/Madame[18]
  Secretary General

[18] *Madame* is the correct form for a foreigner; *Madam* is the proper form for an American.

ambassador to U.S.

His/Her Excellency Lee A. Roe   Excellency:
Ambassador of (country)   Dear Mr./Madame[19]
(address)   Ambassador:

minister to U.S.

The Honorable Lee A. Roe   Sir/Madame:[19]
Minister of (department)   Dear Mr./Madame[19] Minister:
(address)

ambassador, U.S.

The Honorable Lee A. Roe   Sir/Madam:
American Ambassador   Dear Mr./Madam Amassador:
    (*or* The Ambassador of
the United States of America)
(address)

chargé d'affaires, U.S.

The Honorable Lee A. Roe   Dear Sir/Madam:
United States Chargé d'Affaires   Dear Mr./Ms. Roe:
(foreign address of U.S. embassy)

ROMAN CATHOLIC CLERGY AND RELIGIOUS

pope

His Holiness the Pope   Your Holiness:
    Most Holy Father:

or

His Holiness Pope John Paul II
Vatican City
00187 Rome
ITALY

cardinal

His Eminence John   Your Eminence:
    Cardinal Foley   Dear Cardinal Foley:
Archbishop of (place)
(address)

---

[19] *Madame* is the correct form for a foreigner; *Madam* is the proper form for an American.

apostolic delegate

The Most Reverend	Your Excellency:
James R. Hoff	Dear Archbishop Hoff:
Archbishop of (place)	
The Apostolic Delegate	
(address)	

archbishop and bishop

The Most Reverend	Your Excellency:
James R. Hoff	Dear Archbishop
Archbishop (*or* Bishop)	(*or* Bishop) Hoff:
of (place)	
(address)	

monsignor

The Right Reverend	Right Reverend Monsignor:
Monsignor Paul B. Lee	Dear Monsignor Lee:
(address)	

abbot

The Right Reverend	Right Reverend Abbot:
Paul Lee, O.S.B.	Dear Reverend Abbot:
Abbot of (place)	
(address)	

provincial superior

The Very Reverend	Very Reverend Father Fox:
Neil J. Fox, S.J.	Dear Father Provincial:
(address)	

priest

The Reverend	Reverend Father:
Neil J. Fox, O.F.M.	Dear Father Fox:
(address)	Dear Father:

mother superior

The Reverend Mother	Reverend Mother:
Superior	Dear Reverend Mother:
(address)	

or

Reverend Mother Mary
Burke, O.S.U.
(address)

751

sister

Sister Mary Jane, O.S.F.   Dear Sister Mary Jane:
(address)

or

Sister Alice Bihn, R.S.M.   Dear Sister Alice Bihn:
(address)   Dear Sister:

brother

Brother Anselm, O.S.B.   Dear Brother Anselm:
(address)

or

Brother Anton Bain, S.V.D.   Dear Brother Bain:
(address)   Dear Brother:

permanent deacon

Rev. Mr. David T. Pahl   Dear Mr. Pahl:
(address)

or

Mr. David T. Pahl
(address)

JEWISH CLERGY

rabbi with doctor's degree

Rabbi F. M. Birnbaum, D.D.   Dear Rabbi Birnbaum:
(address)   Dear Dr. Birnbaum:

or

Dr. F. M. Birnbaum
(address)

rabbi without doctor's degree

Rabbi F. M. Birnbaum   Dear Rabbi Birnbaum:
(address)

S

PROTESTANT CLERGY

Episcopal bishop

The Right Reverend
    Marc T. Clifford
Bishop of (place)
(address)

Right Reverend Sir:
Dear Bishop Clifford:

Episcopal dean

The Very Reverend
    Allen C. Wise
Dean of (place)
(address)

Very Reverend Sir:
Dear Dean Wise:

Lutheran bishop

The Reverend James R.
    Hicks, Bishop

Dear Bishop Hicks:

or

The Reverend James R. Hicks
Bishop, (synod)
(address)

Methodist bishop

The Reverend Carl W. Lukas
Bishop of (place)
(address)

Reverend Sir:
Dear Bishop Lukas:

or

Bishop Carl W. Lukas
(address)

minister with doctor's degree

The Reverend Dr. Lee A. Roe

Reverend Sir:
Dear Dr. Roe:

or

The Reverend Lee A. Roe, D.D.
(address)

minister without doctor's degree

The Reverend Lee A. Roe
(address)

Reverend Sir:
Dear Mr./Ms. Roe:

EDUCATION OFFICALS

president of a college or university

Lee A. Roe, Ph.D.   Dear Dr. Roe:
President, (name of college)   Dear President Roe:
(address)

or

Dr. Lee A. Roe
President, (name of college)
(address)

or

President Lee A. Roe
(name of college)
(address)

dean of a college or university

Lee A. Roe, Ph. D.   Dear Dean Roe:
                                      Dear Dr. Roe:

or

Dr. Lee A. Roe
Dean, (name of school or division)
(name of college)
(address)

or

Dean Lee A. Roe
(name of school or division)
(name of college)
(address)

professor

Professor Lee A. Roe   Dear Professor Roe:
Department of (subject)   Dear Dr. Roe:
(name of college)   Dear Mr./Ms. Roe:
(address)

or

Lee A. Roe, Ph.D.

or

Dr. Lee A. Roe
Department (*or* Professor) of (subject)
(name of college)
(address)

or

Prof. Lee A. Roe
Department of (subject)
(name of college)
(address)

superintendent of schools

Mr./Ms./Dr. Lee A Roe   Dear Mr./Ms./Dr. Roe:
Superintendent of (city) schools
(address)

member of board of education

Mr./Ms. Lee A. Roe   Dear Mr./Ms. Roe:
Member, (name of city)
    Board of Education
(address)

principal

Mr./Ms./Dr. Lee A. Roe   Dear Mr./Ms./Dr. Roe:
Principal, (name of school)
(address)

PROFESSIONALS

lawyers

Mr./Ms. Lee A. Roe   Dear Mr./Ms. Roe:
Attorney-at-Law
(address)

or

Lee A. Roe, Esq.[20]
(address)

S

---

[20] Do not use a courtesy title such as Ms. or Dr. before a name if a title follows the name.

physicians and others with doctoral degrees

Dr. Lee A. Roe   Dear Dr. Roe:
(address)

or

Lee A. Roe, M.D.[21]
(address)

MILITARY PERSONNEL

army (USA), air force (USAF), and marine corps (USMC) officers

Major General Lee A. Roe, USA   Sir:
                                     Dear General Roe:

or

Maj. Gen. Lee A. Roe, USA
(address)

or

navy (USN) and coast guard (USCG) officers

Commander Lee A. Roe, USN   Sir:
                                     Dear Commander Roe:

or

Cmdr. Lee A. Roe, USN
(address)
                                     [For officers below the rank of
                                     commander, use *Dear Mr./Ms.*]

enlisted personnel

Private Lee A. Roe, USA   Dear Private Roe:

or

Pvt. Lee A. Roe, USA
(address)

---

[21] Do not use a courtesy title such as Ms. or Dr. before a name if a title follows the name.

Seaman Lee A. Roe, USCG   Dear Seaman Roe:

or

Smn. Lee A. Roe, USCG
(address)

INDIVIDUALS

woman—title preference unknown

Ms. Lee A. Roe   Dear Ms. Roe:

or

Lee A. Roe   Dear Lee Roe:
(address)

individual— name known, gender unknown

Lee A. Roe   Dear Lee Roe:
(address)

individual name and gender unknown

(title of individual)   Sir or Madam:
(name of organization)   Dear Sir or Madam:
(address)

two men

Mr. Lee A. Roe   Gentlemen:
Mr. James P. Kyle   Dear Mr. Roe and Mr. Kyle:
(address)   Dear Messrs. Roe and Kyle:

two women

Ms. Lee A. Roe   Dear Ms. Roe and Ms. Hunt:
Ms. Mary L. Hunt   Dear Mses. (*or* Mss.) Roe and Hunt:
(address)

or

Mrs. Lee A. Roe   Dear Mrs. Roe and Mrs. Hunt:
Mrs. Mary L. Hunt   Dear Mesdames
(address)   (*or* Mmes.) Roe and Hunt:

or

Miss Lee A. Roe   Dear Miss Roe and Miss Hunt:
Miss Mary L. Hunt   Dear Misses Roe and Hunt:
(address)

or

Miss (*or* Ms.) Lee A. Roe   Dear Miss (*or* Ms.) Roe
Mrs. Mary L. Hunt   and Mrs. Hunt:
(address)

COUPLES

married couple— no special title

Mr. and Mrs. John A. Roe   Dear Mr. and Mrs. Roe:
(address)

married couple— husband with special title

Dr. and Mrs. John A. Roe   Dear Dr. and Mrs. Roe:
(address)

married couple— wife with special title

Dr. Jane H. Roe   Dear Dr. and Mr. Roe:
Mr. John S. Roe
(address)

married couple— each with special title

Col. John S. Roe, USMC   Dear Colonel and Dr. Roe:
Dr. Jane H. Roe
(address)

[The woman's name may be placed before the man's.]

married couple—wife retains maiden name

Mr. John S. Roe   Dear Mr. Roe and Ms. (*or* Miss) Alt:
(address)   Ms. (*or* Miss) Jane H. Alt

ORGANIZATIONS

organization of men

(name of organization)   Gentlemen:
(address)

organization of women

(name of organization)   Mesdames:
(address)   Ladies:

organization of men and women

(name of organization)	Ladies and Gentlemen:
(address)	Gentlemen and Ladies:
	Gentlemen:

or

Sales Manager	Sir or Madam:
(or other title)	Madam or Sir:
(name of organization)	Dear Sir or Madam:
(address)	Dear Madam or Sir:

Social-Business letters

S65 There are three types of social-business letters:

A. Letters between high-level executives on matters beyond ordinary business, such as corporate policy or issues of social responsibility.

B. Official letters of praise, concern, or condolence written to someone in or outside of the organization; for example, a letter to an employee retiring after years of faithful service.

C. Letters to business associates in or outside of the company on purely social matters.

S66 Social-business letters differ in form from typical business letters in several ways:

A. The inside address is placed at the bottom of the letter, beginning on the fifth line below the writer's typed name or title (whichever is last).

B. The salutation is followed by a comma rather than a colon. In less formal letters, the person's first name alone may be used in the salutation.[22]

C. In less formal letters the full signature is typed but the first name alone is signed.

---

[22] The full name, of course, is typed in the inside address.

D. Reference initials and notations related to copies, enclosures, and so on, are ordinarily omitted.

Personal letters

S67   Personal letters are a form of correspondence dealing with non-business matters.[23] Letters of apology, condolence, invitation, praise, thanks, and continuing correspondence between friends are typical personal letters.

S68   Personal letters should be typed or written on white or light-colored stationery. The paper may be a single unfolded sheet varying in size from 5 1/2 x 7 inches to 8 1/2 x 11 inches, or the stationery may be in the form of a booklet.

S69   It is advisable to use a dark typewriter ribbon or blue, black, or blue-black ink.

S70   Letters should be clean—free of smudges, visible erasures, mistakes, crossouts, corrections, and strike-overs.

S71   Typewritten letters have indented or blocked paragraphs. (There is a line-space between paragraphs of block-form letters.) Handwritten letters have indented paragraphs. See L5 and model in S80.

S72   The letter is centered on the paper so that the margins are balanced around it. The margins should never be less than half an inch wide; they may, of course, be wider if the message is short.

S73   Writing should not be crowded at the bottom of the page. If necessary, start another page rather than destroy the appearance of the letter by cramped writing.

s

---

[23] See S1, S65.

S74 With booklet paper and a message long enough to run four pages, start at page 1 and go straight through to page 4. When the message is shorter, write on page 1; on pages 1 and 3; or on pages 1, 3, and 4.

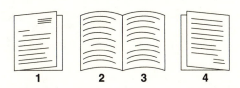

S75 It is customary to begin the letter with a heading in the upper right-hand corner. Write your street address on the first line; the city, state, and ZIP code on the second line; and the date on the last. The date alone is sufficient if the recipient is certain to know your address or if the address is printed on the stationery.

S76 The recipient's address (inside address) is not part of the heading of the letter.

S77 The salutations *Dear Friend, Dear Miss, Sir,* or *Madam* are inappropriate.

S78 A comma, not a colon, follows the salutation.

S79 The complimentary close should be in harmony with the salutation and tone of the letter.

A. *Sincerely yours* and *Yours sincerely* are the most formal.

B. *Cordially yours, Affectionately yours, Your loving daughter,* and similar expressions, suggest various degrees of affection and intimacy. A thank-you note may close with *Gratefully yours.*

S

S80   Model personal letter:

Ozark Park
Kimberling City, MO 65807
June 21, 1991

Dear Bob,

     The directions you gave us for getting to the Park were helpful, all right. If we hadn't had them, we might find ourselves in Arkansas now — and still going. The detours we had to make were many, as you said, and rough; but we got along without trouble and arrived on time.

     Will you do me a favor, Bob? Phone Mother and tell her we're all well. I should have written a letter to her yesterday but was too late for the mail. If she asks whether there's anything we want, tell her there is — some candy. Not chocolates, though; the weather is too warm.

     Be sure to let us know when you're coming. We'll meet you at the train.

                   Yours truly,
                   Tom

S

Letters of application and résumés

S81   For most unskilled or part-time jobs, an individual applies in person to the personnel manager or to whoever does the hiring. For most skilled jobs a two-part written application is necessary: a letter of application and a résumé.

Letters of Application

S82   The primary objective of a letter of application is to interest the prospective employer enough to schedule the applicant for an interview.

S83   If possible, the letter should be directed to a specific person rather than to a company or to an office. A letter addressed to an individual is more likely to get results.

If you do not know the name of the personnel manager or the person in charge of hiring, you should call the company or check the appropriate directory. If necessary, confirm the spelling of the person's name before writing.

S84   There are two kinds of letters of application:

A. Letters for solicited jobs. These letters are in response to specific advertised job vacancies. Through notices in newspapers, in journals, on bulletin boards, and so on, an employer is actively looking for personnel.

B. Letters prospecting for a job. These job-inquiry letters are sent without a known job opening. They are written asking for consideration if and when a position becomes available.

S85   Begin a soliciting letter by mentioning the job you are applying for and by identifying your source for this particular opening (ad, posted notice, and so on). Include the date of any advertisement. If someone suggested that you apply, include that information. Mention why you are interested in working with this company.

s

S86   Begin a prospecting letter by stating what position you are interested in and why you are interested in working with this particular company. Mention any company characteristics or policies that you admire.

S87   The body of the letter should summarize your qualifications for the job. Mention any special courses, training, or experience that qualify you for this particular job. (Summarize or comment on these; do not merely repeat what is in the résumé.) Include anything that makes you distinctive from other candidates for the job. Be sure to respond to the particular concerns in the advertisement.

S88   Be specific; generalities do not impress. Be positive, but do not exaggerate your abilities or accomplishments.

S89   The conclusion should refer to your résumé and indicate when you are available for an interview. Give precise information on how you can be reached. List any dates and times when you will not be available.

S90   A letter of application should be typed on good-quality paper and be free of errors and noticeable corrections. It should be brief, not exceeding one page, and be centered on the page. The style should be business-like but natural, clear, and concrete.

S91   A letter of application follows the conventions of a formal business letter.[24]

S

---

[24] See S1-64.

(11 line spaces)

506 St. Antoine St.
Detroit, MI 48226
April 11, 1990

(4 line spaces)

Roy F. Pirnot
Manager Editor
Daily Tribune
210 E. 3rd St.
Royal Oak, MI 48067

(1 line space)

Dear Mr. Pirnot:

(1 line space)

In response to your notice of April 6 to the U. of D. Placement Office, I would like to be considered for the position of editorial assistant.

(1 line space)

I will graduate next month from the University of Detroit with a major in journalism and mass communications. For the past three years I have been on the staff of the Varsity News (student newspaper). I have also worked for the Grosse Pointe News and Dearborn Today Magazine. My experience with these publications has provided me with important skills and has taught me how to adapt to different situations. With my educational background and this experience, I sincerely believe I am qualified for the position of editorial assistant.

(1 line space)

My résumé is enclosed. I can be reached at 961-8076 after 3:00 P.M. on weekdays and can arrange my schedule for an interview at your convenience. I appreciate your consideration and look forward to hearing from you.

(1 line space)

Sincerely,

(3 line spaces)

Paul C. Lucas

(1 line space)

Enclosure

S92   For many temporary or part-time jobs, a letter of application is sufficient. For full-time employment a résumé should be included with a letter of application.

Résumés

S93   Whereas a letter of application presents a summary of qualifications and indicates your interest in a particular job, a résumé is basically a list of accomplishments.

S94   A résumé[25] is an essential part of most job applications. It presents those items from your personal history that are relevant to the job you are seeking. It does so in a well-organized manner, in correct language, and in an effective format.

The customary divisions of a résumé are identification, education, work experience, personal data, and references.

IDENTIFICATION

S95   Type your name, home address (and, if appropriate, your school or business address), and telephone number(s).

S96   If you intend to use the résumé for one particular job application (and not for various purposes), you may include the heading "Position Sought:" below your name and address and identify the job you are seeking.[26]

EDUCATION

S97   List significant data from your educational history. Include the following:

names of schools attended, with dates

s

---

[25] A résumé is sometimes referred to as a *personal data sheet* or a *vita* (from the Latin word meaning "life").

[26] Whether or not the position is mentioned in the résumé, it is always mentioned in the letter of application.

[If you have graduated from college, do not mention your high school unless there were outstanding achievements.]

date of graduation
scholarships, honors
courses related to the job application
grades [but only if they are above average]
special workshops, training
co-curricular activities related to the job application
[In some cases these activities come under Work Experience.]

This education information is particularly important if you do not have much work experience.

WORK EXPERIENCE

S98 The work-experience section lists jobs you have had that show your qualifications for the present position. You may mention the most recent job first and then work back in time, or you may mention the most important job first and work to the least important. For each job mention the following:

job title
dates of employment
employer
specific responsibilities
accomplishments

Include in this section volunteer work, community service, and other activities related to the position you seek.

S99 Be positive in your presentation, but do not offer evaluations of your accomplishments. Instead, be objective; let your accomplishments speak for themselves.

S100 Use action verbs, words like *planned, assisted* (rather than *duties included*) in your presentation.

S

PERSONAL DATA

S101 The personal-data section includes birth date, special interests or activities, social skills, work habits, memberships in clubs and organizations. Do not include height, weight, color of hair unless such considerations bear directly on the job sought. Since there are laws prohibiting job discrimination on the basis of sex, race, religion, and marital status, none of these items should be mentioned unless they bear directly on the job qualification. Ordinarily do not include a photograph.

REFERENCES

S102 The reference section lists the names, addresses, and telephone numbers of three people who have agreed to endorse your application. (Always get permission from those whose names you want to use.) Include their positions if these suggest your qualifications for the job.

S103 Keep in mind that potential employers will want precise information from your references on the quality of your work, your attitude and reliability, and so on. Accordingly, select people who will strongly endorse you.

S104 Although it is better to list the names and addresses of references, you may simply state "References are available on request."

FORM

S105 There is no single accepted form for a résumé. There are, however, some general guidelines. The résumé is typed in block style with major sections single-spaced and a line-space between sections. It is arranged on the page to provide quick and easy reading, and should not exceed one page unless there are extensive qualifications that need to be mentioned. The models on the next page illustrate many of the common characteristics of the résumé.

S

Norman X. Baxter

ADDRESS   Home   Business
            2551 Fenwick Rd.   Microtek, Inc.
            Cleveland, Ohio 44118   8370 Dow Circle
            932-4548   Cleveland, Ohio 44136
                                          234-8040

POSITION SOUGHT
  Computer programer

RÉSUMÉ
Paul C. Lucas
506 St. Antoine St.
Detroit, MI 48226
961-8076

Education   University of Detroit
1986-90   Bachelor of Arts degree, May 1990
                 Major: Journalism and Mass Communications
                 Minor: Political Science and Economics
                 Grade point average: 3.6
                 Dean's List: 1987-90

Experience
1988-90   Worked part-time as a reporter for Grosse
                 Pointe News.
                 On staff of the Varsity News (student newspaper
                 at the University of Detroit); wrote feature
                 articles and edited.
1986-87   Worked during two summers for Dearborn Today
                   Magazine; edited copy and proofread.
1985-86   Worked part-time at Waldenbooks, shelved and
                   inventoried books.

Personal Data   Born (January 5, 1968) and raised in Detroit.
                 Interested in fiction writing and photography.
                 Type 60 words per minute and have experience
                   with word-processors.
                 Wrote short stories for high-school literary
                   magazine.
                 Play piano and guitar.

References   Arthur B. Sax, Editor
                 Grosse Pointe News
                 96 Kercheval
                 Grosse Pointe Farms, MI 48236
                 882-6900

                 Dr. Alice J. Merkle
                 Smith Media Center
                 University of Detroit
                 4001 W. McNichols
                 Detroit, MI 48221
                 927-1173

S

S106 Proofread your résumé. In fact, it is sensible to proof-read the résumé several times. Errors make the writer appear careless and irresponsible and may result in a job lost.

S107 Never send a résumé without a job-application letter.

S108 It is courteous to send a brief thank-you letter a week or so after an interview to express your appreciation and your continuing interest in the job. In addition, such a letter will make a good impression and will keep your name in the mind of the interviewer.

Memos

S109 Unlike business letters, business memoranda (memos) are used to communicate *within* an organization. Although a memo may be long, most them are brief, conveying information on a single page on a specific topic.

S110 The heading *MEMORANDUM* appears at the top of the page. If the heading is not printed on the stationery, it is typed (ordinarily centered) in all-capital letters on the seventh line from the top on plain paper or on the third line below a letterhead.

S111 The memo is designed for quick assimilation. In place of certain formalities of a business letter (return address, inside address, salutation, complimentary close), a memo heading consists of the name of the addressee, the writer's name, the subject, and the date of the communication.

S112 The guide words are typed beginning on the third line below the heading *MEMORANDUM*. Each guide word is typed in all-capital letters and followed by a colon.

S113 All entries following guide words are blocked left (that is, aligned vertically) two spaces after the longest guide word and colon.

S114 The *To* and *From* lines contain the name and department or position of the individuals. Ordinarily personal titles (*Mr., Ms., Mrs., Miss*) are not used.

S115 The person sending the memo may sign his initials at the end of the line where his name appears.

S116 The subject line should be as precise as possible. A line such as "Sales Figures" is too general; "Declining Sales Figures for March 1990" is more meaningful.

S117 Ordinarily skip one line between guide-word entries.

S118 The memo begins on the third line below the last guideline entry.

S119 The body of the memo is typed single-spaced, with a line-space between paragraphs. Paragraphs may be blocked or indented.

S120 The first paragraph of a memo is devoted to a brief, clear presentation of the issue at hand and any conclusions.[27] Any succeeding paragraphs provide additional details, reasons, and so on.

S121 The writer's name or initials (with signature above) may be typed on the fourth line below the message. This is frequently done when the sender's name does not appear in the heading.

S122 Any initials, enclosure notation, or copy notation placed below the memo follow the format of a business letter.[28]

S

---

[27] Even though the subject is mentioned in the subject line, it should also be mentioned in the first paragraph of the memo. Clarity is essential.
[28] See S45-52.

S123 Model memorandum:

(6 line spaces)

MEMORANDUM

(2 line spaces)

TO: ARMCO Employees

(1 line space)

FROM: Sydney L. Bermbaugh, Maintenance Supervisor

(1 line space)

DATE: May 1, 1990

(1 line space)

SUBJECT: Parking Lost Resurfacing

(2 line spaces)

The reconstruction and resurfacing of portions of the main parking lot will begin on the morning of May 7 and should be completed by the afternoon of May 11.

(1 line space)

This repair work means the temporary closing of the entrance off Milan Avenue and the unavailability of parking spaces 12 through 30 and 72 through 95. Alternate parking for those affected will be available in designated areas at the back of the Galaxy Publishing Co. parking lot.

(1 line space)

Thank you for your cooperation as we continue to do battle with settling ground and potholes.

S

Word processing

In general

T1 A word processor is a computer program that provides flexibility and efficiency in writing and revising. Original material can be deleted or relocated; new material can readily be inserted. With any of these changes, the program instantly reformats the text so that there is always a "clean" copy. A word processor also facilitates storage and retrieval of information and simplifies some mechanical procedures.

T2 Computer science has its own distinctive terminology. A few basic terms are described here.

Hardware is the equipment used in computer work: keyboard, screen, central processing unit, disk drives, printer, and so on.

Software is the programs that run the hardware. The software determines whether the hardware will process words, organize files, play games, and so on.

A *word processor* is a computer with a software program facilitating writing.

A *disk* (*disc*) is a small plastic or metal plate on which information is stored magnetically. It contains the programs that run a computer and the stored text of documents produced on a computer.

To *boot* is to start up a computer or to load the first piece of software that starts a computer.

A *document* is anything prepared on a computer, such as a letter, an essay, a spreadsheet, or a picture.

T
U

A *cursor* is a blinking marker on a computer screen that indicates the point where the writer is working.

Wraparound is a term indicating the automatic placement of any text extending beyond the right margin onto the next line.

Memory is the capacity of a computer to store information. This information comes from the software program being used and the document being created.

Save is the command directing a computer to make a permanent copy of a document. Until a document is saved, it can be lost by a computer shut-down, a move to another program, or a power surge or failure.

Backup refers to the practice of copying a file (or set of files) to a second or backup (floppy) disk in order to protect against losing the file and hours of hard work.

A *byte* is a basic unit of storage. Large amounts of memory are indicated by kilobytes (1,024 bytes), megabytes (1,048,576 bytes), ans so on. A disk that can hold 500K bytes, for example, is capable of storing approximately 500,000 characters or close to one thousand pages of information.

Hard copy is a printout of a document.

A *database* is a collection of information so organized that a computer program can quickly select pieces of data.

DOS is an acronym for disk operating system.

A *modem* is a device for converting data from a computer or a terminal to data that can be transmitted over communication lines or, in reverse process, for converting data from communication lines to a computer or terminal.

An *on-line* service is a database service accessed through a modem.

A *daisy-wheel* printer makes fully formed characters one at a time by rotating a circular print element made up of a series of spokes.

A *dot matrix* printer makes characters out of combinations of very small dots.

T
U

774

A *laser* printer is a non-impact device that makes characters by means of a laser beam.

A *surge protector* helps avoid damage—and data loss—from the normal peaks and valleys in the flow of electricity, as when heavy equipment uses the same electric line.

Selection and use

T3 In choosing to work with a word processor, select software before hardware. Then choose hardware that is compatible with the selected software.

Selecting software

T4 In order to select the proper software program, you should know exactly what features you need for your work. Typical concerns in selecting a program are the following:

Does the program have underlining, boldface, italics, small capitals?

Does it have all required alphabets, accent marks, math symbols?

Does it check spelling?

Does it handle equations, illustrations, computer graphics?

Does it generate tables and lists?

Does it permit single-spaced and double-spaced text on the same page (necessary with some styles of block quotations and for pages with footnotes)?

Does it automatically place footnotes on the correct page?

Does it alphabetize a list?

Does it permit columns?

Does it locate selected words or symbols and change them?

T
U

Does it measure space in inches or characters or in both? If it provides only proportional spacing, it may cause complications with certain types of formatting.[1]

Does the program automatically renumber a sequence running through a text (for example, footnote superscripts) when a new number is inserted into that sequence?

Does the program permit working with several documents on the screen at the same time and transferring material from one to the other?

T5 Even if the program does all that you want, does it perform these functions quickly and efficiently?

T6 It is important to select a word processor with a good tutorial. A considerable effort is always required to learn a new program, especially one of the better and more complicated ones. This effort can be considerably shortened by a good tutorial program.

T7 If at all possible, work with different software programs before you commit yourself to any one of them. Good word-processor programs include WordPerfect, Nota Bene, Word Star, and Microsoft Word. Because new software programs are continually being developed, you need to conduct a careful investigation. Check a bookstore or library for a current writer's and buyer's guide to word-processing software.

Selecting hardware

T8 Choose hardware that is compatible with the selected software. Various programs will work only on certain computers and with certain printers. Also make sure that your equipment can be upgraded with any new technology; in this way you can ward off obsolescence. In

---

[1] Not all word-processing programs readily produce the spacing required by some research-paper formats; for example, the spacing between ellipsis points, the spacing between various elements in a bibliography entry. In such cases, compensate as best you can to approximate proper format.

T
U

making these decisions, consult someone knowledge-able in the field.

T9 In selecting a printer, keep in mind any quality require-ments for the finished product. A dot matrix printer does not produce a dark print-like quality unless the double-strike feature is used. A daisy-wheel printer pro-vides "letter quality" printouts. Laser printers produce outstanding copy and are excellent for graphics.

T10 Make certain that the printer is able to produce all required alphabets, accent marks, and math symbols and that its typeface has true descenders (that is, the letters *g, j, p, q, y* descend below the baseline of the rest of the type).

T11 Once you have selected hardware and software, read the manuals and systematically learn how to use the equipment. In other words, make the most of the re-sources at hand.

Writing the first draft

T12 As you begin the first draft, it is helpful to set up a separate file for different components; for example, thesis-1, outline-1, text-1. (When you are ready to re-vise, create a second set of files; for example, thesis-2, outline-2, text-2. In this way you can combine and revise the second set without losing the first set.)

T13 A word-processing program makes outlining an easy task. You can efficiently insert new divisions, rearrange and delete others. Unlike corrections added to a hand-written or typed outline, you can make major changes on a computer and still have an uncluttered copy.

T14 To guard against accidental loss of data, save material after every page or two. Periodically put material on a backup disk or tape.[2]

---

[2] If you are using a mainframe computer, frequently save your mate-rial. In doing this, you are putting your work on a tape or a disk in the mainframe and will not lose it if the computer crashes.

T
U

T15   Make a hard copy of any draft. First of all, you will need it when you revise. Secondly, disks are vulnerable to malfunction or damage;[3] a hard copy is relatively permanent.

Revising

T16   One of the outstanding features of a word processor is that it simplifies revision. The composition of most documents can be done as quickly on a typewriter, but revision is a different matter. The computer, on the other hand, invites revision. Changes can be made very simply, and the result is a "clean" copy—quite unlike pages of tediously handwritten or typed corrections.

T17   Obviously there will be some ongoing revision as the first draft is typed. Wording and phrasing may be changed, ideas rearranged, and so on. For a major revision it is advisable to run off a double-spaced hard copy and make all changes there.

One reason for working from a hard copy is that it allows you to scan the entire document easily and to examine larger sections than you can on the twenty-or-so lines of a computer screen. It is also true that mechanical errors such as punctuation and spelling stand out more clearly on a printed page. Finally, there is danger that in revising entirely on the computer you might erase some earlier versions that you would later like to use.

T18   When all the changes are made on the hard copy, you can return to the keyboard and easily make all corrections: rearrange sentences, paragraphs, insert new material, delete material, add connectives, and so on.

---

[3] Disks can be ruined by being too close to a magnetic field (such as the speakers in a stereo or the screen on a personal computer) or by being exposed to excessive heat or moisture.

T19 Always keep successive hard-copy drafts until you have finished the paper. You may decide, after all, to return to an earlier version.

T20 If you work without a hard copy and change a paragraph or an example while working at the keyboard, move the original material to the end of the composition and store it there until you have have completed the paper. Do not erase anything until the paper is completed. It is possible, for instance, that the rejected material may be useful in another part of the paper.

T21 Software programs have special features. You may be able to check spelling,[4] length of sentences, repetition of particular words or phrases, the number of monosyllabic and polysyllabic words, clichés, weak verbs (like *is*, *was*), grammar problems, and so on. Many of these editorial changes may be made with the text on the screen.

Printing the final copy

T22 Specific requirements for the final copy should be double-checked: margins, spacing, running head, page numbers, title, bibliography format, and so on.[5]

T23 Do not justify the right-hand margin unless your instructor allows it.

T24 Because many word processors have propotional spacing, it is difficult to observe the precise spacing requirements of various style sheets. If lines are justified, there is a further distortion (this is one reason why most

---

[4] Spelling checkers will not identify words spelled correctly but used incorrectly (for example, *its* and *it's*, *their* and *there*). Even with a spelling checker you need to proofread for spelling errors.

[5] For guidelines in preparing the final copy of an essay, see M87-98. For directives and models on the format and documentation of a research paper, see N114 (MLA), N123 (APA), N140 (University of Chicago).

T
U

instructors do not favor a justified margin). When you are asked, for example, to skip two spaces after periods, you should adopt a consistent approximation. Particular care is necessary in preparing bibliographies.

T25 Use a standard typeface with good legibility. Do not use script or gothic type.

T26 Good paper and a quality printer enhance the appearance of the final product. The paper should be sixteen- or twenty-pound weight, not ordinary computer paper. Sheet-fed paper or razor-cut continuous forms provide the best results. (Perforated continuous-forms paper leaves ragged edges.)

T27 Check the ribbon to see that it makes a dark impression. The ribbon on a dot-matrix printer wears out quickly.

T28 Show your instructor a sample printout to see if both the printing and paper are acceptable. Printouts should have both uppercase and lowercase letters (not just capitals), descenders (*g,j,p,q,y* descending below the baseline of the rest of the type), and enough dots per character-space for easy readability.

T29 With continuous-forms computer paper, make certain that you separate the pages and tear off the tractor feed. It is very disconcerting for anyone to receive a paper that has not been properly assembled.

T30 Proofread the printed copy. If corrections cannot be done so that they are practically undetectable, return to the computer and print out the necessary pages.

T31 Store all important documents on disk.[6] Label them accurately and, if necessary, keep a list of the file names.

T
U

---

[6] Take care of disks. The information on them can be scrambled by exposure to magnetic fields, moisture, or excessive heat.

Glossary of usage

This glossary is a guide to the proper use of words and phrases frequently misused. Its scope is necessarily limited. If you cannot locate a particular word or phrase here, begin by checking the index. For further information on these words and phrases and on others not discussed in this book, consult a dictionary.

a, an

Use the indefinite article *a* before words beginning with a consonant or a consonant sound: *a controversy, a hymn, a university, a year.* Use the indefinite article *an* before words beginning with a vowel or vowel sound: *an enemy, an heir, an honorable peace, an orange.* Although *a* is preferred before words beginning with *h* in an unaccented syllable (*a historical event*), *an* is also acceptable (*an historical event*). The form of the indefinite article before abbreviations and acronyms depends on how the abbreviation or acronym is pronounced: *She received an M.A. degree. That is a NASA project.*

affect, effect

Although either word can function as a noun or a verb, *affect* is almost always used as a verb while *effect* is regularly used as a noun. As a verb, *affect* means "to influence": *Her behavior affected my decision.* As a noun, *affect* means "a feeling or an emotion": *One can learn much about affect from behavior.* (*Affect* can also mean "to pretend": *He affected the mannerisms of British aristocracy.*) As a noun, *effect* means "a consequence or a result": *One effect of the drought was higher prices.* As a verb, *effect* means "to bring about": *The accident effected a complete change in her behavior.* See C172.

aggravate, irritate

Aggravate means "to make worse"; *irritate* means "to annoy." *Anne was irritated when George aggravated a pulled leg muscle.*

among, between

Among is used to show a relationship involving three or more people or things. *Between* is used to show a relationship involving two. However, *between* is also used to show the relationship of one to many or to avoid the awkward use of *among. He sank a well between those three trees.* See C339.

amount, number

Amount refers to a total mass or quantity. *Number* refers to something that can be counted. *The amount of food left over from the picnic will depend on the number of people who come.*

angry See **mad, angry.**

anxious, eager

In conversation these words are sometimes used interchangeably. However, in some informal contexts and in all formal situations, a distinction is necessary. Use *anxious* to stress concern and *eager* to emphasize expectancy. *The captain of the disabled ship was anxious to avoid the enemy. The Joneses were eager to leave on their vacation.*

any more, anymore

The two-word form is used in referring to a particular thing. The one-word form is an adverb of time. *The avocados are reasonably priced, but we don't need any more. I don't like to jog anymore.*

apt See **liable, likely, apt.**

as

The conjunction *as* has multiple uses, and this sometimes leads to a lack of clarity. *As* may safely be used in the sense of *while.* If the conjunction is used to indicate a causal connection, it frequently must be changed to *because* or *since* to avoid ambiguity. *She took a walk because* (not *as*) *she was restless.* See C366.

as, like

As is used as a preposition or a conjunction. *Like* is used only as a preposition. *Do as I say* (not *Do like I say*).

T
U

782

as if, as though

These expressions are interchangeable. In formal use they are followed by the subjunctive. See C113.

assume, presume

Both words are verbs indicating an act of taking something for granted. To *assume* is to suppose something with or without a basis in fact. To *presume* is to regard something as true because there is some reason for it and because there is no reason to the contrary. Another common meaning of *presume* is to take too much for granted or to act without authority. *I would not presume to speak for you.*

awhile, a while

Awhile is an adverb. The words *a while*, an article and a noun combination, usually function as the object of a preposition. *Stay awhile. Stay for a while.*

bad, badly

Bad is an adjective; *badly* is an adverb. The usage problem revolves around the use of these words with the verb *feel*. With intransitive *feel* referring to the tactile sense, use the adverb: *I feel badly*. With *feel* as a linking verb referring to one's health, use the adjective: *I feel bad*. See C163-64. (For the use of *good* and *well*, see **good**.)

because See **since, because.**

because of See **due to, because of.**

beside, besides

The preposition *beside* means "next to" or "apart from." *Besides* is an adverb meaning "moreover" or "in addition to." *He left the tractor beside the barn. There were, besides, other reasons for going. Besides the ancient Greek philosophers, she studied Hegel and Kant.* See C329.

between See **among, between.**

bi-, semi-

Bi- means "two" as in *biennial* (every two years). *Semi-* means "half" as in *semiannual* (every half year). Sometimes *bi-* is also used to mean "twice" as in *bimonthly* (twice a month). When this

T
U

secondary meaning leads to ambiguity, *semi-* should be used (as in *semimonthly*).

can, may   See C82 and C89.

capital, capitol

Capitol refers to the building where the legislature meets. In all other senses use *capital: capital city, capital gains, capital idea, capital punishment, capital for the venture,* and so on.

center around

This expression should be avoided. One thing cannot logically center around something else. Use instead *revolve around* or *center on. The issue revolves around our commitment to the company.*

compare to, compare with

Compare to is used in the general sense of *liken: As a student, he can be compared to a runner getting his second wind. Compare with* puts two things side by side for closer analysis: *He will present a series of lectures comparing nineteenth century Russian drama with French drama of the same period.* Since *compared to* usually involves figurative language, whereas *compared with* involves more literal, everyday language, the uses calling for *with* greatly outnumber those for *to.*

complement, compliment

To *complement* means to "add to" or to "complete." To *compliment* means to "praise." *The oriental rugs complemented the antique furniture. She complimented the fashion designer on her fall show.* As an adjective, *complimentary* can also mean "free." *They received complimentary tickets.*

consist in, consist of

To *consist in* is to inhere or reside in as a characteristic; to *consist of* is to be made up of or composed of. In some instances, either expression is acceptable. *Charity consists in kindness to others. Brass is an alloy consisting chiefly of copper and zinc. That stand of trees consists chiefly of* (not *in*) *pine. The job consists in* (or *of*) *teaching basic skills to the handicapped.*

T
U

continual, continuous

Continual means "frequently recurring." *Continuous* means "unceasing." *She was amazed at the continual flood of third-class mail. The continuous motion of the sea made her queasy.*

converse, obverse, reverse

The adjective *converse* means "opposite" or "contrary"; *obverse* means "forming a counterpart"; *reverse* means "turned around backward," the opposite of *obverse. No grade-school teacher is avaricious; conversely, avaricious people are not grade-school teachers. The obverse side of the coin bears the image of John Kennedy; the reverse side shows an American eagle.*

convince, persuade

Convince means "to cause someone to believe something." *Persuade* means "to move someone to do something." *Her arguments convinced everyone. I persuaded him to invest in my fledgling company.*

credible, creditable

Credible means "believable"; *creditable* means "praiseworthy" or "deserving of credit." *Because his stories are so fantastic, they are not credible. Finishing third, the debate team gave a creditable performance.*

data

Data means "facts." Opinion is divided as to whether this word, plural in form, should be followed by a singular or a plural verb. *The data are inconclusive. The data is obsolete.*

differ from, differ with

Differ from means "to be unlike"; *differ with* means "to disagree." *Military weapons today differ from those used in World War II. I hate to differ with you on such a basic issue.* See C332-33.

different from, different than

Use *different from* in simple comparisons involving a noun or pronoun. Use *different than* in more complex situations (usually involving a complete or elliptical clause). *Sheila is different from her sister in many ways. Shorty is playing a different style of basketball than the rest of us.* See C330-31.

T
U

discreet, discrete

Discreet means "cautious" or "tactful." *Discrete* means "separate and distinct." *Megan was discreet in her inquiry. The fundamental hypothesis of the atomic theory is that matter consists of discrete particles.*

disinterested, uninterested

Disinterested means "impartial"; *uninterested* means "without concern or interest." *The mediator in binding arbitration must be a disinterested party in the proceedings. His job consumes his life; he is uninterested in everything else.*

due to, because of

Due to means "as a result of" or "caused by." The expression functions as an adjective and appears after linking verbs or after nouns. *Many physical ailments are ultimately due to improper diet. Health problems due to vitamin deficiency can be readily resolved.* In adverbial situations *because of* replaces *due to. The game was delayed because of* (not *due to*) inclement weather. See C351. This distinction notwithstanding, the two expressions are used interchangeably in most contemporary writing.

eager See **anxious, eager**.

effect See **affect, effect**.

ensure, insure

These two words are sometimes used interchangeably. Careful speakers and writers, however, distinguish *ensure* (to make certain) and *insure* (to guarantee against financial loss). *The new telephone system will ensure easy access to all parts of the country. It is increasingly difficult for amusement parks to insure themselves against potential injury claims.*

et al., etc.

Et al. is the abbreviation for the Latin *et alii* or *et aliae* and means "other people." *Etc.* is the abbreviation for the Latin *et cetera* and means "other things." (Obviously, *and etc.* is a redundancy and should be avoided.) *The research of Forsythe, Petkash, Libens, et al., is impressive. Some students were without books, paper, pencils, etc., for their first class.* In general, it is better to avoid these abbreviations (except in technical notes and bibliographies) and use expressions such as *and others, and so forth, and so on.* See F1.

T
U

every one, everyone

Every one refers to each person, place, or thing of a particular group and is typically followed by *of*. *Everyone* means "everybody" and is never followed by *of*. *Every one of his scientific demonstrations turned out to be a disaster. Everyone enjoyed his scientific demonstrations.*

farther, further

Farther refers to physical distance; *further* means "in addition." *He drove ten miles farther than he had planned. We must discuss this question further.* (There is a tendency in informal speech to use *further* in place of *farther*.)

fewer, less

Fewer is used in referring to items that can be counted. *Less* is used in referring to total quantities. *There are fewer children per family now than there were twenty years ago. We have less time than I expected.* See C257, C283.

former, latter

Former means "preceding" or "the first of two things just mentioned." *Latter* means "the second of two things just mentioned." *Although Kathy likes both steak and lobster, she prefers the former to the latter.*

further See **farther, further.**

good, well

Good is always an adjective. *Well* is an adverb when it indicates manner; it is an adjective when it refers to health. *He is a good speaker. He speaks well. She looks good* [attractive appearance]. *She looks well* [general health]. *I feel good* [vitality]. *I feel well* [general health]. See C163-64.

got, gotten

The past participle of *get* is *got* or *gotten*. *Have got* emphasizes possession; *have gotten* emphasizes recent acquisition. Ordinarily an idea can be better expressed without *got* or *gotten*. *The family has got* (better *owns*) *two cars. He recently has gotten* (better *received*) *a raise.*

T
U

hanged, hung

Hang, hung, hung means "to suspend." *Hang, hanged, hanged* means "to put to death by suspension and strangulation." *Jesus hung on a cross. Tom Dooley was hanged from an oak tree.* See C168.

healthful, healthy

Healthful refers to whatever promotes good health. *Healthy* describes someone or something that has good health. *Healthy* can also mean "large" or "vigorous." *The Caribbean islands provide a healthful climate. She is healthy for her age. He has a healthy appetite.*

herself See **myself, herself, himself, yourself.**

himself See **myself, herself, himself, yourself.**

historic, historical

Historic means "important to history." *Historical* means "relating to history in a general way." *The landing on the moon in 1969 was a historic event. She likes to read historical novels.*

hopefully

Hopefully means "in a hopeful manner." Because *hopefully* is an adverb, it can only modify a verb, adjective, or other adverb. Other uses should be avoided. *She spoke hopefully of a new era. Hopefully they will come* is not correct since they are not coming *with hope.* The sentence should be rewritten: *I hope they will come.*

hung See **hanged, hung**.

if, whether

If frequently introduces an adverb clause indicating possibility or condition. *If he comes tomorrow, we can start painting the house. If I were you, I would stop smoking.* In some instances either *if* or *whether* may introduce a noun clause. However, *whether* is generally preferred—especially when alternatives are involved. *He can't decide whether he should go or stay. We can't determine whether she is telling the truth.*

imply, infer

Imply means "suggest"; *infer* means "come to a conclusion." *The teacher implied that we were not making an effort. I infer from your comments that you are in favor of higher taxes.*

T
U

insure See **ensure, insure.**

irritate See **aggravate, irritate.**

its, it's

Its is a pronoun in the possessive case and is never written with an apostrophe. *It's* is a contraction for *it is. The copy machine flashes all of its red lights when it's overworked.*

kind of, sort of

Both of these modifying expressions are colloquial. In formal situations use *somewhat, rather, fairly,* and so on. See C268.
[Of course, these words have a standard use when followed by a noun. *This kind of work is tiring. That sort of behavior is inappropriate.*]

latter See **former, latter.**

lay See **lie, lay.**

lend, loan

Both verb forms are acceptable; *lend,* however, is preferred in some cases. *Loan* is also used as a noun. *Please lend* (or *loan*) *me your pen for a few minutes. "Friends, Romans, countrymen, lend me your ears." My loan from the bank must be paid within a year.*

less See **fewer, less.**

liable, likely, apt

Liable implies danger or legal responsibility. *Likely* and *apt* both mean "probable," but the latter word includes the notion of a natural or known tendency. *You are liable to fall from the catbird seat. If you go into Mrs. Brown's apple orchard, you are liable to a charge of trespassing. She is a likely candidate for office. Because of his mercurial disposition, he is apt to be socially embarrassing.*

lie, lay

Intransitive *lie, lay, lain* means "to recline." Transitive *lay, laid, laid* means "to put or place." Because *lay* is a legitimate form for both verbs, it requires special attention. *The snow lay on the mountains.* [In this sentence *lay* is the past of *lie,* not the present of *lay.*] See C166.

like See **as, like.**

likely   See **liable, likely, apt.**

loan   See **lend**.

mad, angry
In formal use *mad* means "insane." In colloquial use *mad* and *angry* are synonyms.

majority, plurality
Majority means "more than half." In an election when there are more than two candidates and no one receives a majority, *plurality* may mean either the vote margin of victory or the total number of votes received by the winner.

may, might
May indicates greater likelihood than *might*. See C84. *I may go to the game tonight. I might go to the game tonight.* Other distinctions between these two words are discussed in C81-87.

myself, herself, himself, yourself
The *-self* pronouns are reflexive or intensive and always refer to an antecedent. These words are not a substitute for the ordinary personal pronouns; for example, *myself* should not be used in place of *I* or *me. We saw it ourselves. She herself drove the truck. No one except me* (not *myself*) *was at home.*

number   See **amount, number**.

obverse   See **converse, obverse, reverse**.

parameter
In scientific parlance *parameter* means "a variable or arbitrary constant." The word is technical and should not be confused with words like *perimeter* or *boundary. This country must live within the limits* (not *parameters*) *of its budget.*

percent, percentage
Both *percent* and *percentage* refer to a part of the whole. *Percent* is used with a definite figure. [In formal writing—other than technical and business writing—the word should be used instead of the symbol (%).] *Percentage* is not accompanied by a definite figure but usually has a qualifying adjective. *He was supported by 40 percent of the electorate. A significant percentage of last year's crop was lost because of beetle infestation.*

persuade See **convince, persuade**.

plurality See **majority, plurality**.

practicable, practical
Practicable means "capable of being done." *Practical* carries the further notion of "useful" or "sensible." *Many regard building supersonic commercial airplanes as practicable but not practical.*

presume See **assume, presume**.

previous to, prior to
In most instances these expressions are wordy substitutes for *before* and should be avoided.

principal, principle
As a noun *principal* means "a chief official" or "a sum of money." As an adjective it means "most important." *Principle* is a noun only and means "rule" or "axiom." *The principal lectured the students on their poor behavior. In his court case with Antonio, Shylock forfeited even his principal. Her principal reason for studying Latin was to please her father. "Do unto others as you would have them do unto you" is a principle worthy of practice.*

prior to See **previous to, prior to**.

provided, providing
Both words (ordinarily followed by *that*) are acceptable as subordinating conjunctions meaning "on condition." *Provided* is preferred in formal situations. Neither word should be used when *if* suffices. *You may go to the party provided that you return by midnight. The reunion will be a success if your relatives come.*

raise, rise
Raise means "to lift." Because it is a transitive verb, it always has a direct object. *Rise* means "to get up" or "to emerge." Because it is intransitive it never has an object. See C169.

reason is because
The phrase is ungrammatical (an adverb clause after a linking verb) and redundant. Use *reason is that*. See C355. *The reason why negotiations collapsed is that* (not *because*) *both governments are unstable.*

T
U

relation, relative

Both words can mean "kinship through blood or marriage." In such instances *relative* is clearer and therefore preferred because it doesn't carry the baggage of multiple meanings that *relation* does.

reverse See **converse, obverse, reverse**.

rise See **raise, rise**.

semi- See **bi-, semi-**.

set, sit

Set means "to place or put." *Sit* means "to be seated." The first word is regularly transitive, the second regularly instransitive. For exceptions see C167. *The trainer sets the schedule. The house sits on a hill.*

shall, will

As a future-tense helping verb, *will* is now in general use for all persons (*I, you, he, she, it, we, they*). *Shall* is used in first-person questions and in statements of obligation, especially in legal matters. *I will do what you say. Shall we dance? This bank's loan shall be repaid in quarterly installments.* See C64-69.

should, would

Should is used with all persons to express obligation or expectation. *Would* is used with all persons to express a wish (or promise), a customary action, or a condition. *You should do your homework. If all goes according to plan, we should finish this project within a year. Would that your mother were here! I would regularly finish my chores and then go off to school. If she would just relax, she could become an outstanding golfer.* See C70-80.

since, because

As a conjunction, *since* can indicate cause or time. In sentences that could indicate either cause or time, avoid ambiguous *since* in favor of *because* (for cause) or *ever since* (for time).

> *Since they left, I have been unhappy.* [ambiguous]
> *Because they left, I have been unhappy.* [clearly cause]
> *Ever since they left, I have been unhappy.* [clearly time]

T
U

sit See **set, sit.**

so, so that

In formal writing *so* is usually followed by *that* when it introduces a purpose clause. In other uses as a conjunction, *so* stands alone. *He worked overtime so that his family could have a vacation. They came, so I left.*

so, very

So is not a precise modifier nor is it an adequate substitute for *very* without some kind of explanation. [Colloquial use only:] *She is so ambitious. She is so ambitious that she works during the day and goes to school at night. She is very ambitious.* Both *so* and *very* are overworked and often may be omitted without loss of meaning.

someplace, somewhere

In referring to a specific place not definitely known, *someplace* is acceptable and *somewhere* more formal. *Somewhere* is the proper word in making an indefinite reference. *I'm looking for a house somewhere* (or *someplace*) *in the suburbs. He will be happy somewhere over the rainbow.*

sort of See **kind of, sort of.**

such a

Such a should not be used adverbially as a substitute for *very*. *Such a* should be followed by a result clause introduced by *that*. *It was a very cold winter.* [Incorrect:] *It was such a cold winter.* [Correct:] *It was such a cold winter that many animals died.*

sure and, sure to

The expression *sure and* is incorrect in sentences like *Be sure to see that movie.* In such instances the predicate is not compound.

that, which, who

That may be used to refer to persons as well as to places or things; *which* refers to places or things (or to a group of people); *who* refers to persons. See A46-48. *That* introduces restrictive clauses. *Which* can introduce either restrictive or nonrestrictive clauses (although many writers limit *which* to nonrestrictive clauses). See C252. *This is the team that will win the World Series. This team, which has so much potential, will win the World Series.*

T
U

this kind of, these kinds of

Preferred usage calls for consistent singulars or plurals through-out phrases like the following: *this kind of game*; *these kinds of birds*.

till, until

Both of these words have the same meaning and are accept-able. The form *'till* is incorrect; *'til* is acceptable only in infor-mal writing.

to, too

To can be a preposition or an infinitive marker. *Too* is an adverb meaning "also" or "excessively." *She was unable to come to the party. You too can win a fortune. He is too aggressive.*

toward, towards

Although both forms are acceptable, *toward* is more common in formal writing.

try and, try to

The expression *try and* is incorrect in sentences like *Try to reach that luggage rack.* In such instances the verb is not compound.

uninterested See **disinterested, uninterested.**

unique

Strictly speaking, this word (and a few others) does not have a comparative or superlative form. There are no degrees of uniqueness. Do not write, for example, *very unique.* See C284.

until See **till, until.**

use, utilize

Use means "to put into action or service." *Utilize* means "to make use of in a practical or profitable way." In most instances, *use* is the proper choice. *You must use* (not *utilize*) *your talents. Their skill is not being utilized* (or *used*) *to the fullest.*

way, ways

Ways is a colloquial substitute for *way*. *We have a long way* (not *ways) to go.*

well See **good, well.**

whether See **if, whether.**

T
U

794

which See **that, which, who.**

who See **that, which, who.**

will See **shall, will.**

would See **should, would.**

wrack, wreak
Wrack means "to cause pain or suffering." *Wreak* (pronounced rēēk) means "to inflict or deliver a damaging blow." *She was wracked with doubts about her business investments. Hurricane Gilbert wreaked havoc on coastal towns.* [not *wrecked havoc,* which is redundant]

yourself See **myself, herself, himself, yourself.**

Sentence exercises

The sentence exercises in this section review basic problems of grammar, usage, style, and diction. The exercises are arranged as follows:

1. sentence sense   Exercises   1-3
2. punctuation between clauses   Exercises   4-6
3. punctuation of introductory phrases   Exercises   7-9
4. punctuation of series   Exercises 10-12
5. punctuation of nonrestrictive appositives and modifiers   Exercises 13-15
6. punctuation of independent and parenthetical elements   Exercises 16-18
7. punctuation with quotations   Exercises 19-21
8. dangling and misplaced modifiers   Exercises 22-24
9. plurals and possessives   Exercises 25-27

V

1. Sentence sense

Review these rules: B1-5, D1-20.

V1 Rewrite these word groups, correcting any half-sentences or runovers. (In addition to changing punctuation and capitalization, you may need to modify wording.) If a group contains no half-sentences or runovers, write *correct*.

1. No one can swim the river at flood stage, it is then a muddy, rushing ocean carrying logs, dead animals, beer cans, barn roofs, and even whole houses in its swollen tide.
2. The chaplain walked slowly through the hospital ward. Thinking that behind every patient there was an interesting story, perhaps a tale to freeze or warm the heart.
3. The smell of pancakes drifted into the tent on a vagrant breeze, the mouthwatering aroma of sizzling bacon and fresh coffee.
4. It was shortly after noon when Curlett's horse was shot, horse and rider had been running fast to clear a stone wall north of Winchester when the shot came from the woods.
5. Quoting Nicholas Murray Butler, a prominent educator, as saying that many people's tombstones should read: "Died at thirty, buried at sixty."
6. The most ignorant are often the most conceited, unless

v

people know that there is something more to be known, their inference is, of course, that they know everything.

7. Everyone laughed at the fact. His red hair stood up in peaks, like a rooster's comb.

8. The most important specimen of Anglo-Saxon literature, *Beowulf,* was probably composed by the collecting and re-fashioning of older lays. Accounting for the curious inter-mingling of pagan and biblical elements.

9. The teacher was impressive; she treated ten pages of text without once consulting her textbook.

10. Exposition is one of the four major forms of writing or speaking it attempts to give the reader or listener a clear understanding of some topic.

V2 Rewrite these word groups, correcting any half-sentences or runovers. (In addition to changing punctuation and capitalization, you may need to modify wording.) If a group contains no half-sentences or runovers, write *correct.*

1. After a winter of being sealed up, the cottage was dark and smelled of dead fish, Mother refused to walk into it until Dad had aired out the rooms and built a fire.

2. Jack asked the pilot what caused the vapor trails to stream out behind planes at high altitudes, he gave a long and complicated explanation, too difficult for Jack or, indeed, for any of the others to understand.

3. I was listening; but doctors get into the habit of studying people, and so I watched his face, it was flushed with suppressed excitement.

4. Charles W. Beebe used a bathysphere to explore the ocean floor. Being a hollow steel ball with thick quartz windows, equipped with powerful electric lights.

5. The Benson boy was the laziest lad in town, shuffling along, leaning against fences. Always on the shady side of the street.

6. For an instant the plane shot out of a puffy cloud into a blue-domed pocket of air. Before heading straight into the sheer white wall of another cloud. Which towered up like a mountain in its path.

v

7. As the quartet's star, Oscar doubling as guitar soloist and also played keyboard and sang.

8. A duster pilot lives dangerously. Flying at a low altitude over fields, avoiding high-voltage lines at the ends of fields, and working with chemicals that may be injurious to his health.

9. To slip the landing net deftly beneath the big black bass and hoist quickly before it explodes in another fit of action.

10. For ten solid hours she worked eagerly and steadily, answering telephone calls and filling orders, this was her big chance to prove to her employer that she was the person for the job.

V3   Rewrite these word groups, correcting any half-sentences or runovers. (In addition to changing punctuation and capitalization, you may need to modify wording.) If a group contains no half-sentences or runovers, write *correct.*

1. Major Randolph heard him. So did Jane Raidl.

2. We looked at it many times. The diploma with the yellow cover.

3. That you may come to realize that the greatest breeder of interest in anything is a healthy curiosity.

4. August Saint-Gaudens, one of America's most famous sculptors, whose statues are in prominent places in the largest cities of the United States.

5. To mention that James Marshall discovered the gold that started the rush of forty-nine to California.

6. Even though a figure of speech has been said to be "the essential stuff of poetry."

7. The fact that the writer, to make dialogue sound natural, must give not only what was said but also how it was said.

8. Self-conscious because of his youth, Harold Tucker—editor of the *Democratic Press*—he wore somber suits and had his hair dyed gray.

9. Prosperity tries the fortunate, adversity the great.

10. Before giving a shine to his boots, removing the thick, dry layers of mud.

V

2. Punctuation between clauses

Review these rules: C388-98, C403, C409, D43-46, D56-59, D78-80.

V4 Rewrite these sentences, correcting any mistakes in punctuation. If a sentence contains no mistakes, write *correct*. Do not make two sentences out of any of these.

1. While he was warming up in the bullpen he suddenly felt a small muscle or tendon snap in his shoulder. Pain took hold.
2. As she began to write home seemed very, very far away.
3. The Memorial Day parade was a dismal affair because of the rain however, we have July Fourth to look forward to.
4. Ted Tracy signed his contract this morning he broke his leg in a game this afternoon.
5. The excitement of the day kept her awake I am told.
6. In today's critical circumstances anything that weakens a portion of the free world becomes the business of free people everywhere.
7. In thus braving Martin's wrath, his brother was taking what is called a calculated risk and hoping for the best.
8. Cole launched headlong into the sea of politics and he went on to win office after office in the next ten years.
9. Marilyn was reared on an Iowa farm and before moving to California, she taught fourteen years at Jonas College, a women's school, where she lectured in mathematics.
10. That was his trouble: a swelled head and so none of the class wanted him as valedictorian.

V5 Rewrite these sentences, correcting any mistakes in punctuation. If a sentence contains no mistakes, write *correct*. Do not make two sentences out of any of these.

1. Curtin comes from a wealthy family and has had a college education yet he has little sense of responsibility and is now just a beachcomber on the Florida coast.
2. The elaborate directions that were enclosed in the princess's invitation told me that I should present myself at the back

door of the palace in the uniform of a street cleaner and that I should speak to no one but simply obey the instructions of the palace guard who would admit me and explain what I must do and all of this rigmarole I decided to put up with out of love.

3. As she drove to her friend's party, Louise realized, that for the first time in her life, she was thoroughly jealous.

4. As a pitcher he showed pinpoint control as a man he showed none.

5. Friendship can be bought with money and often is but then it seldom proves worth the price.

6. Mrs. Turvy didn't answer a word she just remained there quietly, impassively, as if she enjoyed sitting on an ant hill.

7. There was one football game on the television set in front of him and another on the radio at his ear for George hated to miss anything.

8. Fortunately, when the day of the examination came he found himself well prepared.

9. Melanie has a freak memory, she is one of those people who remember that Frédéric Bartholdi designed the Statue of Liberty.

10. Obviously it was somebody's error but it certainly wasn't ours.

V6 Rewrite these sentences, correcting any mistakes in punctuation. If a sentence contains no mistakes, write *correct*. Do not make two sentences out of any of these.

1. It is dangerous and exciting work for lack of oxygen or a vicious shark may put an end to the diver's career.

2. Knowledge of previous failures worries him I have heard.

3. Yes, it's quite true, at the masquerade I thought Marie was someone else.

4. That only two golfers, Heggeman and I, were interested in the tournament was obvious.

5. Although the paintings were sold as originals we later learned, they were forgeries.

6. While you are trying to fix the engine I'll walk down the road to get help.

V

7. Napoleon's New France was a dream-empire, that would extend its arms round the whole Gulf of Mexico and the Caribbean, taking in not only the islands but also Louisiana and the Floridas.

8. After the dozen or so guests had all been properly introduced to each other their host came forward and told them that dinner would be served at eight o'clock.

9. World War II accounted for a slight rise in the number of steam locomotives manufactured but, the days of steam were numbered.

10. Since all writers know that naturalness of dialogue requires getting away from the monotonous repetition of "he said" and "she said" I'm sure you will find this exercise in variety helpful.

3. Punctuation of introductory phrases

Review these rules: C310, D54-67, D69-71.

V7 Rewrite these sentences, correcting any mistakes in the punctuation of introductory phrases. If a sentence contains no mistakes, write *correct.*

1. Keeping tabs on the comings and goings of the class during the summer, is a tedious task even for Mildred.

2. Keeping tabs on the comings and goings of the class during the summer, Mildred showed herself an interested and efficient secretary.

3. Just before leaving for the party we heard the phone ringing shrilly.

4. As a matter of fact what seems—even smells and tastes—like sushi is simply a very good imitation.

5. By the second act Alf was sound asleep, his ample chin cushioned on his ample chest.

6. Well, to tell the truth, is usually the best policy; and, of course, it's always the only thing to do.

7. After breakfast she walked resolutely to her typewriter and began to peck out Chapter 4.

8. To the north of the playing field is a hospital.

9. In brief I owe you a great deal, my friend— thirty thousand dollars, isn't it?
10. Talking to ordinary people about ordinary things he considered beneath his dignity, poor fellow.

V8 Rewrite these sentences, correcting any mistakes in the punctuation of introductory phrases. If a sentence contains no mistakes, write *correct*.

1. Speaking for myself I would like to hire you; but the boss's daughter-in-law is looking for a job right now.
2. To see the city drive around Allenport with some other visitor, for natives almost never know the points of interest in their own town.
3. On the other hand the very climate that produces all the lush beauty of the Gulf Coast also drives people very nearly to frenzy with heat and humidity.
4. On our way to the baseball game we met the Sutters.
5. Cooing and gurgling in its crib the baby managed to entertain itself quietly for ten minutes, but then began firing toys and rattles out a nearby window.
6. Having to change the tire in the pelting rain was the last straw.
7. Lying awake he heard the rain rattling like tons of bird shot on the tin roof of the cottage.
8. In the meantime definite word had reached the *Sturgeon* that a submarine tender was standing by two degrees to the west. Of course, that ended all our worries.
9. With everything she had blazing at the sky the little old lady went down before we fully realized she had been hit. Without five full minutes' warning, we had lost our ship.
10. In many parts of this country people are starving.

V9 Rewrite these sentences, correcting any mistakes in the punctuation of introductory phrases. If a sentence contains no mistakes, write *correct*.

1. Yes I'll be down as soon as I have finished shaving.
2. Disturbed by the unethical practices of some of its members, the American College of Surgeons decided to wage open warfare on the wrongdoers.

V

3. At four o'clock, Janet Weston excused herself and went to her room.

4. To study all night in preparation for the examination was an imprudent thing for Trix to do after her recent illness.

5. During this same period, the new administration was trying to resolve a new doubt about the UN—that is whether the UN Charter tends to override the Constitution in certain areas.

6. For heaven's sake if you're going to play that thing, can't you play it quietly?

7. Minutes after Germaine said that Alec Hill's new racer was seen roaring through the dusk.

8. Despairing of the prospect of finding riches in the Seward River area Ben loaded his donkey and set out for the wilds.

9. Against the many benefits of the program are the exorbitant monthly rates.

10. Diverting mass resentment away from the living ruler to the dead, is a cunning trick often used by dictatorships.

4. Punctuation of series

Review these rules: D28-42 and D81.

V10 Rewrite these sentences, correcting any mistakes in punctuation. If a sentence contains no mistakes, write *correct*.

1. The detective's watchful eyes scanned the crowd, on the alert for a tall man in a tan suit, wearing a yellow, and white tie and a soiled, panama hat.

2. Chickens and pigs and geese wandered amicably around the barnyard together, poking about and rooting and pecking for corn other grain and vegetables.

3. Beyond, to the west and north, the forest of pine and fir began, a great ragged, blanket of darkest green, rising on, and up to far-distant peaks touched now with early snow.

4. Gillian, Plater, Thomas, have gone through three years of high school without making anyone notice them.

5. Gillian, and Plater, and Thomas, have gone through three years of high school without making anyone notice them.

V

6. The Switzer Mattress Company opened an office at 3508 Sag Street Rusty Springs Indiana on January 15 1985.

7. The police officer smiled, put her foot negligently on the curb and, pulled out her pad of tickets.

8. Your small son has got his history mixed up. From his belt hang, powder horn bullet pouch and short ramrod; but in the holster swings a modern, dark-handled revolver.

9. Franklyn always says grace devoutly before meals sits down, and complains long, and loud about the food, then rises, and piously says grace again.

10. Yes, it was quicksand—sucking treacherous, death-trap, quicksand—and Jergen was in it up to her waist. She called to us for help.

V11 Rewrite these sentences, correcting any mistakes in punctuation. If a sentence contains no mistakes, write *correct*.

1. She will fly directly to Rome; but while she is there, she intends to fly on successive weekends, to Paris, France, Cairo, Egypt, Athens, Greece, and, to be sure, back to New York.

2. George Sanders Jr. received his M.A. from Georgetown University on June, 1, 1990.

3. With a twinkle in his eye, Mr. Traynor said he thought SOS meant sink, or swim; but Eileen, who has no sense of humor, and almost prides herself on the lack, corrected him indignantly, saying that it meant save our ship or, save our souls.   Mr. Traynor blinked.

4. At baseball camp we batted, and threw, and slid under the alert eyes of the coaches.

5. How on earth are you going to lose weight if you keep eating hot, fudge sundaes?

6. She talked about losing weight; but, alas, she continued to eat rich, calorie-packed desserts.

7. Robert Cunningham of San Jose, California and Green Bay, Wisconsin is an unusual person in the world of auto racing.

V

8. When the war ended, Joe went to college to play football, Mary to nursing school and Henry to the college of embalmers.

9. Glenn Miller was king of jazz in the late '30's, and early '40's, in the East from Boston's Plaza, to Miami's Copa.

10. Mrs. Jardonek found herself sitting before the usual banquet fare: fruit cocktail clear soup roast chicken with peas and carrots and, mashed potatoes.

V12 Rewrite these sentences, correcting any mistakes in punctuation. If a sentence contains no mistakes, write *correct.*

1. Jake was a short, and stocky, lad with ears which seemed to lean forward to catch every whisper.

2. Mr. Watkins owns twenty-five automobiles, ranging from a 1914 Bentley through a choice selection of Stanley Steamers Bugattis Jaguars, Duesenbergs Citroëns Stutz Bearcats Rolls Royces Fiats and, other famous makes.

3. On July 31, 1876 the Coast Guard Academy, then known as the "School of Instruction" of the Revenue Cutter Service, was established by law.

4. They topped the rise and, descending into a shallow valley, turned left onto a wide road. The trees above their heads were filled with azaleas, and apple blossoms.

5. Short, and dumpy, tall, and lanky, male, or female, I needed a secretary at once.

6. He walked uncertainly, warily as if he were afraid; then he paused on the edge of the circle.

7. In Brazil Argentina and Chile, it is small wonder that the housewife is dissatisfied, faced as she is with steep prices and limited choice of commodities.

8. The day was fair the sun glinted on sails in the lagoon, and there was music in the air.

9. I was dressed in a sou'wester, a red, plaid, jacket, and a pair of sailor pants.

10. Color, cutting and clarity as well as carat weight, contribute to a diamond's beauty and value.

5. Punctuation of nonrestrictive appositives and modifiers

Review these rules: C202-5, C302-8, D48-53.

V13 Rewrite these sentences, correcting any mistakes in the punctuation of restrictive and nonrestrictive appositives and modifiers. If a sentence contains no mistakes, write *correct*.

1. William Nicholas Windlestone was the second son of Sir Nicholas William Windlestone an eccentric country gentleman, who detested children and singing birds.
2. At Olympia in the Peloponnesus site of the original Olympic Games stood one of the original wonders of the world, the great statue of Zeus by Phidias.
3. Aviation engineers have a special unit of measure, the "stapp." Named for Colonel John Paul Stapp who is famous for his numerous rides on an experimental rocket sled, a "stapp" is the force exerted on a body by an acceleration of one G for one second.
4. Winthrop has four fine three-year-old stallions. One of them which resembles Secretariat very much is being conditioned for Santa Anita next year.
5. Lay aside other considerations and face the fact, that in the great basin about the Persian Gulf, lies the world's richest concentration of crude oil.
6. Jean Monnet, the indefatigable little Frenchman who first proposed the Schumann Coal-Steel Company, is called "Mr. Europe."
7. Christina Rossetti the sister of Dante Rossetti has been called the greatest woman poet in the English language.
8. The Defarges husband and wife came lumbering under the starlight, in their public vehicle, to the gates of Paris.
9. Hester crossed the yard to the garage, that housed the car, and while she backed the Ford Escort down the driveway, she reflected, unhappily, on the little scene she had just witnessed between Ambrose and her father.
10. Gil MacDougal tired and bleeding slumped against the rail, wishing that Jared would return with the doctor.

v

V14 Rewrite these sentences, correcting any mistakes in the punctuation of restrictive and nonrestrictive appositives and modifiers. If a sentence contains no mistakes, write *correct.*

1. I twisted around to look after her, but all I could see from where I stood was Bernice, walking along at the front end of the litter and Sandra, at the rear end.

2. Charles Evremonde, called Darnay, was accused by the public prosecutor as an emigrant, whose life was forfeit to the Republic, under the decree, which banished all emigrants on pain of death.

3. Alexander the Great succeeded his father Philip on the throne of Macedon in 336 B.C.

4. The only one of the students, who was ever interested in any sort of studying, was Cheryl.

5. Mr. Delmar Van Alsteyne cashier for the great shipping firm of Leith and Ackley sat in his little private office with an open ledger in front of him and a smile on his wizened face.

6. Were the elephant and the donkey symbols of the Republicans and Democrats invented in 1870 by the cartoonist, Thomas Nast?

7. It is said of Edwin Booth, Shakespearean tragedian, that he did not act Hamlet—he lived it.

8. It was very interesting to hear Carlita tell about Elkanah Watson the person most active in promoting the Erie Canal.

9. Charles Wilkes lieutenant in the American Navy was the first man to identify Antarctica as a continent. More than one hundred years ago.

10. The sun which was now far below the horizon, left the mountaintop in darkness.

V15   Rewrite these sentences, correcting any mistakes in the punctuation of restrictive and nonrestrictive appositives and modifiers. If a sentence contains no mistakes, write *correct*. Since these ten sentences are a continous passage, pay attention to proper paragraphing.

1. "What's going on back there?" called Graves the pilot and captain of the bomber who distracted by the shouts had looked up from his instruments and cut in on the intercom.
2. "There's a bomb, still hanging in the bay, and the doors haven't closed," cried O'Toole.
3. After a thoughtful pause, the pilot's voice crisp and authoritative came over the headphones: "As you know, the co-pilot Lieutenant Hawkins caught himself a piece of flak during the last bomb run.
4. I can't leave either the controls or the lieutenant who is bleeding pretty badly.
5. I am asking for a volunteer, someone, to work the bomb loose.
6. He'll have to work fast without gloves I guess to jettison the thing; and, guys, it's cold outside."
7. The pilot continued: "I'll keep the plane level while someone—Mr. Hero as far as I'm concerned—eases that bomb, down through the door.
8. We're over water now the North Channel, so nobody below will be hurt."
9. Before the captain's voice was off the air, O'Toole's Irish brogue, trembling a little with the thought, that this could be his last flight, rumbled, "I'm your man."
10. A second later O'Toole had shed his gloves and cumbersome parachute his last safeguard and gingerly crept into the plane's belly, to the steel struts and hooks of the bomb rack.

v

6. Punctuation of independent and parenthetical elements

Review these rules: D47, D51, D54, D56, D61, D92, D94, D102, D104-6.

V16 Rewrite these sentences, correcting any mistakes in the punctuation of independent and parenthetical elements. If a sentence contains no mistakes, write *correct*.

1. Colonel Buxton they said was out on the prairies Indian-fighting; and though this is hard to believe they also said he thought Grant was still president and would send him reinforcements any day.

2. Slam that screen door just once more my dear young fellow, and you'll find yourself grounded let me tell you for the rest of the afternoon!

3. Prices being what they are I'd like to know how for goodness' sake she was able to get flying lessons at ten dollars an hour.

4. To tell you the truth, I stayed away because I did not want to have to explain myself over again to well you know who.

5. No one here I imagine knows what it is to be two feet from a stick of dynamite when it explodes and yet live to tell the tale; but believe it or not that's just what happened to me not quite a year ago.

6. But really officer don't you think "reckless driving" is to say the least a rather strong expression for what I was doing?

7. Since he had a camera, I wore my most attractive sports outfit; but no he wasted all the film on that silly old boat of his.

8. The incriminating papers disposed of Fleugel once more locked the desk and rapidly and silently left the office.

9. You would think that someone of the hundreds of people on the beach would have noticed that the swimmer was in trouble; I must report unfortunately that not one of them did.

10. Tell me tell me the truth where did you hide the treasure?

V17 Rewrite these sentences, correcting any mistakes in the punctuation of independent and parenthetical elements. If a sentence contains no mistakes, write *correct*.

1. Now and this was my final clue the measurements showed that this cabinet must have a secret compartment, one big enough to hold shall we say Mr. Dachetti a black briefcase?
2. Sling that hammock between these two beeches slave and then trot into the kitchen and make at least a gallon of ice-cold lemonade with mint and maraschino cherries in it.
3. To me at least it seemed a good time to propose marriage; but as luck would have it a millionaire got the same idea at the same time.
4. I have always contended the opinion of the rest of the world notwithstanding that a girl is no less attractive in the right work clothes than she is in the right formal gown.
5. That being the case you ought to accustom yourself to your condition and not deny your handicap.
6. Pete I think you, and Martha ought to let the boy be, ought to let him do as he likes in this one matter; for it is his vocation let us remember and not ours that he is struggling with.
7. Now Marge you know that the San Francisco fire of 1906 caused greater financial loss than the Chicago fire of 1871.
8. His Eminence Arthur Cardinal Carrington, D.D. Ph.D. will speak at the alumni banquet on the topic of responsible stewardship.
9. Are you by chance in the market for a dozen boxes of used correcting tape?
10. Didn't Susan Drake—she went to medical school after college, you remember—become a noted surgeon in Chicago?

V18 Rewrite these sentences, correcting any mistakes in the punctuation of independent and parenthetical elements. If a sentence contains no mistakes, write *correct*.

1. Vidas Barzukas Jr. is following in the footsteps of Vidas Barzukas Sr.
2. The discussion having ended on a sour note I slipped away as soon as I could.

V

3. But boss I had intended to go down to the Chanticleer a little before twelve.

4. All right Ernestine I'll buy anything that sells for a profit.

5. Shep we have to do something about those dogs. You know we'll have to do something quick don't you?

6. Dealers in surplus supplies seldom hit it that lucky; in fact one informal survey showed that only thirty percent of surplus deals were at all successful.

7. "You seem shocked my dear," said the colonel uneasily. "Never heard of such impudence have you?"

8. Lady Elspeth, shaking like an aspen—or is it asp; I can never remember—opened her mouth and began to chirp like a chicken.

9. Curiously Dr. Conant dates the dawn of the atomic age from the first explosion of an atomic device by the Russians.

10. Suddenly with a dash of surprising speed, Bobo leaped forward across Kiva's path.

7. Punctuation with quotations

Review these rules: D74-75, D84-85, D117-32.

V19 Rewrite these groups of sentences, using quotation and other punctuation marks correctly. Start new paragraphs and adjust the capitalization wherever necessary. If a group of sentences contains no mistakes, write *correct*.

1. Veronica stood at the head of the stairs and called I'll be down in a second; then she added, thanks for the beautiful corsage!

2. Here is an old story you may not have heard: A rookie knocked a double clear out to the center-field wall. Next day he saw in the paper that he had not received credit for a hit. That afternoon he walked up to the official scorer and asked, why he had not been credited with a hit. Don't worry about it said the scorer mildly; it was just a typographical error. Whaddaya mean, error! yelled the rookie. Nobody laid a hand on that ball, and you know it!

3. Go down the road, he drawled, Until you come to a farmhouse marked State Experimental Farm. When you come

to that, turn around, 'cause you've gone too far. [Use quotation marks with State Experimental Farm.]

4. What, in the name of heaven, did she mean by, "May live to regret calling a woman old"?

5. The manager said, with a sad smile, we can't win them all; but it was clear he had wanted with all his heart to win this one.

6. I then slipped the water skis off, said the lifeguard in a matter-of-fact, emotionless tone, and skidded along behind the boat on my heels! We girls were surprised, of course; but since he was handsome and since he seemed to have said heels carefully and deliberately, why, we believed him.

7. The title of this poem by Holmes may recall a short story. It is "The Last Leaf."

8. Every time you putt short like that, said the pro, someone in the foursome will always say You've got to hit them harder, or Never up, never in. Why do people insist on the obvious?

9. Chuck called and said, that Maury will go. He said to tell you that, he and Maury will bring the dogs and meet you right after dark at the Three Corners grocery.

10. Is the faucet dripping? she asked. No he said drowsily from under a pillow. It is dripping, she insisted. I can't hear a thing. This last remark faded into a snore.

V20 Rewrite these groups of sentences, using quotation and other punctuation marks correctly. Start new paragraphs and adjust capitalization wherever necessary. If a group of sentences contains no mistakes, write *correct*.

1. No, the reviewers were not kind to my brainchild. Can you imagine them using such expressions as—and I quote verbatim—intellectual froth, lukewarm religiosity, and ersatz emotions?

2. Mrs. Crowthers said You put that gun down and come over here by me; then the robber smiled at her sheepishly.

3. The mayor said We all heard Willet with our own ears. We heard him say Don't get the idea I'm running for office.

4. My check's on the way, he said. Tomorrow's the day we really "go for broke." Why don't you ride over with us?

5. There's our turn Nachtrab said. We're going too fast said the reporter. Turn anyway Nachtrab shouted.

6. Have you heard their story asked Murdock grimly? No? Well you'd better listen then.

7. Five days later Troy told her that "He would not be able to see her again."

8. John Simpson stood there and for a moment did not utter a word. Then he said take your hands off that dog. He belongs to me.

9. She held up her hand as the stranger started to speak again. Let me ask you something else, she said. How much do you think land costs here?

10. Helga turned and said, that Maurice must go. They agreed, That his usefulness was at an end.

V21 Rewrite these groups of sentences, using quotation and other punctuation marks correctly. Start new paragraphs and adjust the capitalization wherever necessary. If a group of sentences contains no mistakes, write *correct.*

1. We're shoving off Mike said to him aloud. Three days, boy. Give me three days, and I'll have you home. It can't be done, Mike, Johnny moaned. We'll go aground on the rocks in the passage.

2. She approached the well-dressed woman. Good morning, Dorothy she said. Her friend did not recognize her and stammered, But I do not know—you must be mistaken. No, I am Susan Spieker. Her friend uttered a cry of surprise, Oh! Susan! How you have changed!

3. Very well, whispered the old man. You have asked, Why did I do it? I am an old man. Life is still sweet to me; I will suffer anything to keep it.

4. Cape Cod is the bared and bended arm of Massachusetts said Thoreau; the shoulder is at Buzzard's Bay, the sandy fist at Provincetown.

5. She called these "expenses:" two tickets to the symphony concert, a new dress, and dinner for two.

6. Yes, it is true Davis answered that Avery's exact words were tell Mother not to worry about me. I will come back tomorrow morning.

V

7. What do you think she meant when she said, All of you will be sorry?

8. Have you been in New York long asked Eddie. Just arrived yesterday he said. For a vacation? Well, for a little rest now, but I may stay here. Are you looking for a job? I don't know yet. My father said: Son, take your time. Don't be too quick to settle on a career.

9. I wish girls weren't afraid to dance with me, said Buggsy. It's partly the way you ask them, said Jack. Didn't I hear you say to Linda, Come on, snake, let's slither?

10. Don't you think it odd that Natalie said that every one of the witnesses told the identical story? asked Gilbert.

8. Dangling and misplaced modifiers

Review these rules: C312-20.

V22 Rewrite these sentences, correcting any dangling, misplaced, or squinting modifiers. If a sentence contains no mistakes, write *correct*.

1. After pedaling uphill on a bicycle for two miles, the shady tree at the side of the road promised coolness and rest.

2. When six years old, my father had a job refereeing football games for the Big Ten.

3. Blue-petaled and green-stemmed, my sister prepared a bouquet of flowers as a centerpiece for the dinner table.

4. Jack shouted quickly to throw the ball to first base.

5. For days after the accident, she steered between the cars parked on either side cautiously, to avoid any children who might suddenly dart out into the street.

6. He slipped out to smoke the stolen cigarette that he had taken from his father's room behind the garage.

7. With a delightful French accent and a very European mustache, Jane found the waiter very attractive.

8. Although weary, the little green pill did not not induce sleep until shortly before dawn.

9. To be eaten with relish, one must apply the tenderizer several hours before the guests arrive; for no one likes tough meat, even if offered by a charming host.

10. To be understood, the tutor gave me an intensive course in the language spoken in this region of the Himalayas.

V23 Rewrite these sentences, correcting any dangling, misplaced, or squinting modifiers. If a sentence contains no mistakes, write *correct*.

1. It was unnerving to watch the stubby winged plane trying to glide unsuccessfully to a landing.
2. Granted that Shane is not brilliant, still he can turn out something better than this doodle, can't he?
3. She thought, for relaxation, of playing the piano.
4. Mother put Dad's shirt into the new washer, which was greasy from his hours of working on the car.
5. Coasting down the hill, the brakes suddenly locked; and the car screeched to a reluctant stop, leaving a trail of smoking rubber behind it.
6. Grimacing, screaming, and writhing on the canvas, the TV announcer pretended to believe that the flabby old wrestler was really in pain.
7. When nervous, food should never be eaten until calmness returns; for anxiety is an enemy to digestion.
8. With no thought at all of his years of faithful service, the old nag found himself, far from retirement to lush pastures, forced to work harder than ever.
9. If shaken, you will find that the sugar does not all settle to the bottom and the drink tastes much better.
10. The principal signaled me quietly to enter her office.

V24 Rewrite these sentences, correcting any dangling, misplace, or squinting modifiers. If a sentence contains no mistakes, write *correct*.

1. After a long and painstaking search, Johnson found the gear in the upstairs closet that had been missing since last year.
2. While flying north over the Dakota prairies last summer, many wheat farmers were harvesting abundant crops.
3. When halfway to the garage, remembering that murder had been done there, a chill of terror seized Thurmann.

4. After an hour she dissuaded the man from jumping off the building by a chain of logical arguments.

5. He almost supplied himself with enough film for his travels to become a second Ansel Adams.

6. It was rather amusing to watch the small puppy trying to wriggle unsuccessfully out of Aunt Sarah's firm grasp.

7. There's much more to ice fishing than lowering merely a baited hook through a hole in the ice.

8. To wash down breast of guinea hen, a bottle of Montrachet, 1906, will do wonders.

9. What? You mean that Alvin read that nine-hundred-page book written by Henry Fielding in one day!

10. Although wide awake at midnight, sleep came swiftly once she was in bed.

9. Plurals and possessives

Review these rules: C183-91, D158-78, I4-12.

V25 Rewrite these sentences, correcting any mistakes in plurals or possessives. If a sentence contains no mistakes, write *correct*.

1. The tornadoes ripped off the rooves of several houses and those of two churchs. They tore away the two cupola's of the courthouse and the arches at the ends of Youree Bridge.

2. Echos of Cass' crys for help mocked at him from the canyon walles.

3. John's and Maury's dinner jacket gets a lot of use, since they have to share it.

4. On the college's three campus, there are seven librarys, all richly endowed, and several with reading roomes for the use of alumnuses and alumnas only.

5. Although the meteorologist forecast includes clear skies for the morning, she offers only thunderstormes for the afternoon, so the Allen's had better give some thought to canceling their' picnic.

6. He roamed through the back street's and alley's of Dublin, looking for allies in his personal war; and soon he had a

v

trio of bullies with him—McShane, O'Dowd, and the younger McClellan—all vicious brutes.

7. Six cupsful of rice in one of these ordinary pots? For goodness' sake!

8. Now the result of all these kids foolishness was one badly cut thigh, one broken arm, two badly damaged outboard motors, and ten years subtracted from six parent's lives.

9. He told me why sopranoes are so particular about the pianos that are used to accompany them in there soloes. Singers surely have worries.

10. My sister-in-laws are both Latvian's, so you can imagine how they feel about events in the Baltic countries these days.

V26 Rewrite these sentences, correcting any mistakes in plurals or possessives. If a sentence contains no mistakes, write *correct*.

1. Its true that mosquitoes at that resort are just as uncommon as deers.

2. Between halfes the Wolfs, the soccer team from Liverpool, ate hot potatos, which they called murphies. England is certainly a very strange country!

3. I know how determined some female relatives can be; for I have a full complement of mother-in-laws, sister-in-laws, aunts, grandmotheres, and assorted female cousins.

4. You ought to see the Davises fence after Tom, Mike, and Joe's axes did their work yesterday.

5. The students' English teacher is in one of her crises about parentheses, but no one can tell whether she's for them or against them.

6. Joe, can you tell me how many sacksful of cement weigh a ton?

7. Among the recent editions of classics are Shakespeares plays, Keats and Shelleys poetry, Milton's *Paradise Lost*, Twains *Huckleberry Finn* and many of Dickens novels.

8. Many young girls think of themselves as the Jane Austen's, the Florence Nightingale's, the Meryl Streep's, and the Gladys Knight's of the future.

9. Sir Humphrey spent his vacation hunting. Last year he bagged ten grouses and six quails.

10. With it's fine observatory, the University of Ponce provides astonomers the opportunity to study the spiral nebula's in the constellation of Orion.

V27 Rewrite these sentences, correcting any mistakes in plurals or possessives. If a sentence contains no mistakes, write *correct*.

1. The commander-in-chiefs of the British and American army corpses—the British First Corps and the American Second—met in a farm house to reconsider the days' battle plan.

2. Millie was a person who was willing to take chances. Returning from the Orient, she failed to declare two Kashmir scarfs, six rare topazs, and a dozen uncut diamondes.

3. Now that I am an alumni of the school of baby sitting, I can say unequivocally that two-year-old's behavior is very unpredictable.

4. According to the judge's verdict, Agnes's house, Robert's land, and the children's ponies must be sold at public auction.

5. Tanya, when you come, bring five copys of each of the librettoes of the operas we have been studying.

6. Off Port Amboy were two rocky reefes which were a menace to shippes and the ruin of many fine skippers.

7. The Smith's garage is crammed with old wooden chairs, benches, and their two son-in-law's scuba diving gears.

8. Martha asked her mother how many cupsful of sugar and how many whites of egges should be put into the cake batter.

9. The doctor's examination disclosed two cracked vertebraes.

10. Although it was anothers' farfetched idea, we agreed to make the trip to the crossroades to see two small chaletes.

10. Faulty references and omissions

Review these rules: C7-35, C152-53, C183-84, C218-42, C262, C322-23, C364-65, D158-71.

V28 Rewrite these sentences, correcting any faulty references and omissions, and any faulty possessives. If a sentence contains no mistakes, write *correct*.

1. When the director finally ended the rehearsal, the hungry cast hurried out of the auditorium, pulling on its coats, sweaters, and gloves.
2. Talking fast to the two elderly sisters at the same time, the salesperson convinced them that if she bought the VCR to use with the other's new television set, she would not regret the purchase.
3. Last night's lecture on assistance to third-world nations was the best of all the presentations that was given at the conference.
4. Uncle Toby is so huge that on a bus he can give his seat to a fat and thin woman at the same time.
5. You claim the principal is hardhearted, but I think she is more than willing to listen if not sympathize with troublesome students.
6. The ship's prows were lined up with faultless precision as they moved down the Thames in the coronation manuevers.
7. Pick out someone to accompany you, but do not merely choose whomever walks into the room first.
8. I've seen many scatterbrained youngsters, but I haven't seen any quite so flighty as him.
9. It was, after all, a natural urge, as much to be expected as turning a flower's face to the sun.
10. The driver with the broken wrist stood beside his automobile. It had been wrecked when he drove through a red light and skidded on the wet pavement.

V29 Rewrite these sentences, correcting any faulty references and omissions, and any faulty possessives. If a sentence contains no mistakes, write *correct*.

1. "Each girl will take out their books, open it to page sixty, and write out all the sentences." That's how Ms. Smith talks to those students of her's.
2. How can one do their best work when he has to suffer interruptions all the time?

3. Using the same racing car, same tires, same kind of gasoline, Duke Nolan drove the ten laps as fast, but less recklessly, than the other drivers.

4. The number of fans who were present for the game was surprising.

5. The janitor gouged a chunk of skin out of his thumb while repairing a broken window. It had been smashed before, and the doctor had put splints and bandages on it.

6. It's my daughter Cathy running onto the field, isn't she?

7. Each of the girls have asked whom you were talking to.

8. He was one of those people who mistakes attention for affection, one of those who, at a party, put lamp shades on their heads and pretend they're great comics.

9. I don't want just any mattress; I want a genuine Snor-Rest mattress, on which, it says in the paper, they give a year's money-back guarantee.

10. Children's voices came shrilly through the dormitory windows and compelled each sleeper to jam a pillow over their ears.

V30 Rewrite these sentences, correcting any faulty references and omissions, and any faulty possessives. If a sentence contains no mistakes, write *correct*.

1. The company withdrew their product from the market because of poor sales.

2. The black and white cat were both found by some children playing in an abandoned house.

3. The class is giving their first party for the seniors next Friday at Fleebie Putterton's home.

4. In this book, it explains how American scientists constructed the first atomic pile under a stadium in Chicago.

5. She has neither respect nor pride in her daughter's ambitions.

6. Whose books are these? Neither Kathy nor Melanie left theirs.

7. Dukas's *The Sorcerer's Apprentice* was written in 1897. It's polish and thematic originality have been praised by musicians and audiences of every nation and age.

V

8. Jim is one of the members of the team who has potential to play professional sports.

9. In the answer section to the quiz, it says that Wyoming and Colorado are the only two states that have straight boundary lines on all four sides.

10. When Mother took the twin's birthday sweaters (Aunt Alice had given them each a bright red one) back to Jansen and Hansen, a rather stuffy clerk tried to say they were not theirs but had been bought elsewhere.

11. Case of pronouns

Review these rules: C152-53, C211-22, C243-55, C339.

V31   Rewrite these sentences, correcting any mistakes in the case of pronouns. If a sentence contains no mistakes, write *correct*.

1. You might think that those peculiar neighbors of ours would give Ellen and I some of the pompano they caught; but no, not them.

2. If you have any doubt about me being angry, just put your head here.

3. His wife was deeply shocked by his, a man who could swim for miles, refusing to go in after the little girl.

4. "I don't care whom you are," shouted the manager; "one more tantrum and I'll find a singer whom I can count on."

5. With she and her sister absent, we are powerless to make any decisions whatever, sir.

6. And whom do you suppose the master of revels singled out as "most beautifully costumed"? Why, my sister and me.

7. And who do you suppose then led the grand march all around the Athenaeum? Why, my sister and I.

8. "Just between you and me," asked Joan, "is there any chance of Harry showing up here tonight?"

9. Then the precocious little fellow astounds Aubrey and I by remarking, quite without emphasis, "God gave John and I these shoes through the agency of our parents."

10. One must always either obey Rose or quarrel with her, she being the termagant that she is.

V

V32 Rewrite these sentences, correcting any mistakes in the case of pronouns. If a sentence contains no mistakes, write *correct.*

1. Gentlemen, me and Mr. Eglin have come to apologize for Mr. Eglin's strange behavior.
2. Invite whomever you like, my dear; it's your party, and you know who will enjoy it most.
3. Between you and I it is quite clear that you are much stronger than him.
4. There's little danger of us turning Communist; we're far too rich to find it alluring.
5. List all those whom you know are having trouble with English grammar and composition.
6. How many players have you chosen for your team? Just them, or they over in the corner of the field, too?
7. You must choose between Mack and I. No, not Tony. It is not him about whom I am concerned.
8. Elaine and her both being uncertain what college to enter, they decided to make a short visit to a few during the semester break.
9. The principal insisted that us seniors wear summer formals to the graduation exercises.
10. Do you approve of me going to the concert next Wednesday, and do you approve of Maruca going with me?

V33 Rewrite these sentences, correcting any mistakes in the case of pronouns. If a sentence contains no mistakes, write *correct.*

1. Whom do you suppose will settle the question of who is the legitimate ruler of the island?
2. Terry Lefevre tried to squeeze through the pack. LeMay and her almost collided.
3. Just among them five players, whom would you think ought to bat .300 this season?
4. The head of the English Department gave Glennis and I permission to interview the university's only published poet.
5. Your description is not at all clear; nevertheless, I know the girl whom you mean.

V

6. Some say that Hillman's father did not approve his deciding upon writing as a career.
7. Mrs. Erbs scolded you because she took you to be I.
8. Unfortunately for us, Willard was a person who we thought to be trustworthy and reliable.
9. When it comes to working on the auction, him and Jane will do whatever you ask.
10. At the second session, it was announced that we might nominate whoever we wished for the office of president.

12. Principal parts and tenses

Review these rules: A68-73, C53-55, C62, C111-12, C135-37.

V34 Rewrite these sentences, correcting any mistakes in principal parts or tense. If a sentence contains no mistakes, write *correct*.

1. Stealing was bad enough, but what he done was to steal from a poor old woman who would of used the money to pay her rent and who was instead throwed out on the street by the building supervisor.
2. You should not have slided into third base before the left fielder had threw the ball.
3. Our car crawled along on its blowed-out tire for two miles, and the terrific friction slowly ground the rubber to shreds.
4. You lied, didn't you, when you said you had only lended the Russian a blank computer disk?
5. I give that boy two dollars in the morning, and by noon he had spended every nickel of it.
6. The witness, who said he had saw the accident, certainly perspired in the courtroom when the lawyer wrang from him a confession that he had lied from top to bottom.
7. Louis had swam across that river thirty times without a mishap, but today his luck runned out.
8. They had drank all the pop in the refrigerator and still wanted more.
9. As the robot approached, Percival shaked with fear and hided in a darkened corner.
10. She sung the national anthem before every athletic contest in the Forum for the last ten years.

V

V35   Rewrite these sentences, correcting any mistakes in principal parts or tense. If a sentence contains no misakes, write *correct*.

1. The trout stream in which we meant to fish had overflown its banks and sewn destruction for five hundred yards on either side.
2. The youngster stood before the president, shaked his hand, and then run back to his mother and father who had rose from their seats in surprise.
3. If I had bought more coal last summer when prices were down, we could of lit a good fire on these cold spring days.
4. Gladys come in, sank down in an easy chair, drunk three glasses of lemonade, and then fell asleep.
5. The thief had weaved in and out of traffic for twenty blocks, the police in wild pursuit, before they finally catched him and drug him from the car.
6. We all set down at a long table set up on the lawn and attackted a magnficent beef roast, with potatoes that were simply drownded in natural gravy.
7. Without thinking, she neatly splited the infinitive and could only wonder why her teacher looked askance.
8. He busted his nose and then bleeded half to death.
9. Why do you keep asking whether I swum the entire distance under water?
10. It is almost certain that none of his clients would of called Sir Anthony a softhearted man.

V36   Rewrite these sentences, correcting any mistakes in principal parts or tense. If a sentence contains no mistakes, write *correct*.

1. Characteristically, Jacques tryed to scare off his opposition by dark and mysterious insinuations about the future.
2. We would have told her: send some of your best people to us for training as you had ought to have done long ago.
3. In any other circumstances Joe could of been deeply interested; but, as it was, he shaked with rage at the stupidity of the arrogant speaker.
4. If I had boughten the car last fall, I would of paid less for it.

V

5. The alarm sounded through the little ship, and when they heared it, the passengers run for the lifeboats.

6. A heavy gale put the *Kon-Tiki* through a severe test of sturdiness and could of sank her without leaving a trace.

7. The subject having been brung up by Jost, we spent the evening talking about all kinds of game and birds: deer, bear, quail, grouse, pheasants, and woodchuck.

8. On her maiden voyage the $7,500,000 *Titanic* sunk after colliding with an iceberg off Newfoundland.

9. Tomas had shook with fright until he realized that his fear was groundless.

10. They had rode along in shocked silence after hearing the news report that Rosita Dias had drownded in Lake Erie.

13. Verbs confused

Review these rules: C166-78.

V37 Rewrite these sentences, correcting any use of the wrong verb. If a sentence contains no such misuse, write *correct*.

1. You left me hire a rank amateur, when you knew the fellow had never laid a brick before in his life.

2. Pockworth is such a stingy person that she would rather loose a quarter than give one away. You see, she may get the lost quarter back.

3. Leave the poor fellow be; it's obvious that his mind has been effected by our kindness in letting him work twelve hours a day.

4. Tagler raised up from behind the table and cautiously peered over its top to where Mitalen laid on the kitchen floor, just as the raiders had let her when they ran out of the house.

5. Bit by bit, for ten years, the prisoner had chipped out a tunnel under the wall; but it was death that effected his ultimate escape.

6. We loosened the cinch, which was cruelly cutting the horse's belly, and removed the rein that would not leave him crop grass.

V

7. The angry mob would not listen to reason, and so they hanged the man before the sheriff arrived.

8. The sun came probing through the raised tent flaps and coaxed Lupita from the cot on which she had laid for ten hours.

9. The crowd was much effected by the sight of Caesar's body.

10. From the day that Griswold was sentenced to be hanged, his eyes seldom raised from the floor of his cell.

V38   Rewrite these sentences, correcting any use of the wrong verb. If a sentence contains no such misuse, write *correct*.

1. Prince Hal was deeply affected when he came upon his old friend Falstaff, who was laying on the battlefield pretending to be dead—the old fraud!

2. Jill had just rose to register a protest, when the woman in the row behind her whispered hoarsely, "Sit down, you fool. Save your objections for something important."

3. You can see where the poor, hunted thing laid down to rest—there, near those bushes, where the grass is crushed.

4. The plan was to lay in ambush for anyone who should happen to lose his way, drawn aside by our confusing road sign. We lay there for the better part of a day.

5. Leave them to themselves, then, Mrs. Adams; and leave us have no more to do with such discourteous little beasts as porcupines. Look, one of them is about to raise its quills again. I say, let them be.

6. At the buzzer, Maruca left go a long, desperate shot that bounced off the rim.

7. On the floor laid the final messy debris of an ice-cream cone, let there without a second thought by a toddler who had grown tired of holding it.

8. A second later all the tools lay scattered across the floor.

9. Harley was deeply effected by her tears. "I'll let you go this time," he said bitterly, "but next week I must have an answer."

10. Since the Stevensons will be late, you may as well set awhile and relax.

v

826

V39 Rewrite these sentences, correcting any use of the wrong verb. If a sentence contains no such misuse, write *correct*.

1. Though Anita had laid the book aside, she lay sleepless wondering whether her mother would take the failure laying down.
2. Loosen his shoes. Since his toes are frozen, the tight laces may effect his circulation and cause gangrene.
3. After the tidal wave, the beautiful villa laid in ruins.
4. Since you have asked my opinion, my advice is to leave the child be until nature and the passage of time affect a cure.
5. After John recovered consciousness, the orderly told him to lie there quietly and rest.
6. Affection so effects the human heart that a little kindness often effects more than harsh discipline.
7. Leave the trail at the first fork, and then strike out across the mountain for Gill Lake, which lays just on the other side of the divide.
8. The bailiff said, "Raise and lift up your right hand."
9. When she heard the doorbell ring, she sat the packages down in the kitchen and hurried through the hallway.
10. Leave us put Walt Whitman's *Leaves of Grass* aside for a time and turn our attention to the poems of Emily Dickinson.

14. Subject-verb agreement

Review these rules: C7-35.

V40 Rewrite these sentences, correcting any mistakes in agreement. If a sentence contains no mistakes, write *correct*.

1. The crew on that Great Lakes freighter are made up of individuals from thirty different states; and each of them, believe me, stubbornly maintain that his state is the only place to live.
2. The crew on that Great Lakes freighter are from thirty different states; but all of them are solidly American and show common background, interests, and standards.
3. A number of people was gathered in the little office of the parking lot, demanding their keys of an inebriated attendant

who thought it was fun to keep his customers waiting.

4. After the robbery frightened Mrs. Tull out of her job, each usher and concession operator were asked to take a turn selling tickets.

5. The understanding of foreign politics and diplomacy are beyond me; for example, why, in the Korean War, did we use a blockade that kept our allies on Formosa from attacking our enemies in China?

6. The number of people that comes here diminishes each summer, and the natives are wondering what to do for a living when the tourist trade dies.

7. There's at least two people in this town who would like to see me leave—the tavern keeper and the manager of the local gambling casino.

8. A second unit, the Fifty-ninth Sharpshooters, were expected to arrive at any moment.

9. A mighty jolly fellow and a good boss are our president, J. Michaels Wenterwetterbum.

10. Bread and butter is good, especially with jelly or jam.

V41   Rewrite these sentences, correcting any mistakes in agreement. If sentence contains no mistakes, write *correct.*

1. Either that cat or I have to go; there's not room for us both.

2. The cat, not I, has to go; after all, I'm a person.

3. German measles have kept me out of school for two weeks, and so I'm afraid my mathematics has suffered to the point where I'll need some coaching.

4. It was three hours before we detected one of the three subs that was lying in wait for us.

5. Geoffrey Chaucer's *The Canterbury Tales* seem to be one of those books that defies translation into modern English.

6. The only one of the statues that were intact was Meunier's *The Prodigal Son.*

7. The old Chinese proverb "better to light one candle than to curse the darkness," together with many other proverbs, are quoted in the book I have here.

8. Each and every one of the secret documents stolen by the spies were photographed on microfilm.

V

9. The number of people who are giving up the habit of smoking from fear of cancer are increasing from year to year.
10. Rebecca heard that not only Mr. and Mrs. Gunnar but also the local police inspector were present at the wedding.

V42 Rewrite these sentences, correcting any mistakes in agreement. If a sentence contains no mistakes, write *correct.*

1. This year there has been a large number of people interested in the Currier and Ives prints.
2. The last three chapters of this absorbing novel was written by Roberta L. Peters.
3. I'm confident that either Michelangelo or Titian were Venetians. Do you remember which was the Venetian?
4. The buzzer having sounded the code signal, we took it for granted that either Cass or Hartley were at the door.
5. There's several plans to be considered before the committee make a decision.
6. I have heard that neither the Barrymores nor Judith Anderson have ever acted on this stage.
7. Mrs. Garth writes that Charlotte Armstrong, as well as Barbara and Susan, is driving down for the holidays.
8. Sometimes a few kind words, at other times an unselfish deed draw sinners to repentance.
9. Every boy and girl in that village believe that salamanders live in fire.
10. The rest of the bins in this grocery store is loaded with bananas and apples that needs to be thrown out or given to the local zoo.

15. Adjectives and adverbs

Review these rules: C162-65, C263-74.

V43 Rewrite these sentences, correcting any mistakes in the use of adjectives and adverbs. If a sentence contains no mistakes, write *correct.*

v

1. No, I'm not insensitive. I have a cold; and so, no matter how sweetly the bouquet smells, I won't hardly notice it's in the room. But thank you just the same.
2. The ex-president remarked that he felt sort of badly about losing the election, but was some relieved that he could now hunt and fish as he pleased, without worries.
3. We were told not to walk so heavy because of the recent damage to the floor.
4. Somewheres the sun was shining; somewheres the sky was blue; but there wasn't scarcely any joy in Mudville, for mighty Casey had struck out.
5. Even though I was not a detective, it appeared strange to me that, although nobody had been in the room, the poison in the bottle was now most gone.
6. Crebers stated real confident that she could sell enough tickets by herself to fill the lower floor of McFarlane Auditorium; but, once the sales began, she sold only seven.
7. Ted has a real mellow trumpet, which he plays very good; and you don't hardly have to coax him to play for you.
8. Rest confidently, ma'am, that my men and I will allow nobody to rob you.
9. The dialogue in the first act went real good; but in the second act Timothy ran truly to form and entered just after Ellen said he was already dead—causing all of us to blow our lines.
10. While it is true that the problem of money loomed largely before my mind, I think I was also worried some about my daughter's illness, slight though it was.

V44 Rewrite these sentences, correcting any mistakes in the use of adjectives and adverbs. If a sentence contains no mistakes, write *correct*.

1. I never played tennis this morning, I was feeling badly— too badly to do very good at a vigorous game like tennis.
2. Now Julie was sort of glad she had come, since nowheres else had she ever received such flattering attention as the camp counselors were giving her here. She felt so well

about the whole thing, in fact, that she couldn't hardly keep up the show of being displeased, thwarted, and imposed upon.

3. The man, deeply embarrassed but unable to control himself, was crying so effusively that we barely couldn't make out what he was saying through his sobs.

4. I thought you did very good at the party, especially when you played the piano so nice.

5. The teacher got upset because I never wrote my name on the paper this morning; but, anyways, she knew it was my paper because she couldn't read the handwriting.

6. The taller man was most kind, going out of his way more than a block to show us our hotel and behaving most courteous the whole time.

7. "Do good to them that hate you" sounds easy until you sit in front of Tommy Samuels in class and have him torture you all day long and get you into trouble with teachers.

8. They sure told that waiter that they were dissatisfied; then they turned around and very politely asked for real hot coffee.

9. Everyone knew that Robinson was feeling rather despondently, for the fire had wiped out everything.

10. I didn't say nothing in reply. I decided I would wait patient for her next move.

V45 Rewrite these sentences, correcting any mistakes in the use of adjectives and adverbs. If a sentence contains no mistakes, write *correct*.

1. I know you don't feel well. I suggest that you lie quiet on the sofa for an hour or so.

2. The tour wasn't working out very good; Moscher spoke disparagingly of ancient monuments.

3. "No," I kept saying, "I don't have hardly one for myself."

4. Cipriano was embarrassed, for when he found that the steers had broken into Shorty's winter pasture, he couldn't think of no explanation to give to his boss.

5. I was finally admitted to the secret laboratory and was so confused by its intricacy that I most lost my way.

v

6. Marsha felt some worse after looking at the woman lying prostrate under the car.

7. He behaved so bad that he wasn't allowed to participate in any more of the group's activities.

8. Scarcely nobody called for his services; anyways, he knew he needed a vacation.

9. I always feel badly when I think of the times I failed to help my mother around the house.

10. This is the kind of give-away program that makes sense, for our own interests are served at the same time. In other words, we are sort of making an investment which will pay us premiums in the future.

16. Comparison of adjectives and adverbs

Review rules C276-301.

V46 Rewrite these sentences, correcting any mistakes involving the comparison of adjectives and adverbs and related matters. If a sentence contains no mistakes, write *correct.*

1. Sorry, friend; this is all the farther I can go without collapsing.

2. The graduation class of Loyola Academy in their white jackets and black trousers looked far handsomer than the caps and gown worn by our class at Pickworth Prep.

3. Hunters saw less deer in the forests this winter because the terriblest famine in years had decimated what had once been the numeroust herd on record.

4. One of, if not the bravest, police officers on the force, Sergeant Jan McCarthy was killed today in a shoot-out with criminals.

5. This air conditioner cools, filters, and dehumidifies the air to our complete satisfaction, even though it costs the least of all the others now on the market.

6. Though Sarah had had no previous experience at horseback riding, she leapt into the saddle as expertly as somebody else with a lifetime of taming bucking broncos to her credit.

v

7. Of the ten men on the Wolves' pitching staff, the new rookie's curve ball was far faster than the others.

8. Stage plays are supposed to have great impact, but this one is just as dull as any other mediocre movie I have ever seen.

9. Whispering along at trolling speed, our new outboard motor was easily the most quietest of the twenty other motors churning up Lake Tranquil that afternoon.

10. This is all the longer I can wait, but I am sure you will find my plan more agreeable than any other company.

V47　Rewrite these sentences, correcting any mistakes involving the comparison of adjectives and adverbs and related matters. If a sentence contains no mistakes, write *correct*.

1. To the faculty she seems a nobody, but she is the most popular of any student in the school.

2. Well, I must say, Egbert Flandule, that your sense of humor is rather unique and most unpleasant!

3. I'm sorry to report, Mr. Ludwin, that your son is doing badder and badder every day. Frankly, he behaves the sillyest of any student I've ever had.

4. I agree: they are both lovely girls. I simply say that Erica is the most intelligent and do not see why that should not weigh in her favor.

5. Heath and Claxton are flashy players, but Anatoly is the steadier performer and the best in the long run. *Sports Review* rates him better than either of the others.

6. Your speech was simpler and shorter than anyone else, but you still received the first prize.

7. Less headlines are given to the activities of the United Nations every year. Does that say anything about its role in world affairs?

8. The staircase in the Supreme Court Building is more circular than the one in the old Senate Building.

9. Steve Grant is one of, if not the last sourdough, in Alaska today.

10. It is clear that the carbon arc gives better light than the incandescent lamp or neon tubes.

V48 Rewrite these sentences, correcting any mistakes involving the comparison of adjectives and adverbs and related matters. If a sentence contains no mistakes, write *correct*.

1. Of all the other writing instruments sold in the United States the ballpoint pen is in most demand.
2. Julia Lawton, an aggressive salesperson, has sold more typewriters than anyone in her department.
3. It is true, of course, that a boy can be a successful farmer without a high school education, but his chances are much more better if he has a diploma.
4. I've heard that President Eisenhower played the guitar as well as any other gypsy in the world.
5. I listened to her for an hour; that was all the longer I could stay without being late for my appointment.
6. Three weeks before, Kuszman had written a letter to his son, Vlad. Writing was a major task for Kuszman; he had taken the best part of three days to compose the letter.
7. Of the three jet airplanes, this one is faster and more expensive.
8. To the traveler in India, the city of Lahore is perhaps the most interesting of all the others.
9. The lathe operator at my father's shop is more experienced than any machinist in town.
10. Of all the huge trucks strung out along the highway, the diminutive driver of the tank-trailer seemed to be the least politest.

17. Errors of idiom

Review these rules: A87-92, A119, C206-11, C220-21, C245-49, C321-352.

V49 Rewrite these sentences, correcting any errors of idiom. If a sentence contains no mistakes, write *correct*.

1. It had been more than three minutes since the swimmer had dived beneath the barge besides the dock, but no one had come up.

2. Neither the majestic heights of the mountains or the awesome depths of the gorge made the expected impression on Madge and myself.

3. That there kind of book is just right for children; but I prefer any of them that deal with sports.

4. "Sorry as I am to differ from you, sir," answered the caddy, "I can only repeat that you'll overshoot the green with a seven iron."

5. Osric, he surely is a busy child. Now, Osric, where did you get that rattlesnake at?

6. Them sweet sentiments, although obviously insincere, seemed to comfort Aunt Ag; and I couldn't help thinking how different she was than the rest of the McMahon family.

7. I don't recall of ever receiving a worse rebuke than the one an old lady once gave myself and my sister for laughing at a foreigner's faulty English.

8. Let's us do our best to make this here program a success.

9. You should of seen the looks on their faces when I told them I wanted off at the next corner.

10. My signature has lately begun to differ so greatly with what it once was that the bank called me the other day and questioned a check I had signed.

V50 Rewrite these sentences, correcting any errors of idiom. If a sentence contains no mistakes, write *correct*.

1. The three troopers climbed cautiously up through the scrub oak toward the bare hilltop, leading their mounts and talking softly between themselves.

2. Let's us not make a big to-do about all this until we've searched. Perhaps you've only misplaced your wallet, and then you'll feel very foolish if you accuse someone of stealing same. Besides, it is unjust to do so.

3. The murderous-looking jet was radically different from anything McPherson had ever flown before, but he nonchalantly climbed in it as though he had been flying those kind for years.

4. Neither the mother, who had been with the boy since seven o'clock, or the nurse, who was summoned by the doctor at ten, left the sickroom all night.

5. If you don't give us them tools, me and Marsha won't be able to fix the railing on the porch.

6. We weren't exactly proud of ourselfs when we dropped the untied bucket in the well.

7. As Pat surveyed the defendant's table, she saw that Abel was sitting besides Otto Liscomb, his Chicago attorney.

8. Your reaction was very different than what I expected. Indeed, I expected disagreement on every point of the agenda.

9. An unkempt stranger arriving at this here café in Panama would attract little attention. It was near the docks and, therefore, patronized neither by the tourist or by the native socialite.

10. We didn't know where we were at when Judy and him suddenly appeared on the scene.

V51 Rewrite these sentences, correcting any errors in idiom. If a sentence contains no mistakes, write *correct*.

1. Clark called Susie and myself at eight o'clock. "Joe, we and the others are safe enough until it is discovered that we failed to deposit the money," he said.

2. This report, obviously, is incomplete; it doesn't state where the crime was committed at.

3. Strictly between us, this lower-priced coat is no different in quality than that more expensive one.

4. What bothers President Drake and myself is the prevailing idea that the important thing in education is preparing to pass examinations.

5. Rani should neither give her telephone number or her address to every young man who asks her.

6. Undoubtedly, that there is the most enlightening article I've read in months.

7. Before he stepped on to the boat, he made one of those kind of speeches that made us wish for a speedy departure.

8. Because of an argument among two members of our tennis team, the coach levied a fine on all of us.

9. She has considerable interest and enthusiasm for the guitar she bought off a friend.

10. Gunder strode across the lawn and went in the house. "Where is your father at?" he snarled at Annie.

18. Conjunctions and clauses

Review these rules: C353-73.

V52 Rewrite these sentences, correcting any mistakes in the use of conjunctions that introduce clauses. If a sentence contains no mistakes, write *correct.*

1. It was the wettest, windiest, and loneliest lighthouse on the coast; but Aspenbacker volunteered for it on account of because she wanted to be alone and write the great American novel.
2. Being as making a boxer out of me was your idea, Mac, it seems that paying my hospital bills should be your responsibility.
3. I don't think the tents will be sufficient protection against a hungry panther except we also post an armed lookout.
4. While the fish are not biting well, I intend to try my luck.
5. The reason that you regularly get lost is because you have not bothered to fix north in your mind.
6. That you collect odd coins does not give you the right to walk off with the loose change at the bottom of my father's easy chair.
7. As Mrs. Buncroop is leaving, let us express our gratitude by singing "The Old Gray Mare."
8. While the fire escape is inspected, hoodlums tamper with it so much that we never quite trust it.
9. The reason you think you don't like work is because you have never tried it.
10. She read in the paper where the new highway would finally be opened while her neighborhood street would be closed.

V53 Rewrite these sentences, correcting any mistakes in the use of conjunctions that introduce clauses. If a sentence contains no mistakes, write *correct.*

1. As I am leaving on vacation tomorrow, I want to be assured that all urgent matters have been taken care of.
2. The prisoner jerked the guard into the cell, put a knife across his throat, and hissed, "Except you give us liberty, we will give you death."

v

3. I never go fishing without I think of my father, who always used large hooks on account of he wanted to catch a really big fish and, as a result, never caught anything at all.

4. While in Montana, in June, daylight comes early, you will have to hurry to get through the pass before night falls.

5. The reason Mako wears patched clothes is because he has not had a job for a year.

6. Being as he was Stalin's choice as successor, Malenkov for a time ruled the USSR.

7. Except you pass the final examination in physics, you will have another failure on your report card.

8. Because libraries are arsenals of ideas should not make us run from them like scared rabbits.

9. The reason Emory doesn't read is on account of because he has never been guided to interesting books.

10. The big event of the year is when the Robinson and Zeller families have their picnic at Lake Woebegone.

V54 Rewrite these sentences, correcting any mistakes in the use of conjunctions that introduce clauses. If a sentence contains no mistakes, write *correct*.

1. Being that you—not I, certainly—are deciding, you must make up your mind now.

2. She cannot afford a new car except she gets a substantial trade-in for the old one.

3. It seems to me as if they should buy a full-size car on account of their family is growing.

4. He is totally blind, being as he was injured in a recent explosion at the factory.

5. While she was only ten years old, Nicole got a part in the high school play as she was smart and self-possessed for her age.

6. Professor Chauncey Tinker was told that he would lose his sight, except he gives up his long hours of reading and writing.

7. One reason why we have brought our Mercedes to you for repairs is because you are said to know German automobiles better than a German mechanic.

V

8. I read in the paper where neither Thompson or Jarrell has a chance to be elected.
9. Never leave your car parked on a slope without you first put on the emergency brake.
10. Because you are busy does not give you the right to be discourteous.

19. Unified sentences

Review these rules: K1-7.

V55 Rewrite the numbered entries to give them greater unity either by putting related ideas into one sentence (with proper subordination and coordination) or by putting marginally related ideas into separate sentences. If an entry is already unified, write *unified.*

1. Jane, the girl who lives next door, has beautiful blue eyes and is majoring in political science.
2. Before the day is over, everyone in this town knows everything that has happened in it; and what the Conklins had for dinner is of far greater interest than the most astounding political upheaval in Washington or London.
3. My uncle lives in Missouri and has some unusual views on politics.
4. Nutrasweet is like sugar in some ways. Nutrasweet is unlike sugar in other ways.
5. My sister is a noted violinist. My brother plays professional basketball. My mother and father have co-authored a book. All I can do is boil water.
6. In 1985 Mexico City suffered one of the severest earthquakes in its history, just seven years before the five hundredth anniversay of Columbus's arrival in the Americas.
7. At daybreak the general counted his troops by the thousands; but when the sun had set, where were they?
8. At the center of the campus is an impressive library. It contains several hundred thousand books. It also subscribes to and circulates most of the current periodicals.

V

9. Oliver Wendell Holmes was richly endowed with intelligence and charm; and his major work, *The Common Law*, still remained in print some one hundred years after its first publication.

10. The evening news announced that our local talk-show host had died—an attractive and articulate person, well-liked by the entire city, her parents having been raised in extreme poverty.

V56   Rewrite the numbered entries to give them greater unity either by putting related ideas into one sentence (with proper coordination and subordination) or by putting marginally related ideas into separate sentences. If an entry is already unified, write *unified*.

1. There were flattering introductions by locally well-known people. Then Dr. Tischer gave the main address. But he spoke for only five minutes. So a question-and-answer period took up most of the time.

2. The college is small. It has a fine liberal arts program. I think I will go there.

3. Many college freshmen come to realize one thing. They realize that they do not know how to study. And now they find themselves under pressure to produce.

4. I come home from school about three o'clock, and I always have a sandwich and a glass of milk.

5. My mother thinks I am uncoordinated. She thinks I am slow. She would be surprised to see me in action in the school gym.

6. Alicia Rodriguez lives next door, and she has stuffed animals and dolls that fill an entire room and closet.

7. This is where the Duggans live. It is a cheerful little house. It has a nice view.

8. There was some disturbance in the gym, but Knox quieted it before the noise reached the coaches' office.

9. Julie began singing lessons in high school, and, as she was the daughter of the ambassador to Italy, she went to that country with her father, going to Italian schools and frequenting Italian opera, and we may presume that her

living abroad gave her a knowledge of Italian music that was later of service to her.

10. I'm going to have a birthday party and invite all of my friends—except Margo, who is visitng relatives in Spain.

V57 Rewrite the numbered entries to give them greater unity either by putting related ideas into one sentence (with proper coordination and subordination) or by putting marginally related ideas into separate sentences. If a sentence is already unified, write *unified*.

1. Kuchinski has built a great body by lifting weights. He hasn't done anything to improve his mind. It is a pity.

2. I entered the room, and Pamela was still sitting quietly and staring blankly into space.

3. Franz Liszt was one of the towering figures of nineteenth century music. He as an original composer. He was also a piano virtuoso.

4. Nadine is a girl in my class, and in our last intramural basketball game she amazed everyone with her shooting ability.

5. When our ten-year-old Jeep had bounded over the rocky terrain and almost slid down a muddy decline into the valley where the Lost River flows, we piled together, near a shimmering birch, our tent, duffel bags, cooking equipment, fishing rods, and food supplies before making an exploratory hike of the area where we were to fish for three days.

6. A woman is wearing a yellow dress and just fell overboard and is calling for help.

7. Mrs. Rossi was carrying two armfuls of groceries. She did not see the curb. Suddenly she went sprawling. The groceries went sprawling.

8. I do things now, and they gladden or depress my former teachers.

9. On January 12, 1990, died Alexander Agostino, leaving behind him the memory of many charities and a large

family, of whom three were girls, one of them, Alice, the eldest, being a lawyer later became a federal judge.

10. Jared Jessup, author of the gloomy *It's the Pits*, was hospitalized four times for acute depression—that is, if my information is correct.

20. Coherent sentences

Review rules K8-28.

V58 Rewrite these sentences, correcting any mistakes in coherence. (You may need to reposition modifying words, phrases, or clauses; add parallel structure; use proper connectives; supply clear references between pronouns and antecedents; correct needless shifts in idea, voice, tense, person, or number; and so on.) If a sentence is already coherent, write *coherent*.

1. Not only did Sabina enjoy swimming, but also hiking was liked by her.
2. Some people enjoy picnics in public parks, but not me.
3. The roads of Shawnee County were not in good repair, and I kept to my customary sixty miles per hour for more than an hour.
4. I will either meet you at the Hollenden Hotel or at Link's Restaurant.
5. Just as Marshall High School is known for its athletic teams, so the students of East High School are prominent in debating.
6. To write her off as ineffective is avoidng the basic question—why is she ineffective?
7. The gardener and maintenance man is quitting because he thinks he has too much work to do.
8. Lance is a slow learner, and he leads his class.
9. A little waif, sad and with tangled hair, sold me some flowers.
10. Myra was respected by everyone whose opinion really mattered and by the dean of the college too.

v

V59 Rewrite these sentences, correcting any mistakes in coherence. (You may need to reposition modifying words, phrases, or clauses; add parallel structure; use proper connectives; supply clear references between pronouns and antecedents; correct needless shifts in idea, voice, tense, person, or number; and so on.) If a sentence is already coherent, write *coherent*.

1. My aunt, who is proud of her five cats, is troubled with ticks and fleas.
2. Bravely the child spoke to the butler; but instead of getting an answer, he slammed the door in her face.
3. I was told every Friday to report to the kitchen and wash the floor.
4. Growing tall very quickly, the coaches said he would soon be a prospect for the basketball team.
5. Catherine brought us sandwiches and coffee; but, best of all, we were given the new publication deadlines by her.
6. The Hartmanns had planned a brief vacation in New York with the Sibels, but they had to drop their plan when they found that they would have to stay in town because of their daughter's illness.
7. The police are searching for Olga Massino, the daughter of P. J. Massino, a rich industrialist, who has been missing for six days.
8. Diesel engines are used in some cars, but most use gasoline.
9. As Maura was smiling, I realized that she distrusted me.
10. Military training teaches a person obedience, to be alert, and how to command others.

V60 Rewrite these sentences, correcting any mistakes in coherence. (You may need to reposition modifying words, phrases, or clauses; add parallel structure; use proper connectives; supply clear references between pronouns and antecedents; correct needless shifts in idea, voice, tense, person, or number; and so on.) If a sentence is already coherent, write *coherent*.

1. If anyone sees a burglary in progress, you should call the police immediately.
2. In literature class Alfred never understood the difference between verbal irony and dramatic irony, and the definition of satire also made no sense to him.
3. I realize how uninformed I am and the advantage an educated person has over one who is not.
4. She sat looking out the window; and when her son comes with her dinner, she takes no notice—though all of it is eaten when he returns for the tray in an hour.
5. Resourcefulness and being patient conquer all things.
6. She thought the chemistry examination would be easy; still it really wasn't very difficult.
7. The Mohawk, judging that it is safe once more to move, slowly raises his head above the marsh grass and peers toward the knoll; but suddenly there was a shot, and he drops once more to the ground and remains perfectly motionless.
8. Tall, articulate, and trouble-shooter for the boss, J. Clayton Trump suddenly appeared in the doorway.
9. They all thought that one of them had the key; and when they reached the cottage, no one did.
10. Make yourself comfortable until 8:30 P.M. when the lecture will begin.

21. Emphatic sentences

Review these rules: K29-49.

V61 Rewrite these sentences, making them emphatic. (You may need to use the active voice, make statements positive, arrange ideas in the order of climax, eliminate wordiness, call attention to important ideas by unusual word order or by repetition, and so on.) If a sentence is already emphatic, write *emphatic.*

1. Clearly Oscar has talent: he develops computer programs, repairs furniture, and plays the harmonica.

v

2. Although the hike took no more than three hours, we were all tired and weary.

3. What I want is to go to the basketball game which is being played by the city's two top high-school teams.

4. In the tornado Beth and Sam Hearns were both killed and their car was damaged beyond repair.

5. Boundless and constant is the love of a mother for her children.

6. She did not think that studying history was of any value.

7. Tear gas choked the robbers, drove them out of the building, and poured into all the rooms on the first floor.

8. It is easy to forgive the offense; it may be beyond my capability to forget it.

9. Bells were rung, horns were blown, flags were waved from all the boats along the shore.

10. The football game was exciting; the weather was perfect; the crowd was enthusiastic; and the hot dog buns were fresh.

V62 Rewrite these sentences, making them emphatic. (You may need to use the active voice, make statements positive, arrange ideas in the order of climax, eliminate wordiness, call attention to important ideas by unusual word order or by repetition, and so on.) If a sentence is already emphatic, write *emphatic.*

1. Relentlessly the dentist drilled into Smagala's tooth.

2. She did not pay any attention to the fact that her companion did not feel well.

3. We found a message scrawled in the dirt and the remains of a fire in a small opening concealed by a heavy growth of spruce near the foot of the mountain on the eighth day of the search.

4. You seem to need money for movies, money for games, money for food, money for dates. Can't you do anything that doesn't require money?

5. The fact that he had not succeeded came as a surprise to no one.

6. In the back of her cab she found a wallet, a machine gun, and a stick of gum.

7. The meeting was called to order by the chairman, and the minutes were read by the recording secretary.

8. The rich Mr. Endright was fatally shot under the brilliant lights of the marquee, waiting for his chauffeur to bring around the limousine.

9. All my debts can be paid and some money provided for a rainy day by this ten-thousand-dollar prize.

10. When Mr. Mercer set out for the office, he always kissed his wife and three children, all lined up in the front hallway; took his coat from the closet and put it on; adjusted his glasses; picked up his briefcase with its important papers; opened the front door; turned once more to his family and declared, with a kind of grim gaiety, as though were going into battle, "Well, I'm off"; and disappeared into the great outdoors of East Rutherford Avenue. These things he did every working morning, always in that order, with a routine that never, never failed.

V63 Rewrite these sentences, making them emphatic. (You may need to use the active voice, make statements positive, arrange ideas in the order of climax, eliminate wordiness, call attention to important ideas by unusual word order or by repetition, and so on.) If a sentence is already emphatic, write *emphatic*.

1. The decision was not disputed by any of the players, even though it meant that their top scorer would not be allowed to play in the next two games.

2. The light of the sun reaches even those who are wicked.

3. Australia was the last habitable continent to be discovered and developed, lying far from the early trade routes between the East and the West and near no other lands but islands inhabited by natives.

4. After a thorough examination by the doctor, a diagnosis was made.

5. A man who was wearing a yellow shirt and brown shorts entered the shop where bicycles are sold and came out in something less than fifteen minutes with a pogo stick.

6. "You are behaving foolishly, quite foolishly," she hissed with venom.

V

7. The ominous sound of thunder was heard by the crew, and the boat was quickly made secure before the storm struck.

8. Be advised that you are not to discharge your rifles until you have established eye contact with the enemy.

9. I have a skillet and, more importantly, some perch to fry in it.

10. The charges against Burgess were possession of drugs, running a stop light, and jumping bail.

22. Word choice

Review these rules: K75-98, K125-28.

V64 Rewrite the following sentences, replacing the italicized words with more particular ones. Try to suit your words to the subject matter.

1. Badly crippled, Joel *moved* down the corridor.
2. The skiff *moved* suddenly.
3. The bug *moved* across the pond.
4. The elephant *moved* through the jungle.
5. The speedboat *moved* down the river.
6. The panhandler *moved* sidewise up to me.
7. The baby *moved* about on hands and knees.
8. They made *a lot of money* selling programs.
9. The *object* of this meeting is to establish a booster club.
10. They bought this *house* because neither of them can climb stairs.

V65 Rewrite the following sentences, replacing the italicized words with more particular ones. Try to suit your words to the subject.

1. Mr. Snoop was *talking*.
2. Mrs. Timid was *talking*.
3. The crowd was *talking*.
4. The baby was *talking*.
5. The security guard was *talking*.
6. The twenty sixth-graders were *talking*.
7. Honesty is *something* that we expect of all our employees.
8. The passage at the mouth of the bay was *large*.

V

9. His appetite was *large*.
10. The neighbors did not believe in using *negative reinforcement* with their youngest child.

V66 Revise these sentences by improving diction. (You may need to use more precise language, recast overworked phrases, correct mixed metaphors, establish consistent language, and so on.)

1. George is in bad shape.
2. Rebecca is a lawyer, but I don't know what her line is.
3. The perpetrator of the crime was apprehended as he exited the establishment.
4. Beyond a shadow of a doubt that boy is a chip off the old block.
5. It was a great party—great people, great food, great music, and great conversation.
6. She was already walking a fine line and then lightning struck.
7. One aspect of the decision is the elimination of some middle-level jobs.
8. Media Inc. has adopted the movie for television.
9. The art dealer knew immediately that the painting was a phony.
10. As a politician, Jeffrey already had two strikes against him, and then came the last straw.

V

Index

body, S85–87
conclusion, S89
kinds of, S84
objective, S82
See also Business letters.
Apposition. *See* Appositives.
Appositive adjectives, C261
Appositives, C197–205
agreement with head word, C198–99
definition of, C197
diagraming, J24
figures (numbers) between dashes, D101
introduced by *or, namely,* and so on, C200
not affecting agreement of predicate verb, C9
as part of proper name, D50
restrictive and nonrestrictive, C202–5
punctuation, D48–50, D83, D97–101, D106
test of, C205
Apt, liable, likely, U
Archbishop as form of address in business letters, S38, S64
Argument, P1–91
brief. *See* Brief (of argument)
deductive reasoning in, P28–29, P30
definition of, P1
evidence in, P23–25. *See also* Evidence.
exposition, description, narration in, P2, P44
fallacies, P58–91
ad hominem, P83
ambiguity of terms, P74–75
begging the question *(petitio principii),* P61–62
defective induction, P76–77
either-or, P80
false analogy, P78–79
false appeal to common knowledge or consent, P69–71
false assumption, P67–68
false causality *(post hoc, ergo propter hoc),* P65–66
mistaking the question *(ignoratio elenchi),* P59–60
non sequitur, P82
reductive, P81
unfair implication, P72–73
vicious circle, P63–64
inductive reasoning in, P26–27, P30, P37
issues in, P19–21, P44, footnote 10
non sequitur, P82
persuasion in, Q1, footnote 1,

planning, P3–43
propaganda in, P84
bandwagon, P91
card stacking, P89
misrepresentation, P90
misuse of authority, P87
red herring, P86
stereotype, P85
transfer, P88
sources of proof in, P31–43
analogy, P39–40
authority, P32–33
cause and effect, P34–35
circumstances, P36
common experience, P38
general truths or principles, P31
specific instances, P37
statements of a witness, P41–43
thesis in, P3–13
action, P5, P47
avoiding extravagant terms, P9
based on the issues, P19
conciseness of, P13
debatability, P8
offering to prove too much (error), P12
recapitulation, P44, footnote 10, P56
stated definitely, P10
stated in single declarative sentence, P7
stating only certain truths as certain, P11
truth in, P4
types, P31–44
written requirement for, P6
writing, P44–57
action thesis, P47
body, P50–57
conclusion, P56–57
introduction, P48–49
oral, P44, footnote 10
Argumentative paragraph, topic sentence in, L16
Army, capitals for, H122–23
Around for *nearly* or *about,* C343
Art, works of
capitals for titles of, H126
italics preferred to quotation marks for titles of, D151
Articles *(a, an, the),* A98, A103–4
with each of two or more adjectives or nouns, C262
restrictive modifiers, C307
the, first word in headings and addresses

C

G

N

O

P

Q

at end of literary title set off on line by itself, D27
with parentheses, D112–13
with quotation marks, D129
Quotation marks, D117–42
acts, alliances, charters, reports, statutes, and treaties (error), D134, H138–39
articles (essays), D132
artistic works, D151
ballets, D151
Bible and its books, canons, divisions, parts, revisions, and versions (error), D149, H23, H25–26
Book of Common Prayer and its parts (error), D135
books, D131, D144
catechisms, confessions of faith, and creeds (error), D135, H34
chapters, D132
church services and devotions (error), D135
for clearness, D136
dialogue, D124
directories, manuals, and similar reference works (error), D147, H134
direct quotations, D117
dialogue, D124
prose and verse quoted in themes, D123
within a quotation, D118
in research paper, N92–93
uninterrupted quotation of more than one paragraph, D122
uninterrupted quotation of more than one sentence, D121
essays, D132
expressions on different language level from rest of composition, D139
Gospel, Gospels (error), H27
indirect quotations, D120
letters used for names (error), D156
Mass and its parts (error), D135, H68
Missal and its parts (error), D135, H33
motion pictures, D144
musical works, D132, D151
mysteries of the rosary (error), D135
operas, D151
with other punctuation marks, D127–29
paintings, D151
pamphlets, D144
parables and biblical discourses (error), D135, H29–30
plays, D144
poems, D132
prayers (error), D135, H31
radio programs, D144
reference works (error), D147, H134
sacred writings (error), D149, H23, H25–27
short stories, D132
single, D118, D141
something mentioned as part of a larger work, D131
statues, D151
technical words or terms, D138
television programs, D144
titles of essays, M93–96
words directed by a person to himself, or unspoken thoughts (error), D119
words followed by their definition of or explanation, D137
words that need setting off for clearness, D136
words used ironically, D140
works of art, D151
Quotations
in business letters, S33
direct, D117–19, D121–30
block, N109, N114, N118, N123, N140
brackets in, D115
broken by ellipsis points, D21–22
broken by *he said* expressions, D130
capitals for, D125–26, H5–7
colon before, D84
comma before, D74
diagraming, J42–43
in dialogue, D124
in narrative compositions, R50–51
quotation marks with. *See* Quotation marks.
from a secondary source, N135
indirect
capitals for, H8
comma before (error), D75
in narrative compositions, R51
with quotation marks, D120
within quotations, D118, D141

R

Race and races, capitals for, H140–42
Radio programs
capitals for, H126, H131–32
italics preferred to quotation marks, D144
Radio station names
abbreviation for, F15
capitals for, H118, H121

W